Prosecuting International

This book discusses the legitin
regime. It explains the develop
criminal law enforcement in h
through the Nuremberg and To … prosecutions of
atrocities in the former Yugoslavia, Rwanda and Sierra Leone. The modern regime of prosecution of international crimes is evaluated with regard to international relations theory. The book then subjects that regime to a critique on the basis of legitimacy and the rule of law, in particular selective enforcement, not only in relation to who is prosecuted, but also to the definitions of crimes and principles of liability used when people are prosecuted. It concludes that although selective enforcement is not as powerful as a critique of international criminal law as it was previously, the creation of the International Criminal Court may also have narrowed the substantive rules of international criminal law.

ROBERT CRYER is Senior Lecturer in Law at the University of Nottingham. He is the book review editor of the *Journal of Conflict and Security Law*. He teaches international law, criminal law, theory of criminal law, theory of international law, humanitarian law, international criminal law and the law of collective security. He has taught in the United Kingdom, Germany, Austria, Malaysia and South Africa.

CAMBRIDGE STUDIES IN INTERNATIONAL AND COMPARATIVE LAW

Established in 1946, this series produces high quality scholarship in the fields of public and private international law and comparative law. Although these are distinct legal sub-disciplines, developments since 1946 confirm their interrelation.

Comparative law is increasingly used as a tool in the making of law at national, regional and international levels. Private international law is now often affected by international conventions, and the issues faced by classical conflicts rules are frequently dealt with by substantive harmonisation of law under international auspices. Mixed international arbitrations, especially those involving state economic activity, raise mixed questions of public and private international law, while in many fields (such as the protection of human rights and democratic standards, investment guarantees and international criminal law) international and national systems interact. National constitutional arrangements relating to 'foreign affairs', and to the implementation of international norms, are a focus of attention.

The Board welcomes works of a theoretical or interdisciplinary character, and those focusing on new approaches to international or comparative law or conflicts of law. Studies of particular institutions or problems are equally welcome, as are translations of the best work published in other languages.

A list of books in the series can be found at the end of this volume.

Prosecuting International Crimes

Selectivity and the International Criminal Law Regime

Robert Cryer

CAMBRIDGE
UNIVERSITY PRESS

CAMBRIDGE UNIVERSITY PRESS
Cambridge, New York, Melbourne, Madrid, Cape Town, Singapore, São Paulo, Delhi

Cambridge University Press
The Edinburgh Building, Cambridge CB2 8RU, UK

Published in the United States of America by Cambridge University Press, New York

www.cambridge.org
Information on this title: www.cambridge.org/9780521824743

First published 2005

A catalogue record for this publication is available from the British Library

ISBN 978-0-521-82474-3 hardback

Transferred to digital printing 2008

To my parents

Contents

Preface and acknowledgements

This project is the outcropping of work undertaken at two universities, Nottingham and Manchester: first at Nottingham, as a research student, next at Manchester as a lecturer and, finally, back at Nottingham as an academic. From my early days at Nottingham, I owe a debt of gratitude to my supervisors Nigel D. White and Dino Kritsiotis, and to David Harris and the School of Law for granting me a scholarship to pursue my interest in international criminal law.

At Manchester, aside from providing a first-rate intellectual environment, my colleagues were supportive and kind. Particular thanks ought to be recorded to Margot Brazier, Neil Duxbury, Angus McCulloch and John Murphy. Since my return to Nottingham I have received help, support and advice from colleagues, especially Di Birch, Peter Cartwright, Matthew Happold, Robert McCorquodale, Andrew Simester and Dirk van Zyl Smit. Matthew and Robert have also been kind enough to read and comment on parts of this work, as have Richard Burchill and Sangeeta Shah. I have imposed the vast majority of the manuscript of this book on Nigel White, who has given freely of his time to read and comment on it, even though he must be rather tired of seeing some of the material again. I would also like to thank two anonymous reviewers for Cambridge University Press for their helpful comments. One in particular gave a set of exceptionally detailed suggestions, which has been invaluable. I have discussed the issues in this book with too many people to mention individually, but I am grateful to them all.

A great deal of the rewriting of this book was undertaken during a very pleasant stay in the Institut für Völkerrecht in the University of Göttingen. I would like to thank all the members of the University for making me so welcome. Special thanks go to Heike Kreiger for being such an excellent host in Germany. At Cambridge University Press, I would like to thank Finola O'Sullivan, Brenda Burke and Jane O'Regan for all their help and patience.

Parts of the section on Sierra Leone in chapter 1 draw upon an article published in the *International and Comparative Law Quarterly* in 2001. An early version of chapter 6, alongside some of the introduction to chapter 5, appeared in the 2001 *Journal of Conflict and Security Law*. I have attempted to keep the book up to date to Easter 2004, but have managed to include some later material where it has been possible.

Cases

Treaties

Abbreviations

AD	*Annual Digest of Public International Law Cases*
AJCL	*American Journal of Comparative Law*
AJIL	*American Journal of International Law*
Alb LR	*Albany Law Review*
All ER	*All England Reports*
AP	Additional Protocol
Arizona JICL	*Arizona Journal of International and Comparative Law*
ASIL	American Society of International Law
ASP	Assembly of States Parties
AUJILP	*American University Journal of International Law and Politics*
BCE	Before Common Era
BFSP	*British Foreign and State Papers*
BUILJ	*Boston University International Law Journal*
BYBIL	*British Yearbook of International Law*
Cal LR	*California Law Review*
CWRJIL	*Case Western Reserve Journal of International Law*
CE	Common Era
CLF	Criminal Law Forum
CLJ	*Cambridge Law Journal*
CLP	*Current Legal Problems*
CMR	*Court Martial Reports*
Columbia JTL	*Columbia Journal of Transnational Law*
Columbia LR	*Columbia Law Review*
Connecticut JIL	*Connecticut Journal of International Law*
Cornell ILJ	*Cornell International Law Journal*
Cr App R	*Criminal Appeal Reports*

Crim LR	*Criminal Law Review*
CSCE	Conference on Security and Cooperation in Europe
CWILJ	*California Western International Law Journal*
CWRILJ	*Case Western Reserve International Journal*
CYBIL	*Canadian Yearbook of International Law*
De Paul LR	*De Paul Law Review*
Dickinson JIL	*Dickinson Journal of International Law*
DJCIL	*Duke Journal of Comparative and International Law*
DJILP	*Denver Journal of International Law and Policy*
ECHR	European Court of Human Rights
EIA	*Ethics and International Affairs*
EJCCLCJ	*European Journal of Crime, Criminal Law and Criminal Justice*
EJIL	*European Journal of International Law*
Emory ILR	*Emory International Law Review*
EPIL	Rudolf Bernhardt *et al.* (eds.), *Encyclopaedia of Public International Law* (New York: Elsevier, 1995)
FA	*Foreign Affairs*
FEC	Far Eastern Commission
FFWA	*Fletcher Forum of World Affairs*
Fordham ILJ	*Fordham International Law Journal*
FRY	Federal Republic of Yugoslavia
GA	General Assembly
GC	Geneva Convention
GYBIL	*German Yearbook of International Law*
Harvard HRLJ	*Harvard Human Rights Law Journal*
Harvard ILJ	*Harvard International Law Journal*
HRLJ	*Human Rights Law Journal*
HRLR	*Human Rights Law Review*
HRQ	*Human Rights Quarterly*
IA	*International Affairs*
ICC	International Criminal Court
ICCPR	International Covenant on Civil and Political Rights
ICJ	International Court of Justice
ICLQ	*International and Comparative Law Quarterly*
ICRC	International Committee of the Red Cross
ICTR	International Criminal Tribunal for Rwanda
ICTY	International Criminal Tribunal for the former Yugoslavia

ILA	International Law Association
ILC	International Law Commission
ILM	*International Legal Materials*
ILQ	*International Law Quarterly*
ILR	*International Law Reports*
ILSAJICL	*International Law Students' Association Journal of International and Comparative Law*
IMT	International Military Tribunal
IP	*International Politics*
IRRC	*International Review of the Red Cross*
Israel LR	*Israel Law Review*
IYBHR	*Israel Yearbook on Human Rights*
JACL	*Journal of Armed Conflict Law*
JCSL	*Journal of Conflict and Security Law*
JHIL	*Journal of the History of International Law*
JICJ	*Journal of International Criminal Justice*
KCLJ	*King's College Law Journal*
L. Ed.	Lawyer's Edition
LCP	*Law and Contemporary Problems*
LJ	Law Journal
LJIL	*Leiden Journal of International Law*
LLAICLR	*Loyola & Los Angeles International and Comparative Law Review*
LNTS	League of Nations Treaty Series
LPICT	*Law and Practice of International Courts and Tribunals*
LQR	*Law Quarterly Review*
LR	Law Reports
LRTWC	*Law Reports, Trials of War Criminals*
LSI	*Law and Social Inquiry*
Mich LR	*Michigan Law Review*
Military LR	*Military Law Review*
MJIL	*Michigan Journal of International Law*
MLR	*Modern Law Review*
MPYBUNL	*Max Planck Yearbook of United National Law*
MULR	*Melbourne University Law Review*
NELR	*New England Law Review*
NI	*The National Interest*
NILR	*Netherlands International Law Review*
Nordic JIL	*Nordic Journal of International Law*
NYIL	*Netherlands Yearbook of International Law*

NYLSJICL	*New York Law School Journal of International and Comparative Law*
NYUJILP	*New York University Journal of International Law and Policy*
OJLS	*Oxford Journal of Legal Studies*
OLA	UN Office of Legal Affairs
OLR	*Oregon Law Review*
OTP	Office of the Prosecutor
Pace ILR	*Pace International Law Review*
PCIJ	Permanent Court of International Justice
PREP Com	Preparatory Committee for an International Criminal Court/Preparatory Commission
Proc.	Proceedings
Proceedings ASIL	*Proceedings of the American Society of International Law*
RADIC	*African Review of International and Comparative Law*
RdC	*Receuil des Cours, l'Académie de Droit International*
Rep.	
RIAA	*Reports of International Arbitration Awards*
RIDMDG	*Révue Internationale de Droit Militaire et Law Droit de la Guerre*
RIDP	*Révue International de Droit Penal*
SALJ	*South African Law Journal*
SAYBIL	*South African Yearbook of International Law*
SCSL	Special Court for Sierra Leone
SDJJ	*San Diego Justice Journal*
SFOR	Stabilisation Force
SFRY	Socialist Federal Republic of Yugoslavia
SOFA	Status of Forces Agreement
TGS	*Transactions of the Grotius Society*
TILJ	*Texas International Law Journal*
TLCP	*Transnational Law and Contemporary Problems*
TLR	*Texas Law Review*
TS	Treaty Series
Tulane LR	*Tulane Law Review*
TWC	*Trials of War Criminals*
UCDJIL	*University of California, Davis, Journal of International Law*
UKTS	*United Kingdom Treaty Series*
UNTAET	United Nations Transitional Authority in East Timor

UNTS	*United Nations Treaty Series*
UNWCC	United Nations War Crimes Commission
UPLR	*University of Pennsylvania Law Review*
USCMA	*United States Court Marital Appeals*
Vil. LR	*Villanova Law Review*
VJIL	*Virginia Journal of International Law*
VJTL	*Vanderbilt Journal of Transnational Law*
WCR	*World Court Reports*
Yale JIL	*Yale Journal of International Law*
Yale LJ	*Yale Law Journal*
YBIHL	*Yearbook of International Humanitarian Law*
YBILC	*Yearbook of the International Law Commission*

Introduction

This is a book about international criminal law. More specifically, this book is an investigation of the regime of international criminal law enforcement that has been created since the late 1980s. This is a regime which involves both national and international forums for the prosecution of international crimes. This study is essentially in two parts: part I (chapters 1–3) explains the development of the regime, and some of the problems it has encountered. Having established the existence of the regime, part II (chapters 4–6) will evaluate the regime from the point of view of its legitimacy and compliance with the rule of law, with respect both to who is prosecuted and the approaches taken to the applicable substantive law.

There are a number of different understandings of the content of 'international criminal law'. There is no single right answer as to what is included in 'international criminal law': the phrase may mean different things to different people. Writers such as M. Cherif Bassiouni take an 'omnibus' approach to the subject, including any crime which fulfils one of ten criteria, encompassing having a treaty which includes a duty or right to extradite.[1] This is a very broad approach. The approach taken in this book is narrower than Bassiouni's. International criminal law is taken to be that body of international law that imposes criminal responsibility directly upon the individual, without the necessary interposition of national legal systems.[2] This was something accepted by the Nuremberg International Military Tribunal (hereafter, Nuremberg IMT)

[1] M. Cherif Bassiouni, *Introduction to International Criminal Law* (Ardsley: Transnational, 2004), pp. 114–15.

[2] *Accord* Bruce Broomhall, *International Justice and the International Criminal Court: Between Sovereignty and the Rule of Law* (Oxford: Oxford University Press, 2003), pp. 9–10.

in its famous pronouncement that 'crimes against international law are committed by men, not abstract entities, and only by punishing individuals who commit such crimes can the provisions of international law be enforced . . . individuals have international duties which transcend the national obligations of obedience imposed by the individual state'.[3] This position has received no convincing academic challenge for half a century.[4] Critics of international criminal law are now limited to castigating statesmen for their invocation of the concept, which they feel will fail on *realpolitik* grounds, rather than denying that States accept it.[5] Debates now more fruitfully centre on the contours of individual liability under international law, rather than its existence.

Limiting the discussion to those rules of international law that directly impose criminal responsibility on individuals involves the exclusion of two other types of rules sometimes referred to under the general rubric of 'international criminal law'. The first of these is the controversial concept of international crimes of States, originally in Article 19 of the ILC Draft Articles on State Responsibility,[6] but dropped from the final Articles sent to the General Assembly in 2001.[7] Although the type of conduct covered by Article 19 overlaps with the offences dealt with in international criminal law, the transposition of criminality onto a collective entity such as the State is still highly controversial. However,

[3] 'Nuremberg IMT: Judgment and Sentence' (1947) 41 AJIL 172, 221.

[4] The most serious challenge to the existence of international criminal law in this sense of the word was Georg Schwarzenberger, 'The Problem of an International Criminal Law' (1950) 3 CLP 263.

[5] See Alfred P. Rubin, *Ethics and Authority in International Law* (Cambridge: Cambridge University Press, 1997). His criticisms (for example, of the hypocrisy of States) are well founded, but do not undermine the existence of the concept of individual responsibility. As Colin Warbrick points out, there is no principled reason in international law why there cannot be individual responsibility for crimes under international law, and enforcement by international courts; Colin J. Warbrick, 'The United Nations System: A Place for International Criminal Courts?' (1995) 5 TLCP 237, 261.

[6] For the first reading, see Report of the International Law Commission on the Work of its Forty-Eighth Session UN GAOR 51st Sess. Supp. No. 10, p. 131. See, generally, Nina H. B. Jørgensen, *The Responsibility of States for International Crimes* (Oxford: Oxford University Press, 2000); Geoff Gilbert, 'The Criminal Responsibility of States' (1990) 39 ICLQ 345; Krystina Marek, 'Criminalising State Responsibility' (1978–1979) 14 *Revue Belge de Droit Internationale* 460; Shabtai Rosenne, 'State Responsibility and International Crimes: Further Reflections on Article 19 of the Draft Articles on State Responsibility' (1997–1998) 30 NYUJILP 145.

[7] See James Crawford, *The International Law Commissions' Articles on State Responsibility: Introduction, Text and Commentaries* (Cambridge: Cambridge University Press, 2002), pp. 16–20, 35–8.

the reason it falls outside the scope of this work is that it does not relate to individual, but to State, responsibility.[8]

The second exclusion is those crimes set up by treaty regimes which require States to prohibit conduct as part of their national law. Treaties of this nature, such as the 1988 Vienna Convention Against the Illicit Trafficking in Narcotic Drugs and Psychotropic Substances[9] do not create individual responsibility under international law, but place a duty on the State to criminalise the conduct municipally.[10] They are therefore different to the international crimes under discussion herein, as international law does not criminalise such crimes in and of itself. Equally, the two types of crime have certain aspects of national enforcement in common, so reference to those crimes is made where relevant.[11] In one instance, individual peacetime acts of torture contrary to the 1984 Convention Against Torture,[12] a treaty crime may have jumped the gap to the status of an international crime. The assertion that individual acts of torture entail individual liability in international law is still controversial.[13]

Treaty crimes were excluded from the jurisdiction of the ICC. This is another reason for excluding them from this work. Those crimes have been excluded from the regime of international criminal law enforcement that is our focus. Although certain acts of terrorism and perhaps peacetime individual acts of torture are sufficiently serious to rise to the level of the most serious crimes of concern to the international community of States as a whole, the same cannot be said for all treaty crimes such as interference with submarine cables.[14] Treaty crimes such as drug trafficking are also often controversial, and not universally accepted.[15]

[8] See also Broomhall, *International Justice*, pp. 13–19. [9] 1019 UNTS 175.

[10] See further Broomhall, *International Justice*, pp. 12–14.

[11] Report of the ILC on the Work of its Forty Fifth Session, Report of the Working Group on a Draft Statute for an International Criminal Court, UN GAOR 48th Sess. Supp. No. 10, pp. 100–32, UN Doc. A/48/CN.4/Ser.A/1993/Add.1. For an attempt to rationalise both types of international crime into one taxonomy see Barbara Yarnold, 'Doctrinal Basis for the International Criminalisation Process' (1994) 4 *Temple International and Comparative Law Journal* 85.

[12] Which, if committed in an armed conflict, is a war crime. Widespread or systematic torture against a civilian population is a crime against humanity.

[13] In favour, see Antonio Cassese, *International Criminal Law* (Oxford: Oxford University Press, 2003), pp. 117–19; against, Bruno Simma and Andreas Paulus, 'The Responsibility of Individuals for Human Rights Abuses in Internal Conflicts: A Positivist View' (1999) 93 AJIL 302, 313.

[14] Contrary to the 1982 United Nations Convention on the Law of the Sea, 516 UNTS 205, Article 113.

[15] 1988 Vienna Convention Against the Illicit Traffic in Narcotic Drugs and Other Psychotropic Substances, Article 1.

These exclusions leave only four categories of crime to be discussed in detail: genocide, crimes against humanity, war crimes and the crime of aggression. These four remain as they have been accepted in the latter half of the twentieth century as the 'core' international crimes which international law itself criminalises. This choice is also supported by the fact that to the present day they are the only crimes which have been punished before international criminal tribunals (ICTs). All four are present in some form in the 1998 Rome Statute.[16] They are also the crimes which comprised the streamlined ILC Draft Code of Crimes Against the Peace and Security of Mankind.[17] The Draft Code declared (in Article 1) that 'Crimes against the peace and security of mankind are crimes under international law and punishable as such, whether or not they are punishable under national law'.

Although I am personally in favour of accountability, it is not the purpose of this book to engage in a detailed evaluation of the policy decision to 'give justice a chance'.[18] There is a rich literature on the question of the appropriateness of the decision to engage in a prosecutorial response to situations involving international crimes.[19] The purpose of this book is to show that many States have also taken the view that accountability

[16] Rome Statute, Article 5.

[17] Draft Code of Crimes Against the Peace and Security of Mankind, in Report of The International Law Commission on the Work of its Forty-Eighth Session, UN Doc. A/51/10, Articles 16–20.

[18] Leila Nadya Sadat, *The International Criminal Court and the Transformation of International Law: Justice for a New Millennium* (Ardsley: Transnational, 2002), pp. 72–5.

[19] For a sample of such literature, see Susan Dwyer, 'Reconciliation for Realists', (1999) 13 EIA 81; Desmond Tutu, *No Future Without Forgiveness* (London: Rider, 1999); John Dugard, 'Reconciliation and Justice: The South African Experience', (1998) 8 TLCP 277; Kader Asmal, 'Truth, Reconciliation and Justice: The South African Experience in Perspective' (2000) 63 MLR 1; Carlos S. Nino, *Radical Evil on Trial* (New Haven: Yale University Press, 1996); Martha Minow, *Between Vengeance and Forgiveness* (Boston: Beacon Press, 1998); Mark J. Osiel, 'Why Prosecute? Critics of Punishment for Mass Atrocity' (2000) 22 HRQ 118; Gary J. Bass, 'War Crimes and the Limits of Legalism' (1999) 97 Mich LR 2103; Juan E. Méndez, 'National Reconciliation, Transnational Justice and the International Criminal Court' (2001) 15 EIA 25; Steven R. Ratner, 'New Democracies, Old Atrocities: An Inquiry in International Law' (1999) 87 Georgetown LJ 707; Naomi Roht-Arriaza, *Impunity In Human Rights Law and Practice* (Oxford: Oxford University Press, 1995); Stephen Cohen, 'State Crimes of Previous Regimes: Knowledge, Accountability and the Policing of the Past' (1995) 20 LSI 7; Richard J. Goldstone, 'Justice as a Tool for Peace-Making: Truth Commissions and International Tribunals' (1996) 28 NYUJILP 485; Anthony D'Amato, 'Peace *v.* Accountability in Bosnia' (1994) 88 AJIL 500 *contra* the correspondence in (1994) 88 AJIL 717, (1995) 89 AJIL 93, (1995) 89 AJIL 94; Anonymous, 'Human Rights in Peace Negotiations' (1996) 18 HRQ 249; Oliver Schuett, 'The International War Crimes Tribunal for Former Yugoslavia and the Dayton Peace

is the appropriate response to international crimes, and that they have set up a regime to effectuate that decision. This book will then evaluate the operation of that regime with respect to critical principles derived from concepts of legitimacy and the rule of law.

To do this, the book will proceed to show the development of international criminal law in chapter 1, where there will also be a demonstration that some of the problems noted later in the book have a considerable historical pedigree. Chapter 2 explains the framework of jurisdiction and duties to extradite or prosecute to show the problems that have characterised the enforcement of international criminal law and State reluctance to prosecute. The regime created to ensure accountability for international crimes is introduced in chapter 3, alongside a defence of the view that it deserves to be called a 'regime' in the sense in which the term is used in international relations theory. Chapters 4–6 are evaluations of the legitimacy of the attempts to prosecute international crimes from the point of view of legitimacy and the rule of law. This evaluation focuses on critiques of selective enforcement of the law, from both the point of view of whom is prosecuted (chapter 4) and how expansive a view of the ambit of international criminality is taken (chapters 5–6). In these chapters the Nuremberg and Tokyo IMTs are evaluated alongside the ICTY, ICTR, ICC and Special Court for Sierra Leone, as they provided the foundations of the international criminal law regime which became more solid in the 1990s, and critiques of those tribunals were at the forefront of the minds of the creators of that regime. We shall see the extent to which the architects of the modern regime managed to avoid the problems identified in relation to what had gone before.

Much of what follows is critical of aspects of the regime. This is not because I am unhappy such a regime exists; on the contrary I agree fully with Gerry Simpson that 'an international war crimes regime founded on a concern for consistency, legality and impartiality would be

Agreement: Peace Versus Justice?' (1997) 4 IP 91; Lisa Schmandt, 'Peace With Justice: Is It Possible for Former Yugoslavia?' (1995) 30 TILJ 335; Payam Akhavan, 'The Yugoslav Tribunal at a Crossroads: The Dayton Peace Agreement and Beyond' (1996) 18 HRQ 259; Payam Akhavan, 'Can International Criminal Justice Prevent Future Atrocities?' (2001) 85 AJIL 7; W. Michael Reisman, 'Institutions and Practices for Restoring and Maintaining Public Order' (1995) 6 DJCIL 175; Ruti Teitel, *Transitional Justice* (New York: Oxford University Press, 2000); Neil J. Kritz, *Transitional Justice: How Emerging Democracies Reckon With Former Regimes* (Washington, DC: US Institute of Peace, 1995).

a valuable addition to the international legal system'.[20] My critique of the international criminal law regime is born not of a desire to undermine the regime, but to ask what it could have been, and might still be.

[20] Gerry J. Simpson, 'War Crimes, A Critical Introduction', in Gerry J. Simpson and Timothy L. H. McCormack (eds.), *The Law of War Crimes: National and International Approaches* (The Hague: Kluwer, 1997), p. 1, p. 3.

Part I The development of the international criminal law regime

1 The development of international criminal law

Introduction

This chapter will trace the development of international criminal law and its enforcement mechanisms. Writing on the development of international criminal law after 1998 carries with it certain risks. It is all too simple to write a 'Whig history'.[1] Such a tale would be inaccurate. We cannot forget the role of contingency and pure chance. Had different choices been made in the twentieth century the situation could be considerably different, for better or for worse. Nonetheless, developments in international criminal law have occurred since the 1990s at a pace that is unprecedented.

There are a number of histories of international criminal law.[2] It could be said that there is a small academic cottage industry engaged in discovering earlier and earlier examples of what might be termed prosecutions of international crimes. The greatest endeavours in this regard were those of Georg Schwarzenberger.[3] There is a particular reason for discussing the historical aspects of international criminal law. Many of

[1] In more modern, albeit less evocative, terms, construct a linear progress narrative. As Martti Koskenniemi notes, the popularity of the title 'From Nuremberg to the Hague' in writings reflects the attractions of the progress narrative in international criminal law, Martti Koskenniemi, 'Between Impunity and Show Trials' (2002) 6 MPYBUNL 1, 34–5.

[2] For examples see Timothy L. H. McCormack, 'From Sun Tzu to the Sixth Committee: The Evolution of an International Criminal Law Regime', in Timothy L. H. McCormack and Gerry J. Simpson (eds.), *The Law of War Crimes: National and International Approaches* (The Hague: Kluwer, 1997), p. 31; M. Cherif Bassiouni, 'From Versailles to Rwanda in Seventy-Five Years: The Need to Establish an International Criminal Court' (1997) 10 Harvard HRLJ 11; Howard Levie, *Terrorism in War: The Law of War Crimes* (New York: Oceana, 1992), chapter 1.

[3] Beginning with 'The Breisach War Crimes Trial of 1474', *Guardian (Manchester)*, 23 September 1946, and continuing with Georg Schwarzenberger, 'The Judgment of Nuremberg' (1947) 21 Tulane LR 329, 329–31.

the problems, debates and solutions mooted are by no means novel. To proceed today in ignorance of what has been identified and discussed before is needlessly to retrace the footprints of the past.

Nonetheless, this chapter makes no claim to comprehensiveness. Neither is it a history of the laws of armed conflict. Others have told that story.[4] A third qualification is that the author is a lawyer, not a historian, and therefore this chapter cannot profess historiographic sophistication.[5] Instead, by an analysis of the history of international criminal law it is hoped to cast some light on the development of the subject, and the perennial nature of some of the questions surrounding it.

A final caveat before moving on to history: much of what follows is, until the twentieth century, focused primarily on developments in Europe. This is not because of a conscious or (it is hoped) unconscious Eurocentrism. Histories of international law have rightly been criticised for an excessive focus on Europe.[6] There is some merit in such critiques.[7] The law of armed conflict has a cosmopolitan history.[8] The history of international criminal law is also not solely European.[9] It is not fully the case that '[m]ost of the modern law of war relating to the repression of war criminality has evolved, historically, in a European setting . . . though borrowing, substantially, from Koranic law through long and close contact with the Moslem civilisation . . . the law relating to war criminality owes most to the ethos of mediaeval Christendom'.[10] Nonetheless, much of the literature, in English at least, does tend to focus on Europe. An attempt will be made to refer to developments

4 Geoffrey Best, *Humanity in Warfare: The Modern History of the International Law of Armed Conflicts* (London: Methuen, 1983); Geoffrey Best, *War and Law Since 1945* (Oxford: Oxford University Press, 1994).

5 International lawyers are not necessarily good historians, see Best, *Humanity*, pp. 27–8. For modern developments in international legal historiography, see Ingo J. Hueck, 'The Discipline of the History in International Law: New Trends and Methods in the History of International Law' (2001) 3 JHIL 194.

6 See Yasuaki Onuma, 'When was the Law of International Society Born? An Inquiry into the History of International Law From an Intercivilisational Perspective' (2000) 2 JHIL 1.

7 There is little about the extra-European world in the standard history of international law. Arthur Nussbaum, *A Concise History of the Law of Nations* (New York: Macmillan, revised edn., 1954).

8 See, generally, Hilaire McCoubrey, *International Humanitarian Law* (Aldershot, Ashgate, 2nd edn., 1998), pp. 8–17; Leslie C. Green, *The Contemporary Law of Armed Conflict* (Manchester: Manchester University Press, 2nd edn., 2000), pp. 20–2; Surya Subedi, 'The Concept in Hinduism of Just War' (2003) 8 JCSL 239.

9 There have been attempts, for example, to conceptualise an Islamic international criminal law. Farhad Malekian, *The Concept of Islamic International Criminal Law: A Comparative Study* (London: Graham & Trotman, 1994).

10 Gerald I. A. D. Draper, 'The Modern Pattern of War Criminality' (1976) 6 IYBHR 9, 10.

outside Europe, although this will necessarily be limited by the availability of material dealing with such developments. That said, the time for qualifications is over: it is apposite to proceed to matters of substance.

Antiquity

This is roughly the period prior to the fifth–sixth century BCE. In the empires of Egypt, Babylon, Assyria and that of the Hittites (1400–1150 BCE) there was restraint on warfare.[11] There is also evidence of limits on combat in the Christian Old Testament.[12] Nonetheless, as with most forms of religiously based law at the time, the form of sanction remained more divine than earthly. If the tale of Wen-Amon is taken as indicative of concepts of jurisdiction over crime, then no clear concept of overarching criminal rules comparable to international criminal law can be seen.[13] The events recounted by Wen-Amon in a papyrus found in Egypt and dating back to *c.*1000 BCE relate to a disagreement between that writer and the Prince of Dor over authority to prosecute actions by foreigners on a foreign ship. The tension between the vision of international society as one composed of bounded entities and one in which there is a global community with values and a common criminal law is one that continues to this day, and has characterised debate about the International Criminal Court (ICC).[14]

Further to the East, possible analogues to international criminal law have been thought traceable to Confucionist thought in the fifth century BCE. Although Mencius and Motzu (both disciples of Confucius) spoke in the language of criminality in relation to unjust wars, it appears that neither had a legal concept of crime in mind.[15] The indiscriminate use of the potent rhetoric of crime (in particular, international crime) remains popular to this day.[16]

[11] David J. Bederman, *International Law in Antiquity* (Cambridge: Cambridge University Press, 2001), esp. chapter 1, pp. 242–63.

[12] *Ibid.*, pp. 244–6; Leslie C. Green, 'The Judaic Contribution to Human Rights' (1990) 28 CYBIL 3, 20–2.

[13] This forms the basis of the argument in Alfred P. Rubin, *Ethics and Authority in International Law* (Cambridge: Cambridge University Press, 1997), pp. 1–4.

[14] See Bruce Broomhall, *International Justice and the International Criminal Court: Between Sovereignty and the Rule of Law* (Oxford: Oxford University Press, 2003); Frederic Mégret, 'Epilogue to an Endless Debate: The International Court's Third Party Jurisdiction and the Looming Revolution of International Law' (2001) 12 EJIL 247.

[15] Keishiro Iriye, 'The Principles of International Law in the Light of Confucian Doctrine' (1967–I) 120 RdC 1, 50–1.

[16] For a critical analysis of this trend, see William A. Schabas, *Genocide in International Law: The Crime of Crimes* (Cambridge: Cambridge University Press, 2000), pp. 9–11.

Ancient Greece

One important development with contemporary resonance occurred in classical Greece. This is the purported universality of the laws of war asserted by Xenophon.[17] There is little evidence that prior to this time (fifth century BCE) this concept was a feature of thinking about crime. The concept of the universal applicability of international criminal law is now a commonplace assumption.

Xenophon also reports the earliest process referred to expressly as a precedent for modern international criminal law. This was the treatment of Athenian prisoners captured after they fell into the hands of the victorious Spartan commander, Lysander.[18] The Athenian prisoners were accused of having committed and planned various violations of the (Greek) law of war such as cutting off the hands of Spartan prisoners and throwing those prisoners into the sea. Lysander drew together those allied against the Athenians, and it was decided to execute all Lysander's prisoners, except for Adeimantos, either for the reason that he refused to support the order to cut off prisoners' hands[19] or he had betrayed the Athenians to the Spartans.[20] This indicates a problem with over-reading this action as a precedent. The facts remain heavily contested, and it remains questionable if the disposition of the cases could really be considered a judicial one.[21] The bringing together of allies at the end of a conflict to determine the fate of their captured enemies, nonetheless, has relevance in international criminal law, being repeated after the Second World War.

Ancient India

It has been said that there were the functional equivalents of war crimes trials undertaken by States in Ancient India. Evidence for this may be found in the Maharabharata, which said that violators of the law of war were classed as outcasts and stripped of privileges.[22] Further details

[17] Xenophon, *Hellenica, Anabasis, Cyropaedia* (Cambridge, MA: Harvard University Press, 1932), p. 293, cited in Bederman, *International Law in Antiquity*, p. 246. McCormack refers to Herodotus' *History* for such a point; McCormack, 'From Sun Tzu' p. 33.

[18] G. Maridakes, 'Un precécedent du Procès du Nuremberg tiré de l'histoire de la Grèce ancienne' (1952) 5 Revue Hellénique de Droit International 1, cited in McCormack, 'From Sun Tzu', p. 33.

[19] McCormack, *ibid.*

[20] Kraske, 'Klassiches Hellas und Nurnberger Prozess' (1953–1954) 4 *Archiv de Völkerrechts* 183, pp. 183–9, cited in Robert K. Woetzel, *The Nuremberg Trials in International Law* (New York: Praeger, 1960), pp. 18–19.

[21] *Ibid.*

[22] See K. R. R. Sastry, 'Hinduism and International Law' (1966–I) 117 RdC 502, 570–1, citing Mahabharata, Santi-Parva, 9.6–9.10.

remain scant.[23] As with all the above, these are not legal precedents.[24] The idea that international law in the modern sense is traceable back to ancient society is highly questionable.[25]

The Middle Ages

Religious approaches

The Articles of War promulgated by the Roman Emperor Maurice in the 6th century CE not only contained prohibitions on the methods of war, but also graded punishments for their violation.[26] There are restraints on the waging of war contained in the Koran, which have been interpreted to mean that there are obligations on commanders to mete out punishments.[27] Again, evidence is scant in relation to the application of those penalties.[28] Still, the responsibility of commanders in relation to the conduct of their troops is something that has been a constant theme of what we now consider international criminal law.[29]

The religious connection to punishment for violations of the limits on war making was also present in the Christian world. By the ninth century CE, the use of penitential books and decrees was fairly widespread in Northern Europe. These were lists of peoples' sins, along with the penance that they were required to undergo to expiate those sins.[30] As early as the late seventh century CE, in the Penitential of Theodore, Archbishop of Canterbury, we can see discussions of superior orders.[31] There were penitential decrees issued after the Battle of Soissons (923) and the Battle of Hastings (1066).[32] The first decree, issued in 924, applied to both sides in the conflict and thus stands out as a comparatively rare

[23] There is no mention of this aspect of the Mahabharata in the section on the laws of war in C. Joseph Chacko, 'India's Contribution to International Law' (1958–I) 93 RdC 117, 135–42.

[24] William S. Armour, 'Customs of Warfare in Ancient India' (1922) 8 TGS 71, 83–84.

[25] Bederman, *Antiquity*, p. 4.

[26] McCormack, 'From Sun Tzu', pp. 35–6.

[27] See Sobhi Mahmassani, 'International Law in Light of Islamic Doctrine' (1966–I) 117 RdC 201, 295.

[28] McCormack, 'From Sun Tzu', p. 36.

[29] W. Hays Parks, 'Command Responsibility for War Crimes' (1973) 62 Military LR 1.

[30] Gerald I. A. D. Draper 'Penitential Discipline and Public Wars in the Middle Ages', in Michael A. Meyer and Hilaire McCoubrey (eds.), *Reflections on Law and Armed Conflicts: Selected Works on the Laws of War by the late Professor Colonel G. I. A. D. Draper, OBE* (The Hague: Kluwer, 1998), p. 20.

[31] Draper, 'Penitential Discipline', p. 23.

[32] See Gerald I. A. D. Draper, 'The Penitential Decrees and the Battles of Soissons and Hastings', in Michael A. Meyer and Hilaire McCoubrey (eds.), *Reflections on Law and Armed Conflicts: Selected Works on the Laws of War by the late Professor Colonel G. I. A. D. Draper, OBE* (The Hague: Kluwer, 1998), p. 26.

example of impartiality in the selection of those deserving of punishment. It seems unlikely that a similarly objective approach would have been taken if the battle had been between Christians and non-Christians, though.

The events in and following the Battle of Hastings included not only conflict between combatants of considerable savagery, but also killings, devastation, despoliation and also rape of the civilian population until 1070. In that year, the Norman bishops issued penitential decrees demanding penance of those who had fought under William the Conqueror. This contrasting decree, which imposed penance on the victors alone (an inversion of the 'victor's justice' argument) may be explained by the possibility that the bishops thought 'the miseries of the defeated Saxons were sufficiently great without the added impositions of penance'.[33] Or it could have reflected the politics of the church at the time.[34] Since the penitentials, as did the Islamic system, relied on parochial visions of the world, they cannot be considered universal, even though the substantive principles were similar.

By the thirteenth–fourteenth century, we can begin to see an increase in the use of penal sanctions for violations of the laws of war. The laws of war at this time were almost entirely based on national laws, such as John's Constitutions to be Made in the Army of 1215.[35] Fifty-three years later, in 1268, we encounter a proceeding sometimes claimed as an early trial for what might now be termed 'aggression', then described in terms of beginning an 'unjust war'. This is the trial and execution of Prince Conradin von Hohenstaufen by Charles of Anjou.[36] However, in fact, the trial was for waging war as a rebel, closer to treason than aggression. It is also questionable if the proceedings deserve to be called a trial.[37]

The law of arms

Somewhere around this time, certainly by the fourteenth century, the closest analogue to modern international criminal law, the enforcement

[33] Draper, 'Penitential Decrees', p. 32. [34] Draper, 'Penitential Decrees', p. 32.

[35] Theodor Meron, 'Medieval and Renaissance Ordinances of War: Codifying Discipline and Humanity', in Theodor Meron, *War Crimes Law Comes of Age* (Oxford: Oxford University Press, 1998), p. 1, pp. 1–2. The Statute of Westminster 1279 allowed for punishment of 'soldiers according to the laws and customs of the realm', see McCormack, 'From Sun Tzu', p. 37.

[36] It is cited as such in M.Cherif Bassiouni, *Crimes Against Humanity in International Criminal Law* (The Hague: Kluwer, 2nd rev. edn., 1999), p. 517.

[37] Schwarzenberger, 'The Judgement of Nuremberg', 329–30, although Gentili was more sanguine; Alberico Gentili, J. Rolfe (trans.), *Three Books on the Law of War* (Washington: Carnegie Institute of International Peace, 1933), p. 323.

of the laws of war through the laws of arms, or *jus militare*, developed.[38] Direct parallels between what we now consider international law and the pre-1648 law of nations should not be drawn uncritically. The two sets of laws are based on different conceptual frameworks.[39] Nor should an excessively dewy-eyed view of the law of arms, and its parent, the law of chivalry, be taken. As Theodor Meron has rightly pointed out: '[c]hivalry had many formal, vain and excessive aspects . . . often based on exaggerated notions of honour.'[40] Also the law of chivalry did not make for humane wars.[41] Nonetheless, this period was vastly influential in the formation of the law of war crimes, and the law then and now has considerable overlaps.

The first and most important of these is that there was a return to a conception of the law that applied beyond national or allegiance-based boundaries. Drawing upon Roman ideas of *jus gentium*, the law common to all countries, the early theorists of the law of arms, such as John of Legano, considered that the law of arms applied throughout Christendom.[42] In this concept of expanded application is an early, partial, analogue to the idea of the universal applicability of international criminal law.

In coming to these conclusions much can be gleaned from two cases, the dispute between the Black Prince and the Marshal d'Audreham and the trial of the Seigneur de Barbasan by Henry V.[43] The former case, which dealt with violation of parole by a prisoner of war, was heard before a panel of twelve knights in 1367. His acquittal, on grounds of the technical rules of parole, was treated as a precedent in other States.[44] The later trial of Barbasan, in 1420, before Henry V for the murder of John the Fearless, is very interesting. The act was described by Keen as 'tantamount to a war crime'.[45] Also Barbasan did not owe allegiance to Henry, showing the enforceability of the law beyond the normal ties of allegiance;[46] the law applied to all knights. Secondly, Barbasan appealed

[38] Maurice H. Keen, *The Laws of War in the Late Middle Ages* (London: Keegan Paul, 1965), chapter 1.

[39] See David Kennedy, 'Primitive Legal Scholarship' (1986) 27 Harvard ILJ 1, 1–7.

[40] Theodor Meron, *Bloody Constraint: Crimes and Accountability in Shakespeare* (New York: Oxford University Press, 1998), p. 6.

[41] For a particularly critical view, see Amos S. Hershey, 'The History of International Relations During Antiquity and the Middle Ages' (1911) 5 AJIL 901, 927.

[42] Keen, *The Laws of War*, pp. 7–19.

[43] Keen, *The Laws of War*, pp. 48–54.

[44] Keen, *The Laws of War*, pp. 52–3.

[45] Keen, *The Laws of War*, p. 50.

[46] Jurisdiction being based at the time on allegiance rather than territoriality; see Malcolm Shaw, 'Territory in International Law' (1982) 13 NYBIL 61, 62.

his sentence successfully to an international panel of heralds, experts in chivalric lore.

The herald's judgment bound Henry, not as a sovereign, but as a knight.[47] Yet it showed that 'in war the rules of honour applied universally . . . [in Christendom] . . . binding princes and men at arms equally. Offences against those rules could therefore be tried by anyone who had a right to try the offences of soldiers, whatever the offender's allegiance.'[48] This is an interesting precursor to the Nuremberg IMT's statement that 'individuals have international duties which transcend the national obligations of obedience imposed by the individual State'.[49] It might be objected that at the time, the law applied only to a limited class of fighters rather than to all people. The idea that war crimes may be committed only by limited classes of people endured until recently.[50]

There were some institutional developments at this time. One was the introduction of joint commissions where, in an attempt to ensure impartiality in a truce, both parties would agree that disputes (which appeared to be criminal in nature) would be adjudicated upon by joint panels. An example of this was the 1453 Austro-Burgundian truce. This created a system by which a group of five judges was to be empanelled, two by the plaintiff, three by the defendant, to ensure at least the perception of impartiality.[51] The Nuremberg IMT was criticised by some for failing to appoint a German judge.[52] Similar considerations have informed the discussions on the mixed composition of tribunals for the prosecution of the remainder of the Khmer Rouge responsible for international crimes in Cambodia.[53]

The similarities with modern international criminal law enforcement do not end here.[54] Although joint (or at times fully third-party)

[47] Keen, *The Laws of War*, p. 50.

[48] Keen, *The Laws of War*, p. 53. Meron, *Bloody Constraint*, p. 6, states that the 'system was quite international'.

[49] 'Nuremberg IMT, Judgment and Sentence' (1947) 41 AJIL 172, 221.

[50] *Prosecutor* v. *Akayesu*, Judgment, ICTR-96-4-A, 1 June 2001, para. 435.

[51] Keen, *The Laws of War*, p. 38.

[52] Hans Ehard, 'The Nuremberg Trial Against the Major War Criminals and International Law' (1949) 46 AJIL 223, 243. See also Leo Gross, 'The Punishment of War Criminals: The Nuremberg Trial', in Leo Gross (ed.), *Selected Essays on International Law and Organisation* (Ardsley, Transnational, 1984), p. 133, p. 142.

[53] On the early debates, see Suzannah Linton, 'Cambodia, East Timor and Sierra Leone, Experiments in International Criminal Justice' (2001) 12 CLF 185, 187–202; Aaron J. Buckley, 'The Conflict in Cambodia and Post-Conflict Justice', in M. Cherif Bassiouni (ed.), *Post Conflict Justice* (Ardsley: Transnational, 2002), p. 635.

[54] Keen, *The Laws of War*, p. 38.

commissions had considerable powers to issue binding decisions, they had no powers to enforce those judgments, orders and awards. That authority was retained by the contesting powers.[55] *Plus ça change*. It is difficult to read of these commissions and not be reminded of Antonio Cassese's comment about the ICTY, that it 'remains very much like a giant without arms and legs – it needs artificial limbs to walk and work. And these artificial limbs are state authorities. If the cooperation of States is not forthcoming, the ICTY cannot fulfil its functions.'[56] Similar comments could be made about the ICC regime. The ICC has to work almost solely through the mediation of domestic legal systems.

The von Hagenbach trial

This brings us to what is one of the most famous trials (to international criminal lawyers) before the twentieth century.[57] This is the trial of Peter von Hagenbach. The case arose from an occupation of the Burgundian city of Breisach, which had been pledged to Charles the Bold as security for a loan of 100,000 gold florins by Sigismund, the Archduke of Austria. Charles appointed von Hagenbach as governor, and proceeded to attempt to annex Breiasch. Von Hagenbach imposed a regime on the area 'which shocked even the by no means over-tender sensibilities of late medieval Europe'.[58]

After five years of suffering his regime, and after complaints, *inter alia*, to Frederick III and Charles, a coalition rose against von Hagenbach. He was tried on 9 May 1474 in Breisach's marketplace. The trial was before a panel of twenty-eight judges, appointed by allied towns who had fought Charles and von Hagenbach. Archduke Sigimund appointed the presiding judge and prosecutor. At the trial, von Hagenbach was convicted, stripped of his knighthood and sentenced to death,[59] the sentence being carried out in front of a large crowd.

[55] Keen, *The Laws of War*, pp. 38–9.

[56] Antonio Cassese, 'On the Current Trends Towards Criminal Prosecution and Punishment of Breaches of International Humanitarian Law' (1998) 9 EJIL 2, 13.

[57] The standard reference for international criminal lawyers remains Georg Schwarzenberger, *International Law as Applied by International Courts and Tribunals, II: The Law of Armed Conflict* (London: Stevens & Sons, 1968), chapter 39. See also Richard Vaughan, *Charles the Bold: The Last Valois Duke of Burgundy* (London: Longman, 1973), esp. pp. 268–86.

[58] Hilaire McCoubrey, 'War Crimes Jurisdiction and a Permanent International Criminal Court: Advantages and Difficulties' (1998) 3 JACL 9, 11.

[59] Vaughan states '[t]he execution was resolved on first; the trial was a mere formality'; *Charles the Bold*, p. 284.

Timothy McCormack criticises the 'tendency by some commentators to make too much of the Hagenbach trial by characterising it without qualification as the "first international war crimes trial" and then relying on it as an international legal precedent for more contemporary developments'.[60] Discussion of the von Hagenbach trial often comes with the musty smell of antiquarianism. As McCormack points out, there are questions as to the international nature of the tribunal, and whether von Hagenbach's acts can be analogised to war crimes or crimes against humanity.[61] Schwarzenberger was mindful of these problems.[62] Others have not been so careful.[63]

Perhaps the largest problem with drawing direct precedential value from the trial[64] is that the law was not 'international' in the way we now see international law.[65] It is possible that the trial was conducted pursuant to the law of arms. After all, von Hagenbach was stripped of his knighthood prior to his execution, and there was considerable discussion of oaths at the trial.[66] Yet there is evidence to point that the law used was imperial law. The first charge upon which he was tried (beheading three or four Thann citizens on 3 July 1473) was expressly based on the law of the Holy Roman Empire.[67] It may also be that in terms of the definition of the offences, little store was put on precisely which law was to be used, as his guilt was pre-ordained.[68] Either way, the law used was certainly not international law in the modern sense.

Nevertheless, there are a number of aspects of the trial of von Hagenbach that indicate many of the arguments and claims made today in relation to international criminal law are of long standing. The first of these is that the various allies had various different ideas about what

60 McCormack, 'From Sun Tzu', p. 38. Schwarzenberger occasionally falls into this trap, see *International Law*, pp. 516–17.

61 McCormack, 'From Sun Tzu', p. 38. See also Hilaire McCoubrey, 'The Concept and Treatment of War Crimes' (1996) 1 JACL 121, 123 and Woetzel, *The Nuremberg Trials*, pp. 19–21.

62 Schwarzenberger, *International Law*, pp. 463–6.

63 See, for example Justice Norman Birkett, 'International Legal Theories Evolved at Nuremberg' (1947) 23, IA 317, 317. Birkett was one of the judges at the Nuremberg IMT.

64 Which, according to Levie, *Terrorism in War*, p. 11, the US Chief of Counsel for War Crimes did. It was also, as Levie notes, cited in the judgment of *US* v. *von Leeb* (the *High Command Trial*) 11 TWC 1, 476.

65 McCormack, 'From Sun Tzu', p. 38.

66 McCoubrey, 'War Crimes Jurisdiction', p. 11.

67 Vaughan, *Charles the Bold*, p. 285.

68 Vaughan, *Charles the Bold*, pp. 284, 285, describes the trial as 'a mere formality' and a 'beastly ritual'.

should be done with von Hagenbach. The authorities in Breisach, where he was being held, were willing to hand him over to Charles to prosecute him. Those in Berne, however, where many of von Hagenbach's offences had occurred, wanted to arrange his trial and punishment themselves.[69]

The question of disagreement among allies as to how to deal with captured enemies who are suspected of international offences is a continuing theme in international criminal law, and one to which we shall return. The question arose in particular in relation to the First and Second World Wars,[70] but has also recently been raised in relation to those detained at Guantánamo Bay in Cuba by the United States, some of whom are to be prosecuted for international offences.[71] Other States allied to the United States have suggested that they be sent to their country of nationality for trial. The United States has rejected these calls, preferring to keep control of any trial processes.

The flip side of this sort of debate about the correct venue for trying those suspected of international crimes also has a historical echo in the von Hagenbach trial. Part of his defence was that he did not recognise any other judge but the Duke of Burgundy.[72] The tactic of denying the legitimacy of the tribunal, and claiming that it has no right to try the defendant, is one which has been repeated regularly in international trials and forms a staple of Slobodan Milošević's defence before the ICTY.[73] The more specialised form of this claim, made by von Hagenbach, was that the only person appropriate to convoke a tribunal to try him would be Charles, as the person to whom von Hagenbach owed allegiance. A similar plea, *jus de non evocando*, was raised in the *Prosecutor* v. *Tadić* Interlocutory Appeal. There, the defence suggested that there was a human right to be tried in front of a home court. The plea was, unsurprisingly, unsuccessful.[74] Similar arguments underlie much of the US opposition to the ICC.[75]

[69] Vaughan, *Charles the Bold*, p. 284. [70] See below, pp. 36–42.

[71] See Ruth Wedgwood, 'Al Qaeda, Terrorism and Military Commissions' (2002) 96 AJIL 328; Harold H. Koh, 'The Case Against Military Commissions' (2002) 96 AJIL 337.

[72] Schwarzenberger, *International Law*, p. 465.

[73] See, for example, *Prosecutor* v. *Milošević*, Decision on Preliminary Motions, IT-99-37-T, 8 November 2001, paras. 5–17; Koskenniemi, 'Between Impunity', 1.

[74] See *Prosecutor* v. *Tadić*, Decision on Interlocutory Appeal on Jurisdiction, IT-94-1-AR72, 2 October 1995, paras. 61–64; José E. Alvarez, 'Nuremberg Revisited: The *Tadić* Case' (1996) 7 EJIL 245, 258–9.

[75] This point is also made by Don Murray, 'Judge and Master', CBS, News Viewpoint, 18 July 2002, available at http//:www.cbc.ca/news/viewpoint/vp_murray/20020718.html.

One of the most commented-on parallels between the von Hagenbach trial and more modern trials of international crimes is that of superior orders.[76] In von Hagenbach's defence, Hans Irmy declared '[h]e had no right to question the orders which he was charged to carry out, and it was his duty to obey'.[77] The question of superior orders is one which continues to raise difficulties and controversy.[78]

The issue of superior orders in the von Hagenbach trial raises an issue which will be discussed in greater depth later. This is the law and politics of obtaining co-operation on evidence from abroad. Von Hagenbach had requested that the tribunal adjourn so he could seek Charles' evidence that he had, indeed, been acting under orders. This request was refused.[79] It may have been that such evidence would not have been forthcoming, von Hagenbach sometimes went beyond his orders[80] and Charles had left von Hagenbach high and dry before.[81] Still, the point is an important one, and a tribunal that does not do its best to assist a defendant obtain access to relevant materials runs the risk of being seen as weighted towards the prosecution. Such claims were made in the *Tadić* Case,[82] although they were not accepted by the ICTY. The evidential regime set up by the ICC Statute may make it difficult to obtain certain types of evidence.

The final aspect of this is *tu quoque*. The defence has never been accepted in an international tribunal as a legal defence *per se*.[83] Perhaps the closest this claim has got to being considered law was Grotius' *The Rights of War and Peace*, where it is said that any person duly authorised may try offences so far as they are not responsible for similar offences

[76] Schwarzenberger, *International Law*, pp. 465–6; Birkett, 'International Legal Theories', 317. The von Hagenbach trial was not the first airing of these issues, see, for example, Honoré Bonet (G. W. Coupland trans.), *The Tree of Battles* (Cambridge, MA: Harvard University Press, 1949 originally 1386), pp. 169–70. Superior orders were also mentioned in penitential decrees nearly 400 years before Bonet.

[77] Schwarzenberger, *International Law*, p. 465. [78] See below, pp. 292–301.

[79] Schwarzenberger, *International Law*, p. 465.

[80] See Vaughan, *Charles the Bold*, pp. 98, 99, 265, 271. This is also the implication of the memoirs of Phillippe de Commynes, S. Kinser (ed.), I. Cazeaux (trans.), *The Memoirs of Phillippe de Commynes* (Columbia: University of South Carolina Press, 1969), p. 300. Equally, Commynes is not always accurate in his discussion of these matters, having clear sympathy for Charles; *ibid.*, p. 176 and (editor's) n 57.

[81] Vaughan, *Charles the Bold*, p. 255.

[82] *Prosecutor* v. *Tadić*, Judgment, IT-94-1-A, 15 July 1999, paras. 29–55. See generally Gabrielle Mcintyre, 'Equality of Arms – Defining Human Rights in the Jurisprudence of the International Criminal Tribunal for the former Yugoslavia' (2003) 16 LJIL 269.

[83] Although the Nuremberg IMT came close, in relation to Admiral Dönitz, to accepting a cognate plea, see below, pp. 200–1.

themselves.[84] Practice has not borne this out.[85] Also, Grotius' ideas here come from his rather idiosyncratic view of how authority to punish is grounded.[86] Finally, it is questionable if Grotius intended this to apply to prosecutions by States.[87]

To return to von Hagenbach, in relation to the claim that he had 'outraged married women, virgins and even nuns', von Hagenbach replied that he 'had only done what many others in the courtroom had done, paying good money for it'.[88] The tribunal did not accept this claim.

It would be wrong to assert that the von Hagenbach trial has any precedential value in the legal sense. It does not. But many of the facts, arguments and claims surrounding the proceedings are ones which have shown remarkable longevity. That is not to say that they are necessarily intractable, but that they are older than is sometimes thought.

The end of the age of chivalry and the 'classical' period of the law of nations

Not long after the von Hagenbach trial, the system of chivalry began its inevitable decline. By 1500, the age of chivalry was dying, even if the law of arms was not quite dead.[89] The law of arms relied on a common religious outlook, the ideals of a particular style of fighting and a concept of filial obligation to other members of the fighting class of knights. It could not survive the age of religious schism, the development of new weaponry and the increasing proletarianisation of fighting forces.[90] That

[84] Hugo Grotius, A. C. Campbell (trans.), *The Rights of War and Peace* (London: M. Walter Hill, 1901), p. 226.

[85] Equally it was only after Grotius (1583–1645) that a fuller concentration on State practice became the more accepted form of international legal analysis. See Hersch Lauterpacht, 'The Grotian Tradition in International Law' (1946) 23 BYBIL 1, 4–5; Nussbaum, *A Concise History*, pp. 164–74.

[86] See Takashi Furukawa, 'Punishment', in Yasuaki Onuma (ed.), *A Normative Approach to War: Peace, War and Justice in Hugo Grotius* (Oxford: Clarendon, 1993), p. 221, pp. 224–5.

[87] Grotius, *The Rights of War and Peace*, p. 247; see Quincy Wright, 'The Law of The Nuremberg Trial' (1947) 41 AJIL 38, 46.

[88] Vaughan, *Charles the Bold*, p. 285. It is possible here that he was claiming that he had committed no crime, as what he and others had done was paid for prostitutes. Given his shocking and infamous treatment of women (*ibid.*, p. 283), either way von Hagenbach's plea seems highly unlikely.

[89] See Robert C. Stacey, 'The Age of Chivalry', in Michael Howard, George J. Andreopoulos and Mark Schulman (eds.), *The Laws of War: Constraints on Warfare in the Western World* (New Haven: Yale University Press, 1994), p. 27, p. 27.

[90] Meron, *Bloody Constraint*, pp. 6–7. This is not to say that non-knights did not engage in fighting prior to this date (Stacey, 'Age of Chivalry', p. 30), but that they had become the dominant part of fighting forces by this time.

is not to say that the laws of war disappeared. Indeed, many of the foundational principles of those laws arose during the period 1550–1700.[91]

Doctrine

The start of the sixteenth century was the era of great writers on the law of war, in particular Vitoria,[92] Ayala,[93] Belli,[94] Gentili[95] and, of course, Grotius.[96] These writers exercised a considerable influence on the doctrine of international law, although it is less certain how much they affected practice.[97] It should also be said that their views on what was permitted to a victorious belligerent, and generally by the laws of war, was very broad, providing little actual restraint.[98] Beginning with Vitoria, and going through to Grotius though, we must be very careful about drawing glib analogies between their ideas about law and modern international criminal law. Their underlying ideas about law were highly different to those prevalent in the post-Vattelian legal order.[99]

Some, including Sir Hersch Lauterpacht, claim to be able to trace international criminal law back to Vitoria.[100] However, the idea that there is a specific criminal phase in the Vitorian conception of international law takes things too far. Vitoria viewed a prince waging war as a judge.[101]

91 Geoffrey Parker, 'Early Modern Europe', in Michael Howard, George J. Andreopoulos and Mark Schulman (eds.), *The Laws of War: Constraints on Welfare in the Western World* (New Haven: Yale University press, 1994), p. 40, p. 41.

92 See Francisco de Victoria, John P. Bate (trans.), *De Indis et de Iure Belli Relectiones* (Washington, DC: Carnegie Institute for International Peace, 1917). For a very sympathetic treatment of Vitoria and the law of war, see James B. Scott, *The Spanish Origins of International Law I: Francisco de Vitoria and his Law of Nations* (Oxford: Clarendon, 1934), pp. 195–241.

93 See Baltasar Ayala, John P. Bate (trans.), *Three Books on the Law of War and on the Duties Connected with War and on Military Discipline* (Washington, DC: Carnegie Institute for International Peace, 1912).

94 See Pierini Belli, Herbert C. Nutting (trans.), *A Treatise on Military Matters and Warfare* (Oxford: Clarendon, 1936).

95 See Alberico Gentili, James C. Rolfe (trans.), *De Iure Belli Libri Tres* (Oxford: Clarendon, 1933).

96 Grotius, *The Rights of War and Peace*; see Gerald I. A. D. Draper, 'Grotius' Place in the Development of Legal Ideas About War', in Hedley Bull, Benedict Kingsbury and Adam Roberts (eds.), *Hugo Grotius and International Relations* (Oxford: Clarendon, 1990), p. 177.

97 Bederman, for example, thinks that Vattel had a greater impact on practice than Grotius; David J. Bederman, *International Law Frameworks* (New York: Foundation Press, 2001), pp. 3–4.

98 See Lauterpacht, 'The Grotian Tradition', 11–12; Scott, *The Spanish Origins*, p. 197.

99 See Kennedy, 'Primitive Legal Scholarship', *passim*.

100 Hersch Lauterpacht, 'The Law of Nations and the Punishment of War Crimes' (1944) 21 BYBIL 58, 61.

101 Scott, *The Spanish Origins*, p. 210, see also Kennedy, 'Primitive International Law', 31–40.

Even James Brown Scott saw this as a fiction.[102] Still, the idea that a victor is the judge is the underlying basis of 'victor's justice' claims today.

It could be thought that a prototype of international criminal law could be found in the works of Alberico Gentili. At times, Gentili may imply criminality in the law of nations. He cites Paolo Giovanni's description of Salassus' order to kill Spanish surrenderees as a 'crime' with considerable approval.[103] However, there is no clear discussion of the nature of criminality and there is no distinction between national and international law in his work.[104] As a result, it is difficult to draw broad conclusions from Gentili about the development of law.

Similar considerations to those applicable to Vitoria may apply to some of Grotius' writings. Grotius writes, in a phrase that could easily be taken to refer to an incipient form of international criminal law,[105] '[i]t is proper to observe that kings and those who are possessed of sovereign power have a right to exact punishment not only for injuries affecting immediately themselves or their own subjects, but also for gross violations of the law of nature and of nations, done to other states and subjects'.[106] Again, though, we have the problem that his concept of punishment is not one of criminal responsibility here. It is clear that for Grotius in this instance the punishment is the 'punishment of hostilities'; a just war may be entered into against the malefactors.[107]

Lauterpacht places Grotius alongside Vitoria as one of the founders of international criminal law, on the basis of his statement that 'in order to warrant their [PoWs'] execution it is necessary that a crime shall previously be committed, such a crime however, as a just judge would hold punishable by death'.[108] This is a more convincing quote; Grotius is referring to 'punishment' in the criminal sense. In the paragraph cited, Grotius refers back, for further details to book II, chapter XX, which deals expressly with criminal punishment, as opposed to the waging of war against wrongdoers.[109] However, it is difficult to draw clear conclusions

[102] *The Spanish Origins*, p. 210. [103] Gentili, *De Iure Belli*, p. 223.
[104] Kennedy, 'Primitive International Law', 64–5.
[105] And is so taken by Meron; Theodor Meron, 'The Common Rights of Mankind in Gentili, Grotius and Suàrez' (1991) 85 AJIL 110, 112.
[106] Grotius, *The Rights of War and Peace*, p. 247.
[107] Grotius, *The Rights of War and Peace*, p. 247; see also p. 248.
[108] Lauterpacht, 'The Law of Nations', 61, citing *The Rights of War and Peace*, book III, chapter XVI. I; the phrase appears in book III, chapter XI. I (pp. 359–60).
[109] Grotius, *The Rights of War and Peace*, p. 360. On Grotius and punishment generally, see Furukawa, 'Punishment'.

on what Grotius meant as his work is at times contradictory.[110] Against his comment repeated above, we can place the fact that Grotius considered it acceptable to kill any person in enemy territory, be they an enemy national or not, or a combatant or not.[111] Such doubts did not trouble François de Menthon, who referred to Grotius in his speech at the Nuremberg IMT.[112]

Practice

In contrast to the writers mentioned already, Ayala and Belli, two military professionals, concentrated on concepts of military discipline, a focus more in line with practical developments. Much practice at this time was based around codes of war, which stretches back at least to 1158, but it was in 1590 that the first permanent code of war was issued, by the Dutch Republic.[113] The codes or articles of war tended to include disciplinary offences relating to, for example, cowardice or sleeping on guard, but also contained prohibitions of robbery and the like. They mixed such offences with law of arms (when that remained relevant) and customary law.[114]

The codes tended to include draconian penalties; in the English Parliamentary army's articles of war of 1642, there were forty-two offences for which the death penalty was available.[115] The ordinances include offences such as rape (Ordinances of War promulgated by Richard II in 1583) and pillage (1639 Lawes and Ordinances of Warre of Thomas, Earl of Arundel).[116] It would also appear that at times there were attempts to monitor compliance. For example, judicial enquiries were entered into in 1574 and 1576 to investigate what would now be termed war crimes.[117]

It is true that the ordinances of war, and the proceedings brought under them were national, rather than international in nature. Although they referred, as a residuary source, to the law of arms or the customs of war, the locus of their binding force was strictly national, or allegiance-based. This should not lead us to discount them entirely

[110] See, for example, Lauterpacht, 'The Grotian Tradition', 5.

[111] Grotius, *The Rights of War and Peace*, p. 292 and book III, chapter IV. See Naoya Kasai, 'The Laws of War', in Yasuaki Onuma, *A Normative Approach to War: Peace, War and Justice in Hugo Grotius* (Oxford: Clarendon, 1993), pp. 244, 258–62, 266–8.

[112] 4 *Trial of German Major War Criminals*, p. 369.

[113] Parker, 'Early Modern Europe', p. 234, n. 6.

[114] Theodor Meron, *Henry's Wars and Shakespeare's Laws: Perspectives on the Laws of War in the Late Middle Ages* (Oxford: Clarendon, 1993), p. 142.

[115] Parker, 'Early Modern Europe', p. 47. [116] Meron, *Henry's Wars*, chapter 8.

[117] Parker, 'Early Modern Europe', p. 52.

on this ground. Many war crimes trials are prosecuted under national codes of military justice, and there is nothing inherently wrong with proceeding in this way.

1700–1914

During this period, there were further examples of codes of war[118] and, perhaps, more examples of trials for violations of these codes (although it may be that this is explainable on the basis that more records of such trials are available). Many of the examples of these codes and prosecutions come from the wars in America, in particular the American War of Independence and the American Civil War. The difficulty in grounding an international criminal law in a decentralised legal order also became clearer during this period.

Doctrine

That legal order was only fully conceptualised in this period, with Emerich de Vattel's *The Principles of the Law of Nations* (1758).[119] Prior writers, up to and including Christian Wolff had assumed the existence of a supranational authority;[120] Criminal law traditionally requires some sense of hierarchical authority;[121] Vattel rejected the idea of such an authority, although he did not reject the idea of offences against the law of nations.

Later scholars began to suggest an international criminal court. The first such proposal made to States came from Gustav Moynier in 1872.[122] The underlying idea in favour of an international court was a feeling that for matters related to war, national judges might not be independent.[123] Time has not wearied this idea, nor necessarily should it have.[124]

118 McCormack, 'From Sun Tzu', pp. 40–2.

119 Emerich de Vattel, Charles G. Fenwick (trans.), *Principles of the Law of Nations* (New York: Carnegie Institute for International Peace, 1916). Vattel was highly influential; see Henry S. Maine, *International Law* (London: John Murray, 1888), pp. 126, 130.

120 Christian Wolff (trans. Joseph H. Drake), *Jus Gentium Methodo Scientifica Pertractatum* (Oxford: Carnegie Foundation for International Peace, 1934).

121 James Crawford, 'The ILC's Draft Statute for an International Criminal Tribunal' (1994) 88 AJIL 140, 140.

122 See Christopher Keith Hall, 'The First Proposal for a Permanent International Criminal Court' (1998) 322 IRRC 57.

123 Hall, 'The First Proposal', 60.

124 See Eyal Benvenisti, 'Judicial Misgivings Regarding the Application of International Law: An Analysis of Attitudes of National Courts' (1993) 4 EJIL 159.

To overcome this aged but unbowed critique, the court was to be empanelled by both belligerents, and by neutral States.[125]

In a provision that presages Article 75 of the ICC Statute,[126] Article 7(1) of the proposed Statute would have permitted the court to award compensation to victims.[127] The analogy is by no means perfect, however, as the draft Convention (Article 7(2)) would have required the complaining government to seek the compensation. Therefore, unlike in Article 75 of the ICC Statute, there was no autonomous right for any victim to ask for compensation.[128]

The proposal fell on deaf governmental ears and doubtful academic ones.[129] Admittedly James Lorimer made a similar suggestion twelve years later, this time in the context of a more comprehensive scheme for an international legislature and international court system.[130] He was considered a 'lonely figure' for having made such a suggestion.[131] Even so, he identified one of the greatest problems in international criminal law, and one that will be a considerable part of what follows: the question of who defines the relevant law.

The tepid reception which greeted proposals for an international criminal court did not mean that there was no support for criminal responsibility for violations of the law of war. In 1880, the Institute of International Law affirmed that belligerents had the right to prosecute those violations.[132] The law of war was also undergoing a period of codification and progressive development during this time, with the 1868 St Petersburg Declaration[133] and the 1899 and 1907 Hague conferences.[134] It may have been too much to expect that there would

125 Hall, 'The First Proposal', 60.

126 On which see David Donat-Cattin, 'Article 75', in O. Triffterer (ed.), *Commentary on the Rome Statute of the International Criminal Court* (Baden-Baden: Nomos, 1999), p. 965.

127 The draft convention is printed as an appendix to Hall, 'The First Proposal', 72–4.

128 For other analogies to the situation just prior to the creation of the ICC Statute, see Hall, 'The First Proposal', 66–71.

129 Hall, 'The First Proposal', 63–4.

130 James Lorimer, *The Institutes of the Law of Nations: A Treatise of the Jural Relations of Separate Political Communities* (London: William Blackwood, 1884), p. 279.

131 Georg Schwarzenberger, 'The Problem of an International Criminal Law' (1950) 3 CLP 263, 296.

132 Institute of International Law, *Manual of the Law of War on Land* (Oxford: Institute of International Law, 1880).

133 1868 St Petersburg Declaration Renouncing, in Time of War, The Use of Explosive Projectiles Under 400 Grammes in Weight 58 BFSP (1867–1868) 16.

134 See Best, *Humanity in Warfare*, chapter 3.

also be strides forward in enforcement mechanisms in a time of development of the primary rules.[135]

Practice

The American War of Independence began on 19 April 1755. Three sets of articles of war promulgated on the American side – the Massachusetts' Bay Congress Articles and the American Articles of War of 30 June 1755 and 20 September 1776 – contained provisions that amount to a form of command responsibility.[136] These articles also conceptualised a number of offences as against the law of nations, rather than domestic crimes.[137] In the war itself, pillage was especially prevalent, and there were a number of prosecutions of soldiers for this offence.[138] Violent offences were also frequent on both the American and British sides. Prosecutions occurred for offences such as murder, attacking civilians and rape.[139] Offences against prisoners of war (PoWs) were also common, and there were some trials of those accused of mistreatment of such prisoners.[140]

In 1812, Arbuthnot and Ambritser, two British men who were said to have encouraged the Creek Indians to fight the United States, thus levying war against it in an uncivilised manner, were tried in the United States.[141] The charges were apparently based on international law.[142] What is most interesting is the reaction in the United Kingdom to the trial. There was an extraordinary level of public consternation expressed that the United States should exercise jurisdiction over British nationals

[135] Human rights law also went through a period of standard setting prior to entering an enforcement phase; see Hurst Hannum, 'Human Rights', in Christopher C. Joyner (ed.), *The United Nations and International Law* (Cambridge: Cambridge University Press, 1997), p. 131, p. 134.

[136] See McCormack, 'From Sun Tzu', p. 40. See also George L. Coil, 'War Crimes of the American Revolution' (1978) 82 Military LR 171, 193–7.

[137] Wright 'The Law of the Nuremberg Trial', 55–56, n. 66a.

[138] See Coil, 'War Crimes', 173–4.

[139] Coil, 'War Crimes', 175–8. See also Elbridge Colby, 'War Crimes' (1924–1925) 23 Mich LR 483, 500–1; Elbridge Colby, 'War Crimes and Their Punishment' (1923–1924) 8 *Minnesota Law Review* 40, 42.

[140] Coil, 'War Crimes', 191.

[141] William Winthrop, *Military Law and Precedents* (Washington, DC: Government Printing Office, 2nd edn., 1896), p. 464; see McCormack, 'From Sun Tzu', pp. 40–1; Jordan J. Paust, 'My Lai and Vietnam: Norms, Myths and Leader Responsibility' (1972) 57 Military LR 99, 113–15.

[142] McCormack, 'From Sun Tzu', p. 41.

for offences against international law.[143] The current US opposition to the ICC seems, ironically, to be based on similar ideas to the British criticism, which was rejected by the United States.[144] Further examples of prosecutions for war crimes in the United States may be found in the 1846–48 Mexican War, where such offences were prosecuted before military commissions pursuant to an order of General Scott.

Some of the most famous developments in the law of war, and a clear affirmation of the criminality of violations of that law, came about during the American Civil War.[145] This came from General Army Order 100, better known as the Lieber Code.[146] In addition to setting out detailed (although not always entirely humane) regulations for the conduct of troops in the conflict, the Code also provided for criminal responsibility for infractions of its dictates.[147] The most famous case brought for violations of the Lieber Code, as a codification of the laws of war, was the trial of Captain Henry Wirz, commander of the infamous Andersonville PoW camp.[148] As is so often the case the primary, and rejected, defence was superior orders.[149] There were also criticisms of the process, with some saying that Wirz was the victim of victor's justice.[150]

The Lieber Code was extraordinarily influential, being reissued unamended by the US government for the war with Spain,[151] used at the

[143] McCormack, 'From Sun Tzu', p. 41.

[144] For a useful work on the US position on the ICC, see Sarah B. Sewell and Carl Kaysen, *The United States and the International Criminal Court* (New York: Rowman & Littlefield/American Academy of Arts and Sciences, 2000). See also David P. Forsythe, 'The United States and International Criminal Justice' (2002) 24 HRQ 974.

[145] Despite its name, the law applicable to the conflict was that applicable to international conflicts, as there had been recognition of belligerency by the central government, See John Bassett Moore, *International Law Digest, I* (Washington, DC: Government Printing Office, 1906), pp. 184–93; see also *Ford* v. *Surget* (1878) 97 US 605, *Coleman* v. *Tennessee* (1878) 97 US 509.

[146] General Order No. 100 (New York: van Nostrand, 1863), see, for example, George B. Davis, 'Doctor Francis Lieber's Instructions for the Government of Armies in the Field' (1907) 1 AJIL 13; Theodor Meron, 'Francis Lieber's Code and Principles of Humanity' (1998) 35 CJTL 269.

[147] General Order 100, Articles 25, 37, 44, 47, 71.

[148] For a highly critical, at times polemic, review, see Lewis L. Laska and James M. Smith, '"Hell and the Devil", Andersonville and the Trial of Captain Henry Wirz, C. S. A., 1865' (1975) 68 Military LR 77; for a more factual account, see McCormack, 'From Sun Tzu', p. 42.

[149] Laska and Smith, '"Hell and the Devil"', 125.

[150] See generally Laska and Smith, '"Hell and the Devil"'.

[151] Charles Stockton, *Outlines of International Law* (New York: Charles Scribner, 1914), p. 300.

attempt to codify the laws of war in Brussels in 1874[152] and influencing a number of other States' codes of the laws of war.[153] The code also had an indirect effect in the 1899 Hague Conference.[154]

The aftermath of the American Civil War also gave rise to a number of cases which affirmed that liability for violations of the laws of war were not based solely in the domestic order. For example, in *Dow* v. *Johnson*[155] it was said: '[w]hat is the law which governs an army invading an enemy's country? It is not the civil law of the invaded country; it is not the civil law of the conquering country; it is military law - the law of war.'[156] James Brierly asserted that such cases stand for authority that the US Supreme Court accepted that war crimes jurisdiction was a special jurisdiction granted by international law, rather than simply an aspect of domestic criminal law.[157]

Courts-martial and military courts were also used for offences committed by American and Filipino fighters involved in the war in the Philippines of 1899–1902.[158] The decision to prosecute US personnel was taken because of public outcry at allegations of atrocities.[159] There were therefore only a few trials of US service members, and sentences, where they were imposed, bordered on the derisory: 'Prosecutors were at times complacent . . . [and] . . . the army's *esprit de corps* led some of the judges to identify with the accused and show a fraternal readiness to excuse and mitigate their actions'.[160] As a result, comparisons with the later Leipzig proceedings (see below) are not wholly inapposite.[161]

[152] Charles G. Fenwick, *International Law* (New York: Century, 1924), p. 74. Lorimer, *The Institutes*, p. 302, went as far as to say it was the basis of all subsequent codifications.

[153] See Jordan J. Paust, 'Dr. Francis Lieber and the Lieber Code' (2001) 95 Proceedings ASIL 112, 114.

[154] See C. A. Hereshoff Bartlett, 'Liability for Official War Crimes' (1919) 35 LQR 177, 181–3; Paust, 'Dr. Francis Lieber', 114; George B. Davis, 'Appendix' (1913) 7 AJIL 466. On the 1899 Hague Conference generally, see William I. Hull, *The Two Hague Conferences and Their Contributions to International Law* (Boston: Ginn & Co., 1908).

[155] 100 US 158.

[156] *Dow* v. *Johnson*, p. 636. See generally George A. Finch, 'Jurisdiction of Local Courts to Try Enemy Persons for War Crimes' (1920) 14 AJIL 218.

[157] James Brierly, 'The Nature of War Crimes Jurisdiction', in Hersch Lauterpacht and C. Humphrey M. Waldock (eds.), *The Basis of Obligation in International Law and other Papers by the Late James Leslie Brierly* (Oxford: Clarendon, 1958), p. 297, pp. 303–4.

[158] Levie, *Terrorism in War*, p. 16.

[159] Gunaël Mettreaux, 'US Courts-Martial and the Armed Conflict in the Philippines (1899–1902): Their Contribution to National Case Law on War Crimes' (2003) 1 JICJ 135, 137. See also Robert Maguire, *Law and War: An American Story* (New York: Columbia, 2000), pp. 51–67.

[160] Mettreaux, 'US Courts-Martial', 148.

[161] Mettreaux, 'US Courts-Martial', 148–9.

Other countries also engaged in prosecutions for violations of the law of war. Levie, for example, notes Article V of the 1881 Convention of Pretoria, which provided that 'sentences passed on persons who may be convicted of offences contrary to the rules of civilised warfare committed during recent hostilities, will be carried out'. Apparently some trials, which ended in acquittals, were engaged in under this provision.[162] There were also prosecutions of British, Australian and Boer combatants for war crimes.[163] A year later, in 1882, Egypt tried and convicted Ahmed Arabi for perfidious use of a white flag.[164] Prosecution was not solely limited to American incentives.

The 1899 Hague Declarations made no express provision for criminal punishment. Nor did the 1864 Geneva Convention,[165] or the 1907 Hague Conventions, in particular Hague Convention IV Respecting the Laws and Customs of War on Land.[166] Bassiouni claims that there was an implicit acceptance in Hague Convention IV that violations of the Rules were criminal.[167] The Nuremberg IMT declared violations of those rules criminal in 1946,[168] but this is most likely to have been on the more general basis that violations of the law of war in general were criminal rather than an inference drawn from any provision of the treaty itself.[169] The only provision of the treaty that dealt with the matter of responsibility was Article 3, which dealt with State responsibility.

In 1906, the 1864 Geneva Convention was updated to include a precursor to the grave breaches regime of later Geneva Conventions, Article 28(1). This article required parties to ensure their criminal laws covered various violations of the 1864 Convention. Hague Convention X of 1907,[170] drafted at the same conference as Hague Convention IV, contained a similar provision in Article 21. The customary underpinning of

[162] Levie, *Terrorism in War*, p. 15; See also Lord Cave, 'War Crimes and Their Punishment' (1922) 8 TGS xix, xxv.

[163] McCormack, 'From Sun Tzu', p. 42.

[164] Levie, *Terrorism in War*, p. 15.

[165] 1864 Convention for the Amelioration of the Condition of Wounded in Armies in the Field, 1 Bevans 7.

[166] TS No. 539.

[167] M. Cherif Bassiouni, *International Crimes, Digest/Index of International Instruments 1815–1985* (New York: Oceana, 1986), p. 174.

[168] 'Nuremberg IMT, Sentence and Judgment', 248. The IMT said that the matter was 'too well settled to admit of argument'.

[169] The influence of the Lieber Code on the Hague Conventions and the fact that the code contained criminal provisions should not be underestimated on this point.

[170] Hague Convention X for the Adaptation to Maritime Warfare the Principles of the Geneva Convention, 1 Bevans 694.

criminality is therefore important, as it is difficult to imply criminality from the terms of Hague Convention IV itself.[171]

The First World War

During and until shortly after the First World War, the Allies took a strong, albeit at times illiberal, line on international criminal liability.[172] From the statements made during and just after the war, it would appear that there would be a systematic reckoning for international crimes. Although there were some domestic trials of German nationals,[173] and the (in)famous German trial of Captain Fryatt for using his ship to ram German submarines[174] the later post-war actions of the Allies did not bear out their rhetoric.[175]

The first statements from the Allies came in relation to the genocide perpetrated by the Ottoman Empire against the Armenians.[176] On 24 May 1915 Russia, France and the United Kingdom issued a declaration in which they said that 'the connivance and often assistance of Ottoman authorities . . . [in the killings were] . . . crimes of Turkey against humanity and civilization', and promised personal responsibility for those implicated.[177] In relation to German defendants, Allied rhetoric was even more strident, after the war Lloyd George promised to 'hang the Kaiser'.[178]

The Commission on the Responsibility of the Authors of the War

Come the end of war in 1918, expectations were high for international criminal accountability. The Allies set up the Commission on the Responsibility of the Authors of the War and on the Enforcement

[171] See Cyril M. Picciotto, 'War Crimes' (1916) 1 International Law Notes 69, 70.

[172] Whatever its rhetorical force, Lloyd George's electoral rallying-cry of 'hang the Kaiser' betrayed little respect for the presumption of innocence.

[173] See Levie, *Terrorism in War*, pp. 18–20; McCormack, 'From Sun Tzu', p. 44.

[174] See James B. Scott, 'The Execution of Captain Fryatt' (1917) 11 AJIL 865.

[175] See M. Cherif Bassiouni, 'World War I, "The War to End All Wars" and the Birth of a Handicapped International Criminal Justice System' (2002) 30 DJILP 244.

[176] See generally, Vakhan N. Dadrian, 'Genocide as a Problem of National and International Law: The World War I Armenian Case and its Contemporary Legal Ramifications' (1989) 14 Yale JIL 221.

[177] FO/371/2488/51010. On British statements see Gary J. Bass, *Stay the Hand of Vengeance: The Politics of War Crimes Tribunals* (Princeton: Princeton University Press, 2000), pp. 112–17.

[178] On academic views at the time, see Matthew Lippman, 'Towards an International Criminal Court' (1995) 3 SDJJ 5, 5–11.

of Penalties (thereafter, 'the Commission') in January 1919. This was a fifteen-member commission, made up of representatives of the United Kingdom, United States, France, Italy, Belgium, Greece, Poland, Romania, Serbia and Japan.[179] Its mandate was to investigate the responsibility for the start of the war, violations of the laws of war and what tribunal would be appropriate for trials.[180]

The Commission reported at the end of March 1919, with a number of imaginative suggestions. Unsurprisingly, given its composition, the Commission found that the outbreak of war was entirely the fault of the Central Powers,[181] despite the fact that they also accepted that the question was complex and 'might be more fitly investigated by historians and statesmen than by a tribunal'.[182] They also determined that there were cases to answer in relation to violations of the laws of war and humanity. They gave an illustrative list of those offences.[183] They recommended that high officials, including the Kaiser, be tried, not only for issuing unlawful orders, but also on the basis of command responsibility.[184]

Further to this, the Commission suggested the setting up of an Allied 'High Tribunal' with members from all of the Allied countries. This was to try violations of the laws and customs of war and the laws of humanity. The Commission also recommended that the law applied by the tribunal ought to be '[t]he principles of the law of nations as they result from the usages established among civilised peoples, from the laws of humanity and from the dictates of public conscience'.[185] In other words, the proposals contained a clear affirmation of liability directly under international law, rather than domestic legal orders incorporating such offences. This aspect was criticised both by the American and Japanese members of the Commission. The American members said that they knew 'of no international statute or convention making violation of the laws and customs of war – not to speak of the laws or principles of humanity – an international crime'.[186] They would have

179 On the Commission generally, see Bassiouni, *Crimes Against Humanity*, pp. 63–7; Lippman, 'Towards', 12–17.

180 Report of the Commission to the Preliminary Peace Conference, reprinted in (1920) 14 AJIL 95, p. 95.

181 Report, 107. 182 Report, 119. 183 Report, 114–15.

184 Report, 116–17, 121. The American members of the commission dissented from the last two points, 129, 135–7.

185 Report, 122.

186 Report, 146. The American representatives considered the 'principles of humanity' to be too vague for criminal law; Report, 144–5.

preferred national military commissions, acting under domestic implementing laws, to prosecute such offences. The Japanese representatives questioned 'whether international law recognizes a penal law applicable to those who are guilty'.[187] The majority clearly considered there to be a separate phase of international criminal law, albeit one which did not include aggression as a crime.[188] Nonetheless, for situating the locus of liability for war crimes in the international legal order the report stands as a clear example of what might now be considered modern international criminal law.

Post-war trials

If the Commission's proposals had been implemented, the history of international criminal law might have taken a different route. They were not. The first peace treaty with Turkey, the Treaty of Sèvres (1920)[189] contained a provision (Article 230) by which Turkey was obliged to hand over those responsible for the atrocities to the Allies. However, the treaty was never ratified, and was replaced by the Treaty of Lausanne (1923),[190] which had no equivalent provision on punishment, and was accompanied by a declaration of amnesty. There were a few Turkish national trials of high-ranking officials instigated under Allied, particularly British, pressure.[191] Unsurprisingly, these caused political turmoil in Turkey,[192] and the process began to be wound down. As a result of this, the United Kingdom took a number of suspects into custody,[193] while further Turkish courts-martial appeared to be tilting towards acquittal.[194] All attempts at prosecution ceased in 1921. The death knell of any possible further accounting was sounded in 1923, with the Treaty of Lausanne.

The story of the Leipzig trials is a similar one. It all started so well. The initial plans were set out in the 1919 Treaty of Versailles, and broadly followed the Commission recommendations.[195] Perhaps the least satisfactory aspect was Article 227. This Article provided that the Kaiser was to be 'publicly arraigned' for 'a supreme offence against international

[187] Report, 152. [188] Report, 118.

[189] TS No. 11 (1920). See generally, David Matas, 'Prosecuting Crimes Against Humanity: The Lessons of World War I' (1989–1990) 13 Fordham ILJ 86.

[190] 1923 8 LNTS 11. [191] See generally Bass, *Stay the Hand*, pp. 117–30.

[192] Bass, *Stay the Hand*, pp. 124–6. [193] Bass, *Stay the Hand*, p. 128.

[194] Bass, *Stay the Hand*, pp. 128–30; Dadrian 'Genocide', 291–2.

[195] Similar provisions were included in a number of other treaties signed by the central powers.

morality and the sanctity of treaties' before an international tribunal. This was not a truly criminal proceeding, the offence being a 'moral' one,[196] and even though it promised the Kaiser a defence the article itself had at least some of the trappings of an act of attainder. It was never implemented as the Netherlands refused to hand the Kaiser over to the Allies.[197]

More satisfactory were Articles 228 and 229. In Article 228, provision was made for the prosecution of German suspects by the Allies and, in a sentence designed to ensure that shielding prosecutions were not entered into,[198] 'notwithstanding any proceedings or prosecution before a Tribunal in Germany or in the territory of her Allies'. Prosecutions were to be before the military tribunals of the victim or, if the charges related to victims of more than one State, mixed military commissions made up of members from those States.[199] Sensibly, Articles 228 and 229 also included obligations on Germany to hand over suspects, along with all relevant evidence. None of it worked.[200]

The Allies began by creating a list of suspects to try. From a starting point of around 3,000 people, the list was whittled down to 896. This was still considered too many by Germany.[201] Later, in 1920, Germany offered a compromise, trying suspects nationally in Leipzig. This was reluctantly conceded by the Allies, who submitted a list of forty-five people they wanted tried, and reserving their right to begin trials if they were unhappy with the German proceedings.

The trials themselves were not, from the point of view of the Allies, a success.[202] From the number of proceedings that were brought,[203] their tenor and extraordinary lenience when convictions were recorded, quite serious questions can be asked about the *bona fides* of the prosecutions. Belgium and France withdrew their delegations in protest at the proceedings, considering them little more than a sham. Sir Ernest Pollock, the British Solicitor-General, was more impressed with those trials in which the United Kingdom took an interest.[204] He was the only one.[205]

[196] James Garner, 'Punishment of Offences Against the Laws and Customs of War' (1920) 14 AJIL 90, 91. This follows the Commission conclusion that aggression was not an international crime at the time.

[197] See Bassiouni, 'World War I', 269–73; Bass, *Stay the Hand*, pp. 76–8.

[198] See now ICC Statute, Article 17(2).

[199] Treaty of Versailles, Article 229.

[200] See generally Bass, *Stay the Hand*, chapter 3.

[201] Geo. Gordon Battle, 'The Trials Before the Leipsic Supreme Court of Germans Accused of War Crimes' (1921–1922) 8 *Virginia Law Review* 1, 5.

[202] Cave, 'War Crimes', xxviii–xxix.

[203] In the end, there were twelve.

[204] Battle, 'The Trials', 9.

[205] Bass, *Stay the Hand*, p. 81.

The most famous of the trials at Leipzig were the *Dover Castle* (1922) and *Llandovery Castle* (1922) Cases.[206] Both related to the sinking of ships and which superior orders were used to acquit the defendants of certain charges (although not, in the latter Case, of the charge of firing on the shipwrecked). Although the decisions in some of the Leipzig trials may have been defensible, and the fact they occurred at all can be considered a start on the road to reckoning, it is difficult to end a survey of them without citing Leo Gross' pithy summary: '[t]he Versailles experiment taught the Allies at least one lesson, namely how *not* to set about trying German war criminals.'[207]

In some ways, the Leipzig trials can be said to have a broader legacy. This is the fear that a State is unlikely to engage in active prosecution of its own nationals before its own courts, and that therefore international supervision or proceedings are needed, or prosecution before another State's courts. Even so, this was not a new idea at the time of Leipzig.

The inter-war period

After the First World War, the idea of an international criminal court regained currency, with proposals for an international tribunal coming from a League of Nations Advisory Committee in 1921, as a means of overcoming the problems encountered in prosecuting offences from that war.[208] The President of that Committee, Baron Deschamps, was particularly supportive of the proposal; however, the committee was not unanimous.[209] As a result the committee recommended only that the League consider the issue.[210] The League Committee dealing with it was more than a little dismissive, being sceptical of international criminal law and considering discussion '[p]remature'.[211]

Consideration of a court then fell into the unofficial arena, with the International Law Association (ILA) drafting a statute for an international criminal court in 1926.[212] Other bodies, such as the

[206] *Dover Castle* (1922) 16 AJIL 704; *Llandovery Castle* (1922) 16 AJIL 708.

[207] Gross, 'The Punishment', p. 136.

[208] McCormack, 'From Sun-Tzu', pp. 51–2. These were not taken up. *Ibid.* p. 52. See also Lord Phillimore, 'An International Criminal Court and the Resolutions of the Committee of Jurists' (1922–3) 3 BYBIL 79.

[209] See McCormack 'From Sun Tzu', pp. 51–2.

[210] McCormack, 'From Sun Tzu', p. 52.

[211] McCormack, 'From Sun Tzu', p. 52.

[212] *Report of the 34th Conference* (ILA) 1927; see McCormack, 'From Sun Tzu', p. 53, for criticism, see James Brierly, 'Do We Need an International Criminal Court?' (1927) 8 BYBIL 81.

Inter-Parliamentary Union, the International Congress of Penal Law and Pan-American conference also recommended the creation of a court.[213] The assassination of King Alexander of Yugoslavia in 1934 led to the most advanced proposal. The League of Nations drafted, adopted and opened for signature a statute for an international criminal court. The court was to enforce the (separate) convention for the prevention of terrorism.[214] The convention remained without State support.

The Second World War

In the Second World War international criminal law came into its own. There were a few trials during the war on the Allied side – for example, the Kharkhov trials by the USSR[215] in late 1943. Preparations were made during the war for trials in both the European and Pacific theatres. The *Yamashita* Case (*US* v. *Yamashita*), for example, was prepared before the end of the war, but the prosecutors waited for the Japanese surrender to begin the trial.[216] It is with the post-war efforts at justice that we see an incipient system of international criminal law being brought into being.

The European sphere and the Nuremberg IMT

During the war, the Allies issued many statements relating to violations of the law of war and promising punishment for such offences in Europe.[217] The most important of these in the European sphere of the war was the Moscow Declaration of 1 November 1943. In this:

> the . . . [United States, United Kingdom and USSR] . . . speaking in the interests of the 32 United Nations . . . decla[red] . . . at the time of the granting of any armistice to any government that may be set up in Germany, those German

[213] UNWCC, *The History of the United Nations War Crimes Commission* (London: HMSO, 1948), pp. 439–40.

[214] 1937 Convention for the Creation of an International Criminal Court, (1938) League of Nations Official Journal Special Supp. 156. See generally Manley O. Hudson, 'The Proposed International Criminal Court' (1938) 32 AJIL 549.

[215] For a rather uncritical discussion of these trials, see George Ginsburgs, 'The Nuremberg Trial: Background', in George Ginsburgs and Vladimir N. Kudriavatsev (eds.), *The Nuremberg Trial and International Law* (Dordrecht: Martinus Nijhoff, 1990), p. 9, pp. 25–7.

[216] See below p. 47.

[217] See, for example the statements of Roosevelt and Churchill 25 October 1941, *Punishment for War Crimes, the Inter Allied Declaration Signed at St James's Palace on 13th January and Relative Documents* (London: HMSO, 1942), p. 15, Declaration of St James' Palace 13 January 1942, *ibid.*, p. 1; 144 BFSP 1072; See generally UNWCC, *The History*, pp. 87–94.

officers and men and members of the Nazi party who have been responsible for, or have taken a consenting part in the atrocities, massacres and executions, will be sent back to the countries in which their abominable deeds were done in order that they may be judged and punished according to the laws of the liberated countries and of the free governments which will be erected therein . . . *the above declaration is without prejudice to the Case of the major criminals whose offences have no particular geographical location and who will be punished by a joint declaration of the governments of the Allies.*[218]

This did not amount to a legally binding commitment to punish the 'major criminals' by judicial process. By its own terms, the Declaration did not apply to these 'major criminals', who would be punished by a 'joint declaration of the . . . Allies'. The Declaration was not seen by the Allies as ruling out an executive decision to punish them. Churchill's original view was that extrajudicial firing squads were the best option, and it was only because of an unlikely alliance between the United States and the USSR that he was persuaded otherwise.[219]

This ambiguity did not prevent the Moscow Declaration providing the political backdrop to the creation of the Nuremberg IMT, and it was cited in the latter's founding instrument.[220] It is interesting to note the parallels between this declaration and the approach taken in the Declaration and the proposed actions in relation to minor and major offenders against international law (and the Kaiser for aggression) in the aftermath of the First World War. Minor offenders were to be sent back for trial in the *locus delicti*, whereas major offenders, or those whose offences were not geographically limited, were to be dealt with by joint action.

A month before the Moscow Declaration, the Allies had set up the United Nations War Crimes Commission (UNWCC), to investigate war crimes and, later, to advise on the process for punishment.[221] The

218 Declaration of Moscow 1 January 1943, 9 (US) *Dept. of State Bull.* 310 (No. 228, 6 November 1943). See UNWCC, *The History*, pp. 107–8, emphasis added.

219 See, for example, Anne Tusa and John Tusa, *The Nuremberg Trial* (Macmillan: London, 1983), pp. 24, 50–1; Bradley Smith, *Reaching Judgment at Nuremberg* (London: André Deutsch, 1977), pp. 23–4; Arieh Kochavi, *Prelude to Nuremberg: Allied War Crimes Policy and the Question of Punishment* (Durham, NC: North Carolina University Press, 1998). For Russian statements see Ginsburgs, 'The Nuremberg Trial', p. 28.

220 1945 Agreement for the Prosecution and Punishment of the Major War Criminals of the European Axis Powers and Charter of the International Military Tribunal, 82 UNTS 279. Preamble.

221 See generally, UNWCC, *The History*; M. E. Bathurst, 'The UN War Crimes Commission' (1945) 39 AJIL 565. On the effectiveness of the UNWCC see Tusa and Tusa, *The Nuremberg Trial*, pp. 22–3; Telford Taylor, *The Anatomy of the Nuremberg Trials* (London: Bloomsberg, 1993), pp. 26–8; Kochavi, *Prelude to Nuremberg*, pp. 104–7.

sixteen-member commission was ineffectual. It had been set up as a covering mechanism by the Allies (in particular the United Kingdom), who wished to be seen to be 'doing something' about the reports of war crimes.[222] However, the governments in exile had little authority or power to help, and the other Allies had little interest supplying the commission with evidence, personnel or support. This lack of support contributed to the resignation of Sir Cecil Hurst from the UNWCC.[223] The body itself 'was criticised for its decision not to include the Holocaust within its purview . . . [and] . . . [b]y the time Nuremberg was in the works, the UNWCC was unceremoniously killed off'.[224]

The Nuremberg IMT, which formed the cornerstone of the Allied prosecution policy by the end of the war, was a creature created by treaty, the 1945 London Agreement.[225] The negotiations for the London Agreement were tense, as the Allies had very different ideas about the nature and purpose of the trial. The Americans and Soviets, for example, entertained considerable mutual suspicion. The Soviets thought the only utility of the trial was to set the punishment of the already guilty. The Americans wanted some semblance of a fair trial. There were also differences in approach between the civil and common lawyers. That agreement was reached at all is testimony to the more diplomatic members of the delegations.[226]

Otto Kranzbühler, counsel for Karl Dönitz, questioned if the Nuremberg IMT was truly international, opining that it was merely a joint occupation court.[227] The ICTY took a similar view in the *Tadić* Case, where the Trial Chamber in that Case described the Nuremberg IMT as not 'truly international . . . [instead being] . . . multinational in nature, representing only part of the world community'.[228] If this statement is taken as denying the international nature of the Nuremberg IMT, it conflates the question of whether or not the Nuremberg IMT was an international court with that of whether it was truly global in scope. In retrospect, although only the Allies were represented on the bench, it appears that the Nuremberg IMT was an international court, as it was not in practice

222 Tusa and Tusa, *The Nuremberg Trial*, p. 22.

223 Tusa and Tusa, *The Nuremberg Trial*, p. 23.

224 Bass, *Stay the Hand*, p. 149.

225 1945 London Agreement for the Prosecution and Punishment of the Major War Criminals of the European Axis Powers and Charter of the International Military Tribunal 8 UNTS 279.

226 See generally Tusa and Tusa, *The Nuremberg Trial*, chapter 5.

227 Otto Kranzbühler, 'Nuremberg Eighteen Years Afterwards' (1963–1964) 13 De Paul LR 333, 337.

228 *Prosecutor* v. *Tadić*, Opinion and Judgment, IT-94-1-T, 7 May 1997, para. 1.

subordinated to the Control Council,[229] and the London Agreement was adhered to by a number of States which were not occupying powers.[230]

The creation of the Nuremberg IMT was extraordinary: an international criminal tribunal applying international law directly. This, in most ways, is the defining aspect of international criminal law, the direct imposition of liability without any intercession of domestic legal orders; the Nuremberg IMT can therefore be said to be the first pure example of such liability in the modern legal world.[231] The statement of the Nuremberg IMT that individuals have duties beyond domestic law[232] and the fact that crimes against humanity were criminal, according to Article 6(c) the IMT's Charter 'whether or not in violation of domestic law of the country where perpetrated' are entirely unambiguous affirmations of the international responsibility of individuals.

The Tribunal had eight judges, four principal judges (one for each of the major Allies (France, the USSR, the United Kingdom and the United States) and four alternates (understudies drawn from the same States). The indictment was received by the Tribunal on 10 October 1945, at its official seat of Berlin. It contained four main charges based on Article 6 of the IMT's Charter. Count one was the overall conspiracy, which was dealt with at trial by the United States. Count two was Crimes Against Peace. This count was dealt with by the United Kingdom. Count three was war crimes, Count four Crimes Against Humanity. The prosecution of these offences was split between France and the USSR, France dealing with the Western zone of conflict, the USSR with the East. Twenty-four defendants were arraigned before the Tribunal.[233] There

[229] Schwelb is a little less sure; see Egon Schwelb, 'Crimes Against Humanity' (1946) 23 BYBIL 178, 208–10.

[230] Nineteen States other than the four major powers adhered to the London agreement.

[231] Some doubted that such liability existed in 1945; see Herbert Kraus, 'The Nuremberg Trials of the Major War Criminals: Reflections After Seventeen Years' (1963–1964) 13 De Paul LR 233, 243–4; Elizabeth Zoller, 'The Status of Individuals Under International Law', in George Ginsburgs and Vladimir Kudriavtsev (eds.), *The Nuremberg Trial and International Law* (Dordrecht: Martinus Nijhoff, 1990), p. 99, p. 100. But see Hans Kelsen, 'Collective and Individual Responsibility in International Law with Particular Regard to the Punishment of War Criminals' (1942–1943) 31 Cal LR 530, 532–8; Justice Birkett considered it one of the theories that 'evolved at Nuremberg'; Birkett, 'International Legal Theories', 325.

[232] Nuremberg IMT Judgment, 221.

[233] Hermann Göring, Rudolf Hess, Joachim von Ribbentrop, Wilhelm Keitel, Ernst Kaltenbrunner, Alfred Rosenberg, Hans Frank, Wilhelm Frick, Julius Streicher, Walter Funk, Hjalmar Schacht, Karl Dönitz, Willem Raeder, Baldur von Schirach, Fritz Saukel, Alfred Jodl, Franz von Papen, Arthur Seyss-Inquart, Albert Speer, Konstantin von Neurath, and Hans Fritzsche. Martin Bormann was tried *in absentia*, Gustav Krupp was declared mentally incapable of standing trial, Robert Ley committed suicide in custody, prior to the beginning of the trial.

were also prosecutions of six criminal organisations.[234] Having received the indictment, the Tribunal moved to the city with which it is now associated, Nuremberg.

The trial took place over ten months, and 403 open sessions. In the end three of the defendants (Shacht, Fritzsche and von Papen) were acquitted, three of the six indicted organisations (the Gestapo, the SS and the Leadership corps of the Nazi party) were declared criminal. Of the remaining defendants, twelve were sentenced to death and seven to periods of imprisonment ranging from ten years to life. The Soviet judge, Major-General Nikitchenko, dissented from all the acquittals and the life sentence for Rudolf Hess. He would have declared all the defendants and organisations guilty, and sentenced Hess to death.

What actually happened at Nuremberg has been overshadowed by the legacy it left.[235] The Nuremberg legacy is a curate's egg; allegations of victor's justice, and selective justice do have some purchase, as we will see later. The trial process also had some faults,[236] the crimes against peace charge was, in truth, *ex post facto*,[237] the crimes against humanity charge was of uncertain provenance and, on some matters, the judgment was less than candid.[238] On the other hand, we cannot forget that modern international criminal law finds its first real practical example in the Nuremberg IMT and, contrary to the view of Hans Kelsen,[239] the effect on international law of the IMT's Charter and judgment was profound.[240]

[234] See Taylor, *The Anatomy of the Nuremberg Trials*, pp. 501–33; Stanislaw Pomorski, 'Conspiracy and Criminal Organisations', in George Ginsburgs and Vladimir Kudriavtsev (eds.), *The Nuremberg Trial and International Law* (Dordrecht: Martinus Nijhoff, 1990), p. 213. For a modern suggestion of a return to organisational criminality, see Nina H. B. Jørgensen, 'A Reappraisal of the Abandoned Nuremberg Concept of Criminal Organisations in the Context of Justice in Rwanda' (2001) 12 CLF 371.

[235] W. Bosch, *Judgment on Nuremberg: American Attitudes Towards the Major German War Crimes Trials* (Durham, NC: North Carolina University Press, 1970), p. 239; M. Cherif Bassiouni, 'Nuremberg Forty Years Afterwards: An Introduction' (1986) 18 CWRILJ 261, 262; M. Cherif Bassiouni, 'The Nuremberg Legacy: Historical Assessment', in Belinda Cooper (ed.), *War Crimes: The Legacy of Nuremberg* (New York: TV Books, 1999), p. 291.

[236] See, for example, David Overy, 'The Nuremberg Trials: International Law in the Making', in Phillipe Sands (ed.), *From Nuremberg to the Hague: The Future of International Criminal Justice* (Cambridge: Cambridge University Press, 2002), p. 1, pp. 23–5.

[237] See below, pp. 241–3. [238] See Taylor, *The Anatomy of the Nuremberg Trials*, pp. 639–40.

[239] Hans Kelsen, 'Will the Judgment in the Nuremberg Trial Constitute a Precedent in International Law?' (1947) 1 ILQ 153.

[240] For a general assessment of Nuremberg, see Matthew Lippman, 'Nuremberg Forty-Five Years Later' (1991) 7 Connecticut JIL 1, 37–64.

There were plans for a second IMT at Nuremberg, which was intended to prosecute the industrialists who had been involved in the Nazi programme. However, the plans foundered owing to the incipient Cold War rivalry that undermined any attempt at development of international criminal law until the last decade of the twentieth century.[241] It has been suggested that this second IMT was sacrificed to the wish of some of the Allies to ensure that businessmen who were being courted for the reconstruction of Germany were not subject to prosecution.[242]

International tribunals were not the only or most prevalent response to international crimes in the European sphere of the Second World War. Many more Axis personnel were prosecuted at the national level. In Germany, this was pursuant to Control Council Law 10.[243] The closest followers of this law were twelve US trials that took place in Nuremberg, known as the 'subsequent proceedings'. These included trials of Nazi doctors and judges, the *Einsatzgruppen* (extermination squads) and members of the German High Command. These trials have had a considerable influence on international criminal law.[244] Proceedings in the British zone of Germany were carried out under the Royal Warrant of 1946;[245] French and Soviet proceedings were less influenced by Control Council Law 10. There were also a number of trials in the Netherlands, Poland and other occupied countries.[246] Although there were many such trials, the later practice of the Allies has been criticised for releasing many of those held in Germany before their sentences had been fully served.[247]

With the IMT and other proceedings we can see the beginning of attempts in practice to co-ordinate prosecution of offenders at the national and international levels. Control Council Law 10 had provisions giving priority to the IMT over domestic prosecutions.[248] The impact of the factual and legal determinations of the IMT on domestic trials was

[241] See Donald Bloxham, *Genocide on Trial: War Crimes Trials and the Formation of Holocaust History and Memory* (Oxford: Oxford University Press, 2001), pp. 24–5.

[242] Bloxham, *Genocide*, pp. 162–72; Tom Bower, *Blind Eye to Murder: Britain, America and the Purging of Nazi Germany – A Pledge Betrayed* (London: Little, Brown & Co., 1997).

[243] *Official Gazette of the Control Council for Germany*, No. 3, 31 January 1946.

[244] See Levie, *Terrorism in War*, pp. 72–98; Matthew Lippman, 'The Other Nuremberg: American Prosecutions of Nazi War Criminals in Occupied Germany' (1992) 3 *Indiana International and Comparative Law Review* 1.

[245] See Anthony P. V. Rogers, 'War Crimes Trials Under the Royal Warrant: British Practice 1945–1949' (1990) 39 ICLQ 780.

[246] See Levie, *Terrorism in War*, pp. 98–139; Istvan Deak, 'Post-World War II Political Justice in a Historical Perspective' (1995) 159 Military LR 137.

[247] Bloxham, *Genocide*, pp. 162–72; Bower, *Blind Eye to Murder*.

[248] Control Council Law 10, Articles 2(3), 3(3), 4(3).

variable, but not negligible.[249] There was also co-ordination, as promised in the Moscow Declaration, the highest-ranking offenders (or at least some of them) being prosecuted in international proceedings, with those considered less important being left to domestic trials. Similar policies are at work in the ICTY and ICTR.[250]

The Pacific sphere and the Tokyo IMT

Whereas the Allies spoke of 'punishment' for Nazis from early on in the Second World War, declarations on the Pacific sphere did not expressly mention individual liability until late on.[251] There were some statements relating to prosecution of international crimes from the United States in 1942,[252] but the first important multilateral declaration came in 1943. This was the Cairo Declaration of 1 December, in which the United Kingdom, United States and China promised to 'restrain and punish the aggression of Japan' and to eject Japan from the territories it had conquered.[253] Although some later US declarations were contradictory as to whether individual liability would be imposed,[254] in May 1944 the UNWCC set up a Far East division.[255]

The most important of the declarations was the Potsdam Declaration of 25 July 1945.[256] In this, the United States, United Kingdom and China set out their terms of surrender for Japan.[257] The most important part

[249] See Adam Basak, 'The Influence of the Nuremberg Judgment on the Practice of the Allied Courts in Germany' (1977–1978) 9 *Polish Yearbook of International Law* 161.

[250] See Richard J. Goldstone, 'The International Tribunal for Former Yugoslavia, A Case Study in Security Council Action' (1995) 6 DJICL 5, 7; Michael Bohlander, 'Last Exit Bosnia – Transferring War Crimes Prosecution from the International Tribunal to Domestic Courts' (2003) 14 CLF 59.

[251] Protests relating to violations of the laws of war were issued, though. R. John Pritchard and Sonia M. Zaide (eds.), *The Tokyo War Crimes Trial* (New York: Garland, 1981), *Vol 20. Judgment*, pp. 48,648, 48,669, 48,683.

[252] See Roosevelt's comments, and Vice President Wallace's address, 'America's Part in World Reconstruction', both quoted (without citation) in John Piccigallo, *The Japanese on Trial* (Austin, TX: Texas University Press, 1979), p. 4.

[253] Elizabeth Kopelman, 'Ideology and International Law: The Dissent of the Indian Justice at the Tokyo War Crimes Trial' (1991) 23 NYUJILP 373, 386 notes that this is not phrased in terms of individual liability.

[254] Solis Horwitz, 'The Tokyo Trial' (November 1950) *International Conciliation* 465, 478. On the period in question, see Joseph B. Keenan and Brendan F. Brown, *Crimes Against International Law* (Washington, DC: Public Affairs Press, 1950), chapter 1.

[255] See Bathurst, 'The UN War Crimes Commission', 570.

[256] 13 US Dept. of State Bulletin (29 July 1945), p. 137. Annex A-1 Vol. 7, p. 1. By this time, the Allies in Europe had already agreed (in principle) to an international tribunal for the major war criminals in Europe.

[257] The USSR adhered to the declaration later, on its entry into the Pacific war (9 August 1945).

of this Declaration was Principle 10, which promised that 'stern justice shall be meted out to all war criminals including those who have visited cruelties upon our prisoners'. This does not clearly mandate an international judicial process but, given the timing and its reference to 'stern justice', some form of trial seemed likely.[258] On 11 August, the United Kingdom, United States, China and the USSR clarified what General MacArthur's powers, as Supreme Commander for the Allied Powers (SCAP) would be, by defining them to include the power to 'take such steps as he deems proper to effectuate the surrender terms'.[259]

On 14 August 1945, the Japanese government accepted the Potsdam Declaration; the instrument of surrender was signed on 2 September 1945.[260] On 21 September, the US Joint Chiefs of Staff ordered the investigation and arrest of all war crimes suspects. General MacArthur was mandated to set up international courts for their trial. At this point, although the directives were 'known and approved' by the other Allies, they constituted unilateral action by the United States.[261]

The United States, United Kingdom and Soviet Union agreed to create the 'Far Eastern Commission' (FEC) by declaration on 27 December.[262] This set up a body of eleven States with the four major Allies having a veto power. It issued directives for the occupation to the Allied Council for Japan. The declaration also officially delegated the power to General MacArthur to implement their directives and the terms of surrender.[263] The nature of this was that the Allies granted the power to General MacArthur to act on their behalf to implement the surrender terms and any further directives they gave him. The instrument of surrender amounted to a treaty between the Japanese authorities and the Allies. The Allies then delegated the powers that they had in international law to punish war crimes and those conceded to it by Japan to General MacArthur, subject to their right to issue directives to him.

Under the powers granted to him, General MacArthur ordered the creation of the Tokyo IMT 'in order to implement the term of surrender

258 That earlier statements were equivocal was shown by the fact that many were surprised by this part of the declaration. See Bernard V. A. Röling and Antonio Cassese, *The Tokyo Trial and Beyond: Reflections of a Peacemonger* (Cambridge: Polity Press, 1993), p. 2.

259 13 US Dept. of State Bulletin (12 August 1945), p. 206.

260 13 US Dept. of State Bulletin (9 September 1945), p. 364 Annex A-2, pp. 7–11. It was signed by Japan and General MacArthur, on behalf of the United States, United Kingdom, USSR, China and the other united nations at war with Japan.

261 See Bathurst, 'The UN War Crimes Commission', 383; Horwitz, 'The Tokyo Trial', 480.

262 13 US Dept. of State Bulletin (27 December 1945), pp. 1027–32. China concurred in the communiqué.

263 *Ibid.*, Article VII B.5.

which required the meting out of stern justice to war criminals' on 19 January 1946.[264] The trial began with the lodging of the indictment with the Tokyo IMT, which occurred on 29 April 1946. The indictment contained fifty-five counts, and the section on Crimes Against Peace alone contained over 750 individual charges. Counts 1–36 related to Crimes Against Peace and conspiracies to commit that crime.[265] Counts 37–52 related to killings in an aggressive war. Conventional war crimes, Crimes Against Humanity and their conspiracies were left to the last three Counts (53–55). The Tribunal consisted of eleven judges, drawn from the victor nations in the Pacific sphere.[266] There were twenty-eight defendants, of whom twenty-five remained at the time of the judgment.[267]

The trial took over two-and-a-half years. The sheer magnitude of evidence necessitated such a long trial: 4,336 exhibits were admitted, 419 witnesses testified in person and 779 witnesses gave evidence by affidavit. All this led to a 1,218-page majority judgment, which upheld ten counts of the indictment, finding all the accused guilty, albeit not as charged. It sentenced seven defendants to death, one to twenty years imprisonment one to seven years imprisonment and the rest to incarceration for life. In addition to this there were three dissents, one concurring judgment and one separate opinion, all of which varied in length and quality.

The main aspect of the trial was the focus on the crimes against peace and conspiracy charges. This was ill-advised: these were the two most controversial charges at Nuremberg, and turned out to be even

[264] Special proclamation, Establishment of an International Military Tribunal for the Far East, 19 January 1946, T. I. A. S. No. 1589 3. MacArthur was exercising powers delegated to him (and not to the United States), and he was acting as an agent of the Allied nations. See *Hirota* v. *MacArthur* 335 US 876; 93 L. Ed. 1903 at 1904.

[265] The various itemised conspiracies under this heading are described by Ian Brownlie as 'incredibly artificial'; Ian Brownlie, *International Law and the Use of Force By States* (Oxford: Clarendon, 1963), p. 203.

[266] These being, Sir William Webb (Australia), E. Stuart McDougall (Canada), Ju-ao Mei (China), Henri Bernard (France), Delfin Jaranilla (Philippines), Bernard V. A. Röling (Netherlands), Erima H. Northcroft (New Zealand), I. M. Zaryanov (USSR), Lord Patrick (United Kingdom), John P. Higgins (replaced by Major-General Myron C. Cramer) (United States) and Radhabinodh M. Pal (India).

[267] The defendants were Kenji Dohihara, Koki Hirota, Seishiro Itagaki, Heitaro Kimura, Iwane Matsui, Akira Muto, Hideki Tojo, Sadao Araki, Kingoro Hashimoto, Shunroko Hata, Kiichiro Hiranuma, Naoki Hoshino, Okinori Kaya, Koichi Kido, Kuniaki Koiso, Jiro Minami, Takasumi Oka, Hiroshi Oshima, Kenryo Sato, Shigetaro Shimada, Toshi Shiratori, Teiichi Suzuki, Yoshijiro Umezu, Shigenori Togo, Mamoru Shigemitsu. Yosuke Matsuoka and Osami Nagano died during the trial. Shumei Okawa was declared mentally unfit to stand trial and was removed from the trial. See Tokyo IMT Judgment Transcript, pp. 48, 425.

more so at Tokyo. The prosecution claimed that there had been a wide-ranging conspiracy to go to war with, *inter alia*, the United Kingdom and United States since 1928. Later on, even some of the prosecutors admitted that there was no conclusive evidence of a plan going back that far.[268]

The prosecution had taken a conspiracy theory approach to history in their presentation of the case, and the majority opinion adopted that framework. They were taken to task for their simplistic approach by Judge Radhabinodh Pal, the Indian judge. Pal gave another interpretation of Japanese history, one influenced by his understandable dislike of European colonialism in East Asia.[269] If the majority was ready to take the prosecution at face value, Pal was ready to believe anything the defence told him.[270] The Dutch judge, Bernard Röling steered a middle path. Röling gave a more subtle reading of the facts, showing it was quite late, and partially as a result of Allied actions, that plans for war had ensued. Röling did not shy, however, from accepting the responsibility of some of the Japanese leaders for the war.[271]

Less controversially, the majority also found a number of the defendants responsible for war crimes such as the Bataan death march and the rape of Nanking. There were some questions, raised by Judge Röling, about whether five of the defendants, including Mamoru Shigemitsu and Koki Hirota, should have been convicted, although he also thought that other defendants (Oka, Sato and Shimada) had been wrongfully acquitted of some of the war crimes charges.[272]

Judge Pal, on the other hand, said that no war crimes at all could be placed at the door of the defendants, a position which was far less defensible than his discussion of crimes against peace.[273] To Pal, the trial was victor's justice, and selective.[274] Pal incurred the wrath of one of his fellow judges, Delfin Jaranilla, for his dissent, not least as Jaranilla had been on the Bataan death march, and was unsympathetic to both Pal

[268] Horwitz, 'The Tokyo Trial', 499. See also Piccigallo, *The Japanese on Trial*, p. 212.

[269] See Levie, *Terrorism in War*, p. 152.

[270] For contrasting views, see Kopelman, 'Ideology', 418–21 and the works cited therein; Arnold Brackman, *The Other Nuremberg: The Tokyo War Crimes Trial* (New York: William Morrow & Co., 1987), p. 391; Levie, *Terrorism in War*, pp. 151–2.

[271] Dissenting Opinion of Judge Röling, p. 50.

[272] Dissenting Opinion of Judge Röling, pp. 178–249.

[273] See Levie, *Terrorism in War*, pp. 151–2. He also took a radically sceptical view of witness evidence in sex offences; see Kelly D. Askin, *War Crimes Against Women: Prosecution in International Tribunals* (The Hague: Kluwer, 1997), pp. 181–5.

[274] See below, pp. 206–7.

and the defendants.[275] Jaranilla criticised the sentences on the ground that they were over-lenient and insufficiently exemplary.[276] It should be questioned whether Jaranilla should have sat when he was a victim of one of the crimes charged.

The trial itself took place in the former War Ministry buildings in Tokyo. It seems likely that the reason for the choice of this venue was an indelicate attempt to bring home to the world the complete defeat of the Japanese military forces and government. The theatrical aspects of the trial did not go unnoticed. *Time* magazine described the trial as resembling 'a third string road company of the Nuremberg show'.[277] This aura did not escape the notice of at least two of the judges, Judge Röling, for instance, considered that there were too many 'Hollywood' touches.[278] The negative aspects of the theatrical atmosphere were criticised by Judge Pal in his dissent, who criticised the trial as a crude public morality play.[279]

Considerable doubts have been expressed about the conduct of the proceedings.[280] There were provisions for fair trial in the Tokyo IMT's Charter,[281] but the trial was not conducted in accordance with even the limited rights of defence granted in the Charter and international law at the time. Two of the judges, Judge Pal and Judge Bernard both included stinging critiques of the conduct of the trial in their dissents.[282] Bernard went as far as to say that 'the procedure followed by the Prosecution and by the Tribual . . . did not permit me to formulate a definite opinion', and refused to enter any decision on the guilt or innocence of the defendants.[283] Pal was, as ever, scathing.[284]

History has not been kind to the Tokyo IMT. It is almost as if the Nuremberg and Tokyo IMTs are related in the manner that Dorian Gray was to his painting. Whilst the missteps at Nuremberg have not truly

[275] See Concurring Opinion of Judge Jaranilla, pp. 28–35.

[276] Concurring Opinion of Judge Jaranilla, pp. 32–5, see Röling and Cassese, *The Tokyo Trial*, pp. 29–30.

[277] 20 May 1946, p. 24.

[278] Röling and Cassese, *The Tokyo Trial*, p. 20.

[279] Dissenting Opinion of Judge Pal, pp. 1234–5.

[280] See, for example, Gordon Ireland, 'Uncommon Law in Martial Tokyo' (1950) 4 *Yearbook of World Affairs* 54; John Appleman, *Military Tribunals and International Trials* (Indianapolis: Bobbs Merrill, 1954), pp. 252–7, 317. M. Cherif Bassiouni, 'Nuremberg 40 Years Afterwards' (1986) 80 Proceedings ASIL 59, 59, 64.

[281] Tokyo IMT Charter, Article 13.

[282] Dissenting Opinion of Judge Pal, pp. 280–8, Dissenting Opinion of Judge Bernard, pp. 18–20.

[283] Dissenting Opinion of Judge Bernard, p. 20.

[284] Dissenting Opinion of Judge Pal, pp. 346–8.

undermined the image of the trial as basically fair, the Tokyo proceedings have been secreted away, and appear worse after time.[285] The Tokyo trial is now almost totally ignored,[286] something explained by Röling as following from embarrassment at the trial on the part of some of the prosecuting States.[287] The fact that the dissents had openly stated some of the IMT's faults and, on the part of Pal, put the prosecuting nations in the dock, did not endear the Tribual to its creators.[288]

There were also a large number of trials at the national level in the Pacific sphere. The earliest of these, the US prosecutions of Generals Yamashita and Homma in the Philippines, predated the Tokyo IMT[289] and came very quickly after the Japanese defeat. Later, there were a number of trials by the United States[290] and United Kingdom[291] and other States.[292] A particularly interesting trial was the trial of Admiral Someyu Toyoda before a panel of judges from Australia and the United States. The general view of this trial seems positive, suggesting that it was considered more independent than some of the earlier prosecutions,

[285] Gerry J. Simpson, 'War Crimes: A Critical Introduction', in Timothy L. H. McCormack and Gerry J. Simpson (eds.), *The Law of War Crimes: National and International Approaches* (The Hague: Kluwer, 1997), p. 2, states that Nuremberg is shadowed by its 'morally and legally defective twin at Tokyo'.

[286] See Chihiro Hosoya, 'Preface', in Chihiro Hosoya, Yasuaki Onuma, Nisuke Ando and Richard Minear (eds.), *The Tokyo Trial: An International Symposium* (Tokyo: Kodanasha International, 1986), p. 1, p. 7. See also Arnold Brackman, *The Other Nuremberg*, pp. 19, 22.

[287] Röling, in Röling and Cassese, *The Tokyo Trial*, p. 81, suggests that the US government 'were perhaps a bit ashamed of what happened there . . . with all the . . . awkward events'.

[288] See Simpson, 'War Crimes', p. 26. Richard Minear, *Victor's Justice: The Tokyo War Crimes Trial* (Princeton: Princeton University Press, 1971), p. 33, repeats claims that the United States deliberately prevented publication of Judge Pal's dissent in Japan while they were in occupation.

[289] *US* v. *Yamashita* 327 US 1, 4 CRTWC 1. For critical reviews, see A. Frank Reel, *The Case of General Yamashita* (Chicago: University of Chicago Press, 1949); Lawrence Taylor, *A Trial of Generals: Homma, Yamashita, MacArthur* (South Bend, Indiana: Icarus, 1981), pp. 149–68; Parks, 'Command Responsibility', 22–38.

[290] See George E. Erickson, 'US Navy War Crimes Trials (1945–1949) 5 *Washburn Law Journal* 255; Timothy Maga, *Judgment at Tokyo: The Japanese War Crimes Trials* (Lexington: Kentucky University Press, 2001); Robert W. Miller, 'War Crimes Trials at Yokohama' (1948–1949) 15 *Brooklyn Law Review* 19; Levie, *Terrorism in War*, pp. 155–72.

[291] See Pritchard, 'International Military Tribunal', pp. 136–9; Levie, *Terrorism in War*, pp. 173–6.

[292] R. John Pritchard, 'The International Military Tribunal for the Far East and the Allied National War Crimes Trials in Asia', in M. Cherif Bassiouni (ed.), *International Law, III: Enforcement* (Ardsley: Transnational, 2nd edn., 1999), p. 109, pp. 134–6, Levie, *Terrorism in War*, pp. 176–84; Piccigallo, *The Japanese on Trial*.

perhaps because of its international composition.[293] Again we can see the creation of a co-ordinated approach between national and international fora, assisted by the fact that those controlling the latter were also going to use the former types of trial.

All the defendants tried before the Tokyo IMT were from the Class A category, those suspected of crimes against peace. Those falling into the B and C categories (i.e. not suspected of crimes against peace) were prosecuted before national panels. As in Germany, there have been critiques of the release policies of the Allies.[294] The day after the death sentences were carried out on those sentenced to capital punishment by the Tokyo IMT, seventeen 'Class A' suspects were released without indictment.[295] All those remaining in prison were released within ten years, irrespective of sentence. Such releases strengthened the view 'that politics, not justice was at stake here, that even after Japan's surrender, the war was continued for a while to satisfy the Allied desire for revenge against the Japanese leaders'.[296]

The Cold War

At the start of the Cold War, there were moves to entrench the law identified at Nuremberg. The first of these was General Assembly Resolution 95(I) (1946), which '[a]ffirm[ed] the principles of international law recognised by the Charter of the Nürnberg Tribunal and the Judgment of the Tribunal'. Resolution 95(I) also directed the ILC to formulate those principles.[297] Despite some early doubts,[298] this Resolution now forms

[293] That was the intention; see Parks, 'Command Responsibility', 69–73, esp. 70. The idea that international composition of a tribunal is likely to lead to a more objective judgment is one that runs through international law; see Oscar Schachter, 'The Invisible College of International Lawyers' (1977) 72 *Northwestern University Law Journal* 217, 223.

[294] R. John Pritchard, 'The Gift of Clemency Following the British War Crimes Trials in the Far East 1946–1948' (1996) 7 CLF 15.

[295] See Kentaro Awaya, 'In the Shadows of the Tokyo Trial', in Chihiro Hosoya, Yasuaki Onuma, Nisuke Ando and Richard Minear (eds.), *The Tokyo Trial: An International Symposium* (Tokyo: Kodanasha International, 1986), p. 79, p. 83.

[296] Röling, 'Introduction', in Chihiro Hosoya, Yasuaki Onuma, Nisuke Ando and Richard Minear (eds.), *The Tokyo Trial: An International Symposium* (Tokyo: Kodanasha International, 1986), p. 18.

[297] UN Doc. A/64/Add.1. See Arthur Kuhn, 'International Criminal Jurisdiction' (1947) 41 AJIL 430.

[298] See, e.g. Hans Ehard, 'The Nuremberg Trial Against the Major War Criminals and International Law' (1949) 46 AJIL 223, 242.

the backbone of the case for the contention that the innovations at Nuremberg amounted to customary law.[299] The ILC reported with its formulation of those principles in 1950.[300]

In Resolution 280 (1948) the General Assembly asked the ILC to 'study the desirability and possibility of establishing an international judicial organ for the trial of persons charged with genocide or other crimes'.[301] In 1950, two Special Rapporteurs gave conflicting reports on the current desirability of an international criminal court.[302] After this, the question was passed to a committee of seventeen State representatives in the General Assembly, which produced two draft statutes in 1951 and 1953.[303] Because of the Cold War, these proposals were stillborn, and in 1954 the question was shelved pending the drafting of a definition of aggression.[304]

Substantive law developed at this time. Just prior to the postponement of the international criminal court project, there had been the Genocide Convention (in 1948) and the four Geneva Conventions of 1949.[305] There were some prosecutions for international crimes at this time, almost all of Nazis.[306] Prosecutions were undertaken in this time in Germany,[307]

[299] Report of the Secretary General Pursuant to Paragraph 2 of Security Council Resolution 808, UN Doc. S/25704, paras. 34–35.

[300] 1950 YBILC 852.

[301] UN Doc. A/RES/280B (1948). In 1948, the Genocide Convention had suggested the possibility of such a tribunal in Article VI.

[302] Report of the International Law Commission on the Question of International Criminal Jurisdiction, UN GAOR 5th Sess. UN Docs. A/CN.4/ 15 and 20. See Bengt Broms, 'The Establishment of an International Criminal Court', in Yoram Dinstein and Mala Tabory (eds.), *War Crimes in International Law* (The Hague: Martinus Nijhoff, 1996), p. 183, pp. 183–4.

[303] Report of the Committee on International Criminal Jurisdiction, UN Doc. A/2136 and Report of the 1953 Committee on International Criminal Jurisdiction, UN Doc. A/2638.

[304] GA Resolution 898, UN Doc. A/2890. See Leila Sadat-Wexler, 'The Proposed International Criminal Court: An Appraisal' (1996) 20 Cornell ILJ 665, 679–83.

[305] See Roger S. Clark, Clark, 'Offences of International Concern: Multilateral State Treaty Practice in the Forty Years Since Nuremberg' (1988) 57 Nordic JIL 49.

[306] Gillian Triggs, 'Australia's War Crimes Trials: A Moral Necessity or Legal Minefield?' (1987) 16 MULR 382; Gillian Triggs, 'Australia's War Crimes Trials: All Pity Choked', in Timothy L. H. McCormack and Gerry J. Simpson (eds.), *The Law of War Crimes: National and International Approaches* (The Hague: Kluwer, 1997), p. 123; J. Martin Wagner, 'US Prosecution of Past and Future War Criminals and Criminals Against Humanity: Proposals for Reform Based on the Canadian and Australian Experiences' (1989) 29 VJIL 887.

[307] See Dirk de Mildt, *In the Name of the People: Perpetrators of Genocide in the Reflection of their Post-War Prosecution in West Germany* (The Hague: Martinus Nijhoff, 1996).

but the most famous were probably the *Eichmann*[308] Case in Israel (*Attorney-General of Israel* v. *Eichmann*) and the *Barbie* (*Fédération Nationale des Déportes et Internes Résistants et Patriots* v. *Barbie*) and *Touvier* trials in France.[309] Outside what might have been considered 'unfinished business' from the war crimes programmes related to the Second World War, there were a considerable number of prosecutions in the United States for what amounted to war crimes, although they were prosecuted as violations of the Uniform Code of Military Justice.[310] The best known of these were the *Calley* (1969) and *Medina* (1971) Cases,[311] both of which arose from the My Lai massacre.[312] The Argentine prosecutions of the leading members of the *junta* in the 1980s were also under domestic law, although the acts amounted to international crimes.[313]

Prosecutions were the exception rather than the rule, and this led some to question if there was any commitment to international criminal law after Nuremberg.[314] There was some truth in this. A number

[308] 36 ILR 18; see Helen Silving, 'In re Eichmann: A Dilemma of Law and Morality' (1961) 55 AJIL 307; Peter Papadatos, *The Eichmann Trial* (London: Stevens, 1961); Hannah Arendt, *Eichmann in Jerusalem: A Report on the Banality of Evil* (Harmondsworth: Penguin, 1994).

[309] *Fédération Nationale des Deportes et Internes Résistants et Patriots* v. *Barbie* 78 ILR 125. Leila Sadat-Wexler, 'The Interpretation of the Nuremberg Principles by the French Court of Cassation: from Touvier to Barbie to Back Again' (1994) 32 CJTL 289; Guyora Binder, 'Representing Nazism: Advocacy and Identity at the Trial of Klaus Barbie' (1989) 98 Yale LJ 1321.

[310] See Gary D. Solis, 'Military Justice, Civilian Clemency: The Sentences of Marine Corps War Crimes in South Vietnam' (2000) 10 TCLP 59. See generally, Benjamin Ferencz, 'War Crimes Law and the Vietnam War' (1968) 17 *American University Law Review* 403; Telford Taylor, *Nuremberg and Vietnam: An American Tragedy* (Chicago: Quadrangle Books, 1970).

[311] *US* v. *Calley* (1969) 41 CMR 96; (1973) 46 CMR 1131; (1973) 48 CMR 19; *US* v. *Medina* (1971) 43 CMR 243.

[312] See Norman G. Cooper, 'My Lai and Military Justice – To What Effect?' (1973) 59 Military LR 93; Matthew Lippman, 'War Crimes, The My Lai Massacre and the Vietnam War' (1993) 1 SDJJ 295 and Kevin Bilton and Michael Sim, *Four Hours in My Lai* (Harmondsworth: Penguin, 1993); W. Baird (ed.), *From Nuremberg to My Lai* (London: Heath & Co., 1972); Alfred P. Rubin, 'Legal Aspects of the My Lai Incident' (1970) 49 OLR 260; Jordan J. Paust, 'Legal Aspects of the My Lai Incident: A Response to Professor Rubin' (1971) 50 OLR 138.

[313] Luis Moreno-Ocampo, 'The Nuremberg Precedent in Argentina' (1990) 11 NYLSJICL 357; Carlos S. Nino, *Radical Evil on Trial* (Yale: Yale University Press, 1996); Anthony Garro, 'Nine Years of Transition to Democracy in Argentina: Partial Failure or Qualified Success?' (1993) 31 CJTL 1; Anthony Garro and Henry Dahl, 'Legal Accountability for Human Rights Violations in Argentina: One Step Forward and Two Steps Back' (1987) 8 HRLJ 283.

[314] Eugene Davidson, *The Nuremberg Fallacy: Wars and War Crimes Since World War II* (New York: Macmillan, 1973).

of academics, including Cherif Bassiouni,[315] Robert Woetzel[316] and ex-Nuremberg prosecutor Benjamin Ferencz[317] sought to keep the project for an international criminal court going, but irrespective of the fortitude with which they put forward their views, State officials heard their calls *pianissimo*, if at all. Attempts by unofficial bodies, such as the Russell Tribunal for Vietnam, to apply international criminal law did not have much practical effect.[318]

Suggestions for the prosecution of Saddam Hussein in the aftermath of the Gulf Conflict in 1990–1 came to nothing.[319] In the end, the lack of movement on an international criminal court was reflected in the excision of material relating to Nuremberg from standard textbooks,[320] and few could criticise Ian Brownlie for writing, in the fourth edition of his *Principles of Public International Law*, that 'in spite of extensive consideration of the problem in committees of the General Assembly, the likelihood of setting up an international criminal court is very remote'.[321]

The International Criminal Tribunal for the Former Yugoslavia (ICTY)

It took the atrocities of the Yugoslav wars of dissolution[322] to elicit an international penal response. The history behind the creation of the ICTY reveals certain similarities and differences to that preceding the Nuremberg and Tokyo IMTs. One similarity to the two IMTs created in

315 See, for example, M. Cherif Bassiouni, *A Draft International Criminal Code and Draft Statute for an International Criminal Tribunal* (Dordrecht: Martinus Nijhoff, 1987).

316 Julius Stone and Robert K. Woetzel, *Towards a Feasible International Criminal Court* (Geneva: World Peace Through Law Institute, 1970).

317 Benjamin Ferencz, *The International Criminal Court: A Step Towards World Peace* (New York: Oceana, 1980).

318 For a different view, see Richard Falk, 'Keeping Nuremberg Alive', in Richard A. Falk, Friedrich V. Kratchowil and Saul H. Mendlovitz, *International Law: A Contemporary Conception* (Boulder: Westview, 1985), p. 494.

319 See William V. O'Brien, 'The Nuremberg Precedent and the Gulf War' (1991) 31 VJIL 391; Louis R. Beres, 'Toward Prosecution of Iraqi Crimes Under International Law: Jurisprudential Foundations and Jurisdictional Choices' (1991–1992) 22 CWILJ 127.

320 Colin Warbrick, 'International Criminal Law' (1995) 44 ICLQ 466, 466.

321 Ian Brownlie, *Principles of Public International Law* (Oxford: Clarendon Press, 4th edn., 1990), pp. 563–4.

322 For an early discussion of the application of international law to the conflict, see Jordan J. Paust, 'Applicability of International Criminal Law to Events in Former Yugoslavia' (1994) 9 AUJILP 499.

the aftermath of the Second World War was that the history of the ICTY begins with public denunciations of the atrocities.[323] The first relevant resolution was Security Council Resolution 764,[324] which demanded compliance with humanitarian law in former Yugoslavia. When this had no practical effect, the Security Council passed Resolution 771.[325] This required the parties to the conflict to cease their breaches of humanitarian law and gave a list of such violations. It also contained a request to States to submit any 'substantiated information' on these violations in their possession to the Security Council.[326]

In the face of the continued violations of humanitarian law the Security Council passed Resolution 780.[327] This created a Commission of Experts to investigate and gather evidence of the violations of humanitarian law in former Yugoslavia.[328] Like the UNWCC, the Commission was hamstrung by State ambivalence and lack of finance.[329]

Between the submission of the Commission of Experts' interim and final reports, the Security Council took the decision to take steps in Resolution 808 to bring into being an international criminal tribunal.[330] To begin the process of creating the tribunal, the resolution asked the Secretary General to prepare a report within sixty days on how to establish an international criminal tribunal. When the Secretary General reported back, he included a draft statute for the tribunal. This was adopted

[323] On the following resolutions and the events leading up to the creation of the ICTY, see John C. O'Brien, 'The International Tribunal for Violations of International Humanitarian Law in the Former Yugoslavia' (1993) 77 AJIL 639, 639–42; Virginia Morris and Michael P. Scharf, *An Insider's Guide to the International Criminal Tribunal for Former Yugoslavia* (Ardsley: Transnational, 1995), chapter 2; M. Cherif Bassiouni and Peter Manikas, *The Law of the International Criminal Tribunal for Yugoslavia* (Ardsley: Transnational, 1996), chapter 2; Michael P. Scharf, *Balkan Justice: The Story Behind the First International Trial Since Nuremberg* (Durham, NC: North Carolina University Press, 1997), chapter 4; On the response of other organisations or UN bodies, see Payam Akhavan, 'Prosecuting War Crimes in the Former Yugoslavia: A Critical Juncture for the New World Order' (1993) 15 HRQ 262.

[324] UN Doc. S/RES/764. [325] UN Doc. S/RES/771.

[326] As Morris and Scharf note, *An Insider's Guide*, p. 23, the lack of definition of 'substantiated information' led to conflicting State interpretations of the type of information requested.

[327] UN Doc. S/RES/780.

[328] On the Commission, see M. Cherif Bassiouni, 'The United Nations Commission of Experts Established Pursuant to Security Council Resolution 780' (1994) 88 AJIL 784; William J. Fenrick, 'In the Field With UNCOE: Investigating Atrocities in the Territory of Former Yugoslavia' (1994) 34 RIDMDG 33; Scharf, *Balkan Justice*, chapter 3.

[329] See Bassiouni, 'From Versailles', 39 ('there is an uncanny resemblance between the problems facing the Commission of Experts and those of the UNWCC') and 41.

[330] UN Doc. S/RES/808.

unanimously by the Security Council in Resolution 827, which created the ICTY.[331]

In the Secretary General's report accompanying the ICTY Statute the possibility of using a treaty to set up the ICTY was canvassed, as this would be 'the approach which, in the normal course of events, would be followed in establishing an international tribunal'.[332] In the circumstances, the Secretary General thought this would take too long and, tellingly, there was 'no guarantee that ratifications . . . [would be] . . . received from those States which should be parties to the treaty'.[333] As a result the Secretary General recommended the creation of the ICTY by the Security Council, on the basis of its Chapter VII powers.[334]

The Security Council established the ICTY by Resolution 827. In the meeting preceding the passing of that Resolution, Brazil and China both questioned whether the Security Council had the authority to set up an international criminal tribunal under Chapter VII,[335] but neither considered their reservations fundamental enough to vote against the Resolution. The legality of the creation of the Tribunal has caused some controversy, and was challenged by the defendant in the *Tadić* Case.[336]

The first ground of challenge was that the Security Council was not mandated by the framers of the Charter to create a tribunal.[337] The framers never considered the matter,[338] but the Charter is not an originalist document, to be interpreted solely in accordance with the will of the drafters in 1945.[339] As Oscar Schachter said, 'the Charter is surely not

331 UN Doc. S/RES/827.

332 Report of the Secretary General Pursuant to Security Council Resolution 808, UN Doc. S/25704, para. 19. The CSCE had previously suggested a treaty for the creation of the ICTY, and had drafted one. See UN Doc. S/RES/25307.

333 *Ibid.*, para. 20.

334 *Ibid.*, para. 22. See Adam Roberts 'The Laws of War: Problems of Implementation in Contemporary Conflicts' (1995) 6 DJCIL 11, 64.

335 S/PV, 3217, pp. 20–2.

336 *Prosecutor* v. *Tadić*, Decision on Interlocutory Appeal on Jurisdiction, IT-94-1-AR72, 2 October 1995, para. 33.

337 *Prosecutor* v. *Tadić*, *ibid.* para. 32. See also the comments of Brazil at UN SCOR 47th Sess. S/PV. 3175, p. 4, and China at S/PV. 3217, pp. 20–1.

338 Hazel Fox considers this an important argument against the lawfulness and legitimacy of the ICTY; Hazel Fox, 'The Objections to Transfer of Criminal Jurisdiction to the UN Tribunal' (1997) 46 ICLQ 434, 435.

339 Brian Urquhart, 'The United Nations and International Security after the Cold War', in Adam Roberts and Benedict Kingsbury, *United Nations, Divided World* (Oxford: Oxford University Press, 2nd edn., 1993), p. 81, p. 91; Rosalyn Higgins, 'The Development of International Law Through the Political Organs of the United Nations' (1965) 69 Proceedings ASIL 116, 119.

to be construed like a lease of land or an insurance policy, it is a constitutional instrument whose broad phrases were designed to meet changing circumstances for an undefined future'.[340] The Charter grants the Security Council authority to determine, within broad parameters, what response to make to specific threats to international peace and security. Christopher Greenwood is correct, 'there seems no reason in principle why the Security Council, if it considers that the creation of a judicial instrument is necessary for it to effectively perform its functions in respect of peace and security, should not create such an instrument'.[341]

The legal basis for the Security Council's creation of the ICTY was generally supported by States[342] (particularly in the General Assembly)[343] and has been entrenched by the repetition of the actions for the ICTR[344] and the provisions of the ICC Statute allowing the Council to send cases to the ICC.[345] As the ICTY was set up by an organ of an international organisation under the powers delegated to it by States under a treaty, its basis is international. The method of creation of the ICTY is more reminiscent of the method of creation of the Tokyo IMT than it is of the Nuremberg 'precedent'. As the jurisdiction, practice and record of the ICTY will be the subject of comment later in this book, no more need be said here.[346]

The International Criminal Tribunal for Rwanda (ICTR)

Soon after the creation of the ICTY, another conflict arose that shocked many States, to which the response from the Security Council showed

[340] Oscar Schachter, 'Review of Kelsen, The Law of the United Nations' (1951) 60 Yale LJ 189, 193.

[341] Christopher J. Greenwood, 'The Development of International Humanitarian Law by The International Criminal Tribunal for the Former Yugoslavia' (1998) 2 MPYBUNL 97, 104.

[342] See Paul C. Szasz, 'Centralized and Decentralized Law Enforcement, The Security Council and the General Assembly Acting Under Chapters VII and VIII', in Jost Delbrück (ed.), *Allocation of Law Enforcement Authority in the International System* (Berlin: Duncker & Humblot, 1995), p. 17, p. 33.

[343] GA Resolution 48/88, UN Doc. A/RES/48/88, welcomed the creation of the ICTY.

[344] See below, pp. 54–6. [345] See below, p. 225.

[346] For general accounts, see William J Fenrick, 'The Development of the Law of Armed Conflict through the Jurisprudence of the International Criminal Tribunal for the Former Yugoslavia' (1998) 3 JACL 197; Kelly D. Askin, 'Reflections on Some of the Most Significant Achievements of the ICTY' (2003) 37 NELR 903; Geoffrey R. Watson, 'The Changing Jurisprudence of the International Criminal Tribunal for the Former Yugoslavia' (2003) 37 NELR 871; Mark A. Drumbl, 'Looking Up, Down and Across: The ICTY's Place in the International Legal Order' (2003) 37 NELR 1037. A very useful symposium can be found in (2004) 2 JICJ 353–597.

the impact of the creation of the ICTY. In Rwanda, genocide was perpetrated in full view of the United Nations. Early in the genocide ten UN peacekeepers had been killed. Within a fortnight this had led to the reduction of the UN peacekeeping force from over 1,500 to 270 by virtue of Resolution 912.[347] The Council began its action in response to the atrocities in Rwanda quietly. As in Yugoslavia, it began by condemning violations of humanitarian law (not genocide, which was conspicuously absent from the statement) in Rwanda, but only in a Presidential statement.[348] Fear of the spectres of selectivity and Eurocentrism helped give momentum to the drive to set up a tribunal for Rwanda.[349] Stung by criticism after the Rwandan Patriotic Front (RPF) had asked for an international tribunal, the Security Council mandated the Secretary General to investigate the Rwandan situation.[350]

The Secretary General's Special Rapporteur for Rwanda broke the UN linguistic taboo surrounding the description of the killings in Rwanda as genocide. Soon after, the Security Council passed Resolution 925,[351] which acknowledged that genocide had occurred.[352] From this, the Security Council (not without reservations) went on to create a Commission of Experts for Rwanda.[353] As in Yugoslavia, in between the submission of the interim and final report of the Commission, the Security Council, responding to many calls for an international tribunal, including one from the new government of Rwanda,[354] passed Resolution 955.[355] This created the ICTR, and annexed its Statute. The Statute was drafted not by the Secretary General, but by New Zealand and the United States, with input from the (new) Rwandan government.[356] The legal authority

347 UN Doc. S/RES/912.

348 UN Doc. S/PRST/1994/21. See Jaana Karhilo, 'The Establishment of the International Criminal Tribunal for Rwanda' (1995) 64 Nordic JIL 683, 689–90.

349 Antonio Cassese, 'From Nuremberg to Rome: International Military Tribunals to the International Criminal Court', in Antonio Cassese, Paula Gaeta and John R. W. D. Jones (eds.), *The Rome Statute of the International Criminal Court: A Commentary* (Oxford: Oxford University Press, 2002), p. 3, p. 14.

350 Resolution 918, UN Doc. S/RES/918. See Karhilo, 'The Establishment', 689.

351 UN Doc. S/RES/925.

352 Virginia Morris and Michael P. Scharf, *The International Criminal Tribunal for Rwanda* (Ardsley: Transnational, 1998), pp. 59–64.

353 Resolution 935, UN Doc. S/RES/935. See Morris and Scharf, *The International Criminal Tribunal for Rwanda*, p. 65.

354 Letter Dated 28 September 1994 from the Permanent Representative of Rwanda to the United Nations Addressed to the President of the Security Council, UN Doc. S/1994/1115.

355 UN Doc. S/RES/955. See Morris and Scharf, *The International Criminal Tribunal for Rwanda*, pp. 65–73.

356 Roy S. Lee, 'The Rwanda Tribunal' (1996) 9 LJIL 37, 39.

did not come from the consent of Rwanda, but Chapter VII of the UN Charter.[357]

The legal basis of the ICTR is therefore the same as that of the ICTY.[358] In *Prosecutor* v. *Kanyabashi*, the defendant challenged the creation of the tribunal on the basis of an alleged lack of a threat to international peace and security and a suggestion that the Security Council could not create a court. The ICTR dealt with his contentions in a rather summary fashion, refusing to second-guess the Council at all.[359] The Trial Chamber claimed that the determination of a threat to the peace was totally within the discretion of the Security Council,[360] and that as Article 41 of the UN Charter was not exhaustive, the Security Council could choose to create the Tribunal.[361]

The legality of the ICTR's creation was perhaps less controversial, given that the precedent had already been set in 1993. In the Security Council, both Brazil and China repeated their reservations about the legality of the creation of international courts by the Security Council.[362] Again, however, they did not vote against the creation of the court.[363] One country outside the Security Council queried the creation of the ICTR. This was Kenya; after discussions with the Security Council, Kenya officially accepted the legality of the Tribunal.[364] The power of the Security Council to create such tribunals pursuant to Chapter VII appears to have been confirmed by the creation of the ICTR. As with the ICTY, since the record of the ICTR will be discussed later, further comment here would be superfluous.[365]

[357] Larry Johnson, 'The International Tribunal for Rwanda' (1996) 67 RIDP 211, 215; Lee, 'The Rwanda Tribunal', 41.

[358] Secretary General's Report, paras. 8–9.

[359] *Prosecutor* v. *Kanyabashi*, Decision on the Defence Motion on Jurisdiction ICTR-96-15-T, 18 June 1997, paras 17–32; Virginia Morris, 'International Decisions, *Prosecutor* v. *Kanayabashi*' (1998) 92 AJIL 66. See similarly *Prosecutor* v. *Karemera*, Decision, ICTR-98-44-T, 25 April 2001, para. 25.

[360] *Prosecutor* v. *Kanyabashi*, para. 20. [361] *Ibid*.

[362] S/PV.3453 pp. 6–7, 7 resp. See Daphna Schraga and Ralph Zacklin, 'The International Criminal Tribunal for Rwanda' (1996) 7 EJIL 501, 505.

[363] China abstained on Resolution 955, on different grounds (that more consultation to accommodate Rwanda should have been undertaken. (S/PV. 3453, p. 7)).

[364] Letter Dated 11 October 1995 From the Permanent Representative of Kenya to the United Nations Addressed to the President of the Security Council, UN Doc. S/1995/861. See Morris and Scharf, *The International Criminal Tribunal for Rwanda*, pp. 656–7.

[365] Although see generally, José E. Alvarez, 'Crimes of Hate/Crimes of State, Lessons from Rwanda' (1999) 24 Yale JIL 365; Christina M. Carroll, 'An Assessment of the Role and Effectiveness of the International Criminal Tribunal for Rwanda and the Rwandan National Justice System in Dealing With the Mass Atrocities of 1994' (2000) 18 BUILJ 163.

The International Criminal Court (ICC)

After 1954, nothing of note about an international criminal court occurred in official fora until 1989. Then, in response to the request of a coalition of sixteen Caribbean and Latin American States (led by Trinidad and Tobago), the General Assembly asked the ILC to look at the possibility of an international criminal court to enforce the draft code of offences against the peace and security of mankind.[366] Their reason for suggesting this extraordinary act of revival was not the protection of human rights, or the enforcement of international criminal law in the sense it is used in this book, but to create a collaborative measure for enforcing national laws based on the 1988 Vienna Convention Against the Illicit Trafficking in Narcotic Drugs and Psychotropic Substances.[367] This was suggested as a means for countries whose judicial systems were unable to cope with the power and influence of rich drug barons, and to ensure that prosecution occurred in an independent forum, less subject to the pressures that could be brought to bear on national politicians, judges and prosecutors. The suggestion coincided with an upturn in academic interest in the idea.[368]

Some progress had been made by 1992,[369] when the General Assembly asked the ILC to begin work on a draft statute,[370] but many States remained sceptical, and some were actively opposed.[371] The debates in the ILC were 'going around in circles and getting nowhere'.[372] By 1993,

[366] GA Resolution 44/39, UN Doc. A/RES/44/39. Before this, Professor Bassiouni had been asked, by the UN Mission for Human Rights, to prepare a draft statute for a court to implement the Apartheid convention (UN Doc. E/CN.4/1416) (1980). Nothing was done about his proposal. See M. Cherif Bassiouni and Christopher Blakesley, 'The Time has Come for an International Criminal Court' (1992) 25 VJTL 151, 157.

[367] 1019 UNTS 175.

[368] John Dugard, 'Obstacles in the Way of an International Criminal Court' (1997) 56 Cambridge LJ 329, 330, notes a political upturn towards the idea in the 1980s. See also William N. Giniaris, 'The New World Order and the Need for an International Criminal Court' (1992–1993) 16 Fordham ILJ 88.

[369] See Benjamin Ferencz, 'An International Criminal Code and Court: Where They Stand and Where They're Going' (1992) 30 CJTL 375.

[370] GA Resolution 47/33, UN Doc. A/RES/47/33. On the ILC's efforts see James Crawford, 'The Work of the International Law Commission', in Antonio Cassese, Paula Gaeta and John R. W. D. Jones (eds.), *The Rome Statute of the International Criminal Court: A Commentary* (Oxford: Oxford University Press, 2002), p. 23.

[371] Ferencz, 'An International Criminal Code', 387–90; Michael P. Scharf, 'The Jury is Still Out on an International Criminal Court' (1991) 1 DJCIL 135; Michael P. Scharf, 'Getting Serious About an International Criminal Court' (1994) 6 Pace ILR 103, 103–4.

[372] Ferencz, 'An International Criminal Code', 390. This was partially as a result of the United States deliberately raising problems, but not answers, in an effort to stall matters, Scharf, 'Getting Serious', 105.

and partially as a result of the creation of the ICTY, States (particularly the United States) began to become more flexible.[373] Concern had been expressed about the selective nature of *ad hoc* responses.[374] The quick creation of the ICTY also showed that such an institution could be created, and the Statute provided a template, at least concretising the issues involved in the creation of an international criminal court.[375]

Media coverage of international crimes in Yugoslavia and Rwanda, alongside the creation of the ICTY also stimulated interest in civil society, especially in the NGO community, which played a generally positive role in the development of the ICC Statute.[376] 'What started out in 1993 as mostly a public relations ploy, namely to create an *ad hoc* tribunal to appear to be doing something about human rights violations in Bosnia without major risk, by 1998 had become an important global movement for international criminal justice'.[377] In 1993, the shifting views of many, although by no means all, States led the ILC to come up with a draft statute that borrowed heavily from that of the ICTY.[378]

In response, the General Assembly asked the ILC to complete its work on the statute by 1994.[379] The ILC adopted a draft statute on time,[380] the General Assembly set up an *ad hoc* committee of States to look at the matter,[381] then in 1995 set up the Preparatory Committee for an

373 Scharf, 'Getting Serious', 106–7.

374 Ian Brownlie, *Principles of International Law* (Oxford: Oxford University Press, 5th edn., 1998), p. 568.

375 On this, see Robert Cryer, 'Human Rights and the Question of International Courts and Tribunals', in Michael Davis, Wolfgang Dietrich, Dieter Sepp and Bettina Scholdan (eds.), *International Intervention in the Post-Cold War World* (Armonk, New York: M. E. Sharpe, 2003), p. 60.

376 On this, see William R. Pace and Jennifer Schense, 'The Role of Non-Governmental Organisations', in Antonio Cassese, Paula Gaeta and John R. W. D Jones (eds.), *The Rome Statute of the International Criminal Court: A Commentary* (Oxford: Oxford University Press, 2002), p. 105.

377 David Forsythe, *Human Rights in International Relations* (Cambridge: Cambridge University Press, 2000), p. 221 *contra* David J. Scheffer, 'Three Memories of the Year of Origin, 1993' (2004) 2 JICJ 353, 353–7.

378 *Report of the ILC on the Work of its Forty-Fifth Session*, Report of the Working Group on a Draft Statute for an International Criminal Court, UN Doc. A/48/CN.4/Ser.A/1993/Add.1, pp. 100–32. See James Crawford, 'The ILC's Draft Statute'. For criticism, see Scharf, 'Getting Serious', 109–18.

379 GA Resolution 48/31, UN Doc. A/RES/48/31.

380 *Report of the ILC on the Work of its Forty-Sixth Session*, UN Doc. A/49/10. See J. Crawford, 'The ILC Adopts a Statute for an International Criminal Court' (1995) 89 AJIL 404; Sadat-Wexler, 'The Proposed International Criminal Court', 685–726.

381 GA Resolution 49/53; UN Doc. A/RES/49/53; M. Cherif Bassiouni, 'Observations Concerning the 1997–8 Preparatory Committee's Work', in M. Cherif Bassiouni (ed.),

International Criminal Court (PREPCOM). This was mandated to look at the ILC Draft and to try to come up with a consolidated text of proposals for an international conference to create a treaty for an international criminal court.[382] This was done for the Rome Conference on an International Criminal Court, which met in June–July 1998 and which adopted the Rome Statute of the International Criminal Court.[383] In accordance with Article 126, the Rome Statute came into force on 1 July 2002, shortly after the deposit of the sixtieth instrument of ratification.[384] To prepare for this eventuality, the Preparatory Commission (also called PREPCOM) worked on a number of matters, including the Elements of Crimes and Rules of Procedure and Evidence for the ICC.[385]

The International Criminal Court: Observations and Issues Before the Preparatory Committee; and Administrative and Financial Implications 13 *Nouvelles Etudes Pénales*, (Chicago: Erès, 1997), p. 5, pp. 8–9, claims that this was a stalling movement by recalcitrant States.

382 GA Resolution 50/46; UN Doc. A/RES/50/46; the mandate was extended by GA Resolution 51/207, UN Doc. A/RES/51/207, On the PREPCOM's work, see *Report of the Preparatory Committee on the Establishment of an International Criminal Court*, UN Doc. A/51/22; Adriaan Bos, 'From the International Law Commission to the Rome Conference (1994–1998)', in Antonio Cassesse, Paula Gaeta and John R. W. D. Jones (eds.), *The Rome Statute of the International Criminal Court: A Commentary* (Oxford: Oxford University Press, 2002), p. 35 and Christopher Keith Hall, 'The First Two Sessions of the Preparatory Committee on the Establishment of an International Criminal Court' (1997) 91 AJIL 177; Christopher Keith Hall, 'The Third and Fourth Sessions of the Preparatory Committee for an International Criminal Court' (1998) 92 AJIL 124; Christopher Keith Hall, 'The Fifth Session of the Preparatory Committee on the Establishment of an International Criminal Court' (1998) 92 AJIL 331. Christopher Keith Hall, 'The Sixth Session of the UN Preparatory Committee on the Establishment of an International Criminal Court' (1998) 92 AJIL 548; Andreas Zimmerman, 'The Creation of a Permanent International Criminal Court' (1998) 2 MPYBUNL 169.

383 A/CONF.183/9. On the drafting process, see Philippe Kirsch and John T. Holmes, 'The Rome Conference on an International Criminal Court: The Negotiating Process' (1999) 93 AJIL 2; M. Cherif Bassiouni, 'Negotiating the Treaty of Rome on the Establishment of an International Criminal Court' (1999) 32 Cornell ILJ 443; Immi Tallgren, 'We Did It? The Vertigo of Law and Everyday Life at the Diplomatic Conference on the Establishment of an International Criminal Court' (1999) 12 LJIL 683. For a US view, see David J. Scheffer, 'The United States and the International Criminal Court' (1999) 93 AJIL 12.

384 Ten instruments were simultaneously deposited on 11 April 2002, taking the number from fifty-six to sixty-six.

385 On the work of the PREPCOM, see Philippe Kirsch and Valerie Oosterveld, 'The Post-Rome Preparatory Commission', in Antonio Cassese, Paula Gaeta and John R. W. D. Jones (eds.), *The Rome Statute of the International Criminal Court: A Commentary* (Oxford: Oxford University Press, 2002), p. 93; Christine Byron and David Turns, 'The Preparatory Commission for the International Criminal Court' (2001) 50 ICLQ 420; Christopher Keith Hall, 'The First Five Sessions of the Preparatory Commission for the International Criminal Court' (2000) 94 AJIL 773.

Other developments in the post-Cold War era

Alongside, and at times inspired by, developments in international enforcement of international criminal law, there has since 1990 also been increasing activity at the national (or in one case part-national, part-international) level dealing with international crimes. Early in the final decade of the twentieth century, the programmes of prosecutions of Nazis continued in a few States (Canada and the United Kingdom in particular), with the *Finta* (*R.* v. *Finta*) and *Sawoniuk* (*R.* v. *Sawoniuk*) Cases.[386] Both related to local police officials in Eastern Europe, who were prosecuted for their parts in the Holocaust. Finta was acquitted in a controversial 1994 decision of the Canadian Supreme Court, Sawoniuk was convicted and his appeal dismissed in 2001.[387] In France, the issue of Vichy France was finally faced head-on in the *Papon* Case.[388] Prosecutions of Nazis became more difficult and, owing to the advanced age of the defendants and suspects, were all but brought to an end by the turn of the millennium.[389] These prosecutions did not reignite the debate about prosecution of international crimes more generally. It was after the creation of the ICTY and ICTR that there was a clear movement towards prosecution of international crimes. Many of these were of suspects from former Yugoslavia and Rwanda, a point that will be returned to in chapter 2. Not all were, however. Ethiopia began prosecutions of the former *Derg* government in the 1990s.[390] Of the attempts at prosecuting international crimes, the 1999 arrest and extradition proceedings involving Augusto Pinochet, ex-Head of State of Chile must also be noted.[391]

[386] 104 ILR 285; see David Matas, 'The Case of Imre Finta' (1994) 34 *University of New Brunswick Law Review* 281; Matthew Lippman, 'The Pursuit of Nazi War Criminals in the United States and in Other Anglo-American Legal Systems' (1998) 29 CWILJ 1; Irwin Cotler, 'War Crimes Law and the Finta Case' (1995) 6(2d) *Supreme Court Law Review* 577.

[387] *R* v. *Sawoniuk* (2001) 2 Cr App R. 220.

[388] Richard J. Golsan (ed.), *The Papon Affair: Memory and Justice on Trial* (London: Routledge, 2000).

[389] The investigative unit created in pursuance of the British War Crimes Act 1991 has been disbanded Luc Reydams, *Universal Jurisdiction, International and Municipal Legal Perspectives* (Oxford: Oxford University Press, 2003), p. 205.

[390] See Julie V. Mayfield, 'The Prosecution of War Crimes and Respect for Human Rights: Ethiopia's Balancing Act' (1995) 9 Emory ILR 553; T. Sverdrup Engelsjøhn, 'Ethiopia – War Crimes and Violations of Human Rights' (1995) 34 RIDMDG 9; Wondwossen L. Kidane, 'The Ethiopian "Red Terror" Trials', in M. Cherif Bassiouni (ed.), *Post Conflict Justice* (Ardsley: Transnational, 2002), p. 667.

[391] See generally, Fiona Webber, 'The Pinochet Case, The Struggle for the Realisation of Human Rights' (1999) 26 *Journal of Law and Society* 523; Michael Byers, 'The Law and

In the post-Rome era, there have been a number of other developments in international criminal law, primarily at the national level, although often with an international element. The primary examples of such developments are the prosecutions in Sierra Leone, Cambodia, East Timor and Kosovo. There have also been further examples of domestic trials, for example in Indonesia. Whether these represent an advance or retrenchment of international criminal law remains a matter of dispute.[392]

Sierra Leone[393]

Although the conflict in Sierra Leone began in 1991, it was not until mid-2000 that any real moves were made towards accountability. Then in response to a request from the Government of Sierra Leone to the UN Secretary General for assistance in setting up a court to try offences committed in its civil war,[394] the Security Council passed Resolution 1315. In contradistinction to the resolutions creating the ICTY and ICTR, Resolution 1315 does not provide the legal basis of the Special Court for Sierra Leone.[395] The Resolution requested that the Secretary General negotiate with Sierra Leone, and recommend further action to the Council. The Secretary General did this, producing the Report of the Secretary General on the Establishment of a Special Court for Sierra Leone on 4 October 2000.[396] This report, to which was annexed a draft Agreement between the United Nations and Sierra Leone and a draft Statute for the Special Court, provided the basis for negotiations in the Security Council.

Politics of the Pinochet Case' (2000) 11 DJICL 415; Neil Boister and Richard Burchill, 'The *Pinochet* Precedent. Don't Leave Home Without It' (1999) 10 CLF 405; David Turns, 'Pinochet's Fallout, Jurisdiction and Immunity for Criminal Violations of International Law' (2000) 20 *Legal Studies* 566; Hazel Fox, 'The First Pinochet Case, Immunity of a Former Head of State' (1999) 48 ICLQ 207, Hazel Fox, 'The Pinochet Case No. 3' (1999) 48 ICLQ 687.

392 For a more sanguine view see Laura A. Dickinson, 'The Promise of Hybrid Courts' (2003) 97 AJIL 295. A balanced view is given in Antonio Cassese, *International Criminal Law* (Oxford: Oxford University Press, 2003), pp. 344–6.

393 This section draws upon Robert Cryer, 'A Special Court for Sierra Leone?' (2001) 50 ICLQ 435.

394 S/2000/786.

395 It was, nonetheless, described by the UK Representative to the Security Council as 'a good, firm step to set up a court', see BBC News, 'War Crimes Tribunal for Sierra Leone', 14 August 2000, http://news.bbc.co.uk/hi/english/world/africa/newsid/879000/879825.stm.

396 *Report of the Secretary-General on the Establishment of a Special Court for Sierra Leone*, 4 October 2000, UN Doc. S/2000/915. On this see Michaela Frulli, 'The Special Court for Sierra Leone: Some Preliminary Comments' (2000) 11 EJIL 857.

The Security Council responded to the Report in a letter to the Secretary General dated 22 December 2000,[397] which asked the Secretary General to make certain alterations to the draft Agreement and Statute. After some more alterations, an agreement was signed between the United Nations and Sierra Leone, which formed the legal basis of the Special Court for Sierra Leone, on 16 January 2002.[398] In the Sierra Leonean domestic sphere, the legal basis is the Special Court Agreement, 2002, Ratification Act 2002.[399]

The Court itself is neither fully national nor international, it is a 'treaty-based sui generis court of mixed jurisdiction and composition'.[400] It is fully a part of neither UN nor Sierra Leonean legal systems. The judicial arm of the court is made up of a trial chamber and an appeals chamber, both of which are composed of judges appointed separately by the Secretary General and the Sierra Leonean government.[401] Similarly, while the prosecutor was appointed by the Secretary General, his deputy was appointed by Sierra Leone.[402] The Registrar is a UN official.[403] The Special Court has jurisdiction over those who 'bear the greatest responsibility for serious violations of international humanitarian law and Sierra Leonean law committed in the territory of Sierra Leone since 30 November 1996'.[404]

The nature of the court, being set up by treaty between the United Nations and Sierra Leone, means not only that primacy is limited to Sierra Leone courts, but so is the duty to co-operate with the Court.[405] The Security Council could have decided to impose a duty to co-operate

[397] UN Doc. S/2000/1234.

[398] Agreement Between the United Nations and the Government of Sierra Leone on the Establishment of a Special Court for Sierra Leone (2001). On the special Court, see Suzannah Linton, 'Cambodia, East Timor and Sierra Leone: Experiments in International Criminal Justice' (2001) 12 CLF 185, 231–41; Jennifer L. Poole, 'Post-Conflict Justice in Sierra Leone', in M. Cherif Bassiouni (ed.), *Post Conflict Justice* (Ardsley: Transnational, 2002), p. 593; Stuart Beresford, 'The Special Court for Sierra Leone: An Initial Comment' (2001) 14 LJIL 365; Nicole Fritz and Alison Smith, 'Current Apathy for Coming Anarchy: Building the Special Court for Sierra Leone' (2001) 25 Fordham ILJ 391.

[399] *Supplement to Sierra Leone Gazette* CXXX, 7 March 2002.

[400] Sierra Leone Report, para. 9. The Court considers itself a fully international tribunal, see *Prosecutor* v. *Taylor*, Decision on Immunity, SCSL-2003-01-I, 31 May 2004.

[401] Agreement, Article 2, Special Court Statute, Article 12, See Cryer, 'A Special Court', pp. 437–8.

[402] Agreement, Article 3, Special Court Statute, Article 15.

[403] Agreement, Article 4, Special Court Statute, Article 16.

[404] Agreement, Article 1(1), Special Court Statute, Article 1.

[405] Agreement, Article 17; See Frulli, 'The Special Court', 861–2.

on all States, in line with those relating to the ICTY and ICTR, but it did not.[406] The implications of this became very clear in 2003 when, as part of the deal that persuaded the President of Liberia, Charles Taylor, who had been indicted by the Special Court, to leave power, Nigeria offered him 'exile' there, apparently beyond the reach of the Special Court.

The Court has jurisdiction over three sets of crimes, two international, one national. The first set is crimes against humanity (Article 2). The Special Court is also given jurisdiction over violations of Common Article 3 and Additional Protocol II by Article 3 of its Statute. Article 4 of the Statute grants the Court jurisdiction over three named violations of international humanitarian law. According to the Secretary General's report, as there was no evidence of genocide in Sierra Leone, and the Security Council did not mention genocide in Resolution 1315, the Secretary General did not include genocide in the jurisdiction of the Court.[407] This, along with the determination that the conflict was non-international, in spite of external intervention, in particular through Liberian support for the Revolutionary United Front (RUF), is a determination which ought to have been left to the Special Court. It involves the application of law to facts yet to be found and, as such, should not have been determined by fiat prior to the setting up of the Special Court.[408] Article 5 refers to crimes under Sierra Leonean law. Offences included are those under the 1926 Prevention of Cruelty to Children Act and crimes of arson under the 1861 Malicious Damage Act.

Although the Sierra Leonean conflict began in 1991, practical constraints dictate that it would be impossible for the Court to prosecute offences going back to the beginning of the conflict. So the Secretary General decided that 30 November 1996, the date of the Abidjan Peace Agreement, should mark the starting point of the Court's jurisdiction. The date was chosen as it was apolitical, captured the majority of the most serious crimes and would not result in an unmanageable caseload for the Court.[409] As the conflict in Sierra Leone was ongoing at the time of the creation of the Court, the jurisdiction of the Special Court for the future is open-ended.[410]

406 Frulli, 'The Special Court', 862. 407 Sierra Leone Report, para. 13.

408 This led to an interesting preliminary motion which asserted that, as the conflict was international, the Special Court had no jurisdiction under Articles 3 and 4 over war crimes, as they were framed in terms of internal conflicts. The motion was rejected, see *Prosecutor* v. *Fofana*, Decision on Preliminary Motion on Lack of Jurisdiction Rationae Materiae: Nature of the Armed Conflict, SCSL-2004-14-AR72(E) 25 May 2004.

409 Sierra Leone Report, para. 27. 410 Sierra Leone Report, para. 28.

Certain provisions of the Lomé Peace Accord could have caused problems for the Court. Particularly important in this regard was Article IX, which amounted to an amnesty for crimes prior to the date of the signing of the Accord (7 July 1999). The status of amnesties under international law is debatable,[411] although it would seem that since the advent of the Rome Statute, the tide may have begun to turn against their legality under international law. This trend is bolstered by the Report, which unambiguously rejects the legality of the Lomé amnesty.[412] The Report notes that when the Secretary General's representative signed the Lomé Accord, he appended a disclaimer asserting that the amnesty in Article IX did not apply to international crimes.[413] The Secretary General goes further than claiming the non-opposability of the amnesty to the United Nations, however, declaring that 'the United Nations has consistently maintained the position that amnesty cannot be granted in respect of international crimes'.[414] The Report also states that the amnesty shall be denied legal effect 'to the extent of its illegality under international law'.[415] Therefore, the amnesty is considered not to affect the jurisdiction of the Special Court over international crimes.[416] The rejection of the Lomé amnesty does not extend to crimes under Sierra Leonean law under the jurisdiction of the Special Court.

Although the Special Court is certainly better than nothing, and there are positive aspects to it,[417] it is rather difficult to shake off the feeling that Sierra Leone has received an ersatz response from the United Nations.[418] The crucial issue of financing is one which may hugely limit the Special Court, as it is financed through voluntary contributions, rather than through the UN general or peacekeeping budget.[419] This led to delays in setting up the Court, and considerably limit its practical mandate.[420] Given that one of the prime defendants, Foday Sankoh, has now died, and another, Charles Taylor, is at the time of writing, safe in

[411] See Diane Orientlicher, 'Settling Accounts: The Duty to Prosecute Human Rights Violations of a Former Regime' (1991) 100 Yale LJ 2537; John Dugard, 'Dealing With the Crimes of a Past Regime: Is Amnesty Still an Option?' (1999) 12 LJIL 1001.

[412] Sierra Leone Report, paras. 22–24.

[413] Sierra Leone Report, para. 23.

[414] Sierra Leone Report, para. 22. The United Nations, in the past, has supported amnesty provisions, for example in Haiti; see Michael P. Scharf, 'Swapping Amnesty for Peace: Was There a Duty to Prosecute International Crimes in Haiti?' (1996) 31 TILJ 1.

[415] Sierra Leone Report, para. 24.

[416] Sierra Leone Statute, Article 10.

[417] See Dickinson, 'The Promise'.

[418] See generally Fritz and Smith, 'Current Apathy'.

[419] Sierra Leone Statute, Article 6.

[420] Report of the Planning Mission for the Establishment of the Special Court for Sierra Leone, UN Doc. S/2002/246. paras. 28–29. See generally Avril McDonald, 'Sierra Leone's Shoestring Special Court' (2002) 845 IRRC 121.

Nigeria, the Special Court cannot be said to have had an auspicious start. This is particularly the case when the difficulties relating to the motions relating to perceived bias on the part of the then-President of the Special Court, Geoffrey Robertson, are taken into account.[421] On the other hand, the Court has issued some interesting preliminary motions,[422] including some relating to the rather sensitive matter of the relations between the Court and the Truth and Reconciliation commission of Sierra Leone.[423]

Cambodia

The Special Court has, at least, made a start. Nearly twenty-five years after the end of the Khmer Rouge regime in Cambodia, there is still no existing forum for the prosecution of the remnants of that regime.[424] A process is under way to create tribunals for such prosecutions, and there is an agreement between the United Nations and Cambodia on the setting up of those tribunals, but as yet none has been established.

There were some *in absentia* proceedings against Pol Pot and Ieng Sary in 1979, by the government that overthrew them. But these 'were mere show trials with no regard for due process'.[425] Politics, both domestic and international, meant that no real progress on accountability was made until 1997, when the Cambodian Prime Ministers, Hun Sen and Norodom Ranidhh, wrote to the Secretary General, asking for international

421 See, for example, *Prosecutor* v. *Sesay, Kallon and Gbao*, Decision on the Disqualification of Justice Robertson from the Appeals Chamber, SCSL-2004-15-AR15, 13 March 2004.

422 See, for example, *Prosecutor* v. *Kallon and Kamara*, Decision on Challenge to Jurisdiction: Lomé Accord Amnesty, SCSL-2004-15 AR 72(E) and SCSL-2004-16-AR72(E), 13 March 2004; *Prosecutor* v. *Taylor*, Decision on Immunity; *Prosecutor* v. *Fofana* Decision on Preliminary Motion on Lack of Jurisdiction Materiae: Illegal Delegation of Powers by the United Nations, SCSL-2004-14-AR72(E), 25 May 2004.

423 *Prosecutor* v. *Gbao*, Decision on Appeal by the Truth and Reconciliation Commission ('TRC') and accused against the decision of Judge Bankole Thompson on 3 November 2003 to deny the TRC's request to hold a public hearing with Augustine Gbao, SCSL-2004-15-PT109, 7 May 2004.

424 As with many of the previous belated efforts at prosecution, some of the leaders are now dead, most notably Pol Pot. On the early history of Cambodia and international criminal law, see Hurst Hannum, 'International Law and the Cambodian Genocide: The Sounds of Silence' (1989) 11 HRQ 82; Stephen Marks, 'Forgetting the Policies and Practices of the Past: Impunity in Cambodia' (1994) 18 FFWA 17; David Chandler, 'Will There be a Trial for the Khmer Rouge?' (2000) 14 EIA 67; Steven R. Ratner, 'The Cambodia Settlement Agreements' (1993) 87 AJIL 1; Balakrishnan Rajagopal, 'The Pragmatics of Prosecuting the Khmer Rouge' (1998) 1 YBIHL 189.

425 *Report of the Group of Experts for Cambodia Established Pursuant to General Assembly Resolution 52/135*, UN Doc. A/53/850-S/1999/231 Annex, para. 43.

assistance in prosecuting offences committed between 1975 and 1979.[426] The General Assembly responded in December of that year by setting up the Group of Experts for Cambodia.[427] The Commission decided that the dilapidated and corrupt nature of the Cambodian justice system made domestic trials, even with international involvement and assistance, unlikely to succeed or be perceived as just.[428] They concluded that these problems were sufficiently serious to rule out a domestic tribunal under UN control, which would also involve delay, as an agreement to set up such a tribunal would take too much time, and '[t]he Cambodian Government might insist on provisions that might undermine the independence of the court'.[429] The Commission therefore recommended that the Security Council set up an analogous tribunal to the ICTY.[430]

This was unacceptable to the Cambodian government, which wanted domestic trials.[431] It was not only cynics that suggested that this was so that Hun Sen, Cambodian Prime Minister and ex-Khmer Rouge member, could influence the proceedings according to his political preferences.[432] The compromise was negotiations on a mixed UN–Cambodian tribunal, of the type the Commission had decided not to recommend, but had seen as better than purely domestic trials. The Commission's fears came true. Delay and rancour characterised the negotiations.[433] Cambodia also passed its law creating joint tribunals precipitately in 2001.[434] As further negotiations between the parties failed to solve the problems identified with the law, Hans Corell, Under-Secretary General for Legal Affairs broke off negotiations in early 2002.[435]

[426] Letter of 21 June 1997 to the Secretary General, UN Docs. A/51/930, S/1997/488.

[427] GA Res 52/135, UN Doc. A/52/135. On the commission, see Steven R. Ratner, 'The United Nations Group of Experts for Cambodia' (1999) 93 AJIL 948 and Buckley, 'The Conflict in Cambodia', pp. 646–9.

[428] Cambodia Report, paras. 126–138.

[429] Cambodia Report, paras. 185–192; the quote comes from para. 190.

[430] Cambodia Report, paras. 139–184.

[431] Letter from Hun Sen, Prime Minister of Cambodia, 3 April 1999.

[432] Steven R. Ratner, 'Accountability for the Khmer Rouge, A (Lack of) Progress Report', in M. Cherif Bassiouni (ed.), *Post Conflict Justice* (Ardsley: Transnational, 2002), p. 613, pp. 614–17.

[433] Ratner 'Accountability', p. 616. See also Daniel Kemper Donovan, 'Joint UN–Cambodia Efforts to Establish a Khmer Rouge Tribunal' (2003) 44 Harvard ILJ 551, 558–64.

[434] Law on the Establishment of Extraordinary Chambers in the Courts of Cambodia for the Prosecution of Crimes Committed during the Period of Democratic Kampuchea 7 August 2001. See generally, Linton 'Cambodia, East Timor', 189–202.

[435] See Helen Jarvis, 'Trials and Tribulations: The Latest in the Long Quest for Justice for the Cambodian Genocide' (2002) 34 *Critical Asian Studies* 607; Ben Kiernan, 'Cambodia and the United Nations – Legal Documents' (2002) 34 *Critical Asian Studies* 611, 611–12.

Having taken considerable persuading, pursuant to General Assembly Resolution 57/228,[436] Corell returned to negotiations in January and March 2003, which ended in the promulgation of a draft agreement in March. The agreement provides for Extraordinary Cambodian Tribunals, with UN involvement and international personnel. It is largely based on the 2001 Cambodian Law.[437] The tribunals will have jurisdiction over offences committed by 'senior leaders of Democratic Kampuchea and those who were most responsible for' serious violations of Cambodian law, international humanitarian law and custom and treaties accepted by Cambodia committed between 17 April 1975 and 6 January 1979.[438] These are defined in Article 9 of the Draft Agreement as genocide, crimes against humanity (as defined in the Rome Statute), grave breaches of the Geneva Conventions and other crimes referred to in the Cambodian Law of August 2001.

Each of the two main chambers (a Trial Chamber and an Appeals Chamber) are to be made up of a mixture of international and Cambodian judges. The Trial Chamber is composed of three Cambodian judges and two international judges.[439] The Appeals Chamber is made up of four Cambodian judges and three international judges.[440] The preponderance of Cambodian judges has given rise to fears that the chambers will not be impartial.[441] To attempt to counter this, qualified majorities are required for decisions, in each Chamber, to ensure that a decision cannot go through without the concurrence of at least one international judge.[442] This may not be a sufficient guarantee of effectiveness, as the requirements leave room for sclerosis in the proceedings.[443]

Investigations are the responsibility of two investigating judges, one Cambodian, one international.[444] They are to work together, but if they cannot agree on whether to investigate, the investigation must proceed, unless either or both of the judges request the matter be settled by a Pre-Trial Chamber.[445] This is to be empanelled in a similar fashion to the Trial Chamber, and the same rules on majorities apply as to

436 UN Doc. A/RES/57/228.

437 For analysis, see Donovan, 'Joint UN–Cambodia Efforts', 564–7.

438 Agreement Between the United Nations and the Royal Government of Cambodia Concerning the Prosecution Under Cambodian Law of Crimes Committed During the Period of Democratic Kampuchea, Adopted by GA Resolution 228/B, UN Doc. A/57/RES/288B, Articles 1 and 2.

439 Agreement, Article 3(2)(a).

440 Agreement, Article 3(2)(b).

441 See Ratner, 'Accountability', pp. 616.

442 Agreement, Article 4.

443 Ratner, 'Accountability', p. 616.

444 Agreement, Article 5(1).

445 UN–Cambodia Agreement, Articles 5(4), 7.

that Chamber.[446] If there is no qualified majority to stop the investigation, it is to proceed.[447] This provision is a mechanism of ensuring that deadlock in the Chamber will not prevent investigation. Prosecutions are the responsibility of two prosecutors, again one international, one Cambodian.[448] Differences between them are dealt with in the same way, *mutatis mutandis*, as those between investigating judges.[449] The default position is that prosecutions shall continue.

The amnesty granted to Ieng Sary in 1996 is also dealt with in the draft agreement.[450] It is clear that there was no agreement between the United Nations and Cambodia on this issue. Cambodia was concerned that prosecution of Ieng Sary would lead to renewed armed opposition to the government by the Khmer Rouge. The United Nations was opposed to the use of amnesties. Article 11 therefore throws the problem to the Chambers. Article 11(1) states that Cambodia will not ask for amnesty or pardon for those investigated or prosecuted under the agreement. Article 11(2) deals with the more complex issue of existing pardons. It reads, in full:

> [t]his provision is based upon a declaration by the Royal Government of Cambodia that until now, with regard to matters covered in the law, there has been only one Case, dated 14 September 1996, when a pardon was granted to only one person with regard to a 1979 conviction on the charge of genocide. The United Nations and the Royal Government of Cambodia agree that the scope of this pardon is a matter to be decided by the Extraordinary Chambers.

Although it is no surprise that Ieng Sary is a likely defendant, it is nonetheless quite extraordinary to see a provision in an international agreement on prosecution that deals with one individual, assumes that that person will be prosecuted and raise a particular defence.

As a final point on the agreement, it should be noted that as the agreement is to be between Cambodia and the United Nations, the obligation to co-operate with the Chambers in Article 25 is limited to Cambodia. This comes not only from the text but the nature of bilateral treaty relations. The experience of the Sierra Leone Special Court shows that if effective prosecution is to occur, an obligation to co-operate limited to one country is insufficient. A number of possible Khmer Rouge

446 UN–Cambodia Agreement, Article 7(2)(4).

447 UN–Cambodia Agreement, Article 7(4).

448 UN–Cambodia Agreement, Article 6(1).

449 UN–Cambodia Agreement, Articles 6(4), 7.

450 There may be others, but the agreement seems to refer basically to this one, Article 11.

suspects are on the Cambodian–Thai border, and may seek to avoid arrest this way. Other States are likely to have relevant evidence. Currently, though, it cannot be said with any certainty that the agreement will be brought into effect quickly, and the possibility that Khmer Rouge officials may escape prosecution is still present.

East Timor and Kosovo

In two territories over which the United Nations has exercised governmental authority, programmes of accountability have been adopted. These are, strictly speaking, national efforts, as although both efforts were initiated by the United Nations, the authority exercised to set them up was that of the national legal system, which at that time was controlled by that organisation.[451] In both, the United Nations was faced with a dysfunctional or absent judicial system on arrival, and has had to construct one all but from scratch.

In Kosovo, trials are currently taking place of a number of suspects accused of international crimes. These are occurring in tandem with prosecution of high-level offenders before the ICTY. Although initially it was suggested that any trials take place in a special court for War Crimes and Ethnic Crimes, this idea was dropped on cost grounds.[452] Trials are therefore taking place in purely domestic courts, albeit courts made up of a mixed national–international bench.[453] This is considered imperative, as the bias of each ethnic group make impartial decision making without an international presence a desideratum rather than a realistic prospect.[454] Although this, along with the possibility of removing any case to another venue or ensuring the presence of international judges,[455] may represent the only option available, critiques abound. Not least, in most jurisdictions, the presence, or perception, of bias in

[451] In East Timor, pursuant to Security Council Resolution 1272, in Kosovo, Security Council Resolution 1244. On these see Boris Kondoch, 'The United Nations Administration of East Timor' (2001) 6 JCSL 245; Michael J. Matheson, 'United Nations Governance of Postconflict Societies' (2001) 95 AJIL 76; Ralph Wilde, 'From Danzig to East Timor and Beyond: The Role of International Territorial Administration' (2001) 95 AJIL 583.

[452] See John R. W. D. Jones and Steven Powles, *International Criminal Practice* (Oxford: Oxford University Press, 3rd edn., 2003), pp. 26, 28–9.

[453] See UN Mission in Kosovo, Regulations 2000/6 and 2000/24. See generally Hansjörg Strohmeyer, 'Collapse and Reconstruction of a Judicial System: The United Nations Missions in Kosovo and East Timor' (2001) 95 AJIL 46; Hansjörg Strohmeyer, 'Making Multilateral Interventions Work: The UN and the Creation of Transitional Justice Systems in Kosovo and East Timor' (2001) 25 FFWA 107.

[454] Cassese, *International Criminal Law*, p. 344.

[455] UNMIK Regulation 2000/64.

relation to one judge on a panel is enough to impugn proceedings, here, as in Cambodia, international representation is an institutional recognition of such bias.[456]

The trials themselves have been heavily criticised for both their lackadaisical standards of justice[457] and weak or Delphic reasoning.[458] Sadly, '[t]he use of internationalized panels in Kosovo has not to date made significant progress towards ending impunity for international crimes in the region. Nor have the judgments of the internationalized panels made any real contribution to jurisprudence in this field'.[459]

The situation faced by the United Nations when it entered East Timor was even worse. There was nothing upon which to build.[460] Trials began, however, under the authority of the UN Transitional Authority in East Timor's Regulations 2000/11 and 2000/15. Regulation 2000/15 largely reflects the law set down in the ICC Statute.[461] It remains contentious, though, as the East Timorese were not included in the consultation process preceding this regulation.[462] There have been considerable problems finding qualified, but untainted, local judges, lawyers, translators and prosecutors. A conspicuous lack of funding has exacerbated the problem.[463] The output of the Courts has not been impressive, there has been considerable 'undercharging' in the cases and in those judgments that have been issued there has been a lack of reasoning and analysis.[464] There have also been a number of cases related to East Timor undertaken, under considerable pressure, by Indonesia, although as at Leipzig and in many cases since, the *fides* of the prosecutions appears undermined by

[456] Jones and Powles, *International Criminal Practice*, p. 28. In the United Kingdom, the possibility of perception of bias on the part of one of a five-judge panel in the *Pinochet* litigation was enough to cause a rehearing before another panel, see *R* v. *Bow Street Stipendiary Magistrate ex parte Pinochet Ugarte* [No. 2] [1999] All ER 577.

[457] See, a little intemperately, Edwin Villmoare, 'Ethnic Crimes and UN Justice in Kosovo: The Trial of Igor Simić' (2002) 37 TILJ 373.

[458] Silvia de Bertodano, 'Developments in Internationalized Courts' (2003) 1 JICJ 226, 238–41.

[459] de Bertodano, 'Developments', 241.

[460] See Linton, 'Cambodia, East Timor', 202–3; Suzannah Linton, 'Rising From the Ashes: The Creation of a Viable Criminal Justice System in East Timor' (2001) 25 MULR 122, 123–9.

[461] For discussion, see Claus Kress, 'The 1999 Crisis in East Timor and the Threshold of the Law on War Crimes' (2003) 13 CLF 409; Kai Ambos and Steffen Wirth, 'The Current Law of Crimes Against Humanity: An Analysis of UNTAET Regulation 15/2000' (2002) 12 CLF 1; Linton, 'Rising', 144–73.

[462] Linton, 'Rising', 138, 150. [463] de Bertodano, 'Developments', 231.

[464] de Bertodano, 'Developments', 232–3.

the acquittal rate and lenient sentencing that has characterised those proceedings.[465]

Iraq

The most recent attempts to ensure accountability for international crimes have related to Saddam Hussein and the deposed Ba'ath party in Iraq. The Iraqi governing coalition, under powers delegated to them by the Coalition Provisional Authority as occupiers, have promulgated a Statute for a Special Tribunal for the prosecution of Ba'ath crimes, with jurisdiction going back to 1968.[466] The Tribunal is to be essentially a national tribunal, with some international involvement.[467] It has jurisdiction over genocide, crimes against humanity and war crimes,[468] alongside some Iraqi national crimes, including a domestic analogue to aggression.[469]

International reaction has not been especially positive to the Tribunal; although few openly question whether Ba'ath crimes ought to be prosecuted, the mechanism is far from perfect. Certain pre-trial rights of the defence have not been adopted and there are questions about how impartial a domestic tribunal may be, given the record of the Iraqi judiciary and the general opprobrium in which Saddam Hussein is held, including by some of those appointed to the Tribunal.[470] The legitimacy of the Tribunal is also considered by some to be compromised by the relationship between the Iraqi Governing Coalition and the US/UK 'Authority' in Iraq.[471] Two thousand five hundred years after Lysander, the ghost of victor's justice has been raised again, as although Ba'ath crimes are to be prosecuted, the jurisdiction of the Special Tribunal is structured so

465 David Cohen, *Intended to Fail: The Trials Before the ad hoc Human Rights Court in Jakarta* (Berkley: International Centre for Transitional Justice, 2003).

466 Statute of the Iraqi Special Tribunal, Articles 1(b).

467 Statute of the Iraqi Special Tribunal, Articles 6(b), 7(n). For criticism, see Michael P. Scharf, 'Is it International Enough? A Critique of the Iraqi Special Tribunal in Light of the Goals of International Criminal Justice' (2004) 2 JICJ 330; Yuval Shany, 'Does One Size Fit All? Reading the Jurisdictional Provisions of the New Iraqi Special Tribunal in the Light of the Statutes of the International Criminal Tribunals' (2004) 2 JICJ 338.

468 Statute of the Iraqi Special Tribunal, Articles 11–13.

469 Statute of the Iraqi Special Tribunal, Article 14(c). For critique, see Claus Kress, 'The Iraqi Special Tribunal and the Crime of Aggression' (2004) 2 JICJ 347.

470 See Danilo Zolo, 'The Iraqi Special Tribunal: Back to the Nuremberg Paradigm?' (2004) 2 JICJ 313.

471 José E. Alvarez, 'Trying Hussein: Between Hubris and Hegemony' (2004) 2 JICJ 319, 326–7.

that it is impossible to try any international crimes committed by the occupying powers.[472]

Conclusion

The present is a time of uncertainty for international criminal law. Although there have been many steps forward in the creation of a regime of prosecution around such offences, cost and political expediency have begun to exact a toll on efforts to ensure prosecution. It appears likely that immunity from prosecution may have been offered to Charles Taylor to step down in Liberia, and before the armed conflict in Iraq in 2003 to Saddam Hussein and his deputies.[473] Prosecution is by no means certain for any particular individual offence. Indeed, this chapter, by concentrating on instances of prosecution, ignores the vast majority of international crimes which have remained unpunished. As Gerry Simpson aptly reminds us, 'each war crimes trial is an exercise in selective justice to the extent that it reminds us that the majority of war crimes go unpunished'.[474] The foregoing must be understood in that context. Non-prosecution is the traditional response to international crimes.

It is hoped that this chapter has not only introduced the institutions but also some of the prosecutions that will form the basis for the discussion that follows, but has also shown that a number of the questions, problems and debates that characterise the pursuit of international criminal justice are of considerable historical pedigree. Who should be prosecuted, for which crimes, according to what law, with what defences, by whom, sentenced to what and, indeed, prosecuted for what purpose, are questions which have been answered differently at different times by different people.

Of particular note in this regard are the responsibility of commanders and the issue of superior orders. As we shall see, these issues remain controversial. Questions of selectivity of enforcement and 'victor's justice' are perennial. The question of obtaining evidence when prosecutions are undertaken abroad and fear that nationality States will be unduly lenient have been relatively constant over time.

[472] Alvarez, 'Trying Hussein', 326–7.

[473] P. Spiegel and R. Khalaf, 'Rumsfeld Hints at Iraq Amnesty', *Financial Times*, 20 January 2003; Richard Norton-Taylor and H. Smith, 'US Offers Immunity to Saddam', *Guardian*, 20 January 2003.

[474] Simpson, 'War Crimes', p. 8.

2 International criminal law: State rights, responsibilities and problems

Introduction

Chapters 2 and 3 will explain and evaluate the moves made by a number of States and international organisations towards a regime of international criminal law enforcement. These moves stem from decisions taken in the 1990s to promote accountability in individual situations, which slipped their moorings and led to a commitment by some States and parts of the United Nations to a broader sweep of accountability. This decision was based on a realisation that 'there is a risk of losing substantive justice when we revert to individual States because often it becomes contingent on the willingness of States to fulfil, among other things, their international obligation to punish international crimes'.[1] To effectuate their policy shift towards accountability, those States have attempted to overcome some of the challenges presented to international criminal law by an international society based on sovereignty, although not to the same extent as was done by the Security Council in relation to the former Yugoslavia and Rwanda.[2] They have also taken steps to create a common international criminal law between themselves.

As we shall see in chapter 3, the existence of such a regime for international crimes involving international and domestic courts can now confidently be asserted. As Judges Higgins, Kooijmans and Buergenthal put it: 'the international consensus that the perpetrators of international

[1] Ferraro Mantovani, 'The General Principles of International Criminal Law: The Viewpoint of a National Criminal Lawyer' (2003) 1 JICJ 26, 28.

[2] In this respect, the 'internationalised' tribunals in East Timor, Sierra Leone and Kosovo are in the same position as national courts. The Special Panels in East Timor have had considerable problems relating to mutual legal assistance from Indonesia; see William W. Burke-White, 'A Community of Courts: Toward a System of International Criminal Law Enforcement' (2002) 24 MJIL 1, 73.

crimes should not go unpunished is being advanced by a flexible strategy, in which newly established international criminal tribunals, treaty obligations and national courts all have their part to play.'[3] This chapter seeks to divine some of the problems that this regime needs to overcome for it to prove more effective than the inter-State regime of repression of international crimes. This chapter is not a comprehensive evaluation of all legal issues and problems relating to the prosecution of international crimes: for example, immunities before national and international courts will not be dealt with. This is not to minimise their importance,[4] but to allow us to concentrate more on the direct steps that have been taken to persuade States to prosecute international crimes more diligently.

This chapter focuses on the most important actors in the regime for the prosecution of international crimes, national courts. They are intended to take the bulk of the enforcement load, as is shown by the complementarity which is set up in the Rome Statute.[5] This is set out in the preamble of the Rome Statute, and its Article 1. The preamble affirms 'that the most serious crimes of concern to the international community as a whole must not go unpunished and that their effective prosecution must be ensured *by taking measures at the national level* and by enhancing international cooperation' (emphasis added), and emphasises 'that the International Criminal Court established under this Statute shall be complementary to national criminal jurisdictions'. If the point had not been made clearly enough, the parties, out of an abundance of caution,

[3] *Case Concerning the Arrest Warrant of 11 April 2000 (Democratic Republic of Congo* v. *Belgium)* ICJ General List 121 (*Yerodia* Case), Separate Opinion of Judges Higgins, Kooijmans and Buergenthal, para. 51. For an early study, see Lyal S. Sunga, *The Emerging System of International Criminal Law* (The Hague: Kluwer, 1997). More recently, see Burke-White, 'A Community of Courts'; William W. Burke-White, 'Regionalization of International Criminal Law Enforcement: A Preliminary Exploration' (2003) 38 TILJ 729; Jonathan Charney, 'International Criminal Law and the Role of Domestic Courts' (2001) 95 AJIL 120.

[4] The literature on immunities is large; see, for example, Andrea Bianchi, 'Immunity Versus Human Rights: The Pinochet Case' (1999) 10 EJIL 237; J. Craig Barker, 'The Future of Former Head of State Immunity After *ex parte Pinochet*' (1999) 48 ICLQ 937. The correct position is summed up by Lady Fox, that current international law does not grant material immunity to those committing international crimes, but personal immunities may still be available before national courts; Hazel Fox, *The Law of State Immunity* (Oxford: Oxford University Press, 2002), chapter 12. An exemplary analysis is Dapo Akande, 'International Law Immunities and the International Criminal Court' (2004) 98 AJIL 407. There is no procedural immunity before international courts; see, for example, *Prosecutor* v. *Taylor*, Decision on Immunity, SCSL-2003-01-I, 31 May 2004.

[5] For more detailed discussion, see chapter 3.

also included the phrase 'shall be complementary to national criminal jurisdictions' with reference to the ICC in Article 1 of the Statute. This chapter concentrates on three areas: jurisdiction, duties to prosecute and incorporation/harmonisation. The reason for choosing these subjects is, for jurisdiction and duties, to show who may, and who must prosecute, so when we turn to selectivity later (chapter 4) we may differentiate when the critique is on the basis of legality or legitimacy. Incorporation/harmonisation is included as it shows the general lackadaisical attitude taken towards international criminal law on the part of States, the importance of some form of supervisory mechanism and one of the appropriate criticisms of extraterritorial jurisdiction.

Jurisdiction

Prosecutions of international crimes are often undertaken outside the *locus delicti*, therefore special attention must be given to extraterritorial jurisdiction.[6] The reason for this is there has traditionally been concern about prosecutions of international crimes by territorial or nationality States. The question of jurisdiction must be approached from the standpoint of treaty and customary international law.

The 'traditional' principles of jurisdiction

There are two entirely uncontroversial grounds of jurisdiction in international law, territoriality and nationality. Both have important roles to play in the repression of international crimes. Territoriality is now the fundamental principle of jurisdiction: the right to assert territorial jurisdiction is a right inherent in sovereignty.[7] The appropriateness of prosecuting international crimes in the vicinity of their perpetration where possible is broadly accepted.[8] That is not to say that the territorial principle raises no problems in international criminal law. As the offences are prosecuted where they are committed, there is sometimes an excessive willingness to convict, in particular where political opponents are on trial. The 1979 *in absentia* trial of Pol Pot and Ieng Sary is an example of this. So are a number of trials of alleged war criminals in

[6] On jurisdiction generally, see Michael Akehurst, 'Jurisdiction in International Law' (1972–1973) 46 BYBIL 145.

[7] *Island of Palmas Case* (1928) 2 RIAA 829, 838.

[8] See, for example, José E. Alvarez, 'Crimes of Hate/Crimes of State: Lessons From Rwanda' (1999) 24 Yale JIL 365.

the former Yugoslavia, including the *in absentia* proceedings against Bill Clinton, Tony Blair and Jaques Chirac in relation to Kosovo.[9] Alternatively, prosecutions by the compatriots of the offender are often suspected of excessive lenience or willingness to acquit, if there is a prosecution at all.[10]

The second generally accepted principle of jurisdiction is nationality.[11] This allows States to exercise jurisdiction over offences committed by their nationals abroad. States are considered to have an interest in regulating the conduct of their nationals abroad, in particular where that State prohibits the extradition of its nationals. It extends also to those with a sufficiently strong tie to the country at the time of the offence, such as foreign nationals serving in the armed forces of another country or a permanent residency at the time of the offence.[12] There is no doubt that the principle has a role to play in the repression of international crimes. In particular, in relation to armed conflicts overseas, the main source of jurisdiction a State may assert over its armed forces is based on nationality jurisdiction. This type of jurisdiction formed the basis of, for example, the *Calley* and *Medina* Cases in the United States.[13]

These trials also display one often-heard critique of trials for international crimes based on nationality jurisdiction. As before, the critique is one of partiality: that the affinity between the courts and the accused, or political interference in the process on behalf of the accused, leads to unwarranted leniency or unjustified acquittals.[14] This is exacerbated when the offence is committed against foreigners who are unlikely to have a strong domestic contingency in the forum State to push for accountability, and provide a counterpoint to domestic constituencies

[9] See, for example, Jann K. Kleffner, 'Acquittal of Five Croatian Serbs Accused of War Crimes' (2000) 3 YBIHL 465; Suzannah Linton, '*Baković, Topić and Majić*' (2000) 3 YBIHL 463; Jann K. Kleffner, 'Case Against NATO Leaders' (2000) 3 YBIHL 493.

[10] Osiel notes that in many transitional States, prosecution may not be a vote-winner; Mark J. Osiel, 'Ever Again: Legal Remembrance of Administrative Massacre' (1995) 144 UPLR 463, 590–9. See also Christine van den Wyngaert, 'War Crimes, Genocide and Crimes Against Humanity – Are States Taking Their Obligations Seriously?', in M. Cherif Bassiouni (ed.), *International Criminal Law, III: Enforcement* (Ardsley: Transnational, 2nd edn., 1999), pp. 227, 228.

[11] See Akehurst, 'Jurisdiction', 156–7.

[12] See Robert Y. Jennings and Arthur Watts, *Oppenheim's International Law* (London: Longmans, 9th edn., 1992), pp. 1156–7.

[13] *US* v. *Calley* (1969) 41 CMR 96; (1973) 46 CMR 1131; (1973) 48 CMR 19; *US* v. *Medina* (1971) 43 CMR 243.

[14] On the Philippines see above p. 29; on *Calley* and *Medina* see the literature cited above, p. 50.

opposed to trying any of 'our boys' for faraway crimes, or crimes against enemy nationals. This type of critique is often, and rightly, directed at the Leipzig trials. In the Vietnam War, Jordan Paust summed up the underlying idea that often leads to critiques of nationality-based prosecution of international crimes: 'those of us who are quick to judge sometimes ignore the fact that men are both good and bad whether they are of our nationality or that of the enemy.'[15] This followed the *Calley* and *Medina* trials, and a decision by the US government to not prosecute further violations as the issue was politically 'too hot'.[16] The experiences of the Indonesian domestic trials for offences committed in East Timor provide a modern example of partiality towards the accused where prosecutions of nationals have been undertaken.

A third principle of jurisdiction that has sometimes been asserted as a basis for jurisdiction over international crimes is the protective principle. This is at least one explanation of the jurisdiction of Israel in the *Eichmann* Case. Both the District Court of Jerusalem and the Supreme Court of Israel relied on the protective principle of jurisdiction as a subsidiary source of jurisdiction.[17] Normally the protective principle is viewed as giving jurisdiction over attacks on the security of the State, perjury in relation to proceedings in the State and offences against the integrity of governmental functions such as counterfeiting currency and conspiracies to violate immigration or customs rules, rather than international crimes.[18] Another problem for the arguments in *Eichmann* is that Israel did not exist at the time of Eichmann's offences.[19] However, an assertion of jurisdiction over international crimes on the basis of protective jurisdiction was made by the Dutch Cour de Cassation in *Rohrig, Brunner and Heinze* in 1950.[20] As with *Eichmann*, the claim was mixed with ones of jurisdiction on the basis of passive personality or universality. It is possible to conceptualise some, although not all, international crimes as being justifiable under this head. Jurisdiction over aggression, for example, could certainly be subsumed under the protective principle.

[15] Jordan J. Paust, 'My Lai and Vietnam: Norms, Myths and Leader Responsibility' (1972) 57 Military LR 99, 101.

[16] Paust, 'My Lai', 125.

[17] *Attorney-General of Israel* v. *Adolph Eichmann* (1968) 36 ILR 18, 54–57, 304.

[18] Frederick A. Mann, 'The Doctrine of Jurisdiction in International Law' (1964–1) 111 RdC 9, 94; Louis Henkin, 'International Law, Politics, Values and Functions' (1989-IV) 216 RdC 9, 288; Akehurst, 'Jurisdiction', 157–9.

[19] See James E. S. Fawcett, 'The Eichmann Trial' (1962) 38 BYBIL 181, 190–2; David Lasok, 'The Eichmann Trial' (1962) 11 ICLQ 35, 364.

[20] (1950) 17 ILR 393, 396.

Passive personality jurisdiction, jurisdiction based on the nationality of the victim rather than the perpetrator, is generally of uncertain legality, having largely been rejected in the *Lotus* Case (1927).[21] In the 1930s, the Harvard Draft Restatement on jurisdiction rejected the lawfulness of the passive personality principle, and it remains controversial.[22] However, there is an undoubted right of belligerents to prosecute war crimes committed by enemy forces against them. This was confirmed, for example, in *Rohrig* and is generally accepted. The most controversial assertion of passive personality jurisdiction in the context of international crimes was in *Eichmann*. The controversy was not over whether the prosecution of international crimes committed against nationals was unlawful, but the status of Eichmann's victims as Israeli nationals.[23] International law goes beyond the normal ideas of passive personality jurisdiction to allow jurisdiction to be asserted over war crimes committed against allied States.[24] This overlaps with, is sometimes confused with and may be subsumed under, universal jurisdiction. The overlap may be shown by the assertion of passive personality and universal jurisdiction in the *Eichmann* Case.[25]

The relationship between Eichmann's victims and Israel has also given rise to a complaint that could be more broadly applicable to passive personality jurisdiction. This was the claim made by Dr Robert Servatius (Eichmann's counsel) that the judges, as representatives of the victims, could not give him a fair trial.[26] In this instance, the suggestion can be rejected; Eichmann had a fair trial. The point is made strongly by Georg Schwarzenberger:

> the Bench, composed of three judges, each of whom might have been one of the six million victims of the 'Final Solution', impressively draws the line between a neutrality which civilisation does not permit in its everlasting struggle with savagery and barbarism and that impartiality which even a savage or barbarian may expect in a civilised community.[27]

The more general point stands, though, that possible questions of fair trial may arise in highly charged proceedings for international crimes in a forum State representing the victims of the crime. This type of

[21] *SS Lotus (France* v. *Turkey)* (1927) PCIJ Rep. Series A, No. 10, dissenting opinion of Judge Moore.

[22] 'Harvard Research Draft Convention on Jurisdiction With Respect to Crime' (1935) 29 AJIL Supplement 443, 578–9.

[23] Fawcett, 'The Eichmann Trial', 190–2; Lasok, 'The Eichmann Trial', 364.

[24] Akehurst, 'Jurisdiction', 160.

[25] *Attorney General of Israel* v. *Adolph Eichmann*, 304.

[26] Fawcett, 'The Eichmann Trial', 181, 183; Lasok, 'The Eichmann Trial', 359.

[27] Georg Schwarzenberger, 'The Eichmann Judgment: An Essay in Censorial Jurisprudence' (1962) 15 CLP 248, 249. See also Fawcett, 'The Eichmann Trial', 183.

problem is best addressed through the application of human rights law standards to the proceedings rather than the law of jurisdiction.[28] In addition, Article 75 of Additional Protocol I grants all persons undergoing trial during a conflict for offences related to that conflict certain judicial guarantees, and PoWs and civilians have additional rights in this regard.[29] Violations of those rights of PoWs and civilians are grave breaches of the relevant Convention.[30] Denying basic fair trial rights in time of war to those entitled to them under the Geneva Conventions is a war crime according to Additional Protocol I and the Rome Statute.[31]

Universal jurisdiction

It is a truism that the traditional principles of jurisdiction have not ensured the impartial or comprehensive prosecution of international crimes. According to James E. S. Fawcett '[e]ven before the Second World War there was a strong doubt as to the efficacy of the exercise of exclusive jurisdiction over war crimes by one State, based on the nationality of the victim or offender or the locality of the offence'.[32] One of the primary reasons Kofi Annan gave for the necessity of an international criminal court was the inadequacy of leaving international crimes to be prosecuted on the basis of nationality or territoriality jurisdiction. Speaking in 1998, to the Rome Conference that adopted the International Criminal Court Statute, Annan said:

> [g]radually the world has come to realise that relying on each State or army to punish its own transgressors is not enough. When crimes are committed on such a scale we know that the State lacks either the power or the will to stop them. Too often, indeed, they are part of a systematic State policy, and the worst criminals may be at the pinnacle of State power.[33]

We shall return to the Rome Statute in chapter 3.

The failure of national jurisdictions acting alone to effectively suppress international crimes has also led to two developments in national jurisdiction – the creation of treaties by which States agree to exercise jurisdiction on an expanded basis and the rise of universal jurisdiction legislation and jurisprudence. As Judges Higgins, Kooijmans and Buergenthal noted in their joint opinion in *Yerodia*, through loose use of

[28] See, for example, Article 14 of the International Covenant on Civil and Political Rights 999 UNTS 171.
[29] GCIII, Articles 99–108 and GC IV, Articles 71–75, 126.
[30] GCIII, Article 130, GC IV, Article 147.
[31] API, Article 85(4)(e), Rome Statute, Article 8(2)(a)(vii).
[32] Fawcett, 'The Eichmann Trial', 204. [33] UN Doc. L/Rom/6.r1.

language, the two are sometimes confused.[34] There are many treaties which could be evaluated with respect to their jurisdictional provisions; here, we shall concentrate only in detail on those that overlap with, or are expressed as referring to, core international crimes. These are the Torture Convention (1984), the Geneva Conventions (along with Additional Protocol I) and the Apartheid Convention (1973).[35]

Treaties and the universality principle

Article 5 of the 1984 UN Convention Against Torture is frequently invoked as an example of a treaty provision setting up universal jurisdiction, Article 5 provides that, in addition to territorial, nationality and, if appropriate, passive personality jurisdiction, 'each state party shall likewise take such measures as may be necessary to establish jurisdiction over such offences in cases where the alleged offender is present in any territory under its jurisdiction and it does not extradite him'.[36] It is often said that this grants universal jurisdiction over torture.[37] On its terms, this is quite possible, but we should note that there is the limit that the suspect be present in the jurisdiction seeking to prosecute,[38] and there is still the matter of whether treaties alone can create universal jurisdiction without universal ratification.

To investigate this, it is useful to refer to discussions which occurred in relation to other treaties with similar jurisdictional provisions. The precedents used in the negotiation of this provision were those in the terrorist 'suppression conventions' of the 1970s.[39] Louis Henkin gave an accurate and succinct explanation of the international legal nature of the jurisdictional provisions in those Conventions. It deserves quotation in full. Speaking of the terrorist conventions Henkin said that they:

> may be seen as pooling the jurisdiction of different States and supplementing them by extended co-operation in extradition, clearly they have also revised and extended traditional bases of jurisdiction. As such they may constitute

[34] *Yerodia*, para. 41.

[35] On other conventions, see Neil Boister, *Penal Aspects of the UN Drug Conventions* (The Hague: Kluwer, 2000).

[36] UN Convention Against Torture and Other Cruel, Inhumane or Degrading Treatment and Punishment, 1465 UNTS 85.

[37] For example, see Nigel S. Rodley, *The Treatment of Prisoners Under International Law* (Oxford: Oxford University Press, 2nd edn., 1999), p. 129.

[38] Luc Reydams, *Universal Jurisdiction* (Oxford: Oxford University Press, 2003), pp. 64–7.

[39] J. Herman Burgers and Hans Danelius, *The United Nations Convention Against Torture: A Handbook on the Convention against Torture and Other Cruel, Inhumane or Degrading Treatment and Punishment* (Dordrecht: Martinus Nijhoff, 1988), pp. 57–60, 72–3.

declarations by the parties that the extensions are permissible under international law. At least, they constitute undertakings by the parties to accept such exercises of jurisdiction as permissible inter se and to waive any objections they might otherwise have as territorial States or as States of nationality of the accused . . . The anti-terrorist conventions, of course, do not bind States not party to them.[40]

Henkin goes on to explain that broader jurisdiction would come about only if the Conventions could be considered custom. As they are not, Henkin concludes that affected third parties could protest jurisdiction. This must be correct. Although parties to such treaties may 'pool' jurisdiction, by agreeing to waive their rights of protest with respect to other parties, those treaties cannot affect the rights of non-parties or impose an obligation on them not to protest an excessive claim of jurisdiction. Any assertion of broader jurisdictional rights must rely on a collateral assertion that customary international law permits such jurisdiction. This argument can be made with some force for torture, at least since the *Furundžija* decision.[41]

The relation of these treaties to general international law was also alluded to, although not discussed in depth, in some of the opinions in *Yerodia*. Judge Guillaume referred to the treaties as ensuring 'universal punishment of the offences in question is assured, as the perpetrators are denied refuge in all States'.[42] He fails to explain how this may be. More subtle is the joint opinion of Higgins, Kooijmans and Buergenthal. Referring to suggestions that 'the great international treaties on crimes and offences evidence universality as a ground for the exercise of jurisdiction' the three comment that 'this is doubtful'.[43] They note that the parties did not argue the customary status of the Conventions in any detail, and thus express no opinion on the matter.[44]

Michael P. Scharf asserts that there is a right to assert jurisdiction founded on treaties against non-parties.[45] He argues on the basis that

[40] Henkin, 'International Law', 301.

[41] *Prosecutor* v. *Furundžija*, Judgment, IT-95–17/1-T, 10 December 1998, para. 156. See also the discussion in *R* v. *Bow Street Stipendiary Magistrate, ex parte Pinochet Ugarte* [No. 3]. *Amnesty International Intervening* [1999] 2 All ER 97, 109 (*per* Lord Browne-Wilkinson), 177 (*per* Lord Millett). But see 147 (*per* Lord Hope). For comment, see Rosanne van Albeek, 'The *Pinochet* Case: International Human Rights Law on Trial' (2000) 71 BYBIL 29, 33–6.

[42] Separate Opinion of President Guillaume, para. 9.

[43] Joint Opinion of Higgins, Kooijmans and Buergenthal, para. 26.

[44] Joint Opinion of Higgins, Kooijmans and Buergenthal, paras. 41–42.

[45] Michael P. Scharf, 'Application of Treaty-Based Jurisdiction to Nationals of Non-Party States' (2001) 35 NELR 363.

although many of the conventions are not customary, there is a separate right to assert jurisdiction on a universal basis against non-parties.[46] The argument is flawed. It relies for its validity on three bases. First, the *Lotus* principle of freedom of States to assert jurisdiction in the absence of a prohibitive rule to the contrary.[47] This argument will be rejected later. Second, that there is no right of a third State that is violated when prosecution of one of its nationals or an offence on its territory occurs.[48] As Henkin observes, territorial and nationality States have rights related to non-intervention which are violated when there is an excessive claim of extraterritorial jurisdiction. Third, Scharf identifies practice that he claims supports a right to use treaties as a basis for universal jurisdiction. The practice identified in support of the alleged right involves that of two States, the Netherlands and United States, and does not support any general right to assert such jurisdiction. In each case, the jurisdiction based on the treaty can be explained other than by universal jurisdiction. Scharf's more limited point – that where there is jurisdiction this may be asserted without the consent of the State of nationality – however, is clearly correct.

The most famous treaty regime is the grave breaches regime of the Geneva Conventions. Article 49 of Geneva Convention I sets out the general rule: 'Each High Contracting Party shall be under the obligation to search for persons alleged to have committed, or to have ordered to be committed, such grave breaches and shall bring such persons, regardless of their nationality, before its own courts [or hand them over to another High Contracting Party].'[49] This is a very broad assertion of jurisdiction, relating not only to a duty to prosecute, but on the basis of what is in practice, almost indistinguishable from, universal jurisdiction.[50]

[46] Scharf, 'Application', 374. [47] Scharf, 'Application', 366–8.

[48] Scharf, 'Application', 377.

[49] Geneva Convention I for the Amelioration of the Condition of the Wounded and Sick in Armed Forces in the Field 75 UNTS 31, Article 49; Geneva Convention II for the Amelioration of the Condition of the Wounded, Sick and Shipwrecked Members of Armed Forces at Sea 75 UNTS 85, Article 50; Geneva Convention III Relative to the Treatment of Prisoners of War 75 UNTS 135, Article 129; Geneva Convention IV Relative to the Protection of Civilian Persons in Time of War 75 UNTS 287, Article 146.

[50] See, for example, Hersch Lauterpacht, 'The Problem of the Revision of the Law of War' (1952) 29 BYBIL 360, 362; Gerald I. A. D. Draper, 'The Geneva Conventions of 1949' (1965-II) 114 RdC 63, 167; Horst Fischer, 'Grave Breaches of the 1949 Geneva Conventions', in Gabrielle Kirk McDonald and Olivia Swaak-Goldman (eds.), *Substantive and Procedural Aspects of International Criminal Law, I: Commentary* (The Hague: Kluwer, 2000), pp. 63, 69. See generally, Richard R. Baxter, 'The Municipal and International Legal Bases of Jurisdiction Over War Crimes' (1951) 28 BYBIL 382.

There is a minority view, admittedly held by eminent authority, that the obligation is only to implement legislation and prosecute in case the State becomes a belligerent.[51] This view cannot be squared with the Conventions.[52] Indeed Röling ends his discussion by appearing to accept that the drafters intended and did bring about universal jurisdiction but that, in his eyes, they were wrong to do so.[53]

Although the matter is now of little import because of the near-universal acceptance of the Conventions, and the likelihood that the grave breaches regime is customary,[54] it may be noted that they did not provide for application to non-parties to the Conventions. The obligation is to search for and extradite or prosecute those who have committed grave breaches *of the Conventions*. Article 50 of GCI defines the acts as those 'committed against persons or property protected by the convention'. Therefore although jurisdiction is available to all parties in relation to all grave breaches, wherever they are committed, for there to be grave breaches the Conventions must have been applicable to the conflict in which the acts occurred. This requires a conflict involving high contracting parties (Common Article 2). Therefore there is no non-party effect envisaged in the Conventions.

The Apartheid Convention,[55] by virtue of the fact that its clear targets were highly unlikely to become parties to the treaty, is an example of a treaty that sought to create universal jurisdiction opposable to non-party States.[56] After setting up a duty to prosecute acts of apartheid in Article IV, Article V of the treaty states that 'Persons charged with the acts enumerated in Article II of the present Convention may be tried by a competent tribunal of any State to the Convention which may acquire jurisdiction over the person of the accused'. Had the Convention ever been used as a basis of a prosecution, the question of jurisdiction would

[51] Bernard V. A. Röling, 'The Law of War and the National Jurisdiction Since 1945' (1960-II) 100 RdC 329, 359–63; Derek W. Bowett, 'Jurisdiction: Changing Patterns of Authority Over Activities and Resources' (1982) 53 BYBIL 1, 12.

[52] See Richard van Elst, 'Implementing Universal Jurisdiction Over Grave Breaches of the Geneva Conventions' (2000) 13 LJIL 815, 821–3. See also *Yerodia*, Separate Opinion of Judges Higgins, Kooijmans and Buergenthal, paras. 28–32 (although the question here was whether the obligation to search for was territorially limited), paras. 46, 61.

[53] Röling, 'The Law of War', 363.

[54] The Grave Breaches regime was held to be customary in *Prosecutor* v. *Tadić*, Opinion and Judgment, IT-94-1-T, 7 May 1997, para. 577; Higgins, Kooijmans and Buergenthal are uncertain, Joint Opinion of Higgins, Kooijmans and Buergenthal, paras. 41–42.

[55] International Convention for the Suppression and Punishment of the Crime of Apartheid 1015 UNTS 243.

[56] See Reydams, *Universal Jurisdiction*, pp. 59–61.

doubtlessly have been raised,[57] not least as the question of jurisdiction was controversial in the drafting of the Convention. Again, the question of whether true universal jurisdiction could be said to exist would be one of customary law rather than treaty law (unless the Convention were to be ratified by all States).[58] To the extent that the definition in Article II of the Convention overlaps with crimes against humanity,[59] universal jurisdiction may be found under general international law anyway, but beyond the overlaps it is questionable if the Convention can be considered customary. It is general international law and the 'core' crimes to which we must now turn.

Universal jurisdiction and the 'core' crimes

There is a common theme in the traditional heads of jurisdiction. They are granted by international law to a State to protect its national interests.[60] The treaty regimes are best seen as a mutual concession of jurisdiction to achieve joint purposes, although this concession may evidence some level of consensus that there is a broader interest in repression. 'Pure' universal jurisdiction is the customary right of States to exercise jurisdiction over a limited set of offences, wherever such offences occurred, by whom such offences are committed and irrespective of any other jurisdictional link to the prosecuting State.[61] The underlying idea of universal jurisdiction is that such crimes are sufficiently serious that they amount to an attack on the international legal order itself,[62] an order in which States all have an interest in upholding;[63]

[57] On which see Roger S. Clark, 'Apartheid', in M. Cherif Bassiouni (ed.), *International Criminal Law, I, Crimes* (Ardsley: Transnational, 2nd edn., 1999), p. 643, pp. 653–8.

[58] Apartheid itself was doubtlessly a violation of the *jus cogens* prohibition of racial discrimination (Louis Henkin, *International Law: Politics and Values*, The Hague: Kluwer, 1995, p. 39).

[59] On which, see later.

[60] Brigitte Stern, 'Better Interpretation and Enforcement of Universality Jurisdiction', in Christopher Joyner (ed.), *Reining in Impunity for International Crimes and Serious Violations of Fundamental Human Rights* (St Agne, Erès, 1998), p. 175, p. 177.

[61] See the Princeton Principles on Universal Jurisdiction, Article 1(1). The Principles will not receive detailed consideration here as, by their own terms, they are a mixture of codification and progressive development, not a clear restatement of custom. On universal jurisdiction generally, see Reydams, *Universal Jurisdiction*; Willard B. Cowles, 'Universality of Jurisdiction Over War Crimes' (1945) 33 Cal LR 177; Kenneth C. Randall, 'Universal Jurisdiction Under International Law' (1988) 65 TLR 785.

[62] The conceptualisation is traceable to Frederick Mann; Mann, 'The Doctrine of Jurisdiction', 95. See also Rosalyn Higgins, *Problems and Process: International Law and How We Use It* (Oxford: Clarendon, 1994), pp. 58–9.

[63] On the idea, see Arthur Watts, 'The Importance of International Law', in Michael Byers (ed.), *The Role of Law in International Politics* (Oxford: Oxford University Press, 2000), p. 5, p. 7.

thus, almost by analogy with the protective principle, States may prosecute such offences.[64] Beyond this, there is authority for the idea that national courts are acting as organs of global justice in prosecuting international crimes in case-law.[65] Similar claims are often made in doctrine.[66]

As a preliminary matter, it is necessary to explain the distinction drawn by some between universal jurisdiction in the 'pure' sense (as it is defined above, sometimes called universal jurisdiction *in absentia*) and 'territorial jurisdiction over extraterritorial events' where a suspect is found in the territory of the State asserting jurisdiction, and prosecuted without any other jurisdictional link. The basic practical difference is that a State cannot request extradition on the basis of the latter principle. The distinction was drawn by a number of judges in the *Yerodia* Case and may, as a matter of practical politics, be a sensible limitation on the concept of universal jurisdiction.[67] To exercise jurisdiction over a crime allegedly committed by a person with no other link to the prosecuting State other than having been later found on the territory still requires an assertion of universal jurisdiction over the crime. Normally custody of a person does not give jurisdiction over offences they have committed elsewhere. That is one reason for the existence of extradition.

There are two possible exceptions to this, both relating to matters coming under the heading of international criminal law *lato sensu*: piracy and the suppression Conventions. It is therefore worth investigating these, as it might be thought that the concept of universal jurisdiction inevitably

[64] The analogy is drawn by Antonio Cassese, 'When May Senior State Officials Be Prosecuted for International Crimes: Some Comments on the *Congo* v. *Belgium* Case' (2002) 13 EJIL 853, 859.

[65] *In re Rauter*, 114 LRTWC 89, 109; *Demjanjuk* v. *Petrovsky* 776 F. 2d 571, 583 (USCA 6th Circuit 1985); cert. den. 475 US 1016 (1986), 628 F. Supp. 1370; F1 F. 2d 1254 (1986), *Eichmann*, Supreme Court, para. 12; *Fédération Nationale des Déportes et Internes Résistants et Patriots* v. *Barbie* (1985) 78 ILR 125, p. 131; *Yerodia*, Separate Opinion of Judges Higgins, Kooijmans and Buergenthal, para. 51 (although the paragraph does not offer whole-hearted support for the view), 72–5; Dissenting Opinion of Judge *ad hoc* van den Wyngaert, paras. 86–87.

[66] See, for example, Antonio Cassese, 'International Criminal Justice: Is it Needed in the Present World Community?', in Gerard Kreijen *et al* (eds.), *State Sovereignty, and International Governance* (Oxford: Oxford University Press, 2002), p. 239, p. 258; Neil Boister, 'Transnational Criminal Law?' (2003) 14 EJIL 953, 968–74; Roger O'Keefe, 'Customary Crimes in English Courts' (2001) 72 BYBIL 293, 335; Anthony Sammons, 'The "Under-Theorization" of Universal Jurisdiction: Implications for Legitimacy on Trials of War Criminals by Domestic Courts' (2003) 21 *Berkley Journal of International Law* 111, 137–8; Georges Abi-Saab, 'The Proper Role of Universal Jurisdiction' (2003) 1 JICJ 596, 596–7, 601.

[67] See, for example, Cassese, 'When May Senior State Officials', 856–7.

involves presence.[68] Turning first to piracy, it is possible that prior presence in the forum State is a prerequisite to the assertion of universal jurisdiction over suspected pirates.[69] Different versions of Oppenheim, for example, express different opinions on the matter.[70] However, confusion may have arisen because of the statement in Article 105 of the Law of the Sea Convention that the courts of the arresting State may exercise jurisdiction over pirates. This should not be read as granting exclusive jurisdiction to those courts.[71] It is also important that the suspect is not voluntarily in the State prosecuting, but will have been brought there by the arresting State. The judges dealing with the matter in *Yerodia* appeared to consider piracy to be a crime of pure universal jurisdiction.[72]

The second possible example is the limits contained in treaties that a person must be present in a jurisdiction for prosecution to be undertaken on the basis of expanded treaty-based jurisdiction, an example of which is Article 5(2) of the Torture Convention. The reason for this is that there is a duty to prosecute in such instances, and it is nonsensical to speak of a duty to prosecute all offences everywhere on every State party to the Convention. The nexus of voluntary presence in the jurisdiction cannot thus be seen as an inherent aspect of universal jurisdiction.

A case for jurisdiction is best made on the basis of State practice. A secondary argument linked to this could be made that, to the extent that international crimes are also subject to *jus cogens* prohibitions, this could lead to the existence of universal jurisdiction.[73] As *jus cogens* norms

68 The suggestion is made in Campbell Maclachlan, 'Pinochet Revisited' (2002) 51 ICLQ 959, 965 and Abi-Saab, 'The Proper Role', 600–1.

69 In support of such a requirement, see Cassese, 'When May Senior State Officials', 857, against, see Benjamin A. Wortley, 'Pirata Non Mutat Dominum' (1947) 245 BYBIL 258, 262. On piracy generally, see Alfred P. Rubin, *The Law of Piracy* (Ardsley: Transnational, 2nd edn., 1998).

70 Compare Lassa Oppenheim, Ronald F. Roxburgh (ed.), *International Law – A Treatise* (London, Longmans, Green & Co., 3rd edn., 1920), p. 434: 'the pirate is considered the enemy of every State, and can be brought to justice anywhere', with Jennings and Watts, *Oppenheim's International Law*, p. 753, 'it is for the courts of the state which has carried out the seizure to impose the penalties to be imposed'.

71 See, for example, Robin Churchill and A. Vaughan Lowe, *The Law of the Sea* (Manchester: Manchester University Press, 3rd edn., 1999), p. 210.

72 Separate Opinion of President Guillaume, para. 12, Separate Opinon of Judges Higgins, Kooijmans and Buergenthal, paras. 54, 61; the Separate Opinion of Judge Koroma, para. 9, is ambiguous.

73 *Prosecutor* v. *Furundžija*, Judgment, IT-95-17/1-T, 10 December 1998, para. 156; *Pinochet [No. 3]*, 177 (Lord Millet); M. Cherif Bassiouni, 'Universal Jurisdiction for International Crimes: Historical Perspectives and Contemporary Practice' (2001) 42 VJIL 1, 28.

involve *erga omnes* obligations there is some mileage in this argument.[74] The argument supports the idea of the community interest in the suppression of international crimes being converted into a national interest of States for the purposes of jurisdiction. Nonetheless, although the prohibitions on genocide and crimes against humanity are *jus cogens*, that is not the case for all war crimes.[75] Many war crimes are also subject to universal jurisdiction, so *jus cogens* reasoning cannot supply a complete answer to the question of universal jurisdiction.

There is considerable academic support for universal jurisdiction over the core crimes.[76] State practice is more equivocal, but offers just about sufficient support to ground a right to do so in custom.[77] This exceptional form of jurisdiction probably covers war crimes, crimes against humanity and genocide. Aggression is a considerably more difficult case. Any discussion of universal jurisdiction must now take place against the backdrop of the ICJ decision in the *Yerodia* Case. Although the court's decision expressly avoided the question of universal jurisdiction,[78] the separate and dissenting opinions of a number of the judges referred to in detail. Of those who dealt with the matter, four were against the existence of universal jurisdiction[79] and five expressly in favour.[80] The most detailed opinion on the matter, that of Judges Higgins,

[74] See, for example, Maurizio Ragazzi, *The Concept of International Obligations* Erga Omnes (Oxford: Oxford University Press, 1997), p. 50.

[75] See Bartram S. Brown, 'The Evolving Concept of Universal Jurisdiction' (2001) 35 NELR 383, 393. A very limited view of what war crimes amount to violations of *jus cogens* may be found in Rafael Nieto-Navia, 'International Peremptory Norms (Jus Cogens) and International Humanitarian Law', in Lal Chand Vohrah *et al.* (eds.), *Man's Inhumanity to Man: Essays in Honour of Antonio Cassese* (The Hague: Kluwer, 2003), p. 595.

[76] See, for example, Randall, 'Universal Jurisdiction', 788–90; Cowles, 'Universality'; Ian Brownlie, *Principles of International Law* (Oxford: Oxford University Press, 6th edn., 2003), pp. 303–5; Christopher C. Joyner, 'Arresting Impunity: The Case for Universal Jurisdiction in Bringing War Criminals to Accountability' (1996) 59 LCP 153; Christopher L. Blakesley and Otto Lagodny, 'Finding Harmony Amidst Disagreement Over Extradition: Jurisdiction, the Role of Human Rights, and Issues of Extraterritoriality Under International Criminal Law' (1991) 24 VJTL 1, 35. See generally, A. Hays Butler, 'Universal Jurisdiction: A Survey of the Literature' (2000) 11 CLF 353. See also the authors cited in the Amnesty International Study, *Universal Jurisdiction: The duty of States to Enact and Implement Legislation* (London: Amnesty International, 2001), AI Index IOR 53/02–018/2001, chapter 3, pp. 8–9. See, however, Alfred P. Rubin, 'Actio Popularis, Jus Cogens and Offences Erga Omnes' (2001) 35 NELR 265.

[77] For a contrary view, see Bassiouni 'Universal Jurisdiction'.

[78] *Yerodia*, paras. 41–46. See also Separate Opinion of Judge Koroma.

[79] President Guillaume, Judges Ranjeva, Rezek and Bula-Bula.

[80] Judges Koroma, Higgins, Kooijmans, Buergenthal and van den Wyngaert; Judge al-Khasawneh appears to support the principle, but is not express about it.

Kooijmans and Buergenthal, relies partially on the *Lotus* presumption in favour of freedom of State action.[81] Although their conclusion (that universal jurisdiction does exist) is correct, the reasoning is rather more questionable.

Relying on the *Lotus* principle to ground universal jurisdiction is problematic. The *Lotus* principle is immensely controversial.[82] It is quite possible that the *Lotus* Case is quoted in this regard to say something it did not. The fate of the *Lotus* principle is an object lesson in avoiding making broad pronouncements only to qualify or reject them. The PCIJ began 'far from laying down a general prohibition to the effect that States may not extend the application of their laws, and the jurisdiction of their courts to persons, property and acts outside their territory, [international law] leaves them in this respect a wide measure of discretion which is only limited in certain cases by prohibitive rules'.[83] Torn from its context, this seems unequivocal; however, the Permanent Court did not decide between this position and the idea that absent a permissive rule a State could not assert jurisdiction.[84] If, this notwithstanding, the PCIJ's views have been accurately reflected since, as James Brierly rightly complained:

> their reasoning was based on the highly contentious metaphysical proposition of the extreme positivist school that the law emanates from the free will of sovereign independent States, and from this premiss they argued that restrictions on the independence of States cannot be presumed. Neither, it may be said, can the absence of restrictions; for we are not entitled to deduce the law applicable to a specific state of facts from the mere fact of sovereignty or independence.[85]

Finally, at the practical level, the statement simply does not reflect the way in which States argue about jurisdiction, which is on the basis that a positive right must be shown to assert jurisdiction.[86]

[81] Separate Opinion of Judges Higgins, Kooijmans and Buergenthal, paras. 49–52.

[82] See Mann, 'The Doctrine of Jurisdiction', 35; Henkin, 'International Law', 278–80.

[83] *Lotus*, p. 19.

[84] *Lotus*, p. 20. See Separate Opinion of President Guillaume, para. 14; Joint Opinion, para. 49.

[85] James L. Brierly, 'The "Lotus" Case' (1928) 44 LQR 154, 155–6. See further, Ole Spiermann, 'Lotus and the Double Structure of International Legal Argumentation', in Laurence Boisson de Chazournes and Phillipe Sands (eds.), *International Law, The International Court of Justice and Nuclear Weapons* (Cambridge: Cambridge University Press, 1999), p. 131.

[86] Brierly, 'The "Lotus" ', 156. Vaughan Lowe, 'Jurisdiction', in Malcolm Evans (ed.), *International Law* (Oxford: Oxford University Press, 2003), p. 329, p. 335–6.

It must be conceded at the start that there is not a huge number of cases actually resting on universal jurisdiction. However, as we shall see later, the nature of universal jurisdiction is that States have a right, not a duty, to assert it. Therefore a smaller amount of practice is required than to establish a duty to do so. The first clear example is the *Eichmann* Case.[87] Recently, there has been a swing towards accepting that the *Eichmann* Case was based on passive personality jurisdiction.[88] The District Court engaged in a detailed discussion of Israel's right to use passive personality jurisdiction[89] and the Supreme Court declared that they were in complete agreement with the lower court's opinion on the matter.[90] But the manner in which they explained their excursus on universal jurisdiction leaves a narrow view of the *Eichmann* Case outside in the cold: 'if in our judgment we have concentrated on the international and universal character of the crimes . . . one of the reasons for our so doing is that some of them were directed against non-Jewish groups.'[91] The right of Israel to act on this basis was accepted by the US Court of Appeal for the 6th circuit in the *Demjanjuk* Case.[92]

More recent cases include the *Pinochet* cases in Spain.[93] These asserted universal jurisdiction over Pinochet on the basis of a questionable reading of his acts as genocide, despite the fact that the defendant was not present in the jurisdiction.[94] In both this Case and the later *Montt* Case in Spain (which also accepted that universal jurisdiction *in absentia* over genocide existed),[95] the Spanish courts declared that they would take

87 Above p. 50.

88 An example is the Dissenting Opinion of van den Wyngaert, para. 44. It may explain President Guillaume's comment that Israel was a 'special case', para. 12.

89 District Court, paras. 31–38.

90 Supreme Court, para. 12.

91 Supreme Court, para. 12.

92 *Demjanjuk* v. *Petrovsky* 776 F. 2d 571 (USCA 6th Circuit 1985); cert. den. 475 US 1016 (1986), 628 F. Supp. 1370; 784 F. 2d 1254 (1986). See James W. Moeller, 'United States Treatment of Alleged Nazi War Criminals: International Law, Immigration law and the Need for International Co-operation' (1985) 25 VJIL 793; Rena Hozore Reiss, 'The Extradition of John Demjanjuk: War Crimes, Universality Jurisdiction and the Political Offense Doctrine' (1987) 20 Cornell ILJ 281.

93 Case 19/97, November 4 1998, Case 1/98 November 5 1998, *reprinted in* (1999) 2 YBIHL 505. For general works on this, see Antoni Piragu Sole, 'The Pinochet Case in Spain' (2000) 6 ILSAJICL 653; Reydams, *Universal Jurisdiction*, pp. 184–8; María del Carmel Márquez Carrasco and Loaquín Alcaide Fernández, 'In Re Pinochet' (1999) 93 AJIL 690.

94 The genocide charges were not proceeded with in the United Kingdom because of the dubious interpretation of the scope of genocide in the Spanish cases.

95 Decision of 13 December 2000, *reprinted in* (2000) 3 YBIHL 691; see Michael Cottier, 'What Relationship Between the Exercise of Universal and Territorial Jurisdiction?', in Horst Fischer, Claus Kreß and Sascha Rolf Lüder (eds.), *International and National Prosecution of Crimes Under International Law* (Berlin: Arno Spitz, 2001), p. 843.

jurisdiction only where the territorial State had shown itself unwilling to prosecute. This idea that universal jurisdiction is subsidiary, coming into play only if the territorial jurisdiction was unwilling or unable to prosecute was reiterated in the *Guatemalan Generals* Case in 2003.[96]

It has been suggested that such a limit forms a part of universal jurisdiction.[97] However, the approach of the Spanish court was based on a dubious interpretation of the Genocide Convention's jurisdictional provisions and an application of the complemantarity provisions of the Rome Statute to inter-State overlaps of jurisdiction, when the principle does not apply as a matter of law.[98] That is not to say that it is a useful pragmatic limit on universal jurisdiction. Nonetheless, the broader Spanish approach to universal jurisdiction seems to have been accepted by Mexico, who extradited an Argentine ex-General (Ricardo Miguel Carvallo) to Spain on the basis of its exercise of universal jurisdiction.[99] Belgian Courts have also asserted universal jurisdiction over Pinochet in spite of his absence from the forum State.[100] More controversially, there was an attempt to assert such jurisdiction over Ariel Sharon, Prime Minister of Israel, by Belgium, which led to a formal protest from Israel.[101] In the Netherlands, the 2001 *Bourtese* Case affirmed universal jurisdiction over crimes against humanity, even where the defendant was not present in the forum.[102]

There are a considerable number of pieces of national legislation which also assert universal jurisdiction without expressly requiring the voluntary presence of the defendant in the forum State. These include the criminal codes of Azerbaijan,[103] Belarus,[104] the Czech Republic,[105] Ethiopia,[106] Finland,[107] Hungary[108] and Paraguay.[109] Other States have implemented the Rome Statute by legislation including universal

[96] Decision of 25 February 2003. For criticism, see Hervé Ascensio, 'Are Spanish Courts Backing Down on Universality? The Supreme Tribunal's Decision in *Guatemalan Generals*' (2003) 1 JICJ 690.

[97] Antonio Cassese, 'Is the Bell Tolling for Universality? A Plea for a Sensible Notion of Universal Jurisdiction' (2003) 1 JICJ 589, 593.

[98] Ascensio, 'Are Spanish Courts', 693–8; although it may be a sensible development.

[99] *Carvallo*, decision of 11 January 2001.

[100] *In re Pinochet, reprinted in* (1999) 2 YBIHL 475, 483. See Luc Reydams, 'Belgian Tribunal of First Instance' (1999) 93 AJIL 700.

[101] On the *Sharon* Case generally, see Antonio Cassese, 'The Belgian Court of Cassation v. the International Court of Justice: The *Sharon and Others* Case' (2003) 1 JICJ 437.

[102] *Bourtese*, Decision of 20 November 2001, *reprinted in* (2000) 3 YBIHL 677, 688.

[103] Criminal Code, Article 12(3).

[104] Penal Code of Belarus No. 28, 2000, Article 6(3).

[105] Criminal Code, section 19.

[106] Penal Code 1957, Article 17(1).

[107] Finnish Penal Code, Chapter 1, section 7, Decree on the application of Chapter 1, section 7 of the Penal Code (627/1996), section 1(2)(3).

[108] Criminal Code, 1978, section 4(1)(c).

[109] Law No. 1160/97, Article 8.

jurisdiction over international crimes without expressly creating a requirement of voluntary presence. These include Australia,[110] Canada,[111] Germany[112] and New Zealand.[113] Until political pressure from the United States led Belgium to alter its legislation, a similar basis of jurisdiction was incorporated into Belgian law.[114] Some have taken the Belgian alteration of its legislation to signify the death of universal jurisdiction *in absentia*.[115] The problem with such a view is that it assumes that Belgium's actions were accompanied by *opinio juris* that universal jurisdiction *in absentia* is unlawful, when the stated reason for limiting the reach of its extraterritorial jurisdiction was that the statute had been abused.[116]

The United Kingdom accepts the legitimacy of the exercise of such jurisdiction. The UK International Criminal Court Act 2001 permits extradition to States prosecuting on the basis of universal jurisdiction.[117] In an *amicus curiae* brief to the US Supreme Court in 2004 the United Kingdom, Australia and Switzerland maintained that universal criminal jurisdiction exists over serious crimes such as serious war crimes, genocide and crimes against humanity.[118] The United States may be taken to have accepted universal jurisdiction without a link of voluntary presence when it asked a number of States to prosecute Pol Pot in the 1990s.[119] Although the US position on the ICC could be taken as casting some doubt on its view, it is probable that it does not, as the legal argument was that it is not lawful to delegate jurisdiction to an international body without the consent of the State of nationality.[120] Finally, although it is UN, rather than State practice, UNTAET

[110] Australian Criminal Code Act 1985, sections 1, 15(4) as amended by the International Criminal Court (Consequential Amendments Act 2002).

[111] Crimes Against Humanity and War Crimes Act 2001, section 6. The act is ambiguous on this point.

[112] Code of Crimes Against International Law, section 1.

[113] International Crimes and International Criminal Court Act 2000, sections 8, 9, 10, 11.

[114] See generally Steven R. Ratner, 'Belgium's War Crimes Statute. A Postmortem' (2003) 97 AJIL 888 on the Law of 16 June 1993, as amended in 1999. On the later amendments, see Luc Reydams, 'Belgium Reneges on Universality: The 5 August 2003 Act on Grave Breaches of International Humanitarian Law' (2003) 1 JICJ 679; on the US threats, see George P. Fletcher, 'Against Universal Jurisdiction' (2003) 1 JICJ 580, 584.

[115] Cassese, 'Is the Bell Tolling', 589. [116] Reydams, 'Belgium', 679.

[117] International Criminal Court Act, 2001 Ch. 17, section 72.

[118] *Sosa* v. *Alvarez-Machain*, No. 03–339, Brief of the Governments of the Commonwealth of Australia, the Swiss Federation and the United Kingdom as *Amici Curiae*, p. 6. The footnote to the position accepts that there is still room for some doubt, however.

[119] David J. Scheffer, 'Opening Address' (2001) 35 NELR 233, 254–6.

[120] Burrus M. Carnahan, 'International Criminal Court' (1999) 2 YBIHL 424, 425.

regulation 2000/15 asserts universal jurisdiction over international crimes.[121]

There are more instances where States have asserted universal jurisdiction over those already in their territory. Sometimes this is because it is considered a formal requirement. For example, in France complaints relating to Bosnia and Rwanda were rejected on the ground that the putative defendant was not in the country.[122] The same occurred in relation to French attempts to investigate Pinochet.[123] Early cases in Germany, such as *Tadić* and *Djajić* asserted that it was necessary to have some link to Germany to prosecute genocide extraterritorially, but that the voluntary presence of the suspect in Germany was sufficient.[124] This is not always the case however; in the later *Jorgić* Case the question was left open in relation to war crimes.[125] In addition, the possibility of overload of the German legal system was part of the motivation for the imposition of the requirement, rather than a serious evaluation of international law.[126] The German Code of Crimes Against International Law does not impose such a requirement. As we saw above, the Spanish Courts moved to accept such a requirement in the *Guatemalan Generals* Case.

There have been other uses or assertions of universal jurisdiction over international crimes committed by persons who later are found in the forum State. An interesting example of the use of a treaty was the *Cvjetković* Case in Austria,[127] as it implied universal jurisdiction into the Genocide Convention when there is no functioning territorial judiciary. As there is no basis for this in the Genocide Convention, its

[121] UNTAET Regulation 2000/15, section 2.

[122] See Brigitte Stern, '*In re* Javor, *In re* Munyeshaka' (1999) 93 AJIL 525; Reydams, *Universal Jurisdiction*, pp. 135–9.

[123] Brigitte Stern, '*In re* Pinochet' (1999) 93 AJIL 696.

[124] Tadić was transferred to the ICTY prior to judgment; *Djajić* No. 20/96. Supreme Court of Bavaria, 3d Strafsenat, 23 May 1997. See generally, Kai Ambos and Steffen Wirth, 'Genocide and War Crimes in Former Yugoslavia Before German Courts', in Horst Fischer, Claus Kreß and Sascha Rolf Lüder (eds.), *International and National Prosecution of Crimes Under International Law* (Berlin: Arno Spitz, 2001), p. 769; Albin Eser 'National Jurisdiction over Extraterritorial Crimes within the Framework of International Complementarity', in Lal Chand Vohrah *et al.* (eds.), *Man's Inhumanity to Man: Essays in Honour of Antonio Cassese* (The Hague: Kluwer, 2003); p. 279, pp. 282–3.

[125] *Jorgić*, OLG Dusseldorf, 26 September 1997; Christopher J. M. Safferling, 'Public Prosecutor v. Djajić' (1998) 92 AJIL 528.

[126] Ambos and Wirth, 'Genocide and War Crimes', pp. 781–3.

[127] *Dusko Cvetjković*. Beschluss des Oberstern Gerichtshofs Os99/94–6, 13 July 1994. See Axel Marschik, 'European National Approaches to War Crimes', in Timothy L. H. McCormack and Gerry Simpson (eds.), *The Law of War Crimes: National and International Approaches* (The Hague: Kluwer, 1997), p. 65, pp. 79–82; Reydams, *Universal Jurisdiction*, pp. 99–101.

international acceptability must rest on customary law. Belgium has taken action on the basis of universal jurisdiction in relation to offences in Rwanda.[128] In the 'Butare four' case, convictions on the basis of common Article 3 and Additional Protocol II were entered on this basis.[129] Again there is no treaty-based jurisdiction, so the basis needs to be customary. The same provisions were invoked in Switzerland in the *Niyontenze* Case, again dealing with Rwanda.[130]

There are a number of States who have asserted jurisdiction over non-nationals who commit international offences and later come to the jurisdiction in their legislation. As with universal jurisdiction *in absentia*, many of these post-date the Rome Statute, and were influenced by it, although there is no part of the treaty that either requires or permits the assertion of such jurisdiction. The Netherlands,[131] South Africa[132] and the United Kingdom[133] have examples of this sort of legislation.

From the above survey, certain conclusions can be drawn. The first is that there is increasing support for the assertion of universal jurisdiction by States. This level of support is sufficient to suggest that the customary case for universal jurisdiction over core crimes may be made. The existence of universal jurisdiction was used by the Special Court for Sierra Leone as an integral part of its reasoning in the *Kallon and Kamara* appeal decision on the Lomé amnesty.[134] Both the ICTY and ICTR have

[128] See Reydams, *Universal Jurisdiction*, pp. 102–18; Luc Reydams, 'Universal Jurisdiction Over Atrocities in Rwanda: Theory and Practice' (1996) 1 EJCCLCJ 18, 35–8.

[129] Reydams, *Universal Jurisdiction*, pp. 109–12. See also Luc Reydams, 'Belgium's First Application of Universal Jurisdiction: The Butare Four Case' (2002) 1 JICJ 428. For a helpful discussion of the cases relating to non international armed conflict, see Sonja Boeleart-Suominen, 'Grave Breaches, Universal Jurisdiction and Internal Armed Conflicts: Is Customary Law Moving Towards a Uniform Enforcement Mechanism for All Armed Conflicts' (2000) 5 JCSL 63.

[130] Tribunal Militaire Division 2, Lausanne, 30 April 1999. See Luc Reydams, 'Prosecutor v. Niyontenze' (2002) 96 AJIL 231; William A. Schabas, 'National Courts Finally Begin to Prosecute the "Crime of Crimes": Genocide' (2003) 1 JICJ 39, 47–9.

[131] International Crimes Act, section 2(1)(a).

[132] Implementation of the Rome Statute for the International Criminal Court Act No. 27 of 202, section 4(3). On the draft bill, see Hennie Strydom, 'South Africa and the International Criminal Court' (2002) 6 MPYBUNL 345.

[133] International Criminal Court Act, section 68(1); War Crimes Act 1991 section 1(1); on the latter see Theodor Meron, 'International Criminalization of Internal Atrocities' (1995) 89 AJIL 554, 573. Christopher Greenwood, 'The War Crimes Act 1991', in Hazel Fox and Michael A. Meyer (eds.), *Armed Conflict and the New Law, II: Effecting Compliance* (London: British Institute of International and Comparative Law, 1993), p. 215, p. 217.

[134] *Prosecutor* v. *Kallon and Kamara*, Decision on Challenge to Jurisdiction: Lomé Accord Amnesty, SCSL-2004–15-AR 72(E) and SCSL-2004–16-AR72(E), 13 March 2004, paras. 67–71.

accepted the existence of universal jurisdiction.[135] The difficult question is whether or not States are entitled to assert such jurisdiction in the absence of the voluntary presence of the suspect in the forum State.

There is less evidence for the proposition that a defendant may be prosecuted on the basis of universal jurisdiction absent his or her voluntary presence in the forum State, but this may simply be because it is rare that States will seek to exercise such jurisdiction. That is not fatal to a claim that there is a right to do so. The question is largely linked to the question of whether or not States may ask for extradition on this basis. It is difficult to fault the opinion of Higgins, Kooijmans and Buergenthal on this point, where they note that 'if the underlying purpose of designating certain acts as international crimes is to authorise a wide jurisdiction to be asserted over persons committing them, there is no rule of international law . . . which makes illegal co-operative acts designed to secure the presence within a State wishing to exercise jurisdiction'.[136] As we saw in relation to the other examples of universal jurisdiction *lato sensu*, such limitations were created for specific reasons not applicable here. There are a number of States that assert such jurisdiction, and it may cautiously be suggested that they are acting lawfully in doing so for the limited category of crimes we are investigating. If there is no distinction between the types of universal jurisdiction, the case is, naturally, stronger.

It should be pointed out that, on the basis of similar evidence, Luc Reydams concludes that universal jurisdiction *in absentia* does not exist.[137] Reydams states that in 'the few precedents (*Sharon, Ndombasi* [*Yerodia*] and *Pinochet*) the States of nationality of the suspects protested vigorously, and not just on immunity grounds'.[138] There is some truth in this, but in *Yerodia* the Democratic Republic of Congo expressly dropped its objection to Belgium's assertion of universal jurisdiction as it did not wish to prejudice the developing law of universal jurisdiction.[139] In *Pinochet*, the United States pointedly refrained from protesting the

[135] *Prosecutor* v. *Tadić*, Decision on Interlocutory Appeal on Jurisdiction, IT-94-1AR72, 2 October 1995, para. 62. *Prosecutor* v. *Ntuyuhaga*, Decision on the Prosecutor's Motion to Withdraw the Indictment ICTR-96-40-T, 18 March 1999 (in relation to genocide).

[136] Joint Separate Opinion, para. 58.

[137] Reydams, *Universal Jurisdiction*, p. 224. Antonio Cassese has moved to this view; see Cassese, 'Is the Bell Tolling', 595.

[138] Reydams, *Universal Jurisdiction*, p. 230.

[139] On which, see William A. Schabas, 'Introduction', in Reydams, *Universal Jurisdiction*, pp. x–xi.

decision of the UK courts, and Chile's protests in that case must also be taken alongside the expressions of support from other States. Israel may have protested the decision to investigate in *Sharon*, but had used universal jurisdiction without voluntary presence itself in both *Eichmann* and *Demjanjuk*, which rather undermines any protest on that ground.[140]

Problems of universal jurisdiction

There are a number of critiques that can be made of universal jurisdiction, and they have a bearing on the political landscape in which international criminal law is, or is not, enforced. As Bruce Broomhall observes '[u]niversal jurisdiction will not become a reliable pillar of the international rule of law until these difficulties are squarely faced . . . [and prosecutions on the basis of universal jurisdiction are] . . . a magnet for domestic and international controversy'.[141]

The first critique is that the exercise of universal jurisdiction is a form of neo-colonial intervention. This is linked to ideas of selectivity, that international crimes are prosecuted only where there is a political reason for doing so. Some of the attempted exercises of universal jurisdiction have been by ex-colonial powers. Spain has asserted jurisdiction over offences in Chile. The Netherlands has been involved in cases relating to (what was then) Surinam.[142] Most famously, the *Yerodia* litigation involved a post-colonial State (the Democratic Republic of Congo, DRC) and its former colonial power, Belgium.[143] The most outspoken critic was the Congolese *ad hoc* judge, Judge Bula-Bula. Bula-Bula considered the assertion of universal jurisdiction by Belgium to be part of a Belgian practice of neo-colonial interference, which began with Belgian involvement in the killing of Patrice Lumumba.[144] President Guillaume was only slightly more diplomatic: '[to accept universal jurisdiction] . . . would be to . . . encourage the arbitrary for the purposes of the powerful, purportedly acting for an ill-defined "international community".'[145]

140 On immunities, Israel had more of a point.

141 Bruce Broomhall, *International Justice and the International Criminal Court: Between Sovereignty and the Rule of Law* (Oxford: Oxford University Press, 2003), p. 105. See also Steven R. Ratner, 'Belgium's War Crimes Statute'.

142 See Pita J. C. Schimmelpennick van der Oije, 'A Surinam Crime Before a Dutch Court: Universal Jurisdiction or a Post-Colonial Injustice?' (2001) 14 LJIL 455.

143 See Maclachlan, 'Pinochet Revisited', 965. For an interesting reversal of such rhetoric, see Brown, 'The Evolving Concept', 391.

144 *Yerodia*, Separate Opinion of Judge *ad hoc* Bula-Bula, paras. 9–14.

145 *Ibid.*, Separate Opinion of President Guillaume, para. 15. See also Judge Rejek, para. 10; Boister, 'The ICJ in the Belgian Arrest Warrant Case: Arresting the Development of International Criminal Law' (2002) 7 JCSL 293, 307.

It is easier to make than to refute allegations of neo-colonialism,[146] and neo-colonial intervention should be condemned. But at least part of the reason for the fact that ex-colonial States have been involved in such action is because either victims or perpetrators have found their way to the old colonial power and victims have persuaded independent magistrates in those countries to investigate. The governments of those States have not been involved in the initial decision to prosecute. Where they have been involved in the proceedings, as often as not those States' governments have been unenthusiastic.[147]

The correct response to suggestions that neo-colonial ideals underpin particular prosecutorial efforts is to call for impartial prosecution of international crimes, wherever they are committed.[148] Amnesty International, whose views on universal jurisdiction are more assertive than many international lawyers',[149] accept that in an ideal world the territorial or perhaps nationality State would take responsibility for prosecution.[150] That this was not the case in *Yerodia* was raised by Judge *ad hoc* van den Wyngaert as a reason the DRC did not come before the Court with 'clean hands'.[151] Although undiplomatic, there is truth in the general assertion that universal jurisdiction may have its most appropriate role in acting where the territorial or perhaps nationality State does not, even if the subsidiarity criterion applied in Spain is not established in international law. The appropriate role for universal jurisdiction may well be to ensure, rather as the ICC is intended to do, that the most interested States prosecute international crimes fairly by leaving a back-up role for others if those States do not prosecute.[152]

However, overlapping jurisdictional claims are a possible source of tension. This perhaps explains President Guillaume's description of a dystopian 'judicial chaos' which would, in his eyes, follow from the acceptance of universal jurisdiction.[153] There is no hierarchy established between the forms of jurisdiction. This has been a problem for Tanzania,

[146] See the ILA Report, p. 422, where it is noted that most cases are in OECD States, but that there is no evidence that prosecutions were carried out on frivolous or political grounds.

[147] This was certainly the Case in the Pinochet litigation.

[148] Boister, 'The ICJ', 313–14; ILA Report, p. 422.

[149] As we will see, including my own.

[150] Amnesty International, *Universal Jurisdiction*, Introduction, p. 31.

[151] Dissenting Opinion of Judge *ad hoc* van den Wyngaert, see Boister 'The ICJ', 307.

[152] See similarly, 'David A. Tallman, 'Universal Jurisdiction: Lessons From the Belgian Experience', in Jane E. Stromseth (ed.), *Accountability for Atrocities: National and International Responses* (Ardsley: Transnational, 2003), p. 375.

[153] *Yerodia*, Separate Opinion of President Guillaume, para. 15.

which has been faced with Rwandan (territorial jurisdiction) and Belgian (universal jurisdiction) extradition requests for Bernard Ntuyuhaga. It is also, in some ways, what was at issue in the *Pinochet* litigation, as Chile claimed it should be able to try him,[154] while the 'implicit assumption in the Spanish–English effort was that Chile had no protected right' to do so in preference to their courts.[155] Bassiouni is a supporter of the creation of a hierarchy of jurisdictional claims.[156] It would be a sensible, but difficult development,[157] and the problem of overlapping jurisdiction remains despite the hints of subsidiarity suggested in the Spanish and Austrian cases.

Some scholars have suggested other difficulties involved in universal jurisdiction. One of these is the possibility that prosecutions on the basis of universal jurisdiction may not be made with sufficient respect for basic due process rights.[158] Aside from the speculative nature of the suggestion, a number of responses to such a claim spring to mind. First, that is precisely why we have due process rights in international human rights law, and in humanitarian law.[159] Michael Akehurst's statement covers the point admirably: referring to the 'fear that in some other countries courts are biased and punishments inhuman' Akehurst retorts that 'there are other rules of international law which guarantee a minimum international standard for the treatment of aliens, so one cannot invoke the possibility of jurisdiction's being abused as a reason for denying jurisdiction altogether'.[160]

The likelihood that partiality will be a greater problem when prosecutions occur on a universal basis rather than any other basis is low. States

154 See written submissions of Chile, as reported by Lord Hutton in *Pinochet*, 164.

155 Ruth Wedgwood, 'International Criminal Law and Augusto Pinochet' (2000) 40 VJIL 829, 832–3.

156 M. Cherif Bassiouni, 'Policy Considerations on Inter-State Cooperation in Criminal Matters', in M. Cherif Bassiouni (ed.), *International Criminal Law, II: Procedural and Enforcement Mechanisms* (Ardsley: Transnational, 2nd edn. 1999), p. 3, p. 9, ranking them as territoriality, nationality, passive personality, protective and universal.

157 Chirstopher Blakesley, 'Extraterritorial Jurisdiction', in M. Cherif Bassiouni (ed.), *International Criminal Law, II: Procedural and Enforcement Mechanisms* (Ardsley: Transnational, 1999), p. 33, p. 82.

158 Madeline Morris, 'Universal Jurisdiction in a Divided World' (2001) 35 NELR 337, 352–3; Henry Kissinger, 'The Pitfalls of Universal Jurisdiction' (2001) (July–August) FA 86. For a response, see Kenneth Roth, 'The Case for Universal Jurisdiction' (2001) (October–November) FA 150.

159 Gerald I. A. D. Draper, *The Red Cross Conventions* (London, Stevens & Co., 1958), p. 95, considers the contribution of the Geneva Conventions to the protection of those suspected of violations to be equal to their role in protecting others affected by war.

160 Akehurst, 'Jurisdiction', 165.

with territoriality or passive personality jurisdiction are no more likely to prosecute with scrupulous regard for international standards; there are grounds for believing that at times they are less so.[161] Where universal jurisdiction *in absentia* forms the basis of an extradition request, protection for the putative defendant is offered by the ability of a requested State to refuse extradition on the basis that the defendant's fair trial rights would not be respected in the requesting jurisdiction.[162] If the prosecution is based on an excessive assertion of universal jurisdiction, such as one on the basis of an extremely broad interpretation of the relevant crime, the rules on double criminality will also be relevant.[163]

George Fletcher, who fears that 'there is no guarantee whatsoever against hounding an accused in one court after another until the victims are satisfied that justice has been done', brings a more solid objection.[164] In the absence of a general international version of the *non bis in idem* principle that appropriately balances the rights of defendants, victims and international society in general,[165] there is the possibility of such an outcome. However, the point is overstated, as States are not generally over-enthusiastic about using universal jurisdiction.[166] There is also again Akehurst's point that the possibility of abuse does not mean that the principle of jurisdiction is fatally flawed. In addition, many extradition treaties allow *non bis in idem* as a reason for non-cooperation.[167] Given the reasonable point made by Fletcher, though, perhaps the approach of the Spanish courts in the *Guatemalan Generals* Case

[161] See, for example, Jordan J. Paust, 'Antiterrorism Military Commissions: Courting Illegality' (2001) 23 MJIL 1; Jordan J. Paust, 'Antiterrorism Military Commissions: The Ad Hoc DOD Rules of Procedure' (2002) 23 MJIL 677.

[162] See, for example, Leslie C. Green, 'Political Offences, War Crimes and Extradition' (1962) 11 ICLQ 329; Christine van den Wyngaert, 'The Political Offence Exception to Extradition: How to Plug the "Terrorists' Loophole" Without Departing from Fundamental Human Rights' (1989) 19 IYBHR 297; John Dugard and Christine van den Wyngaert, 'Reconciling Extradition with Human Rights' (1998) 92 AJIL 187.

[163] On the importance of protections contained in extradition law in prosecuting international crimes, see Christopher L. Blakesley, 'Autumn of the Patriarch: The Pinochet Extradition Debacle and Beyond – Human Rights Clauses Compared to Traditional Protections Such as Double Criminality' (2000) 91 *Journal of Crime, Criminal Law and Criminology* 1.

[164] George P. Fletcher, 'Against Universal Jurisdiction' (2003) 1 JICJ 580, 582.

[165] See Cristine van den Wyngaert and Guy Stessens, 'The International *Non Bis in Idem* Principle: Resolving Some of the Unanswered Questions' (1999) 48 ICLQ 779.

[166] Abi-Saab, 'The Proper Role', 600–1.

[167] Although this can be limited to where the requested or requesting State has prosecuted; see Geoff Gilbert, *Transnational Fugitive Offenders in International Law: Extradition and Other Mechanisms* (The Hague: Martinus Nijhoff, 1998), pp. 181–2.

may show a useful mechanism for ensuring that universal jurisdiction is used in a manner that is sensitive to respect for the defendant. The complementarity regime of the ICC may provide a useful analogy here, even if the principle is not directly applicable to State jurisdiction as a matter of law.

There have been suggestions that there could be some form of governmental control over prosecutions on the basis of universal jurisdiction, such control to be exercised if there were serious repercussions for international relations.[168] This begs the question of precisely what such repercussions are, and who is to define them. It is more than likely that a balancing exercise, or a veto for executive authorities, would ensure impunity for those offenders from powerful States, as relations with powerful nationality States would be more 'fundamental' than those of States with lesser political 'clout'. This raises the spectres of selectivity, with which we shall concern ourselves at some length later. The Joint Opinion of Higgins, Kooijmans and Buergenthal took as one of its basic conditions for the exercise of universal jurisdiction that prosecutions are initiated by independent authorities.[169]

The specific reason given by Luc Reydams for the inadvisability of adopting universal jurisdiction is that it would be inappropriate to subject every person in the world to a set of rules which, *inter alia*, they could not reasonably know about.[170] There is some truth in this in relation to domestic criminal law, which alongside common crimes such as murder and theft also often reflects legitimate societal idiosyncrasies. As far back as 1928 James Brierly castigated as intolerable 'the suggestion that every individual is or may be subject to the laws of every State at all times and in all places'.[171] The answer can, again, be found in Michael Akehurst's classic treatment of jurisdiction. Commenting on Brierly's disquiet, Akehurst replied '[b]ut surely it is intolerable only if the laws vary from place to place; if they are the same in all countries the individual suffers little hardship'.[172] International criminal law on the core crimes in particular may provide a common criminal law of humanity which could overcome this critique.[173]

[168] Morris, 'Universal Jurisdiction', 333.

[169] *Yerodia*, Separate Opinion of Judges Higgins, Kooijmans and Buergenthal, para. 59.

[170] Reydams, *Universal Jurisdiction*, p. 224.

[171] Brierly, 'The Lotus Case', 161.

[172] Akehurst, 'Jurisdiction', 165.

[173] See below, pp. 172–3. David Hirsch considers international criminal law to be an incipient form of cosmopolitan law; David Hirsch, *The Law Against Genocide: Cosmopolitan Trials* (London: Glasshouse, 2003). A similar point to the above may also

There are also practical problems which are common to extraterritorial prosecutions, but which arise in a particularly acute form in prosecutions based on universal jurisdiction. The most pressing is gaining custody of the accused and gaining sufficient evidence to ensure a fair trial. Absent assistance given on the basis of comity, inter-State co-operation is based on a highly incomplete network of mostly bilateral treaties. The problems of obtaining defendants have led to States at times engaging in unlawful activities such as abduction (as in the *Eichmann* Case), or other forms of unlawful rendition (such as occurred in the *Barbie* Case).[174] For fair trials to occur, both the prosecution and defence need to be able to call on other States to co-operate in the provision of evidence. The *Demjanjuk* Case in Israel also saw another problem, where unreliable evidence is provided by another State (in that instance, the then USSR) overzealous in its pursuit of a conviction.[175] The ILA accepted that obtaining evidence might be the biggest problem when prosecuting international crimes outside of the *locus delicti*.[176]

This is exacerbated by the fact that mutual legal assistance regimes are the exception rather than the rule. This is an aspect of the primarily bilateral international regime that exists in relation to international criminal co-operation.[177] There are some multilateral treaty obligations to provide assistance to other parties prosecuting offences under those treaties. Examples of these include Article 88 of Additional Protocol I and Article 9 of the Torture Convention. They do not appear to have been used. Even where there are Mutual Legal Assistance regimes, their operation is difficult, even when States are willing to hand over evidence, and that is not always the case.[178] Cultural and language factors also make trials outside the *locus delicti* difficult.[179] Evidential insufficiency

be found in Henry J. Steiner, 'Three Cheers for Universal Jurisdiction – Or is it Only Two?' (2004) 5 *Theoretical Inquiries in Law* 199, 204–7.

174 On Eichmann, see Helen Silving, 'In re Eichmann: A Dilemma of Law and Morality' (1961) 55 AJIL 307; on Barbie, see Guyora Binder, 'Representing Nazism: Advocacy and Identity at the Trial of Klaus Barbie' (1989) 98 Yale LJ 1321, 1327.

175 See Matthew Lipmann, 'The Pursuit of Nazi War Criminals in the United States and Other Anglo-American Legal Systems' (1998) 29 CWILJ 1, 89–99.

176 ILA Report, pp. 418, 419, reports anecdotal evidence to that effect.

177 Phillip B. Heyman, 'Two Models of National Attitudes Towards International Cooperation in Law Enforcement' (1990) 31 Harvard ILJ 99, 100. In Europe, though, see Council Decision 2003/335/JHA, of 8 May 2003, on the investigation and prosecution of genocide, crimes against humanity and war crimes OJ 118/12 (14 May 2003).

178 ILA Report, p. 418.

179 Robert Cryer, 'Witness Evidence Before International Criminal Tribunals' (2003) 3 LPICT 411, 420–9.

led to acquittals in *Demjanjuk, Cvetjković* and in the Swiss Case of *Gabrez* (In re Gabrez).[180]

Partially because of the problems above, the fact remains that there is a relative paucity of prosecutions on this basis. But the comparatively small use of universal jurisdiction 'is not because it is not available as a matter of international law; rather it is because States most often are not eager to deal with crimes – however odious, committed by foreigners, against foreigners, outside their territory'.[181] It may be that the recent upswing is evidence of a slow, but nonetheless identifiable shift in practice. Still, universal jurisdiction and its utilisation remain controversial, and have caused considerable tension between States.

Duties to extradite or prosecute?

The question of whether or not there is a general duty to extradite or prosecute international crimes is one which has been thought to provide an answer to the so-called 'impunity gap' that affects international criminal law. In theory, this seems sensible: if States were obliged to prosecute international crimes, then they would. Also, an implemented duty to prosecute international crimes would also provide a strong counter-argument to those who claim that the use of universal jurisdiction, in particular, is selective (or, more specifically, neo-colonial). Nevertheless, there are two problems with placing too much emphasis on a postulated duty alone. The first is the difficulty involved in establishing such a duty. The second is that it may be that a duty, without some form of supervision of the implementation of that duty has, in practice, made little difference to the level of prosecution.

The answer to the question of whether or not there is a duty incumbent on all States to extradite or prosecute international crimes needs to be dealt with at a number of levels. Not only does the position under treaty law and under customary international law have to be investigated, but also precisely upon which States any duty falls. It is quite likely that greater obligations fall upon the *locus delicti* or the State of nationality of the offender than fall upon States with less of a link to the crime. We shall begin by looking at treaties expressly imposing

[180] *In re Gabrez* Military Tribunal, Division 1, Lausanne, 18 April 1997, noted Andreas Ziegler, 'International Decisions: In re G' (1998) 82 AJIL 78. See Reydams, *Universal Jurisdiction*, p. 196. It would appear that some of the lessons were learned by the *Niyontenze* Case, see Reydams, *Universal Jurisdiction*, p. 200.

[181] Sern, 'Better Interpretation', p. 178.

duties to prosecute offences domestically, then human rights treaties as they have been read as implying such a duty. We shall then move to investigate whether customary law expressly provides a basis for an obligation to prosecute, and the possibility that the normative status of some of the rules on international crimes could provide a foundation for one.

Treaties

To turn to treaties other than the Rome Statute (which will be evaluated in chapter 3), the classic example of a duty to extradite or prosecute can be found in the Grave Breaches regime of the Geneva Conventions. The Grave Breaches provisions are phrased in the imperative: 'Each High Contracting Party shall be under the obligation to search for persons alleged to have committed, or to have ordered to be committed, such grave breaches and shall bring such persons, regardless of their nationality, before its own courts [or hand them over to another High Contracting Party].'[182] This is a very broad duty, relating not only to prosecution, but on the basis of what is practically indistinguishable from universal jurisdiction.[183] However, the duty could realistically relate only to suspects who are in the territory of the High Contracting Party.

The Genocide Convention does not mention trials before national courts outside the *locus delicti*, but for such courts there is a duty to prosecute.[184] Articles IV and VI both say that *genocidaires* 'shall be' tried and punished by the territorial State. There is one statement by the ICJ that implies that the Convention may require more of third States. In the Preliminary Objections decision in the *Bosnia Genocide* Case, '[t]he Court note[d] that the obligation each State thus has to prevent and to punish the crime of genocide is not territorially limited by the Convention'.[185] Antonio Cassese considers that this 'may among other things entail for States the general duty to set up appropriate judicial mechanisms or procedures for the universal repression of those crimes'.[186]

[182] Geneva Convention I, Article 49; Geneva Convention II, Article 50; Geneva Convention III, Article 129; Geneva Convention IV, Article 146.

[183] See e.g. Lauterpacht, 'The Problem of the Revision', 362; Draper, 'The Geneva Conventions', 167.

[184] Convention on the Prevention and Punishment of Genocide, 78 UNTS 277.

[185] *Case Concerning the Application of the Convention on the Prevention and Punishment of Genocide (Bosnia-Herzegovina* v. *Yugoslavia)* Preliminary Objections (1996) ICJ Rep. 616, para. 31.

[186] Antonio Cassese, *International Criminal Law* (Oxford: Oxford University Press, 2003), p. 303.

The Court's statement has a tenuous relationship with the text of Article VI, which merely states that 'Persons charged with genocide or any of the other acts enumerated in Article III shall be tried by a competent tribunal of the State in the territory of which the act was committed, or by such international penal tribunal as may have jurisdiction with respect to those Contracting Parties which shall have accepted its jurisdiction'. It says nothing about other courts. It may be that the Court was inducting their conclusion from the fact that they accepted that the obligations in the Genocide Convention were *erga omnes* obligations.[187] The Court relied in part on its earlier statement in the *Reservations* Case referring to the 'universal character both of the condemnation of genocide' and of the co-operation required 'in order to liberate mankind from such an odious scourge' (Preamble to the Convention).[188] The reasoning is problematic, as it implies a duty to act from an interest in preventing genocide. There is no evidence of State practice assuming such a duty from the nature of the obligation.

As there is no treaty directly dealing with crimes against humanity there obviously is no treaty-based duty to prosecute crime against humanity *per se*.[189] However, for both genocide and crimes against humanity involving torture there is a duty to prosecute acts of torture at least under the heads of territorial, nationality and passive personality jurisdiction placed on parties to the Torture Convention.[190] The extent to which this obligation is customary is uncertain.[191]

Human rights law

Where treaties do not directly cover the ground, advocates of a more general duty to prosecute have turned to the interpretation of human rights treaties to found that duty. Since States have a duty to 'respect and ensure'[192] the rights granted in the various Human Rights Conventions, it could be that the latter clause implies a duty to prosecute certain serious violations of human rights. All acts constituting genocide and crimes against humanity would be serious violations of human rights, as

[187] *Bosnian Genocide* Case, para. 31.

[188] *Reservations to the Convention on the Prevention and Punishment of Genocide* Opinion (1951) ICJ Rep. 15, p. 23.

[189] The problems related to the absence of such a treaty is the subject of M. Cherif Bassiouni, 'Crimes Against Humanity: The Need for a Specialized Convention' (1994) 31 CJTL 457.

[190] Torture Convention, Article 5.

[191] See *Yerodia*, Separate Opinion of Higgins, Kooijmans and Buergenthal, paras. 42–43.

[192] International Covenant on Civil and Political Rights 999 UNTS 171, Article 2.

would most war crimes. There is some support for the idea that human rights law imposes a duty to prosecute such acts in the practice of the UN Human Rights Committee, the European Court and Commission of Human Rights and from the famous *Velasquez-Rodriguez* Case before the Inter-American Court of Human Rights.[193] Any duty, however, can be put only on those States party to the relevant Conventions, and are limited to those human rights violations that relate to persons either in their territory, subject to its jurisdiction,[194] or under their control.[195]

In the *Velasquez-Rodriguez* Case, the Inter-American Court held that a violation of the right to life had occurred, in part because of the failure to 'ensure' the right to life by investigating and punishing those responsible.[196] The body that has gone furthest towards recognising a duty to prosecute on territorial States has been the Inter-American Commission on Human Rights, which declared, *inter alia*, Chile's amnesty to be incompatible with the Inter-American Convention on Human Rights, and that for compliance with the Convention to be achieved, perpetrators had to be punished.[197] The Chilean amnesty was imposed by the Pinochet regime itself, and Chile's investigation commission was hobbled by its lack of power. The reaction of human rights bodies to more nuanced decisions not to prosecute, such as South Africa's, may not be

193 On the Human Rights Committee and European bodies, see Orientlicher, 'Settling Accounts', 2568–82; Alastair Mowbray, 'Duties of Investigation Under the European Convention on Human Rights' (2002) 51 ICLQ 437; Jessica Gavron, 'Amnesties in the Light of Developments in International Law and the Establishment of the International Criminal Court' (2002) 51 ICLQ 91, 94–100. On *Velasquez-Rodriguez* v. *Honduras*, Inter-American Court of Human Rights, Judgment of July 29, 1988 (1989) 28 ILM 29, see Orientlicher, 'Settling Accounts', 2576–9; Kai Ambos, 'Impunity and International Criminal Law' (1997) 18 HRLJ 1, 6–7. But see Michael P. Scharf, 'Swapping Amnesty for Peace: Was There a Duty to Prosecute International Crimes in Haiti?' (1996) 31 TILJ 1, 26–8; Andrea O'Shea, *Amnesty for Crime in International Law and Practice* (The Hague: Kluwer, 2001), pp. 228–66.

194 ICCPR, Article 2(1).

195 See, for example, European Convention on Human Rights, ETS No. 5, Article 1, *Banković* v. *Belgium* Application No. 52207/99, Admissibility Decision of 12 December 2001, on which see Matthew Happold, 'Bankovic v. Belgium and the Territorial Scope of the European Convention on Human Rights' (2003) 3 HRLR 77.

196 *Velasquez-Rodriguez*, paras. 166, 175–7.

197 *Garay Hermosilla et al.*, Case No. 10.843, 1996 Report of the Inter-American Commission on Human Rights, 156, pp. 182–3; *Irma Reyes et al.*, Case 11,228, *ibid.*, 196, pp. 219–20. A detailed analysis of the Inter-American organs' treatment of amnesties can be found in Douglas Cassel, 'Lessons From the Americas: Guidelines for International Response to Amnesties for Atrocities' (1996) 59 LCP 197, see in particular 215–16. See generally, Dinah Shelton, *Remedies in International Human Rights Law* (Oxford: Clarendon, 1999), pp. 322–7.

the same,[198] especially when civil remedies are still available.[199] Care must also be taken not to take decisions relating to relatively wealthy States with the resources to prosecute acontextually, when other States simply cannot possibly embark on large-scale accountability processes.

Frequently arguments based on substantive rights are added to by reference to the right to a remedy. Angelika Schlunck's conclusion on the effects of the cases relating to the right to a remedy, is an accurate one: '[a]ccording to the individual circumstances of the case, the right to a remedy can be interpreted as including a state obligation to prosecute. The right to a remedy does not absolutely require criminal prosecution of human rights offenders.'[200] A final argument against the decisions being taken as requiring prosecution of all international crimes is that States have not interpreted them as requiring the prosecution of every international crime.

Most of the cases dealing with postulated duties to prosecute international crimes deal with offences referable to State officials. Obligations to respect and ensure rights may also not require that international crimes committed by armed opposition groups be fully prosecuted so long as due diligence is exercised during an investigation.[201] The cases on this matter are rather equivocal about the content of the duty to prevent actions by insurgents. For State responsibility in general to be incurred for failing to prevent the actions of insurgents, the standard is one of negligence.[202] As can be seen, there are problems with any unqualified assertion that human rights law imposes an all-encompassing duty to prosecute all international crimes.

Customary law

In addition to express duties in treaties, and attempts to imply a duty from human rights treaties, those seeking to found a duty in international law have turned to customary international law. This is said to

[198] See John Dugard, 'Dealing With the Crimes of a Past Regime: Is Amnesty Still an Option?' (1999) 12 LJIL 1001, 1009–10.

[199] René Provost, *Human Rights and Humanitarian Law* (Cambridge: Cambridge University Press, 2002), pp. 112–14.

[200] Angelika Schlunck, *Amnesty versus Accountability: Third Party Intervention Dealing With Gross Human Rights Violations In Internal and International Conflicts* (Berlin: Arno Spitz, 2000), p. 44.

[201] Liesbeth Zegveld, *The Accountability of Armed Opposition Groups in International Law* (Cambridge: Cambridge University Press, 2002), pp. 170–3, 196–207.

[202] Michael Akehurst, 'State Responsibility for the Wrongful Acts of Rebels – An Aspect of the Southern Rhodesian Problem' (1968–9) 43 BYBIL 48, 48–50.

cover, in addition to duties based on treaties, genocide, war crimes not amounting to Grave Breaches of the Geneva Conventions and crimes against humanity. A customary duty would bind all States other than persistent objectors, getting around the question of whether or not a State had ratified the relevant treaty. The General Assembly has promulgated resolutions relevant to the possibility of a duty.[203] The most important of these, Resolutions 2840 and 3074, could be thought to give rise to a duty. These came about in relation to the fear in the 1970s that statutes of limitation in Germany would lead to crimes by those not already prosecuted (in particular people hiding in other States) becoming time-barred. Resolution 2840 states that refusal to co-operate in the arrest, extradition, trial and punishment of persons accused of international crimes is contrary to the purposes of the UN Charter and international law. Resolution 3074 built on this, and is worth quoting at length:

> 1. War Crimes and Crimes Against Humanity, wherever they are committed, shall be subject to investigation and . . . [perpetrators] . . . *shall* be subject to tracing, arrest, trial and, if they are found guilty, to punishment.
> 2. Every State has the *right* to try its own nationals for war crimes and crimes against humanity.
> 3. Persons . . . [suspected of such crimes] . . . *shall* be subject to trial . . . as a general rule in the countries in which they have committed these crimes' (emphasis added).

Opinion differs on the effect of Resolutions 2840 and 3074. Some commentators consider the Resolutions to be constitutive of a duty to extradite or prosecute.[204] Amnesty International put considerable stress on Resolution 3074 when making the case for the mandatory exercise of universal jurisdiction.[205] Others consider the Resolutions as merely evidence of an emerging customary rule.[206] It is, of course, axiomatic that General Assembly Resolutions are not, in themselves, an independent formal source of law. They may, however, act as evidence, of States' *opinio juris*,[207] or alter the way in which States view their rights and obligations,

203 GA Resolution 2840, UN Doc. A/8429, p. 88; GA Res. 3074, UN Doc. A/9030, p. 78.

204 Jordan Paust, *International Law as Law of the United States* (Durham, NC: Carolina Academic Press, 1996), p. 405.

205 Amnesty International, *Universal Jurisdiction*, chapter 3, pp. 10–11.

206 Michael P. Scharf, 'National Prosecutions: Report of the Rapporteur', in Christopher Joyner (ed.) *Reining in Impunity for International Crimes and Serious Violations of Human Rights* (St Agne: Erès, 1998), p. 125, p. 128.

207 See generally, Blaine Sloane, 'General Assembly Resolutions Revisited' (1987) 58 BYBIL 39; David J. Harris, *Cases and Materials on International Law* (London: Stevens, 5th edn.,

thus catalysing change.[208] The ICJ gave a succinct explanation of the significance of General Assembly Resolutions in the *Legality of the Threat or Use of Nuclear Weapons* Opinion:

> General Assembly Resolutions, even if they are not binding, may sometimes have normative value. They can, in certain circumstances, provide evidence important for establishing the existence of a rule or the emergence of an *opinio juris*. To establish whether this is true of a given General Assembly Resolution, it is necessary to look at its content and the conditions of its adoption; it is also necessary to see whether an *opinio juris* exists as to its normative character.[209]

The two most important clues a General Assembly Resolution may give as to its status are its wording and its voting record. As to its wording, Resolution 3074 is at some points framed in the imperative – for example, 'perpetrators shall' be subject to trial. So the resolution could be taken to imply a general duty to prosecute war crimes and crimes against humanity. The inclusion of 'as a general rule' injects ambiguity as to the scope of the obligation, however. Resolution 3074 does not claim to be declaratory of international law, it merely 'proclaims' the principles it contains.

To turn to the voting pattern, there were 94 positive votes and none against. There were 29 abstentions. This level of abstention could possibly be dismissed if the Resolution were to proclaim a permissive right, although this is by no means certain. The contention that this Resolution forms the bedrock of a duty to extradite or prosecute international crimes must fail on the basis of the ambivalence of a significant number of States. If this were not enough, there is no evidence that States have considered themselves under any obligation to extradite or prosecute on the basis of the Resolution.

At least until recently, the strongest argument against the use of either of the General Assembly Resolutions to establish a duty to extradite or prosecute suspects is State practice.[210] A fairly strong case can still be made that despite the trend away from the use of amnesties, States have not denied that they have amnestied international crimes, but have considered amnesties compatible with their international duties, including under human rights law. This is a position that in some instances

1998), pp. 58–64 and the literature cited therein; Vladimir-Djuro Degan, *Sources of International Law* (The Hague: Kluwer, 1997), pp. 194–200.

208 See Maarten Bos, 'The Recognised Manifestations of International Law' (1977) 20 GYBIL 9, 65–70.

209 *Legality of the Threat or Use of Nuclear Weapons* [1996] ICJ Rep. 4, pp. 254–5, para. 70.

210 A summary of which was given in a US 'non-paper' at the pre-Rome PREPCOM.

appears to have been supported by the United Nations.[211] On this basis, Michael P. Scharf asserted in 1996 that 'a "rule" that is so divorced from the realities of State practice is unlikely to achieve substantial compliance in the real world, and, therefore, cannot be said to be a binding rule at all, but rather an aspiration'.[212]

On the other hand, there are possible examples of States who have asserted a duty to prosecute offenders. The first is Ethiopia, in relation to crimes of its *Derg* regime.[213] This related to offences by its nationals and on its territory. The second example is Belgium, who submitted to the ICJ that there was a 'general obligation on States under customary international law to prosecute perpetrators of crimes'. It conceded, however that where such persons were non-nationals, outside of its territory, there was no obligation but rather an available option.'[214]

There is evidence that UN practice in relation to accountability has altered in respect of the obligations incumbent on States for international crimes committed on their territories. The Secretary General refused to accept amnesties for international crimes in Sierra Leone and Angola and, in the former case, condemned such amnesties as unlawful and, to the extent of their illegality, void.[215] The ILA was therefore right in averring that 'international practice offers considerable, but not yet conclusive, support for' the argument that amnesties will always violate international law.[216] This was reflected in the negotiations for the Rome Statute where, although some States were prepared to say that prosecution was the only appropriate response to international crimes, this was not accepted by all States.[217] A significant trend towards that

[211] See Dugard, 'Dealing', 1003; Scharf, 'Letter of the Law: The Scope of the International Legal Obligation to Prosecute Human Rights Crimes' (1996) 59 LCP 41, 57–59. This was also the position of Lord Lloyd in the first *Pinochet* Appeal, *R.* v. *Bow Street Stipendiary Magistrate, ex parte Pinochet Ugarte* [1998] 4 All ER 897, 929.

[212] Scharf, 'Swapping', 41.

[213] See Julie V. Mayfield, 'The Prosecution of War Crimes and Respect for Human Rights: Ethiopia's Balancing Act' (1995) 9 Emory ILJ 553, 570.

[214] *Yerodia* Case, Separate Opinion of Higgins, Kooijmans and Buergenthal, para. 8.

[215] *Report of the Secretary-General on the Establishment of a Special Court for Sierra Leone*, 4 October 2000, UN Doc. S/2000/915, para. 24.

[216] International Law Association Committee on International Human Rights Law and Practice (Menno Kamminga), 'Final Report on the Exercise of Universal Jurisdiction in Relation to Gross Human Rights Abuses', in ILA, *Report of the Sixty-Ninth Conference, Held in London* (London: ILA, 2000), pp. 403, 416. On selected recent practice, see Christine Bell, *Peace Agreements and Human Rights* (Oxford: Oxford University Press, 2000), pp. 259–91.

[217] See Daryl Robinson, 'Serving the Interests of Justice: Amnesties, Truth Commissions and the International Criminal Court' (2003) 14 EJIL 481, 483. See also John Dugard,

position must be acknowledged, sufficient for some to suggest an emerging customary rule requiring prosecution of some of those responsible for international crimes.[218]

This position also seems to have been adopted by the Special Court for Sierra Leone who, in the *Kallon and Kamara* decision opined 'that there is a crystallising international norm that a government cannot grant amnesty for serious violations of crimes under international law is amply supported by materials placed before the Court [but the view] that it has crystallised may not be entirely correct . . . it is accepted that such a norm is developing under international law'.[219] Even so, it is extremely unlikely that any duty could be deduced that required prosecution of every single international crime, but the precise principles upon which decisions on who should be prosecuted and for what are very unclear. This militates against any quick conclusion that there is as yet such a duty to prosecute in positive law.

The above relates to the possible obligation on States to prosecute international crimes committed on their territories.[220] There is almost no evidence of any State practice confirming prosecution on a universal jurisdictional basis as a customary duty rather than a right.[221] Even the most ardent supporters of such a duty are forced to concede this point.[222] The view that there is no general duty to prosecute on the

'Possible Conflicts of Jurisdiction With Truth Commissions', in Antonio Cassese, Paula Gaeta and John R. W. D. Jones (eds.), *The Rome Statute of the International Criminal Court: A Commentary* (Oxford: Oxford University Press, 2002), p. 693; Michael P. Scharf, 'The Amnesty Exception to the Jurisdiction of the International Criminal Court' (1999) 32 Cornell ILJ 507; Mahnoush Arsanjani, 'The International Criminal Court and National Amnesty Laws' (1999) 63 Proceedings ASIL 65.

218 Robinson, 'Serving the Interests', 491, 493–5 characterises such a duty for nationality and territoriality as either current or emerging custom. For a more sceptical view, see Provost, *Human Rights*, pp. 110 15. See also Yasmin Naqvi, 'Amnesty for War Crimes: Defining the Limits of International Recognition' (2003) 851 IRRC 583.

219 *Prosecutor* v. *Kallon and Kamara*, Decision on Challenge to Jurisdiction: Lomé Accord Amnesty, SCSL-2004–15-AR72(E) and SCSL 2004–16-AR72(E), 13 March 2004.

220 All the opinions supporting universal jurisdiction in *Yerodia* framed such jurisdiction in terms of a right, rather than an obligation.

221 See p. 108 and the explanatory memorandum which accompanied the Dutch ICC implementing legislation, which asserted that there was an obligation to assert universal jurisdiction over ICC crimes; see Jan K. Kleffner, 'The Impact of Complementarity on National Implementation of Substantive International Criminal Law' (2003) 1 JICJ 86, 91, n. 19.

222 M. Cherif Bassiouni and Edward M. Wise, *Aut Dedere Aut Judicare: The Duty to Extradite or Prosecute in International Law* (The Hague: Martinus Nijhoff, 1995), p. 45. They note, *ibid.*, that even the treaty duty under the Geneva Conventions remained (in 1995) effectively a dead letter.

basis of universal jurisdiction in customary international law is correct. If there is a duty to extradite or prosecute beyond those in the treaties mentioned above or the Rome Statute, then it must be found elsewhere in international law.

Jus cogens *approaches*

Cherif Bassiouni has suggested that the duty can be derived not from practice, but from either the nature of international society or the *jus cogens/erga omnes* status of the prohibitions of international crimes. To begin with, Bassiouni suggests that international society has developed to the extent that there is a common interest in the repression of international crimes which, when combined with the right they all have to prosecute them, gives rise to a duty either to prosecute or extradite.[223] This is questionable; it implies a duty to extradite or prosecute from common interest and a permissive right. More importantly, as Bassiouni recognises, it rests on the presumption of the international society being a *civitas maxima*, which is hotly contested.[224] Although there is a pronounced trend towards accountability, to derive normative conclusions from the assertion that there has been a move towards new values in the international community is premature.[225]

Perhaps a more convincing argument for a duty would be from the nature of the crimes under consideration. The prohibitive norms they encapsulate are in many, although not by any means all, instances *jus cogens*.[226] From this, Bassiouni implies that there is a duty to suppress such crimes and assist in bringing perpetrators to justice by extraditing or prosecuting them. In this, he is joined by Lord Hope in the *Pinochet* Case,[227] Guy Goodwin-Gill[228] and, for genocide, Shabtai Rosenne and

223 Bassiouni and Wise, *Aut Dedere*, pp. 49–50.

224 Bassiouni and Wise, *Aut Dedere*, pp. 26–37.

225 See, for example, Edward M. Wise, '*Aut Dedere Aut Judicare*: The Duty to Extradite or Prosecute', in M. Cherif Bassiouni (ed.), *The International Criminal Court: Observations and Issues Before the 1998 Preparatory Committee; and Administrative and Financial Implications* (Chicago: Erès, 1997), pp. 27–8.

226 M. Cherif Bassiouni, 'International Crimes, *Jus Cogens* and *Obligatio Erga Omnes*', in Joyner (ed.), *Reining in Impunity*, p. 133. See also Lauri Hannikainen, *Peremptory Norms (Jus Cogens) in International Law* (Helsinki: Finnish Lawyers' Publishing Company, 1988), p. 286. All *jus cogens* norms also involve *erga omnes* obligations. Some doubt must exist about the *jus cogens* nature of the prohibitions encapsulated in certain war crimes.

227 *Pinochet [No. 3]*, 147.

228 Guy S. Goodwin-Gill, 'Crime in International Law: Obligations *Erga Omnes* and the Duty to Prosecute', in Guy S. Goodwin-Gill and Stefan Talmon (eds.), *The Reality of*

the ICJ in the *Bosnia Genocide* and *Reservations* Cases.[229] The question that needs to be answered here is whether a duty to extradite or prosecute any offence follows from the fact that the prohibitions of those offences are *jus cogens*. Although some doubt may be expressed on the matter, it must remain the case that the fact that the prohibitions of many international crimes have reached the level of *erga omnes* obligations or *jus cogens* norms does not give rise to a duty to exercise universal jurisdiction.

To generate a duty to prosecute for a third State from the rules prohibiting the crimes themselves, one of two positions must be adopted. Either the rule itself must impose the obligation, or the status of the rule somehow acts so to require action by third States. Regarding the first position, this simply begs the question of whether there is such a duty. There is no evidence that States have ever considered the prohibitions contained in international criminal law to have this secondary effect for third States.

It is true that the effects of *jus cogens* go beyond the invalidity of a treaty incompatible with such a norm. The essence of a *jus cogens* rule is such that it renders illegal any act conflicting with it.[230] The problem here is whether a third State, by not prosecuting those suspects of international crimes whose activities are alleged to have violated *jus cogens* norms, is itself also violating international law. In contradistinction to most rules of international law, the primary addressee of the prohibitions of international criminal law is the individual *qua* a person, rather than a State functionary.[231] When that person is acting in an official capacity so as to engage State responsibility in accordance with the usual rules of international law,[232] the State on whose behalf the person is acting also becomes liable.[233] In certain circumstances, such

International Law: Essays in Honour of Ian Brownlie (Oxford: Oxford University Press, 1999), p. 199, pp. 213–20.

229 *Yearbook of the International Law Commission*, 1963, I, 74. For the ICJ's statements see p. 103 and Vincent Chetail, 'The Contribution of the International Court of Justice to International Humanitarian law' (2003) 850 IRRC 235, 250–2.

230 Hannikainen, *Peremptory Norms*, p. 7.

231 Pierre-Marie Dupuy, 'International Criminal Responsibility of the Individual and International Responsibility of the State', in Antonio Cassese, Paula Gaeta and John R. W. D. Jones (eds.), *The Rome Statute of the International Criminal Court: A Commentary* (Oxford: Oxford University Press, 2002), p. 1085, p. 1086.

232 In particular, Articles 4–7 of the ILC Rules, Attachment to General Assembly Resolution 56/83, UN Doc. A/Res/56/83. See James Crawford, *The International Law Commission's Articles on State Responsibility: Introduction, Text and Commentaries* (Cambridge: Cambridge University Press, 2002), pp. 91–109.

233 See *Prosecutor* v. *Furundžija*, Judgment, IT-95–17/1-T, 10 December 1998, para. 142; *Bosnia Genocide* Case, para. 32. On the link between individual and State responsibility,

as where international crimes affect other States, punishment by the territoriality or nationality State can be ordered as reparation.[234]

For a third party to become responsible by virtue of complicity in the act, we have to look to the law of State responsibility. If the State exercised control over the offender, then it would become liable, as the primary State.[235] If a State assists another in violating its obligations, then it may become responsible for that act of assistance if the assisted State's acts would be unlawful if done by the assisting States.[236] There may be some scope for deriving a duty here, where States have allowed leaders to go into exile where they have committed crimes which are subject to duties to prosecute on the basis of nationality or territoriality. Nigeria in relation to Charles Taylor may be an example. However, the relevant violation of international law has already occurred in such situations, and the law is too undeveloped in relation to the link between individuals and third States to make certain conclusions.

In relation to *jus cogens/erga omnes* norms, there are third-party duties. These are summed up in Article 41 of the ILC rules. This reads:

> 1. States shall cooperate to bring to an end through lawful means any serious breach within the meaning of article 40.
> 2. No State shall recognize as lawful a situation created by a serious breach within the meaning of article 40, nor render aid or assistance in maintaining that situation.
> 3. This article is without prejudice to the other consequences referred to in this Part and to such further consequences that a breach to which this Chapter applies may entail under international law.

see André Nollkaemper, 'Concurrence Between Individual Responsibility and State Responsibility in International Law' (2003) 52 ICLQ 615; Marina Spinedi, 'State Responsibility v. Individual Responsibility for International Crimes' Tertium non Datur?' (2002) 13 EJIL 895; Hazel Fox, 'The ICJ's Treatment of Acts of the State, and in Particular, the Attribution of Acts of Individuals to the State', in Nisuke Ando, Edward McWhinney and Rüdiger Wolfrum (eds.), *Liber Amoricum Shigeru Oda* (The Hague: Kluwer, 2001), p. 147.

234 See Nollkaemper, 'Concurrence', 636–8.

235 ILC Articles, Article 8; the precise level of control is a matter of controversy; see Crawford, *The International Law Commission's Articles*, pp. 110–13. See also Nina H. B. Jørgensen, 'State Responsibility and the 1948 Genocide Convention', in Guy S. Goodwin-Gill and Stefan Talmon (eds.), *The Reality of International Law: Essays in Honour of Ian Brownlie* (Oxford: Oxford University Press, 1999), p. 273; and André J. J. de Hoogh, 'Articles 4 and 8 of the 2002 ILC Articles on State Responsibility, the *Tadić* Case and attribution of Acts of Bosnian Serb Authorities to the Federal Republic of Yugoslavia' (2001) 72 BYBIL 255.

236 ILC Articles, Article 16; see Crawford, *The International Law Commission's Articles*, pp. 145–51. For an earlier discussion, see John Quigley, 'Complicity in International Law: A New Direction in the Law of State Responsibility' (1987) 58 BYBIL 77.

The commission of international crimes by State officials will give rise to the consequences for other States in situations where they involve a 'gross or systematic failure by the responsible State to fulfil the obligation',[237] in this instance, not to commit international crimes. If this criterion is fulfilled, States have duties to 'cooperate to bring to an end' any serious breach, and not recognise the situation as lawful. It may be asked if these duties can give rise to a duty to prosecute for third States. The duty to co-operate to bring to an end the violations relates for the most part to political co-operation, not judicial means.[238] The question remains whether failing to prosecute a person could amount to recognising the situation created as lawful.

That seems unlikely, despite the statement of the ICJ in the *Bosnia Genocide* Case. In three other decisions of international tribunals, no such duty was implied from the nature of the obligations. The first of these was the decision of the ICTY in the *Furundžija* Case. In that case, the Trial Chamber stated that 'one of the consequences of the *jus cogens* character bestowed by the international community upon the prohibition of torture is that every State is *entitled to* investigate, prosecute and punish or extradite individuals accused of torture'.[239] This deals with precisely the issue under discussion, but is framed in the permissive, rather than the mandatory form.

Next is the decision of the European Court of Human Rights in *Al-Adsani* v. *United Kingdom*.[240] This dealt with immunities in a civil case in a third State, but also discussed the consequences of the *jus cogens* status of the prohibition of torture. In this case, a bare majority (9–8) held that there was no obligation flowing from the prohibition of torture to grant a civil remedy in relation to extraterritorial acts.[241] They were also unwilling to hold that immunity was removed in civil suits.[242] Although the Court was expressly not dealing with criminal actions, unwillingness to draw additional duties on States from the *jus cogens* nature of the prohibition is telling. The main dissent, subscribed to by six members of the Court, denied the difference between civil and

[237] ILC Articles, Article 40; there is, however, also the difficult issues of intent and where the threshold of Article 40 is not reached; see Nollkaemper, 'Concurrence', 622–3, 633–5.

[238] The examples used in the authoritative Crawford, *International Law Commission's Articles*, p. 252, are of non-recognition of certain acts of Apartheid South Africa, not prosecutions.

[239] *Furundžija*, para. 156, emphasis as in Akande, 'International Law Immunities', 27–8.

[240] Application No 35763/77, 105 ILR 24.

[241] *Al-Adsani*, para. 40.

[242] *Al-Adsani*, para. 67.

criminal proceedings, but did not deal with the question of whether an obligation to prosecute could be drawn from the *jus cogens* nature of the prohibition of torture.[243] The same applies to the dissent of Judge Louciades.[244]

Judge Ferrari-Bravo's Dissent dealt with precisely this question, saying that as torture was contrary to *jus cogens* '[i]t follows that every State has a duty to *contribute* to the punishment of torture and cannot hide behind formalist arguments to avoid having to give judgment,' (emphasis in the Dissent). He quickly explained himself: 'I say to "contribute" to punishment and not, obviously, to punish, since it was clear that the acts of torture had not taken place in the United Kingdom, but elsewhere.'[245] This is a clear rejection of the idea that the *jus cogens* nature of a prohibition creates a duty to prosecute on third States. The case has been criticised, in particular on the ground that the distinction between the substance and enforcement of *jus cogens* rules can be overdrawn.[246] This may be correct, but there is simply no evidence beyond unsupported statements that the rules on *jus cogens* can be stretched as far as to require prosecution in third States. As Christian Tams has said, steps 'which slowly extend the effects of *ius cogens* beyond its initial field of application in the law of treaties, are taken individually and on the basis of appreciation of the particular context'.[247] As yet, there is no consensus that *jus cogens* rules can do the work Bassiouni would like them to on this point.

This can be seen from the final case in an international forum that falls for discussion, the *Yerodia* Case.[248] The comments of some of the judges are illuminating. As the majority judgment avoided the question of universal jurisdiction, nothing can be drawn from that part of the

[243] *Al-Adsani*, Dissenting Opinion of Judges Rozakis and Caflisch, Joined by Judges Wildhaber, Costa, Cabral Barreto and Vajić.

[244] *Al-Adsani*, Dissenting Opinion of Judge Louciades.

[245] *Al-Adsani*, Dissenting Opinion of Judge Ferrari-Bravo, paras. 1–2.

[246] See, for example, Alexander Orakhelashvili, 'State Immunity and International Public Order' (2002) 45 GYBIL 227, 257–8 and, asserting a duty, 263. It may be that the reference is to where a treaty already created a duty, see 266.

[247] Christian J. Tams, 'Well-Protected Enemies of Mankind' (2002) 61 CLJ 246, 248.

[248] The Case has generated a large body of literature, for example, Cassese, 'When May Senior State Officials'; Steffen Wirth, 'Immunity for Core Crimes? The ICJ's Judgment in the Congo v. Belgium Case' (2002) 13 EJIL 877; Chanaka Wickremasinghe, 'Arrest Warrant of 11 April 2000 (Democratic Republic of the Congo v. Belgium) Preliminary Objections and Merits, Judgment of 14 February 2002' (2003) 52 ICLQ 775; Alain Winants, 'The *Yerodia* Ruling of the International Court of Justice and the 1993/1999 Belgian Law on Universal Jurisdiction' (2003) 16 LJIL 491.

decision.[249] The same can be said for the four judges who rejected universal jurisdiction *in absentia*.[250] More can be gleaned from the opinions of the six judges who came out in support of universal jurisdiction.[251]

None of the judges accepting universal jurisdiction framed it as an obligation,[252] despite a number of the judges alluding to the concept of *jus cogens*. The closest any judge came to asserting that position was Judge Koroma, who referred to 'what Belgium considers to be its international obligation'.[253] Three points need to be made. First, this was not Belgium's position in relation to customary law, which was that it was entitled to assert such jurisdiction. Second, Judge Koroma does not adopt the view that Belgium would be correct in claiming that asserting jurisdiction was an obligation, he simply reports that Belgium considered itself obliged. Finally, elsewhere in his opinion Judge Koroma refers to universal jurisdiction being 'available' and Belgium being 'entitled' to assert it.[254] The Joint Separate Opinion of Higgins, Kooijmans and Buergenthal is clear, dealing from the start with 'the question whether States are *entitled* to exercise jurisdiction' (emphasis added).[255] Judge al-Khasawneh's opinion is a little difficult to decipher on this point, as he does not discuss jurisdiction in depth. Judge Al-Khasawneh does accept that a Minister of Foreign Affairs is liable to prosecution outside his or her home jurisdiction for international crimes.[256] He also states that 'the effective combating of grave crimes has arguably assumed a *jus cogens* character',[257] but at no point is there an implication that this means that there is a duty to prosecute on third States.

Judge van den Wyngaert's opinion is clear. Judge Van den Wyngaert castigates the majority judgment for not taking into account the development of international criminal law and the need for accountability.[258] The opinion is clear that the rules relating to war crimes and crimes against humanity are in a 'higher order of norms'.[259] Judge Van

[249] *Yerodia*, paras. 41–45.

[250] *Yerodia*, Separate Opinion of President Guillaume; Opinion of Judge Rezek, para. 6; Opinion of Judge Ranjeva paras. 11–12; Opinion of Judge Bula-Bula *passim*.

[251] Separate Opinion of Judge Koroma, paras. 8–9; Joint Separate Opinion of Higgins, Kooijmans and Buergenthal, paras. 19–65; Dissenting Opinion of Judge Al-Khasanawneh, paras. 1–8; Dissenting Opinion of Judge van den Wyngaert, paras. 40–67.

[252] See Wickremasinghe, 'Arrest Warrant', 780.

[253] Koroma Separate Opinion, para. 8.

[254] Koroma Separate Opinion, paras. 9, 8.

[255] Joint Separate Opinion, para. 19.

[256] Al-Khasawneh Dissenting Opinion, para. 1.

[257] Al-Khasawneh Dissenting Opinion, para. 7.

[258] Van den Wyngaert Dissenting Opinion, paras. 5–6, 27.

[259] Van den Wyngaert Dissenting Opinion, para. 26.

den Wyngaert is also clearly aware of the importance of distinguishing rights and duties.[260] The opinion refers at all times to the 'entitlement' or 'permissibility' of universal jurisdiction,[261] even when citing the ICJ's 1951 comment.[262]

There is no evidence that the status of the rules relating to some international crimes leads to a duty to prosecute those crimes on third States. If such a rule existed, then most States would be in consistent violation of it most of the time.[263] This in itself provides a reason for doubting the utility of postulating a duty on third States from the status of the primary rules. International law is a normative system, and therefore its prescriptions do not, and should not, simply reflect State practice. Nonetheless, they should also not move impossibly far away from it, or they are unlikely to influence practice.[264] A duty on third States derived solely from the *jus cogens* status of some international criminal law prohibitions is at the utopian rather than the apologetic end of debate.[265]

Existing treaty-based duties to prosecute on the basis of universal jurisdiction, such as those in the Geneva Conventions, have not led to diligent prosecutions of international crimes.[266] In practice, Grave Breaches are rarely prosecuted at all, for a variety of reasons, practical and political. On this basis, it may be said that the enforcement mechanism set up by the Geneva Conventions has not proved effective. What applies to the Geneva Conventions applies *a fortiori* to the enforcement of other international crimes. This is one of the major arguments in favour of an ICC. As Hermann von Hebel explains: 'The apparent contradiction between the norms and non observances of these norms shows the need for better methods of enforcement.'[267] It will be argued below that encouraging domestic prosecution as well as ensuring international prosecution

[260] Van den Wyngaert Dissenting Opinion, paras. 5, 51, 60–62.

[261] Van den Wyngaert Dissenting Opinion, paras. 43, 47, 60.

[262] Van den Wyngaert Dissenting Opinion, para. 60.

[263] This is conceded by Bassiouni (see Broomhall, *International Justice*, p. 111).

[264] See Bruno Simma and Andreas Paulus, 'The Responsibility of Individuals for Human Rights Abuses in Internal Conflicts: A Positivist View' (1999) 93 AJIL 302, 303.

[265] On this generally, see Martti Koskenniemi, *From Apology to Utopia: The Structure of International Legal Argument* (Helsinki: Finnish Lawyers' Publishing Company, 1989).

[266] Antonio Cassese, 'On the Current Trends Towards Criminal Prosecution and Punishment of Breaches of International Criminal Law' (1998) 9 EJIL 2, 5–6.

[267] Hermann A. M. von Hebel, 'The International Criminal Court – A Historical Perspective', in Hermann A. M. von Hebel, Johan G. Lammers and Johen Schukking (eds.), *Reflections on the International Criminal Court: Essays in Honor of Adriaan Bos* (The Hague: T. M. C. Asser Instituut, 1999), p. 13, p. 14.

when necessary will, and should, amount to one of the major roles that the ICC takes on. It suffices for the moment to note that the difference in levels of prosecution of international crimes where there is a clear obligation to prosecute (such as Grave Breaches of the Geneva Conventions) and those where there is not (such as crimes against humanity) is small, if even discernible. It is therefore difficult to disagree with the ILA final report on universal jurisdiction that the absence of systematic international supervision is a major problem for international criminal law.[268]

Incorporation into domestic law and harmonisation

The general torpor of States in relation to prosecution of international crimes, if not their actual reluctance to do so, can be seen from the general level of implementation of international crimes into national legal systems. In addition, concentration on international criminal law as it has been incorporated and interpreted in national law (prior to the Rome Statute) demonstrates that traditionally there have been problems of consistency between States. As we noted above, the use of extraterritorial jurisdiction is far less problematic if the law applied is uniform across States.

It would be simple if the status of international criminal law in national criminal law could be dealt with at the level of theory, namely in relation to the debate surrounding the monist/dualist positions.[269] If monism prevailed, questions of States' legislation's conformity with international law would not arise. Unfortunately, neither monist or dualist theories can adequately explain all aspects of international law. Monism cannot rationalise aspects of international practice (for example the UK and Commonwealth States' insistence on implementing legislation for treaties),[270] or the idea of non-self-executing treaties. Dualism,

[268] ILA Final Report, p. 18.

[269] On this debate, see, for example, Hans Kelsen, *Principles of International Law* (London: Stevens, 2nd edn., 1967), pp. 553–88; Luigi Ferrari-Bravo, 'International and Municipal Law: The Complementarity of Legal Systems', in Ronald St J. Macdonald and Douglas M. Johnson, *Structure and Process of International Law* (Dordrecht: Martinus Nijhoff, 1986), p. 715; L. Erades (Malgosia Fitzmaurice and C. Flinterman, (eds.)), *Interactions Between International and Municipal Law: A Comparative Case Law Study* (The Hague: T. M. C. Asser Instituut, 1993), pp. 549–945; Alfred P. Rubin, *Ethics and Authority in International Law* (Cambridge: Cambridge University Press, 1997), pp. 83–124, 150–62. Gerald Fitzmaurice, 'The General Principles of International Law Considered From the Standpoint of the Rule of Law' (1957) II 92 RdC 5, pp. 70–80.

[270] See Erades, *Interactions*, pp. 699–841 (a survey of various States' approaches), in particular pp. 840–1 (concluding that ex-British colonies almost all consider themselves to require implementing legislation).

on the other hand has been hard pressed to accommodate the practice of a great number of States which apply customary international law and treaties directly in the municipal sphere,[271] the rise of the EU, and more importantly, the place of individuals,[272] both as the bearers of rights (for example, in human rights treaties), and duties (under international criminal law).

A failure to implement international obligations domestically when there is a duty to do so in international law is a violation of international law. It does not, however, prevent individual liability arising under international law. International criminal law, it must be said, has an implicit monist bent, as its demands are directed to individuals, and liability arises irrespective of national law. The direct effect of international law was upheld by the Nuremberg IMT,[273] and has found acceptance in State practice.[274]

There are three ways in which States discharge their obligations to implement international criminal law, when they choose to implement it at all. Some States, such as the United Kingdom, Canada, the United States, the Netherlands, Sweden and Switzerland, use implementing legislation, creating the offence in national law. Others rely on the direct applicability of international law in the national legal system,[275] while the remainder of those prosecuting merely use analogous national or military offences (for example the United States in the prosecution of William Calley).[276] Not all these methods are necessarily acceptable.[277] When there is a duty to prosecute international crimes, implementing those crimes into the domestic legal order with narrower definitions

[271] Erades, *Interactions*, pp. 565–679. [272] Erades, *Interactions*, p. 528.

[273] Nuremberg IMT Judgment, p. 221.

[274] See, for example, the *British Manual of Military Law* (Part III) (London: HMSO, 1958), para. 1. It is worthwhile noting that this part of the manual was drafted by Sir Hersch Lauterpacht, an unabashed monist.

[275] Malaysia has done this on one occasion: *Stanislaus Kroftan* v. *Public Prosecutor* (1967) 1 *Malaysian Law Journal* 133.

[276] (1973) 48 CMR (1973) 22 USCMA 534.

[277] See Axel Marschik, 'The Politics of Prosecution: The European National Approach to War Crimes', in Timothy L. H. McCormack and Gerry J. Simpson (eds.), *The Law of War Crimes: National and International Approaches* (The Hague: Kluwer, 1997), p. 73. For an extended discussion of the place of humanitarian law in national law, see Michael Bothe, Thomas Kurzidem and Peter Macalister-Smith, *National Implementation of Humanitarian Law* (Dordrecht: Martinus Nijhoff, 1990). The ICRC is of the opinion that 'in most cases normal penal legislation . . . is inadequate to ensure repression of breaches of the Geneva Conventions', ICRC 1969 Comments, CE/Com/IV/14.

than those in international law is a violation of that duty, as it could lead to acquittals which would not be warranted under international law.

The ILA report on universal jurisdiction noted that one of the major problems was the absence in many States of legislation implementing international crimes.[278] Courts have shown themselves unwilling to rely on customary international law to found liability even in systems where customary law is automatically incorporated into the domestic legal system. Examples of this can be seen in the United Kingdom, in the *Pinochet* Case,[279] and in Australia, the *Nulyarimma* Case.[280] Although the ILA's commentary was made with respect to the use of universal jurisdiction, it is more broadly applicable to legislation domesticating international crimes. The legislation that is in place in many States is a mélange of disparate provisions, usually based on some, but often not all, treaties to which a State is party. Legislation is rarely based on customary international law.[281] The absence of domestic legislation is the dominant trend, even where there are duties to implement.

Some States have incorporated the Geneva Conventions,[282] but the legislation of some countries with respect to the Geneva and Genocide Conventions is non-existent, or is otherwise unsatisfactory.[283] It has been said that there is an 'alarming degree of failure', in legislative implementation of the Geneva Conventions.[284] Of those that have incorporated the Geneva Conventions, practice is, in Michael Bothe's words 'so far . . . mediocre'.[285] Many countries have not defined the crimes adequately

[278] ILA Report, pp. 412–14.

[279] *Pinochet [No. 3]*. Although see Roger O'Keefe, 'Customary Crimes in English Courts' (2001) 72 BYBIL 293.

[280] *Nulyarimma* v. *Thompson* (1999) 165 ALR 621; see Andrew D. Mitchell, 'Is Genocide a Crime Unknown to Australian Law? *Nulyarimma* v. *Thompson*' (2000) 3 YBIHL 362; Kristen Daglish, 'The Crime of Genocide: *Nulyarimma* v. *Thompson*' (2001) 50 ICLQ 404.

[281] Although see later, pp. 182–3 on the Canadian Crimes Against Humanity and War Crimes Act.

[282] For example, the UK Geneva Conventions Act 1957, as amended by the 1995 Geneva Conventions (Amendment) Act 1997. See Peter Rowe and Michael A. Meyer, 'The Geneva Conventions (Amendment) Act 1995: A generally Minimalist Approach' (1996) 45 ICLQ 476.

[283] A useful comparative study may be found in van Elst, 'Implementing'.

[284] K. Drzewicki, 'National Legislation as a Measure for Implementation of Humanitarian Law', in Fritz Kalshoven and Yves Sandoz (eds.), *Implementation of International Humanitarian Law* (Dordrecht: Martinus Nijhoff, 1989), p. 109, p. 109.

[285] Michael Bothe, 'The Role of National Law in the Implementation of International Humanitarian Law', in Christoph Swinarski (ed.), *Studies and Essays on International Humanitarian Law in Honour of Jean Pictet* (Geneva: ICRC, 1984), p. 301, p. 307.

or accepted jurisdiction widely enough. For example, the US legislation was issued forty years late,[286] and failed to criminalise Grave Breaches wherever they occur, as required by the Conventions.[287]

A similar tale could be told about the Genocide Convention. For example, by the time of the genocide in Rwanda (1994), and despite Rwanda's accession to the Convention on 16 April 1975, it had still not introduced national legislation prohibiting genocide.[288] In relation to genocide, Jordan Paust goes as far as to claim that the US legislation 'demonstrates that national legislative efforts can be quite disingenuous and dangerous'.[289] This is almost certainly overstated in relation to the specific legislation,[290] nonetheless, the debates in the Senate preceding the passage of that legislation were characterised by 'pettiness', and national implementation is subject to domestic political pressures that may impact on whether or not international crimes are accurately reflected in domestic law.[291] As we saw earlier, where extraterritorial jurisdiction is used, it is important to have definitions consistent with those in international law.

The problem of consistency can also be seen in relation to national attempts to determine custom. Owing to the often vague nature of customary law, particularly before the ICTY and ICTR began to issue clear guidance, courts have come to different conclusions about the scope of international crimes. Courts have had particular difficulty with crimes against humanity. Until recently, there was no broadly accepted detailed codification of their definition, meaning that criticisms of

286 The United States ratified the Conventions in 1955, the legislation entered into force in 1996.

287 See Mark Zaid, 'Remarks' (1997) 91 Proceedings ASIL 275.

288 See Carla Ferstman, 'Domestic Trials for Genocide and Crimes Against Humanity: The Example of Rwanda' (1997) 9 RADIC 857, 863.

289 Jordan Paust, 'Threats to Accountability after Nuremberg: Crimes Against Humanity, Leader Responsibility and National Fora' (1995) 12 *New York Law School Journal of Human Rights* 555, 562. See also Bunyan Bryant and Robert H. Jones, 'The United States and the Genocide Convention' (1975) 16 Harvard ILJ 683.

290 The limitation that provoked the comment (that the mental element of genocide required a 'substantial' part of the group to be sought to be destroyed) has been largely accepted; see, for example, *Prosecutor* v. *Krstić*, Judgment, IT-98-33-A, 19 April 2004, para. 8.

291 Laurence J. le Blanc, 'The Intent to Destroy Groups in the Genocide Convention: The Proposed US Understanding' (1984) 78 AJIL 369, 378; Samantha Power, *A Problem From Hell: America and the Age of Genocide* (London: Flamingo, 2003), pp. 61–85. On the United Kingdom's rather belated ratification and implementation, see A. W. Brian Simpson, 'Britain and the Genocide Convention' (2002) 73 BYBIL 4, 43–64.

inconsistency are more applicable.[292] Two jurisdictions, Canada and France have attempted prosecutions for crimes against humanity, and run into problems. In Canada, definitional problems abounded in *R.* v. *Finta*,[293] and in spite of overwhelming evidence, the courts did not record a conviction. Despite the Statute being fairly clear that the provision concerned merely granted the court jurisdiction over the international law concept of crimes against humanity, the Canadian Supreme Court read it as creating a separate national offence.[294]

This misconception led the Supreme Court down various legal blind alleys, including confusing national and international legal approaches, and then using a standard in excess of that required in Canadian law.[295] In particular, by requiring the defendant to realise that the acts were inhumane, the Court went far beyond what international law required. In addition the Supreme Court required an unnecessary criterion, namely that the acts 'shock the conscience of right thinking persons'.[296] The results of these errors were serious. The case led to an abandonment of the attempt to prosecute Nazi offences in Canada. The government position paper released to explain its resort to extradition and denaturalisation in relation to those offences was express: '[in *R.* v. *Finta*] the court established a higher standard of proof for the prosecution of war crimes and crimes against humanity than is recognised at international law. For the World War II cases, this decision has made the prosecution of these crimes much more difficult and less likely.'[297]

If the majority in *Finta* acted in good faith, at times the French cases seem little less than perverse. Prior to 1992, when a statute was brought in to try to clear up some of the confusion caused by the courts, the courts were notionally applying the definition in Article 6(c) of the Nuremberg IMT Charter. However, 'the definition of crimes against humanity arrived at by the French courts through the twenty year

[292] Although attention here focuses on crimes against humanity in national jurisdictions, issues also arise from the 'general part' of international criminal law, which deals with the principles of liability.

[293] *R.* v. *Finta* 104 ILR 285. On this Case, see Irwin Cotler 'R. v. Finta' (1996) 90 AJIL 460; Irwin Cotler, 'Bringing Nazi War Criminals in Canada to Justice: A Case Study' (1997) 91 Proceedings ASIL 262; Irwin Cotler, 'War Crimes Law and the Finta Case' (1995) 6(2d) *Supreme Court Law Review* 577; David Matas, 'The Case of Imre Finta' (1994) 34 UNBLJ 281; Christopher Amerasinghe, 'The Canadian Experience', in M. Cherif Bassiouni (ed.), *International Criminal Law, III: Enforcement* (Ardsley: Transnational, 2nd edn., 1999), p. 243; Lippman, 'The Pursuit of Nazi War Criminals', 29–32.

[294] Cotler, 'War Crimes Law', 607–11.

[295] See Cotler, 'War Crimes Law', 623–7.

[296] *Finta*, p. 357. See Cotler, 'War Crimes Law', 618.

[297] Cited in Cotler, 'R. v. Finta', 461.

litigation that the *Touvier* and *Barbie* Cases went through was really quite different from anything found in 6(c) of the Nuremberg Charter'.[298] This was because the courts added a particular requirement to the definition of crimes against humanity, which had no place in the international definition, and no coherent rationale.[299] The requirement was that the crime against humanity must have been committed in furtherance of a common plan instigated by a state practising a hegemonic ideology.[300] This was introduced in the *Barbie* Case,[301] but reached its zenith in the *Touvier* litigation.[302] In addition to such a requirement being entirely extraneous to any international definition of crimes against humanity, it is vague, and the courts did not elaborate the meaning of their innovation.[303] As Leila Sadat-Wexler comments, the requirement made the French definition of crimes against humanity so 'distant from its international meaning as to arguably remove it from the province of international law'.[304] It must also be remembered that both of these jurisdictions have a stable political system and a well-developed and professional judiciary, and thus labour under none of the limitations that many other societies experience.

Conclusion

Although the prosecution of international crimes through national courts is, and has traditionally been, the normal method of proceeding when such prosecutions have occurred, a number of problems have accompanied their use. The problems do not relate to the absence of jurisdiction; all States have jurisdiction over international crimes, at the least, by those who are present in their territories. Still, there are problems associated with most of the principles of jurisdiction, which often relate to real or perceived bias, and practical problems such as the

298 Leila Sadat-Wexler, 'Prosecutions for Crimes Against Humanity in French Municipal Law: International Implications' (1997) 91 Proceedings ASIL 270, 271. See also Leila Sadat-Wexler, 'The Interpretation of the Nuremberg Principles by the French Court of Cassation: From Touvier to Barbie and Back Again' (1995) 32 CJTL 289.

299 See Claire Finkelstein, 'Changing Notions of State Agency in International Law: The Case of Paul Touvier' (1995) 30 TILJ 261, 268; Sadat-Wexler, 'The Interpretation of the Nuremberg Principles', 337–55.

300 See Sadat-Wexler, 'Prosecutions', 271–3.

301 Judgment of 20 December 1985 Cass. Crim. 1986 JCP II G No. 20,655.

302 Particularly Decision of 13 April 1992, cited in Sadat-Wexler, 'The Interpretation of the Nuremberg Principles', 293.

303 *Ibid.*, 359. 304 *Ibid.*, 273.

gathering of evidence in a primarily bilateral system. The major failing in prosecuting international crimes has been the failure to prosecute by either territorial States or States of nationality. That failure has been frequently, although not always, a violation of international law, but one which has been largely condoned. Those failures have led other States, which have taken the rhetoric of international criminal law seriously and decided that the prosecution of international crimes is at least a moral imperative, to assert broader jurisdiction over such offences. These prosecutions also have problems, including those of evidence and assertions of partiality. Also, until at least the late 1990s those prosecutions showed that the absence of authoritative definitions of international crimes led to dissonant interpretations of those crimes, which both risked unfairness to defendants, and had a fractious relationship with claims that international criminal law had a unified content.

These problems were known to States in the 1990s, when the feeling that international crimes should be prosecuted gained strength, perhaps as the result of the near-accidental creation of two international criminal tribunals, the ICTY and ICTR. The decision in favour of accountability reached its high point in 1998, with the negotiation of the Rome Statute. It is to those three tribunals that discussion turns now. Chapter 3 is an appraisal of how well those tribunals have responded, or may in future respond, to the problems noted in this chapter, and is intended to form its complement.

3 International Criminal Tribunals and the regime of international criminal law enforcement

Chapter 2 was in part dedicated to discussion of some of the problems related to the repression of international crimes by national courts. This chapter is intended to complete the picture of the regime of international criminal law enforcement as it exists in the twenty-first century, and the mechanisms that have been employed to attempt to transcend the problems mentioned above. As a result, there will be little discussion in this chapter of the Nuremberg and Tokyo IMTs: the two IMTs sat in the countries where the defendants were found, and as the convening powers of those tribunals had control over all the relevant areas the practical problems discovered in chapter 2 were of less relevance.

This chapter will thus seek to build upon the discussion of the problems identified in chapter 2 and discuss the manner in which the ICTY, ICTR and the ICC respond to the difficulties that have been identified in what might be termed the 'bilateral enforcement mechanisms' for dealing with violations of international criminal law.[1] As we saw, it has not proved very effective. The practical problems relating to the use of extraterritorial jurisdiction apply to all the more recent international criminal tribunals, as all the trials occur outside the *locus delicti*; almost every piece of evidence and every defendant has therefore to be supplied by, or through the medium of, States. As we will see, those setting up the international courts and tribunals took some innovative steps, and some perhaps serendipitous developments have come about as a result of their existence and practice. Nevertheless, some of the problems still remain, and may do so, unless equally inventive means of circumventing them can be found.

[1] As mentioned in chapter 2, the 'internationalised' tribunals are in basically the same position as national courts here.

The definition of a regime adopted here is Steven Krasner's, a 'set of implicit or explicit principles, norms, rules and decision making procedures around which actors' expectations converge in a given area of international relations'.[2] Some gloss needs to be added to this. Krasner's definition has been criticised, with some justification, on the basis that it does not contain any criterion of effectiveness, thus including 'paper regimes' which do not affect behaviour in the concept of a regime.[3] Robert Keohane has critiqued the critics on the basis that to identify effectiveness requires complex causative evaluation.[4] The difficulties of causation are overstated in this regard,[5] and Keohane admits a minimal threshold for a regime, that 'states recognize these agreements as having continuing validity'.[6] This is rather anaemic, as it does not exclude simple rhetorical commitment. In the circumstances, it is not necessary to decide who, in any objective sense (if any such sense exists) is 'right', as Keohane would probably also concede that a regime that fulfils the more exacting requirements of the criterion of effectiveness is a stronger regime. Thus discussion will also centre on effectiveness.[7]

Interdisciplinary research using regime theory has been criticised on the basis of its technocratic focus on the existence and effectiveness of international regimes, rather than on their legitimacy and the aims they serve. From the international law angle, the most vigorous critic is Martti Koskenniemi, in particular in his *Gentle Civilizer of Nations*.[8] He has a point; at times, such work does take certain aims (such as furthering free-trade agendas) as read, and there is a concerning tendency in the

[2] Steven Krasner, 'Structural Causes and Regime Consequences: Regimes as Intervening Variables', in Steven Krasner (ed.), *International Regimes* (Ithaca: Cornell University Press, 1983), p. 1, p. 1. For a discussion of the UN as a system, see Nigel D. White, *The United Nations System: Toward International Justice* (Boulder: Lynne Reiner, 2002), chapter 1.

[3] Volker Rittberger, 'Research on International Regimes in Germany: The Adaptive Internalization of an American Social Science Concept', in Volker Rittberger (ed.), *Regime Theory and International Relations* (Oxford: Clarendon, 1993), p. 3, pp. 9–10.

[4] Robert O. Keohane, 'The Analysis of International Regimes: Towards a European–American Research Programme', in Volker Rittberger (ed.), *Regime Theory and International Relations* (Oxford: Clarendon, 1993), p. 22, pp. 27–8.

[5] See Friedrich Kratchowil, 'How Do Norms Matter', in Michael Byers (ed.), *The Role of Law in International Politics: Essays in International Law and International Relations* (Oxford: Oxford University Press, 1999), p. 35.

[6] Keohane, 'The Analysis of International Regimes', p. 28.

[7] It might also be noted that effectiveness is one of the tests that Joseph Raz postulates for the existence of a legal system; see Joseph Raz, *The Concept of a Legal System* (Oxford: Clarendon, 1970), pp. 205–8.

[8] Martti Koskenniemi, *The Gentle Civilizer of Nations: The Rise and Fall of International Law 1870–1960* (Cambridge: Cambridge University Press, 2001), pp. 494–509.

work of scholars such as Anne-Marie Slaughter to denigrate sovereign equality.[9]

Regime theory does not have to link itself to such American-focused 'normatively tinged' sociologies. Regime theory has been used for a variety of projects which reject the more parochial uses to which it has been turned.[10] Early work on regimes, such as Robert Keohane's classic *After Hegemony* made it clear that regime analysis was sensitive to claims that it was overly focused on technical matters of co-operation to the exclusion of its moral aspects. Keohane is express that it is not taken as a given that co-operation is always a good thing: 'Since the point is often missed, it should be underlined: Although international regimes may be valuable to their creators, they do not necessarily improve world welfare. They are not *ipso facto* "good".'[11] Moral analysis is also necessary.[12] For this reason, later parts of this book will look into the legitimacy of the regime investigated in this part, by looking at the critiques of international criminal law based on selectivity. In relation to the aims of the regime, promoting accountability for international crimes is eminently supportable.[13]

The fact that the two UN tribunals have a very different role and relationship with national courts than the ICC necessitates that they be dealt with separately for the most part. This chapter will begin with the two UN tribunals, as although they are not to be permanent features of the regime of international criminal law enforcement they came chronologically before the ICC, and influenced the creators of the Rome Statute. They provide an interesting contrast to the ICC, and show another way that the regime could have developed. Again, as with chapter 2, this chapter does not purport to be a comprehensive survey of all legal issues that have arisen or may arise in relation to the tribunals, but seeks to focus on a number of key issues. These will be co-operation, calibration of

[9] Koskenniemi, *The Gentle Civilizer*, pp. 488–9.

[10] See Rittberger, 'Research on International Regimes', pp. 6–7.

[11] Robert Keohane, *After Hegemony* (Princeton: Princeton University Press, 1984), p. 73.

[12] On this aspect of regime theory, see Andrew Hurrell, 'International Society and the Study of Regimes: A Reflective Approach', in Volker Rittberger (ed.), *International Regimes and International Relations* (Oxford: Clarendon, 1993), p. 49, pp. 67–9.

[13] Some doubt the deterrent aspect of international criminal law, see, for example, David Wipmann, 'Atrocities, Deterrence and the Limits of International Justice' (1999) 23 Fordham ILJ 473; Jan Klabbers, 'Just Revenge? The Deterrence Argument in International Criminal Law' (2001) 12 *Finnish Yearbook of International Law* 249. It is likely, nonetheless, that deterrence is no more or less effective at the national and international level.

efforts between different jurisdictions and incorporation/harmonisation of international criminal law.

Two special cases: Rwanda and the former Yugoslavia

Primacy

In relation to two conflicts a radically different approach was taken to all other post-war international crimes. This approach was to be one of international prosecution, and was decided on by the Security Council. The Council also took the view that the most appropriate forum for the high-profile cases was an international court. In these two exceptional cases, the international courts enjoy an authority superior to national courts. The ICTY and ICTR are considered to be in a 'vertical' relationship with national jurisdictions.[14] This 'high water mark' of the priority of international courts is known as 'primacy'.[15] Although Article 9(1), ICTY Statute (8(1) ICTR Statute) accepts that concurrent jurisdiction exists between national courts and the UN Tribunals, Article 9(2) ICTY Statute (8(2) ICTR Statute) gives the right to the UN tribunals to 'formally request national courts to defer to the competence of the International Tribunal'. It is clear that the 'request' is binding.[16] This places the UN tribunals in a hierarchically superior position to national jurisdictions, as they may demand they derogate their competence to them. As Judge Sidhwa put it: 'the rule obliges States to accede to and accept requests for deferral on the ground of suspension of their sovereign rights to try the accused themselves.'[17]

Thus for crimes committed in the conflicts in former Yugoslavia and Rwanda, a break was made from the traditional bilateral system of

[14] See Göran Sluiter, *International Criminal Adjudication and the Collection of Evidence. Obligations of States* (New York: Intersentia, 2002), pp. 81–8.

[15] On which, see Bartram S. Brown, 'Primacy or Complementarity: Reconciling the Jurisdiction of National Courts and International Criminal Tribunals' (1998) 23 Yale JIL 383, 385; José E. Alvarez, 'Nuremberg Revisited: The Tadić Case' (1996) 7 EJIL 245, 252, 256; Virginia Morris and Michael P. Scharf, *An Insider's Guide to the International Criminal Tribunal for Former Yugoslavia* (Ardsley: Transnational, 1995), pp. 125–32; Virginia Morris and Michael P. Scharf, *The International Criminal Tribunal for Rwanda* (Ardsley: Transnational, 1998), pp. 312–25.

[16] See, for example, *Prosecutor* v. *Tadić*, Decision on the Request of the Prosecutor for a Formal Request for Deferral, IT-94-T, 8 November 1994; *Prosecutor* v. *Tadić*, Decision on Interlocutory Appeal on Jurisdiction, IT-94-1-AR72, 2 October 1995, Separate Opinion of Judge Sidhwa, para. 83. Luisa Vierucci, 'The First Steps of the International Criminal Tribunal for Yugoslavia' (1995) 6 EJIL 134, 136–42.

[17] *Tadić*, *ibid*.

co-operation in criminal matters. Pursuant to Article 25 of the UN Charter and Article 29 of the ICTY Statute (28 ICTR Statute) there is an obligation on all UN member States to co-operate with the tribunals. By virtue of their creation under Chapter VII, the ICTY and ICTR are entitled to require the transfer of any person in any UN member State to them for the purpose of prosecution.[18] So where the UN Tribunal has jurisdiction, and has taken an interest in that individual, a duty is created for the custodial State. The duty is to transfer the suspect/indictee to the UN tribunal concerned, irrespective of its own preferred course of action. This became a matter of controversy when Rwanda was forced to transfer Theoneste Bagosora to the ICTR despite its strong preference in favour of prosecuting him domestically. It does have the advantage, nonetheless, of settling at the start the appropriate jurisdiction to try the suspect.

The ICTY has accepted that there is a role for domestic courts in the prosecution of international crimes committed in the former Yugoslavia. This has become particularly important given the completion strategy that has been imposed on the ICTY by the Security Council in Resolution 1503.[19] By virtue of Rule of Procedure 11*bis*, a Trial Chamber can suspend the ICTY indictment against the accused, and order transfer to the *locus delicti*, the State which originally transferred him or another willing State.[20] This recognises the concurrence of jurisdictions, but also the primacy of the ICTY. The ICTY retains the right to decide if it is appropriate and the relevant Trial Chamber can, at any time up to conviction or acquittal of the accused, order return to the ICTY to stand trial.

For the ICTR, this process of surrender was originally a one-way street. For indictees in custody at the ICTR who had made their initial appearance, transfer to a requesting State was not possible until 2002. In *Prosecutor* v. *Ntuyuhaga*[21] Belgium had indicated its willingness to try the defendant.[22] The Prosecutor agreed that the most sensible course of action was that Belgium do so. Thus she sought to withdraw the indictment she had over him in the ICTR, and to transfer him to Belgium to stand trial there. The ICTR, in a controversial decision, which did little for relations between that body and Belgium, determined that although

[18] Article 9, ICTY Statute, Article 8, ICTR Statute.

[19] See generally, Michael Bohlander, 'Last Exit Bosnia – Transferring War Crimes Prosecution from the International Tribunal to Domestic Courts' (2003) 14 CLF 59.

[20] ICTY Rules of Procedure and Evidence, IT/32/Rev.31, Rule 11*bis*(A).

[21] *Prosecutor* v. *Ntuyuhaga*, Decision on the Prosecutor's Motion to Withdraw the Indictment, ICTR-98-40-T, 18 March 1999.

[22] The reason for this was that the crime with which he was charged before the ICTR was the killing of ten Belgian peacekeepers.

it could (and did) withdraw the indictment, at that point its jurisdiction over the (ex-)indictee ended, and he had to be released.[23] The ICTR rejected Belgium's arguments that the ICTR could transfer him directly despite the absence of an express provision in the Statute or Rules for this. The decision was not unassailable. The Security Council could not have contemplated that co-operation between States and the tribunal should only be one-way when their jurisdictions, although not equal, are concurrent.[24] However, on 6 June 2002 the ICTR adopted its own Rule of Procedure 11*bis* which allowed the ICTR to transfer a detainee to the arresting State or another State, provided the arresting State did not object.[25]

In relation to which States the two UN tribunals may ask to defer, the ICTR Statute is clear: they may ask any UN member State (or State who has specifically accepted the obligation) to defer to them.[26] With respect to the ICTY, the position was a little confused, Article 9 of the ICTY Statute merely mentioning that the ICTY could ask 'national courts' to defer. Despite there being no express limitation in this language,[27] certain members of the Security Council gave interpretative statements that limited the obligation, in particular, by saying that the obligation to defer was limited to the States of the former Yugoslavia alone.[28] That said, there is doubt whether these should be taken as authoritative interpretations for all purposes.[29] The statements themselves were not

[23] *Ntuyahaga*.

[24] See *Amicus Curiae* Arguments, reported in 'A Sign of the Times' (1999) 58 *Ubutabera* 8.

[25] The problem of contests over defendants was noted at least as far back as 1997; see Madeline H. Morris, 'The Trials of Concurrent Jurisdiction: The Case of Rwanda' (1996–1997) 7 DJCIL 349, 362–6; Frederik Harhoff, 'Consonance or Rivalry? Calibrating the Efforts to Prosecute War Crimes in National and International Tribunals' (1996–1997) 7 DJCIL 571, 583–5.

[26] Article 8, see *Ntuyuhaga*, 'the primacy recognised by the statute is clear inasmuch as the Tribunal may request any national jurisdiction to defer investigation or ongoing proceedings'.

[27] Brown, 'Primacy or Complementarity', 407.

[28] See S/PV.3217, UK, p. 11; they claimed that primacy would be exceptionally invoked only over non-former Yugoslav States. Russia (p. 28) went the furthest, denying the automatic binding nature of the orders; none of the others adopted this, nor have the Tribunals.

[29] John C. O'Brien, 'The International Tribunal for Violations of International Humanitarian Law in the Former Yugoslavia' (1993) 77 AJIL 639, 657–8 claims that the Tribunal should consider them an integral part of the Statute as they must be presumed to have been agreed to by the Council. Michael P. Scharf, 'Comments' (1994) 88 Proceedings ASIL 251, 252 explains that no representative had been empowered to respond to them, as the statements were not expected at the meeting. *Prosecutor* v.

identical, nor did they agree with each other here,[30] and seem to contradict the clear wording of the Statute. The approach taken by the ICTY in the Rules of Procedure shows they considered the duty to be incumbent on all States,[31] and the duty extending to all States was affirmed by the ICTY in the *Tadić* Case[32] in which Germany also accepted that it was under a duty to defer.[33] The duty thus extends to all States who are UN members or who have accepted the obligation.

There are limits to the rights of the tribunals to require the transfer of cases. After all, the tribunals have concurrent jurisdiction with national courts: they are not intended to prevent national jurisdictions prosecuting offences from the Yugoslav and Rwanda conflicts. Their right to demand deferral is notionally limited to where it is justified.[34] The situations when deferral is justified are given in Rule 9 of the Rules of Procedure. They are when the act is being charged as an ordinary (not an international) offence,[35] where the proceedings are not fair or impartial, or 'what is in issue is closely related to, or otherwise involves, significant factual or legal questions which may have implications for investigations or prosecutions before the Tribunal'.[36] The first two may be quite narrow, focusing on the national proceedings, but the last is a very broad provision, effectively allowing the tribunal (on the request of the Prosecutor) to demand transfer of an individual case whenever it wants to, making the limits more illusory than real.[37]

Normally, for deferral proceedings the government to whom the order is to be made is heard as *amicus curiae*,[38] but this is not necessary, nor is

Tadić, Judgment, IT-94-1-A, 15 July 1999, paras. 298–304, found that for determining if crimes against humanity required a discriminatory *animus*, the statements made in the Security Council were not to be considered controlling.

30 Brown, 'Primacy or Complementarity', 400–2.

31 *Ibid.* See ICTY and ICTR Rules of Procedure, 9–10.

32 *Tadić* deferral.

33 *Ibid.* Transcript, pp. 30–1. See Vierucci, 'The First Steps', 140–2.

34 Morris and Scharf, *The International Criminal Tribunal for Rwanda*, pp. 315–16.

35 For criticism of this in the context of Article 10(2), see Howard Levie, 'The Statute of the International Tribunal for the Former Yugoslavia: A Comparison with the Past and a Look to the Future' (1995) 21 *Syracuse Journal of International Law and Commerce* 1, 15.

36 ICTY/ICTR, Rule 9(i–iii).

37 In *Tadić* deferral, para. 11, the ICTY accepted a declaration by the OTP that the proceedings in Germany relating to Tadić were 'closely related to, or may have implication and common significant factual or legal questions, for the investigations or prosecutions before the Tribunal' was conclusive, as the decision was for the Prosecutor alone.

38 The governments were heard, for example, in the *Karadžić and Mladić* and *Tadić* Cases; see Faisa Patel-King and Anne-Marie la Rosa, 'The Jurisprudence of the Yugoslavia Tribunal 1994–1996' (1997) 8 EJIL 123, 127–8.

(in theory) the consent of the government to the transfer.[39] As can be seen, this is a very wide inroad into State sovereignty, given that the UN tribunals can take any case they wish to try away from any national (or sub-national) authority,[40] at any stage of the national proceedings. As Morris and Scharf say, this is both 'extraordinary and unprecedented'.[41]

The UN Tribunals' powers extend further than this, even to the situation where a national court has pronounced judgment. Once a defendant has been tried by one of the tribunals, national courts are prevented from retrying that person for the same crimes.[42] The converse does not always apply. Article 10 ICTY Statute (9 ICTR Statute) gives the tribunals the 'unprecedented power to render a national judicial process invalid'.[43] Obviously, as this is a matter of some sensitivity, and as the principle of *non bis in idem* is an important protection for the defendant, the circumstances for this are limited. The UN tribunals may retry a person only if the crime is characterised as an ordinary crime, or the proceedings are not fair or impartial, or are designed to shield the accused from the tribunal's jurisdiction.[44] Here a clear hierarchy is put in place between national jurisdictions and the UN tribunals, with the authority to make these decisions being placed in the international tribunals. Not only are the tribunals given the right to determine that they are the appropriate forum for the prosecution of offences in that conflict, but pursuant to 11*bis* the Tribunal can go a little further, to pass the suspect to other

[39] No comment was made by the FRY in the *Erdemović* deferral proceedings. Orders were made in each instance. The ICTR has heard governments, for example, in *Procesutor* v. *Musema*, Decision of the Trial Chamber in the Application by the Prosecutor for a Formal Request for Deferral by Switzerland in the Matter of Alfred Musema, ICTR-96-5-D, 12 March 1996; *Prosecutor* v. *Bagosora*, Decision of the Trial Chamber on the Application by the Prosecutor for a Formal Request for Deferral by the Kingdom of Belgium and in the matter of Theoneste Bagosora, ICTR-96-7-D, 17 May 1996; see Morris and Scharf, *The International Criminal Tribunal for Rwanda*, pp. 322–5.

[40] Rule 9 was amended in 1995 to give the ICTY the right to issue orders to sub-State entities to defer; this was introduced to deal with the post-Dayton position in Yugoslavia.

[41] Morris and Scharf, *An Insider's Guide*, p. 126.

[42] Article 10(1) ICTY Statute, Article 9(1) ICTR Statute, Joint Rule of Procedure 13; *Prosecutor* v. *Tadić*, Decision of the Defence Motion on the Principle of *Non Bis in Idem*, IT-94-1-T, 14 November 1995, para. 13. See Patel-King and la Rosa, 'The Jurisprudence', 150; Jelena Pejić and Liz Egan, 'Prosecuting War Crimes in the former Yugoslavia: The Two Tiers and the Linkage' (1995) 1 *East European Human Rights Review* 11, 18.

[43] Karl Arthur Hochkammer, 'The Yugoslav War Crimes Tribunal: The Compatibility of Peace, Politics and International Law' (1995) 28 VJTL 119, 153.

[44] Article 10(2), ICTY Statute, Article 9(2), ICTR Statute; see Morris and Scharf, *An Insider's Guide*, pp. 134–5; Morris and Scharf, *The International Criminal Tribunal for Rwanda*, p. 317; Levie, 'The Statute', 15.

jurisdictions than the arresting State, provided that the latter State does not object.

Co-operation

Obviously, although the tribunals have the right to demand the presence of defendants, this would be useless unless there were a concomitant duty to demand the passing on of evidence. The second manifestation of the superiority of the UN tribunals over national jurisdictions is thus based on Article 29 of the ICTY Statute (28 ICTR Statute).[45] This states that: '1. States shall cooperate with the International Tribunal . . . 2. States shall comply without undue delay with an request for assistance or an order issued by a Trial Chamber . . .'; for both tribunals, the obligation is bolstered by the Security Council Resolutions which established them. Resolutions 827 and 955 declare that 'all States shall cooperate fully with . . . [the tribunal] . . . all States shall take any measures necessary under their domestic law to implement the provisions of the present resolution and the statute including the obligations of States to comply with requests for assistance or orders issued by a trial chamber'.[46] As can be seen, the basis of this obligation is a Chapter VII resolution of the Security Council, gaining its force from Article 25 of the UN Charter.[47] There is some question about the precise nature of the obligation: the Secretary General has claimed that every order by the tribunals is an enforcement measure.[48] It is doubtful that the Security Council can delegate the power to decide on further enforcement measures, and it is better to see the power being merely the issuance of orders, which are binding on States as a result of the Chapter VII resolutions.[49] This is

[45] See generally Sluiter, *International Criminal Adjudication*, pp. 145–55 and Rachel Kerr, *The International Criminal Tribunal for the Former Yugoslavia: An Exercise in Law, Politics and Diplomacy* (Oxford: Oxford University Press, 2004), chapter 6.

[46] This creates not only an obligation to comply with the orders, but a separate duty to introduce implementing legislation to ensure they may comply with any orders. See *Prosecutor* v. *Blaškić*, Decision of the President on the Defence Motion Filed Pursuant to Rule 64, IT-95-14-T, 2 April 1996, para. 7: 'since 1993 all States have been under an unquestionable obligation to enact implementing legislation necessary to permit them to execute warrants and requests of the Tribunal.'

[47] See S/PV. 3453, pp. 3, 6. Morris and Scharf, *The International Criminal Tribunal for Rwanda*, p. 638; Christopher Greenwood, 'The Development of International Humanitarian Law by the International Criminal Tribunal for the Former Yugoslavia' (1998) 2 MPYBUNL 97, 106.

[48] Report of the Secretary General Pursuant to paragraph 5 of Security Council Resolution 808. UN Doc. S/25704, para. 23.

[49] Kenneth Gallant, 'Securing the Presence of Defendants Before the International Tribunal for Former Yugoslavia; Breaking with extradition', in Roger S. Clark and

the position taken by the ICTY,[50] ICTR[51] and later on, by the Secretary General.[52]

Nonetheless, the nature of the obligation being based in Chapter VII of the UN Charter leads to certain important features. First, all UN member States are under an obligation to comply with the requests, irrespective of whether or not they were in the Security Council and voted for the tribunals. In *Prosecutor* v. *Blaškić*, the ICTY described the obligation as novel and unique: the 'obligation set – out in the clearest of terms – in Article 29 is an obligation on every member State of the United Nations *vis-à-vis* all other member States. Thus it is an *erga omnes* obligation . . . [and every UN member State] . . . has a legal interest in the fulfilment of the obligation.'[53] All UN member States are thus under an obligation to provide the legal assistance, including the handing over of evidence, that the Tribunals request. There is no reciprocal duty on the Tribunals to assist national jurisdictions in their investigations and prosecutions, a considerable break from the traditional inter-State system, but not one which is designed to encourage domestic prosecutions at the national level. The Tribunals have, consistent with this, not always been supportive of domestic efforts, particularly in the former Yugoslavia.[54]

The obligation to comply with requests from the Tribunals trumps other international legal obligations by virtue of Article 103 of the UN Charter. Very importantly, 'there are no specified grounds on which a State may refuse to comply with an order or request from

Madeline Sann (eds.), *The Prosecution of International Crimes* (New Brunswick: Transaction, 1995), p. 343, p. 351.

50 See *Prosecutor* v. *Mrksić, Radić, Sljivancanin and Dokmanović*, Decision on the Motion for Release by the Accused Slavko Dokmanović, IT-95-13a-PT, 22 October 1997, para. 35.

51 *Prosecutor* v. *Kanyabashi*, Decision on the Defence Motion on Jurisdiction, ICTR-96-15-T, 18 June 1997, para. 34.

52 Letter from the Secretary General to FRY, 24 April 1994.

53 *Prosecutor* v. *Blaškić*, Judgment on the Request of the Republic of Croatia for Review of the Decision of Trial Chamber II of 18 July 1997, IT-95-14-AR108*bis*, 29 October 1997, para. 26. Christopher C. Joyner, 'Strengthening Enforcement of International Humanitarian Law: Reflections on the International Criminal Tribunal for Former Yugoslavia' (1995) 6 DJCIL 79, 91 overstates the position, claiming that orders are equivalent to *jus cogens* as they overcome other obligations. The correct basis for this trumping is Article 103 of the UN Charter.

54 In practice, the ICTY has engaged in some assistance, such as that provided under the 'rules of the road' agreement and the training of domestic prosecutors. It has also begun to take part in training of domestic lawyers in the prosecution of war crimes, see Press Release cc/P.I.S./849–3, 20 May 2004. Their actions in this area are somewhat overdue; see David Tolbert, 'The International Criminal Tribunal for the Former Yugoslavia: Unforeseen Successes and Foreseeable Shortcomings' (2002) 26(2) FFWA 7, 12–16.

the International Tribunal'.[55] National law impediments are simply not applicable: '[C]ompliance by States with any requests from the Tribunal for judicial assistance is obligatory and not subject to interpretation.'[56] The unconditional nature of the obligation is particularly important for two matters: obtaining defendants despite the normal restrictions on extradition, and gaining possession over documents subject to national security restrictions.

For surrender, Rule of Procedure 55 gives the Tribunal the right to demand transfer, and 58 leaves no doubt about the obligation: 'The obligation in Article 29 of the Statute shall prevail over any legal impediment to surrender or transfer the accused or a witness to the tribunal which may exist under the national law or extradition treaties of the State concerned.' With respect to national security protected documents, Rule of Procedure 54 allows the tribunals to demand documents. Although customary international law protects these from disclosure,[57] the ICTY asserted the right to these documents in the *Blaškić* Case, on the ground that they would be required for trial and there was no specific limit in Article 29 on the obligation.[58] Although the ICTY accepted that some measures for confidentiality would need to be taken, the decision on whether the documents had to be transferred lay, at all times, with the Tribunal.[59]

The Tribunals have a very broad competence to issue orders. Rule 54 states: '[a]t the request of either party, or *proprio motu*, a judge or Trial Chamber may issue such orders, summonses, subpoenas, warrants and transfer orders as may be necessary for the purposes of an investigation or for the preparation or for the conduct of the trial.' This is an

[55] *Blaškić*, AR108, para. 63.

[56] Joyner, 'Strengthening', 89. See also Robert Kushen and Kenneth J. Harris, 'Surrender by the United States to the International Tribunals for former Yugoslavia and Rwanda' (1996) 90 AJIL 510, 511. This is the position taken by the United Nations, Letter from Hans Corell to Biljana Plavsić, 21 January 1997.

[57] *Blaškić* AR108, para. 29.

[58] *Blaškić* AR108, paras. 62–68. See generally, Hennie Strydom, 'The Legal Authority of the International Criminal Tribunal for ex-Yugoslavia to Order the Disclosure of Evidence' (1997) 22 SAYBIL 76; Ruth Wedgwood, 'International Criminal Tribunals and State Sources of Proof: The Case of Tihomir Blaškić' (1998) 11 LJIL 635; Jacob Katz Cogan, 'The Problem of Obtaining Evidence for International Criminal Courts' (2000) 22 HRQ 404, 415–23. A useful comparison of the UN tribunals and the ICC is Thomas Henquet, 'Mandatory Compliance Powers *vis-à-vis* States by the *ad hoc* Tribunals and the International Criminal Court: A Comparative Analysis' (1999) 12 LJIL 969.

[59] *Blaškić* AR108, paras. 67–8. Wedgwood is mildly critical of this, for rejecting legitimate State interests; 'International Criminal Tribunals', 644–5.

open-ended provision granting very wide discretion to the Tribunals to require co-operation, which has been used for orders on various subjects, including evidence gathering.[60]

This does not mean that there are no limits to the Tribunals' authority to issue orders. One particularly important limit is that they are not permitted to issue subpoenas or binding orders to State officials in relation to their official duties. The ICTY decided that this was the position in *Blaskić* because such persons were acting for the State, which can choose how to implement its obligations to the tribunals.[61] This includes soldiers in their national forces, but not those in international forces under UN mandate, or those acting in their private capacity.[62] The importance of this is that it prevents the Tribunals from compelling individuals to account for State actions even where they, at a high level, are making the relevant decisions. Limited classes of people, such as ICRC representatives, are also immune from appearing before the court as witnesses.[63]

An interesting issue arises with respect to the orders of the Tribunal relating directly to defendants and witnesses.[64] The power to pierce the State veil and deal directly with individuals is a very wide power,

[60] See for example, *Prosecutor* v. *Krsmanović and Djukić*, Order for Provisional Detention, IT-96-20. For criticism, see Paul J. I. M. de Waart, 'From Kidnapped Witness to Released Accused "for Humanitarian Reasons": The Case of the Late Djorde Djukić' (1996) 9 LJIL 453. *Prosecutor* v. *Tadić*, Decision on Prosecution Motion for Protective Measures for Witnesses, IT-94-1-T, 10 August 1995, para. 8; see Andre Klip, 'Witnesses Before the International Criminal Tribunal for Former Yugoslavia' (1996) 67 RIDP 267, 281–2; *Prosecutor* v. *Lajić*, Order for the Withdrawal of Charges Against the Person Named Goran Lajić and for his Release, IT-95-8, 17 June 1996. In addition, Article 98 gives the Trial Chamber the power to order the presence of witnesses, and Rules 39 and 40 give the Prosecutor the right to ask States for certain measures to be taken.

[61] *Blaškić* AR108, paras. 38–44.

[62] *Blaškić* AR108, para. 49; see Wedgwood, 'International Criminal Tribunals', 642, 653; Greenwood, 'The Development', 108–9; Danesh Sarooshi, 'The Powers of the United Nations International Criminal Tribunals' (1998) 2 MPYBUNL 141, 161.

[63] Such as that of ICRC officials and, in certain circumstances, war correspondents, see *Prosecutor* v. *Simić, Tadić and Zarić*, Decision on the Prosecution Motion under Rule 73 for a Ruling Concerning the Testimony of a Witness, IT-95-9-PT, 27 July 1999; *Prosecutor* v. *Brđjanin and Talić*, Decision on Interlocutory Appeal, IT-99-36-AR73.9, 11 December 2002. Robert Cryer, 'Witness Evidence Before International Criminal Tribunals' (2003) 3 LPICT 411, 414–15; Steven Powles, 'To Testify or not to Testify – Privilege from Testimony and the Ad Hoc Tribunals: The Randal Decision' (2003) 16 LJIL 511; Steven Powles, 'International Criminal Courts: Practice, Procedure and Problems: Privilege From Testimony at the ICTY' (2003) 2 LPICT 467.

[64] See, for example, Françoise J. Hampson, 'The International Criminal Tribunal for the Former Yugoslavia and the Reluctant Witness' (1998) 47 ICLQ 50.

normally associated with courts considered to have supranational powers.[65] Obviously, all criminal courts do this to the extent that they give out sentences, but with the UN tribunals, the matter goes further. Originally, there was some doubt whether the orders of the Tribunals actually bound individuals.[66] Since then, opinion has swung to the view that Article 29 orders are directly binding upon them.[67] This was settled by the *Blaškić* Case, where the ICTY Appeals Chamber said that, although requests would normally go through the State, where the authorities prevented the Tribunal from fulfilling its mandate, 'the International Tribunal may enter into direct contact with an individual subject to the sovereign authority of a State. The individual, being within the ancillary (or incidental) criminal jurisdiction of the International Tribunal, is duty bound to comply with its orders, requests and summonses.'[68] It would thus seem that going through the State is a concession made by the Tribunals, but not one that is legally necessary.

The final aspect of the Tribunals' extraordinary power is the ability of the Prosecutor to investigate on a State's territory without the consent of that State. Article 18(2) of the ICTY Statute (17(2) ICTR Statute) gives the Prosecutor the power to 'question suspects, victims and witnesses, to collect evidence and to conduct on-site investigations. In carrying out these tasks, the Prosecutor may, as appropriate, seek the assistance of the State authorities concerned.'[69] Two points need to be made. First, this gives the Prosecutor the right to undertake investigations, and perform official investigations on the territory of the States concerned, without the further consent, or knowledge, of the State concerned.[70] Second, the Prosecutor can ask the Trial Chamber to make other demands for help.[71] These are very wide powers, giving the prosecutor the right to

[65] Laura R. Helfer and Anne-Marie Slaughter, 'Toward a Theory of Effective Supranational Adjudication' (1997) 107 Yale LJ 273, 289.

[66] See Andre Klip, 'Witnesses Before the International Criminal Tribunal for the Former Yugoslavia' (1996) 67 RIDP 267, 268–9, 275 (implying that the duties apply to States alone).

[67] See Sarooshi, 'The Powers', 158; *Amicus Curiae* Brief Submitted by the Max Planck Institute for Comparative Public Law and International Law, IT-95-14-PT, para. 391.

[68] *Blaškić* AR108, para. 55. See Sluiter, *International Criminal Adjudication*, pp. 77–9; Shuichi Furuya, 'Legal Effect of the International Criminal Tribunals and Court Upon Individuals: Emerging International Law of Direct Effect' (2000) 47 NILR 111, 123–9.

[69] See generally, Morris and Scharf, *An Insider's Guide*, pp. 192–4; Morris and Scharf, *The International Criminal Tribunal for Rwanda*, pp. 452–4.

[70] See Louise Arbour, 'The Crucial Years' (2004) 2 JICJ 396, 398.

[71] Joint Rule of Procedure 39.

perform some police functions on the territory of a sovereign State.[72] On the other hand, this is difficult when a State does not wish this to happen, as with the FRY in relation to Kosovo. The refusal of the FRY to allow the Prosecutor into Kosovo to investigate in 1999 led to a Security Council resolution specifically deploring that refusal.[73]

In spite of the strong obligations, the ICTY has had a mixed record of compliance from States.[74] In cases including the transfer of Duško Tadić from Germany, co-operation has worked well. On other occasions, for example in the case of the 'Vukovar three', States have resisted surrender, particularly where the accused are holding States' nationality. The continued failure of Serbia and Montenegro and/or the Republika Sprska to hand over Radovan Karadžić and Ratko Mladić remains a strong reminder of the difficulties in obtaining co-operation which affect the Tribunals that are, in the oft-quoted words of Antonio Cassese 'like a giant without arms and legs'.[75] The failure of (what was then) the FRY to transfer indictees to the ICTY led to adverse statements from the President of the Security Council[76] and a condemnatory Security Council resolution.[77] The primacy of the UN Tribunals should, in theory, end the difficulties associated with overlapping jurisdiction in the cases it takes, but without having power to enforce its judgments when faced with State contumacy, it is difficult, although not impossible, to gain custody of defendants.[78] Help has been given by States such as the United States and United Kingdom withholding aid or insisting on the retention of sanctions on the FRY until it transferred Slobodan Milošević.[79] NATO forces working in Bosnia-Herzegovina have also sometimes arrested suspects pursuant to rights granted under the Dayton Agreement, the consent

[72] See, for example, Anne Bodley, 'Weakening the Principle of Sovereignty in International Law: The International Criminal Tribunal for the Former Yugoslavia' (1999) 31 NYUJILP 417, 417.

[73] UN Doc. S/RES/1207, see Kerr, *The International Criminal Tribunal*, p. 141.

[74] See generally, Jackson Nyamuya Maogoto, *State Sovereignty and International Criminal Law: Versailles to Rome* (Ardsley: Transnational, 2003), pp. 175–89.

[75] Antonio Cassese, 'On the Current Trends Toward Criminal Prosecution and Punishment of Breaches of International Humanitarian Law' (1998) 9 EJIL 2, 13.

[76] S/PRST/1996/23, 8 May 1996.

[77] S/RES/1207, 17 November 1998.

[78] See generally Kerr, *The International Criminal Tribunal*, chapter 7; Susan Lamb, 'The Powers of Arrest of the International Criminal Tribunal for Former Yugoslavia' (1999) 70 BYBIL 165; Arbour, 'The Crucial Years', 397; Mark B. Harmon and Fergal Gaynor, 'Prosecuting Massive Crimes With Primitive Tools: Three Problems Encountered by Prosecutors in International Criminal Proceedings' (2004) 2 JICJ 403, 408–12.

[79] Kerr, *The International Criminal Tribunal*, pp. 124–5.

of Bosnia-Herzegovina and the relevant Security Council Resolutions.[80] When the United Nations was acting as the transitional authority in Eastern Slavonia, it assisted the ICTY by facilitating transfer of suspects.[81]

Because of actions taken to overcome the reluctance of certain States to co-operate, the ICTY has had to deal with claims of irregular rendition by luring or abduction.[82] The lawfulness of luring was raised by Slavko Dokmanović. The Trial Chamber dealing with his application claimed (inaccurately) that luring was not contrary to international law.[83] Allegations of kidnapping have caused the ICTY some consternation.[84] It is easy to see why: as a body that is enforcing international norms, it is sensitive to claims that it is violating human rights. In the end, the Appeals Chamber was forced to face the issue squarely when dealing with Dragan Nikolić, a defendant before the Tribunal who claimed he had been abducted from Serbia.[85]

Turning first to State rights not to have police functions exercised on their territory without consent, the Chamber determined that 'the

[80] Security Council Resolution 1031 and Article 9, General Framework Agreement, Article IV(4) Annex 4, and Article 10, Annex 1-A of the Dayton Peace Agreement. See Nico Figa-Talamanca, 'The Role of NATO in the Peace Agreement for Bosnia and Herzegovina' (1997) 7 EJIL 164, 171–2; Paola Gaeta, 'Is NATO Authorised or Obligated to Arrest Persons Indicted by the International Criminal Tribunal for the Former Yugoslavia?' (1998) 8 EJIL 174, 175–8 and Kerr, *The International Criminal Tribunal*, pp. 154–69. For criticism, see Walter Gary Sharp, 'International Obligations to Search for and Arrest War Criminals: Government Failure in the former Yugoslavia?' (1996–7) 7 DJCIL 411.

[81] See *Prosecutor* v. *Mrksić, Radić, Sljivancanin and Dokmanović*, Decision on the Motion for Release by the Accused Slavko Dokmanović, IT-95-13a-PT, 22 October 1997; see Michael P. Scharf, '*The Prosecutor* v. *Slavko Dokmanović*: Irregular Rendition and the ICTY' (1998) 11 LJIL 369, 373–6.

[82] See generally, Özlem Ülgen, 'The ICTY and Irregular Rendition of Suspects' (2003) 2 LPICT 441.

[83] *Dokmanović*, para. 57.

[84] A Trial Chamber originally refused Stevan Todorović an evidentiary hearing on his arrest, *Prosecutor* v. *Simić, Tadić, Zarić and Todorović*, Decision Stating Reasons for Trial Chamber's Order of 4 March 1999 on Defence Motion for Evidentiary Hearing on the Arrest of the Accused Todorović, IT-95-9, 4 March 1999; *Prosecutor* v. *Simić, Tadić, Zarić and Todorović*, Decision on Appeal by Stevan Todorović Against the Oral Decision of 4 March 1999, Written Decision of 25 March 1999 of Trial Chamber III, IT-95-9-A, 19 October 1999; *Prosecutor* v. *Simić, Tadić, Zarić and Todorović*, Decision, IT-95-9-T, 23 November 2003. The (ICTY's) problem went away when Todorović pleaded guilty. See James Sloan, '*Prosecutor* v. *Todorović*: Illegal Capture as an Obstacle to the Exercise of International Criminal Justice' (2003) 16 LJIL 85.

[85] At trial level, it was found that the abduction could not be attributed to the Prosecutor. *Prosecutor* v. *Nikolić*: Decision on Defence Motion Challenging the Exercise of Jurisdiction by the Tribunal, IT-94-2-PT, 9 October 2002. See James Sloan, '*Prosecutor* v. *Dragan Nikolić*: Decision on Defence Motion on Illegal Capture' (2003) 14 LJIL 541.

damage caused to international justice caused by not apprehending fugitives accused of serious violations is comparatively higher than the injury, if any, caused to the sovereignty of a State by a limited intrusion into its territory, particularly when the intrusion occurs in default of the State's cooperation'.[86] Moving to the more sensitive issue (for the ICTY) of the defendant's human rights, the Chamber opined that unless the violations of human rights were egregious, (and abduction *simpliciter* was not) then setting aside jurisdiction would be disproportionate, as 'the correct balance must . . . be maintained between fundamental rights of the accused and the essential interests of the international community in the prosecution of persons charged with serious violations of international humanitarian law'.[87] Thus, rather like States, the ICTY has at times condoned the use of unlawful methods of rendition where international crimes are involved and there is no other way of obtaining suspects. In some ways, this shows the considerable problems that bedevil obtaining international assistance, whatever the formal obligations imposed on States.

The passing on of evidence has also been somewhat sporadic. As Rachel Kerr has said, 'although there existed a binding obligation to comply with all requests originating from the Tribunal . . . [it] in practice worked on the basis of voluntary compliance'.[88] Some States have, like the USSR in relation to John Demjanjuk, been overzealous in their attempts to obtain convictions. In the *Tadić* Case, the now notorious matter of Dragan Opacić threatened the legitimacy of the proceedings.[89] Opacić, a convict in Bosnia, was transferred to the ICTY to give evidence against Tadić, and obtained witness protection measures that included anonymity. Having been proved to have perjured himself, Opacić claimed that he had been forced to do so by the Bosnian government, who had wanted to ensure the conviction of a Bosnian Serb.[90] However, greater problems have arisen with relation to States refusing to hand

[86] *Prosecutor* v. *Nikolić*, Decision on Interlocutory Appeal Concerning Legality of Arrest, IT-94-2-AR73, 5 June 2003, para. 26.

[87] *Nikolić* (Appeal), para. 30.

[88] Kerr, *The International Criminal Tribunal*, p. 128.

[89] Defence counsel have also argued that they are hampered by lack of co-operation; see Mark S. Ellis, 'Achieving Justice Before the International War Crimes Tribunal: Challenges for the Defense Counsel' (1996–7) 7 DJCIL 519, 533–6. See generally, Sluiter, *International Criminal Adjudication*, pp. 130–8.

[90] *Prosecutor* v. *Tadić*, Opinion and Judgment, IT-94-1-T, 7 May 1997, para. 33. See Kerr, *The International Criminal Tribunal*, p. 109, Michael P. Scharf, *Balkan Justice: The Story Behind the First International War Crimes Trial Since Nuremberg* (Durham, NC: Carolina Academic Press, 1997), pp. 199–200.

over evidence, in particular evidence sensitive from the point of view of national security. The obligations of States with regard to this type of evidence was dealt with in the *Blaškić* Case, but orders to Croatia were not complied with. After the wartime President of Croatia Franjo Tudjman died, however, Croatia's attitude to co-operation altered, and reams of evidence useful to the defence was made available.[91]

The problem of sensitivity of national security evidence and the unwillingness of States to pass evidence to the ICTY has not been limited to States of the former Yugoslavia. Richard Goldstone recalls the diplomatic efforts required to obtain evidence for the ICTY in its infancy.[92] It has been plausibly contended that the United States and other Western States have been reluctant to hand over some intelligence information.[93] Although co-operation has become far better from those States, particularly since the Kosovo conflict, the suspicion remains that this co-operation is born of political expediency rather than a sense of obligation on the part of those States. This has led to a number of officials being permitted to testify before the Tribunal only by giving a prepared statement and being able to limit the matters on which they may be questioned.[94] In the *Todorović* Case, requests for information about his arrest by SFOR addressed to that force led to a considerable cooling of relations between SFOR and the ICTY, despite the best efforts of the Office of the Prosecutor to protect SFOR.[95] As we shall see, the relationship between the Office of the Prosecutor, in particular, and NATO States, has led to some suspicions about whether that organ can be fully objective in appraising NATO actions. As can be seen, despite the strength of the regime on paper, obtaining evidence for the ICTY has not been easy, although perhaps easier than for domestic courts trying similar crimes.

The ICTR has had more practical success, but problems have still manifested themselves.[96] Uganda has complained about the fact that the

[91] *Prosecutor* v. *Blaškić*, Judgment, IT-95-14-A, 29 July 2004, paras. 4–6. See Harmon and Gaynor, 'Prosecuting Massive Crimes', 413–21; Jacob Katz Cogan, 'International Criminal Courts and Fair Trials: Difficulties and Prospects', (2002) 27 YJIL 111, 122–4; on evidence and appeals, see Richard May and Marieke Wierda, *International Criminal Evidence* (Ardsley: Transnational, 2002), pp. 299–323.

[92] Richard J. Goldstone, *For Humanity: Reflections of a War Crimes Investigator* (New Haven: Yale University Press, 2000), pp. 89–93.

[93] Katz-Cogan, 'International Criminal Courts', 122–4.

[94] See, for example, *Prosecutor* v. *Blaškić*, Decision of Trial Chamber I on Protective Measures for General Phillipe Morillion, Witness of the Trial Chamber, IT-95-14-T, 12 May 1999.

[95] Katz Cogan, 'International Criminal Courts', 124–7; Sloan, '*Prosecutor* v. *Todorović*', 93–6.

[96] See generally Maogoto, *State Sovereignty*, pp. 210–23.

ICTR has primacy over it for crimes under ICTR jurisdiction committed by Rwandans in Uganda,[97] but as a UN member it had no choice but to accept the ICTR's power.[98] Co-operation between the ICTR and most States in Africa has been quite good,[99] although at times the ICTR and Rwanda have clashed over defendants they both wish to try and Rwanda has used its position as the *locus delicti* to exercise influence on the ICTR.[100]

A problem did arise in relation to the surrender of Elizaphan Ntakirutimana from the United States.[101] In contravention of Article 28 of the ICTR Statute, which requires unqualified obedience to requests for surrender, a local magistrate in Texas refused to order Ntakirutimana's surrender on the ground that he believed the evidence supplied with the request was insufficient to warrant extradition, and because he considered the agreement between the United States and the ICTR to surrender suspects to be unconstitutional. The US government was unhappy with the decision, and successfully sought to overturn it, but the whole case shows the difficulties that co-operation can generate even where a government is willing.[102]

A more serious problem has arisen when Rwanda has used the fact that almost all the evidence required for the ICTR to be successful

[97] 'The Ugandan Government considers that its judicial system has primary and supreme jurisdiction and competence over any crimes committed on Ugandan territory'. Letter Dated 31 October 1994 from the *Charge d'Affaires* A. I. of the Permanent Mission of Uganda to the United Nations Addressed to the President of the Security Council, UN Doc. S/1994/1230.

[98] Morris and Scharf, *The International Criminal Tribunal for Rwanda*, p. 296.

[99] See Catherine Cissé, 'The End of a Culture of Impunity in Rwanda' (1998) 1 YBIHL 161, 169–70.

[100] See Madeline Morris, 'The Trials of Concurrent Jurisdiction: The Case of Rwanda' (1997) 7 DJCIL 349, 362–3.

[101] See *In the Matter of the Surrender of Elizaphan Ntakirutimana* 1997 LEXIS 20714 (S. D. Tex., Laredo Div. December 17 1997). See generally, Ivo Josipović, 'Implementing Legislation for the Application of the Law on the International Criminal Tribunal for the Former Yugoslavia and Criteria for its Evaluation' (1998) 1 YBIHL 35, 59–60; Göran Sluiter, 'To Cooperate or not to Cooperate?: The Case of the Failed Transfer of Ntakirutimana to the Rwanda Tribunal' (1998) 11 LJIL 383; Jordan J. Paust, 'The Freeing of Ntakirutimana in the United States and "Extradition" to the ICTR' (1998) 1 YBIHL 205. On the US agreements at issue in the case, see Kenneth J. Harris and Robert Kushen, 'Surrender of Fugitives to the War Crimes Tribunals for Yugoslavia and Rwanda: Squaring International Legal Obligations with the US Constitution' (1996) 7 CLF 561.

[102] *Ntakirutimana* v. *Reno* (184 F. 3d 419 US Court of Appeals, 5th Circuit); see Mary Coombes, 'International Decisions: In re Surrender of Ntakirutimana' (2000) 94 AJIL 171; Göran Sluiter, 'The Surrender of Ntakirutimana Revisited' (2000) 13 LJIL 459. As Sluiter notes, 464–6, the appeals decision itself is, like the first instance decision it overturned, somewhat parochial.

is located within its borders to pressurise the ICTR into adopting an attitude favourable to the Rwandan government. When the ICTR has taken action with which Rwanda has disagreed, it has threatened to suspend co-operation with the Tribunal.[103] This reached its apogee in the *Barayagwiza* affair.

The affair came about when the Appeals Chamber in *Prosecutor* v. *Barayagwiza*[104] determined that the Tribunals had had a residual power to refuse to hear a Case where there had been serious violations of human rights prior to trial.[105] As they found such violations in his case, the Appeals Chamber determined that Barayagwiza should not be prosecuted before the ICTR and set free. Rwanda was apoplectic at this development, and suspended all co-operation with the ICTR.[106] Given that almost all the witnesses and pieces of evidence are located in Rwanda, the Tribunal is singularly dependent on Rwandan co-operation for its effectiveness. Four months after the first ruling, the Appeals Chamber revisited its decision on somewhat questionable grounds (although the first decision was by no means unassailable), and decided that the prosecution of Barayagwiza could go ahead before the ICTR.[107] Two of the judges involved in both decisions (Vohrah and Nieto-Navia) expressly denied that the Rwandan suspension of co-operation had had an impact on their decision. The Prosecutor also issued a similar statement. As William Schabas has commented, the decisions give rise to a suspicion that the relevant actors protest too much.[108]

The Rome regime

The extraordinary regime set up for the former Yugoslavia and for Rwanda is, whatever its merits, exceptional. The 'vertical' enforcement system they represent applies only in relation to two situations, and it is

[103] See Christina M. Carroll, 'An Assessment of the Role and Effectiveness of the International Criminal Tribunal for Rwanda and the Rwandan National Justice System in Dealing with the Mass Atrocities of 1994' (2000) 18 BUILJ 163, 180–1; William A. Schabas, 'Prosecutor v. Barayagwiza' (2000) 94 AJIL 563, 565. A more sanguine view may be found in Jean Marie Kamatali, 'The Challenge of Linking International Criminal Justice and National Reconciliation: The Case of the ICTR' (2003) 16 LJIL 115, 119–20.

[104] *Prosecutor* v. *Barayagwiza*, Decision, ICTR-97-19-AR72, 19 November 1999.

[105] *Barayagwiza*, paras. 70–77.

[106] Carroll, 'An Assessment', 180–1.

[107] *Prosecutor* v. *Barayagwiza*, Decision (Prosecutor's Request for Review or Reconsideration) ICTR-97-19-AR72, 31 March 2000.

[108] Schabas, 'Prosecutor v. Barayagwiza', 568–71.

unlikely that any similar tribunals will be set up by the Security Council in the near future. Although they have certainly achieved a fair level of effectiveness and fulfil the other criteria for the identification of a regime – that of including a set of explicit rules and decision making procedures around which expectations converge – the exceptional, *ad hoc* nature of these Tribunals means that they can be considered only a temporary, limited regime.[109] The coming into force of the Rome Statute, however, can be said to have created a fully-fledged regime of international criminal law enforcement, one that involves both national courts and the ICC itself.

The regime has substantive rules which structure expectations, not only of behaviour, but also of the appropriate reaction to violations of those rules. In addition to the ICC being itself a decision making organ, the Rome Statute also contains decision making procedures for the Prosecutor,[110] and to a certain extent national courts, through the principle of complementarity, which also serves to provide priority rules for the decision making fora. In a particularly interesting development, the ICC regime is intended to a large extent to superintend one set of decision making fora (national prosecutors and courts) by threatening the use of another (the ICC Prosecutor and Chambers).

As Arthur Stein has noted, 'all regimes designed to deal with dilemmas of common interests must specify strict patterns of behaviour and insure that no one cheats. Because each actor requires assurances that the other will also eschew its rational choice, such collaboration requires a degree of formalization. The regime must specify what constitutes cooperation and what constitutes cheating, and each actor must be assured of its own ability to spot others' cheating immediately.'[111] The Rome Statute creates such a regime. Further than that, the system of complementarity creates a strong interest in States not to cheat by failing to prosecute. Although the regime is not global, as the Rome Statute only applies

[109] As Krasner notes, 'Regimes must be understood as something more than temporary arrangements that change with every shift in power or interests'; Krasner, 'Structural Causes', p. 2. At p. 3 Krasner distinguishes regimes from agreements, the latter being '"one shot" arrangements'. Although the Tribunals are not permanent, the fact that they have lasted over ten years does mean they cannot be dismissed as entirely temporary arrangements.

[110] See Article 53 of the ICC Statute; Chris Gallavin, 'Article 53 of the Rome Statute of the International Criminal Court: In the Interests of Justice?' (2003) 14 KCLJ 179.

[111] Arthur A. Stein, 'Coordination and Collaboration: Regimes in an Anarchic World', in Steven Krasner (ed.), *International Regimes* (Ithaca: Cornell University Press, 1983), p. 115, pp. 128–9.

to its parties, it is a gradually expanding one, and one which may be expected to have some practical effects on non-parties. This is, *inter alia*, because to ensure that their nationals do not come before the ICC, non-State parties will have to prosecute offences subject to the jurisdiction of the ICC themselves.

To begin with an issue which was the subject of considerable discussion in chapter 2, duties to prosecute; parties to the Rome Statute may well have accepted an obligation to prosecute international crimes, at the very least those occurring on their territories or by their nationals. The expectation of the Rome Statute is that the normal reaction to international crimes is to be prosecution. This sets a 'strict pattern of behaviour'. The preamble to the Rome Statute 'Recall[s] that it is the duty of every State to exercise its criminal jurisdiction over those responsible for international crimes' (preambular para. 6). There is considerable ambiguity about this provision, as to whether it refers to an obligation to prosecute on the basis of nationality and territoriality jurisdiction or universality.[112] As it is a preambular statement, rather than a substantive provision, and bearing in mind the disagreement about whether or not prosecution is the only possible response, it is too much to base a duty to prosecute on the basis of universality on the preamble.[113] This is particularly the case because the ICC itself can exercise jurisdiction, absent a Security Council referral, only on the basis of nationality or territorial jurisdiction. Nonetheless, the normal expectation is now that international crimes must be prosecuted by States on the basis of either nationality or territoriality.

The extent to which the ICC may contribute to ensuring prosecution of international crimes will rely in large part on whom it may seek, or threaten to seek, to prosecute. To understand the role the ICC is taking on (and thus the Rome regime for the enforcement of international criminal law), we need to engage in an excursus on the principle of complementarity and the powers of the ICC.

[112] Morten Bergsmo and Otto Triffterer, 'Preamble', in Otto Triffterer (ed.), *Commentary on the Rome Statute of the International Criminal Court: Article by Article* (Baden-Baden: Nomos, 1999), p. 1, p. 13. See also Tuiloma Neroni Slade and Roger S. Clark, 'Preamble and Final Clauses', in Roy S. Lee (ed.), *The International Criminal Court: Issues, Negotiations, Results* (The Hague: Kluwer, 1999), p. 421, p. 427.

[113] Frank Jarasch and Claus Kreß go as far as claiming that preambular para. 6 crystallises a customary duty to prosecute crimes on the basis of territoriality or by their nationals; Frank Jarasch and Claus Kreß, 'The Rome Statute on the German Legal Order', in Claus Kreß and Flavia Lattanzi (eds.), *The Rome Statute and Domestic Legal Orders: 1* (Baden-Baden: Nomos, 2000), p. 91, p. 109.

Complementarity

The relationship between States, their courts and the ICC is different to that relating to national jurisdictions and the UN Tribunals, and different again to the bilateral inter-State regime of extradition and mutual legal assistance. Of course, one of the most important issues is that, as a treaty-based court, the Rome Statute does not (and cannot) impose duties on non-parties.[114] Thus, unless the Statute becomes as widely ratified as the UN Charter (or the Security Council imposes a duty),[115] the number of States subject to duties under the Statute will be smaller than that under the UN Tribunals' Statutes.

While the UN Tribunals' relationship to national jurisdictions is defined by primacy, the ICC's relationship to them is one of 'complementarity'.[116] The term has been criticised as being of unstable meaning, at least during the drafting of the Rome Statute.[117] That as it may be, 'complementarity' is a useful term if it is taken as having a descriptive rather than a normative function. Mahnoush Arsanjani explains the basic descriptive meaning of complementarity: '[t]he ICC is not intended to replace national courts, but operates only when they don't.'[118] This was settled early on in the ILC Drafts.[119] The reason for this is that

[114] 1969 Vienna Convention on the Law of Treaties, 1155 UNTS 331, Article 34. See Anthony Aust, *Modern Treaty Law and Practice* (Cambridge: Cambridge University Press, 2000), chapter 14.

[115] Indeed, '[m]ost delegations agreed that the Security Council, acting under Chapter VII of the Charter of the United Nations and referring a situation to the Court, obligated all States to cooperate'; John T. Holmes, 'The Principle of Complementarity', in Roy S. Lee (ed.), *The International Criminal Court: Issues, Negotiations, Results* (The Hague: Kluwer, 1999), p. 41, p. 71. Sluiter considers the question to depend on the wording of the Security Council resolution; Sluiter, *International Criminal Adjudication*, pp. 70–2.

[116] For early literature on the principle, see generally Adriaan Bos, 'The Role of an International Criminal Court in the Light of the Principle of Complementarity', in Eric Denters and Nico Schriver (eds.), *Reflections on International Law from the Low Countries: Essays in Honour of Paul de Waart* (The Hague: Kluwer, 1998), p. 249; Jeffrey Bleich, 'Complementarity', in M. Cherif Bassiouni (ed.), *The International Criminal Court: Observations and Issues Before the Preparatory Committee; and Administrative and Financial Implications* (Chicago: Erès, 1997), p. 231.

[117] Immi Tallgren, 'Completing the International Criminal Order: The Rhetoric of International Repression and the Notion of Complementarity in the Draft Statute for an International Criminal Court' (1998) 67 Nordic JIL 107, 110, 120.

[118] Mahnoush H. Arsanjani, 'The Rome Statute for an International Criminal Court' (1999) 93 AJIL 22, 24–5; see similarly Philippe Kirsch, 'Keynote Address' (1999) 32 Cornell ILJ 437, 438.

[119] James Crawford, 'The ILC Adopts a Statute for an International Criminal Court' (1995) 89 AJIL 404, 410. On the history of the provisions in the Rome Statute, see Oscar Solera, 'Complementary Jurisdiction and International Criminal Justice' (2002) 845 IRRC 145.

criminal law is traditionally seen as a central aspect of sovereignty, over which States have an interest in retaining control.[120] Militating against this is an international interest in seeing international crimes properly prosecuted.[121] The result is a complex mixture of deference, and challenge, to national jurisdictions.[122] The theme of complementarity runs through the Statute, coming in at many places, but it is clear from the very start that it is a major aspect of the ICC.

Unlike the UN Tribunals which effectively (other than where the principle of *non bis in idem* applies)[123] can take a case whenever they want, the ICC can effectively take the case only if certain States are 'unwilling or unable' to investigate or prosecute the offence.[124] Article 17 is express about this, providing that:

> the Court shall determine that a case is inadmissible where (a) the case is being investigated or prosecuted by a State which has jurisdiction over it, unless the State is unwilling or unable to genuinely carry out the investigation or prosecution; (b) the case has been investigated by a State which has decided not to prosecute the person concerned, unless the decision resulted from the unwillingness or inability of the State genuinely to prosecute.[125]

Article 17(2) gives guidelines in order to determine if a State is 'unwilling or unable'. These are (17(2)(a)) if the investigation or prosecution is for the purposes of 'shielding' the defendant from the court, (17(2)(b)), if 'there has been an unjustified delay in the proceedings which in the circumstances is inconsistent with an intent to bring the person concerned to justice', or (17(2)(c)) 'the proceedings were not or are not being

[120] Brown, 'Primacy or Complementarity', 424; John Dugard, 'Obstacles in the Way of an International Criminal Court' (1997) 56 CLJ 329, 336.

[121] Arsanjani, 'The Rome Statute', 25.

[122] For a view suggesting it is too challenging, particularly to non-parties, see Jimmy Gurulé, 'United States Opposition to the 1998 Rome Statute Establishing an International Criminal Court: Is the Court's Jurisdiction Truly Complementary to National Criminal Jurisdictions?' (2001–2) 35 Cornell ILJ 1. For critique of this, see David J. Scheffer, 'Staying the Course with the ICC' (2001–2) 35 Cornell ILJ 47, 56–7, 60, 88–9. A more ambivalent study is Michael A. Newton, 'Comparative Complementarity: Domestic Jurisdiction Consistent with the Jurisdiction of the Rome Statute' (2001) 167 Military LR 20.

[123] See above, pp. 127–32.

[124] Rome Statute, Article 17(1); see generally, Sharon A. Williams, 'Article 17', in Otto Triffterer (ed.), *Commentary on the Rome Statute of the International Criminal Court: Article by Article* (Baden-Baden: Nomos, 1999), p. 383.

[125] Article 17 (1)(c)(d) provide for inadmissibility for *non bis in idem* or insufficient gravity of offence.

conducted independently or impartially, and they were or are being conducted in a manner which, in the circumstances, is inconsistent with an intent to bring the person concerned to justice'.[126]

There is one matter in which the ICC does have power over States, despite the narrowness of the complementarity criteria in Article 17. The decision on whether or not these criteria are fulfilled is with the Court itself; thus, in certain circumstances, it may take a case over the assertion of jurisdiction by a State which is 'unwilling or unable' to genuinely pursue the matter.[127] It may take a case after a national court has pronounced on it, but only where the proceedings were for 'shielding' purposes, or were not conducted impartially, or in a manner inconsistent with an intent to bring the person to justice.[128] Still, these are high standards, which will be difficult for the ICC to fulfil.[129] The determination that a State is 'unwilling or unable' to prosecute offences itself will, in all likelihood be considered impolite by the subject of that determination. This last aspect has led the prosecutor, no doubt eager to avoid inviting State hostility in the critical early phase of the ICC's operation, to declare that '[g]iven the many implications of the principle of complementarity and the lack of court rulings, exhaustive guidelines will probably be developed over the years. As a general rule, however, the *policy of the Office in the initial phase of its operations will be to take action only where there is a clear case of failure to take national action*' (emphasis added).[130]

To ensure that States have a chance to initiate prosecutions themselves and thus invoke complementarity unless the Security Council has passed the situation to the Prosecutor, Article 18 requires the Prosecutor to inform all States party to the Statute and those 'which, taking into account the information available, would normally exercise jurisdiction over the crimes concerned'.[131] Any one of these States, if they wish to

[126] On the negotiation of these, see Holmes, 'The Principle of Complementarity', pp. 48–56.

[127] John T. Holmes, 'Complementarity: National Courts *versus* the ICC', in Antonio Cassese, Paula Gaeta and John R. W. D. Jones (eds.), *The Rome Statute of the International Criminal Court: A Commentary* (Oxford: Oxford University Press, 2002), p. 667, p. 672.

[128] Article 20. See Immi Tallgren, 'Article 20', in Otto Triffterer (ed.), *Commentary on the Rome Statute of the International Criminal Court: Article by Article* (Baden-Baden: Nomos, 1999), p. 419. This largely allows the ICC to avoid Fletcher's critique of universal jurisdiction.

[129] See also, Holmes, 'Complementarity: National Courts', p. 675; for some suggestions on relevant factors, see pp. 675–8.

[130] Paper on some policy issues before the Office of the Prosecutor, available at http://www.icc-cpi.int/library/organs/otp/030905_Policy_Paper.pdf, p. 5.

[131] Article 18.

prevent the Prosecutor acting, must investigate 'its nationals or others within its jurisdiction with respect to criminal acts which may constitute crimes referred to in Article 5 and which relate to the information provided' by the Prosecutor, and notify him of this investigation within a month.[132] If this occurs, then the Prosecutor is entitled to require the State concerned to keep him informed about the investigation.[133] If the Prosecutor can, as a result of his appraisal of the proceedings that triggered complementarity, persuade a Trial Chamber that the State is unwilling or unable to genuinely investigate the offences, then the Prosecutor may continue his investigations.[134]

Together with Article 19,[135] which provides for complementarity challenges by States or accused persons, these provisions make clear that States can, by investigating or prosecuting the matter themselves, remove the matter from the ICC, even if it wants the case. It may be true that Article 18 provides a 'frankly exaggerated protection to the primacy of national jurisdiction',[136] and that 'the overwhelming regulation dictated by Articles 18 and 19, is liable to substantially hamper any serious investigation'.[137] Equally, what is set up (for States parties, at least) is a system of oversight of their prosecutions, with the possibility of having the embarrassment of an adverse decision on complementarity and the transfer of proceedings to the international level if proceedings are not conducted properly. This is a huge development; as was noted in chapter 2, one of the problems related to the prosecution of international crimes was the absence of a system of oversight. In addition, we noted that duties to prosecute international crimes in treaties have been

[132] Article 18(2). [133] Article 18(5).

[134] Article 18(2)(3). Either party can appeal a decision of the Trial Chamber on this (Article 18(4)). It may be noted that this also prioritises the obligation; the first obligation is on the State to investigate, rather than initially to send the accused to the Court. This secondary obligation becomes relevant only if the investigation is unsatisfactory.

[135] On which see Holmes, 'Complementarity: National Courts', pp. 681–3; Simon N. Young, 'Surrendering the Accused to the International Criminal Court' (2000) 71 BYBIL 317, 324–8.

[136] Giuliano Turone, 'The Powers and Duties of the Prosecutor', in Antonio Cassese, Paula Gaeta and John R. W. D. Jones (eds.), *The Rome Statute of the International Criminal Court: A Commentary* (Oxford: Oxford University Press, 2002), p. 1137, p. 1164. See also Hans-Peter Kaul, 'The International Criminal Court: Jurisdiction, Trigger Mechanism and Relationship to National Jurisdictions', in Mauro Politi and Guiseppe Nesi (eds.), *The International Criminal Court: A Challenge to Impunity* (Aldershot, Ashgate, 2001), p. 59, pp. 59–60.

[137] Turone, 'The Powers', p. 1179. See similarly Holmes, 'The Principle of Complementarity', p. 76.

honoured more in the breach, partly because of the fact that there are few adverse international consequences for States who do not prosecute international crimes. The creation of a strong national interest in prosecuting international crimes, in particular those committed by a State's nationals, is therefore a very welcome step. With the creation of the system of oversight and inter-relationship of international and national jurisdictions, we can speak of a regime of international criminal law enforcement, one which not only provides a set of norms and expected behaviours but also sets up a system designed to identify and rectify instances of cheating.

Co-operation

The effectiveness of this regime, however, will be affected to some extent by the ability of the ICC to obtain defendants and evidence when it needs to. As was discussed above, some level of effectiveness is a part of a strong regime – or, if the narrower view is taken, a *sine qua non* of the existence of a regime at all. This chapter is not intended to be an exhaustive discussion of the detail of the nature of obligations to co-operate with the ICC and the evidence gathering process in general. There are other works available that cover that ground more than adequately.[138] It is also not a work on the general aspects of international criminal co-operation. There are other works on that.[139] What is at issue here is the effect the extent of the obligations to co-operate may have on the role the ICC may play. Without defendants, a trial cannot start.[140] Without evidence, courts cannot proceed to a full evaluation of the facts. As we saw in chapter 2, this is a considerable problem for States involved in prosecuting offences extraterritorially.

[138] Sluiter, *International Criminal Adjudication*; Helen Brady, 'The System of Evidence in the Statute of the International Criminal Court', in Flavia Lattanzi and William A. Schabas (eds.), *Essays on the Statute of the International Criminal Court* (Teramo: il Sirente, 1999), p. 279. On the principles of evidence as applied in the ICTY and ICTR, see Richard May and Marieka Wierda, *International Criminal Evidence* (Ardsley: Transnational, 2003).

[139] See, for example, David McClean, *International Co-operation in Civil and Criminal Matters* (Oxford: Oxford University Press, 2002), chapters 5–12; Peter J. Cullen and William C. Gilmore (eds.), *Crimes Sans Frontières: International and European Approaches* (Edinburgh: Edinburgh University Press, 1988).

[140] *In absentia* proceedings are not permitted unless the defendant is disrupting the proceedings (Article 63(2); see William A. Schabas, 'Article 63', in Otto Triffterer (ed.), *Commentary on the Rome Statute of the International Criminal Court: Article by Article* (Baden-Baden: Nomos, 1999), p. 803).

There is a general duty on all States party to the Rome Statute to co-operate with the ICC in Article 86 of the Rome Statute.[141] To begin with obtaining the accused,[142] the ICC has the power to require surrender of suspects from all States party to the Statute. Article 89 of the Rome Statute sets out the obligations of the parties on surrender, subject to the requirements set out in Article 91. Article 91 does not mention any limits such as the political offence limitation, dual criminality, or nationality.[143] It must be considered, therefore, that these limits are inapplicable in relation to the surrender process. Article 102 of the Rome Statute clearly differentiates inter-State extradition and surrender to the ICC.[144] This was included specifically to assist States with entrenched prohibitions on the extradition of nationals to surrender them to the Court.[145]

141 See Claus Kreß, 'Article 86', in Otto Triffterer (ed.), *Commentary on the Rome Statute of the International Criminal Court: Article by Article* (Baden-Baden: Nomos, 1999), p. 1051. On the Rules of Procedure and Evidence Relating to the ICC and co-operation, see Frederick Harhoff and Phakiso Mochochoko, 'International Cooperation and Judicial Assistance', in Roy S. Lee (ed.), *The International Criminal Court: Elements of Crimes and Rules of Procedure and Evidence* (Ardsley: Transnational, 2001), p. 637.

142 On surrender generally, see Bert Swart, 'Arrest and Surrender', in Antonio Cassese, Paula Gaeta and John R. W. D. Jones (eds.), *The Rome Statute of the International Criminal Court: A Commentary* (Oxford: Oxford University Press, 2002), p. 1639; Göran Sluiter, 'The Surrender of War Criminals to the International Criminal Court' (2003) 25 *Loyola of Los Angeles International and Comparative Law Review* 605.

143 There is a reasonable argument that the political offence exception is inapplicable to international crimes. See, for example, Article VII of the Genocide Convention. Geoff Gilbert considers that the exception 'should be applied to war criminals may seem to be stretching the point to absurdity'; Geoff Gilbert, *Aspects of Extradition Law* (Dordrecht: Martinus Nijhoff, 1990), p. 135. There are some old cases that invoked the principle however, see, for example, *in re Kahrs* (1948) 15 ILR 972; *Artukovic* v. *Boyle*, 140 F. Supp. 245. However, the modern trend is undeniably against this position, see *State* v. *Schulmann* (1970) 39 ILR 433; *Quinn* v. *Robinson* 783 2 F. 2d 776, 779; *Demjanjuk* v. *Petrovsky* 784 F. 2d. 1254; 776 F. 2d 571 (USCA 6th Circuit 1985); cert. den. 475 05 1016 (1986), 628 F. Supp. 1370. See also Geoff Gilbert, *Transnational Fugitive Offenders in International Law* (The Hague: Martinus Nijhoff, 1998), p. 393; Leslie C. Green, 'Political Offences, War Crimes and Extradition' (1962) 11 ICLQ 329.

144 See, for example, Phakiso Mochochoko, 'International Cooperation and Judicial Assistance', in Roy S. Lee (ed.), *The International Criminal Court: Issues, Negotiations Results* (The Hague: Kluwer, 1999), pp. 305, 309–10; Claus Kreß, 'Article 102', in Otto Triffterer (ed.), *Commentary on the Rome Statute of the International Criminal Court: Article by Article* (Baden-Baden: Nomos, 1999), p. 1157; Swart, 'Arrest', pp. 1678–80; Young, 'Surrendering', 338–55; Daryl Robinson, 'The Rome Statute and Its Impact on National Law', in Antonio Cassese, Paula Gaeta and John R. W. D. Jones (eds.), *The Rome Statute of the International Criminal Court: A Commentary* (Oxford: Oxford University Press, 2002), p. 1849, pp. 1851–5. For another view, see Gerhard Strijards, 'The Institution of the International Criminal Court' (1999) 12 LJIL 671, 677.

145 The distinction has been used, for example, by Austria, although the position is not so clear in Germany; see Irene Gartner, 'Implementation of the ICC Statute in

There is limit left. The limit is due to the drafters of the Rome Statute being aware of the problems associated with the *Ntakirutimana* litigation. Article 91(2)(c) requires the court to accompany the request with 'such documents, statements or information as may be necessary to meet the requirements for the surrender process in the requested State, except that those requirements should not be more burdensome than those applicable to requests for extradition pursuant to treaties or arrangements between the requested State and other States and should, if possible, be less burdensome, taking into account the distinct nature of the court'.

As a result, some common law States' requirement of the showing of a *prima facie* case has been retained, albeit in attenuated form. Although the requirement may not, in theory, be too burdensome, the *Ntakirutimana* litigation shows this need not necessarily be the case. Unwilling States may use this limitation as a pretext for delaying, perhaps indefinitely, compliance.[146] Civil law States may also feel aggrieved that they have given up their system-specific prohibition on the surrender of nationals, while common law States have retained the status of their requirement of showing a *prima facie* Case.[147] All in all, though, the regime set up by the Rome Statute overcame a large number of problems related to the conditions of extradition, and was perhaps stronger than could have been expected in the pre-Rome negotiations.

When we turn to co-operation with, and assistance to, the Court on matters other than surrender,[148] the general duty to comply is again contained in Article 86.[149] Article 87(5) allows the ICC to make *ad hoc* agreements to co-operate with non-State parties. Article 93 gives a non-exhaustive list of the requests with which the States' parties are required

Austria', in Claus Kreß and Flavia Lattanzi (eds.), *The Rome Statute and Domestic Legal orders: 1* (Baden-Baden: Nomos, 2000), p. 51, pp. 59–61 and Frank Jarasch and Claus Kreß, 'The Rome Statute', pp. 99–104.

146 Swart, 'Arrest', p. 1702.

147 Gilbert suggests both should be abolished: Gilbert, *Transnational Fugitive Offenders*, pp. 178–9.

148 On this generally, see Claus Kreß, Kimberly Prost, Angelika Schlunck and Peter Wilkitzi, 'Part 9', in Otto Triffterer (ed.), *Commentary on the Rome Statute of the International Criminal Court: Article by Article* (Baden-Baden: Nomos, 1999), p. 1045; Phakiso Mochochoko, 'International Cooperation and Judicial Assistance', in Roy S. Lee (ed.), *The International Criminal Court: Issues, Negotiations, Results* (The Hague: Kluwer, 1999), p. 305.

149 In addition, there is a duty under Article 59(1) to take steps to arrest any person subject to a request for arrest from the ICC. There is also a duty under Article 88 to ensure this is possible under national law. This should mitigate the requirement that all requests must be executed in accordance with national law (Article 88).

to comply, which includes finding people or articles, taking and producing evidence, questioning suspects, serving documents, facilitating the voluntary appearance of witnesses and experts,[150] examinations on site, executing searches and seizures, tracing and freezing assets and 'any other type of assistance which is not prohibited by the law of the requested State, with a view to facilitating the investigation and prosecution of crimes within the jurisdiction of the Court'.[151]

The illegality exception to the duty to co-operate on States could be very wide, giving a *de facto* veto for States over any request not expressly mentioned in the Statute. The exception is limited by Article 93(3). This provides that 'where execution of a particular measure detailed in a request under paragraph 1, is prohibited in the requested State on the basis of an existing fundamental legal principle of general application, the requested State shall promptly consult with the Court to try to resolve the matter'. If the matter cannot be resolved by these consultations, the request must be modified by the ICC. The cumulative effect of these two provisions is that the request can be denied only if the national prohibition is based on 'an existing fundamental legal principle of general application'. A problem is that this phrase is hardly free from ambiguity.[152]

A particular weakness in the Rome Statute is the qualified obligation to comply with all requests, qualifications absent in the UN Tribunal regimes.[153] Other than the exclusion in Article 93(3), the most important of these relates to the handing over of evidence which would prejudice a State's national security.[154] In sharp contrast to the UN Tribunals, which have asserted the right to demand such evidence, the Rome Statute imposes an obligation only to consult with the court and to attempt in good faith to find a solution.[155] In the final analysis, a

[150] Unlike the *ad hoc* Tribunals, witnesses cannot be required to appear; see Sluiter, *International Criminal Adjudication*, pp. 253–5.

[151] Article 93(1)(a–h)(l). See Kimberly Prost and Angelika Schlunck, 'Article 93', in Otto Triffterer (ed.), *Commentary on the Rome Statute of the International Criminal Court: Article by Article* (Baden-Baden: Nomos, 1999), p. 1101.

[152] See Sluiter, *International Criminal Adjudication*, pp. 161–3.

[153] On the negotiation of these, see Mochochoko, 'International Cooperation', pp. 310–14.

[154] See Peter Malanczuk, 'Protection of National Security Interests', in Antonio Cassese, Paula Gaeta and John R. W. D. Jones (eds.), *The Rome Statute of the International Criminal Court: A Commentary* (Oxford: Oxford University Press, 2002), p. 1371.

[155] Article 72, Article 93(4). See Wedgwood, 'International Criminal Tribunals', 646–8. For discussion of the matter before, and at, Rome, see Donald K. Piragoff, 'Protection of National Security Information', in Roy S. Lee (ed.), *The International Criminal Court: Issues, Negotiations, Results* (The Hague: Kluwer, 1999), p. 270. Jacob Katz Cogan, 'The Problem of Obtaining Evidence', 425 claims, with some justification, that this Article

State is entitled to refuse the submission of this evidence, and the court cannot demand its production.[156] Its only possible response is to declare that the State is not acting in accordance with the Statute (i.e. that the State is not acting in good faith).[157] Wedgwood sums up the position and its possible effect correctly: '[i]f the State's refusal to turn over national security information is made in good faith, that is the end of the matter, and, potentially, the end of a case.'[158]

The final major limitation on co-operation applies to surrender of persons or evidence to which some form of jurisdictional immunity of a third State applies. Article 98(1) provides that States cannot be required by the ICC to violate obligations relating to State or diplomatic immunity of third parties by co-operating with that Court.[159] The justification for this could relate to the long-standing nature of those rules and fundamental importance of retaining diplomatic relations.[160] A number of States, including the United Kingdom, have interpreted such immunities as having been waived by States party to the Rome Statute,[161] nonetheless the difference between this and the ability of the *ad hoc* Tribunals to trump such immunities of all States pursuant, if nothing else, to Article 103 of the UN Charter is clear.[162]

The above justification does not apply so clearly to the exclusion of the duty to comply in Article 98(2). Article 98(2) reads: 'the Court may not proceed with a request for surrender which would require the requested

is highly deferential to States. See also Sluiter, *International Criminal Adjudication*, pp. 163–7.

156 Article 72(6). Mochochoko, 'International Cooperation', p. 314, asserts that this is the only ground for refusal of surrender of documents. This may not be the case, as there is also, for example, information contained in a bag which has diplomatic protection.

157 Article 72(7)(ii).

158 Wedgwood, 'International Criminal Tribunals', 647. As will be seen, this may have a particularly negative impact on the prosecution of certain offences.

159 See generally, Steffen Wirth, 'Immunities, Related Problems and Article 98 of the Rome Statute' (2002) 12 CLF 429; Dapo Akande, 'International Law Imunities and the International Criminal Court (2004) 98 AJIL 407.

160 See, for example, Eileen Denza, *Diplomatic Law* (Oxford: Oxford University Press, 2nd edn., 1998). Nonetheless, it should be remembered at this point that there is no material immunity for core international crimes; see Dapo Akande, 'The Jurisdiction of the International Criminal Court Over Nationals of Non-Parties: Legal Basis and Limits' (2003) 1 JICJ 618, 638–42; Hazel Fox, 'The Resolution of the Institute of International Law in the Immunities of Heads of State and Government' (2002) 51 ICLQ 119.

161 See Robert Cryer, 'Implementation of the International Criminal Court Statute in England and Wales' (2002) 51 ICLQ 733, 738.

162 For a general analysis along these lines, see Thomas Henquet, 'Mandatory Compliance Powers *vis-à-vis* States by the *Ad Hoc* Tribunals and the International Criminal Court: A Comparative Analysis' (1999) 12 LJIL 969.

State to act inconsistently with its obligations under international agreements pursuant to which the consent of a sending State is required to surrender a person of that State to the Court, unless the Court can first obtain the cooperation of the sending State for the giving of consent for the surrender.' This provision was added primarily to cover the situation of troops abroad under Status of Forces Agreements (SOFAs).[163]

The usual principle under SOFAs is concurrent jurisdiction between the sending and host State.[164] As a result, SOFAs tend to provide for offences on the territory of the host State to be the subject of that State's jurisdiction, the exceptions being disciplinary offences and offences against the security of the sending State.[165] It might thus be asked why the host State should not be able to transfer the accused to the ICC (at least if the offence was committed on its territory). After all, the ICC exists partially as the result of the cession of jurisdiction from the host State. For offences committed in the performance of official duties, however, primary jurisdiction is given to the sending State; it may therefore be argued that there is no right to send a person to the ICC where there is another State with primary jurisdiction. On the other hand, this begs the question of whether international crimes may be considered part of official duties. Irrespective of this, Article 98(2) is not tightly drafted and its interpretation is far from settled.[166]

The United States has attempted to take considerable advantage of this provision by concluding agreements, at times under heavy pressure, with States under which they agree not to surrender US nationals to the court,[167] albeit against advice that these agreements should

[163] Arsanajani, 'The Rome Statute', 411. On SOFAs, see Robert Y. Jennings and Arthur Watts, *Oppenheim's International Law* (London: Longmans, 9th edn., 1992), pp. 1154–64; Gerald I. A. D. Draper, *Civilians and the NATO Status of Forces Agreement* (Leyden: Sitjhoff, 1966); Dieter Fleck (ed.), *The Law of Visiting Armed Forces* (Oxford: Oxford University Press, 2001).

[164] Paul J. Conderman, 'Jurisdiction', in Dieter Fleck (ed.), *The Law of Visiting Forces* (Oxford: Oxford University Press, 2001), p. 99, p. 101.

[165] See Jennings and Watts, *Oppenheim*, p. 1159. NATO Status of Forces Agreement, 1951, UKTS 3 (1955) Cmnd 9363, Article VII.

[166] Fleck considers SOFAs to fall outside Article 98(2), Dieter Fleck, 'Are Foreign Military Personnel Exempt From International Criminal Jurisdiction Under Status of Forces Agreements?' (2003) 1 JICJ 651, 654–64. The problem with this argument is that Article 98(2)'s drafters intended it to cover them.

[167] See, for example, Salvatore Zappalá, 'The Reaction of the US to the Entry into Force of the ICC Statute: Comments on UN SC Resolution 1422 and Article 98 Agreements' (2003) 1 JICJ 114, 126–31; Rosanne van Alebeek, 'From Rome to the Hague: Recent Developments on Immunity Issues in the ICC Statute' (2000) 13 LJIL 485.

be reached 'quietly'.[168] The status of such agreements needs to be approached with reference to three different separate sets of parties. States not party to the Rome Statute are, of course, entitled to make treaties excluding transfer as they see fit without taking the Statute into account.[169] In any case, non-party States are not obliged to co-operate with the ICC. Between State parties, the ICC can order that the sending State transfer the person, or give its consent to the receiving State making such a transfer (under Article 93(1)(l)). This may make agreements that would come under Article 98(2) of little practical effect, given the complementarity regime that governs the relationship between national jurisdictions and the ICC. The fact remains that although the suspect may be passed between the two State parties, they never leave the ambit of the ICC regime.

So the limits on the obligation to co-operate in Article 98(2) may in practice be relevant to agreements between receiving States which are State parties and sending States who are not. The lawfulness of such agreements, particularly those that include suspects who have not been actively 'sent' by the 'sending' State, is distinctly questionable.[170] Whatever the position of an individual agreement under the Rome Statute, we can again clearly see the difference between the ICC co-operation regime, which provides for deference to other treaties entered into by States, and the regime set up for the *ad hoc* Tribunals, for whom inter-State agreements of this nature are, from a legal point of view, simply irrelevant.

Although there is a duty to consult the ICC and attempt to get around any impediment,[171] there are other ways in which a State may avoid complying with an order of the ICC. If the requested State is investigating a different crime, and immediately executing the request could interfere with that investigation, then that State may delay compliance.[172] It may also delay a request if there has been an admissibility challenge, unless the Court determines otherwise.[173] These provisions do not provide

[168] Ruth Wedgwood, 'Fiddling in Rome' (1998) 77 FA 20, 22.

[169] Although signatories are obliged, pursuant to Article 18 of the Vienna Convention on the Law of Treaties, not to take actions which would defeat the object and purpose of the Statute, which may include the making of agreements which would enable the State to leave offences unprosecuted.

[170] The position is likely to depend on the precise terms of such agreements. See Zappalá, 'The Reaction of the US', 126–31; Akande 'The Jurisdiction', 642–6. See also Dominic McGoldrick, 'Political And Legal Responses to the ICC', in Dominic McGoldrick, Peter Rowe and Eric Donnelly (eds.), *The Permanent International Criminal Court: Legal and Policy Issues* (Oxford: Hart, 2004), p. 389, pp. 423–33.

[171] Article 97. [172] Article 94. [173] Article 95.

a reason to refuse the request outright, but with certain types of surrender – for example, where a national of a non-party State accused of a crime within the jurisdiction of the ICC visits a State party, or in relation to perishable evidence (including witnesses open to intimidation) – speed may be of the essence. It cannot be ignored that the assistance must generally be provided through the national procedures put in place. Despite the duty to have sufficient legislation to co-operate with the Court in Article 88, '[i]t must be feared that the fact that, pursuant to the Statute, the domestic laws of the requested State largely determine how requests for assistance will be executed, will often frustrate the proper functioning of the Court', as the national procedure will not provide evidence the ICC can itself use.[174]

In a useful improvement over the ICTY and ICTR Statutes, Article 93(10) allows the ICC to co-operate with a State in its investigations of serious crimes, including international crimes. This, it is to be hoped, presages a more co-operative relationship between national and international fora than has been the case in the *ad hoc* Tribunals' practice. This means that co-operation between States and the ICC need not be one-sided: the ICC may be able to assist States in their own prosecutions, not least by the provision of evidence in the possession of the Prosecutor's office and, no less importantly, by providing advice from those with considerable expertise in what, at the domestic level, is often the arcane discipline of international criminal law. On a practical level, this may give the Prosecutor some leverage with States which want the ICC's help in relation to assistance to the ICC itself.

However, the provisions on the gathering of evidence do not create a strong set of obligations to co-operate, and it will be difficult for the ICC to obtain evidence unless States are willing as well as obliged to co-operate.[175] In sensitive matters, particularly those involving issues considered by States to impact on national security, this may cause many problems for the ICC.[176] A major difficulty with evidence gathering

[174] Swart, 'General Problems', in Antonio Cassese, Paula Gaeta and John R. W. D. Jones (eds.), *The Rome Statute of the International Criminal Court: A Commentary* (Oxford: Oxford University Press, 2002), pp. 1601–2.

[175] See generally, Bert Swart, 'General Problems', p. 1589; see also, albeit less subtly, Jacob Katz Cogan, 'International Criminal Courts and Fair Trials: Difficulties and Prospects' (2002) 27 Yale JIL 111. Katz Cogan concentrates on the defence position; the same is applicable to obtaining sufficient prosecution evidence. In spite of its merits, the piece is at times somewhat overdrawn, see e.g. 111, 133, 139.

[176] Here, Alfred Rubin has a point; see Alfred P. Rubin, 'The International Criminal Court: Possibilities for Prosecutorial Abuse' (2001) 64 LCP 153, 161.

(and suspect gathering) is also the interplay between the provisions on jurisdiction, admissibility and the practicality of implementation. This should be no surprise; the three are intimately linked.[177] The statute was a compromise which involved many inter-related aspects, including the three mentioned above and, as we shall see, the scope of criminal liability. When a crime is committed on the territory of a non-party State by a national of a State party to the Rome Statute, the country where most of the evidence – be it human, written or physical – exists is under no obligation to co-operate, and thus pass on that evidence. Where a crime is committed on the territory of a State party by a non-party national who then returns home, absent foreign travel to a State party, the suspect is highly unlikely to be surrendered to the ICC.

To add to these latter difficulties, which are inherent in the law of treaties, even with respect to State parties, for the ICC to take a case it must have determined that the relevant State(s) are unwilling or unable genuinely to prosecute themselves. This hardly bodes well for the willingness of the national authorities concerned to provide suspects or evidence.[178] For the most part, all judicial assistance requests have to be made through the mechanism of national procedures, and where a State has already been determined by the ICC to be unwilling to prosecute, it is unlikely to be minded to co-operate. In serious cases of this nature the Prosecutor himself has noted that he 'may also be asked to act in a situation where those who have the monopoly of force in a State are the ones to commit the crimes. It goes without saying that in such a case the enforcement authorities in that State will not be at the prosecutor's disposal.'[179]

It might be hoped that the ICC could perhaps circumvent an unwilling executive by directing its orders and requests to individual enforcement bodies, such as the police. The Prosecutor has been establishing relationships with such entities.[180] However, other than requests to international organisations such as INTERPOL or other 'appropriate regional organization[s]' (Article 87(1)(b)), requests are to be directed through diplomatic channels 'or any other appropriate channel' designated by

[177] Hans-Peter Kaul and Claus Kreß, 'Jurisdiction and Cooperation in the Statute of the International Criminal Court: Principles and Compromises' (1999) 2 YBIHL 143, 143–5. On jurisdiction and admissibility, see below.

[178] Paulo Benvenuti, 'Complementarity of the International Criminal Court to National Criminal Jurisdictions', in Flavia Lattanzi and William A. Schabas (eds.), *Essays on the Statute of the International Criminal Court* (Teramo: Sirente, 1999), p. 21, p. 50.

[179] Policy Paper, p. 2. [180] Policy Paper, p. 2.

the relevant State (Article 87(1)(a)). With one possible exception, these 'designated channels' refer to government ministries, usually the ministry of justice, thus ensuring governmental control over requests.

The exception is Finland, whose declaration on ratification states: '[p]ursuant to article 87(1)(a) of the Statute, the Republic of Finland declares that requests for cooperation shall be transmitted either through the diplomatic channel or directly to the Ministry of Justice, which is the authority competent to receive such requests. *The Court may also, if need be, enter into direct contact with other competent authorities of Finland.* In matters relating to requests for surrender the Ministry of Justice is the only competent authority' (emphasis added). For the most part, however, any attempt to achieve more effective compliance with orders and requests by 'disaggregating' States in the manner advocated by Anne-Marie Slaughter would be extremely difficult and unlikely to be welcomed by States.[181]

When a State is unable to prosecute, there are certain special rights for the ICC to investigate. Obviously, where a State has been declared unable to prosecute owing to a complete or substantial collapse of its judicial system, that same system cannot be expected to deal with requests for assistance. As a result, Article 57(3)(d) allows a Pre-Trial Chamber to '[a]uthorize the Prosecutor to take specific investigative steps within the territory of a State Party without having secured the cooperation of that State under Part 9, if, whenever possible having regard to the views of the State concerned, the Pre-Trial Chamber has determined that the State is clearly unable to execute a request for cooperation due to the unavailability of any authority or any component of its judicial system competent to execute the request for cooperation under Part 9'. In such situations, it will often be the case that the judicial arm is not the only part of government that has collapsed.

The Prosecutor is fully aware of the problems that this will raise, as can be seen from the Prosecutor's policy paper. Referring such situations the Prosecutor, Mr Moreno-Ocampo, noted that 'the Prosecutor may be called upon to act in a situation of violence over which the State authorities have no control. His office can be present in the country only at great risk. The protection of witnesses, gathering of evidence and arrest of suspects will be difficult if not impossible'. The paper returns to this

[181] See Anne-Marie Slaughter, 'International Law in a World of Liberal States' (1995) 6 EJIL 503, 512–13, 527–8. For a thorough critique, see José E. Alvarez, 'Do Liberal States Behave Better?: A Critique of Slaughter's Liberal Theory' (2001) 12 EJIL 183.

theme later, noting that '[i]n circumstances such as these the Prosecutor will not be able to exercise his powers without the intervention of the international community, whether through the use of peacekeeping forces or otherwise; the Prosecutor will not be able to establish an office in the country concerned without being assured of its safety. He will also have to be assured that there will be the means available for investigation, protection of witnesses and arrest of suspects.'[182]

A final provision does give limited rights to the Prosecutor directly to execute requests for assistance on the territory of States parties. This applies where the request 'can be executed without any compulsory measures', and it is 'necessary for the successful execution of the request' and extends, *inter alia*, to 'the interview or taking evidence from a person on a voluntary basis . . . and the examination without modification of a public site or other public place'.[183] If the relevant territory is the *locus delicti*, then following all possible consultations with the State involved (which may be none) the Prosecutor can execute the request. If the execution is to take place in any other State, the prosecutor must take into account all reasonable conditions imposed on such execution by the government of that State. The framing of this provision was one of the most controversial at Rome, and it is substantively far weaker than the equivalents in the ICTY and ICTR.[184] Quite serious questions can be asked about whether Article 99(4) can be effective.[185]

These problems are all exacerbated by the fact that, although Article 87 allows the Court to refer a failure to co-operate to the Assembly of States Parties (ASP), there is no provision for compulsory measures against such States. What the ASP will choose to do in the event of non-compliance is not yet clear. Where a situation has been referred to the ICC by the Security Council, the Court may inform the Council of issues relating to non co-operation, and it would be for that body to determine what action was appropriate. The experience of the ICTY and ICTR does not give reason for optimism with respect to vigorous response to non-compliance with orders of the ICC. One aspect of the effectiveness of the ICC's role concerns how seriously States believe the

182 Policy Paper, p. 6. 183 Article 99(4).

184 On the controversy, see Mochochoko, 'International Cooperation', pp. 314–17.

185 See, in particular, Louise Arbour and Morten Bergsmo, 'Conspicuous Absence of Jurisdictional Overreach', in Hermann A. M. von Hebel, Johan G. Lammers and Jolien Schukking, *Reflections on the International Criminal Court: Essays in Honor of Adriaan Bos* (The Hague: T. M. C. Asser Instituut, 1999), p. 129, pp. 137–8; Sluiter, *International Criminal Adjudication*, pp. 320–31, 346–7.

ICC may prosecute offences if they do not; these weaknesses could be problematic.[186] Although the ICC may be expected to be less effective in evidence gathering than the ICTY and ICTR owing to the qualifications to the obligations to comply, the experience of the ICTY and ICTR in gaining evidence is that they have often had to rely on voluntary assistance from third States and their pressure on the territorial or nationality State. This implies that the ICC may not be significantly less effective, at least if it can gain the assistance of such States.[187] Even without such help, it will probably achieve the level of effectiveness of a reasonably strong regime. It is stronger, for example, than the inter-State co-operation mechanisms.

The Prosecutor's role

In some ways, the Prosecutor stands at the centre of the regime of international criminal law enforcement set up in the Rome Statute: in many ways he stands as the guardian of international criminal law for the States parties to the Statute. Like an attentive, albeit slightly intimidating, butler, omnipresent, always prepared to help, the Prosecutor also oversees States' reactions to international criminal law, and may take rectificatory action (taking over the proceedings himself) should they fall short. That said, as a result of the complementarity regime and the likely difficulties in ensuring that adequate evidence can be gathered by both the prosecution and defence, the Prosecutor of the ICC has begun by looking for a co-operative and supervisory role for the ICC in its initial stages.

This role of the Prosecutor is witnessed by the aforementioned Prosecutor's policy document. Page 4 of the document contains the following passage which, if nothing else, displays a keen sense of the art of the possible:

> there is no impediment to the admissibility of a case before the court where no State has initiated any investigation. There may be cases where inaction by States is the appropriate course of action. For example, the Court and a territorial State incapacitated by mass crimes may agree that a consensual division of labour is

[186] On the other hand, part of the role of the ICC is to normalise the prosecution of international crimes at the domestic level, and this may not be negatively impacted upon by the relatively weak co-operation regime, see Robert Cryer, 'Human Rights and the Question of International Courts and Tribunals', in Michael C. Davis *et al.* (eds.), *International Intervention in the Post-Cold War World* (New York: M. E. Sharpe, 2003), p. 60, pp. 62–3, 75.

[187] Although the United States is unlikely to be as quick to offer to help the ICC as it has the ICTY.

the most logical and effective approach. Groups bitterly divided by conflict may oppose prosecutions at each other's hands and yet agree to prosecution by a Court perceived as neutral and impartial. There may also be cases where a third State has extraterritorial jurisdiction, but all interested parties agree that the Court has developed superior evidence and expertise relating to that situation, making the Court the more effective forum. In such cases there will be no question of 'unwillingness' or 'inability' under Article 17.

Although there is a procedure for determining conflicts of extradition and surrender requests from the ICC and other courts in Article 90,[188] in the context of Article 18 the Prosecutor has tried to find a way to make a virtue of the necessity of (in practice) inviting complementarity challenges, having made the following statement of policy:

> The exercise of the Prosecutor's functions under Article 18 of notifying States of future investigations will alert States with jurisdiction to the possibility of taking action themselves. In a case where multiple States have jurisdiction over the crime in question the Prosecutor should consult with those States best able to exercise jurisdiction (e.g. primarily the State where the alleged crime was committed, the State of nationality of the suspects, the State which has custody of the accused, and the State which has evidence of the alleged crime) with a view to ensuring that jurisdiction is taken by the State best able to do so.[189]

Whether this will turn out to be a successful strategy remains to be seen but, bearing in mind what was said above about the problems that can arise from the absence of a hierarchy of jurisdictional claims, this may prove to be a positive contribution to ensuring prosecution. It should be noted that the prosecutor's role here is not necessarily limited to States party to the Rome Statute, as it involves only discussing matters with States.

As we can see, the prosecutor is looking to take on a role in co-ordinating prosecutions of international crimes. There are certain things that may assist in this, and thus, over the longer term, to gain State trust and goodwill for the Prosecutor and the ICC, without which the number of State parties to the Rome Statute will not increase, and the provisions on legal assistance will be very difficult to implement.

Aspects of the Rome Statute will assist the Prosecutor in bringing cases under his watchful eye. The first is the referral mechanism, pursuant to which the Prosecutor may gain cognisance of a situation in which

[188] See Kimberly Post, 'Article 90', in Otto Triffterer (ed.), *Commentary on the Rome Statute of the International Criminal Court: Article by Article* (Baden-Baden: Nomos, 1999), p. 1081.

[189] Policy Paper, p. 5.

international crimes may have been committed. Admittedly, two of the trigger mechanisms do not inspire immediate confidence. The third is revolutionary, however. One of the uninspiring ways has already been mentioned: the right of the Security Council to refer any situation to the prosecutor under Chapter VII of the UN Charter under Article 13(b) of the Rome Statute.[190] The current possibility of the Security Council referring such a situation is low.[191] The second way is by a referral from a State party of a situation under Articles 12(a) and 14.[192] Unfortunately, this will be considered (in all likelihood) an unfriendly act by the States involved in the situation referred. If the practice of the various human rights bodies is used as a guide here, the probability of State referrals is not high.[193] Against this background, the decisions of Uganda to refer the situation in the North of Uganda and of the Democratic Republic of Congo (DRC) to refer itself to the Prosecutor are quite extraordinary.[194]

Nonetheless, as a result of the initial reluctance of States to refer the situation in the DRC, the Prosecutor has declared himself ready to use what amounts to quite a revolutionary innovation in international criminal law. This is the power given to the Prosecutor to initiate investigations *ex proprio motu*.[195] Subject to a Pre-Trial Chamber's determination that there is 'reasonable basis to proceed with an investigation, and that the case appears to fall within the jurisdiction of the Court', the Prosecutor may investigate the offences without requirement of a referral.[196]

190 See generally, Lionel Yee, 'The International Criminal Court and the Security Council: Articles 13(b) and 16', in Roy S. Lee (ed.), *The International Criminal Court: The Making of the Rome Statute* (The Hague: Kluwer, 1999), p. 143, pp. 146–9; Luigi Condorelli and Santiago Villalpando, 'Referral and Deferral by the Security Council', in Antonio Cassese, Paula Gaeta and John R. W. D. Jones (eds.), *The Rome Statute of the International Criminal Court: A Commentary* (Oxford: Oxford University Press, 2002), p. 627, pp. 629–44.

191 The practice of the Security Council so far is evaluated in chapter 4.

192 See Axel Marchesio, 'Article 14', in Otto Triffterer (ed.), *Commentary on the Rome Statute of the International Criminal Court: Article by Article* (Baden-Baden: Nomos, 1999), p. 353; Philippe Kirsch and Darryl Robinson, 'Referral by States Parties', in Antonio Cassese, Paula Gaeta and John R. W. D. Jones (eds.), *The Rome Statute of the International Criminal Court: A Commentary* (Oxford: Oxford University Press, 2002), p. 619.

193 Robert Cryer, 'Commentary on the Rome Statute: A Cadenza for the Song of Those Who Died in Vain?' (1998) 3 JACL 271, 285.

194 ICC Press release, 29 January 2004 (Uganda); ICC Press Release, 19 April 2004 (DRC).

195 See Philippe Kirsch and Darryl Robinson, 'Initiation of Proceedings by the Prosecutor', in Antonio Cassese, Paula Gaeta and John R. W. D. Jones (eds.), *The Rome Statute of the International Criminal Court: A Commentary* (Oxford: Oxford University Press, 2002), p. 657.

196 That is, unless the Security Council has issued a deferral under Article 16 of the Statute. On Article 16, see Yee, 'The International Criminal Court and the Security

This was a controversial addition to the Statute. Like mediocre sophomoric dissertations, the critiques of the powers of the Prosecutor tend towards the overstated.[197] There is no home in the Rome Statute for the bogeyman of such critiques, the 'rogue prosecutor'.[198] Lest we forget, the Prosecutor is under a duty to remain independent, and although there remains a level of discretion in the Prosecutor, that discretion is carefully circumscribed and reviewable.[199] Indeed, perhaps a little too much so.[200] No matter how qualified it is, the addition of the power of independent initiation of investigation is iconoclastic in the positive sense.[201] Leaving referral to States and the Security Council alone would for the most part leave preliminary decisions on whom to prosecute to the vagaries of politics.[202]

It is important when discussing the role of the Prosecutor to remember the principle of complementarity. The point of the ICC is not to prosecute every international crime in the world, nor is it intended to deal with all international crimes in the territory, or committed by a

Council', pp. 149–51; Morten Bergsmo and Jelena Pejić, 'Article 16', in Otto Triffterer (ed.), *Commentary on the Rome Statute of the International Criminal Court: Article by Article* (Baden-Baden: Nomos, 1999), p. 373.

197 Those with a taste for polemic can refer to John R. Bolton, 'The Risks and Weaknesses of the International Criminal Court From an American Perspective' (2000–2001) 41 VJIL 186. Those with a penchant for dyspepsia may turn to Jeremy Rabkin, 'Worlds Apart on International Justice' (2002) 15 LJIL 835.

198 See Giuliano Turone, 'Powers and Duties of the Prosecutor', in Antonio Cassese, Paula Gaeta and John R. W. D. Jones (eds.), *The Rome Statute of the International Criminal Court: A Commentary* (Oxford: Oxford University Press, 2002), p. 1137, pp. 1159–62. As noted at p. 1161, the grounds for refusal of such authorisation are limited and largely apolitical.

199 ICC Statute, Article 42(1). For suggestions about how the prosecutor might look to act, see Allison Marston Danner, 'Enhancing the Legitimacy and Accountability of Prosecutorial Discretion at the International Criminal Court' (2003) 97 AJIL 510. See also Håkan Friman, 'Investigation and Prosecution', in Roy S. Lee (ed.), *The International Criminal Court: Elements of Crimes and Rules of Procedure and Evidence* (Ardsley: Transnational, 2000), p. 493.

200 See Turone, 'Powers and Duties', pp. 1159–61.

201 See Richard Goldstone and Nicola Fritz, '"In the Interests of Justice" and Independent Referral: The ICC Prosecutor's Unprecedented Powers' (2000) 13 LJIL 655; Christopher Keith Hall, 'The Powers and Role of the Prosecutor of the International Ciminal Court in the Global Fight Against Impunity' (2004) 17 LJIL 121; Antonio Cassese, 'The Rome Statute: A Tentative Assessment', in Antonio Cassese, Paula Gaeta and John R. W. D Jones (eds.), *The Rome Statute of the International Criminal Court: A Commentary* (Oxford: Oxford University Press, 2002), p. 1901, p. 1910.

202 Silvia Fernández de Gurmendi, 'The Role of the International Prosecutor', in Roy S. Lee (ed.), *The International Criminal Court: The Making of the Rome Statute* (The Hague: Kluwer, 1999), p. 175, p. 181.

national, of a State party to the Rome Statute. It is not even intended to try a representative sample of such offences. The drafters of the Rome Statute, in seeking to limit the authority of the court when compared to the *ad hoc* Tribunals and their primacy, gave the ICC a slightly different role. Ironically, that role is one which may well have a greater impact on prosecution of international crimes than if the suggestion that international courts should take the lion's share of the cases of international crimes,[203] a role neither they nor the ICC could have taken anyway, had been taken up. The ICC's mandate is to promote domestic prosecutions of international crimes, primarily through the mechanism of complementarity.

The outcome of complementarity is that if the Prosecutor becomes interested in a situation subject to the jurisdiction of the ICC, then although he cannot force the parties to prosecute any offenders, steps can be taken to prompt the relevant States into taking action. This is because States, particularly in relation to offences by their nationals, are more likely to prefer to investigate at the national level, rather than have an investigation proceeded with in public by an independent international investigator.[204] The powers of the Prosecutor to investigate offences and oversee national investigations could be used by a diligent Prosecutor to ensure that offences were investigated in an impartial manner. Important in this regard are the powers of the ICC not only to embarrass States severely by determining them to be unwilling or unable to prosecute, but also to prosecute offences committed by their nationals or committed on their territory (but particularly the former) in a very public forum. The Proscutor's role here is bolstered by Articles 18(3) and 18(5). Article 18(3) allows the Prosecutor to review a deferral to a State after six months 'or at any time when there has been a significant change of circumstances based on the State's unwillingness

203 See Bernard V. A. Röling, 'The Law of War and the National Jurisdiction Since 1945' (1960–II) 100 RdC 329, 355: 'it is for the very reason that war crimes are violations of the laws of war, that is, international law, an international judge should try international offences'.

204 A useful discussion of this is contained in Bruce Broomhall, *International Justice and the International Criminal Court: Between State Sovereignty and the Rule of Law* (Oxford: Oxford University Press, 2003), pp. 86–93. See also Daryl Mundis, 'The Rome Statute and its Impact on National Law', in Antonio Cassese, Paula Gaeta and John R. W. D. Jones (eds.), *The Rome Statute of the International Criminal Court: A Commentary* (Oxford: Oxford University Press, 2002), p. 1849, p. 1860–1. For an early assertion of the likely impact of the Rome Statute on prosecution, see David Turns, 'Prosecuting Violations of International Humanitarian Law: The Legal Position in the United Kingdom' (1999) 4 JACL 1, 3.

or inability genuinely to carry out the investigation'. Further to this, Article 18(5) provides that '[w]hen the Prosecutor has deferred an investigation in accordance with paragraph 2, the Prosecutor may request that the State concerned periodically inform the Prosecutor of the progress of its investigations and any subsequent prosecutions'. States party to the Rome Statute must answer these requests 'without undue delay'.[205] Therefore despite the strong nature of the complementarity regime, the Prosecutor is able to keep up the threat of a complementarity determination being made against a State throughout the prosecution of international crimes in a State. The right to require updates on the prosecutions in a State not only assists the Prosecutor in keeping an eye on national proceedings, but should also serve as a reminder to States that someone is watching and appraising the proceedings. This, in itself, is a strong incentive to prosecute international crimes properly. Thus although the Prosecutor cannot force a State to prosecute, the supervisory aspect of complementarity allows him to make failure to prosecute uncomfortable and risky. This reduces the opportunity for cheating (non-prosecution, or sham/shielding trials, or delays or proceedings inconsistent with an intention to bring the person to justice), and provides a monitoring mechanism by which such cheating may be discovered.

One of the primary problems the ILA identified with universal jurisdiction was the absence of a supervisory mechanism.[206] Mireille Delmas-Marty also considers harmonisation of activity in international criminal law 'indispensable', and that the 'key to harmonization is the acceptance of a State's margin of appreciation, guaranteeing a certain level of discretion, and the organization of a supervisory mechanism avoiding excessive divergence from that margin'.[207] As this quote implies, the problem is one which is also pertinent to all prosecutions of international crimes, but particularly in relation to nationality, territoriality and passive personality jurisdiction. Therefore the creation of a supervisory mechanism (the ICC in general and the Prosecutor in particular) is an extraordinary and welcome step.

[205] Daniel D. Ntanda Nsereko, 'Article 18', in Otto Triffterer (ed.), *Commentary on the Rome Statute of the International Criminal Court: Article by Article* (Baden-Baden: Nomos, 1999), p. 395. Nsereko questions if this obligation applies if the States referred to are not parties to the Statute, p. 399. Young, 'Surrender', 326, mentions only State parties.

[206] ILA Report, pp. 420–1.

[207] Mireille Delmas-Marty, 'The ICC and the Interaction of International and National Legal Systems', in Antonio Cassese, Paula Gaeta and John R. W. D. Jones (eds.), *The Rome Statute of the International Criminal Court: A Commentary* (Oxford: Oxford University Press, 2002), p. 1915, p. 1928.

The granting of authority to the Prosecutor to initiate investigations, albeit with the requirement of the authorisation by a pre-Trial chamber, is a considerable move in international criminal law towards what Sir Gerald Fitzmaurice described in 1976 as an 'integrated system of norms'.[208] The concept of integrated norms relies on the idea that normally systems of rules are bilateral, in that only those States which can directly claim to be affected by a breach of the relevant rule of international law are entitled to demand reparation. In integrated systems of rules, however, the parties to an integrated regime have agreed that there is a common interest in the vindication of the norms involved, and expand the number of States or other parties capable of supervising compliance or considering themselves affected by violations. The latter aspect of integrated norms overlaps, although not entirely, with the concept of *erga omnes* obligations.

Beyond this, though, the creation of an independent third party who exists for the purpose of monitoring compliance, and initiating legal responses to violations, is a very strong form of integration in a regime. Not only have parties agreed that they all have an interest in ensuring the relevant norms are upheld, but they have further empowered an independent third party to oversee compliance (i.e. the practice of national prosecutions), who may initiate proceedings without additional State consent should he determine that it is necessary.[209] The creation of the office of the Prosecutor, with the right to initiate investigations with no State's leave is thus not only a large development in the enforcement of international criminal law, but is also a large part of the constitution of an integrated regime of international criminal law enforcement. This is really a rather strong element of the structure set up by the Rome Statute, which makes the Rome regime worthy of the name.

The caveat that, in the main, this concerns only States party is a large one. If the Security Council does not pass a matter to the Prosecutor then the extent of the ICC's jurisdiction is limited to the territory and nationals of States party, so unless the Statute reaches a near-universal level of acceptance, this will remain a partial solution. It is unfortunate that non-States party may require the Prosecutor to defer to them, and have the right to be informed of an investigation, but are unlikely to be

208 A readily available and helpful discussion of the notion may be found in Joost Pauwelyn, *Conflict of Norms in International Law: How WTO Law Related to Other Rules of International Law* (Cambridge: Cambridge University Press, 2003), pp. 52–69.

209 The Prosecutor, as we have seen, is being careful not to push this aspect of his role too hard in the early days of the ICC, for strong pragmatic reasons.

under a duty to provide the information mentioned in Article 18(5).[210] An obligation to do so could have been created without violating the *pacta tertiis* principle. This is because an obligation could have been made a condition of a non-State party being able to require deferral. As Simon Young has noted, Article 36 of the Vienna Convention on the Law of Treaties requires non-parties seeking to enforce rights to 'do so in the prescribed manner, with the attendant duties and obligations'.[211] There would seem to be nothing objectionable about requiring a State that seeks to prevent the ICC from acting not to remove the case entirely from the effective supervision of that Court.

The fact that the Prosecutor can start investigating only crimes over which the ICC has jurisdiction also shows the link between the substantive law and procedure. The Prosecutor has been granted authority to supervise prosecutions of certain rules of international criminal law. The precise scope of those will be investigated later; for the moment, it suffices to note that the level of authority granted to the Prosecutor and the scope of the law the Prosecutor was to be able to enforce were directly linked in the negotiations for the ICC Statute.[212]

Incorporation and harmonisation of international criminal law

To move on to another major problem noted in chapter 2, a considerable hurdle to the enforcement of international criminal law is the failure of States to live up to their obligations to incorporate international crimes into their domestic legal order. This is particularly important; as Hilary Charlesworth and Christine Chinkin observe; 'the practical value of international standards depends largely on their implementation into domestic legal systems'.[213] Regime theory also accepts the important role that implementation of international norms into national systems and decision making fora plays. There have been calls for greater work on the mechanisms by which international regimes ensure that their norms are brought into domestic orders.[214] The express incorporation of

[210] Turone, 'Powers and Duties', considers the granting of the rights of non-States parties here as 'frankly unacceptable' as they have refused to join the ICC system and are involved in the situation, thus 'might have no other interest than simply preventing justice from being done', p. 1163.

[211] Young, 'Surrender', 338. [212] Kirsch and Robinson, 'Initiation of Proceedings', p. 663.

[213] Hilary Charlesworth and Christine Chinkin, *The Boundaries of International Law: A Feminist Analysis* (Manchester: Manchester University Press, 2000), p. 113.

[214] Freidrich Kratchowil, 'Contract and Regimes: Do Issue Specificity and Variations of Formality Matter?', in Volker Rittberger (ed.), *Regime Theory and International Relations* (Oxford: Clarendon, 1993), p. 73, pp. 88–9.

international criminal law into domestic systems is particularly the case in criminal law, where Courts have shown themselves reluctant to rely directly on customary international law to create domestic crimes.[215] Even where they have done so and where there are no questions of a State's good faith, there are also the problems that accompany differing interpretations of international criminal law in different States. A system of enforcement of norms should have a coherent conception of what those norms are.[216] Otherwise, expectations do not converge on what behaviour is prohibited, or when the obligations for States are triggered.

To look first at the position that existed outside the 'Rome regime';[217] there is at least anecdotal evidence that the creation of the two *ad hoc* Tribunals has, through the increase in interest in international humanitarian law, led to States considering updating their international criminal law legislation.[218] This should not be surprising. Some of the earlier ICTs have had a profound effect on national understanding of customary international law. The Nuremberg Principles, which were developed by the ILC from the Nuremberg Charter and judgment, are widely considered to represent customary international law.[219] The declaration, in the judgment of the Nuremberg IMT that the Hague Convention IV, the rules attached to it and the 1929 Geneva Convention Relative to the Treatment of Prisoners of War are customary has been frequently cited as authoritative.[220] In contrast, the Tokyo IMT's discussion of law, insofar as it was not merely a recapitulation of that pronounced at Nuremberg, has not left such an *imprimatur* on custom, although the *ad hoc* Tribunals have made use of the judgment in relation to superior responsibility.[221]

[215] See above, p. 119.

[216] That is not to say that international criminal law is entirely coherent in its coverage (see Steven R. Ratner, 'The Schizophrenias of International Criminal Law' (1998) 33 TILJ 237), simply that the content of the norms is largely the same.

[217] On the difference between the law inside and outside the Rome Statute, see Leila Nadya Sadat, *The International Criminal Court and the Transformation of International Law: Justice for a New Millennium* (Ardsley: Transnational, 2002), pp. 269–71.

[218] See Theodor Meron, 'Remarks' (1996) 90 Proceedings ASIL 484, 484, and Djiena Wembou, 'The International Criminal Tribunal for Rwanda' (1997) 321 IRRC 685, 692.

[219] See below, p. 243.

[220] Leslie C. Green, *The Contemporary Law of Armed Conflict* (Manchester: Manchester University Press, 2nd edn., 2000), pp. 34, 113, 196, 291; Georges Abi-Saab, 'The 1977 Additional Protocols and General International Law: Some General Reflexions', in Astrid J. M. Delissen and Gerard J. Tanja (eds.), *Humanitarian Law of Armed Conflict: Challenges Ahead* (Dordrecht: Martinus Nijhoff, 1991), p. 115, p. 116.

[221] Before the creation of the UN Tribunals the only references to the law of the Tokyo IMT in the *International Law Reports* are references to the Tokyo Charter, alongside the

Moving forward, it might have been that even without the advent of the Rome Statute, international criminal law was beginning to come together in the 1990s because of the two *ad hoc* Tribunals' Statutes and judgments. It is clear, for example, that the ICTY's Statute has contributed to the development and clarification of customary international law.[222] Its case law, especially the *Tadić* jurisdictional appeal,[223] has often been accepted by States as declaratory of custom.[224]

Decisions by the ICTY have been used by States in the negotiations at Rome,[225] and on the Elements of Crimes.[226] UK courts, when prosecuting crimes under the International Criminal Court Act, are pointed towards the jurisprudence of international courts, including the ICTY and ICTR.[227] There is also evidence that the judgments have been used to assist in the preparation of national military manuals. W. Hays Parks comments that '[i]n my official capacity . . . one of my jobs is to draft substantial portions of the new United States Joint Services Law of War

Nuremberg Charter, in *re Albrecht* (1947) 14 AD 196, 198 and *DPP* v. *Polyukhovic* (1991) 91 ILR 1, 46–7. From the *ad hoc* Tribunals see, for example *Prosecutor* v. *Delalić, Delić Mucić and Landžo*, Judgment, IT-96-21-T, 16 November 1998, paras. 357–358; *Prosecutor* v. *Aleksovski*, Judgment, IT-95-14/1-T, 25 June 1999, paras. 77–78.

222 Theodor Meron, 'War Crimes in Yugoslavia and the Development of International Law' (1994) 88 AJIL 78.

223 *Prosecutor* v. *Tadić*, Decision on Interlocutory Appeal on Jurisdiction, IT-94-1-AR72, 2 October 1995.

224 Theodor Meron, 'The Continuing Role of Custom in the Formulation of Humanitarian Law', in Theodor Meron, *War Crimes Law Comes of Age* (Oxford: Oxford University Press, 1998), p. 262; Christopher J. Greenwood, 'The Development of International Humanitarian Law by the International Criminal Tribunal for the Former Yugoslavia' (1998) 2 MPYBUNL 97, 122–33; Payam Akhavan, 'The Dilemmas of Jurisprudence' (1998) 13 AUJILP 1518; Pamela D Alesky, 'The Yugoslav War Crimes Tribunal and International Humanitarian Law' (1998) 35 IP 1, 13; Sean D. Murphy, 'Progress and Jurisprudence of the International Criminal Tribunal for the Former Yugoslavia' (1999) 93 AJIL 57, 63.

225 See Payam Akhavan, 'Contributions of the International Criminal Tribunals for the Former Yugoslavia and Rwanda to Development of Definitions of Crimes Against Humanity and Genocide' (2000) 94 Proceedings ASIL 270, 280; Theodor Meron, 'The Hague Tribunal: Working to Clarify International Humanitarian Law' (1998) 13 AUJILP 1511, 1538. See also Daryl Robinson, 'Defining Crimes Against Humanity at the Rome Conference' (1999) 93 AJIL 45, 45; Dominic McGoldrick, 'The Permanent International Criminal Court: An End to the Culture of Impunity?' [1999] Crim LR 627, 636; Hermann Von Hebel and Daryl Robinson, 'Crimes Within the Jurisdiction of the Court', in Roy S. Lee (eds.), *The International Criminal Court: The Making of the Rome Statute* (The Hague: Kluwer, 1999), pp. 79, 93.

226 See, for example, Valerie Oosterveld, 'The Elements of Genocide', in Roy S. Lee (ed.), *Elements of Crimes and Rules of Procedure and Evidence* (Ardsley: Transnational, 2001), p. 41, p. 44.

227 ICC Act, section 50(2).

Manual. It is going to be very comprehensive. I can tell you that the cases to date have been absolute gold mines of information to me. They have assisted me very substantially in my drafting.'[228] There have even been comments made to the effect that the ICTY focuses a little too much on elaborating the law and not enough on ensuring justice for the individual defendants.[229] Whatever the merits of that claim, the ICTY has beyond doubt made a significant contribution to the development and elaboration of customary law.

The ICTR's Statute, where it differs from the ICTY's (principally on the express inclusion of war crimes in non-international armed conflict) has successfully militated against the position still quite prevalent at the time, that war crimes were limited to international armed conflicts.[230] There are signs that the ICTR's case law has also affected States' thinking on international crimes.[231] The findings of the ICTR in the *Akayesu* Case were heavily relied on in Switzerland in the *Niyontenze* Case, for example.[232] A further sign that the ICTY and ICTR's cases may have made a significant contribution to the corpus of international criminal law may be found in Article 20(3) of the Special Court of Sierra Leone's Statute, which allows the Special Court to be guided by the decisions of the joint ICTY/ICTR Appeals Chamber. The Special Court has therefore said that it 'will apply the decisions of the ICTY and ICTR for their persuasive value, with necessary modifications and adaptations, taking into account the particular circumstances of the Special Court'.[233]

As should be clear, it might have been that even without the Rome Statute some of the problems of consistency would have been alleviated,

[228] W. Hays Parks, 'Comments' (1998) 13 AUJILP 1531, 1532.

[229] Leslie C. Green, 'Drazen Erdemović: The International Criminal Tribunal for the Former Yugoslavia in Action' (1997) 10 LJIL 363, 376.

[230] See below, pp. 266–7.

[231] Oosterveld, 'The Elements of Genocide', p. 46; For suggestions that the ICC follow some ICTR practice on procedural matters, see Adama Dieng, 'International Criminal Justice From Paper to Practice: A Contribution from the International Criminal Tribunal for Rwanda to the Establishment of the International Criminal Court' (2001–2) 25 Fordham ILJ 688, 700–7.

[232] Luc Reydams, *Universal Jurisdiction: International and Municipal Legal Perspectives* (Oxford: Oxford University Press, 2003), p. 200.

[233] See *Brima, Kamara and Kanu*, Written Reasons for the Trial Chamber's Oral Decision on the Defence Motion on Abuse of Process due to Infringement of Principles of *Nullum Crimen Sine Lege* and Non-Retroactivity as to Several Counts, SCSL-04-16-PT, 31 March 2004, para. 25; see generally, paras. 19–26.

since the ICTs have attempted to create a detailed set of decisions primarily based on custom, and consistent with each other.[234] With both the ICTY and ICTR, however, the effect their jurisprudence might have had in the absence of the Rome Statute is difficult to establish, and the unwillingness of the Kosovan and East Timorese courts to refer to ICTY and ICTR decisions shows that celebration would be premature.

The ICC may be expected to have a greater promotional role for the incorporation of international crimes into domestic legal systems than the *ad hoc* Tribunals. This is because if a State wishes to prevent its nationals (or offences occurring on its territory) from being prosecuted in a very high-profile international forum, then it must prosecute them itself. To do this, it must have the legal means at its disposal to prosecute such offences. Complementarity thus creates an incentive for States to incorporate the crimes enunciated in the Rome Statute.[235] Although using as the basis of prosecutions common national law crimes such as murder would not necessarily be contrary to the Rome Statute, there is a risk that using such crimes might invite complementarity challenges.[236]

There are those who argue that there is a duty to implement the crimes in the Rome Statute.[237] This is doubtful, as such a position relies on inducting an obligation from the preamble of the Statute and the assertion that the fact that many parties have implemented those crimes into their national legal orders is evidence of an agreement between the parties that there is such an obligation. Preambles are useful in interpreting treaties,[238] but it is stretching the normative force of a preamble to use it as evidence of a duty which has no basis in the operative part of

[234] On precedent in the ICTY and ICTR, see Claire Harris, 'Precedent in the Practice of the ICTY', in Richard May *et al.* (eds.), *Essays on ICTY Procedure and Evidence in Honour of Gabrielle Kirk McDonald* (The Hague: Kluwer, 2001), p. 341 and Xavier Tracol, 'The Precedent of Appeals Chambers Decision on the International Criminal Tribunals' (2004) 17 LJIL 67.

[235] For example, ILA Report, p. 414; Darryl Robinson, 'The ICC Statute and Its Impact on National Law', in Antonio Cassese, Paula Gaeta and John R. W. D. Jones (eds.), *The Rome Statute of the International Criminal Court: A Commentary* (Oxford: Oxford University Press, 2002), p. 1849, pp. 1860–1; Katherine L. Doherty and Timothy L. H. McCormack, 'Complementarity as a Catalyst for Comprehensive Domestic Penal Legislation' (1999) 5 UCDJIL 147.

[236] Robinson, 'The ICC Statute', pp. 1861–2; Jann K. Kleffner, 'The Impact of Complementarity on National Implementation of Substantive International Criminal Law' (2003) 1 JICJ 86, 95–100.

[237] Kleffner, 'The Impact of Complementarity', 90–4.

[238] 1969 Vienna Convention on the Law of Treaties, Article 31(2).

the treaty. As for the State practice, it is equally explainable by the fact that the Statute creates a strong practical interest for States to incorporate ICC crimes, rather than a legal obligation to do so.

Whether there is a duty to incorporate or simply a strong pragmatic interest in doing so, the benefits of increased incorporation will accrue from the coming into being of the ICC. Such incorporation may extend beyond the States party. Non-party nationals can become subject to the jurisdiction of the Court if they commit a crime within its jurisdiction on the territory of a State party to the Statute. So, non-party States may consider it expedient to introduce such legislation, to ensure that they can prosecute their nationals for international crimes as defined in the Rome Statute, to prevent them being tried at the international level. There is evidence that this sort of thinking has begun in non-ratifying States.[239]

Another positive aspect of this line of thought could be that a fairly uniform corpus of law is in place over a large number of States, thus alleviating the problems identified above about the non-standard nature of national implementation of international criminal law. There are those, such as José Alvarez, who doubt that international criminal law should be made uniform, and instead ought to reflect local differences.[240] Minor local differences are not of concern; as Delmas-Marty has said, a limited margin of appreciation is perhaps not too objectionable.[241] But there are strong reasons in favour of harmonising the domestic application of international criminal law.

If international criminal law is to be a common criminal law of mankind, wildly divergent interpretations of that law across the globe are an anathema.[242] It is imperative for a regime that the norms are reasonably uniform, otherwise the necessary actors' expectations will not accurately converge, but reflect different understandings of acceptable behaviour. As was found in chapter 2, '[t]he trial of war criminals under local law leads to a diversity of substantive law such that an act may be punished as a war crime in one country but not in

239 See David J. Scheffer, 'A Negotiator's Perspective on the International Criminal Court' (2001) 167 Military LR 1, 15–17; Douglas Cassell, 'The Need to Expand US Domestic Jurisdiction to Prosecute Genocide, War Crimes, and Crimes Against Humanity' (1999) 23 Fordham ILJ 378.

240 José E. Alvarez, 'Crimes of Hate/Crimes of State: Lessons from Rwanda' (1999) 24 Yale JIL 365, 418–36.

241 Delmas-Marty, 'The ICC', p. 1915, p. 1928.

242 See also William A. Schabas, 'National Courts Finally Begin to Prosecute Genocide, the "Crime of Crimes"' (2003) 1 JICJ 39, 63.

another'.[243] Here what is being prosecuted is an international rather than a pure domestic crime. If the idea that national courts are acting as part of the international legal order in prosecuting these crimes has any purchase,[244] the law must surely be at least similar to international law.[245] Perhaps more importantly, where the jurisdiction being asserted is universality or passive personality (to the extent that the latter may be limited to international crimes) considerations of fairness to individuals arise. The criticism that it is inappropriate to subject a person to the laws of many different States is one which has purchase, but may be rejected when the law applicable is uniform, so that substantively the accused is not subject to differing standards or rules that he or she could not reasonably discern.[246] The harmonisation of international criminal law therefore serves to ensure that the applicable law is discoverable and based on generally accepted standards, rather than national idiosyncrasies or aberrations. The Rome Statute has certainly made a contribution to this process.

However, whether this development can be fully welcomed must also depend on an analysis of whether or not the Rome Statute's formulations of the applicable law are accurate restatements of customary international law.[247] The Rome Statute contains very detailed definitions of international crimes and general principles of liability. The French Constitutional Court is of the opinion that the definitions are detailed enough to overcome any *nullum crimen sine lege* issues.[248] Rather like the ILC Articles on State Responsibility, the seductively concrete form of the rules in the Rome Statute invites the conclusion that these rules represent custom.[249] As a treaty drafted at a large multilateral conference,

[243] Richard R. Baxter, 'The Municipal and International Legal Bases of Jurisdiction Over War Crimes' (1951) 28 BYBIL 382, 387–8.

[244] See above, p. 85.

[245] See also Ian Brownlie, *International Law and the Use of Force by States* (Oxford: Clarendon, 1963), p. 207.

[246] Something overlooked by Reydams, *Universal Jurisdiction*, p. 224, when critiquing universal jurisdiction from this angle.

[247] See Robert Cryer, 'General Principles of Liability in International Criminal Law', in Dominic McGoldrick, Peter Rowe and Eric Donnelly (eds.), *The Permanent International Criminal Court: Legal and Policy Issues* (Oxford: Hart, 2004), p. 233, pp. 233–5.

[248] See Beate Rudolf, 'International Decisions: Statute of the International Criminal Court' (2000) 94 AJIL 391, 392–3.

[249] On this aspect of the ILC Articles, see David D. Caron, 'The ILC Articles on State Responsibility: The Paradoxical Relationship Between Form and Authority' (2002) 96 AJIL 857, 867–70. The analogy cannot be exact, however, as the Rome Statute is a treaty.

there is also a fair argument to be made that it will be likely to be treated as an 'artefact of international legal knowledge', a previously agreed form of words to be drawn upon for future use.[250] Care must be taken when doing this, or treating the treaty as reflective of pre-existing custom, as if the relevant treaty contains narrower formulations than customary law, this can stymie the development of custom thereafter.[251]

It is true that Article 10 of the Rome Statute at least attempts to attenuate the force of the Statute on customary international law. However, the legal position of the Rome Statute in relation to custom was perhaps best summed up by the Trial Chamber in the *Furundžija* Case, in their statement that:

> In many areas the Statute may be regarded as indicative of the legal views, i.e. *opinio juris* of a great number of States. Notwithstanding article 10 of the Statute, the purpose of which is to ensure that existing or developing law is not 'limited' or 'prejudiced' by the Statute's provisions, resort may be had *cum grano salis* to these provisions to help elucidate customary international law. Depending on the matter at issue, the Rome Statute may be taken to restate, reflect or clarify customary rules or crystallise them, whereas in some areas it creates new law or modifies existing law. At any event, the Rome Statute by and large may be taken as constituting an authoritative expression of the legal views of a great number of States.[252]

Unfortunately, as we shall see, the definitions of crimes in the Rome Statute only partially reflect pre-Rome customary international law. Although arguments about law were taken very seriously in Rome,[253]

[250] On this process, see Annelise Riles, 'Models and Documents: Artefacts of International Legal Knowledge' (1999) 48 ICLQ 805, 813–14.

[251] See Hugh W. A. Thirlway, *International Customary Law and Codification* (Leiden: Sitjhoff, 1972), pp. 125–6. An interesting question, given the development of international criminal law by the ICTY and ICTR, was if the subject was quite ripe for an attempt at even partial codification in 1998 (although to wait would also not have been advisable, as the chance to establish an ICC could have passed). For a suggestion that the ILC should not have codified the Nuremberg Principles until the Control Council Law 10 courts had ended their work, see Richard R. Baxter, 'The Effects of Ill-Conceived Codification and Development of International Criminal Law', in Faculté de Droit International de l'Université de Genèvé (eds.), *Recueil d'Etudes de Droit International en Homage à Paul Guggenheim* (Geneva: Tribune de Genèvé, 1968), p. 146, p. 152.

[252] *Prosecutor* v. *Furundžija*, Judgment, IT-95-17/1-T, 10 December 1998, para. 227. This was supported in *Prosecutor* v. *Tadić*, Judgment, IT-94-1-A, 15 July 1999, para. 223, but did not go unchallenged; Judge Shahabuddeen reserved his position on the matter (Separate Opinion of Judge Shahabuddeen, para. 3).

[253] See Gerry Simpson, 'Politics, Sovereignty, Remembrance', in Dominic McGoldrick, Peter Rowe and Eric Donnelly (eds.), *The Permanent International Criminal Court: Legal and Policy Issues* (Oxford: Hart, 2004), p. 47, p. 51.

codification by States in a multilateral treaty making context also involves the art of compromise, which may lead to an incomplete or anaemic codification.[254] The ambit of prohibited conduct within the Rome Statute is at times more limited than customary law.[255] Also, the Rome Statute, at least in relation to war crimes, is an incomplete codification of the area. Those war crimes not contained in the Statute will not only become sidelined at the international level, but may also be so in national jurisdictions. States are likely to enshrine versions of international crimes into their national law which are more limited than general international law. As has been said by Bruce Broomhall, 'the resulting incentive of States to take action through national courts . . . [is] circumscribed by the scope of these definitions'.[256] This may render important war crimes not contained in the Rome Statute prone to being overlooked; and that which is overlooked may atrophy.[257]

In relation to the possibility that, despite Article 10, the Rome Statute may lead to a narrowing of custom, this is possible, although the process is by no means easy. Nonetheless, it is noteworthy that in 1930 a number of States were concerned about the inter-relationship of partial codifications (which the Rome Statute is) and the maxim *expressio unius exclusio alterius*. This was on the ground that it could lead to 'a colourable case against a long established rule of customary law on the ground that it was not expressly stated in the convention'; a point to which Jennings adds: 'Such an argument may not be easy to counter when it is remembered how indecisive the evidences of customary law can be.'[258]

It is possible that in certain areas of international criminal law treaties have in the past had a retrograde effect on the law. The definition of genocide contained in the 1948 Convention on the Prevention and

[254] Francis Lieber was of the view that codification was far too important a matter to be left to governments; see Ernest Nys, 'The Codification of International Law' (1911) 5 AJIL 871, 886–7. Lauterpacht was less convinced, see 'Codification and Development of International Law' (1955) 49 AJIL 16, 31–5. He was not entirely consistent on this point, however; see A. W. Brian Simpson, 'Hersch Lauterpacht and the Genesis of the Age of Human Rights' (2004) 120 LQR 49, 68, 73.

[255] See chapters 5 and 6, *passim*; Shahabuddeen in *Prosecutor* v. *Hadžihasanović Alagic and Kubura*, Decision on Interlocutory Appeal in Relation to Command Responsibility, IT-01-47-AR72, 16 July 2003, para. 38.

[256] Broomhall, *International Justice*, p. 77.

[257] Kleffner, 'The Impact of Complementarity', 100, is of the view that those customary crimes outside the Rome Statute may fall into desuetude.

[258] Robert Y. Jennings, 'The Progressive Development of International Law and its Codification' (1947) 24 BYBIL 310, 305.

Punishment of the Crime of Genocide is somewhat narrower than that contained in General Assembly Resolution 96(I).[259] In particular, despite that resolution recognising genocide as an existing crime including the protection of social and political groups, these groups are excluded from the Convention, and the definition in the Convention, rather than the resolution, is taken as customary.[260] It is also arguable that the Trial Chamber in *Čelebići* interpreted Article 86 of Additional Protocol I as having a limiting effect on customary international law.[261] In neither of these instances, though, did the treaty contain a clause similar to Article 10. Nonetheless, as we shall see, at times the ICTY, the ICTR and others have treated the ICC Statute as evidence of a more limited view of custom than asserted by others or adopted language from the Rome Statute uncritically.

In cases where the Rome Statute's definitions are narrower than customary law, and where defences are more widely drawn than international law requires, it is feasible that a person would be entitled to an acquittal under the Rome Statute, or national laws following it, when general international law would not require such a result. This includes the position when the Security Council sends a situation to the ICC rather than setting up an *ad hoc* tribunal with broader material jurisdiction. The Security Council does not have the authority to add crimes to the ICC Statute.[262] In jurisdictions following the Rome definitions and list of crimes, some offences will not be prosecuted with appropriate definitions, while others will not be prosecuted at all.

The reception of the Rome Statute

To test this, admittedly somewhat downbeat, hypothesis, it is worth spending some time investigating how the Rome Statute has impacted

[259] UN Doc. A/64/Add 1.

[260] See, for example, William A. Schabas, *Genocide in International Law: The Crime of Crimes* (Cambridge: Cambridge University Press, 2000), pp. 102–6. For an argument that there has been a parallel *jus cogens* definition of genocide which covers these groups, see Beth van Schaak, 'The Crime of Political Genocide: Repairing the Genocide Convention's Blind Spot' (1996–1997) 106 Yale LJ 2259. Schabas' is the better view, but the point is not which is more appropriate as a definition of genocide, but that codification can lead to a narrowing of pre-existing law.

[261] *Čelebići*, paras. 390–393. On appeal, the Appeals Chamber held that the standards in the post-war jurisprudence and Article 86 were the same, *Čelebići* appeal, paras. 228–239.

[262] Luigi Condorelli and Santiago Villalpando, 'Can the Security Council Extend the ICC's Jurisdiction?', in Antonio Cassese, Paula Gaeta and John R. W. D. Jones (eds.), *The Rome Statute of the International Criminal Court: A Commentary* (Oxford: Oxford University Press, 2002), p. 571.

on definitions of international crimes in documents and cases that post-date 1998. Current indications are that the Rome Statute has, for the most part, appealed to States and others as providing a statement of customary law.[263] To start with the ICTY, despite the cautious phrasing of the *Furunžija* Case, and the doubts expressed on some aspects of the Rome Statute in some other decisions,[264] Chambers have been a little more willing to rely on the Rome Statute without caveat. It has been relied on without comment, for example, in the *Čelebići* appeal,[265] the *Aleksovski* Case,[266] and, at times, the *Kordić and Čerkez* Case.[267] In the latter instance, despite earlier refusals to accept that certain aspects of the Statute amounted to custom,[268] the Trial Chamber referred to one of the most controversial defences (defence of property) in the Rome Statute in Article 31(1)(c), without any comment on the controversy that surrounded it.

Perhaps the strongest affirmation of the normative impact of the Rome Statute in the ICTY came after the Rome Statute entered into force, in the *Hadžihasanović, Alagić and Kubura* decision in 2003.[269] In this decision, the majority held that: 'though by no means legally conclusive of the matter before us, [it] at least casts a major doubt on

[263] Jonathan Charney, 'Progress in International Criminal Law?' (1999) 93 AJIL 452, 454; see also Otto Triffterer, 'Article 10', in Otto Triffterer (ed.), *Commentary on the Rome Statute of the International Criminal Court* (Baden-Baden: Nomos, 1999), p. 315, p. 320. There is no jurisprudence from the ICC, but it can be implied from Article 21(2) of the Statute that the Court is intended to create a consistent body of law, which should have knock-on effects on the consistency of national prosecutions and law. On Article 21, see Margaret MacAuliffe de Guzman, 'Article 21', in Otto Triffterer (ed.), *Commentary on the Rome Statute of the International Criminal Court* (Baden-Baden: Nomos, 1999), p. 435, esp. p. 445.

[264] For example, the Trial Chamber in *Čelebići* seemed uncomfortable with the Rome Statute on command responsibility; *Prosecutor* v. *Delalić, Delić, Mucić and Landžo*, Judgment, IT-96-21-T, 16 November 1998, *Čelebići*, para. 393. See also *Prosecutor* v. *Kupreškić, Kupreškić, Josipović, Papić and Santić*, Judgment, IT-95-16-T, 14 January 2000, para. 580; *Prosecutor* v. *Kordić and Čerkez*, Judgment, IT 95-14/2-T, 26 February 2001, para. 197.

[265] *Prosecutor* v. *Delalić, Delić Mucić and Landžo*, Judgment, IT-96-21-A, 20 February 2001, para. 196. The footnote (to para. 223 of the *Tadić* appeal) repeats that the Statute is evidence of *opinio juris*, but without the limitations in the earlier cases.

[266] *Prosecutor* v. *Aleksovski*, Judgement, IT-95-14/1-A, 24 March 2000, para. 76; *Prosecutor* v. *Aleksovski*, Judgement, IT-95-14/1-T, 25 June 1999, para. 70. In both, it should be noted, the reliance placed on the Statute is, nonetheless, not heavy.

[267] *Prosecutor* v. *Kordić and Čerkez*, Judgment, IT-95-14/2-T, 26 February 2001, paras. 450–452.

[268] *Kordić and Čerkez*, para. 197.

[269] *Prosecutor* v. *Hadžihasanović, Alagić and Kubura*, Decision on Interlocutory Appeal in Relation to Command Responsibility, IT-01-47-AR72, 16 July 2003. For comment, see Christopher J. Greenwood, 'Command Responsibility and the Hadžihasanović Decision' (2004) 2 JICJ 598.

the view embraced by the dissenting Judges. (That the Rome Statute embodied a number of compromises among the States parties who drafted and adopted it hardly undermines its significance. The same is true of most major multilateral conventions.)'[270] Judge Hunt, on the other hand was clear that on the point at hand, the scope of command responsibility, owing to the 'vast differences between the provisions relating to military commanders and those relating to other superiors, and between those provisions and existing instruments such as the Statutes of the *ad hoc* Tribunals . . . the terms of Article 28 of the Rome Statute are of very limited value in determining the customary international law at the time relevant to these proceedings'.[271]

With respect to the majority, their position on this is questionable. Multilateral treaties may amount to evidence of customary international law.[272] However, the decision on whether or not a treaty reflects a particular customary rule needs evidence on the particular provision. As Richard Baxter made clear, 'even in the case of a treaty which speaks of codifying customary international law, there may be internal evidence that it is not in every respect declaratory of customary international law', and where this occurs, to say that the treaty is 'generally declaratory' 'do[es] not help . . . [as this] cast[s]on the interpreter of the treaty the obligation of determining which provisions are declaratory and which are not. The examination for that distinction requires an examination of customary international law, which was the very fact to be proven by reference to the Convention'.[273] The *travaux préparatoires* may be of assistance here, and the majority's strong assertion in relation to the Rome Statute is evidence of a trend towards seeing the Statute as saying more about custom than it does. This is particularly relevant as the majority in that Case used the Rome Statute to bolster their contention that customary law in relation to command responsibility was narrower than the minority intended.

The ICTR, on the other hand, has been rather reticent about the effect of the Rome Statute on customary law. It has noted provisions of the Rome Statute on a number of occasions without either relying

[270] *Hadžihasanović*, para. 53.

[271] *Hadžihasanović*, Separate and Partially Dissenting Opinion of Judge Hunt, paras. 31–32, see also Separate and Partially Dissenting Opinion of Judge Shahabuddeen, para. 38.

[272] See, for example, Mark E. Villiger, *Customary International Law and Treaties: A Manual on the Theory and Practice of the Interrelation of Sources* (The Hague: Kluwer, 2nd edn., 1997), pp. 225–48; Richard R. Baxter, 'Multilateral Treaties as Evidence of Customary International Law' (1965–6) 41 BYBIL 275.

[273] Baxter, 'Multilateral Treaties', 289–90.

heavily on it or referring to its effect on custom.[274] On other occasions, it has been pleaded in support of a position, again without any hint given of the weight accorded to it.[275] In one instance, looking at a controversial area of law (the applicability of command responsibility to civilian leaders), the ICTR has not only considered the Rome Statute 'instructive', but also adopted its controversial stance on a higher threshold of liability for civilians.[276] In this instance, if nothing else, the Rome Statute has impacted upon the decision making processes of the ICTR.

To move on to the reception of the Rome Statute among scholars, although many have noted the differences between the Rome Statute and customary international law,[277] others have been far more willing to accept the Rome Statute definitions at face value when it comes to custom.[278] Some academics have also gone further about the effect of the Rome Statute on international law. Leila Sadat, for example, goes as far as to argue that, in spite of Article 10, the Rome Conference acted in a 'quasi-legislative manner'.[279] Therefore the rules are a ground floor of all international criminal law on the basis not that any custom crystallised at Rome, but that the sources of international law have changed to allow such 'quasi-legislation'. The idea that sometimes a number of States can simply declare the law for everyone is one which has been raised fairly frequently in the post-Cold War era,[280] but is unconvincing. The sources of international law remain those declared in Article 38(1) of the ICJ

[274] *Prosecutor* v. *Rutaganda*, Judgment, ICTR-96-3-T, 6 December 1999, para. 65; *Prosecutor* v. *Musema*, Judgment, ICTR-96-13-T, 27 January 2000, para. 200; *Prosecutor* v. *Akayesu*, Judgment, ICTR-96-4-T, 2 September 1998, para. 577.

[275] *Prosecutor* v. *Semanza*, Judgment, ICTR-97-20-T, 15 May 2003, para. 348; *Prosecutor* v. *Bagilishema*, Judgment, ICTR-95-1A-T, 7 June 2001, para. 91; *Prosecutor* v. *Bagilishema*, Judgment, ICTR-95-1A-A, 3 July 2002; n. 56, however, notes the Prosecution suggestion that Article 28 of the Rome Statute is innovative.

[276] *Prosecutor* v. *Kayishema and Ruzindana*, Judgment, ICTR-95-1-T, 21 May 1999, paras. 227–228.

[277] See, for example, Antonio Cassese, *International Criminal Law* (Oxford: Oxford University Press, 2003), pp. 59–62, 91–4.

[278] Liesbeth Zegveld, for example, refers to the provision on war crimes in non-international armed conflicts as 'thoroughly listing' such offences; Liesbeth Zegveld, *Accountability of Armed Opposition Groups in International Law* (Cambridge: Cambridge University Press, 2002), p. 102.

[279] Leila Nadya Sadat, 'Custom, Codification and Some Thoughts About the Relationship Between the Two: Article 10 of the ICC Statute' (2000) 49 De Paul LR 909, 919 *contra*, for example, Kenneth S. Gallant, 'Jurisdiction to Adjudicate and Jurisdiction to Prescribe in International Criminal Courts' (2003) 48 Vil LR 763, 818–19.

[280] See, for example, Jonathan Charney, 'Universal International Law' (1993) 87 AJIL 529.

Statute.[281] They are an aspect of international order and, indeed, can help to protect foundational principles such as sovereign equality.[282] To argue that there was a revolution in the sources of international law in Rome, but that it was achieved '*sotto voce*, without an explicit or even implicit recognition by the surrounding infrastructures of the international and domestic legal orders'[283] asserts, against the strong evidence to the contrary, that new sources of international law may come about without the clearly expressed assent of States.

Moving next to official reports and internationalised tribunals, the position is mixed. For example, the Statute of the Special Court for Sierra Leone at times ignores, although not completely, the Rome Statute in its definitions of crimes.[284] However, at other times, the Rome Statute is taken rather quickly as an accurate statement of international criminal law. For example, Article 4 of the Special Court's Statute (dealing with war crimes) was 'pragmatically borrow[ed]' from Article 8(2)(e) of the Rome Statute.[285]

Further evidence of use of the Rome Statute may be found in the controversial Report of the Prosecution team looking into possible offences committed by NATO in Kosovo; the more limited definition of the crime of causing excessive collateral damage contained in Article 8(2)(b)(iv) was used to evaluate NATO's actions under customary international law rather than the standards in Additional Protocol I, which were previously thought customary.[286] In the report of the Commission of Experts on Cambodia, Articles 31–33 of the Rome Statute is described as a 'codification' of the defences applicable to international crimes.[287] As we

[281] See, for example, Clive Parry, *The Sources and Evidence of International Law* (Manchester: Manchester University Press, 1965), p. 109; Hugh Thirlway, 'The Sources of International Law', in Malcolm Evans (ed.), *International Law* (Oxford: Oxford University Press, 2003) p. 117, pp. 148–53.

[282] Nico Krisch, 'More Equal than the Rest? Hierarchy, Equality and US Predominance in International Law', in Georg Nolte and Michael Byers (eds.), *United States Hegemony and the Foundations of International Law* (Cambridge: Cambridge University Press, 2003), p. 135, pp. 142–4.

[283] Sadat, 'Custom', 923.

[284] See Cryer, 'A Special Court for Sierra Leone?' (2001) 50 ICLQ 435, 443–5.

[285] See *Prosecutor* v. *Fofana*, Decision on Preliminary Motion on Lack of Jurisdiction Materiae: Nature of the Armed Conflict, SCSL-2004-14-AR72(E), 25 May 2004, para. 28. This is a clear example of the use of the Rome Statute as an artefact of international legal knowledge.

[286] Final Report to the Prosecutor by the Committee Established to Review the NATO Bombing Campaign Against the Federal Republic of Yugoslavia (2000) 39 ILM 1257 paras. 50, 77. For comment see below, pp. 214–20.

[287] Report of the Group of Experts for Cambodia Established Pursuant to General Assembly Resolution 52/135, UN Doc. A/53/850-S/1999/231, para. 82, n. 46.

shall see, this may not be the case. When the Statute for the Cambodian Extraordinary Tribunals was promulgated, the Rome Statute was clearly an inspiration only for the definition of crimes against humanity.[288] Principles of liability and defences are far closer to those in the ICTY/ICTR Statutes.[289] The Courts in Kosovo apply domestic law, not based on the Rome Statute at all.

UNTAET Regulation 2000/15, on the prosecution of serious crimes in East Timor, adopts the definitions of crimes included in the Rome Statute *verbatim*, in particular, treating the list of war crimes as exhaustive.[290] Principles of liability and defences are partially taken from the Rome Statute; section 14, on individual criminal responsibility, section 15 on immunities, section 18 on the mental element and section 19 on exclusion of responsibility are all clearly drawn from the Rome Statute. Only section 16, on command responsibility, and section 21, on superior orders, differ substantially from the equivalent provisions in the Rome Statute. Again, as we shall see, some of the provisions copied here from the Rome Statute are narrower than customary law.[291]

The Statute, of the Iraq Special Tribunal is an interesting mix of the Rome Statute and other provisions. Article 11, on genocide, adopts the definitions from Articles II and III of the 1948 Genocide Convention.[292] Articles 12 and 13, however, are very clearly based on the definitions of crimes against humanity and war crimes in Articles 7 and 8 of the Rome Statute.[293] Notably there are no additional war crimes added to the list in Article 8 of the Rome Statute, despite that list being considered exemplary, rather than exhaustive, of customary war crimes. Like UNTAET Regulation 2000/15, principles of liability are regulated as in Article 25 of the Rome Statute,[294] while command responsibility and superior orders differ from their Rome counterparts.

[288] Draft Agreement Between the UN and the Royal Government of Cambodia Concerning the Prosecution Under Cambodian Law of Crimes Committed During the Period of Democratic Kampuchea, Article 9.

[289] Reach Kram NS/RKM/0801/12, Article 28.

[290] UNTAET Regulation 2000/15, 6 June 2000, Articles 4–6.

[291] In addition, section 18 is narrower than Article 30 of the Rome Statute, in that it does not include the savings clause 'unless otherwise provided' before requiring intention and knowledge for all elements of crimes.

[292] Statute of the Iraqi Special Tribunal, 10 December 2003.

[293] Differences being that certain crimes against humanity, such as Apartheid, are omitted from Article 12, and certain grammatical changes have been made to certain of the war crimes. One substantive difference is that violations of common Article 3 of the Geneva Conventions are rendered prosecutable irrespective of whether the conflict was international or not.

[294] Statute of the Iraqi Special Tribunal, Article 15(1–5).

To turn to States' domestic ICC implementation statutes, at the outset it should be noted that by no means all parties to the Rome Statute have implemented the Rome Statute crimes. Some, such as Finland, have taken the view that in practice, their pre-existing criminal law is sufficient.[295] Of those who have implemented, though, many have simply taken the Rome Statute definitions of crimes *verbatim*.[296] Others have taken implementing the Rome Statute as an opportunity to update their entire domestic legislation dealing with international crimes, drawing, in addition to crimes in the Rome Statute, on customary law, and also harmonising the language of the Rome Statute with their domestic terminology. The Australian International Criminal Court (Consequential Amendments) Act 2002 is a fairly restricted version of this approach.[297] In addition to the crimes contained in the Rome Statute, some of which are modified in line with customary law in the Act,[298] the Act also includes Grave Breaches of Additional Protocol I. Germany has also taken this route, and included not only those crimes in the ICC, but also included others thought to be customary, while also translating the crimes in the Rome Statute into domestic terminology.[299]

The most thoroughgoing incorporation of international crimes into the domestic legal order is Canada's Crimes Against Humanity and War

[295] Finland Progress Report to Council of Europe, Consult ICC/2001 13 Rev., pp. 4–5.

[296] For example, Malta (International Criminal Court Act 2002 cha. 4530 section 13), the United Kingdom (International Criminal Court Act 2002, sections 50, 51), New Zealand (International Crimes and International Criminal Court Act 2000, sections 9–12), South Africa (Implementation of the Rome Statute for the International Criminal Court Act 2002, Act No. 27 of 2002, section 39 and Schedules 1 and 2).

[297] International Criminal Court (Consequential Amendments) Act 2002, Act No. 42 of 2002.

[298] See, for example, ICC Act, Subdivision E, 268.38, which removes the 'clearly' qualifier from the war crime of causing excessive collateral damage in Article 8(2)(b)(iv) of the Rome Statute. The limitation in the Elements of Crimes that the actions must be in the context of a manifest pattern of genocidal conduct or effect destruction themselves is also not included in the Australian Act; see Gideon Boas, 'Implementation by Australia of the Statute of the International Criminal Court' (2004) 2 JICJ 179, 188.

[299] *Völkersträfgesetzbuch*, Federal Gazette 1 (2002) 2254, on which see Gerhard Werle and Florian Jessberger, 'International Criminal Justice is Coming Home: The New German Code of Crimes Against International Law' (2002) 13 CLF 191; Steffen Wirth, 'Germany's New International Crimes Code: Bringing a Case to Court' (2003) 1 JICJ 151. A very useful explanation of the German approach may be found in Andreas Zimmermann, 'Implementing the Statute of the International Criminal Court: The German Example', in Lal Chand Vohrah *et al.* (eds.), *Man's Inhumanity to Man: Essays in Honour of Antonio Cassese* (The Hague: Kluwer, 2003), p. 977.

Crimes Act.[300] After criminalising genocide and crimes against humanity, section 4 of the Act defines them as being genocide or crimes against humanity 'according to customary international law or conventional international law or by virtue of its being criminal according to the general principles of law recognized by the community of nations'.[301] War crimes are similarly defined as being war crimes 'according to customary international law or conventional international law applicable to armed conflicts'.[302] These definitions therefore go quite a long way beyond the Rome Statute, although to ensure that all crimes in the Rome Statute may be prosecuted, section 4(4) states that 'for greater certainty, crimes described in Articles 6 and 7 and paragraph 2 of Article 8 of the Rome Statute are, as of July 17, 1998, crimes according to customary international law. This does not limit or prejudice in any way existing or developing rules of international law'. The exclusion clause at the end of section 4(4), which is clearly based on Article 10 of the Rome Statute, thus allows Canadian courts to treat the Rome definitions as a ground floor of customary law, while allowing them to prosecute broader customary offences (or broader customary definitions of crime also included in the Rome Statute) where appropriate.

Turning to non-party States, at least two non-party States – Indonesia and Congo (Brazzaville) – have used the Rome definitions as a basis of their national legislation.[303] The influence of the Rome Statute and the Elements of Crimes on the US definitions of war crimes in Military Commission Instruction No. 2 is also palpable.[304] The similarity between the elements of Attacking Civilians in the Instruction and those for the same crime in the Elements of Crimes for the ICC is unmistakable. There are also a number of differences in the definitions, but the influence of the Rome Statute is clear.[305]

As can be seen from the foregoing, the Rome Statute has had a large influence on those involved in the drafting of documents dealing with international crimes, in particular domestic legislation, but also for the

[300] Crimes Against Humanity and War Crimes Act, 2000, c. 24. See William A. Schabas, 'Canadian Implementing Legislation for the Rome Statute' (2000) 3 YBIHL 337.

[301] Crimes Against Humanity and War Crimes Act, section 4(3). [302] *Ibid.*

[303] Indonesia: Law 26/2000, see Kleffner, 'The Impact of Complementarity', 110–11; Congo (Brazzaville), Law 8–98 of 31 October 1998 on the definition and repression of genocide, war crimes and crimes against humanity. See Jann K. Kleffner, 'Legislation' (1999) 2 YBIHL 350, 351. Congo (Brazzaville) ratified the Statute only in May 2004.

[304] Department of Defense Military Commission Instruction No. 2, 30 April 2003.

[305] Compare Military Commission Order 2, p. 5 with ICC-ASP/1/3, Elements for Article 8(2)(b)(i).

ICTY and at times the ICTR. The Rome Statute now appears to be forming the default definitions of international crimes when new documents are drafted. As was investigated in chapter 2, one of the reasonable critiques of universal jurisdiction (or passive personality jurisdiction) is that it can subject a defendant to a multiplicity of different sets of norms, and the practice of States in prosecuting international crimes has shown that at times different standards have been applied. The creation of a relatively standard set of definitions which appears to be gaining currency as, if nothing else, the first source of reference for those needing to define jurisdiction over international crimes, does provide an answer to such critiques. Although a person may be subject to a number of different fora for trial (in particular, if universal jurisdiction is being asserted), the law is relatively uniform and discoverable. That, so long as fair trial rights are upheld, largely exhausts what a defendant can legitimately claim prior to conviction.[306] The move towards harmonisation, however, must also be appraised with reference to what the harmonised law is.

Conclusion

As we reach the end of this part, it is worthwhile recapitulating some of the conclusions we have reached so far. As we saw earlier, many of the problems involved in prosecuting international crimes are by no means new. The gathering of evidence, and the questions of fairness in relation both to unfair trials for enemy nationals and undue lenience for home nationals have been quite consistent problems in the prosecution of international crimes – that is, when such crimes have been prosecuted. The vast majority of international crimes have not been prosecuted. There have been a number of reactions to this at the national level, including the development of universal jurisdiction and, in some instances, duties to prosecute international crimes. Universal jurisdiction has nonetheless been controversial, and duties to prosecute have mostly been ignored.

At the international level, there has been a number of developments, beginning in the first half of the twentieth century, in particular at the Nuremberg and Tokyo IMTs. The second wave of international development came about in the 1990s. Although a year before the start of that decade, the question of an international criminal court was revived, there was little impetus behind such a project. This changed after the

[306] If convicted, there are, naturally, a number of prisoners' rights which come into play.

creation of the two *ad hoc* international criminal Tribunals by the Security Council. The ICTY and ICTR showed that international criminal prosecution was possible, and provided a wealth of practice, which either framed the debate for an international criminal court or was taken as providing the answer to some of the problems. It would have been premature to assert that there was a comprehensive regime of international criminal law enforcement at the time.[307] Almost all the developments were *ad hoc* reactions to particular situations.

This could be seen to change with the creation of the International Criminal Court (ICC) in 1998. Although the ICC does not have a universal bailiwick,[308] among its parties it can be said to create a regime of international criminal law enforcement. The ICC is a prospective mechanism designed to endow the prosecution of international crimes at the national or international level with a set of norms and decision making processes.[309] The creation of a Prosecutor with powers to initiate investigations *proprio motu* creates a role in which an independent international official with quite wide powers is given authority by the States party to the Statute authority to oversee their prosecutions of international crimes and, should they be remiss, take remedial action which will ensure the prosecution of offences. This trigger mechanism is perhaps what singles out the ICC regime from almost all other regimes of international oversight, which require some form of trigger from outside the institution itself, and is the hallmark of a strong supranational streak in the ICC. This could lead to a strong regime being created – at the very least, one which fulfils the criterion of effectiveness prevalent in regime theory.

That said, the evidence (and suspect) gathering powers of the ICC are not especially strong,[310] and the strong complementarity regime of the ICC means that it will not, and is not intended to, take the lead role in the prosecution of international crimes; that role is for domestic courts. This is something well understood by the first Prosecutor of the ICC, Luis Moreno Ocampo, who has carefully set a path for the ICC which is

[307] Lyal Sunga, for example, judiciously entitled his 1997 work *The Emerging System of International Criminal Law*; Lyal S. Sunga, *The Emerging System of International Criminal Law* (The Hague: Kluwer, 1997).

[308] The Security Council can pass any situation in the world to the ICC, though, under Article 13(b) of the Rome Statute.

[309] Indeed, one which also defines the relationship between national and international courts through complementarity.

[310] Although the ICC's rights here are not as strong as those enjoyed by the ICTY and ICTR, they are stronger than traditional inter-State co-operation.

designed to maximise its practical role given its powers, while attempting to demonstrate to sceptical States that the ICC will not adopt an unfriendly attitude to them. This has been done by his reassurances that he will not be seeking to push the boundaries of the principle of complementarity, his creation of contacts with prosecutors in States and his attempts to obtain State co-operation and consent to early investigations such as those in the DRC and Uganda.

It is true that the regime set up in the Rome Statute is not a global one, although it has had some effects on non-parties, for two reasons. The first is that the ICC is the living embodiment of the ideals set out in its preamble, *inter alia*, 'such grave crimes threaten the peace, security and well-being of the world', 'the most serious crimes of concern to the international community as a whole must not go unpunished and that their effective prosecution must be ensured by taking measures at the national level and by enhancing international cooperation' and that preventing impunity will 'contribute to the prevention of such crimes'.[311] The creation of a permanent international body which embodies such values cannot but assist in serving to entrench those values, and affect behaviour.[312] These processes are traditionally referred to in relation to parties to an international institution; however, this process can also spill over. For example, it is clear that the experience of the EU was part of the inspiration for the transformation of the Organisation of African Unity (OAU) into the more strongly integrationist African Union (AU). The creation of the ICTY and ICTR doubtlessly spurred the creation of an ICC with far broader geographic jurisdiction, partly as the ideals embodied in those institutions appealed to a number of important international actors.

The spill-over effects of the ICC are also a function of the fact that it has some jurisdiction over non-party State nationals (when they commit crimes on States parties' territories or the Security Council passes jurisdiction to the ICC). This has led some non-party States to adopt legislation ensuring that they could prosecute international crimes. It has also, however, led to some States taking action to ensure that the ICC

[311] Rome Statute Preamble, paras. 3,4,5; see Otto Triffterer, 'Preamble', in Otto Triffterer (ed.), *Commentary on the Rome Statute of the International Criminal Court* (Baden-Baden: Nomos, 1999), p. 1, pp. 9–12; Slade and Clark, 'Preamble and Final Clauses', 426–27.

[312] See Andreas Hasenclever, Peter Mayer and Volker Rittburger, *Theories of International Regimes* (Cambridge: Cambridge University Press, 1997), pp. 142–8. On the ICC, see David Wippman, 'The International Criminal Court', in Christian Reus-Smit, *The Politics of International Law* (Cambridge: Cambridge University Press, 2003), p. 151, pp. 152–3.

could not obtain custody of any of its nationals irrespective of whether they were prosecuted. These latter developments relate to Article 98(2) and militate against any triumphalism. That there has been some third-party effect of the ICC, and the fact that the ideals it embodies have been entrenched for States party does not mean that the regime of international criminal law enforcement is truly global, or likely to become so soon. But there are signs of slow progress in this direction. Nonetheless, the fact that international crimes around the world cannot be prosecuted equally raises the possible critique of selective enforcement of the law, which is investigated in chapter 4.

Finally, in respect of the legitimate concern some have that universal jurisdiction could lead to an arbitrary determination of substantive law, there is evidence that at the least, the Rome Statute is being seen as the starting point for definitions of international crimes. Although harmonisation in such definitions is to be welcomed, this response should not be uncritical, as we also need to evaluate the harmonised law. Chapters 5 and 6 will be dedicated to doing just that, as part of a broader discussion of the legitimacy of this regime in part II of the book.

Part II Evaluating the regime

4 Selectivity in international criminal law

Since we have discussed the emergence of a regime of international criminal law enforcement, it is now time to appraise it. There are various ways in which the regime may be evaluated. It is possible, for example, to approach the regime from the point of view of its ability to protect the human rights of defendants.[1] Although a fruitful line of enquiry, this is not the framework adopted in this book. The method adopted here will be one derived from the rule of law. This seems particularly suited for investigating a legal regime, in that the rule of law is 'an important virtue which legal systems should possess'.[2]

What selective enforcement involves

Timothy McCormack rightly notes that 'there is a dual selectivity on the part of the international community. This selectivity is first found in relation to the acts the international community is prepared to characterise as "war crimes" and secondly, in relation to the particular alleged atrocities the international community is prepared to collectively prosecute.'[3] Chapters 5 and 6 will deal with issues related to the former critique. This chapter deals with the second part of McCormack's critique, selectivity *ratione personae*, although discussion will not be limited solely to collective efforts at prosecution.

[1] Colin Warbrick, 'International Criminal Courts and Fair Trial' (1998) 3 JACL 745; Salvatore Zappalà, *Human Rights in International Criminal Proceedings* (Oxford: Oxford University Press, 2003).

[2] Joseph Raz, 'The Rule of Law and Its Virtue', in Joseph Raz, *The Authority of Law: Essays on Law and Morality* (Oxford: Clarendon, 1970), p. 210, p. 211.

[3] Timothy L. H. McCormack, 'Selective Reaction to Atrocity' (1996–1997) 60 *Albany Law Review* 681, 683.

Kenneth Kulp Davis helpfully explains what selectivity means: 'when an enforcement agency or officer has discretionary power to do nothing about a case in which enforcement would be clearly justified, the result is a power of selective enforcement. Such power goes to selection of parties against whom the law is enforced. Selective enforcement may also mean selection of the law that will be enforced; an officer may enforce one statute fully, never enforce another and pick and choose in enforcing a third.'[4]

Selective enforcement of the law is not inherently wrong. The idea of prosecutorial discretion is established in many legal systems, in particular those in the Common Law or French-styled 'civilian' systems.[5] In 'civilian' systems following the German model the *legalitätprinzip* notionally requires the mandatory prosecution of all offences, but in practice there are frequent exceptions, in particular for minor offences.[6]

The reason for the *legalitätprinzip* is a worthy one: that political influence or expediency should not interfere with the equal application of the law.[7] However, as Kai Ambos notes, practicality means that '[e]ven if a strict mandatory prosecution is called for there are mechanisms of factual discretion since no criminal justice system has nowadays the capacity to prosecute all offences no matter how serious they are'.[8] The question is therefore not whether selective prosecution should occur, as it is essentially impossible that it does not, but when selective enforcement is unacceptable.[9] One answer would be when there is a duty to

[4] Kenneth Kulp Davis, *Discretionary Justice: A Preliminary Enquiry* (Baton Rouge: Louisiana State University Press, 1969), p. 163.

[5] See Brian A Grossman, 'The Role of the Prosecutor in Canada' (1970) 18 AJCL 498; Robert Vouin, 'The Role of the Prosecutor in French Criminal Trials' (1970) 18 AJCL 483; Shigemitsu Dando, 'System of Discretionary Prosecution in Japan' (1970) 19 AJCL 518. For an excellent study of prosecution in regulatory agencies in the United Kingdom, see Keith Hawkins, *Law as Last Resort: Prosecution Decision Making in a Regulatory Agency* (Oxford: Oxford University Press, 2003). In relation to police discretion, see Mike McConville, Andrew Sanders and Roger Leng, *The Case for the Prosecution* (London: Routledge, 1991). For comparison, see more generally the country reports in Louise Arbour, Albin Eser, Kai Ambos and Andrew Sanders (eds.), *The Prosecutor of a Permanent International Criminal Court* (Freiburg: edn. iuscrim, 2000), pp. 197–493 and Kai Ambos, 'Comparative Summary of the National Reports', in Arbour *et al.* (eds.), *The Prosecutor of a Permanent International Criminal Court* (Freiburg: edn. iuscrim, 2000), p. 495, pp. 505–9.

[6] See, for example, Ambos, 'Comparative Summary', pp. 507–9; Hans-Heinrich Jescheck, 'The Discretionary Powers of the Prosecuting Attorney in West Germany' (1970) 18 AJCL 508; Joachim Herrmann, 'The German Prosecutor', in Kenneth Kulp Davis, *Discretionary Justice in Europe and America* (Urbana: University of Illinois Press, 1976), p. 17.

[7] Herrmann, 'The German Prosecutor', p. 18.

[8] Ambos, 'Comparative Summary', p. 525.

[9] Davis, *Discretionary Justice*, pp. 167–8.

prosecute all such offences. It should not be forgotten that whenever a crime goes unpunished, there is an unrighted wrong to the victim and to the relevant society.

The critique of selective enforcement relates at the more general level to arbitrariness, part of which is taking irrelevant criteria into account.[10] This also includes discrimination, which is the taking into account of irrelevant and illegitimate criteria.[11] This includes cases where a political body interferes with a duly authorised prosecutor applying standards applied to all other cases. The underlying value implicated is equality: equality before the law and before courts and tribunals. This is a right accepted at the international level[12] and is clearly an appropriate criterion against which to evaluate a criminal enforcement regime.[13]

There are two aspects of selectivity *ratione personae*; the first legal-, the second legitimacy-based. The legal element of selectivity challenges was explained by the Appeals Chamber of the ICTY in the *Čelebići* appeal. In the course of rejecting Esad Landžo's claim that enforcement was unfairly selective the Appeals Chamber enunciated a general test for a plea of selective enforcement to be accepted at the ICTY. The test was enunciated as requiring the bringing of evidence '(i) establishing an unlawful or improper (including discriminatory) motive for the prosecution and (ii) establishing that other similarly situated persons were not prosecuted'.[14] This is a high threshold, similar to that usually adopted in common law systems.[15]

Proving a motive in particular is very difficult, although an improper, (or unlawful) motive may be evidenced by showing that the prosecutor has violated his or her duty of impartiality.[16] The ICTY, ICTR and

[10] Keith Hawkins, 'The Use of Legal Discretion Perspectives from Law and Social Science', in Keith Hawkins, *The Uses of Discretion* (Oxford: Clarendon, 1992), p. 11, p. 16.

[11] Loraine Gelsthorpe and Nicola Padfield, 'Introduction', in Loraine Gelsthorpe and Nicola Padfield (eds.), *Exercising Discretion: Decision Making in the Criminal Justice System and Beyond* (Portland, OH: Willan, 2003), p. 1, p. 5.

[12] See Articles 14 and 26 ICCPR and Article 21(3) Rome Statute.

[13] Andrew Ashworth, *The Criminal Process: An Evaluative Study* (Oxford: Oxford University Press, 2nd edn., 1999), p. 58.

[14] *Prosecutor* v. *Delalić, Mucić, Delić and Landžo*, Judgment, IT-96-21-A, 20 February 2001 (*Čelebići* Appeal), para. 611.

[15] On which, see Peter Krug, 'Prosecutorial Discretion and its Limits' (2002) 50 AJCL 643; Margaret McGhee, 'Prosecutorial Discretion' (2000) 99 *Georgetown Law Journal* 1057; Wayne R. LaFave, 'Prosecutorial Discretion in the United States' (1970) 18 AJCL 532.

[16] This seems to be the upshot of paras. 602–603 of the *Čelebići* Appeal.

ICC prosecutors all have an obligation to be independent, and not take instruction from any outside source.[17] This standard concentrates on the prosecutor rather than those defining the jurisdiction. It would not have been possible, for example, for Landžo to argue in the *Čelebići* appeal that he could not be prosecuted because no similar tribunal had been set up by the Security Council for Chechnya, for example.[18] The *Čelebići* Appeal decision expressly noted that 'in many criminal justice systems, the entity responsible for prosecutions has finite financial and human resources and cannot realistically be expected to prosecute every offender which may fall within the *strict terms of its jurisdiction*'.[19] The Appeals Chamber thus put the focus on the charging stage, rather than the earlier stage of defining a court's jurisdictional ambit.

Selectivity, legitimacy and the rule of law

The relatively narrow legal limits placed on prosecutorial discretion do not exhaust the ways in which selectivity is used to critique international criminal law. A broader legitimacy/rule of law-based evaluation can be made of international criminal law. Gerry Simpson notes that 'each war crimes trial is an exercise in partial justice to the extent that it reminds us that the majority of war crimes remain unpunished. If Yugoslavia, why not Somalia, if Rwanda, why not Guatemala?'[20] Similar concerns have also led to sharp comments from the more positivistically inclined. Alfred Rubin makes the point pithily: '[u]nless the law can be seen to apply to George Bush (who ordered the invasion of Panama) as well as Saddam Hussein (who ordered the invasion of Kuwait) . . . it will seem hypocritical again.'[21] In a similar key, Ian Brownlie has recently lamented: 'political considerations, power and patronage will continue to determine who is tried for international crimes and who not.'[22] What these critiques share is an ideal of legitimacy and the rule of law.

[17] Article 16(2) ICTY Statute, Article 15(2) ICTR Statute, Article 42(1) Rome Statute.

[18] Indeed, the broader point was also mentioned by the *Čelebići* Appeal, para. 618, that the appropriate remedy to a valid claim of selective enforcement of such serious crimes as international crimes is not the overturning of conviction.

[19] *Čelebići* Appeal, para. 602, emphasis added.

[20] Gerry Simpson, 'War Crimes: A Critical Introduction', in Timothy L. H. McCormack and Gerry J. Simpson (eds.), *The Law of War Crimes: National and International Approaches* (The Hague: Martinus Nijhoff, 1997), p. 1, pp. 8–9.

[21] Alfred P. Rubin, 'International Crime and Punishment' (Fall 1993) 34 NI 73, 74.

[22] Ian Brownlie, *Principles of International Law* (Oxford: Oxford University Press, 6th edn., 2003), p. 575.

The classic definition of the rule of law is Lon Fuller's:

> (1) a system of governance operates through general norms, and all or most of the norms partake of the following properties: (2) they are promulgated to the people who are required to comply with them; (3) they are prospective rather than retrospective; (4) they are understandable rather than hopelessly unintelligible; (5) they do not contradict each other and do not impose duties that conflict; (6) they do not impose requirements that cannot possibly be fulfilled; (7) they persist over substantial periods of time, instead of being changed with disorienting frequency; and (8) they are generally given effect in accordance with their terms, so that there is a congruence between the norms as formulated and the norms as implemented.[23]

Some of these aspects, such as the prohibition on retroactivity, are expressly included in the Rome Statute (Article 22). In this chapter, the focus of debate will be on two criteria, that of generality of norms and of congruence between the norms and their application. Criminal law's claims to legitimacy is undermined when the law is neither general, nor applied evenhandedly. When a law, general on its face, is in practice enforced only against a group or groups, the effect is the same as if it were targeted at those groups by its terms. As Andrew Ashworth notes, it is insufficient to simply look at the law as written: 'we must [also] consider the interaction between the law itself and the discretion in the criminal process if we are to understand the social reality of the criminal law.'[24] In practical terms, the criteria of generality and enforcement in accordance with the law's terms are linked.

These requirements are related to equality. There are few who would claim that as a desideratum, equality of application of the law is inappropriate. Equality of application is by no means exhaustive of the critical principles that ought to be applied to the law, but it is an immensely important one.[25] Equality of enforcement is one of the principles of justice to which Herbert Hart was prepared expressly to adhere. He described a principle of natural justice as one which is designed to 'secure that the law is applied to all those and only those who are alike in the relevant respect marked out by the law itself'.[26]

[23] Lon L. Fuller, *The Morality of Law* (New Haven: Yale University Press, revised edn., 1969), chapter 3, as summarised in Matthew H. Kramer, 'On The Moral Status of the Rule of Law' (2004) 63 CLJ 64, 64. Unlike with Fuller, however, the rule of law is not used here as a test for the existence of a legal system, but a means of appraising the regime described in chapter 3.

[24] Andrew Ashworth, *Principles of Criminal Law* (Oxford: Oxford University Press, 4th edn., 2003), p. 9.

[25] See Ashworth, *The Criminal Process*, p. 166.

[26] Herbert L. A. Hart, *The Concept of Law* (Oxford: Clarendon, 2nd edn., 1994), p. 160.

In a similar fashion, and although he separates equality from the rule of law, Joseph Raz accepts that 'the actions of the police and the prosecuting authorities can subvert the law. The prosecution should not be allowed, for example, to decide not to prosecute for commission of certain crimes, or for crimes committed by certain classes of offenders.'[27] Martin Loughlin also notes that 'as an operative system of rules, legal judgment is quite distinct from political decision making'.[28] Selective enforcement blurs the difference between the two, as it fails to focus on the 'relevant aspect marked out by the law itself', taking into account other factors, such as the political repercussions of an action, and undercutting the general applicability of the law.[29] As far back as Aristotle, discomfort with taking external political reasons into account in legal decision making can be seen.[30]

Thomas Franck's version of legitimacy, which is perhaps the most developed conception of legitimacy at the international level, involves similar principles of coherence and consistency: 'A rule is coherent when its application treats like cases alike and when the rule relates in a principled fashion to other rules of the same system. Consistency requires that a rule, whatever its content be applied in a "similar" or "applicable" instance.'[31] Although Broomhall criticises Franckian legitimacy as being 'incapable of explaining compliance in an adequate way',[32] this is not a reason for rejecting consistency, or the rule of law, which is not solely of instrumental value for ensuring compliance,[33] but a virtue to which a legal system ought to aspire, on the basis of the protection either of liberty or of equality.[34]

There are objections to use of concepts, including legitimacy, which are derived from the rule of law. One is that rule of law standards

27 Raz, 'The Rule of Law', p. 218.

28 Martin Loughlin, *Sword and Scales* (Oxford: Hart, 2000), p. 70.

29 For an excellent discussion of the relationship of law and politics in international criminal law, see Gerry Simpson, 'Politics, Sovereignty, Remembrance', in Dominic McGoldrick, Peter Rowe and Eric Donnelly (eds.), *The Permanent International Criminal Court: Legal and Policy Issues* (Oxford: Hart, 2004), p. 47, pp. 48–50.

30 See Aristotle, *Nicomachean Ethics* (Harmondsworth: Penguin, 1976), p. 181 'all the law considers . . . is the difference caused by the injury'.

31 Thomas M. Franck, *Fairness in International Law and Institutions* (Oxford: Oxford University Press, 1995), p. 38.

32 Bruce Broomhall, *International Justice and the International Criminal Court: Between Sovereignty and the Rule of Law* (Oxford: Oxford University Press, 2003), p. 191.

33 *Accord* Franck, *Fairness*, p. 38.

34 N. E. Simmonds, 'Straightforwardly False: The Collapse of Kramer's Positivism' (2004) 63 CLJ 98, 124–5.

were developed to deal with national affairs, and that therefore they are not appropriate for appraising international law.[35] Although some have applied rule of law standards to international law,[36] it might be thought that 'it is unsuitable and irrelevant' to do so.[37] There are strong reasons for rejecting such a contention in relation to the regime of international criminal law enforcement. International criminal law deals with the criminal prosecution of individuals, in a similar manner to that which occurs at the domestic level. The regime to be appraised also envisages a role for both domestic and international courts, so applying different standards to the national and international level would be inconsistent.

A further reason for the use of the rule of law as a basis for discussion is that it is a form of immanent critique.[38] One of the frequent refrains heard in trials of international crimes, especially in international fora, is the importance of the rule of law. Justice Jackson's opening speech at Nuremberg, which embodies many of the ideals often claimed for international criminal law, contains a ringing endorsement of the rule of law: 'the rule of law in the world, flouted by the lawlessness incited by these defendants had to be restored at the cost to my country of over a million casualties, not to mention those of other nations. I cannot subscribe to the perverted reasoning that society may advance and strengthen the rule of law by the expenditure of morally innocent lives, but that progress in the law may never be made at the price of morally guilty lives.'[39] This is not to say that trials of international crimes are inherently liberal affairs,[40] as they are not.[41] But where such invocations are made, attempts may be made to hold trials up to their own self-proclaimed standards. As Jackson also said, 'the record on which we judge these defendants today is the record on which history will judge

[35] An example might be John Rawls' rejection of applying his *Theory of Justice* at the international level, in John Rawls, *The Law of Peoples* (Cambridge, Mass.: Harvard University Press, 1999).

[36] For example, Ian Brownlie, *The Rule of Law in International Affairs: International Law at the Fiftieth Anniversary of the United Nations* (The Hague: Martinus Nijhoff, 1998); Arthur Watts, 'The International Rule of Law' (1993) 36 GYBIL 15.

[37] Brownlie, *The Rule of Law*, p. 213. It should be noted that Brownlie disagrees with such a position.

[38] On which, see Susan Marks, *The Riddle of All Constitutions* (Oxford: Oxford University Press, 2000), pp. 25–8.

[39] 1 *Trial of Major War Criminals, Nuremberg*, p. 81.

[40] Gary J. Bass, *Stay the Hand of Vengeance: The Politics of War Crimes Trials* (Princeton: Princeton University Press, 2000), p. 8.

[41] Frédéric Mégret, 'The Politics of International Criminal Law' (2003) 14 EJIL 1261, 1268–9.

us tomorrow. To pass these defendants a poisoned chalice is to put it to our lips as well.'[42]

International criminal law is more susceptible to claims of unfair selectivity than domestic law. This not just because international criminal law is more selectively enforced than domestic law (although it is). Arguments about selectivity strike at the rhetoric of international criminal law and its institutions. Jurisdiction over international crimes is said to be universal, jurisdiction over all international crimes inheres in all States. Universal jurisdiction is justified on the basis that it is in the common interest that those who commit international crimes be punished. This is why States can prosecute such crimes no matter where they occur, and by whom they are committed.[43]

The corollary of this is that international criminal law is intended to apply universally, to all people, powerful and weak, rich and poor. Accusations of selective enforcement involve allegations that, contrary to Justice Jackson's statement at Nuremberg that '[t]he wrongs which we seek to condemn and punish have been so calculated, so malignant and so devastating, that civilisation cannot tolerate their being ignored, because it cannot survive their being repeated'[44] such crimes can be ignored where it is considered politically expedient to do so. Modern claims that international crimes are 'crimes against peace and security of mankind'[45] or that 'such grave crimes threaten the peace, security and well-being of the world'[46] show that this idiom is both current, and symbiotic with international criminal law.

Bruce Broomhall is at times critical of attempts to use the rule of law in international criminal law, noting that 'there is no great difficulty in judging international criminal law by the rule of law's formal aspects [such as] prospectivity [and] clarity . . . the rule of law is more than just a bundle of formal qualities. It is also generally understood as a practice and to call at the international level, for the consistent, impartial practice implied by the concept raises profound difficulties, at least as the international system currently exists and is likely to develop.'[47] At other times, Broomhall seems unwilling to reject the relevance of consistency and impartiality entirely, noting at an early stage that impartial,

42 1 *Trial of Major War Criminals, Nuremberg*, p. 51.

43 Rosalyn Higgins, *Problems and Process: International Law and How We Use It* (Oxford: Oxford University Press, 1994), pp. 58–9.

44 1 *Trial of War Criminals, Nuremberg*, p. 49.

45 In the International Law Commission's words.

46 Rome Statute, preamble.

47 Broomhall, *International Justice*, p. 54.

non-discriminatory application of the law is part of the 'formal' aspect of the rule of law.[48] Later, Broomhall comments that 'the concepts of rule of law, accountability, and legality can be expected to form an increasingly entrenched part of international discourse as a standard of legitimacy'.[49] Insofar as Broomhall's concerns remind us that the international system is not one conducive to systematic enforcement, this is correct. But the undoubted difficulty of achieving perfect compliance with the rule of law does not justify a rejection of the desirability of consistency. It simply means that it is harder to achieve than at the national level.

'Victor's justice', tu quoque *and selectivity*

There are two other frequently made arguments about trials of international crimes that tend to include selectivity claims. The first of these, 'victor's justice', can be dealt with quite quickly.[50] Claims of victor's justice are of an omnibus nature, involving a number of interlinked claims. The first is that the trial itself is unfair, in the sense of being biased in favour of the prosecution.[51] The second claim is that criminal acts were also committed by the prosecuting power (*tu quoque*), which is discussed below. The third claim is one of selectivity, that those offences committed by representatives of the prosecuting power are not being prosecuted, and thus the trial reflects the disparity in power between the prosecuting State and the defendants, who were defeated in the conflict to which the prosecution relates.

Although as a legal defence *tu quoque per se* has been all but laid to rest by the *Kupreskić* Case,[52] it remains relevant in two ways. The first is to question the applicable law.[53] When an enemy State is prosecuting a person and both sides engaged in a questionable practice, but prosecutions have not been brought by a State against its own nationals for the

[48] Broomhall, *International Justice*, p. 4.

[49] Broomhall, *International Justice*, p. 189. Broomhall also notes that Franckian versions of legitimacy are very similar to rule of law ideals.

[50] A useful explanation of the claim may be found in Bass, *Stay the Hand*, pp. 8–16.

[51] See, for example, 1 *Trial of Major War Criminals, Nuremberg*, p. 51; Richard H. Minear, *Victor's Justice: The Tokyo War Crimes Trial* (Princeton: Princeton University Press, 1971), pp. 74–124; Bass, *Stay the Hand*, pp. 15–16. As this is a form of evaluation linked to fair trial, it falls beyond the scope of this work.

[52] *Prosecutor* v. *Kupreskić, Kupreskić, Josipović, Papić and Santić*, Judgment, IT-95-16-T, 14 January 2000, paras. 511–520.

[53] For an excellent discussion of *tu quoque*, see René Provost, *International Human Rights and Humanitarian Law* (Cambridge: Cambridge University Press, 2002), pp. 227–35.

conduct, there is scope for raising selectivity in an oblique fashion. The argument is that of the *faux naïf*: if the action was a crime, then doubtlessly the prosecuting States would prosecute its own nationals, too. As they have not, it must be that the conduct was not considered to be unlawful. The prosecuting State is then left with the choice of accepting that this is the case or admitting that prosecutions are indeed selective.

One of the few cases facing this issue squarely is *In re Burghoff*.[54] Burghoff was being tried after the Second World War in the Netherlands for shooting hostages, partly as a reprisal. He was convicted and appealed. Dealing with the fact that the US Military Manual (and to a lesser extent the British one) allowed for hostage taking, the Netherlands Special Court of Cassation responded that '[s]uch provisions ... can only be described as regrettable and arbitrary violations of the accepted norms. It goes without saying that it would be contrary to all principles of law to hold a given act lawful if committed by an Allied soldier and to punish it as a war crime if committed by a German soldier.' The Court continued that it did not know of any examples of US forces taking hostages but, if they had, they would have been war crimes.[55] Despite the strong endorsement of the importance of generality of norms, it might be noted that the Court was referring to hypothetical actions by Allies, not actual actions by Dutch nationals.

Where concrete actions by nationals are suggested, the reasoning for rejecting allegations of selective enforcement become more blurred. The most famous invocation of this type of *tu quoque* was by Otto Kranzbühler, on behalf of Karl Dönitz at Nuremberg.[56] Kranzbühler persuaded Chester Nimitz, Commander in Chief of the US Pacific Fleet, to answer an interrogatory relating to the exercise of unrestricted submarine warfare by the United States in the Pacific sphere. Nimitz agreed that the policy was to wage warfare on such a basis.[57] The judgment on Dönitz for waging unrestricted submarine warfare against neutrals was rather confused.[58] Despite asserting that his actions violated international law 'in view of all the facts proved and in particular of an order of the British Admiralty announced on 8 May 1940, according to which

[54] *In re Burghoff* 16 AD 551. [55] *In re Burghoff*, p. 552.

[56] Telford Taylor, *The Anatomy of the Nuremberg Trials* (London: Bloomsbury, 1993), pp. 566–8.

[57] 18 *Trial of Major War Criminals, Nuremberg*, pp. 26–8.

[58] Telford Taylor goes as far as to describe it as 'absurd', Taylor, *The Anatomy*, p. 631.

all vessels should be sunk at night in the Skagerrak, and the answers to interrogatories by Admiral Nimitz stating that unrestricted submarine warfare was carried on in the Pacific Ocean by the United States from the first day that nation entered the war, the sentence of Dönitz is not assessed on the ground of his breaches of the international law of submarine warfare.'[59] In other words, an unsatisfactory compromise between the judge at Nuremberg (Francis Biddle) who thought Dönitz deserved an acquittal on this charge, and those wanting him convicted, meant that he was convicted, but not sentenced for it.[60]

The second form of *tu quoque* is to attempt to delegitimise the process by bringing to light offences that can be placed at the door of the prosecuting States. Many States have, at some point or another, been involved in conduct that falls foul of international law. Examples of such activities include the Vichy regime in France, as well as France's record in Algeria, the United States in Vietnam and in the Abu Ghraib prison in Iraq, and Europe's record in the colonial period. It is safe to say that most States view reminders of these events as embarrassing. Those suspected of international crimes use *tu quoque* allegations, or the threat of them, as either a means of scaring States off from prosecuting, for fear of charges of hypocrisy, or as a tactic to delegitimise the proceedings when they occur.

An example comes from the Pinochet affair. When General Pinochet issued his first statement after being arrested at the behest of Spain, he took little time to remind the Spanish of their own activities, and response to them, under the Franco regime, saying 'in challenging Chile's reconciliation, Spain ignores its own past. It denies to us the path which it followed. Spain left the Franco years with no recriminations.' To add insult to injury, he continued by referring to when 'our own country obtained its freedom from Spanish colonial domination'.[61] This claim has had some impact on decision makers; for example, in arguing against prosecuting the Kaiser after the First World War, Austin Chamberlain is reported to have said that 'his defence will be our trial'.[62] Some

[59] Nuremberg IMT, Judgment and Sentence, (1947) 41 AJIL 172, p. 305.

[60] Other similar assertions of *tu quoque* in this manner (but not successfully) include *US* v. *von List (The Hostages Trial)* VIII LRTWC 32, p. 63; *US* v. *von Leeb (The High Command Trial)* XII LRTWC 1, pp. 64, 88.

[61] BBC News, 'General Pinochet's Statement in Full', 8 November 1988, available at http://news6.tdho.bbc.co.uk/hi/english/uk/newsid%F209000/209742.stm.

[62] Quoted in Simpson, 'Politics', p. 49.

have claimed that the reason that members of the Saddam Hussein government were not pursued for war crimes after the 1990–1 Gulf conflict was a fear of allegations about Allied conduct in the conflict.[63]

Perhaps the classic example of the use of *tu quoque* and associated arguments of selectivity to attack the legitimacy of the prosecution is the controversial 'defence of rupture' developed by Jacques Vergès and given its most notorious enunciation in the trial of Klaus Barbie.[64] The defence was to attack the actions of the prosecuting State. In the Barbie Case, this focused primarily on France's role in Algeria and Indochina.[65] As the prosecution of Paul Aussaresses in 2002 showed, invoking Algeria still strikes at a raw nerve in France. Aussaresses, a retired French General wrote of torturing Algerians during the Algerian War. He could not be prosecuted for those offences, as they had been amnestied in 1962, so he was prosecuted for complicity in justifying war crimes.[66] Running a defence of rupture is unlikely to either endear the lawyer or the client to the court, or obtain an acquittal, but the real audience is not the bench: it is public opinion, either in the prosecuting State or, and more usually, in third States. Such a defence can fall on sympathetic ears.[67] If it did not, the claim would not be made so frequently.

Selectivity in international criminal law

Although the emergence of the international criminal law regime can be dated to the 1990s, the creation of the regime occurred against a backdrop of claims of selective enforcement of the law. To evaluate the regime fully, it is necessary to look at developments prior to that date, to see the extent to which the modern regime represents an improvement over what went before. State practice reveals highly selective enforcement of

[63] David A. Martin, 'Reluctance to Prosecute War Crimes: Of Causes and Cures' (1994) 34 VJIL 255, 259.

[64] *Fédération Nationale des Déportes et Internes Résistants et Patriots* v. *Barbie* (1985) 78 ILR 125.

[65] Vergès' strategy is the subject of Guyora Binder, 'Representing Nazism: Advocacy and Identity in the Trial of Klaus Barbie' (1989) 99 Yale LJ 1321. His strategy drew strong condemnation from, for example, Alain Finkielkraut; Alain Finkielkraut (Roxanne Lapidus trans.), *Remembering in Vain: The Klaus Barbie Trial and Crimes Against Humanity* (New York: Columbia University Press, 1992).

[66] See Adam Jones, 'Introduction: History and Complicity', in Adam Jones (ed.), *Genocide, War Crimes and the West* (London: Zed Books, 2004), p. 1, p. 6 and Raphaëlle Branche, 'Torture and Other Violations of the Law by the French Army During the Algerian War', in Adam Jones (ed.), *Genocide, War Crimes and the West* (London: Zed Books, 2004), p. 134.

[67] Finkielkraut, *Remembering in Vain*, pp. 36–7.

international crimes, at least until recently.[68] This has occurred in various ways. The Acts brought in by the United Kingdom and Australia for prosecution of offences committed in the Second World War effectively prevent Allied actions being prosecuted.[69] The UK War Crimes Act 1991 was brought in to deal with Axis offenders found in the United Kingdom, and jurisdiction is limited to offences committed 'in a place which at the time was part of Germany or under German occupation'.[70] Although this could notionally cover alleged Allied offences such as the bombing of Dresden, the possibility of such charges is beyond remote.

The Australian War Crimes Amendment Act of 1988 was expressly selective, limiting jurisdiction to the European sphere of the Second World War,[71] where few Australians fought. Earlier drafts, which could possibly have been used to prosecute Australians, were rejected.[72] Although both the UK and Australian Acts have now been supplemented by International Criminal Court Acts for more modern offences, the problem remains for offences prior to the entry into force of those acts, both of which apply only prospectively. The Canadian War Crimes and Crimes Against Humanity Act permits prosecution for offences prior to the Act's coming into force so long as the offences were customary at the time of commission.[73] However, this is possible only for offences committed outside Canada. Allegations of offences committed in Canada (such as suggestions that forcible transfers of Aboriginal children in the 1950s amount to international crimes)[74] are not cognisable under the Act.

[68] See Timothy L. H. McCormack, 'Their Atrocities and Our Misdemeanours: The Reticence of States to Try Their "Own Nationals" for International Crimes', in Philippe Sands and Mark Lattimer (eds.), *Justice for Crimes Against Humanity* (Oxford: Hart, 2003), p. 107.

[69] For an overview, see Gillian Triggs, 'National Prosecutions of International Crimes and the Rule of Law', in Helen Durham and Timothy L. H. McCormack (eds.), *The Changing Nature of Conflict and the Efficacy of International Humanitarian Law* (The Hague: Kluwer, 2000), p. 175, pp. 178–83.

[70] War Crimes Act 1991, section 1(a). See David Turns, 'Prosecution Violations of International Humanitarian Law: The Legal Position in the United Kingdom' (1999) 4 JACL 1, 21–3; Gabriele Ganz, 'The War Crimes Act 1991 – Why no Constitutional Crisis?' (1992) 55 MLR 87; A. T. Richardson, 'War Crimes Act 1991' (1992) 55 MLR 73; Christopher Greenwood, 'The War Crimes Act 1991', in Hazel Fox and Michael A. Meyer (eds.), *Armed Conflict and the New Law: Effecting Compliance* (London: BIICL, 1993), p. 215; Eva Steiner, 'Prosecuting War Criminals in England and France' [1991] Crim. LR 180.

[71] War Crimes Amendment Act 1988, section 5. See generally, Gillian Triggs, 'Australia's War Crimes Trials: A Moral Necessity or Legal Minefield?' (1987) 16 MULJ 382.

[72] Triggs, 'National Prosecutions', p. 179.

[73] Crimes Against Humanity and War Crimes Act, section 6.

[74] See, for example, Ward Churchill, 'Genocide by Any Other Name: North American Indian Reservation Schools in Context', in Adam Jones (ed.), *Genocide, War Crimes and the West* (London: Zed Books, 2004), p. 78, pp. 83–4.

Some case law has effectively prevented prosecution of offences committed on behalf of the prosecuting State. The French incorporation of Article 6(c) of the Nuremberg IMT Charter was held, in the *Boudarel* Case, to be limited only to offences by the Axis powers in the Second World War.[75] This excluded any claims relating to French war crimes in Indochina, such as the allegations Boudarel faced in France. The reasoning in this case was in accordance with the view of the French government, which confirmed the judgment.[76] This has prevented any prosecution for anyone other than Axis officials (which, since the trial of Vichy official Maurice Papon, includes those acting under orders of the Vichy regime). Prior to the *Papon* judgments,[77] the French Court's criterion of the acts being undertaken under the direction of a State following a hegemonic ideology was held, against the historical record, to exclude the crimes committed under the Vichy regime, on the ground that it was not hegemonic.[78] *Papon* was after the first apologies by the French State for the activities of the Vichy regime, and the acceptance that many French people had worked for it.

Prosecutions at the national level have been limited mainly to 'others', either those of discredited past regimes, (such as in Argentina,[79] Ethiopia and France), or foreigners, (mainly Nazis, but now including ex-Yugoslavs and Rwandans). Only very rarely (but increasingly, as Belgian prosecutions of their own peacekeepers show)[80] has a country tried international crimes committed by citizens of that country for offences committed under the current regime. Even when they have done so – as, for example, in the *Calley* Case (*US* v. *Calley*) – there has been great ambiguity of purpose and result. In *Calley*, President Nixon intervened personally to

[75] Judgment of the *Cour de Cassation* 1 April 1993; see Axel Marschik, 'The Politics of Prosecution: European National Approaches to War Crimes', in Timothy L. H. McCormack and Gerry J. Simpson, *The Law of War Crimes: National and International Approaches* (The Hague: Kluwer, 1997), p. 65, pp. 85–6; Leila Sadat-Wexler, 'The French Experience', in M. Cherif Bassiouni (ed.), *International Criminal Law* (Ardsley: Transnational, 2nd edn., 1999), p. 273, pp. 273–4.

[76] See Sadat-Wexler, 'The French Experience', pp. 273–4.

[77] Judgment of *Chambre d'Accusation de la Cour d'Appel de Bordeaux*, 18 September 1996, Judgment *Cass. Crim* 23 January 1997. On the decisions, see Sadat-Wexler, 'The French Experience', pp. 273–4.

[78] See Sadat-Wexler, 'The French Experience', p. 292.

[79] The judgment is reprinted in (1987) 8 HRLJ 368.

[80] *D. A.* v. *Osman* Conseil de Guerre de Bruxelles, arrét du 21 Décembre 1994, Cour Militaire, ch. perm.néerl; arrêt du 24 Mai 1995. On the other hand, Charlesworth and Chinkin question the acquittals in some of the Belgian cases; Hilary Charlesworth and Christine Chinkin, *The Boundaries of International Law: A Feminist Analysis* (Manchester: Manchester University Press, 2000), p. 297.

review the record and effectively ended Calley's sentence.[81] As discussed in chapter 3, it is to be hoped that the complementarity provisions of the Rome Statute will encourage States to prosecute offences by their own nationals. UK prosecutions of soldiers accused of abuses in Iraq provide some evidence for this.

It is arguable that international criminal tribunals have generally increased the willingness of States to prosecute offences. It is evident that most of the recent cases based on universal jurisdiction have related to offences from former Yugoslavia and Rwanda.[82] There is also some evidence of a 'spill-over' effect into prosecutions on the basis of universal jurisdiction. Baltasar Garzón, the Spanish judge responsible for the extradition request for General Pinochet, drew some inspiration from the ICTY.[83]

Prosecutions of offences from Rwanda and former Yugoslavia on the basis of universal jurisdiction have been among the least controversial uses of universal jurisdiction since *Eichmann*, probably as the prosecution of such offences has been very publicly encouraged by the Security Council through the creation of the ICTY and ICTR. Other universal jurisdiction cases, such as those undertaken in Belgium, have been more divisive. As was explained in chapter 2, such prosecutions drew fire in the *Yerodia* Case from Judge Bula-Bula and (more temperately) President Guillaume.[84] There is no evidence that Belgium was acting in bad faith, but the claim of selectivity was considered by those two judges to militate against the recognition of universal jurisdiction. The fear of selective, politically motivated exercises of universal jurisdiction also led Judges Higgins, Kooijmans and Buergenthal to recommend certain safeguards against the abuse of such jurisdiction, including that all prosecutions be initiated by an independent authority.[85] Claims of selectivity have thus influenced the development of the law in this area.

[81] See Alfred P. Rubin, *Ethics and Authority in International Law* (Cambridge: Cambridge University Press, 1997), p. 175. Levie describes this intervention as 'unquestionably a miscarriage of justice and one which will return to haunt the United States'. Howard Levie, *Terrorism in War: The Law of War Crimes* (New York: Oceana, 1992), p. 207.

[82] Jonathan Charney, 'Progress in International Criminal Law?' (1999) 93 AJIL 452, 456; Theodor Meron, 'War Crimes Law Comes of Age' (1998) 92 AJIL 462, 464; Antonio Cassese, 'On the Current Trends Towards Criminal Prosecution and Punishment of Breaches of International Criminal Law' (1998) 9 EJIL 2, 6.

[83] José E. Alvarez, 'Crimes of Hate/Crimes of State: Lessons From Rwanda' (1999) 24 Yale JIL 365, 421.

[84] *Case Concerning the Arrest Warrant of 11 April 2000 (Congo* v. *Belgium) (Yerodia)*, 14 February 2002, ICJ List no. 121, Separate Opinion of Judge *ad hoc* Bula-Bula, paras. 9–14. *Ibid.*, Separate Opinion of President Guillaume, para. 15.

[85] Separate Opinion of Judges Higgins, Kooijmans and Buergenthal, para. 59.

The Nuremberg and Tokyo IMTs

Selectivity is a critique which has plagued international criminal tribunals from their inception to date. Claims have been made in good and bad faith, but it is difficult to deny that some of them have had purchase. The Nuremberg and Tokyo IMTs were open to the criticism, and it has frequently been made. It in no way minimises the crimes of the Nazi or Imperial Japanese regimes to accept these criticisms as largely accurate.[86] The law was applied only to the defeated powers, and selectively in relation to them, too. In his opening speech, Jackson accepted that it was not ideal that the victors tried the vanquished,[87] but declared: '[a]nd let me make clear that while this law is first applied against German aggressors, the law includes, and if it is to serve a useful purpose it must condemn, aggression by any other nations, including those which sit here now in judgment.'[88]

The reason he could say this was that the law and the charges were structured to avoid *tu quoque* allegations. When drafting the provision on crimes against humanity, Jackson was aware that if the jurisdictional limit to war was not introduced, not only could colonialism (embarrassing for France and the United Kingdom), or the Gulags (still a secret in the USSR) be evaluated with reference to the law, but so could the segregationist policies in the United States.[89] Where the law was relatively clear, but involved acts the Allied had also undertaken, such as bombing population centres, charges were for the most part not brought.[90] There was no real intention to subject Allied actions to scrutiny under that law when Nuremberg was created. The fact that the law was not applied to both sides in the Second World War has led many to consider the legacy of the Nuremberg IMT as flawed, and its legitimacy tarnished.[91]

The same applies to the Tokyo IMT, but the story of selectivity in this tribunal is a little more complex, not least as a number of the judges

86 See David Luban, 'The Legacies of Nuremberg' (1987) 54 *Social Research* 779, 809–11.

87 1 *Trial of Major War Criminals, Nuremberg*, p. 51.

88 1 *Trial of Major War Criminals, Nuremberg*, p. 85.

89 Provost, *International Human Rights and Humanitarian Law*, pp. 227–35.

90 Bert V. A. Röling 'The Nuremberg and Tokyo Trials in Retrospect', in M.Cherif Bassiouni and Ved Nanda, *A Treatise on International Criminal Law* (Springfield, IL: Thomas, 1973), p. 590, p. 591. The exception was the charges of waging unrestricted submarine warfare.

91 José E. Alvarez, 'Nuremberg Revisited: the *Tadić* Case' (1996) 7 EJIL 245, 260; Matthew Lippman, 'Nuremberg Forty Five Years After' (1991) 7 Connecticut JIL 1, 37–8; Adam Roberts, 'The Laws of War: Problems of Implementation in Contemporary Conflicts' (1995) 6 DJCIL 11, 26; Hedley Bull, *The Anarchical Society: A Study of Order in World Politics* (London: Macmillan, 2nd edn., 1995), pp. 85–6.

themselves raised the point. Judge Pal was assertive on this point. Pal excoriated the Allied powers for what he saw as their hypocrisy in prosecuting the defendants,[92] on two grounds: their own record of colonialism, and the Hiroshima and Nagasaki bombings.

Pal criticised the United States and its allies for trying to impose a prohibition of aggression that prioritised peace over the interests of those States under colonial domination.[93] He made a point of contrasting European and Japanese actions in the Far East, concluding that Japan was coerced into coming out of isolation 'under terms of treaties obtained by the Western powers from her by methods which, when later on imitated by Japan in relation to her neighbours, were characterised by those very treaty powers as aggressive',[94] and, 'after the Russo-Japanese war, Japan seemed to follow closely the precedents set by Europe in its dealings with China'.[95]

Pal reserved his most critical comments for the atomic bombings, which the prosecution had tried to ignore completely. He considered the Hiroshima and Nagasaki bombings far more iniquitous than anything the defendants were charged with: '[f]uture generations will judge this dire decision . . . [to initiate the bombings] . . . if an indiscriminate destruction of civilian life and property is still illegitimate in warfare, then, in the Pacific war, this decision to use the atom bomb is the only near approach to the directives of the German emperor during the first world war and of the Nazi leaders during the second world war. Nothing like this could be traced to the credit of the accused.'[96] The actions of the prosecutors were publicly damned in Pal's judgment, and those actions dominate discussion about the Pacific sphere of the war.[97]

Pal was not the only judge unhappy with the choice of defendants before the Tokyo IMT. Judge Bernard and President Webb, although they

[92] On this aspect of Pal's dissent, see generally, Elizabeth Kopelman, 'Ideology and International Law: The Dissent of the Indian Justice at the Tokyo War Crimes Trial' (1991) 23 NYUJILP 373.

[93] Dissenting Opinion from the Member From India, Judge Pal, in R. John Pritchard and Sonia M. Zaide (eds.), *The Tokyo War Crimes Trial, 21: Separate Opinions* (New York: Garland, 1981), pp. 238–41. In this respect, Pal also raised the USSR's declaration of war on Japan, claiming it would fall under the definition of aggression proposed by the prosecution; *ibid.*, pp. 241–6.

[94] *Ibid.*, p. 785.

[95] *Ibid.*, p. 795(20). For his survey of pre-war activities, see p. 795 (1–20), especially (rather at odds with this rejection of an objective definition of aggression), p. 785 (15), 'European aggression on China'.

[96] *Ibid.* p. 1,091; see Kopelman, 'Ideology and International Law', 406–9.

[97] See Mark J. Osiel, *Mass Atrocity, Collective Memory and the Law* (New Brunswick: Transaction, 1997), p. 130.

did not challenge the limitation of prosecutions to Japanese defendants, were unhappy about the absence of the Emperor, who had been excluded from the list of possible defendants to ensure a smoother ride for the occupation authorities.[98] Bernard was clear that he considered the non-indictment an unacceptable exercise of discretion: 'the Tribunal did not find itself in a position to control . . . that prosecution be exercised in an equal and sufficiently justified manner regarding all justiciable [persons] . . . The consequences of this inequality are particularly apparent and regrettable in regard to Emperor Hirohito.'[99] President Webb was more diplomatic, opining that 'I do not suggest that the Emperor should have been prosecuted. That is beyond my provenance. His immunity was, no doubt, decided upon in the best interests of all the Allied powers.'[100] Yet he still considered it appropriate to vote against the death sentence for the defendants on the basis that the Emperor, who had overall authority for the initiation of war, was not indicted.

There were absences from the Tokyo IMT of which the judges were unaware in 1948. Members of Unit 731, Japan's chemical and biological weapons unit, who were implicated in human experimentation on PoWs, were not prosecuted. Unit 731 were exempted from trial because the United States wanted their expertise and was willing to trade that expertise for immunity.[101] It is difficult to see this as anything other than an illegitimate use of discretion. The crimes were very serious and the evidence and suspects were available to the prosecuting States. The only argument in favour of not prosecuting was so that one State could

98 M. Cherif Bassiouni, 'From Versailles to Rwanda in 75 Years: The Need to Establish a Permanent International Criminal Court' (1997) 10 Harvard HRLJ 11, 35; Arnold C. Brackman, *The Other Nuremberg: The Untold Story of the Tokyo War Crimes Trial* (New York: William Morrow, 1987), pp. 77–8; Richard Minear, *Victor's Justice: The Tokyo War Crimes Trial* (Princeton: Princeton University Press, 1971), pp. 111–13; John Piccigallo, *The Japanese on Trial* (Austin, TX: University of Texas Press, 1979), p. 16; Peter Li, 'Hirohito's War Crimes Responsibility: The Unrepentant Emperor', in Peter Li (ed.), *Japanese War Crimes: The Search for Justice* (New Brunswick: Transaction, 2003), p. 59.

99 Dissenting Opinion of Judge Bernard, p. 19.

100 Separate Opinion of President Webb, p. 19.

101 Bernard V. A Röling and Antonio Cassese, *The Tokyo Trial and Beyond* (Cambridge: Polity, 1992), p. 18 and Yuki Tanaka, *Hidden Horrors: Japanese War Crimes in World War II* (Boulder, Co: Westview, 1998), pp. 159–60 blame the United States alone; Levie, *Terrorism in War*, pp. 154–5 shares the blame between the United States and USSR. On Unit 731, see Peter Li, 'Japan's Biochemical Warfare and Experimentation in China', in Peter Li (ed.), *Japanese War Crimes: The Search for Justice* (New Brunswick: Transaction, 2003), p. 289. The standard reference work, Sheldon H. Harris, *Factories of Death: Japanese Biological Warfare, 1932–1945 and the American Cover Up* (London: Routledge, 1994), apportions blame in accordance with its title.

further their own biological and chemical warfare programmes. Overall, there was a double imposition of unacceptable selectivity in the Tokyo IMT.

The law was enforced only against the losing nation in the Pacific sphere of the Second World War and only against those not immunised from prosecutions for reasons entirely extraneous to those that guide prosecutorial discretion, such as the availability of evidence. Those immunised were both high ranking and/or responsible for some of the most shocking offences in the conflict. The legacy of the Tokyo IMT has been severely tarnished by the refusal to prosecute such people.

The ICTY and ICTR

Claims of selectivity in the ICTY and ICTR have also arisen, albeit in a different fashion than for the Nuremberg and Tokyo IMTs. For both of these Tribunals, the claim that they were set up to judge the 'losers' is inapposite, as neither was set up by a belligerent, but by the United Nations, the international organisation with the strongest claim to represent international society. Still, the claims of selectivity relating both to the jurisdiction of the Tribunals and to their practice have been made.

Both the ICTY and ICTR were specific *ad hoc* reactions to limited areas and conflicts. Articles 1 and 8 of the ICTY Statute circumscribed that Tribunal's jurisdiction to offences committed on the territory of the former Yugoslavia after 1991. There was no possibility that the ICTY's jurisdiction over the offences in its Statute would apply to actions beyond the old borders of Yugoslavia or before 1 January 1991.[102] The open-ended nature of the ICTY's jurisdiction meant that, more by chance than design, the Tribunal had jurisdiction over the conflicts in Kosovo and the Former Yugoslav Republic of Macedonia.[103]

The position with the Rwanda Statute is slightly different. Article 7 grants the ICTR jurisdiction over offences in Rwanda and offences in

[102] Virginia Morris and Michael P. Scharf, *An Insider's Guide to the International Criminal Tribunal for former Yugoslavia* (Ardsley: Transnational, 1995), chapter VII.

[103] The Security Council has expressly stated that the ICTY has jurisdiction over the Kosovan conflict; SC Resolution 1160, UN Doc. S/RES/1160, SC Resolution 1203, UN Doc. S/RES/1203. *Prosecutor* v. *Multinović, Ojdanić and Šainović*, Decison on Motion Challenging Jurisdiction, IT-99-37-PT, 6 May 2003; *Prosecutor* v. *Multinović, Šainović and Ojdanić*, Reasons for Decision Dismissing the Interlocutory Appeal Concerning Jurisdiction Over the Territory of Kosovo, IT-99-37-AR72.2, 8 June 2004. Sonja Boelaert-Suominen, 'The International Criminal Tribunal for the former Yugoslavia and the Kosovo Conflict' (2000) 837 IRRC 217. On FYR Macedonia, see *In re: The Republic of Macedonia*: Decision on the Prosecutor's Request for Deferral and Motion for Order to the Former Yugoslav Republic of Macedonia, IT-02055-Misc.6, 4 October 2002.

'neighbouring States', if committed by Rwandan citizens. The temporal limit is greater here, being confined to one year (1994).[104] Rwanda was unhappy with the jurisdiction being so limited, it wanted the jurisdiction to begin prior to 1994, to catch those involved in the planning stage of the genocide.[105] This request was refused, according to José Alvarez because 'broader jurisdiction for the ICTR could well have led to inquiries that would have embarrassed the UN as a whole or a particular member of the Security Council'.[106] Rwanda was uncomfortable with allowing the jurisdiction to continue throughout 1994, after the RPF took control of Rwanda in July 1994. This was probably not unrelated to the allegations that the RPF engaged in revenge killings in Rwanda and in (which is now) refugee camps in the Eastern Democratic Republic of Congo.[107] The fact that the jurisdiction of the ICTR is limited to Rwanda (and crimes by Rwandans in the locality) and to 1994 must be seen as rather arbitrary, given that allegations relating to crimes in the area continued into 1995 and beyond.[108] The jurisdiction of Courts and Tribunals is far from an apolitical affair.

After the creation of the ICTY and ICTR, it was said that the Security Council suffered from 'Tribunal fatigue'[109] and thus was unlikely to create any more. This would imply that, rather than showing a commitment to international criminal justice on the part of the Security Council, the ICTY and ICTR were simply limited measures responding to particular situations, selective in that other conflicts (such as those in Liberia or the Congo) remained without similar responses. David Harris' prediction that 'despite the end of the cold war, there is absolutely no guarantee that the international community will not turn a blind eye to the next Rwanda or Yugoslavia'[110] has been proved right.

[104] See Virginia Morris and Michael P. Scharf, *The International Criminal Tribunal for Rwanda* (Ardsley: Transnational, 1998), chapter VII.

[105] Morris and Scharf, *The Internal Criminal Tribunal*, pp. 68–9. The ICTR has been willing to hear evidence relating to pre-1994 conduct, for background and historical context, although the position is slightly different for inchoate offences, for which pre-1994 events may form the basis for charges, provided the offence was consummated after 1994, *Prosecutor* v. *Nahimana, Barayagwiza and Ngeze*, Judgment, ICTR-99-52-T, 3 December 2003, paras. 100–104.

[106] Alvarez, 'Crimes of Hate', 397.

[107] Morris and Scharf, *The International Criminal Tribunal*, p. 69.

[108] Johan Pottier, *Reimagining Rwanda* (Cambridge: Cambridge University Press, 2002), pp. 76–107.

[109] Michael P. Scharf, 'The Politics of Establishing an International Criminal Court' (1995) 6 DJCIL 167, 169.

[110] David J. Harris, 'Progress and Problems in Establishing an International Criminal Court' (1998) 3 JACL 1, 3.

It is true that the Security Council has taken other actions in relation to setting up Tribunals, such as mandating the Secretary-General to negotiate with Sierra Leone to create the Special Court, but these remain the exception rather than the rule. The Security Council has not considered itself under any legal duty to respond to any other conflicts in a similar way. Where there is agreement on the acceptability of a tribunal among the permanent five members of the Security Council, the possibility of an international tribunal is there. Where it is not, either because there is insufficient interest to make proposals for a Tribunal[111] or if the interests of any one of those powers is implicated,[112] then quite simply there will not be a Tribunal. In terms of the gravity of offences, like incidents are not being treated alike, and as such, the *ad hoc* nature of the Tribunals leaves them open to charges of exceptionalism.[113]

This aspect of selectivity was raised by the defendant and *amici curiae* in the Milošević Case.[114] The Trial Chamber dismissed the claim that *ad hoc* reactions relating to one country 'corrupts justice and law', on the basis that all the law requires is that the Tribunal is established by law, and that a fair trial is ensured.[115] In some ways, this avoided the question being asked of the Tribunal. Selectivity is not solely related to law; as we have seen, it also relates to the extent to which the law is general and enforced in accordance with its terms, matters which relate to the legitimacy of the enforcement regime. On that point, *ad hoc* reactions by an executive body such as the Security Council, laudable though they are, fall far short of the ideal.

The creation of the ICTR demonstrates an interesting point about the selectivity argument: States are decidedly sensitive to such critique. This was understood by the RPF when it became the government of Rwanda, and was frustrated at the inconclusive early debates about whether or not to create a Tribunal. To move the process further, the government publicly and rhetorically asked: 'is it because we are Africans that a court has not been set up?'[116] As a Tribunal had been set up for one country, the argument was cleverly made that to fail to create one for another would be discriminatory. This does not prove that the argument was determinative, it was almost certainly not, but had there been no

[111] An example of this type of situation is the conflict in the DRC prior to 2002.

[112] Scharf, 'The Politics', 170.

[113] Alvarez, 'Crimes of Hate', 452–6.

[114] *Prosecutor* v. *Milošević*, Decision on Preliminary Motions, IT-99-37, 8 November 2001, paras. 8–11.

[115] *Milošević*, paras. 8–11.

[116] Morris and Scharf, *The International Criminal Tribunal*, p. 62.

ICTY there could have been no claim of selectivity, and it is highly likely that without the ICTY there would have been no ICTR.[117] The claim of selectivity, and the rhetoric of universal enforcement, is taken seriously by States. This underscores an important point in international criminal law: the idea of a universal crime gives rise to expectations of universal enforcement. Even when the initial turn to the law is made for political reasons,[118] that turning to the law gives rise to an expectation that when similar events occur, the response will be the same.[119]

One significant improvement made by the ICTY and ICTR over the Nuremberg and Tokyo IMTs must be noted – one that makes them less open to claims of selectivity. They may be reactive responses, their jurisdiction limited to the conflicts for which they were created, but unlike the Nuremberg and Tokyo predecessors, the ICTY and ICTR have jurisdiction over all parties to the conflict.[120] In relation to the ICTY, Rubin has asserted that '[the Security Council] made sure that only atrocities by participants in the actual struggle in the former Yugoslavia would be within the Tribunal's purview; their own activities, even as armed "peacekeepers" there, are not'.[121] There is no legal basis for this belief. The legal limitations on the jurisdiction of both Tribunals are geographical and temporal alone.

That said, the law is not the only limitation on prosecutorial policy. The ICTY and ICTR are quite heavily dependent on certain States for assistance and the provision of certain types of evidence, in particular that obtained covertly, such as by intelligence surveillance. The ICTR is particularly dependent on Rwandan co-operation if it is to fulfil its mandate. This has led some commentators to claim that the Tribunals are selective, as in practice the Prosecutor does not act independently of certain States.[122]

117 On the precedential effect of the creation of the ICTY, see Payam Akhavan, 'The International Criminal Tribunal for Rwanda: The Politics and Pragmatics of Punishment' (1996) 90 AJIL 501, 501; Payam Akhavan, 'Justice and Reconciliation in the Great Lakes Region of Africa: The Contribution of the International Criminal Tribunal for Rwanda' (1997) 7 DJCIL 325, 328.

118 As was the case for the creation of the ICTY, the Security Council certainly saw itself to be under no legal duty to act as it did.

119 See Edward P. Thompson, *Whigs and Hunters: The Origins of the Black Act* (Harmondsworth: Penguin, 1990 (1975)), pp. 262–3.

120 Bassiouni, 'From Versailles to Rwanda', 43.

121 Alfred P. Rubin, 'Dayton, Bosnia and the Limits of Law' (Winter 1996/1997) 47 NI 41, 42.

122 An example being Alexander Fatić, *Reconciliation via the War Crimes Tribunal?* (Aldershot: Ashgate, 2000), p. 69.

An unsubstantiated assertion of partiality was also submitted by the defence in the *Krajisnić* Case.[123] As we saw, the Appeals Chamber in the *Čelebići* Case was faced with an innovative claim of unfair selectivity by Esad Landžo, who claimed that he was being singled out for prosecution for an inappropriate reason. Landžo's allegation was that the reason he found himself before the Tribunal was that, unlike similarly placed Serbian defendants who had had their indictments withdrawn, he was prosecuted 'simply because he was the only person the Prosecutor's office could find to "represent" the Bosnian Muslims'. He was, it is said, indicted to give an appearance of 'evenhandedness' to the Prosecutor's policy'.[124] This is an inversion of the normal complaint – that the person is singled out because of discrimination against the national or ethnic group from which the defendant belongs. Landžo's claim was that he was singled out, as a Bosnian Muslim, so the Prosecutor could counter claims that she was biased against Serbs. The Appeals Chamber retorted that given the particularly unpleasant nature of his crimes, he fell under the latter limb of the Prosecutor's declared policy, that she would 'focus on persons holding higher levels of responsibility, or on those who have been personally responsible for the exceptionally brutal or otherwise extremely serious offences'.[125]

As might be expected, Slobodan Milošević dedicated a great deal of time in the early stages of his case before the ICTY to alleging that his prosecution was not impartial. The basis relied on for the similar challenge brought by the *amici curiae* in the case was that the Security Council 'urged' the Prosecutor to collect evidence relating to Kosovo in Resolution 1160. The allegation cannot simply be dismissed as special pleading. Göran Sluiter, for example, has expressed his concern that Resolution 1160 'is improper and casts doubt on the impartiality and independence of the Tribunal'.[126] The Trial Chamber dealing with the Milošević Case dismissed the allegations, saying that the Prosecutor had not acted on the instructions of any government, institution or person in indicting him, Resolution 1160 merely being akin to a domestic government setting general prosecutorial policy.[127] This is not entirely convincing. Governments do not normally suggest that special geographic areas be targeted for investigation. In addition, the fact that three powerful

[123] Decision of 22 September 2000, para. 17. [124] *Čelebići* Appeal, para. 612.

[125] *Čelebići* Appeal, para. 614.

[126] Göran Sluiter, *International Criminal Adjudication and the Collection of Evidence: Obligations of States* (New York: Intersentia, 2001), p. 22.

[127] *Milošević*, Decision, para. 15.

NATO States, which by that time were heavily involved in the Kosovo conflict, are permanent members of the Security Council, raises the question of whether the Council ought to have attempted to set prosecutorial policy.

The Trial Chamber's second response is more satisfactory. The Chamber pointed out that '[w]hat would impugn her independence is not the initiation of investigations on the basis of information from a particular source, such as the Security Council, but whether, in assessing that information and making her decision as to the indictment of a particular person, she acts on the instructions of any government, any institution, or any person' and noted there was no evidence that the Prosecutor had.[128] The argument is not completely beyond reproach; the Security Council did not pass information to the Prosecutor, but urged her to collect some herself.

Still, by the time of Resolution 1160 (31 March 1998) the ICTY's then Prosecutor, Louise Arbour, had expressed her intention to investigate events in Kosovo (on 10 March).[129] In addition, there is no evidence that Arbour took orders from any government. Nonetheless, the flow of information from NATO States that enabled the indictment markedly increased at the time of the Kosovo conflict, and Arbour had discussed the indictment with members of the UK and US government prior to its issuance.[130] The latter may not have been politic from the point of view of perceptions of independence.[131] Nonetheless, the evidence indicates that at best NATO powers were ambivalent about an indictment at the time Arbour presented one for confirmation. Rachel Kerr claims that Arbour presented the indictment over the opposition of the United States and United Kingdom.[132]

Arbour's independence may also be implied from the fact that pursuant to calls from a number of bodies and academics, she ordered a preliminary report on the question of NATO's liability for war crimes in its

[128] *Milošević*, Decision, para. 15. Pursuant to Article 18(1) of the ICTY Statute, the Prosecutor may receive information from State, international organisation and NGOs.

[129] The statement is cited in Rachel Kerr, *The International Criminal Tribunal for the Former Yugoslavia: An Exercise in Law, Politics and Diplomacy* (Oxford: Oxford University Press, 2004), p. 193.

[130] John Hagan, *Justice in the Balkans: Prosecuting War Crimes in the Balkans* (Chicago: Chicago University Press, 2003), p. 122.

[131] For a different view see Kerr, *The International Criminal Tribunal*, pp. 196–8.

[132] Kerr, *The International Criminal Tribunal*, p. 197; For a view in favour of the ambivalence of the United States, see Michael Ignatieff, *Virtual War: Kosovo and Beyond* (London: Chatto & Windus, 2000), pp. 122–5.

campaign over Kosovo. The simple fact that a report was requested raised considerable ire in some (particularly US) quarters.[133] NATO spokesman Jamie Shea, in an attempt to deflect questions about the ICTY and its evaluation of the Kosovo campaign, shot across the ICTY's bow: 'NATO is a friend of the Tribunal . . . [and] . . . would allow Justice Arbour to go to Kosovo and investigate. NATO are the people who have been detaining indicted war criminals for the Tribunal.'[134] The extent to which the ICTY relied on NATO States for evidence and obtaining indictees was clearly being used by Shea in an attempt to influence the Prosecutor.

In July 2000, the new ICTY Prosecutor, Carla del Ponte, made public her decision not to initiate a full investigation into NATO's conduct of the conflict. Just after announcing her decision, del Ponte released the internal report that recommended against any further investigation.[135] The decision and the report have engendered their fair share of controversy[136] and polemic.[137]

The fact that the report itself was released is a useful measure of transparency by the OTP.[138] But the report left many by no means convinced

[133] See Paul R. Williams and Michael P. Scharf, *Peace With Justice: War Crimes and Accountability in the former Yugoslavia* (London: Rowman & Littlefield, 2003), p. 134. The authors are distinctly antipathetic to what they describe (*ibid.*) as a 'pseudo investigation'.

[134] (1999) 125 *Tribunal Update*. It might also be noted that the Security Council could, at a moment's notice, decree the ICTY out of existence, See Leila Sadat-Wexler, 'The Proposed International Criminal Court: An Appraisal' (1996) 29 Cornell ILJ 665, 712.

[135] 'Final Report to the Prosecutor by the Committee Established to Review the NATO Bombing Campaign Against the Federal Republic of Yugoslavia', 8 June 2000, (2000) 38 ILM 1257.

[136] For support of the report (by one of its authors), see William J. Fenrick, 'Targeting and Proportionality during the NATO Bombing Campaign Against Yugoslavia' (2001) 12 EJIL 489; William J. Fenrick, 'The Law Applicable to Targeting and Proportionality After Operation Allied Force: A View From the Outside' (2000) 3 YBIHL 53. For critique, see Eric David, 'Respect for the Principle of Distinction in the Kosovo War' (2000) 3 YBIHL 81; Paolo Benvenuti, 'The ICTY Prosecutor and the Review of the NATO Bombing against the Federal Republic of Yugoslavia' (2001) 12 EJIL 503; Michael Bothe, 'The Protection of the Civilian Population and NATO Bombing on Yugoslavia: Comments on a Report to the Prosecutor of the ICTY' (2001) 12 EJIL 531; Natalino Ronzitti, 'Is the non Liquet of the Final Report by the Committee Established to Review the NATO Bombing Campaign Against the Federal Republic of Yugoslavia Acceptable?' (2000) 840 IRRC 1017.

[137] The FRY issued an attack on del Ponte in a press release entitled 'Carla del Ponte's Legal Amateurishness and Dirty Political Game', 23 June 2000. Michael Mandel, 'Politics and Human Rights in International Criminal Law: Our Case Against NATO and the Lessons to be Learnt From It' (2001–2002) 25 Fordham ILJ 95 is more academic, but only barely more diplomatic.

[138] For critique of the OTP decision, see Williams and Scharf, *Peace With Justice*, pp. 134–5.

of the integrity of the process. A reader of the report does not have to be convinced that NATO did commit war crimes in the Kosovo campaign to have some reservations about the report and its methodology. It is certainly the case that the Kosovo campaign raised a number of difficult issues under international law, in particular to the extent to which States must ensure that targeting is accurate.[139] In favour of the report, it may be noted that it does set out criteria which it is said the Prosecutor applies to decisions to initiate investigations.[140] In relation to the claims of crimes against peace, the report is clearly correct in noting that the ICTY has no jurisdiction over such offences,[141] and its discussion of Depleted Uranium weapons is basically correct.[142] The report does contain some useful discussion of the law, and it may also be the case that in places the law relating to the conduct of hostilities is always simple to apply or entirely clear.[143] However, there are some considerable flaws in the report, sufficient to query whether it ought to have served as the basis of the Prosecutor's decision.[144]

To begin with some of the general aspects of the report, the approach to evidence is unsatisfactory. The report states that despite NATO's response to the requests for information given to it being general and not addressing specific incidents, information provided by NATO was relied on heavily and assumed to be correct.[145] To do this, and yet state that an investigation ought not to be begun, since it was unlikely that sufficient evidence could be acquired despite the ICTY's broad powers to demand the surrender of such evidence, did not inspire confidence in

139 For evaluations, see Peter Rowe, 'Kosovo 1999: The Air Campaign – Have the Provisions of Additional Protocol I Withstood the Test?' (2000) 837 IRRC 147; Anthony P. V. Rogers, 'Zero-Casualty Warfare' (2000) 837 IRRC 165; Sergey Alexevich Egorov, 'The Kosovo Crisis and the Law of Armed Conflicts' (2000) 837 IRRC 183; Konstantin Obradović, 'International Humanitarian Law and the Kosovo Crisis' (2000) 839 IRRC 699.

140 Prosecutor's Report, para. 5. The elaboration of standards is an important aspect of ensuring consistent decision making and allowing for oversight; see Davis, *Discretionary Justice*, p. 190.

141 Prosecutor's Report, paras. 30–34.

142 Prosecutor's Report, para. 26. Benvenuti, 'The ICTY Prosecutor', 511–13 is too harsh here.

143 Prosecutor's Report, para. 90.

144 These include the unattributed inclusion of material from William Fenrick's previously published work, see Mandel, 'Politics and Human Rights', 117. As the furore over the UK government's 'dodgy dossier' on Iraq shows, it undermines confidence in the report. It is certainly bad academic practice (although the report does not claim to be an academic piece of work).

145 Prosecutor's Report, para. 90.

the report's impartiality.[146] Not least, early on in the life of the Tribunal, with early defendants such as *Tadić* and *Blaškić*, the Tribunal initiated investigations in the face of considerable State reluctance to pass over evidence. This criticism applies *a fortiori* to the instances where the report suggests 'on the basis of information presently available' that the OTP should not initiate an investigation.[147] It might be thought that in such circumstances more information ought to be sought through an investigation.

In its decision to recommend against investigation, the report declared that 'in all cases either the law is insufficiently clear' or that the ICTY was unlikely to obtain sufficient information.[148] The approach of the report to the law compares rather badly to the ICTY's previous record in the area and the role the ICTY has willingly taken on of clarifying the law.[149] This role had been encouraged by the OTP in its pleadings before the ICTY.[150] In the early days of the ICTY the law relating to non-international armed conflict was hardly less clear than the law governing the conduct of hostilities. The OTP was happy to bring charges on the basis of that law, and at the time of the report conduct of hostilities offences were at issue in a number of cases before the ICTY.[151] The report is also not entirely consistent on the question of the uncertainties of the law;[152] for example, the report feels confident enough of the law to reject the ICTY decision in *Kupreškić* on proportionality.[153]

At times, the report makes some very fine distinctions of law at odds with its avowed uncertainty. For example, in discussing the attack on the Djakovica refugee convoy, the committee recommends against prosecution as 'the committee is of the opinion that neither the aircrew nor their commanders displayed the degree of recklessness . . . which would sustain criminal charges'.[154] Leaving aside the original statement of the report that recklessness (without qualification) is said to be the *mens rea*

146 Benvenuti, 'The ICTY Prosecutor', 506–7 and Ronzitti, 'Is the non Liquet', 1020, are convincing on this point.

147 Prosecutor's Report, para. 27.

148 Prosecutor's Report, para. 90.

149 Ronzitti, 'Is the non-Liquet', 1020–1.

150 An example being the progressive interpretation of Article 4 of Geneva Convention IV urged by the Prosecution (and accepted by the Trial Chamber) in *Prosecutor* v. *Delalić, Delić, Mucić and Landžo*, Judgment, IT-96-21-T,16 November 1998, paras. 236–243.

151 Such as *Prosecutor* v. *Blaškić* and *Prosecutor* v. *Galić*.

152 Ronzitti, 'Is the non Liquet', 1021.

153 *Prosecutor* v. *Kupreskić, Kupreskić, Jopsipović, Papić and Santić*, Judgment, IT-95-16-T, 14 January 2000, see Prosecutor's Report, para. 52. See Benevenuti, 'The ICTY Prosecutor', 517–18.

154 Prosecutor's Report, para. 70.

of launching attack without taking sufficient precautions,[155] the statement implies that the committee had a substantive (if unenumerated) standard within the concept of recklessness, on the basis of which they were confident enough to recommend against prosecution.

A number of doubts have rightly been raised about the treatment of individual events in the report.[156] For example, the treatment of the bombing of the Chinese Embassy in Belgrade is unsatisfactory. The United States accepted responsibility for the attack, and paid compensation.[157] The report also noted that the United States also dismissed one officer and reprimanded another six, alongside taking action to determine individual responsibility.[158] The report concludes that the aircrew were not responsible (which is probably correct), and also that senior leaders should not be held responsible for accepting intelligence from another agency (again probably correct). However, the report does not deal with the question of those dismissed or reprimanded. Administrative action in such cases would not displace the jurisdiction of the ICC under complementarity, never mind the primary jurisdiction of the ICTY. Tadić was surrendered to the ICTY when already under indictment in Germany. Therefore the decision not even to investigate is out of kilter with past ICTY practice. There are also a number of incidents not mentioned in the OTP report that may have merited discussion, such as the attack on the Luzane bridge.[159]

Although the report is not the complete whitewash some claim it to be,[160] the report leaves the impression that it was prepared to the Prosecutor's order, that being to ensure that the issue went away. Against this, Rachel Kerr suggests that the real reason for the refusal to investigate was that the offences were not as serious as those alleged to have been committed by Serbs and the Kosovo Liberation Army (KLA) in Kosovo, and therefore fell outside the ICTY's mandate, whose remit was serious violations of international humanitarian law.[161] The problem with this

155 Prosecutor's Report, para. 28.

156 Benvenuti, 'The ICTY Prosecutor', 521–4; David, 'Respect', 100–4; Ronzitti, 'Is the non Liquet', 1025–6.

157 Prosecutor's Report, para. 84.

158 Prosecutor's Report, para. 84.

159 David, 'Respect', 103–4.

160 See the comments on the ICTY generally reported in Rodney Dixon, 'New Developments in the International Criminal Tribunal for the Former Yugoslavia' (1995) 8 LJIL 449, 460–2 and Mandel, 'Politics and Human Rights', *passim*. The Russian Foreign Ministry issued a statement accusing the Tribunal of 'political prejudice', in indictment after the prosecutor's refusal fully to investigate NATO, see (2000) 178 *Tribunal Update*.

161 Kerr, *The International Criminal Tribunal*, p. 203.

argument is that when del Ponte reported her decision not to investigate, it was not on that basis. Del Ponte made clear in the Security Council that the report was the basis of her decision,[162] the Prosecutor excluded the idea of an unidentified major premise that the offences were not serious enough.

In addition Kerr's point conflates two issues, whether the allegations were serious enough to warrant investigation and whether they were as serious as those crimes alleged against Serbs and Albanians in the Kosovo conflict. The latter point may be fairly readily conceded; there are no credible allegations of ethnic cleansing that can be directed against NATO. However, that does not mean the offences are not serious, and thus outside the mandate of the ICTY. The allegations in relation to the Djakovica Convoy relate to the possible reckless killing of between seventy and seventy-five people and reckless injuring of one hundred people.[163] The Attack on Koriša village on 13 May 1999 is said to have caused up to eighty-seven civilian deaths and approximately sixty injuries. These are not mere trifles.

By way of comparison, it might be noted that the Prosecutor sought and obtained the deferral of cases relating to the alleged killing of twelve Macedonians by the Macedonian National Liberation Army (NLA) who were found in a mass grave, the killing of five people in the village of Ljuboten and the detention and abuse of five road workers for a number of hours by the NLA.[164] These offences, although serious, are not clearly more serious than those at issue in the NATO cases, and they provide an insight into del Ponte's understanding of the level of 'seriousness' in which the ICTY may be involved.[165]

Despite the criticisms above, the decision not to prosecute was not simply because of an unthinking bias towards NATO States. The difficulties the Tribunal would doubtlessly have encountered had NATO States withdrawn financing and co-operation should not be underestimated. It is clear that the Prosecutor was placed in an unenviable position. Some are of the view that this justifies the Prosecutor in not taking matters further.[166] However, there is an analogous problem at the domestic level: investigation of police brutality. In such cases, it is difficult for a Prosecutor to work as there are continuing relations between the police

[162] UN Doc. S/PV 4150, pp. 21–2. [163] Prosecutor's Report, para. 63.
[164] *In Re Macedonia*, paras. 8, 31, 42.
[165] Again, it is worth noting that del Ponte did not assert that the reason she refused to investigate the NATO cases was that they were insufficiently serious.
[166] Kerr, *The International Criminal Tribunal*, p. 204.

and prosecutors which are imperilled by prosecutions of the investigators and those who hold evidence. Problems with this are considered serious enough by some to suggest the need for an international criminal court.[167] Despite the difficulties the Prosecutor was faced with, it appears that the ICTY (or, more accurately, the OTP) did take into account external factors in coming to its decision. There was no discriminatory motive, but the approach to investigating offences by NATO States and other parties to the Kosovo conflict was disparate, leaving it open to critiques of selective enforcement. Some of the claims were undoubtedly made by interested observers, but the more temperate critiques have purchase on the legitimacy of the Tribunal.

Complaints about selective enforcement have also been made about the ICTR. The claims have been that the ICTR, despite having jurisdiction over both sides party to the 1994 civil war, concentrated solely on the Hutu perpetrators of the genocide, rather than also investigating actions by Tutsis that amounted either to war crimes or crimes against humanity. Again, these critiques are not made by those solely interested in the integrity of the regime of international criminal justice. The first express enunciation of this argument came from the defendant in the *Akayesu* Case in his attempt to show that the ICTR was biased.[168] Specifically, Akayesu alleged 'that the Tribunal is prosecuting only the "losers" in the Rwandan conflict by failing to prosecute the perpetrators of "crimes of extermination of the Hutu" who enjoy "complete immunity" from prosecution'. He further alleged 'that such failure exhibits partiality in the punishment of crimes committed in Rwanda during the relevant period [comparing] this to the contrary situation before ICTY where persons from "both camps", including Croat leaders, have been prosecuted'.[169] The Appeals Chamber responded, in line with the *Čelebići* Case, that there was no evidence that the failure to prosecute demonstrated discrimination. They further opined that even if he had shown discrimination, 'Akayesu has failed to show how such a general allegation relates to his case, that is how the alleged discriminatory prosecution on policy pursued by the Prosecutor was so prejudicial to him as to put in issue the lawfulness of the proceedings instituted against him'.[170]

The idea that the prosecutor acted with a discriminatory animus may easily be dismissed. There is no evidence of such a motive. In the past, the Prosecutor has stated that she was seeking to investigate offences

[167] Krug, 'Prosecutorial Discretion', 663.
[168] *Prosecutor* v. *Akayesu*, Judgment, ICTR-96-4-A, 1 June 2001.
[169] *Akayasu* Appeal, para. 93. [170] *Akayesu* Appeal, paras. 95–96.

committed by Tutsis against Hutus. Interestingly, the possibility of prosecuting Hutus may have lost Carla del Ponte her job as Prosecutor in 2004. As the Barayagwiza affair showed, the ICTR's dependence on Rwandan co-operation means that Rwanda has considerable leverage with the Tribunal. If it was unhappy, Rwanda simply threatened to cut off the ICTR's support. Over 2003 del Ponte made it increasingly clear that she intended to pursue investigations against RPF members for their activities in 1994. The Rwandan government had always been hostile to such suggestions, saying that Tribunal resources were best taken up by prosecuting the 'crime of crimes', genocide. There have been no credible allegations that the actions of the RPF in 1994 amounted to genocide, but the Rwandan government's point is not entirely fatuous; the seriousness of the crime is a relevant criterion to factor in to the decision to investigate or prosecute. But the Prosecutor is the person authorised to take those decisions, not individual governments.

When del Ponte came up for reappointment in 2003 the Rwandan government campaigned very heavily in favour of the Prosecutor's job being split into two, one prosecutor for the ICTY and one for the ICTR. Rwanda also campaigned against del Ponte being reappointed ICTR prosecutor. When the separation of the job occurred, and del Ponte was reappointed only as ICTY Prosecutor,[171] she alleged that improper pressure had been brought on the Security Council by Rwanda with an implicit threat to derail the ICTR with non-co-operation.[172] Del Ponte also alleged that this was because she refused to engage in selective enforcement, by insisting that investigations should go on into actions by the RPF to determine if indictments should be brought. If del Ponte is correct,[173] the entire affair shows the difficulty of ensuring effective, consistent decision making at the international level. The ability to obtain evidence is a relevant aspect of prosecution decision making. However, where the co-operation of suspects or governments sympathetic to them is imperative, it means that in practice the law may be enforced in a disparate manner.

The International Criminal Court

Unlike the tribunals already discussed, the ICC was not set up with one conflict in mind. It is not an *ad hoc* reaction to a single conflict. However, the jurisdictional regime of the ICC, alongside its relationship

171 Resolution 1503, UN Doc. S/RES/1503.

172 BBC News, 'Prosecutor loses Rwanda Role', 28 August 2003, available at http://news.bbc.co.uk/1/hi/world/africa./318905.stm.

173 It should be noted that del Ponte was alleged by Rwanda not to have spent enough time on the ICTR, and it was said that the job was necessarily a full-time one.

with the Security Council, may mean that it may not fully escape claims of selectivity on the basis of its jurisdiction. This is because unless the Security Council acts, the ICC's writ does not run throughout the globe.

Some of the States negotiating at the Rome conference wanted the ICC to be empowered to assert universal jurisdiction as of right. There is no reason in law why this could not have been the case.[174] Politically, though, this was impossible. It was on this issue that the Rome Conference consensus finally failed.[175] As a result, pursuant to Article 12 of the Rome Statute the Court is given jurisdiction first of all over offences committed on the territory of, or by a national of, one of the States party.[176] Even this more limited jurisdiction has provoked controversy; the US view is that by asserting jurisdiction over nationals of non-party States the Rome Statute violates international law.[177]

The US view is unpersuasive. All countries have the right to exercise territorial jurisdiction and there is no evidence of a prohibitive rule of international law which forbids the passing of such jurisdiction to an international organisation that has the necessary fair-trial guarantees.[178] As a result of Article 12 the ICC has jurisdiction over a

174 Andreas Zimmermann, 'The Creation of a Permanent International Criminal Court' (1998) 2 MPYBUNL 169, 205–6; For Rome documents, see A/CONF.183/C.1/L.6, L.53 (Article 7), L.59 (Article 7), L.70.

175 See Elizabeth Wilmshurst, 'Jurisdiction of the Court', in Roy S. Lee (ed.), *The International Criminal Court: The Making of the Rome Statute* (The Hague: Kluwer, 1999), p. 127; See more generally, Eve La Haye, 'The Jurisdiction of the International Criminal Court: Controversies Over the Preconditions for Exercise of its Jurisdiction' (1999) 46 NILR 1; Hans-Peter Kaul, 'Preconditions to the Exercise of Jurisdiction', in Antonio Cassese, Paula Gaeta and John R. W. D. Jones (eds.), *The Rome Statute: A Commentary* (Oxford: Oxford University Press, 2002), p. 583; Hans-Peter Kaul and Claus Kreß, 'Jurisdiction and Cooperation in the Statute of the International Criminal Court: Principles and Compromises' (1999) 2 YBIHL 143; Richard Dicker, 'Issues Facing the International Criminal Court's Preparatory Commission' (1999) 32 Cornell ILJ 471, 473.

176 See Sharon A. Williams, 'Article 12', in Otto Triffterer (ed.), *Commentary on the Rome Statute of the International Criminal Court: Article by Article* (Baden-Baden: Nomos, 1999), p. 329.

177 David J. Scheffer, 'The International Criminal Court: The Challenge of Jurisdiction' (1999) 63 Proceedings ASIL 68, 71; Ruth Wedgwood, 'The International Criminal Court: An American View' (1999) 10 EJIL 93, 99. See also Madeline Morris, 'High Crimes and Misconceptions: The ICC and Non Party States' (2000) 64 LCP 131.

178 On the US position, see, for example, Marcella David, 'Grotius Repudiated: The American Objections to the International Criminal Court and the Commitment to International Law' (1999) 20 MJIL 337; Bartram S. Brown, 'US Objections to the Statute of the International Criminal Court: A Brief Response' (1999) 31 NYUJILP 855; Christopher C. Joyner and Christopher Posteraro, 'The United States and the International Criminal Court: Rethinking the Struggle Between National Interests

larger personal, temporal and geographical range than the *ad hoc* Tribunals, but States can choose to remain outside of this regime to a large extent by not ratifying the Statute or agreeing to its jurisdiction under Article 12(3) and avoiding conflicts with States party to the Rome Statute.[179] Even those who ratify are entitled, by virtue of Article 124, to opt out of the war crimes jurisdiction of the ICC for seven years.[180]

The jurisdictional regime of the ICC means that absent universal ratification of the Rome Statute (which is unlikely at present), or Security Council action, some conflicts – such as the crisis in Darfur, Sudan – will remain outside the remit of the ICC's mandate. This is unfortunate, although it might be questioned if the inclusion of universal jurisdiction in the Statute would have made much practical difference. Although the ICC would then have had jurisdiction over any conflict, it would not have been able to issue binding orders relating to the surrender of suspects or evidence to the State most likely to have such evidence, the nationality or territorial State. The Court might be able to obtain the suspect were he or she to travel to a State party to the ICC, but investigation would be almost impossible in this situation.

The temporal jurisdiction of the ICC may also be open to claims of selectivity. Pursuant to Article 11. '1. The Court has jurisdiction only with respect to crimes committed after the entry into force of this Statute'. In addition '[i]f a State becomes a Party to this Statute after its entry into force, the Court may exercise its jurisdiction only with respect to crimes committed after the entry into force of this Statute for that State, unless that State has made a declaration under article 12, paragraph 3.'[181] This

and International Justice' (1999) 10 CLF 359; Gerhard Hafner, Kristen Boon, Anne Rübesame and Jonathan Hutson, 'A Response to the American View as Presented By Ruth Wedgwood' (1999) 10 EJIL 108; Monroe Leigh 'The United States and the Statute of Rome' (2001) 95 AJIL 124; Sarah B. Sewell and Carl Kaysen, *The United States and the International Criminal Court* (New York: Rowman & Littlefield/American Academy of Arts and Sciences, 2000).

179 Which they have a right to do; Peter Malanczuk, 'The International Criminal Court and Landmines: What are the Consequences of Leaving the US Behind?' (2000) 11 EJIL 77, 78.

180 See Andreas Zimmermann, 'Article 124', in Otto Triffterer (ed.), *Commentary on the Rome Statute of the International Criminal Court: Article by Article* (Baden-Baden: Nomos, 1999), p. 1281. France and Colombia have made such declarations.

181 See Sharon A. Williams, 'Article 11', in Otto Triffterer (ed.), *Commentary on the Rome Statute of the International Criminal Court: Article by Article* (Baden-Baden: Nomos, 1999), p. 323; Stéphane Bourgon, 'Jurisdiction *Ratione Temporis*', in Antonio Cassese, Paula Gaeta and John R. W. D. Jones (eds.), *The Rome Statute of the International Criminal Court: A Commentary* (Oxford: Oxford University Press, 2002), p. 543.

represents a radical change of policy from the previous international criminal Tribunals, which have all been created to deal with conflicts beginning prior to the creation of those Tribunals.[182]

Article 11 was also unnecessary from the point of view of the *nullum crimen sine lege* principle, so long as the conduct prosecuted was contrary to customary law at the time of its perpetration.[183] The reason for the difference between Article 11 and its earlier precedents is related to the fact that in this instance States were setting up an institution that could prosecute their own nationals. Their own past actions could therefore be brought before the ICC. States were unwilling to permit such a result.[184] By way of comparison, it might be noted that US military commission Order 2 on the prosecution of non-US nationals in the 'war on terror', returns to the earlier approach, saying that 'as this document is declarative of existing law, it does not preclude trial for crimes prior to its effective date'.[185]

There is a pragmatic argument in favour of Article 11. The ICC could be overwhelmed by past crimes, and the Court has only limited resources. It could not therefore prosecute every offence back to, say, the Second World War, or even a small sample of them. But the arbitrariness of the date of entry into force may be shown in relation to the conflict in the DRC. The conflict has been ongoing since the 1990s, but the Prosecutor has jurisdiction only over offences committed after 1 July 2002: a crime committed the day before would be outside the jurisdiction of the ICC. This is unfortunate, but it is also true that any date chosen would be similarly arbitrary.

Two of the trigger mechanisms for the ICC's jurisdiction could be criticised as open to abuse. The first of these is State referrals, mentioned in Article 13(a) and 14. The history of such referrals reveals that they have not been apolitical, in that they are considered unfriendly acts, and therefore are not used in relation to Allies or friends.[186] However, the addition of the *proprio motu* powers of the Prosecutor pulls some of the teeth of this critique as the Prosecutor may initiate an investigation where no State has passed on the situation. As William Schabas has

182 Williams, 'Article 12', p. 324. 183 Bourgon '*Temporis*', p. 550.

184 Although William A. Schabas, *An Introduction to the International Criminal Court* (Cambridge: Cambridge University Press, 2nd edn., 2004), p. 70, notes that national courts or *ad hoc* Tribunals could be set up for this, the fact that most such crimes have, as yet, remained unpunished makes it unlikely that they will be now.

185 Department of Defense Military Commission Order 2, 30 April 2003, p. 2.

186 See, for example, Schabas, *An Introduction*, p. 122.

noted, States may also suggest to the Prosecutor that he or she use such powers rather than publicly referring a matter to the ICC.[187]

The self-referral of the situations in Northern Uganda and the DRC have led to concerns that these actions were part of a means to weaken political opponents there. However, 'situations' have to be referred, and this means that all parties in a situation are subject to investigation. It is notable that although the President of Uganda referred the situation 'concerning the Lord's Resistance Army' to the ICC,[188] the Prosecutor has initiated an investigation into 'Northern Uganda'.[189] The decisions to investigate those situations are thus not unfairly selective.

The second possible trigger mechanism that may be criticised as selective is a Security Council referral under Article 13(b). The Security Council may pass any situation to the ICC, irrespective of whether it involves the territory or nationals of a State party, giving the ICC a possible global jurisdiction. This jurisdiction is exercisable only on a contingency outside the power of the Court, a decision of the Security Council. The political nature of the Security Council, and the existence of the veto, mean that certain States (in particular, the permanent five members and their allies and associates) will be protected from this type of referral. This form of jurisdiction is as selective as the decisions of the Security Council to create the ICTY and ICTR. As the Prosecutor has no *proprio motu* powers to investigate unless the situation involves crimes on the territory of, or committed by, nationals of States party to the Statute, the clawback for legitimacy of those powers does not exist. That is not to say that the additional role for the Security Council here is entirely inappropriate, but that there is the possibility of selectivity in it.

The existence of the *proprio motu* powers of the Prosecutor was opposed by the United States on the basis of possible bias or being open to manipulation. This critique could be linked to selective enforcement of the law. The Prosecutor does have discretion, not only in whether to exercise *proprio motu* powers, but also whether to prosecute if the Security Council or a State passes a situation to him or her.[190] This discretion is broad, in that the Prosecutor may refuse to investigate or prosecute on the basis that it is not in 'the interests of justice'.[191] If the Prosecutor decides to do so, however, a Pre-Trial Chamber may refuse to accept the decision, and require the Prosecutor to continue with the investigation or

[187] Schabas, *An Introduction*, p. 122. [188] ICC Press Release, 29 January 2004.
[189] ICC Press Release, 29 July 2004. [190] See Article 53. [191] Article 53(1)(c), 53(2)(c).

prosecution.[192] If the Prosecutor decides to use *prioprio motu* powers, he or she may do so only if a pre-Trial Chamber decides that he or she has a reasonable basis to do so.[193] This level of oversight is quite unprecedented, and provides more than adequate protection against arbitrary action by the Prosecutor. The Prosecutor is also sensitive to questions of legitimacy, has gone out of the way to show transparency, and is working on a publishable set of guidelines.[194]

In one area, the Rome Statute has made it possible for politically motivated selectivity to occur. This is the Security Council's right to demand postponement of action by the Prosecutor under Article 16.[195] Article 16 provides that: '[n]o investigation or prosecution may be commenced or proceeded with under this Statute for a period of 12 months after the Security Council, in a resolution adopted under Chapter VII of the Charter of the United Nations, has requested the Court to that effect; that request may be renewed by the Council under the same conditions.'[196] A political body is thus given the authority to stall the investigation or prosecution of offences for reasons which need not have anything to do with the administration of justice for as long as the Council is prepared to vote for such a resolution.[197] The provision itself was

192 Article 53(3)(b), Rule of Procedure and Evidence 110(2). See Matthew Brubacher, 'Prosecutorial Independence Within the International Criminal Court' (2004) 2 JICJ 71, 85–7.

193 Article 15(3).

194 Such a course is suggested in Alison Marston Danner, 'Enhancing the Legitimacy and Accountability of Prosecutorial Discretion at the International Criminal Court' (2003) 97 AJIL 510, 541–52.

195 See Nabil Elaraby, 'The Role of the Security Council and the Independence of the International Criminal Court: Some Reflections', in Mauro Politi and Guiseppe Nesi (eds.), *The International Criminal Court: A Challenge to Impunity* (Aldershot: Ashgate, 2001), p. 43.

196 See generally Morten Bergsmo and Jelena Pejić, 'Article 16', in Otto Triffterer, *Commentary on the Rome Statute of the International Criminal Court: Article by Article* (Baden-Baden: Nomos, 1999), p. 373; Lionel Yee, 'The International Criminal Court and the Security Council: Articles 13(b) and 16', in Lee, *The International Criminal Court*, p. 143, pp. 149–52; Luigi Condorelli and Santiago Villalpando, 'Referral and Deferral by the Security Council', in Antonio Cassese, Paula Gaeta and John R. W. D. Jones (eds.), *The Rome Statute of the International Criminal Court: A Commentary* (Oxford: Oxford University Press, 2002), p. 627, pp. 644–54.

197 See, for example, Andreas O'Shea, 'The Statute of the International Criminal Court' (1999) 116 SALJ 243, 249. Gabrielle H. Oosthuizen, 'Some Preliminary Remarks on the Relationship Between the Envisaged International Criminal Court and the UN Security Council' (1999) 46 NILR 313, 330; Vera Gowlland-Debbas, 'The Functions of the United Nations Security Council in the International Legal System', in M. Byers (ed.), *The Role of Law in International Politics* (Oxford: Oxford University Press, 2000), p. 277, p. 297.

highly controversial in the drafting of the Rome Statute, partly because many saw any role for a political body in this area as inappropriate.[198] Sir Franklin Berman, head of the UK delegation at Rome, accepts that Article 16 is a 'departure from pure principle', albeit in his view a minor one.[199]

The final compromise was intended to make Article 16 difficult to implement for the Security Council. Any of the permanent five members of the Security Council could veto such a resolution. So a State proposing such a resolution would have to persuade nine other members of the Council, of whom five must be the permanent members, of the advisability of passing it. It was not expected that many Article 16 resolutions would be passed. The drafters had not foreseen that the United States would threaten to veto all resolutions renewing peacekeeping mandates unless the Council passed what became Resolution 1422 in July 2002.[200] Resolution 1422 required a blanket deferral of all investigations 'involving current or former officials or personnel from a contributing State not a party to the Rome Statute over acts or omissions relating to a United Nations established or authorized operation' for a year.

The Resolution was immensely controversial in the Council, and with good reason. Despite the Resolution's protestations to the contrary, Resolution 1422 is not in conformity with Article 16 of the Rome Statute, as that article was intended to refer to specific situations, while Resolution 1422 asks for a general deferral of investigations, including those relating to situations in the future.[201] The fact that there was no

[198] Yee, '*The International Criminal Court*', pp. 149–52.

[199] Franklin Berman, 'The Relationship Between the International Criminal Court and the Security Council', in Hermann A. M. von Hebel, Johan G. Lammers and Jolien Schukking (eds.), *Reflections on the International Criminal Court: Essays in Honor of Adriaan Bos* (The Hague: Kluwer/T.M.C. Asser Instituut, 1999), p. 173, p. 177.

[200] UN Doc. S/RES/1422. On the Resolution, see Robert Cryer and Nigel D. White, 'The Security Council and the International Criminal Court: Who's Feeling Threatened?' (2002) 8 *International Peacekeeping: The Yearbook of International Peace Operations* 143; Marc Weller, 'Undoing the Global Constitution: UN Security Council Action on the International Criminal Court' (2002) 78 IA 693; Carsten Stahn, 'The Ambiguities of Resolution 1422' (2003) 14 EJIL 85; Dan Sarooshi, 'The Peace and Justice Paradox: The International Criminal Court and the UN Security Council', in Dominic McGoldrick, Peter Rowe and Eric Donnelly (eds.), *The International Criminal Court* (Oxford: Hart, 2004), p. 95, pp. 115–20. For a more sympathetic view of Resolution 1422, see Dominic McGoldrick, 'Political and Legal Responses to the ICC', in Dominic McGoldrick, Peter Rowe and Eric Donnelly (eds.), *The International Criminal Court* (Oxford: Hart, 2004), p. 389, pp. 415–22.

[201] Cryer and White, 'Security Council', 148–51; Sarooshi, 'The Peace and Justice Paradox', pp. 117–19.

determination of a threat to international peace and security in Resolution 1422 means that it is also inconsistent with the UN Charter.[202]

In terms of its practical effects on the ICC, Resolution 1422 was not important. In the first year of operation of the Court the Office of the Prosecutor was being set up, and in no position to begin investigations. There were also no allegations of peacekeepers engaging in activities that would implicate the ICC's jurisdiction.[203] The Resolution was renewed in 2003 (in Resolution 1487), but not in 2004, so its effects have now come to an end. The lawfulness of the two Resolutions was highly questionable and the broader challenges they made to the regime of international criminal law enforcement were concerning.

The first of these challenges is that separating off different types of peacekeeper implicates issues of equality before the law. As the representative of Canada explained prior to the adoption of Resolution 1422 'at stake today . . . are issues that raise questions about whether all people are equal before the law; whether everyone in a sovereign State is subject to that State's laws including international laws binding on that State'.[204] The second problem has been explained elsewhere:

> the Resolution can be seen as an attempt to assert the supremacy of political considerations over law in two significant ways: not only by violating both the Rome Statute and the UN Charter, but also by trying to assert the old political order of the veto, secret meetings and self-serving interpretations of 'security', over a newly emerging, but still very weak, legal order based on the enforcement of fundamental laws prohibiting the most heinous crimes. In so doing, the Security Council acted inconsistently with its own movement towards a system of security based increasingly on concerns about justice manifested by its creation of international criminal tribunals and determinations that violations of international humanitarian law constituted threats to the peace.[205]

Despite the ICC being open to certain criticisms of selectivity, and the questionable aspects of the Security Council's early reactions to the coming into force of the Rome Statute, these blemishes should not encourage

[202] Cryer and White, 'Security Council', 151–8; Roberto Lavalle, 'A Vicious Storm in a Teacup: The Action by the United National Security Council to Narrow the Jurisdiction of the International Criminal Court' (2003) 14 CLF 195, 209–10. Stahn, 'The Ambiguities', 86–7, argues that there is an implicit finding of a threat to the peace, but the background to the Resolution shows that this was not the case.

[203] See Lavalle, 'A Vicious Storm', 216–17.

[204] UN Doc.S/PV 4568, p. 4.

[205] Cryer and White, 'Security Council', 169–70. Despite the legal position being different, similar criticisms of the approach of the Council could be made in relation to Resolution 1497.

forgetfulness about the extent to which the Court represents a dramatic leap forward in enforcement of international criminal law. The ICC is considerably less open to criticism on the basis of selectivity than previous Tribunals or many States' practice in this area. To demand perfection would be to demand the impossible, at the domestic or international level.

Special Court for Sierra Leone

The creation of the ICC has not exhausted the examples of Tribunals set up with the assistance of international society. There is also the Special Court for Sierra Leone. The jurisdiction of the Special Court for Sierra Leone is subject to similar critiques as the *ad hoc* Tribunals on the basis that it is a reaction to a single conflict, that in Sierra Leone.[206] There are a number of other countries and conflicts that could have such Courts set up for them. Like the two UN Tribunals, though, the Special Court's jurisdiction applies to both the government and its supporters and to rebels such as the RUF. The Special Court's Prosecutor, David Crane, has adopted an impressively impartial approach to indictment, indicting parties from all sides for their conduct in the conflict. In doing so, he has surprised many Sierra Leoneans, including some in the government.

There is one set of actors in the Sierra Leone conflict who are treated differently. Article 1(b) places primary jurisdiction over any 'peacekeepers and related personnel' in the primary jurisdiction of the sending State so long as they were 'present in Sierra Leone pursuant to the Status of Mission Agreement in force between the United Nations and the Government of Sierra Leone or agreements between Sierra Leone and other governments or regional organisations, or, in the absence of such agreement, provided that the peacekeeping operations were undertaken with the consent of the Government of Sierra Leone'. Insofar as this covers those peacekeepers present pursuant to express agreements this is not too different from Article 98 of the Rome Statute, but it is more expansive than that provision as it includes those peacekeepers who were in Sierra Leone with the consent of its government, but without such an agreement. This related to the Security Council's affirmation that sending States had a responsibility to investigate such offences.[207] Should they prove unwilling or unable to do so the Special Court could prosecute them only should the Security Council expressly authorise the

[206] Special Court Statute, Article 1.
[207] See Robert Cryer, 'A Special Court for Sierra Leone?' (2001) 50 ICLQ 435, 440.

Court to do so.[208] This means that some such persons could be immunised from prosecution owing to the operation of the veto. Article 1(b) was probably unnecessary anyway, as there have been no allegations that peacekeepers are among those who 'bear the greatest responsibility' for crimes in Sierra Leone, and whom it is the mandate of the Special Court to prosecute.[209]

The temporal jurisdiction of the Special Court for international crimes does not reach back to the beginning of the conflict in Sierra Leone in 1991. Instead, the Special Court has jurisdiction from the date of the Abidjan Peace Agreement (30 November 1996) and is ongoing. This is in some respects arbitrary and means that offences predating the Agreement cannot be punished by the Special Court. On the other hand, the date was deliberately chosen as an apolitical one, one which captured most of the serious crimes in the conflict and was based on the strong pragmatic foundation that the Court was not intended to hear a large number of cases, so should not be overburdened.

Conclusion

It would be easy to end this chapter on a negative note. International criminal law has been, and is still, often enforced selectively. There is no question that the enforcement of international criminal law has fallen short of the standard of perfect compliance with rule of law ideals. Despite rule of law concepts being hardwired into international criminal law, these have often been honoured in the breach. Even though the Nuremberg and Tokyo IMTs both explained that they were about bringing the law to bear on high-ranking government officials,[210] the lowliest suspects from the victor States were never put before those courts, nor were they intended to be. The practical necessity of ensuring that some States remain co-operative has limited the practical ability of the ICTY and ICTR to investigate all offences subject to their jurisdiction. The need of those Tribunals to ensure their financing is also a factor, and it is likely to be with the ICC and the Special Court for Sierra Leone. The Special Court, being funded by voluntary contributions rather than assessed (mandatory) ones, is in an especially difficult position in relation to its financers.

Nonetheless, the cup should be seen as half full, rather than half empty. The modern regime of international criminal law enforcement

[208] Special Court Statute, Article 1(c). [209] Special Court Statute, Article 1(a).
[210] For a modern restatement of this, see Article 27 of the Rome Statute.

is far less subject to the criticism that it is selective than earlier attempts to enforce that law. As a result McCormack's comment that: '[t]his self righteous tendency to apply a different set of principles of international justice to one's own nationals, and the corresponding willingness to promote collective international responses when some "other" entity is involved, is as evident in current national positions in relation to the proposed permanent international criminal court as it was in the attitudes of the Allied powers establishing Nuremberg and Tokyo'[211] is a little overstated. The efforts of the 'Like-Minded States' in ensuring the creation of a reasonably strong and effective court should not be ignored. We must remember the massive leap that has occurred from even the mid-1990s as, 'nobody . . . even after the establishment of the ICTY and the ICTR, dared to hope that before the end of the millennium a *permanent* International Criminal Court could be established'.[212]

A considerable number of States have been willing to set up a court that has jurisdiction over allegations of offences by their nationals or on their territory. That the ICC is imperfect from the perspective of the rule of law should not blind us to the extent to which the Court represents a quantum leap beyond what went before. As time goes on, and should more States ratify the Rome Statute, a more global regime may come into being which is less susceptible to such critiques. It is practically impossible for the international criminal law regime to achieve perfect compliance with rule of law standards and be perfectly consistent. National criminal law systems do not achieve full compliance with such standards, and they operate in an environment that is far more conducive to fulfilling such criteria. But there is another form of this critique to which the system may remain vulnerable. It is to this critique that we will now turn.

[211] McCormack, 'Selective Reaction', 719–20.

[212] Otto Triffterer, 'Preliminary Remarks: The Permanent ICC-Ideal and Reality', in Otto Triffterer (ed.), *Commentary on the Rome Statute of the International Criminal Court: Article by Article* (Baden-Baden: Nomos, 1999), p. 17, p. 47.

5 Selectivity and the law: I – definitions of crimes

Introduction

As was shown in chapter 4, selectivity *ratione personae* is a critique that can be (and often has been) levelled at international criminal law. However, this is not to say that States never chose to prosecute their own nationals. With the turn to prosecution that occurred in the 1990s, of which the promulgation of the Rome Statute for the International Criminal Court in 1988 was both cause and effect, selectivity in the sense it was dealt with in chapter 4, appears to be becoming more limited, although it will be by no means eliminated.

However, selectivity bubbles to the surface in a more subtle way, in the parameters of criminal responsibility. Let us return to Kenneth Kulp Davis' explication of selectivity: 'when an enforcement agency or officer has discretionary power to do nothing about a case in which enforcement would be clearly justified, the result is a power of selective enforcement. Such power goes to selection of parties against whom the law is enforced. Selective enforcement may also mean selection of the law that will be enforced; an officer may enforce one statute fully, never enforce another and pick and choose in enforcing a third.'[1] This chapter, and chapter 6, concentrate on a form of selectivity derived from the second aspect of this definition.

The basic contention of these two chapters is that when they are creating what Michael Bothe has termed a 'safe' law enforcement mechanism (one which is unlikely to assert jurisdiction over their nationals' activities),[2] there is a tendency for States to take a different view of the

[1] Kenneth Kulp Davis, *Discretionary Justice: A Preliminary Enquiry* (Baton Rouge: Louisiana State University Press, 1969), p. 163.

[2] Michael Bothe, 'International Humanitarian Law and War Crimes Tribunals: Recent Developments and Perspectives', in Karel Wellens (ed.), *International Law: Theory and Practice* (The Hague: Kluwer, 1998), pp. 581, 593.

law than when there is the possibility of the Tribunal exercising jurisdiction over their nationals (an 'unsafe' mechanism).[3] The trend is for the creators of international criminal courts to take a wider view of the definitions of crimes when they are not to be subject to their jurisdiction than when they are. This includes the contention that when there is the possibility of the court exercising its jurisdiction over its creators, definitional precision is insisted upon, as although States may be content to allow a court to determine the law for other States, they are unwilling to concede to the court a power to make law binding on the States that set it up.[4] It must be remembered that the possibility of leaving definitions to the court was omitted from the ILC Draft Statute for precisely the reason that doing so would amount to giving the court a quasi-legislative role.[5] To move the discussion forward, it is therefore necessary to evaluate the extent to which international courts fall into the 'safe' or 'unsafe' categories.

'Safe' and 'unsafe' Tribunals

The separation of authority was exceptionally clear in the post-war tribunals (the Nuremberg and Tokyo IMTs). In both, those drafting the law and creating the Tribunal were not to be the subjects of investigation or prosecution. The Nuremberg Charter was drafted in the London Conference, which consisted of representatives of the 'Big Four' powers.[6] The possibility of having a German or neutral jurist at the conference was never even considered. In addition to this, because of the comprehensive defeat of Germany the representatives were free to pursue their objective of ensuring 'the conviction and punishment of the Nazi defendants'.[7]

[3] In relation to non-international armed conflicts, this transposes into a court that could exercise jurisdiction over the government participating in negotiations (and its allies) rather than just rebels.

[4] Alain Pellet, 'Applicable Law', in Antonio Cassese, Paola Gaeta and John R. W. D. Jones (eds.), *The Rome Statute: A Commentary* (Oxford: Oxford University Press, 2002), p. 1051, pp. 1056–9.

[5] See James Crawford, 'The ILC Adopts a Statute for an International Criminal Court' (1995) 89 AJIL 404, 411.

[6] See Arieh Kochavi, *Prelude to Nuremberg: Allied War Crimes Policy and the Question of Punishment* (Durham, NC: North Carolina University Press, 1998), pp. 222, 226.

[7] Matthew Lippman, 'Nuremberg: Forty-Five Years Later' (1991) 7 Connecticut JIL 1, 37. See also M. Cherif Bassiouni, *Crimes Against Humanity in International Criminal Law* (The Hague: Kluwer, 2nd rev. edn., 1999), p. 16 ('The facts were to drive the law . . . it was designed to produce a pre-ordained result'); Bradley F. Smith, *Reaching Judgment at Nuremberg*, London: André Deutsch, 1977, p. 62.

In this regard, it is worth mentioning some of the comments made by the drafters; David Maxwell-Fyfe[8] explained: 'I want to make clear in this document what are the things for which the Tribunal can punish the defendants. I don't want it left to the Tribunal to interpret what are the principles of international law that it should apply . . . it should not be left to the Tribunal to say what is or what is not a violation of international law . . . What we want to abolish at the trial is a discussion as to whether the acts are violations of international law or not. We declare what international law is.' Robert Jackson seems to have agreed. Jackson criticised a Soviet proposal as:

> it seems to me to leave the tribunal in the position where it could be argued, and the tribunal might very reasonably say, that no personal responsibility resulted if we failed to say it when we are making an agreement between the four powers which fulfils in a sense the function of legislation. I think there is greater authority in us to declare principles as we see them now than there would be in a court to use new principles that we failed to declare in an organic act setting up the court.[9]

Although the details of the drafting of the Charter of the Tokyo IMT are unavailable, certain points may be raised. The US Chief Prosecutor, without consultation with the other Allies, never mind any neutral or Japanese representatives, drafted the Charter himself.[10] The Charter, in relation to the law applied, was also very similar to the London Charter for the Nuremberg IMT,[11] so in many ways similar policies and attitudes can be presumed to have been at work. As was the case in the London Conference, the law was drafted by the winning side in the war for application to the opposing side in that war, who had little chance to complain about its nature. Together, the two IMTs represent a pair.

The drafting process for the ICTY Statute was partially different. The decision to create the ICTY was taken by the Security Council, which was not a party to the Yugoslav conflict,[12] nor were any of its members. The decision to create the ICTY was formalised in Resolution 808, which asked the Secretary-General of the United Nations to prepare a report

8 Quoted in Robert Jackson, *Report of Robert H. Jackson: US Representative to the International Conference on Military Trials* (Washington, DC: Government Printing Office, 1945), pp. 328–9, 399.

9 *Jackson Report*, p. 311.

10 Solis Horwitz, 'The Tokyo Trial' (November 1950) 465 *International Conciliation* 478, 480.

11 Chihiro Hosoya, 'Preface', in Chihiro Hosoya, Yasuaki Onuma, Nisuke Ando and Richard Minear (eds.), *The Tokyo Trial: An International Symposium* (Tokyo: Kodanasha International, 1986), p. 1, p. 9.

12 That is not to say that the Security Council had been silent on the Yugoslav conflict.

on the creation of a Tribunal, and to write its Statute. The power to make decisions on what was in the Statute was passed by the Security Council (and the States comprising it), to an entirely non-State-based entity, the Office of the Secretary General, (in practice, the UN Office of Legal Affairs, OLA).[13] Cherif Bassiouni gives two reasons for this: first, that the members of the Security Council realised that they would have problems drafting the law themselves. Secondly, they knew that the OLA would be drafting the Statute, so some States knew that they could confidentially influence its contents.[14] The former contention is almost undoubtedly correct, the latter is open to question, given that the reports given by the States were public, and suggestions in their reports were clearly not all taken up.[15] Of course, in an organ such as the Security Council the possibilities of influence cannot be ruled out.

The Secretary General was given an unprecedented power to determine the structure of the Tribunal and the body of law the ICTY was to apply. The final decision making authority for the ICTY was the Security Council. Of course, even though the Security Council was likely to adopt the fruits of the Secretary General's (and OLA's) labours, if the report had gone far beyond what was acceptable it would not have been adopted. Either certain members of the Security Council or the United Nations generally would have (in the former case) either refused to pass the report, or (in the latter) actively opposed the ICTY (and sealed its fate by opposing its funding). This limitation, along with the commitment of the United Nations to human rights,[16] perhaps led the Secretary General to assert that 'the application of the principle *nullum crimen sine lege* requires that the international tribunal should apply rules of international humanitarian law which are beyond any doubt part of customary law so that the problem of adherence of some but not all States to specific conventions does not arise'.[17]

[13] See M. Cherif Bassiouni and Peter Manikas, *The Law of the International Criminal Tribunal for Yugoslavia* (Ardsley: Transnational, 1996), pp. 221–5; Daphna Schraga and Ralph Zacklin, 'The International Criminal Tribunal for Yugoslavia' (1994) 5 EJIL 360, 361–2.

[14] Bassiouni and Manikas, *The Law of the International Criminal Tribunal*, p. 221.

[15] Reports, including suggestions for Statutes, were given by France (UN Doc. S/25266), Italy (UN Doc. S/25300), the Islamic Conference (UN Doc. S/25512), the Russian Federation (UN Doc. S/25536), Canada (UN Doc. S/25594), the Netherlands (UN Doc. S/25716) and the United States (UN Doc. S/25575). The most notable suggestion in a State report, which was not taken up in the Statute, was the US proposal that the Statute determine the conflict to be international (S/25575, Article 10(a)).

[16] See UN Charter, Articles 1(1) and 55.

[17] Report of the Secretary General Pursuant to Paragraph 2 of Security Council Resolution 808, UN Doc. S/25704, para. 34. With respect, the comment of the Secretary General here betrays certain elisions and misconceptions. He conflates the

Although the ICTR's Statute was created by the same body as the ICTY (the Security Council), the way in which the Statute was drafted was very different. Here the Statute was drafted by the United States and New Zealand, with input from Rwanda which, at the time, was a member of the Security Council.[18] This is a relevant factor: not only did parts of the membership of the Security Council retain the right to draft the Statute, but also the State which was to be subject to the jurisdiction of the court was in a position not only to object to any particular formulation of the law but also to attempt to influence the formulation itself.[19] As Rwanda was a non-permanent member of the Security Council, of course, it could not veto the creation of the ICTR, although it did vote against it. Here we see the first example of the creation of an international criminal court where there was not a total separation between the authority creating the tribunal and the State (or nationals thereof) which was to be subject of the Tribunal. However, the ultimate defining authority for the jurisdiction of the ICTR was not Rwanda, but the Security Council.

The most prominent example of unity between the authority to define the law and its possible subjects is the Rome Statute. Here, for the first time, the Statute was not reactive, and all States' nationals at the Rome conference were, at least theoretically, potential defendants before the Court. The negotiations themselves were particularly difficult, and in the end, the Bureau had to create a package deal on which States voted.[20] Because of this unity of authority, Robinson asserted that 'given the interest of participating States in knowing the precise contours of the corresponding obligations . . . [definitions of crimes could be expected to

nullum crimen principle with the adherence of all States to Conventions. In addition, he ignores the fact that the SFRY (and thus all its successors) were parties to all the relevant humanitarian law conventions (the four Geneva Conventions and both Additional Protocols), thus the problem he fears could not arise.

[18] See Roy S. Lee, 'The Rwanda Tribunal' (1996) 9 LJIL 37, 39; Daphna Schraga and Ralph Zacklin, 'The International Criminal Tribunal for Rwanda' (1996) 7 EJIL 501, 504. The Secretary General's initial report on the ICTR (Report Pursuant to Paragraph 5 of Security Council Resolution 955 UN Doc. S/1995/134) is not, like his report on the ICTY, the reflections of the drafter of the Statute.

[19] Schraga and Zacklin, 'The International Criminal Tribunal for Rwanda', 504, note that, more than the ICTY Statute, the ICTR represented a negotiated outcome. One of the reasons Rwanda voted against the Resolution creating the ICTR (SC Resolution 955) was that it included crimes (war crimes and crimes against humanity) that they did not wish to be included in the Statute. See UN Doc. S/PV. 3453, p. 15.

[20] See Philippe Kirsch and John T. Holmes, 'The Rome Conference on an International Criminal Court: The Negotiating Process' (1999) 93 AJIL 2, 5–9. See also David J. Scheffer, 'The United States and the International Criminal Court' (1999) 93 AJIL 12, 20.

be more detailed and] . . . one might expect the definition[s] to be more restrictive than previous definitions'.[21] This would certainly seem to correspond with the opinions of some delegations, who agreed with the US spokesman who asserted: '[t]his court should not . . . be in the business of deciding even what is a crime. This is not the place for progressive development of the law into uncertain areas, or for the elaboration of new and uncertain international criminal law. The court must concern itself with those atrocities which are universally recognized as wrongful and condemned.'[22] A clear contrast can be seen when these comments are compared with those of the drafters of the Nuremberg IMT Charter.

The Special Court for Sierra Leone is a difficult case to call. The Sierra Leonean government was fully engaged in the negotiations for the Court. The basis of the Court is an agreement between the United Nations and Sierra Leone.[23] Sierra Leone thus had the opportunity to reject the Court. The Special Court also had jurisdiction over all offences in Sierra Leone. This would, at first glance place the Court in the 'unsafe' camp, in which it might be expected to have a narrow approach to the applicable law. However, the picture is made more complex by the understanding that most of the Sierra Leonean government had: this was that the Court was intended to prosecute Revolutionary United Front (RUF) leaders and the overthrown junta. This understanding was clear in the request for assistance Sierra Leone sent to the Security Council,[24] which may have been encouraged by the US ambassador to the United Nations, Richard Holbrooke, who noted that '[i]t is very important that the people – Foday Sankoh and his henchmen – who have committed these war crimes be brought to justice'.[25] It is uncertain how widely this understanding was held in the later parts of the negotiation of the Statute of the Special Court, but it is also notable that Sierra Leone retained the right to

[21] Daryl Robinson, 'Defining Crimes Against Humanity at the Rome Conference' (1999) 93 AJIL 43, 43. See also Rosalyn Higgins, 'International Law in a Changing International System' (1999) 58 CLJ 78, 88 who agrees that the ICC will be subject to more political control than the UN Tribunals on the definitions of crimes.

[22] Representative of the US to the General Assembly, 23 October 1997 (Agenda Item 150), cited in Neil Boister, 'The Exclusion of Treaty Crimes from the Jurisdiction of the Proposed International Criminal Court' (1998) 3 JACL 27, 28. Boister also reports that the EC and others agreed with these sentiments.

[23] 2001 Agreement Between the United Nations and Sierra Leone on the Establishment of a Special Court.

[24] UN Doc. S/2000/786.

[25] BBC News, 'Sierra Leone Backs Tribunal Plan', available at http://news.bbc.co.uk/1/hi/world/Africa/855478/stm.

appoint the Deputy Prosecutor, and there has been considerable surprise expressed in Sierra Leone that government supporters such as Sam Hinga Norman are facing the Court.[26] It would thus be ill advised to draw hasty conclusions from provisions in the Statute, as its status cannot easily be determined. Nonetheless, there is evidence that the Special Court was considered quite 'safe'.

Custom, codification, legitimacy and the *nullum crimen sine lege* principle

As this chapter and chapter 6 will necessarily involve the comparison of documents which attempt to codify the applicable law to a greater or lesser extent, some preliminary remarks on codification in criminal law, the *nullum crimen* principle and the extent to which customary international law can live up to it are called for.[27] Criminal codes are usually thought to have a number of benefits – accessability, comprehensiveness, certainty and consistency.[28] These are not entirely uncontroversial. For example, the open-textured nature of language means that absolute certainty is impossible to achieve in practice.[29] In addition, Paul H. Robinson is of the view that criminal codes rarely serve to announce the rules to the public at large.[30] Relatively speaking, a fully codified set of laws is better at achieving accessibility and certainty than one based solely on custom. However, as Andrew Ashworth has perspicaciously pointed out in another context, '[t]he formal virtues claimed for codification should not, however, distract attention away from the issues of *what* is being codified and *why* some parts of the criminal law have been included in

[26] BBC News, 'Sierra Leone Awaits Catalogue of Horror', available at http://news.bbc.co.uk/1/hi/world/africa/3774979.stm.; BBC News, 'Sierra Leone War "Hero" on Trial', available at http://news.bbc.co.uk/1/hi/world/africa/3793727.stm.

[27] On the *nullum crimen* principle, see Susan Lamb, '*Nullum Crimen, Nulla Poena Sine Lege* in International Criminal Law', in Antonio Cassese, Paula Gaeta and John R. W. D. Jones (eds.), *The Rome Statute of the International Criminal Court: A Commentary* (Oxford: Oxford University Press, 2000), p. 733; Machteld Boot, *Genocide, Crimes Against Humanity and War Crimes: Nullum Crimen Sine Lege and the Subject Matter of the International Criminal Court* (New York: Intersentia, 2002), Part 1.

[28] Gráinne de Burca and Simon Gardner, 'The Codification of the Criminal Law' (1990) 10 OJLS 559, 560; Law Commission Report 177, *A Criminal Code for England and Wales*, 1, pp. 7–11. See also Jeremy Horder, 'Criminal Law and Legal Positivism' (2002) 8 *Legal Theory* 221.

[29] De Burca and Gardner, 'The Codification', 560.

[30] Paul H. Robinson, 'Are Criminal Codes Irrelevant?' (1994–5) 68 *Southern California Law Review* 159, 163–9.

the code rather than others'.[31] The purpose of codification can be to hem in courts, preventing the normal process of interpretation.[32]

The reason given for the codification effort in Rome was that it was necessary to live up to the *nullum crimen sine lege* principle. Questions have arisen about whether it is possible or consistent with this principle to rely on custom for prosecutions.[33] There is nothing about relying on customary law that inherently violates the *nullum crimen* principle,[34] the formulation of the principle in the major human rights treaties permits prosecution on the basis of international law, including customary international law.[35] Many of the arguments over customary law relating to international crimes, especially war crimes, also relate to the customary or otherwise nature of treaty provisions rather than on a *tabula rasa*. The content of the rules at issue is no more or less certain than the treaty rules. The customary rule deemed too vague to base a conviction on in *Vasiljević* was the customary parallel to the prohibition of violence to life and person in Common Article 3. Yet treaty norms are frequently incorporated, unaltered, into domestic law.[36]

Care must be taken with custom in this area. Owing to the controversies that surround customary argumentation, the precise position in customary international law is not as easily stated as in a codified set of laws. Claims about customary law are also not always disinterested, as Karnzbühler's argument before the Nuremberg IMT showed.[37]

31 Andrew Ashworth, *Principles of Criminal Law* (Oxford: Oxford University Press, 4th edn., 2003), p. 8, emphasis in the original.

32 William A. Schabas, 'Interpreting the Statutes of the ad hoc Tribunals', in Lal Chand Vohrah *et al.* (eds.), *Man's Inhumanity to Man: Essays in Honour of Antonio Cassese* (The Hague: Kluwer, 2003), pp. 847, 887.

33 See, for example, Colin Warbrick, 'Extradition Aspects of *Pinochet* 3' (1999) 48 ICLQ 958, 965. In the *Vasiljević* Case, a Trial Chamber of the ICTY refused to prosecute an offence of violence to life and person, as it was too vague, *Prosecutor* v. *Vasiljević*, Judgment, IT-98-32-T, 28 November 2002, paras. 193–204. For comment, see Elena Martín Salgado, 'The Judgment of the International Criminal Tribunal for Yugoslavia in the *Vasiljević* Case' (2003) 16 LJIL 321. A more critical view can be found in Antonio Cassese, 'Black Letter Lawyering v. Constructive Interpretation: The *Vasiljević* Case' (2004) 2 JICJ 265, 271–3.

34 Alain Pellet, 'Applicable Law', in Antonio Cassese, Paula Gaeta and John R. W. D. Jones (eds.), *The Rome Statute of the International Criminal Court: A Commentary* (Oxford: Oxford University Press, 2000), pp. 1051, 1057–8.

35 See, for example, 1966 International Covenant on Civil and Political Rights, 999 UNTS 177, Article 15; 1951 European Convention on Human Rights, 213 UNTS 221, Article 7; 1969 Inter-American Convention on Human Rights, PAUTS 36, Article 9.

36 For an example of this, see the UK Geneva Conventions Act 1957, which merely appends the Conventions as a schedule, and criminalises Grave Breaches.

37 See pp. 200–1.

This resurfaced at Rome where, as Timothy McCormack has noted, some States displayed a 'selective and, at times, promiscuous approach to a commitment to customary norms'.[38]

However, the ICTY has showed that the customary law argument can be entered into at a high level in international criminal law. The Secretary General, in the report on the Statute of the ICTY, seemed to consider that only customary law sufficed to satisfy the requirements of the *nullum crimen* principle.[39] This was too cautious with respect to treaty-based norms, but accepts as a basic proposition that customary law suffices. The background to the Secretary General's comment – criticisms of the Nuremberg IMT on the basis that the purported codifications of crimes in the Nuremberg IMT Charter represented violations of the *nullum crimen* principle – shows that the inherent superiority of the codificatory approach cannot simply be presumed. Both customary approaches and written codifications have their pros and cons. Nor can the issue be entirely separated from who is being prosecuted. The United States was probably the strongest proponent of detailed definitions of offences at Rome,[40] yet Military Commission Order 2, which applies to non-nationals, permits the prosecution of unenumerated customary war crimes.[41]

Custom is not always as clear as codified international law, and this does have rule of law and legitimacy implications. One of the criteria in Fuller's concept of the rule of law is that the rules are tolerably clear.[42] This, in itself is related to the question of whether the law can be applied in a non-arbitrary manner.[43] The less vague a law is, the more it conforms to the ideal of the rule of law; however, some vagueness is inherent in language and law, and we ought not to forget Schabas' point that courts ought to have some elbow room in their determinations. Similarly, Thomas Franck notes that determinacy of rules is an aspect of their legitimacy but although written determinacy is preferable, there is another form of determinacy, which he calls 'judicially supplied process determinacy'.[44] In other words, where there is a process by which the

[38] Timothy L. H. McCormack, 'Crimes Against Humanity', in Dominic McGoldrick, Peter Rowe and Eric Donnelly (eds.), *The Permanent International Criminal Court: Legal and Policy Issues* (Oxford: Hart, 2004), p. 179, p. 200.

[39] See n. 17 above.

[40] Pellet, 'Applicable Law', p. 1057.

[41] Military Commission Order No. 2, 30 April 2003, p. 2.

[42] See p. 195.

[43] S. G. Williams, 'Indeterminacy and the Rule of Law' (2004) 24 OJLS 539, 559.

[44] Thomas M. Franck, *The Power of Legitimacy Among Nations* (Oxford: Oxford University Press, 1990), p. 64.

rules may be clarified, this may save the legitimacy of less determinate rules.

Aggression

The first appearance of the crime of aggression was in the Statutes of the Nuremberg and Tokyo IMTs. The formulation was basically the same. Article 6(a) of the London Charter criminalised the 'planning, preparation, initiation or waging of a war of aggression, or a war in violation of treaties, agreements or assurances, or participation in a common plan or conspiracy for the accomplishing of any of the foregoing'.[45] This provision has caused a great deal of controversy.[46]

After the First World War, the 1919 Commission determined that aggression was not contrary to positive international law, although it would be a positive step to make it so.[47] After this, treaties such as the 1923 Draft Treaty of Mutual Assistance and the 1924 League Protocol for the Settlement of International Disputes referred to aggressive war as an international crime. Neither treaty was ratified. In 1927, the League of Nations Assembly unanimously adopted a resolution proclaiming that aggressive war was a crime.[48] This sentiment was repeated in a resolution of the Pan American Conference on 18 February 1928.[49] Sheldon Glueck considered that from these documents 'one may reasonably conclude that the time had arrived in the life of civilised nations when an international custom has developed to hold aggressive war to be an

[45] 1945 London Agreement for the Prosecution and Punishment of the Major War Criminals of the European Axis, 82 UNTS 279. Article 5(a) of the Charter of the International Military Tribunal for the Far East, 2 Bevans 20 is essentially the same.

[46] Benjamin B. Ferencz, 'The Crime of Aggression', in Gabrielle Kirk McDonald and Olivia Swaak-Goldman (eds.), *Substantive and Procedural Aspects of International Criminal Law, I: Commentary* (The Hague: Kluwer, 2000), p. 33; Sheldon Glueck, *The Nuremberg Trial and Aggressive War* (New York: Knopf, 1946); Hans Ehard, 'The Nuremberg Trial Against the Major War Criminals and International Law' (1949) 43 AJIL 223, 236–9; Hans Kelsen, 'Will the Judgment in the Nuremberg Trial Constitute a Precedent in International Law?' (1947) 1 ILQ 153, 155–8; Georg Schwarzenberger, *International Law as Applied by International Courts and Tribunals, II: The Law of Armed Conflict* (London: Stevens & Sons, 1968), pp. 485–94; Sheldon Glueck, *War Criminals, their Prosecution and Punishment* (New York: Knopf, 1944), pp. 37–8; Robert K. Woetzel, *The Nuremberg Trials and International Law* (London: Stevens & Sons, 1962), pp. 163–71; Leo Gross, 'The Criminality of Aggressive War' (1947) 41 *American Political Science Review* 205.

[47] Report of the Commission on the Responsibility of the Authors of the War and on Enforcement (1920) 14 AJIL 95, 118–20.

[48] 'Nuremberg IMT, 'Judgment and Sentence' (1947) 41 AJIL 172, 219–20.

[49] Nuremberg IMT, 'Judgment and Sentence', 220.

international crime'.[50] It seems unlikely that two draft Conventions without a ratification between them, and two non-binding resolutions of non-universal international bodies, could be considered sufficient authority to ground an international crime in positive international law.[51] The Nuremberg IMT limited itself to saying that they evidenced 'the prohibition of aggressive war demanded by the conscience of the world',[52] and using them to interpret the only interwar convention which really had a bearing on the matter, the Kellogg–Briand Pact.[53]

In this Pact, the parties condemned recourse to war and renounced it as an instrument of national policy. The problem with basing the international *criminality* of aggressive war on the Pact is that there is nothing in it to support such a claim. The normal consequence of treaty violation is the violating State coming under a duty to make reparation.[54] On the other hand, the silence of a treaty relating to individual responsibility does not determine whether or not the treaty concerned creates a crime,[55] the issue is one of intent of the parties.[56] Here, the resolutions may be relevant. The problem with this line of argument is, as Glueck had noted prior to his change of heart, 'the great majority of expressions of contemporary public opinion . . . were far from regarding it as an international penal Statute'.[57] The possibility of individual liability did not appear in the 1934 ILA Interpretative Articles for the Pact.[58]

During the Second World War, the crime was not under the mandate of the UNWCC, and it appears that 'only one year before the London Conference three of the big four had gone on record that aggressive war was not in itself a crime'.[59] At the London Conference, there was considerable doubt about the customary basis for charges of aggressive war.[60]

[50] Glueck, *The Nuremberg Trial*, p. 26.

[51] See William Bosch, *Judgement on Nuremberg: American Attitudes Towards the Major German War Crimes Trials* (Durham, NC: North Carolina University Press, 1970), p. 58; Dissenting Opinion of the Member for India, Judge Pal, in R. John Pritchard and Sonia M. Zaide, *The Tokyo War Crimes Trial, 21: Separate Opinions* (New York: Garland, 1981), pp. 70–6; Opinion of Judge Röling, *ibid*, pp. 14–26.

[52] Nuremberg IMT, Judgment, p. 220. The 'conscience of the world' could not be assimilated to State-based *opinio juris*.

[53] 1928 General Treaty for the Renunciation of War as an Instrument of National Policy, (1929) UKTS 29 Cmnd. 3410.

[54] *Chorzow Factory Case* 1 WCR 646, 664, 667–8.

[55] Hague Convention IV does not contain a provision on individual liability. That said, violations of the laws of war have traditionally entailed individual liability.

[56] Woetzel, *The Nuremberg Trials*, p. 166.

[57] Glueck, *War Criminals*, p. 19.

[58] ILA – Report of the 38th Conference (Budapest, 1934), pp. 1–78, esp. pp. 66–8.

[59] Richard Minear, *Victor's Justice: The Tokyo War Crimes Trial* (Princeton: Princeton University Press, 1971), p. 50.

[60] *Jackson Report*, pp. 65–7, 295, 327, 335.

This doubt did not stop the Allies signing the crime into being for the Nuremberg IMT (and accepting it in Tokyo). The Nuremberg IMT (with whom the Tokyo IMT majority concurred) was a little uncomfortable with the inclusion of aggressive war as an international crime. Despite asserting that the London Charter was 'decisive and binding',[61] the Nuremberg IMT went out of its way to attempt to prove that the Charter was in accordance with international law. The separate judgments in the Tokyo IMT are illuminating on this point, as the two dissenting judges asserted that the charge was not part of international law[62] and one of the concurring judges preferred to base the offence on natural law.[63] In all, it is clear that this charge could be accepted only on the basis of an exceptionally broad view of the sources of international law and was, in reality, created *ex post facto*. In that the category of crimes against peace was not established by the time of the two IMTs, there is no point examining whether the definitions given comport with existing international law. Suffice to say that the formulation given to them was very vague, and open to 'interested interpretation'.[64]

After the two IMTs, the position in relation to aggression remained controversial. After the Nuremberg IMT the General Assembly promulgated Resolution 95, which '[a]ffirms the principles of international law Recognised by the Charter of the Nürnberg Tribunal and the Judgment of the Tribunal'.[65] There was some debate at the time about whether this amounted to an acceptance that the Nuremberg law was now customary.[66] It is almost universally accepted now that most of the London Charter represents customary international law.[67] If any clarification on the Nuremberg IMT's Charter were required, both the Secretary General and the ICTY have asserted the customary nature of the Nuremberg Charter.[68] Additional support may be derived from General Assembly Resolution 3314, which reaffirmed individual criminal responsibility for initiating wars of aggression.[69]

[61] Nuremberg IMT, Judgment, p. 216.

[62] Judge Pal, believing that it was not supportable, rejected the charge outright; Dissenting Judgment of Judge Pal, p. 1,226. Judge Röling did not consider it to be legally supportable; Bernard V. A. Röling and Antonio Cassese, *The Tokyo Trial and Beyond* (Cambridge: Polity Press, 1992), p. 67.

[63] Dissenting Judgment of Judge Bernard, p. 10.

[64] Dissenting Judgment of Judge Pal, p. 233. See Latha Varadarajan, 'From Tokyo to the Hague: A Reassessment of Radabinodh Pal's Dissenting Opinion at the Tokyo Trials on its Golden Jubilee' (1998) 38 Indian JIL 233, 236.

[65] GA Resolution 95 (I), UN Doc. A/64/Add.1.

[66] Ehard, 'The Nuremberg Trial', 242.

[67] Ian Brownlie, *International Law and the Use of Force* (Oxford: Oxford University Press, 1963), pp. 191, 193, cites the considerable State practice confirming this.

[68] Secretary General's Report, para. 34.

[69] GA Res 3314, UN Doc. A/9631, Article 5(2).

Neither the ICTY or ICTR Statutes contained a provision granting them jurisdiction over aggression. This may be understandable for the ICTR, given that the conflict was essentially a civil war and that the prohibition of aggression is addressed to inter-State force.[70] This does not explain the absence of any provision in the ICTY Statute; it was not mentioned in any of the State suggestions, or the Secretary General's report. It is probable that, given the contentious nature of the offence, the fact that the Security Council Resolutions leading up to Resolution 808 concentrated on the conduct of the war, not the causes and its absence from State proposals for the ICTY Statute, led the Secretary General (OLA) to assume that inclusion would be too controversial.

The controversy over the inclusion of aggression in international criminal law was clearly manifested in the negotiations leading up to the Rome Statute. The insertion of aggression in the Statute and its definition proved highly controversial.[71] In the *ad hoc* Committee, various definitions were proposed, but some States simply did not want the crime included, whatever its definition.[72] Similar arguments relating to the inclusion and definition of aggression, along with the putative role of the Security Council, plagued the PREPCOM,[73] and by the Rome Conference the outlook for supporters of the addition of aggression to the Rome Statute looked bleak.[74] Although the same issues arose again in Rome, there was strong support for the inclusion of aggression, but this was by no means universal and those seeking its exclusion had a strong legal argument; the absence of a readily available, broadly acceptable, definition. Contrary to the expectations of many, the final package deal at the end of the conference gave the ICC jurisdiction over aggression.[75] However, the ICC is not to assert jurisdiction over the crime unless and until a definition is included by way of amendment to the Statute.[76]

The controversy over the definition of aggression has still not abated and the Statute has a high threshold for alteration, so it is unlikely

[70] The same probably applies to the Sierra Leone conflict.

[71] Herman von Hebel and Daryl Robinson, 'Crimes Within the Jurisdiction of the Court', in Roy S. Lee (ed.), *The International Criminal Court: Issues, Negotiations, Results* (The Hague: Kluwer, 1999), p. 79, pp. 81–5. See generally, Allegra Carpenter, 'The International Criminal Court and the Crime of Aggression' (1995) 64 Nordic JIL 223.

[72] Report of the Preparatory Committee in the Establishment of a Permanent International Criminal Court, UN GAOR Supp. 22 A/51/22 Vol. II, p. 58.

[73] Andreas Zimmerman 'The Creation of a Permanent International Criminal Court' (1998) 2 MPYBUNL 169, 198–204.

[74] Mahnoush H. Arsanjani, 'The Rome Statute for an International Criminal Court' (1999) 93 AJIL 22, 29.

[75] Rome Statute, Article 5(1)(d).

[76] Rome Statute, Article 5(2).

that a definition will be forthcoming in the near future.[77] Furthermore, some interpret Article 5(2) of the Rome Statute as requiring that any definition of aggression must include a requirement that the Security Council declare that aggression has occurred.[78] This requirement would not have a basis in customary law, and would have the same problems of equal application as were noted in chapter 4 in the context of Security Council referrals to the ICC under Article 13(b).[79]

The treatment of aggression in the two IMTs and the ICC would appear to support the contention of this chapter. For the Nuremberg and Tokyo IMTs, the drafters were happy enough to enact the crime, without precedent or definition, in the IMTs' Charters,[80] while in the Rome Statute, even though its customary nature was far more certain, a definition was considered central. No State would have allowed the crime into the Rome Statute and left the ICC to determine its parameters, which is precisely what the IMTs' creators did.

Genocide[81]

Genocide was not expressly included in the IMTs' Statutes. The term was coined only in 1944, so genocide was not charged separately from

[77] See Roger S. Clark, 'Rethinking Aggression as a Crime and Formulating Its Elements: The Final Work-Product of the Preparatory Commission for the International Criminal Court' (2002) 15 LJIL 859; Matthias Schuster, 'The Rome Statute of an International Criminal Court and the Crime of Aggression: A Gordian Knot in Search of a Sword' (2003) 14 CLF 1; William A. Schabas, 'The Unfinished Work of Defining Aggression', in Dominic McGoldrick, Peter Rowe and Eric Donnelly (eds.), *The International Criminal Court: Legal and Policy Issues* (Oxford: Hart, 2004), p. 123; Mauro Politi and Guiseppe Nesi, *The International Criminal Court and the Crime of Aggression* (Aldershot: Ashgate, 2004).

[78] See the discussion of this position in Paula Escarameia, 'The ICC and the Security Council on Aggression: Overlapping Competencies?', in Mauro Politi and Giuseppe Nesi (eds.), *The International Court and the Crime of Aggression* (Aldershot: Ashgate, 2004), p. 133, pp. 139–41.

[79] See also Marja Lehto, 'The ICC and the Security Council: About the Argument of Politicisation', in Mauro Politi and Giuseppe Nesi (eds.), *The International Court and the Crime of Aggression* (Aldershot: Ashgate, 2004), p. 145.

[80] Both of which could not be used against their authors.

[81] See generally, William A, Schabas, *Genocide in International Law: The Crime of Crimes* (Cambridge: Cambridge University Press, 2000); Boot, *Genocide*, pp. 410–53; Matthew Lippman, 'The Convention on the Prevention and Punishment of Genocide: Fifty Years Later' (1998) 15 Arizona JICL 415; Malcolm Shaw, 'Genocide and International Law', in Yoram Dinstein (ed.), *International Law at a Time of Perplexity* (Dordrecht: Martinus Nijhoff, 1989), p. 797; Alexander Kent A. Greenawalt, 'Rethinking Genocidal Intent: The Case for a Knowledge Based Interpretation' (1999) 99 Columbia LR 2259; Guglielmo Verdirame, 'The Genocide Definition in the Jurisprudence of the *ad hoc* Tribunals' (2000) 49 ICLQ 579; Christine Byron, 'The Crime of Genocide', in Dominic McGoldrick, Peter Rowe and Eric Donnelly (eds.), *The International Criminal Court Legal and Policy Issues* (Oxford: Hart, 2004), p. 142.

crimes against humanity, and there was no mention of the word in the Nuremberg IMT judgment. General Assembly Resolution 96(I) declared that 'genocide is a crime under international law, contrary to the spirit and aims of the United Nations and condemned by the civilized world'.[82] The Genocide Convention was promulgated in 1948, and within three years the ICJ had declared it reflective of custom.[83]

Given the conflicts leading up to their creation, the inclusion of genocide in the ICTY and ICTR Statutes was not only uncontroversial, but also inevitable. Both Statutes adopted the definition from Article II of the Genocide Convention *verbatim*.[84] The largest difference of opinion involved in the creation of the ICTR's jurisdiction was the Rwandan contention to the Security Council that genocide should be the only crime in the ICTR's jurisdiction.[85] In the negotiations leading up to the Rome Conference there were a few suggestions that the groups against which the genocidal intent must rest should be extended to cover other groups, such as those defined by reference to gender, culture or social criteria.[86] Whether this would be advisable or not, it was considered that the Convention definition was too settled to reopen and thus at the Rome Conference a 'quick and unanimous' decision was taken to define genocide as in the Convention.[87]

The Elements of Crimes which accompany the Statute have included a limiting element that does not have a clear customary basis. In the *Jelisić* Case, the ICTY accepted that there was no requirement in the Genocide Convention or custom that there be a large-scale set of actions or a broader plan to commit genocide.[88] There was a fear that this could

[82] GA Resolution 96(I), UN Doc. A/64/Add.1 p. 189. The groups protected by the prohibition of genocide in the Resolution are wider than those in the Genocide Convention, including 'political or any other groups'.

[83] *Reservations to the Convention on the Prevention and Punishment of the Crime of Genocide* Case [1951] ICJ Rep. 15.

[84] ICTY Statute, Article 4, ICTR Statute, Article 2.

[85] Virginia Morris and Michael P. Scharf, *The International Criminal Tribunal for Rwanda* (Ardsley: Transnational, 1998), p. 164 said that this was rejected as it would be one-sided, and RPF atrocities had to also be at least theoretically under the ICTR's jurisdiction. See also Schraga and Zacklin, 'The International Criminal Tribunal for Rwanda', 508.

[86] Christopher Keith Hall, 'The Third and Fourth Sessions of the Preparatory Committee for an International Criminal Court' (1998) 92 AJIL 124, 126.

[87] Arsanjani, 'The Rome Statute', 30.

[88] *Prosecutor* v. *Jelisić*, Judgment, IT-95-10-T, 14 December 1999. See also *Prosecutor* v. *Stakić*, Judgment, IT-97-24-T, 31 July 2003, paras. 504–519. There is no mention of a plan as a requirement in *Prosecutor* v. *Krstić*, Judgment, IT-98-33-A, 19 April 2004. The Trial Chamber judgment in *Prosecutor* v. *Krstić*, Judgment, IT-98-33-T, 2 August 2001, is a

lead to the prosecution of individual 'lone *genocidaires*', in the ICC, an improbable scenario, owing to complementarity and the necessity of persuading the Prosecutor to act in an individual instance. However, this fear led to the inclusion of the requirement that the conduct 'took place in the context of a manifest pattern of similar conduct directed against that group or was conduct that could itself effect such destruction'.[89] The advisability of this addition from a criminal law point of view is controversial.[90] Either way, we can see a narrowing of the definition of genocide which is not based on custom, a requirement not considered necessary for the ICTY and ICTR.

Crimes against humanity

Nuremberg and Tokyo IMTs

The first time crimes against humanity were made expressly subject to the jurisdiction of an ICT was in the Nuremberg Charter, Article 6(c) of which criminalised 'murder, extermination, enslavement, deportation, and other inhumane acts committed against any civilian population, before or during the war, or persecutions on political, racial, or religious grounds in execution of or in connection with any crime under the jurisdiction of the Tribunal, whether or not in violation of the domestic law of the country where perpetrated'.[91]

little ambiguous, stating at one point that 'genocide refers to any criminal enterprise seeking to destroy' (para. 550), but this must be read against the background of the comment that 'the gravity and scale of the crime of genocide *ordinarily presume* that several protagonists were involved' (para. 549). See also *Prosecutor* v. *Kayishema and Ruzindana*, Judgment, ICTR-95-1-A, 1 June 2001, para. 138; at para. 163 a 'persistent pattern of conduct' is said not to be an element of genocide.

89 Elements of Crimes for genocide, Common Element 4. See Valerie Oosterveld, 'The Elements of Genocide', in Roy S. Lee (ed.), *The International Criminal Court: Elements of Crimes and Rules of Procedure and Evidence* (Ardsley: Transnational, 2001), p. 41, pp. 45–9.

90 See William A. Schabas, 'The *Jelisić* Case and the *Mens Rea* of the Crime of Genocide' (2001) 14 LJIL 125; Otto Triffterer, 'Genocide: Its Particular Intent to Destroy in Whole or in Part the Group as Such' (2001) 14 L JIL 399.

91 See generally, M. Cherif Bassiouni, *Crimes Against Humanity in International Criminal Law* (The Hague: Kluwer, 2nd edn., 1998); Egon Schwelb, 'Crimes Against Humanity' (1946) 23 BYBIL 178; William J. Fenrick, 'Should Crimes Against Humanity Replace War Crimes?' (1999) 37 CJTL 767; Beth van Schaack, 'The Definition of Crimes Against Humanity: Resolving the Incoherence' (1999) 37 CJTL 787; McCormack, 'Crimes Against Humanity'; Antonio Cassese, 'Crimes Against Humanity', in Antonio Cassese, Paula Gaeta and John R. W. D. Jones (eds.), *The Rome Statute of the International Criminal Court: A Commentary* (Oxford: Oxford University Press, 2000), p. 353; Boot, *Genocide*, pp. 455–535.

Precedents for charging crimes against humanity are thin on the ground before the twentieth century. The first time an analogous concept was used was the famous 'Martens clause',[92] which refers to 'principles of the law of nations, as they result from the laws of humanity, and the dictates of the public conscience'. There is no clear basis for inferring criminal responsibility from this.[93]

In 1915, the Russian, French and British governments protested to Turkey that Turkish massacres of Armenians amounted to 'crimes of Turkey against humanity'.[94] The term was used in a non-technical way.[95] The 1919 Commission was willing to countenance the prosecution on the basis of the laws of humanity,[96] the US members of the Commission dissented on this part, saying that the laws of humanity were too vague to create a judicially enforceable standard.[97] There was, therefore, some evidence of the development of a concept of crimes against humanity, but not one that extended into peacetime.[98]

In the London Conference, there was great debate on crimes against humanity among the delegates. Although little dissent was recorded on the inclusion of such a set of crimes, their definition was controversial.[99] There was disquiet about the applicability of such prohibitions in peacetime, which was mollified by Jackson's inclusion of a limit upon them to those linked with other crimes in the jurisdiction of the court (war crimes or crimes against peace).[100] This was more to do with a fear of allegations of *tu quoque* than fears about *nullum crimen sine lege*. Crimes against humanity extending into peacetime were almost certainly innovative at the time. The Nuremberg IMT convicted defendants for actions

92 1907 Hague Convention IV Respecting the Laws and Customs of War on Land (1910) UKTS 9 Cd. 5030.

93 M. Cherif Bassiouni, 'International Law and the Holocaust' (1979) 9 CWILJ 209, 210.

94 W. G. Sharp to Bryan (28 May 1915), Foreign Relations of the United States 1915: The World War.

95 Timothy L. H. McCormack, 'From Sun Tzu, to the 6th Committee: The Evolution of an International Criminal Law Regime', in Timothy L. H. McCormack and Gerry Simpson, *The Law of War Crimes: National and International Approaches* (The Hague: Kluwer, 1997), p. 31, p. 45.

96 Report of the 1919 Commission, 121.

97 Report of the 1919 Commission, 144. See Lord Wright, 'War Crimes Under International Law' (1946) 62 LQR 40, 48.

98 See Peter Malanczuk, *Akehurst's Modern Introduction to International Law* (London: Routledge, 7th edn., 1997), pp. 354–5.

99 Matthew Lippman, 'Crimes Against Humanity' (1997) 17 *Boston College Third World Law Journal* 171, 178–86.

100 *Jackson Report*, p. 384.

before (but related to) the war,[101] but it clearly had some doubts about peacetime crimes against humanity.

In recent years, opinion has been split about the customary basis of crimes against humanity by 1945. The judges in *DPP* v. *Polyukhovic* split on the question.[102] The Canadian Supreme Court in *R.* v. *Finta* found, 4–3, that crimes against humanity were retroactively, although appropriately, criminalised,[103] and in the United Kingdom, the Hetherington–Chalmers Report said that it was not certain that crimes against humanity were illegal at the time.[104] The *Tadić* judgment asserted that a new category of crime had been created in 1945.[105]

The definition of crimes against humanity in the Tokyo Charter was, initially, practically identical to that in the London Charter.[106] Then, three days before the trial opened, the Prosecution decided to alter the Charter,[107] removing the words 'against any civilian population'. This was done so that the prosecution could assert that killings of enemy combatants by combatants prosecuting an illegal war were themselves illegal.[108] The Tokyo IMT rather half-heartedly rejected these charges, claiming that they were subsumed under the crimes against peace charge.[109] Their reasoning did not deal with the prosecution's contention head on, there was no customary basis for the prosecution's contention. This aspect of the Charter was entirely unjustifiable from a customary point of view, and its late addition did nothing but underscore the prosecution's subjection of the definitions of law to its strategy in Tokyo.

The problem with crimes against humanity post-Nuremberg was not their basis in customary international law, but the contours of their definition. The Nuremberg (and Tokyo) Charter and judgment left many issues uncertain. To Bassiouni, these matters were of such a fundamental nature as to require a multilateral Convention to settle them.[110] At

[101] See Lippman, 'Crimes Against Humanity', 270; Bernard V. A. Röling, 'The Law of War and National Jurisdiction' (1960) 100 RdC 329, 347.

[102] *DPP* v. *Polyukhovic* (1991) 101 ALR 545, Toohey J (majority), pp. 661–2, Brennan J (minority), p. 597.

[103] *R.* v. *Finta* 104 ILR 285, Cory J (majority), p. 402, La Forest J (minority), pp. 336–7.

[104] Thomas Hetherington and William Chalmers, *Report of the War Crimes Inquiry* (London: HMSO, 1989), p. 62.

[105] *Prosecutor* v. *Tadić*, Opinion and Judgment, IT-94-1-T, 7 May 1997, para. 618.

[106] Article 5(c).

[107] Röling and Cassese, *The Tokyo Trial*, pp. 56–7.

[108] Counts 39–43 and 45–52 of the indictment.

[109] Tokyo IMT Judgment, pp. 452–8; Judge Jaranilla dissented on this, Separate Opinion of Judge Jaranilla, pp. 9–10.

[110] M. Cherif Bassiouni, 'Crimes Against Humanity: The Need for a Specialized Convention' (1994) 31 Columbia JTL 457.

the time of the creation of the ICTY and ICTR, there was some legitimate scope for disagreement on the precise definitions of crimes against humanity. The various State proposals for the definition of such crimes preceding the Secretary General's report on the ICTY betray a lack of consensus on the requirements for liability.[111] Debate has centred on the possibility that a nexus to armed conflict was necessary, whether the attack on a civilian population needed to be widespread and/or systematic, if a separate requirement of a policy needed to be shown and if all crimes against humanity required a discriminatory intent on the part of the perpetrator.

ICTY

In spite of the uncertainties mentioned above, the definition of crimes against humanity in the ICTY Statute is relatively short, providing that: '[t]he International Tribunal shall have the power to prosecute persons responsible for the following crimes when committed in armed conflict, whether international or internal in character, and directed against any civilian population: (a) murder, (b) extermination, (c) enslavement, (d) deportation, (e) imprisonment, (f) torture, (g) rape, (h) persecutions on political, racial and religious grounds, (i) other inhumane acts.'[112]

As can be seen, crimes against humanity are limited by Article 5 to crimes committed in armed conflict. The requirement was included, according to Morris and Scharf, because the Security Council had taken jurisdiction over Yugoslavia as an armed conflict, not that the Secretary General considered this to be one of the criteria for a crime against humanity.[113] It must be noted, though, that this amounts to a fault in the ICTY definition.[114] In relation to the contextual requirements for crimes against humanity the Statute is not very helpful resembling, as it does, the Delphic Nuremberg definition. This ambiguity, alongside the question of precisely what was meant by an attack 'directed against a civilian population' and the haziness of parts of the Secretary General's commentary[115] effectively granted the ICTY a high level of latitude in determining what amounted to a crime against humanity.

[111] Virginia Morris and Michael P. Scharf, *An Insider's Guide to the International Criminal Tribunal for Former Yugoslavia* (Ardsley: Transnational, 1995), p. 77.
[112] ICTY Statute, Article 5.
[113] Morris and Scharf, *An Insider's Guide*, pp. 79–80; see also Larry D. Johnson, 'Ten Years Later: Reflections on the Drafting' (2004) 2 JICJ 368, 371–2.
[114] See Morris and Scharf, *An Insider's Guide*, pp. 82–3.
[115] Johnson, 'Ten Years Later', 372; Morris and Scharf, *An Insider's Guide*, p. 199.

On adoption of Resolution 827, the US, French and Russian representatives all mentioned that they interpreted crimes against humanity as requiring a discriminatory intent.[116] Relying on these, the Trial Chamber in the *Tadić* Case controversially interpreted the Statute to require the element of discriminatory *animus* for all crimes against humanity even though it did not agree that the requirement was a part of customary international law.[117] This aspect of the decision has been criticised,[118] and was overturned on appeal.[119] Perhaps more important than the decision in that case is that the decision was left to the ICTY, as were the decisions on other questions relating to the parameters of liability – for example, on whether the conditions of a widespread/systematic nature were cumulative or disjunctive.

The acts enumerated were uncontroversial. Given that the list in the London Charter was illustrative rather than exclusive, a certain degree of leeway is acceptable in adding to the list of modalities by which crimes against humanity can be committed. The list adds imprisonment, torture and rape,[120] these were present in the Control Council Law 10 definition of crimes against humanity, and it would be all but impossible to deny that these acts were inhumane.[121] As with the London Charter, the list is not closed; the ICTY has therefore been granted the opportunity in practice to add more inhumane acts.[122]

ICTR

When compared to the ICTY Statute, the ICTR Statute's definition of crimes against humanity is far more detailed. The ICTR definition repeats the list of acts in the ICTY Statute, and defines them as amounting to crimes against humanity 'when committed as part of a widespread or systematic attack against any civilian population on national, political, ethnic, racial, or religious grounds'.[123] In accordance with custom, there is no nexus to armed conflict.[124] A useful clarification in Article 3 of the

[116] S/PV. 3217 pp. 16, 11, 45, respectively.

[117] *Prosecutor* v. *Tadić*, Opinion and Judgment, IT-94-1-T, 7 May 1997, para. 652.

[118] Larry D. Johnson, 'The International Tribunal for Rwanda' (1996) 67 RIDP 211, 219, says this is what the Statute required; *contra* Robinson, 'Defining', 46.

[119] *Prosecutor* v. *Tadić*, Judgment IT-94-1-A, 15 July 1999, paras. 273–305.

[120] Article 5.

[121] See Morris and Scharf, *The International Criminal Tribunal for Rwanda*, pp. 188–90.

[122] Karl Arthur Hochkammer, 'The Yugoslav War Crimes Tribunal: The Compatibility of Peace, Politics and International Law' (1995) 28 VJTL 119, 162 considers leaving the list open to be problematic, as it is undefined.

[123] ICTR Statute, Article 3.

[124] Röling and Cassese, *The Tokyo Trial*, p. 56. Few States asserted such a nexus at Rome, see Robinson, 'Defining', 45–6; von Hebel and Robinson, 'Crimes', pp. 92–3.

ICTR Statute is that instead of using the vague 'directed at a civilian population' standard, the ICTR Statute requires the acts to be part of a 'widespread or systematic attack'. This clarifies that they are not conjunctive requirements. Morris and Scharf criticise this as possibly being a higher standard than required in the ICTY.[125] This is not the case; in *Tadić* neither side argued about the presence of those requirements under the ICTY Statute, but rather about their cumulative or disjunctive nature.[126]

In stark contrast to the ICTY Statute, the ICTR Statute explicitly provides that crimes against humanity must take place against the background of a discriminatory attack on the civilian population. Although some thought a discriminatory intention was part of the ICTY definition,[127] it is doubtful that this was required in custom at the time.[128] There was no explanation of the addition of a discriminatory *animus* in the Security Council,[129] and theories have abounded about the reasons behind it. Theodor Meron claims that it was inadvertence on the part of the Security Council.[130] Jordan Paust goes further, asserting that as States realised that a permanent court was on the horizon, they sought a limited definition of crimes against humanity which would be a precedent for the future court.[131] This could be supported on the basis that the RPF (the Rwandan government) would want to raise the threshold for crimes against humanity as high as possible to exclude any offences of which they might be accused. This, if true, would be a strong argument in favour of the basic idea of this chapter.

The Appeals Chamber in *Akayesu* took the view that the requirement of a discriminatory attack was not imposed by the Security Council on the basis that customary law required a discriminatory *animus*, but as an appreciation of the Rwandan context analogous to the limitation on the definition of crimes against humanity in the ICTY Statute that they

[125] Morris and Scharf, *The International Criminal Tribunal for Rwanda*, pp. 194–5.

[126] *Tadić*, Opinion and Judgment, paras. 645–646.

[127] Johnson, 'The International Tribunal for Rwanda', 219.

[128] See Morris and Scharf, *The International Criminal Tribunal for Rwanda*, pp. 196–9; McCormack, 'Crimes Against Humanity', pp. 185–6; Robinson, 'Defining', 46–7. *Prosecutor* v. *Tadić*, Judgment, IT-94-1-A, 15 July 1999, paras. 273–305; *Prosecutor* v. *Semanza*, Judgment, ICTR-97-20-T, 15 May 2003, para. 332 (although the case is not without ambiguity).

[129] Johnson, 'The International Tribunal for Rwanda', p. 219.

[130] Theodor Meron, 'International Criminalization of Internal Atrocities' (1995) 89 AJIL 554, 557.

[131] Jordan Paust, 'Panel Discussion' (1995) 89 Proceedings ASIL 311, 311.

must be committed in armed conflict.[132] Another explanation is available, which also does not require an assumption of *mala fides*. In 1994, there was sufficient ambiguity about the definition that the inclusion of the requirement of discrimination for all crimes against humanity was considered to be correct. This is given credence by the statements of some of the Security Council members when Resolution 827 was being passed. The more detailed evaluation of custom which came in the *Tadić* Appeal and in *Kunarac* had not been engaged in by that time. As a result, it would be ill-advised to make too much of the addition.

ICC

In Rome, the question was not whether crimes against humanity should be included in the Statute,[133] but how they were to be defined.[134] The end result was a compromise between those States seeking a very narrow definition and those States (and NGOs) working for a broad, effective definition of the crimes.

Article 7 of the Rome Statute defines a crime against humanity as:

> any of the following acts when committed as part of a widespread or systematic attack directed against any civilian population, with knowledge of the attack:
>
> (a) Murder;
> (b) Extermination;
> (c) Enslavement;
> (d) Deportation or forcible transfer of population;
> (e) Imprisonment or other severe deprivation of physical liberty in violation of fundamental rules of international law;
> (f) Torture;
> (g) Rape, sexual slavery, enforced prostitution, forced pregnancy, enforced sterilisation, or any other form of sexual violence of comparable gravity;
> (h) Persecution against any identifiable group or collectivity on political, racial, national, ethnic, cultural, religious, gender . . . or other grounds as are universally recognized as impermissible under international law, in connection with any act referred to in this paragraph, or any crime within the jurisdiction of the Court;
> (i) Enforced disappearance of persons;
> (j) the crime of Apartheid;
> (k) Other inhumane acts of a similar character intentionally causing great suffering, or serious injury to body or mental or physical health.

[132] *Prosecutor* v. *Akayesu*, Judgment, ICTR-96-4-A, 1 June 2001, paras. 461–469.
[133] Zimmerman, 'The Creation', 172.
[134] See von Hebel and Robinson, 'Crimes', pp. 98–103.

This definition is significantly more detailed than previous formulations. Also, no nexus to armed conflict is required. There is no requirement of discriminatory intent, except for the crime of persecution. But unreserved praise of the definition would be inappropriate. Article 7 raises the threshold for crimes against humanity. This is because 'attack directed against a civilian population' is defined as 'a course of conduct involving the multiple commission of acts . . . against any civilian population, pursuant to or in furtherance of a State or organisational policy to commit such an attack'.[135] As Robinson notes, this amounts to a compromise between those wanting the requirements disjunctively and those wanting them cumulatively.[136] It effectively introduces an additional set of requirements, a 'course of conduct' and a 'policy'.

The requirements come into play in addition to the requirements of widespread nature or systematicity. They are both actually based on those requirements, 'course of conduct' being based on the 'widespread' criterion, while the policy requirement is modelled on the 'systematicity' requirement. Both are intended to be watered-down versions of the criterion they resemble. So a weakened form of conjunctive requirement has been imposed on the definition in the Rome Statute.[137] This is retrogressive from the point of view of customary international law, which requires only that the actions be widespread or systematic.[138] As the *Tadić* judgment explained, in relation to the requirement that the acts are directed against a civilian population 'either a finding of widespreadness . . . or systematicity . . . fulfils this requirement'.[139]

The threshold for crimes against humanity is further raised by the requirement that the widespread or systematic attack needs to be pursuant to a policy. The *Kunarac* Case made it very clear that there was no separate policy requirement for crimes against humanity.[140] It might be argued against this that the *Kunarac* decision came out in 2002, and it would be inappropriate to evaluate the Rome Statute with respect to a later decision. The position was reasonably clear at Rome. The ILC had already adopted such a view,[141] and in 1997 the Trial Chamber in *Tadić* had already effectively abrogated a separate requirement of a policy by

[135] Article 7(2)(a). [136] Robinson, 'Defining', 47.

[137] William A. Schabas, *An Introduction to the International Criminal Court* (Cambridge: Cambridge University Press, 2nd edn., 2004), p. 44.

[138] Schabas, *An Introduction*, pp. 48–50. See Phyllis Hwang, 'Defining Crimes Against Humanity at the Rome Conference' (1998) 22 Fordham ILJ 457.

[139] *Tadić*, Judgment, para. 648.

[140] *Prosecutor* v. *Kunarac, Kovač and Vuković*, Judgment, IT-96-23-A, 12 June 2002, para. 98.

[141] Schabas, *An Introduction*, p. 44.

declaring that 'if acts occur on a widespread or systematic basis that demonstrates a policy to commit those acts'.[142]

The above is consistent with the idea behind this chapter, that where an 'unsafe' Tribunal is created, we see a more cautious approach to the material coverage of international criminal law than where a 'safe' Tribunal is born. The introduction to the Elements of Crimes also supports this contention. Earlier Tribunals (and the Special Court for Sierra Leone) have had quite considerable latitude in interpreting the concept of crimes against humanity. In addition to the more detailed regulation, the Elements contain the following statement: 'Since Article 7 pertains to international criminal law, its provisions, consistent with Article 22, must be strictly construed, taking into account that crimes against humanity as defined in Article 7 are among the most serious crimes of concern to the international community as a whole, warrant and entail individual criminal responsibility, and require conduct which is impermissible under generally applicable international law, as recognised by the principal legal systems of the world.'

The background to this warning was a concern by some Arab States that some of their family law principles could be interpreted as gender-based persecution and by other States who were concerned about the possibility of an activist court.[143] After the *Kupreškić* judgment in 2000 there was also fear that a State's acquiescence in policies of others could lead to a finding of a State policy for the purposes of crimes against humanity.[144] To ensure that consensus could be reached, a high threshold for inaction to suffice for a policy was imposed,[145] and the above-quoted instruction to judges made.[146]

The acts enumerated begin by following the well-established path of the London and Tokyo Charters, Control Council Law 10 and the

[142] *Tadić*, Judgment, para. 653.

[143] Daryl Robinson, 'Elements of Crimes Against Humanity', in Roy S. Lee (ed.), *The International Criminal Court: Elements of Crimes and Rules of Procedure and Evidence* (Ardsley: Transnational, 2001), p. 57, pp. 65, 69–70; Wiebke Rückert and Georg Witschel, 'Genocide and Crimes Against Humanity in the Elements of Crimes', in Horst Fischer, Claus Kreß and Sascha Rolf Lüder (eds.), *International and National Prosecution of International Crimes Under International Law* (Berlin: Arno Spitz, 2001), p. 59, pp. 70–3.

[144] Robinson, 'Elements', p. 67.

[145] Which Cassese believes is incorrect in custom, see Antonio Cassese, 'Crimes Against Humanity', in Antonio Cassese, Paula Gaeta and John R. W. D. Jones (eds.), *The Rome Statute of the International Criminal Court: A Commentary* (Oxford: Oxford University Press, 2000), p. 353, pp. 375–6.

[146] Elements of Crimes for Crimes Against Humanity, n. 6.

two UN Tribunals, mentioning murder, extermination, enslavement and torture.[147] To the well-accepted modality of crimes against humanity and of deportation, the Statute adds 'or forcible transfer of population'. As the condemnation of 'ethnic cleansing' as a crime against humanity evidences, this is nothing new.[148] The ICTY has discussed internal displacements under the rubric of 'other inhumane acts', in Article 5 of its Statute.[149]

The acts enumerated might be thought to represent a broadening of coverage. Antonio Cassese considers that the inclusion of forced pregnancy, Apartheid, enforced disappearance of persons and the inclusion of gender and cultural grounds of discrimination to be in advance of customary international law.[150] To this could be added the definition of torture. If Cassese is correct, it would count as evidence counter to the proposition put forward in this chapter. To investigate the question of the compliance of Article 7 with custom and the *nullum crimen* principle, the following comment made by the Trial Chamber in *Hadžihasanović* should be borne in mind: 'it is critical to determine whether the underlying conduct at the time of its commission was punishable. The emphasis on conduct rather than on the specific description of the offence in substantive criminal law is of primary relevance.'[151]

Unlike the 1984 Torture Convention, there is no requirement that the perpetrator be an official. This is not part of the customary requirements of torture.[152] The position with respect to the purpose of torture is more complex. The Torture Convention states that torture occurs when there are purposes 'such as' interrogation, coercion, intimidation or discrimination.[153] However the Convention accepts in Article 1(2) that its definition is not exhaustive of international law. In addition, as the ICTY

[147] Article 7(1)(a), (b), (c), (e). See generally, Machteld Boot, Rodney Dixon and Christopher Hall, 'Article 7', in Otto Triffterer (ed.), *Commentary on the Rome Statute of the International Criminal Court: Article by Article* (Baden-Baden: Nomos, 1999), p. 117.

[148] Alfred De Zayas, 'International Law and Mass Population Transfers' (1974) 16 Harvard ILJ 207, 252–7, thinks they probably would come under the Nuremberg Principles, and thus be criminal under the law applicable just after the Second World War.

[149] See, for example, *Krstić* Judgment, para. 523. *Stakić*, Judgment, paras. 671–684, treated the offences of deportation and forced displacement (partially on the basis of the Rome Statute), as one crime.

[150] Cassese, 'Crimes Against Humanity', pp. 376–7.

[151] *Prosecutor* v. *Hadžihasanović, Alagić and Kubura*, Decision on Joint Challenge to Jurisdiction, IT-01-47-PT, 12 November 2002, para. 62.

[152] *Kunarac*, Appeal, para. 148.

[153] Convention Against Torture and Other Cruel, Inhumane or Degrading Treatment and Punishment, 1465 UNTS 85, Article 1.

has accurately pointed out, the definition for the purposes of human rights is not necessarily controlling in international criminal law.[154] The Appeals Chamber in *Kunarac* described the customary purposes as 'obtaining information or a confession, or at punishing, intimidating or coercing the victim or a third person, or at discriminating, on any ground, against the victim or a third person'.[155] This is narrower than the Torture Convention, which has an open-ended, *ejusdem generis* list ('such purposes as').[156] The Trial Chamber in *Čelebići* thus included humiliation in the list of purposes.[157] The Appeals Chamber in *Kunarac* should not be read as clearly having rejected such a purpose, as the issue was not raised at appeal level since it had already determined that the defendant's acts were discriminatory. The Trial Chamber in *Kunarac* had noted that they did not need to determine if any other grounds were customary,[158] so the Appeals Chamber decision should not be taken as having settled the matter.

In any event, the ICC definition, in excluding an express requirement of purpose, is not in advance of the law. The reason the requirement was considered unnecessary was that the Elements of Crimes required the victim to be in the custody or control of the defendant, against the background of a widespread or systematic attack on the civilian population on the basis of a policy. It was thought that this would cover the necessary purpose.[159] It is difficult, if not impossible, to conceive of such a situation in which the infliction of severe pain and suffering would not cause intimidation.[160] Therefore the idea of purpose, although not necessary as an aspect of proof, has been taken as subsumed because of the context of crimes against humanity. This is a fairly enlightened approach, but not an overly broad one.

Contrary to Cassese's view, Article 7(1)(g) on sexual offences does not introduce any novel crimes. There is little doubt that rape, sexual slavery

[154] *Kunarac*, Appeal, paras. 147–148. [155] *Kunarac*, Appeal, para. 142.

[156] See Andrew Byrnes, 'Torture and Other Offences Involving the Violation of the Physical or Mental Integrity of the Human Person', in Gabrielle Kirk McDonald and Olivia Swaak-Goldman, *Substantive and Procedural Aspects of International Criminal Law* (The Hague: Kluwer, 2000), p. 197, pp. 215–17.

[157] *Prosecutor* v. *Delalić, Delić, Mucić and Landsžo*, Judgment, IT-96-21-T, 16 November 1998 (*Čelebići*), para. 162.

[158] *Prosecutor* v. *Kunarac, Kovać and Vuković*, Judgment, IT-96-23-T, 22 February 2001, para. 485.

[159] Rückert and Witschel, 'Genocide', pp. 79–80.

[160] As the Appeals Chamber in *Kunarac* noted (at para. 155), knowledge of the fact that the conduct causes one of the prohibited purposes is all that is required; other motivations may be predominant, or even the sole motivation for the conduct.

or enforced sterilisation were pre-existing crimes against humanity.[161] Other sexual violence of comparable gravity would be caught under customary law as 'other inhumane acts'. Both the ICTY and ICTR in the various cases have stated that serious sexual assaults were prohibited as other inhumane acts.[162] The specificity is nonetheless welcome.

Forced pregnancy is not a new crime against humanity. The definition of the offence is 'the unlawful confinement of a woman made forcibly pregnant, with the intent of affecting the ethnic composition of any population or carrying out other grave violations of international law'.[163] Imprisonment or other unlawful forms of deprivation of liberty has long been regarded as a crime against humanity, and is included in Article 7(1)(e) of the ICC Statute. The forcible making of a person pregnant would be rape, a long-standing crime against humanity. Enforced pregnancy is undoubtably inhumane, and would be subsumed under 'other inhumane acts', in custom. The additional intent requirement was placed in the Statute to avoid an impasse between the Vatican and others (including NGOs) due to its possible effect on abortion laws.[164] Avoiding such an eventuality was certainly right, but to add an intent requirement was dangerously close to a discriminatory intent unnecessary for a 'murder-type' crime against humanity; also to make it contingent on being related to other violations of international law has diluted the prohibition, and could possibly make the prosecution of enforced pregnancy without such an intent under other headings more difficult.[165]

The 'enforced disappearance of persons' is beyond doubt a crime against humanity. It was described as such in the 1992 UN Declaration on the Protection of All Persons from Enforced Disappearances,[166] and was included in the 1996 ILC Draft Code.[167] In any case, disappearances

[161] Rape was included in Control Council Law 10; *US* v. *Brandt* 3 TWC 171, 238–9 accepted that sterilisation experiments were crimes against humanity. (See Hall, 'Article 7', p. 144.) Sexual slavery was prosecuted as a crime against humanity of enslavement in *Kunarac* (see Trial Chamber, para. 742).

[162] See, for example, *Prosecutor* v. *Furundžija*, Judgment, IT-95-17/1-T, 10 December 1998, paras. 168–169, 186. See generally, Kelly Dawn Askin, 'Sexual Violence in Decisions and Indictments of the Yugoslav and Rwandan Tribunals: Current Status' (1999) 93 AJIL 97, 99–115.

[163] Rome Statute, Article 7(2)(f).

[164] von Hebel and Robinson, 'Crimes', p. 100; Cate Steans, 'Gender Issues', in Roy S. Lee (ed.), *The International Criminal Court: The Making of the Rome Statute*, p. 357, pp. 365–9.

[165] For example, an attempt to prosecute under 'other inhumane acts' (Article 7(1)(k)).

[166] GA Res. 47/133, UN Doc. A/RES/47/133. See also UN Doc. E/CN.4/1995/36, para. 45, Inter-American Convention on the Forced Disappearance of Persons, 9 June 1994 (1994) 33 ILM 1529.

[167] See generally, Hall, 'Article 7', pp. 151–2.

have a long history of being prosecuted as crimes against humanity. In Nuremberg, Keitel was convicted for promulgating the '*Nacht und Nebel*' decree, which essentially instituted a system of disappearances.[168] Its express inclusion is welcome, but it is in no way in advance of international law. The Trial Chamber in *Kvočka* accepted that forced disappearance was an inhumane act.[169]

Apartheid was declared by the General Assembly to be a crime against humanity in 1965.[170] It was included in both the Non-Applicability,[171] and Apartheid Conventions[172] as such a crime. There were doubts about its customary nature, but it was included in the 1991 Draft Code.[173] Even with its dubious claim to customary status its inclusion in the Statute, as formulated in Article 7(2)(h), is not in excess of custom. Apartheid is defined in Article 7(2)(h) as 'inhumane acts of a character similar to those referred to in paragraph 1, committed in the context of an institutionalized regime of systematic oppression and domination by one racial group over any other racial group or groups and committed with the intention of maintaining that regime'. This is narrower than the Apartheid Convention definition,[174] and it is difficult to envisage any crime covered under this definition that would not be caught under the customary definition of 'persecution-type' crimes against humanity or 'other inhumane acts,' in Article 7(1)(k).

There are elements of the acts enumerated that may be thought to be narrower than custom permits. Article 7(1)(k) prohibits 'other inhumane acts of a similar character intentionally causing great suffering, or serious injury to body or mental or physical health'. The formulation adds the condition beginning 'intentionally causing great suffering'.[175] This is in accordance, *inter alia*, with understanding of its Statute by the ICTY in the *Tadić* Case, which does not expressly include the requirement.[176]

[168] Nuremberg IMT, Judgment, p. 229, See Hall, 'Article 7', p. 151.

[169] *Prosecutor* v. *Kvočka et al.*, Judgment, IT-98-30/1-T, 2 November 2001, para. 208.

[170] GA Resolution 2054, UN Doc. A/6014, p. 16.

[171] 1968 Convention on the Non-Applicability of Statutory Limitations to War Crimes and Crimes Against Humanity, GA Resolution 2931, 754 UNTS 75, Article 1(b). This caused controversy in the negotiations, Robert H. Miller, 'The Convention on the Non-Applicability of Statutory Limitations to War Crimes and Crimes Against Humanity' (1971) 65 AJIL 476, 491–2.

[172] 1973 International Convention on the Suppression and Punishment of the Crime of Apartheid, 1015 UNTS 245, Article 1.

[173] See Lyal S. Sunga, *The Emerging System of International Criminal Law* (The Hague: Kluwer, 1997), pp. 119–23.

[174] Hall, 'Article 7', p. 167.

[175] See Boot 'Article 7', pp. 156–7.

[176] *Tadić*, Judgment, para. 730.

It is narrower than the ICTY's formulation in the *Čelebići* Case, however, omitting the additional protected characteristic of human dignity.[177] The *Čelebići* judgment may not represent international law here, and Article 7(1)(k) is probably broadly coterminous with international law.

The Statute also covers 'persecution-type' crimes against humanity. Article 7(1)(f) defines them as '[p]ersecution against any identifiable group or collectivity on political, racial, national, ethnic, cultural, religious, gender . . . or other grounds that are universally recognized as impermissible under international law, in connection with any act referred to in this paragraph or any crime within the jurisdiction of the Court'. The definition is at once both codificatory, a positive development, and possibly a little retrogressive. The codificatory part is clear from the inclusion of political, racial, religious or ethnic grounds. There are two new categories, and a new catch-all provision. The first of these is cultural grounds: this had previously appeared only in the 1954 and 1991 Draft Codes, but not in the 1996 Code or any Tribunal Statute.[178] The second is gender, which has never appeared previously in definitions of crimes against humanity, although its appearance was overdue. The final ground is a new, catch-all provision, albeit one with a high threshold.[179] Cassese is correct, these aspects of the definition were progressions in 1998. They also represent probably the only example of the Rome Statute's definitions of crimes against humanity going beyond clearly established law.

This development must be seen against a significant limitation on the crimes. To be prosecutable under the Statute, the acts must be connected to acts referred to in the rest of the paragraph, or any other crime in the jurisdiction of the court.[180] This requirement is not present in customary international law,[181] and in practice reduces the persecution-type crimes against humanity to a secondary status.

[177] *Tadić*, Judgment, para. 509. See Boot, 'Article 7', pp. 156–7. See also *Kayishema and Ruzindana*, paras. 148–151; *Prosecutor* v. *Vasiljević*, Judgment, IT-98-32-T, 29 November 2002, para. 234.

[178] Boot, 'Article 7', pp. 147–8.

[179] Boot, 'Article 7', p. 150.

[180] Robinson, 'Defining', 54–5.

[181] *Prosecutor* v. *Kupreškić, Kupreškić, Josipović, Papić and Santić*, Judgment, IT-95-16-T, 14 January 2000, para. 580. Kai Ambos and Steffen Wirth, 'The Current Law of Crimes Against Humanity: An Analysis of UNTAET Regulation 15/2000' (2002) 13 CLF 1, 70–1. Cassese, 'Crimes Against Humanity', p. 376. For a slightly more positive view, see Robinson, 'Defining', 55.

Special Court

Crimes against humanity are defined by Article 2 of the Special Court for Sierra Leone Statute as 'the following crimes as part of a widespread or systematic attack against any civilian population: (a) Murder; (b) Extermination; (c) Enslavement; (d) Deportation; (e) Imprisonment; (f) Torture; (g) Rape, sexual slavery, enforced prostitution, forced pregnancy and any other form of sexual violence; (h) Persecution on political, racial, ethnic or religious grounds; (i) Other inhumane acts.' This definition, consistent with the idea that the Special Court was perceived at the time of its creation as a 'safe' mechanism, gives some discretion to the Court to manoeuvre as it does not define each term in such depth as the Rome Statute. Also its material coverage is essentially that of customary international law; for example, the Statute clearly identifies the widespread or systematic criteria as disjunctive. There is no necessary link to other crimes for persecutive crimes against humanity and there is no requirement that crimes against humanity occur in times of armed conflict. The Special Court's Statute can be read as an implicit critique of the Rome definition.

Conclusion

The story of crimes against humanity is basically in accordance with the theme of this chapter; when the ICC was created there was an increased desire by States to restrain the Court from exercising autonomous judgment on what amounts to a crime against humanity. Creating a detailed elaboration of almost all aspects of crimes against humanity did this, although it cannot be doubted that in many areas definitional precision was a good idea. Crimes against humanity were vaguely defined prior to Rome, low in legitimacy if the yardstick of determinacy were used. There was a price to pay for this clarity. The raising of the threshold for all crimes against humanity meant that the definition was often less inclusive than customary international law. With one or two exceptions, the acts enumerated were quite cautiously defined. States can therefore be seen to have taken a very different approach in drafting the Rome Statute to that taken in the ICTY Statute, Special Court for Sierra Leone Statute and (to a lesser extent) that of the ICTR, where the Tribunals were given the power to explore the parameters of responsibility here. It is also clear that a far less expansive view of customary law was taken than in 1945 for the IMTs, where very vague definitions were imposed, arguably in excess of the international law existing at the time. This applies particularly to the definition in the Tokyo IMT Statute.

War crimes

Discussion of war crimes is made difficult because of the disagreement about the precise relationship of war crimes law to the underlying law upon which it is based, the law of armed conflict (international humanitarian law). There are three views on the extent to which the two areas of law overlap. The first and simplest approach is that all violations of the law of armed conflict are war crimes.[182] The second, responding to the criticism that some violations of the law of armed conflict are minor therefore not appropriately the subject of criminal sanctions, is that all serious violations of the law of armed conflict are criminal.[183] The third, and most exacting view, is that war crimes are limited to those violations of armed conflict to which a parallel secondary rule that ascribes criminal responsibility for its violation is attached.[184] This is the approach taken by the ICTY, for example in the *Tadić* Case,[185] although it must be pointed out that the Appeals Chamber in that decision did not require a great deal of evidence to be convinced of the existence of a secondary rule.

The third approach is defended by Georges Abi-Saab on the basis that the addition of 'serious' is 'question begging' and inappropriate as a distinguishing criterion.[186] In practice, this is likely to be overstated. In UK criminal law, for example, the concept of 'grievous' bodily harm[187] is one which causes juries fewer problems than theory might imply. The ICTY has not had many problems in drawing the distinction.[188] Also,

182 Peter Rowe, 'War Crimes', in Dominic McGoldrick, Peter Rowe and Eric Donnelly (eds.), *The International Criminal Court* (Oxford: Hart, 2004), p. 203, pp. 204–5; Jordan Paust, 'Content and Contours of Genocide: Crimes Against Humanity and War Crimes', in Sienho Yee and Wang Tieya (eds.), *International Law in the Post-Cold World: Essays in Honour of Haopei Li* (London: Routledge, 2001), p. 289, p. 293. US Department of Army Field Manual FM-27, The Law of Land Warfare (1956), p. 178.

183 See, for example, UK Ministry of Defence, *The Law of Armed Conflict* (Oxford: Oxford University Press, 2004), p. 425.

184 Georges Abi-Saab, 'The Concept of War Crimes', in Sienho Yee and Wang Tieya (eds.), *International Law in the Post-Cold War World: Essays in Honour of Haopei Li* (London: Routledge, 2001), p. 99, pp. 112–13.

185 *Prosecutor* v. *Tadić*, Decision on Interlocutory Appeal on Jurisdiction, IT-94-1-AR72, 2 October 1995, para. 94.

186 Abi-Saab, 'The Concept', p. 112.

187 Which is 'really serious harm', *Metheram* [1961] 3 All ER 200.

188 *Tadić*, Decision on Interlocutory Appeal on Jurisdiction, para. 94.

many of the acts prohibited by the law of war – torture, rape, killing of innocents and the like – are *mala in se*. Abi-Saab's point also fails to justify the choice of the third approach rather than the first. Antonio Cassese supports the requirement of a separate criminalising rule on the basis of the *nulllum crimen* principle.[189] The condition sets a higher threshold for criminalisation than the other two approaches, but this is not required by the *nullum crimen* principle. If the principle of criminalisation is set out in advance (that all violations of the laws of armed conflict are criminal, or that all serious violations are) fair warning is given to the subjects of the law that the conduct is criminal. The first approach, and arguably the second, are also clearer than subjecting the existence of the crime to a second-order customary law evaluation, which can prove contentious. Fortunately, it is unnecessary to determine which approach is the accurate reflection of the law. This chapter is concerned with the attitude of States to the ambit of the law, and the different views taken in 'safe' and 'unsafe' Tribunals. The approach taken in each instance may cast light on this. A final point ought to be mentioned. It is quite possible that this debate was considered inapplicable to the law of non-international armed conflicts, which, prior to the 1990s was assumed not to be criminal.[190]

Nuremberg and Tokyo IMTs

Article 6(b) of the London Charter granted the Nuremberg IMT jurisdiction over war crimes, which it defined as 'violations of the laws and customs of war. Such violations shall include, but not be limited to, murder, ill treatment, or deportation to slave labor or for any other purpose of civilian population of or in occupied territory, murder or ill treatment of prisoners of war or persons on the seas, killing of hostages, plunder of public or private property, wanton destruction of cities, towns or villages, or devastation not justified by military necessity.' This was the least controversial crime at the Nuremberg IMT: no one questioned its legality.[191] In relation to the definition itself, it ought to be noted that the list is open-ended and thus the Nuremberg IMT was entitled to add all other violations of the laws and customs of war it thought

189 Antonio Cassese, *International Criminal Law* (Oxford: Oxford University Press, 2003), p. 51.

190 Abi-Saab, 'The Concept', p. 115. See also the explanation of Judge Li's dissent in *Tadić*, Decision on Interlocutory Appeal on Jurisdiction, in Paust, 'Content and Contours', pp. 293–4.

191 Quincy Wright, 'The Law of the Nuremberg Tribunal' (1947) 41 AJIL 38, 59.

were applicable. The definition also considers all violations of the laws of war to be war crimes, supporting the first view of the nature of war crimes mentioned above. The Tokyo Charter granted even further powers to the Tokyo IMT to determine what amounted to a war crime, as its jurisdictional provision defined war crimes as 'violations of the laws and customs of war'. It can be seen that the provision left the decision relating to what amounted to a war crime, and the definitions given to them, entirely to the discretion of the court.[192] Again, this definition equates war crimes and violations of the laws of war.

ICTY

Article 2 of the ICTY Statute grants the Tribunal jurisdiction over grave breaches of the Geneva Conventions. If Article 2 is taken (as it has been by the ICTY)[193] as applying to international armed conflicts alone then there is no question of conformity with customary international law. It is beyond doubt that the examples in Article 2 represent customary war crimes.[194] It is perhaps unfortunate that the Grave Breach provisions of Additional Protocol I (API) were not included. API was not considered undeniably customary, so it was not put in the Statute.[195] As Yugoslavia was a party, this need not have been determinative. In any event, norms from API have played a role, because of the other provision dealing with war crimes in the ICTY Statute, Article 3.

Article 3 grants the ICTY jurisdiction over:

> persons violating the laws or customs of war. Such violations *shall include, but not be limited to*:
>
> (a) employment of poisonous weapons or other weapons calculated to cause unnecessary suffering;
> (b) wanton destruction of cities, towns or villages, or devastation not justified by military necessity;

192 McCoubrey notes that the Tokyo Charter definition may actually be the best of the existing definitions; Hilaire McCoubrey, 'War Crimes Jurisdiction and a Permanent International Criminal Court: Advantages and Difficulties' (1998) 3 JACL 9, 18.

193 With the exceptions – for example *Prosecutor* v. *Tadic*, Decision on Prosecution Motion for Protective Measures for Witnesses. IT-94-1-T, 10 August 1995, paras. 50–53 – and dissenting opinions such as Abi-Saab in *Tadić*, Decisions Separate Opinion; *Prosecutor* v. *Aleksovski*, Judgment, IT-95-14/1-T, 25 June 1999, Dissenting Opinion of Judge Rodrigues.

194 Secretary-General's Report, para. 37, *Tadić*, Decision, para. 83. See more generally, Theodor Meron, 'The Geneva Conventions as Customary Law' (1987) 81 AJIL 348.

195 Schraga and Zacklin, 'The International Criminal Tribunal for Yugoslavia', 364.

(c) attack, or bombardment, by whatever means, of undefended towns, villages, dwellings or buildings;
(d) seizure of, destruction or wilful damage done to institutions dedicated to religion, charity and education, the arts and sciences, historic monuments and works of art and science;
(e) plunder of public or private property (emphasis added).

The acts enumerated, drawn from the 1868 St Petersburg Declaration and the Hague regulations,[196] are prohibited by customary international law.[197] The most important part of the definition is that the list in Article 3 is illustrative. Article 3 extends at least to all serious violations of the customary law of armed conflicts which entail individual liability.[198] This is the view taken by the ICTY in the *Tadić* Case, although the Statute takes the more moderate view that the only criterion is that they are serious.[199] The Appeals Chamber also said that the applicable treaty rules were prosecutable under Article 3. This amounted to a 'creative and progressive' view,[200] but one that is referrable to the text of the Statute and the intention of the creators of the ICTY. In the Security Council, several States expressed the view that Article 3 included all the law applicable to the Yugoslav conflicts, not limiting their comments to those rules with a secondary rule criminalising them.[201]

Article 3 effectively grants the ICTY the right to determine, at least for its purposes, what that customary international law is. It is the ICTY's determinations relating to what is customary that have occasioned controversy. This controversy mostly surrounds its iconoclastic determination, in the *Tadić* Interlocutory Appeal, that the 'laws and customs' of war entailing criminal responsibility include certain violations committed in internal armed conflicts, including, *inter alia*, Common Article 3.[202] The criminality of such violations was contested in some

[196] St Petersburg Declaration, Renouncing, in Time of War, the Use of Explosive Projectiles Under 400 Grammes in Weight 58 BFSP (1867–1868), 16–17; Regulations attached to the Hague Convention IV, UKTS 9 (1910), Cd. 5030. (Article 23(a), (e), 25, 27 and 47).

[197] Nuremberg IMT, Judgment, p. 248; Secretary General's Report, paras. 41–44. On Article 3, see Morris and Scharf, *An Insider's Guide*, pp. 69–72; William J. Fenrick, 'Some International Law Problems Related to Prosecutions Before the International Criminal Tribunal for the Former Yugoslavia' (1995) 6 DJCIL 103, 105–8.

[198] See Morris and Scharf, *An Insider's Guide*, p. 72; Jordan J. Paust, 'Applicable Substantive Law' (1994) 88 Proceedings ASIL 241, 242.

[199] *Tadić*, Decision, para. 94.

[200] William J. Fenrick, 'International Humanitarian Law and Criminal Trials' (1997) 7 TLCP 23, 35.

[201] S/PV. 3217, pp. 11, 15, 19. [202] *Tadić*, Decision, paras. 96–136.

quarters.[203] The most accurate summary of the decision is Colin Warbrick's, that it was 'carefully made, but ambitious'.[204] The point is, though, that the ICTY was granted the authority to make it. It is difficult to disagree with McCoubrey that the formulation in Article 3 of the ICTY Statute 'has much to commend it',[205] and in passing to the ICTY a discretion to determine the extent of the customary law of armed conflict, it enabled the Tribunal to make a lasting contribution to the law.

ICTR

The controversy relating to the classification of the conflict in Yugoslavia[206] played itself out in the ICTY Statute and the discussions around it. This was not the case in relation to the ICTR Statute. The Rwandan conflict was viewed by the Security Council as an internal conflict.[207] The ICTR Statute's provision on jurisdiction over war crimes granted it jurisdiction over 'persons committing or ordering to be committed serious violations of Article 3 common to the Geneva Conventions of 12 August 1949 for the Protection of War Victims, and of Additional Protocol II thereto of 8 June 1977.[208]

Some doubts have been expressed about the inclusion of this provision. Although Common Article 3 is generally accepted as being customary international law, and *jus cogens*, too,[209] the same cannot be

203 Schraga and Zacklin, 'The International Criminal Tribunal for Yugoslavia', 363–5. The *Tadić* Interlocutory Appeal Judgment has generated a huge amount of literature and controversy. Among the fray, see Christopher J. Greenwood, 'International Humanitarian Law and the *Tadić* Case' (1996) 7 EJIL 265; George H. Aldrich, 'Jurisdiction of the International Criminal Tribunal for the Former Yugoslavia' (1996) 90 AJIL 64, 65–7; Theodor Meron, 'The Continuing Role of Custom in the Formation of International Humanitarian Law', in Theodor Meron, *War Crimes Law Comes of Age* (Oxford: Oxford University Press, 1998), p. 262, pp. 263–8 (in favour); Geoffrey R. Watson, 'The Humanitarian Law of the Yugoslavia War Crimes Tribunal: Jurisdiction in *Prosecutor* v. *Tadic*' (1996) 36 VJIL 687, 709–28 (709, 'as bold as it is ill founded'). Judge Li dissented on this point, saying that their decision amounted to an 'unwarranted assertion of legislative power' by the Tribunal; *ibid.*, Separate Opinion of Judge Li, para. 13.

204 Colin Warbrick, 'The United Nations System: A Place for International Criminal Courts?' (1995) 5 TLCP 237, 257.

205 McCoubrey, 'War Crimes Jurisdiction', 19.

206 On which, see Christine Gray, 'Bosnia and Herzegovina: Civil War or Inter-State Conflict? Characterization and Consequences' (1997) 68 BYBIL 155.

207 Morris and Scharf, *The International Criminal Tribunal for Rwanda*, p. 142.

208 ICTR Statute, Article 4. Protocol II being Additional to the Geneva Conventions of 12 August 1949 and Relating to the Protection of Victims of Non-International Armed Conflicts, 1125 UNTS 609.

209 *Case Concerning Military and Paramilitary Activities in and Against Nicaragua (Nicaragua* v. *USA)* Merits (1986) ICJ Rep. 4, p. 114; Theodor Meron, *Human Rights and Humanitarian*

said for Additional Protocol II.[210] There are also arguments asserting the non-criminal nature of the humanitarian law applicable to internal armed conflicts. The first argument can be dealt with quickly. Even if neither Common Article 3 or APII were customary international law, this would be irrelevant in the case of Rwanda. Rwanda was (and remains) a party to the four Geneva Conventions and Additional Protocol II. The second argument has more purchase. Although it is now accepted that the humanitarian law applicable in internal conflicts has penal characteristics, this may not have been the case in 1994. For example, the Red Cross were unconvinced at the time, and commentary dating from the early 1990s (including after the creation of the ICTY) had come to the conclusion that there was no penal responsibility at that time for violations of the law of non-international armed conflict.[211] The Secretary General appears also to have taken this view.[212]

Although the interpretation of the law taken in Article 4 of the ICTR Statute did not necessarily violate the *nullum crimen* principle,[213] it was a progressive one, as might be expected from a 'safe' Tribunal. One of the reasons Rwanda voted against the ICTR Statute was that it contained provisions on war crimes rather than concentrating solely on genocide. The ICTR's discretion in interpreting the law of war crimes is bounded by the provisions in Common Article 3 and APII. It cannot, in contrast to the ICTY, decide on violations of customary international law beyond the provisions in the two documents. This is almost certainly because at the time the ICTR Statute was drafted, common Article 3 and Additional Protocol II were considered exhaustive of the law applicable in non-international armed conflicts. The median position, that the ICTR should prosecute only 'serious' violations of the law, is adopted in Article 4.

Norms as Customary Norms (Oxford: Oxford University Press, 1989), pp. 27–37; Report of the Commission of Experts on Rwanda S/1995/1125, para. 87.

[210] See Meron, *Human Rights*, pp. 71–4, Christopher J. Greenwood, 'Customary Status of the 1977 Geneva Protocols', in Astrid J. M. Delissen and Gerard J. Tanja, *Humanitarian Law of Armed Conflict, Challenges Ahead* (Dordrecht: Martinus Nijhoff, 1991), p. 93, pp. 112–3.

[211] Denise Plattner, 'The Penal Repression of Violations of International Humanitarian Law Applicable in Non-International Armed Conflicts' (1990) 278 IRRC 409, 414. Peter Rowe, 'War Crimes and the Former Yugoslavia: The Legal Difficulties' (1993) 32 RIDMDG 317, 328–33.

[212] Secretary General's Report on the ICTR Statute, para. 12.

[213] Meron, 'International Criminalization'; Greenwood, 'International Humanitarian Law and the *Tadić* Case', 280–1. Morris and Scharf, *The International Criminal Tribunal for Rwanda*, p. 127, note that during the Rwandan conflict the Security Council affirmed individual responsibility for violations of humanitarian law in PRST/1994/21 and Resolution 935.

ICC

War crimes were an exceptionally controversial aspect of the Rome Statute, and were settled only in the final Bureau proposal.[214] This is unsurprising. While a State may be fairly confident that its officials will not commit genocide or crimes against humanity, the same cannot be said for war crimes, which are an omnipresent danger in times of armed conflict. Overall, the Rome Statute takes a different tack to all the previous statutes of ICTs except the ICTR Statute. The Rome Statute contains a closed list of war crimes: there is no discretion in the ICC to add any further war crimes, irrespective of their applicability to the conflict either by virtue of treaty or customary international law. There is no possibility of a *Tadić*-type decision in the ICC.[215] The list in Article 8 is an incomplete codification of custom,[216] in addition, the list can be altered only by an amendment to the Rome treaty, and this has a very high threshold. Thus when evaluating the definition, it must be remembered that it will also be the only one for the foreseeable future. Notably, US Military Tribunal Order 2, relating to perhaps the most 'safe' Tribunals, being limited to the prosecution of non-nationals, allows for the prosecution of an open-ended list of customary crimes.[217]

Article 8 grants the ICC jurisdiction 'in respect of war crimes, in particular when committed as a part of a plan or policy or as part of a large scale commission of such crimes'. This was a compromise between the United States, who wanted the court to deal only with war crimes

[214] For the Pre-Rome discussions and controversies, see, for example, Christopher Keith Hall, 'The Fifth Session of the Preparatory Committee for an International Criminal Court' (1998) 92 AJIL 331, 332–3; Zimmerman, 'The Creation', 187–95. For the Rome proposals, see A/CONF.183/2.Add.1 and A/CONF.183/C.1/L.10, L.4, L.5, L.11, L.13, L.26, L.33, L.40, L.53 (Article 5), L.59 (Article 5*quater*), L.62, L.72, L.74, L.89, L.94. For discussion of the Statute, see Michael Cottier, William J. Fenrick, Patricia Viseur-Sellers and Andreas Zimmermann, 'Article 8', in Otto Triffterer (ed.), *Commentary on the Rome Statute of the International Criminal Court* (Baden-Baden: Nomos, 1991), p. 173; Michael Bothe, 'War Crimes', in Antonio Cassese, Paula Gaeta and John R. W. D. Jones (eds.), *The Rome Statute of the International Criminal Court: A Commentary* (Oxford: Oxford University Press, 2001), p. 379. Thorough discussion of the elements of crimes may be found in Knut Dörmann (with Louise Doswald-Beck and Robert Kolb), *Elements of War Crimes under the Rome Statute of the International Criminal Court: Sources and Commentary* (Cambridge: Cambridge University Press, 2003) and Hermann von Hebel *et al.*, 'The Elements of War Crimes', in Roy S. Lee (ed.), *The International Criminal Court: Elements of Crimes and Rules of Procedure and Evidence* (Ardsley: Transnational, 2001), p. 109.

[215] *Accord*, Schabas, *An Introduction*, p. 54.

[216] For a review of the omissions of the Rome Statute, see Boot, *Genocide*, p. 603.

[217] See p. 240.

when they were committed as part of a plan or policy or as part of a large-scale commission of such offences, and most of the rest of the conference, which wanted no such limit.[218] This limit has been welcomed by various authors.[219] It was right that the US proposal was rejected, as it collapses the definition of war crimes into that of crimes against humanity too easily, and would have led to the court having to prove the additional elements, which are not present in war crimes law, to assert jurisdiction over the offence.[220]

The applicability of the law of armed conflict relies on certain criteria, in particular whether there is an armed conflict, and whether that conflict is of an international or non-international nature.[221] For war crimes, there must also be a link to the conflict. The ICTY has taken these solely as jurisdictional criteria, requiring no knowledge on the part of the suspect of the existence or nature of the conflict.[222] This was not considered acceptable when the ICC Elements of Crimes were being drafted. As a result, the Elements require that the accused was aware of the factual basis that established the conflict. They do not, however, require that a legal evaluation about the existence or nature of the conflict be made.[223]

International armed conflicts

The first set of offences over which the Court is granted jurisdiction was not controversial. Almost all States agreed that Grave Breaches of the Geneva Conventions should be included for international armed

[218] von Hebel and Robinson, 'Crimes', pp. 107–8.

[219] Ruth Wedgwood, 'The International Criminal Court: An American View' (1999) 10 EJIL 93, 94; Antonio Cassese, 'The Rome Statute of the International Criminal Court: Some Preliminary Reflections' (1999) 10 EJIL 144, 149.

[220] Jordan J. Paust, 'The Preparatory Committee's Definition of War Crimes' (1997) 8 CLF 431, 432; Arsanjani, 'The Rome Statute', 33. The *chapeau* prompted the ICRC into issuing a public statement of its concerns; see A/CONF.183/INF/10.

[221] See, for example, Christine Byron, 'Armed Conflicts: International or Non-International?' (2001) 6 JCSL 63.

[222] Kai Ambos, 'Some Preliminary Reflections on the *Mens Rea* Requirements of the Crimes of the ICC Statute and of the Elements of Crimes', in Lal Chand Vohrah *et al.* (eds.), *Man's Inhumanity to Man: Essays in Honour of Antonio Cassese* (The Hague: Kluwer, 2003), p. 11, p. 33.

[223] Common Element 4 to Article 8(2)(a). See also Introduction to Elements of War Crimes. Ambos, 'Some Preliminary', pp. 32–40; Knut Dörmann, Eve la Haye and Herman von Hebel, 'The Context of War Crimes', in Roy S. Lee (ed.), *The International Criminal Court: Elements of Crimes and Rules of Procedure and Evidence* (Ardsley: Transnational, 2001), p. 112; Dörmann, *Elements*, pp. 18–28.

conflicts.[224] They were included in Article 8(2)(a) of the Rome Statute. The inclusion of other Grave Breaches was controversial. An area of contention was the inclusion of the Grave Breaches in API, and they were not included in this part. This is not necessarily a problem, since many Grave Breaches of API are included elsewhere in the definition of war crimes.[225] It is clear that the offences included in Article 8(2)(a) are customarily criminal.[226]

The second set of crimes consists of twenty-six 'serious violations of the laws and customs applicable in international armed conflict, within the framework of international law, namely'.[227] Most of the crimes contained in Article 8(2)(b) are clearly customary. For example, Article 8(2)(b)(xix) restates the prohibition of expanding bullets in Hague Declaration 3[228] while Articles 8(2)(b)(v,vi,xi–xvii) restate provisions of the Hague Rules.[229] Using protected persons to render an area immune from attack is considered a war crime for the purposes of the Statute (Article 8(2)(b)(xxiii)). Such acts are an unfortunately frequent aspect of contemporary conflicts.[230] The criminal proscription of such offences is also customary.[231]

Article 8(2)(b)(xxiv) deals with 'intentionally directing attacks against buildings, material, medical units and transport and personnel using the distinctive emblems of the Geneva Conventions in conformity with international law'. This is based on Articles 19(1) GCI, 18(1)(5) GCII, 11(1) API, which are considered to state the customary rule.[232] There are other welcome additions from API such as intentionally directing attacks against civilians, civilian populations or civilian objects.[233] Another provision drawing on that treaty is Article 8(2)(b)(xxv), which criminalises, 'intentionally using starvation of civilians as a method of warfare by depriving them of objects indispensable to their survival, including wilfully

224 See Zimmerman, 'The Creation', p. 187.

225 Thomas Graditzky, 'War Crime Issues Before the Rome Diplomatic Conference on the Establishment of International Criminal Court' (1999) 5 UCDJIL 199, 202.

226 See p. 266.

227 Article 8(2)(b); 'namely' indicates that this is a closed list.

228 1899 Hague Declaration 3 Concerning Expanding Bullets 32 UKTS (1907) Cd. 3751. This is definitely customary international law, see Hilaire McCoubrey, *International Humanitarian Law* (Aldershot: Dartmouth, 2nd edn., 1998), pp. 232–3.

229 Hague Rules, Annex to Hague Convention IV, Respecting the Laws and Customs of War on Land, 9. UKTS (1910) Cd. 5030.

230 See Anthony P. V. Rogers, *Law on the Battlefield* (Manchester: Manchester University Press, 2nd edn., 2004), pp. 126–9.

231 Rogers, *Law*, p. 128, n. 47.

232 Meron, *Human Rights*, p. 45.

233 Article 8(2)(b)(i)(ii) repeats the Grave Breaches in API Article 85(3)(a), the customary status of which is beyond question.

impeding relief supplies as provided for under the Geneva Conventions'. This is based on Article 54(1) and the core of Article 54(2) of API; both are likely to be customary.[234] The latter part ('wilfully impeding . . .') is based on the Security Council's assertion in relation to Yugoslavia that interference with humanitarian supplies is contrary to Article 23 of Geneva Convention IV. It is probable that this is not in advance of customary international law, and is a useful clarification of the law.[235]

Other parts of customary law included in the Statute are the provisions based on the Geneva Conventions or the customary parts of API, such as Article 8(2)(b)(x).[236] Sexual crimes are covered in Article 8(2)(b)(xxii), namely 'committing rape, sexual slavery, enforced prostitution, forced pregnancy as defined in Article 7(2)(f), enforced sterilisation, or any other form of sexual violence also constituting a grave breach of the Geneva conventions'. Rape and other sexual offences have long been accepted as war crimes,[237] despite often being ignored in practice. This provision develops Article 27 of Geneva Convention IV.[238] Its additions are sexual slavery, forced pregnancy and enforced sterilisation. Some have suggested that these are in advance of existing law.[239] The position is incorrect. The acts added would also amount to the grave breach of 'torture or inhuman treatment . . . [or] . . . wilfully causing great suffering or serious injury to body or health'. Their express inclusion is helpful, and overdue. In a similar, although not identical, vein, Article 8(2)(b)(xxi) contains the prohibition, from Article 75(2)(b) API, of outrages on personal dignity, in particular humiliating and degrading treatment. This is one of the parts of API accepted as customary.[240]

Abi-Saab also criticises Article 8(2)(b)(iii) as being beyond custom. Article 8(2)(b)(iii) prohibits 'intentionally directing attacks against personnel,

[234] Christopher J. Greenwood, 'Customary International Law and the First Geneva Protocol of 1977 in the Gulf Conflict', in Peter Rowe (ed.), *The Gulf War 1990–1991 in International and English Law* (London: Routledge, 1993), p. 68, p. 81.

[235] See Morris and Scharf, *An Insider's Guide*, pp. 71–2, and the Security Council action cited therein (especially Resolution 771).

[236] Subjecting persons in the hands of an adverse party to mutilations or scientific experiments not in their interest, and which cause death or seriously endanger health, which is based on the customary Article 13, GCIII (see Meron, *Human Rights*, p. 45). On experimentation, see Hilaire McCoubrey and Michael Gunn, 'Medical Ethics and the Law of Armed Conflict' (1998) 3 JACL 133, 147–8.

[237] See Meron, 'Rape as a Crime Under International Humanitarian Law' (1993) 87 AJIL 414, 204.

[238] On its customary status, see Meron, *Human Rights*, p. 46.

[239] Abi-Saab, 'The Concept', p. 118; Schabas, *An Introduction*, pp. 62–3.

[240] Meron, *Human Rights*, p. 65; Greenwood, 'Customary', p. 103.

installations, material, units or vehicles involved in a humanitarian assistance or peacekeeping mission in accordance with the Charter of the United Nations, as long as they are entitled to the protection given to civilians or civilian objects under the international law of armed conflicts'. The limited formulation of the prohibition ensures that Article 8(2)(b)(iii) is not novel. The questionable customary status of the 1995 Convention on the Safety of United Nations and Associated Personnel[241] led to its exclusion from the Statute.[242] The war crime of attacking such personnel in the Rome Statute comes into play only if those persons are entitled to protection as civilians, so the provision is simply an application of the unquestioned crime of intentionally attacking civilians and civilian objects.

Another aspect of the Statute that has been wrongfully accused of novelty is the prohibition of 'intentionally launching an attack in the knowledge that such an attack will cause incidental . . . widespread, long term and severe damage to the natural environment which would be clearly excessive in relation to the concrete and direct overall military advantage anticipated', in Article 8(2)(b)(iv).[243] The provision is thought by some commentators to be based on Articles 35(3) and 55 of API, the customary status of which is controversial.[244] This is only partially true; although Article 8(2)(b)(iv) draws language 'widespread, long term and severe' from API, the addition of the proportionality requirement means that the crime is basically the old one of wanton devastation.[245] There is no need to see this as a new crime; in 1996, the ICJ said that States 'must take environmental considerations into account when assessing what is necessary and proportionate'.[246] There is evidence that the offence is in part more restrictively drafted than custom would permit. Those who view Articles 35(3) and 55 of API to be customary could criticise the rule on adding the proportionality requirement to the absolute prohibition

[241] GA Resolution 49/59. 49 UN Doc. A/RES/49/59.

[242] Cottier *et al.*, 'Article 8', pp. 187–9.

[243] Schabas, *An Introduction*, p. 61.

[244] On the controversy, see Greenwood, 'Customary', pp. 86–8; Antonio Cassese, 'The Geneva Protocols of 1977 on the Humanitarian Law of Armed Conflict and Customary International Law' (1984) 3 *University of California Los Angeles Pacific Basin Law Journal* 55, 76–7; George H. Aldrich, 'Prospects for United States Ratification of Additional Protocol I' (1991) 85 AJIL 1, 14; Meron, *Human Rights*, p. 66; Adam Roberts, 'Failures in Protecting the Environment in the 1990–1991 Gulf War', in Peter Rowe (ed.), *The Gulf War 1990–1991 in International and English Law* (London: Routledge, 1993), p. 111, pp. 125–7. The ICJ, in the *Nuclear Weapons* Opinion, reasserted the view that this aspect of API was not customary, [1996] ICJ Rep. 4, para. 31.

[245] Dörmann, *Elements*, p. 167, alludes to this.

[246] *Nuclear Weapons* Opinion, para. 30.

of widespread, long-term and severe damage to the environment.[247] A more solid basis for critique, which does not involve the assertion that those provisions of API are customary, is that if the damage is disproportionate, then the additional requirements are inappropriate additions to the threshold for this offence.[248]

A particularly controversial addition to the Statute was Article 8(2)(b)(viii): 'the transfer, directly or indirectly, by the occupying power of parts of its own civilian population into the territory it occupies, or the deportation or transfer of all or parts of the population of the occupied territory within or outside this territory.' The inclusion of Article 8(2)(b)(viii) led Israel to vote against the Statute. The provision is based on Article 49 of Geneva Convention IV, which represents customary international law.[249] There were two questions raised about Article 8(2)(b)(viii) in Rome.

The first question was whether violation of Article 49 of Geneva Convention IV is a war crime.[250] Parts of Article 49 were included in the grave breach provisions of Geneva Convention IV. The grave breaches provision in API is similar to the language of Article 8(2)(b)(viii) (with the addition of 'directly or indirectly').[251] There is thus evidence that this is a breach separately criminalised, if there is such a requirement. The amount of evidence is more than that accepted in *Tadić* that the law of non-international armed conflict had a criminal aspect. As Schabas notes, the grave breaches provisions are also not exhaustive of criminal violations of the law of armed conflict.[252] The real question is whether the additional language is acceptable.

Ruth Wedgwood queries whether the addition of 'directly or indirectly' is a permissible gloss on Article 49(6) of Geneva Convention IV.[253] The change merely makes express an interpretation of the Geneva Convention IV provision almost universally shared by States. This can be shown in reference to the Israeli policy of settlements, which are an indirect form of transfer.[254] Over a course of years, the General Assembly

247 Bothe, 'War Crimes', p. 400; Cassese, *International Criminal Law*, pp. 60–1.
248 Dörmann, *Elements*, p. 167; Bothe, 'War Crimes', p. 401.
249 Meron, *Human Rights*, p. 46. 250 Schabas, *An Introduction*, p. 61.
251 Article 85(4)(a). Bothe, 'War Crimes' considers the two to be the same.
252 Schabas, *An Introduction*, p. 61.
253 Wedgwood, 'The International Criminal Court', 99.
254 As the government does not forcibly transfer its population, but instead makes relocation to the Occupied Territories economically attractive, see Eyal Benvenisi, *The International Law of Occupation* (Princeton: Princeton University Press, 1993), p. 140.

has condemned indirect transfers as unlawful.[255] The ICJ in the *Wall* Case adopted a similar position, stating:

> [t]hat provision [Article 49(6)] prohibits not only deportations or forced transfers of population such as those carried out during the Second World War, but also any measures taken by an occupying Power in order to organize or encourage transfers of parts of its own population into the occupied territory . . . since 1977, Israel has conducted a policy and developed practices involving the establishment of settlements in the Occupied Palestinian Territory, contrary to the terms of Article 49, paragraph 6.[256]

Nonetheless, to deal with the concerns of Israel and the United States, the Elements of Crimes for this crime require that 'transfer' be interpreted 'in accordance with the relevant provisions of humanitarian law'.[257] The inclusion of this crime was warranted in custom, although its addition was intended by some States as a snub to Israel.[258]

The final provision suggested by some to be new is Article 8(2)(b)(xxvi). This covers '[c]onscripting or enlisting children under the age of fifteen years into the national armed forces or using them to participate actively in hostilities'. The prohibition is based upon Article 77(2) API, which is largely reflective of custom.[259] Article 77(2) of API requires that States 'take all feasible measures in order that children who have not attained the age of fifteen years do not take direct part in hostilities, and, in particular, shall refrain from recruiting them into their armed forces'.[260] One difference is that the adjective 'direct', in API is changed, in the

255 Adam Roberts, 'Prolonged Military Occupations: The Israeli Occupied Territories 1967–1988', in Emma Playfair (ed.), *The Administration of Occupied Territories in International Law* (Oxford: Oxford University Press, 1992), p. 25, pp. 66–8. See also GA Resolution 51/133, UN Doc. A/RES/51/133, GA Resolution 52/66, UN Doc. A/RES/52/66, GA Resolution 53/55, UN Doc. A/RES/53/55, Security Council Resolution 465. The United States views Israeli settlements as contrary to Article 49 of Geneva Convention IV, Letter of H. J. Hansell, Legal Adviser, Department of State to House Committee on International Relations 21 April 1978, (1978) 17 ILM 777. Von Hebel and Robinson, 'Crimes', p. 112 note that only Israel and 'to a certain extent' the United States queried the crime.

256 *Legal Consequences of the Construction of a Wall in the Occupied Palestinian Territories* Opinion, 2004, ICJ List No. 131, para. 120.

257 See Dörmann, *Elements*, pp. 208–14; Herman von Hebel 'Article 8(2)(b)(viii)', in Roy S. Lee (ed.), *The International Criminal Court: Elements of Crimes and Rules of Procedure and Evidence* (Ardsley: Transnational, 2001), p. 158.

258 Graditzky, 'War Crimes', 203.

259 See Meron, *Human Rights*, p. 66; Jenny Kuper, *International Law Concerning Child Civilians in Armed Conflict* (Oxford: Oxford University Press, 1997), pp. 125, 127.

260 The prohibition of recruitment is an example of the general prohibition of allowing children to participate directly in hostilities; the prohibition of enlistment can be similarly justified.

Rome Statute, to 'active'. A strong case can be made that in fact there is no difference between 'active' and 'direct' participation.[261] Even if there was such a difference, that would not take Article 8(2)(b)(viii) out of the realms of custom. Article 4(c) of Additional Protocol II (which applies to non-international conflicts) prohibits recruitment of children or allowing them 'to take part in hostilities'. This provision is considered the customary baseline.[262] The United States did raise the question of whether Article 77(2), said by them to be a 'human rights' principle, was subject to criminal sanction.[263] Most other States disagreed with the United States on this.

The question of whether this was new at Rome depends on the approach taken to whether a separate rule identifying the primary rule with criminal consequences is required, and the level of evidence required for that rule.[264] A majority of the Appeals Chamber of the Special Court for Sierra Leone determined that the parallel provision for non-international armed conflicts was customarily criminal as far back as 1996.[265] This was also the view of the Security Council in 2000, although evidence is rather limited on this point.[266] At the most, the customary law criminalising the use of child soldiers crystallised at Rome.[267] One limit is in excess of API. That is the limit to 'national armed forces', which was added so it would not cover the *Intifada*.[268] This has no precedent in international law, and serves only to exempt certain States' or non-State entities' (the Palestinian Authorities') practices from the scrutiny of the ICC.

Far from being in advance of international law, the Rome Statute is more open to critique on the basis that it is a retrenchment of the law. At times, the Statute adopts rather archaic provisions rather than their more modern counterparts.[269] For example, Article 8(2)(b)(v) prohibits 'attacking, or bombarding, by whatever means, towns, villages,

261 Rogers, *Law*, p. 226.
262 *Prosecutor* v. *Norman*, Decision on Preliminary Motion Based on Lack of Jurisdiction (Child Recruitment) SCSL-2004-14-AR72, 31 May 2004, para. 18.
263 Von Hebel and Robinson, 'Crimes', 117.
264 See Matthew Happold, *Child Soldiers in International Law* (Manchester: Manchester University Press, 2005), chapter 7.
265 *Norman*, paras. 30–52.
266 On 29 June 1998, the Security Council condemned child recruitment and implied that there was criminal responsibility for doing so, *Norman*, para. 4(d).
267 *Norman*, Dissenting Opinion of Judge Robertson, paras. 32–47.
268 Arsanjani, 'The Rome Statute', 34, Cottier *et al.*, 'Article 8', p. 261.
269 Graditzky 'War Crimes', 204.

dwellings or buildings which are undefended and which are not military objectives'. When a similar provision was put in the ICTY Statute, it was criticised as 'very limited'.[270] Similarly Article 8(2)(b)(ix) adopts the prohibition of attacks 'against buildings dedicated to religion, art, science, or charitable purposes, historic monuments, hospitals and places where the sick and wounded are collected'. This has its basis in the Hague Rules,[271] but protection is granted by the Rome Statute only 'provided they are not military objectives'. The Hague Rules apply so long as the buildings 'are not being used for military purposes', which is a narrower exception.[272] For denial of quarter, the Statute (Article 8(2)(b)(xii)) adopts the language of the Hague Rules rather than Article 40 of API, which has a strong claim to customary law status.[273] The same applies to the treacherous killing of an enemy (Article 8(2)(b)(xi)), as defined in the Hague Rules, rather than the definition of perfidy in API.[274]

In general, Hague law violations are not well dealt with in the Rome Statute. Article 8(2)(b)(i) prohibits the intentional targeting of the civilian population. This is beyond doubt a crime; however, the mental element of this crime in custom is wilfulness.[275] Wilfulness includes intention and recklessness.[276] Article 8(2)(b)(i) criminalises only the intentional targeting of civilians. The definition of 'intention' which must be used by the ICC is given in Article 30 of the ICC Statute. Article 30 provides that 'a person has intent where: (a) In relation to conduct, that person means to engage in the conduct; (b) In relation to a consequence, that person means to cause that consequence or is aware that it will occur in the ordinary course of events.' As a result, it would be extremely difficult

[270] William J. Fenrick, 'Attacking the Enemy Civilian as a Punishable Offence' (1997) 7 DJCIL 539, 549.

[271] Although the 1954 Hague Cultural Property Convention 249 UNTS 210 and Articles 53 and 85(4)(d) API are also relevant, see Arsanjani, 'The Rome Statute', 33.

[272] Arsanjani, 'The Rome Statute', 33.

[273] Meron, *Human Rights*, p. 63; Greenwood, 'Customary', p. 106; Cassese, 'The Geneva Protocols', p. 79.

[274] Article 37, see Meron, *Human Rights*, p. 63; Greenwood, 'Customary', pp. 104–5. Equally, the wording of the Elements of Crimes is drawn from API, see Knut Dörmann, 'War Crimes in the Elements of Crimes', in Horst Fischer, Claus Kreß and Sascha Rolf Lüder (eds.), *International and National Prosecution of Crimes Under International Law* (Berlin: Arno Spitz, 2001), p. 95, p. 119.

[275] *Prosecutor* v. *Kordić and Čerkez*, Judgment, IT-95-14/2-T, 26 February 2001; *Prosecutor* v. *Blaškić*, Judgment IT-95-14-T, 3 March 2000; *Prosecutor* v. *Milan Martić*, Decision on Rule 61 Hearing, IT-95-11-R61.

[276] See, for example, Yves Sandoz, Christoph Swiniarski and Bruno Zimmermann, *Commentary to the Additional Protocols* (The Hague: Martinus Nijhoff/ICRC, 1986), para. 3476.

to argue that the concept of wilfulness could be included in the ICC Statute for this crime.

This makes the position of the duties of an attacker perilous. These duties are '(a) to do everything practicable to verify that the objectives to be attacked are military objectives; (b) to take all practicable precautions in the choice of methods and means of warfare with a view to avoiding or, in any event minimizing incidental civilian casualties or civilian property damage'[277] are an integral part of the law in this area.[278] Violation of these duties is good evidence of recklessness.[279] The exclusion of recklessness in this crime is unnecessary from the point of view of custom,[280] and, regrettable as it is, the duties of attackers are not as directly related to intention as defined in Article 30.

Collateral damage has been particularly badly dealt with. The customary rule is that stated in Articles 51(5)(b) and 85(3)(c) API.[281] This prohibits '[launching] an attack which may be expected to cause incidental loss of civilian life, injury to civilians, damage to civilian objects or a combination thereof, which would be excessive in relation to the concrete and direct military advantage anticipated'. The ICC has jurisdiction over 'intentionally launching an attack in the knowledge that such an attack will cause incidental loss of life or injury to civilians or damage to civilian objects or widespread, long term and severe damage to the natural environment which would be clearly excessive in relation to the concrete and direct overall military advantage anticipated'.

Changes from the language of API in the Rome Statute include 'which may be expected' to 'in the knowledge' and of the final part to 'clearly excessive in relation to the concrete and direct overall military advantage anticipated'. It is true that proportionality is a concept that is difficult to apply,[282] but that is no excuse for raising the threshold for liability. The change of the requirement from one 'which may be expected' to it being made 'in the knowledge' is unwelcome. The customary *mens*

[277] *Final Report to the Prosecutor by the Committee Established to Review the NATO Bombing Campaign Against the FRY*, PR/P.I.S./510-E, 13 June 2000, para. 28. Article 57 of Additional Protocol I contains similar duties.

[278] On the link, see Frits Kalshoven, 'Reaffirmation and Development of International Humanitarian Law Applicable in Armed Conflicts: The Diplomatic Conference, Geneva, 1974–1977' (1978) 9 NYIL 107, 115–19.

[279] Dörmann, *Elements*, p. 147.

[280] *Accord* Abi-Saab, 'The Concept', p. 118; Cassese, 'The Rome Statute', 154.

[281] On their customary status, see *Prosecutor* v. *Strugar*, Decision of 22 November 2002, IT-01-42, para. 10; *Blaškić*, Appeal, paras. 157–158; Greenwood, 'Customary', pp. 123–5.

[282] Wedgwood, 'The International Criminal Court', 103.

rea is wilfulness.[283] In derogation of the normal requirements of the Elements of Crimes[284] for this war crime, the prosecution must prove that the defendant made the value judgment that the damage would be 'clearly excessive'.[285] This will be very difficult, and on one interpretation of the Elements, practically unachievable owing to the difficulties of proving a value judgment.[286]

There are two other issues raised by the wording of the provision, the 'overall military advantage', and the requirement that the damage be 'clearly excessive' to that overall military advantage. The use of 'overall' could lead to a dilution of the prohibition: the further away from the individual attack focus lies, the more collateral damage may be thought acceptable. The formulation in the Statute of overall military advantage is not entirely unwarranted; it is in accordance, for example, with a number of 'understandings' on the provisions of API, such as the United Kingdom's.[287] The Elements of Crimes promulgated under Article 9 could represent a move away from the customary standard, by not requiring the 'concrete and direct overall military advantage' to be 'temporally or geographically related to the object of the attack'.[288] Dörmann is of the view that the sentence 'may invite abusive interpretations of the concept of concrete and direct military advantage'.[289]

Moving on to the provision that the damage or casualties be 'clearly' excessive, Fenrick defends the new formulation on the basis that prosecutors would be reluctant to prosecute unless API was clearly breached.[290] This may be the case in practice, but this does not justify the formulation in Article 8(2)(b)(iv). The reasons Fenrick gives are the

283 See *Prosecutor* v. *Galić*, Judgment, IT-98-29-T, 5 December 2003, paras. 58–59; Paust, 'Genocide', p. 302.

284 Elements of Crimes, for Article 8(2)(b)(iv), n. 37.

285 Elements of Crimes for Article 8(2)(b)(iv), n. 37; compare *Galić*, para. 59.

286 Didier Pfirter, 'Article 8(2)(b)(iv)', in Roy S. Lee (ed.), *The International Criminal Court: Elements of Crimes and Rules of Procedure and Evidence* (Ardsley: Transnational, 2001), p. 147, p. 150, states that the drafters of the crime would have not intended the crime to be impossible to prosecute. But some of those drafting the elements clearly wanted to make it as difficult as possible, more difficult than custom requires.

287 Reproduced in Adam Roberts and Richard Guelff, *Documents on the Laws of War* (Oxford: Oxford University Press, 3rd edn., 2000), p. 511; the German declaration is substantially similar, see *ibid.*, p. 505.

288 Elements of War Crimes for Article 8(2)(b)(iv), n. 36.

289 Dörmann, 'War Crimes in the Elements of Crimes', p. 126. Dörmann also notes that other aspects may counterbalance this 'to a certain extent' (p. 126). See also Leila Nadya Sadat, *The International Criminal Court and the Transformation of International Law: Justice for a New Millennium* (Ardsley: Transnational, 2002), p. 165.

290 Fenrick, 'Article 8', p. 197.

difficulties in determining proportionality, and the need to give some discretion to commanders.[291] The inclusion of 'clearly' does not clarify the standard, it simply raises it by reference to an undefined adjective. Prosecutors also may prosecute only when the higher threshold provision of Article 8(2)(b)(iv) is itself clearly breached, which would create a double upsurge in the limits on liability. It would appear possible to argue, in defence to a charge under Article 8(2)(b)(iv), that the defendant determined that civilian casualties were excessive, but not clearly so. The discretion could have been accommodated by adopting, as the ICTY Prosecutor has, the test of the reasonable military commander.[292]

Lastly, for parties to API, violations of that Protocol's (broader) formulation are Grave Breaches, thus there is a duty to prosecute all violations of it. This creates the interesting question of whether the Rome Statute is consistent with the obligations of parties to API under that Protocol. It is relevant in this context to look back at the Kosovan conflict, which showed that States could wage entire campaigns from the air, traditionally a fairly unregulated form of warfare.[293] This makes it imperative to maintain the integrity of what regulation there is. This has not been done in the Rome Statute. Prosecution of this offence will be very difficult indeed, and obtaining evidence may well be rendered impossible by the provisions of national security and co-operation.[294] Decisions on military advantage and the nature of targets require intelligence gathering, and States may refuse to hand over information relating to this on the grounds that it would damage national security.

The Statute grants jurisdiction over violations of the 1925 Gas Protocol, insofar as it covers 'asphyxiating, poisonous or other gases, and all analogous liquids, materials or devices'.[295] Although the Gas Protocol provides the core of the customary prohibition of chemical weapons, it is incomplete. It was expected that the 1993 Chemical Weapons Convention would be included. Reference to the 1993 Convention had been made throughout the Conference, and its inclusion seemed certain.[296] Its exclusion in the final compromise package was as part of the

[291] *Ibid.*

[292] Final Report to the Prosecutor by the Committee Established to Review the NATO Bombing Against the Federal Republic of Yugoslavia, para. 48.

[293] See Chris af Jochnick and Roger Normand, 'The Legitimation of Violence: A Critical History of the Laws of War' (1994) 35 Harvard ILJ 49, 77–9, 81–7; Oscar Schachter, 'UN Law in the Gulf Conflict' (1991) 85 AJIL 452, 456–67.

[294] See, pp. 152–3. [295] Rome Statute, Article 8(2)(b)(xviii).

[296] See A/CONF.183/2/Add.1, Article 5(c)(o) Options 1, 2 and 4; A/CONF.183/2.C.1/L.53, Article 5(o)(v) Options 1 and 2 (these are the only options); L.59, Article 5(o)(v).

quid pro quo for States who were pressing for the inclusion of nuclear weapons in the Statute. They argued that if nuclear weapons were not included, then nor should the poor States' weapons of mass destruction, in particular biological weapons.[297] One important reason why these should be in is that, unlike nuclear weapons, both chemical and biological weapons are the subject of a long-standing express, treaty-based prohibition.

Chemical weapons are, at least partially, covered by the included parts of the Gas Protocol, but in one of the Rome Statute's most significant omissions biological weapons are not covered at all in the Statute. The omission flies in the face of the prohibition, which was included in the 1925 Gas Protocol, and the comprehensive prohibition in the 1972 Biological Weapons Convention,[298] and was a staple of the Statute from the beginning of the Rome Conference.[299] Their exclusion is a serious, unconscionable omission from the Statute.

The exclusion of biological weapons is a specific case of a more general malaise in the Statute when dealing with weaponry. There is an excess of caution on this matter.[300] Article 8(2)(b)(xx) prohibits 'employing weapons, projectiles and material and methods of warfare which are of a nature to cause superfluous injury or unnecessary suffering or which are inherently indiscriminate in violation of the international law of armed conflict, provided that such weapons are the subject of a comprehensive prohibition and are included in an annex to this Statute, by an amendment in accordance with the relevant provisions set forth in Articles 121 and 123'. The prohibition of unnecessary suffering is a cornerstone of humanitarian law, underlying many of the particular rules, and being in itself a customary law prohibition on such methods or weapons.[301] The prohibition does not apply only to those particular instances defined by treaties such as the Gas Protocol.[302]

[297] On the controversies, see von Hebel and Robinson, 'Crimes', pp. 113–16, esp. p. 116.

[298] 1972 UN Convention on Prohibition of the Development, Production and Stockpiling of Bacteriological, Biological and Toxin Weapons and their Destruction 1015 UNTS 164.

[299] See A/CONF.183/2/Add.1, Article 5(o) Options 1, 2 and 4 (iv); A/CONF.183/C.1/L.53, Article 5(o) Options 1 and 2 (v); L.59, Article 5(o)(v).

[300] *Accord* Cassese, *International Criminal Law*, p. 60.

[301] In addition to the customary 1868 St Petersburg Declaration, Article 23(e) Hague Rules contains the prohibition and is undoubtedly customary. See Stafan Oeter, 'Methods and Means of Combat', in Dieter Fleck (ed.), *The Handbook of Humanitarian Law Applicable in Armed Conflicts* (Oxford: Oxford University Press, 1995), p. 105, pp. 111–16.

[302] This was the position of the ICJ in the *Nuclear Weapons* Opinion, paras. 78, 85.

By requiring the prerequisites of a comprehensive prohibition and inclusion in the annex for the specific methods, weapons, etc. with a prohibitively high threshold for addition of such weapons into the Statute,[303] States have robbed the phrase of any autonomous meaning. States have refused to pass to the court any power to declare any weapons as contrary to the general prohibition of weapons causing unnecessary suffering or that are inherently indiscriminate. This is in clear contrast to Article 3(a) of the ICTY Statute.

Non-international armed conflicts

As mentioned above, the Rome Statute does not restrict itself to international conflicts, but also includes some war crimes committed in internal armed conflict.[304] The inclusion of provisions relating to internal armed conflicts was controversial, at least for prohibitions extending beyond Common Article 3.[305] That said, the matter was far less controversial than it would have been prior to the *Tadić* decision. The creation of the ICTR expressly for internal armed conflict, together with the *Tadić* jurisdiction judgment, has revolutionised the law in this area, making some kind of provision far more palatable.

The effect of the *Tadić* Case in the garnering of support for this category of offences cannot be overestimated. The inclusion of offences occurring in internal armed conflict but not under Common Article 3 is a positive step. Article 8(2)(e) grants the ICC jurisdiction over 'serious violations of the laws and customs applicable in armed conflicts not of an international character, within the established framework of international law'. A closed list of twelve violations follows, many of which are 'parallel or identical' to those in Article 8(2)(b).[306]

Article 8(2)(e)(i) (like Article 8(2)(b)(i)) prohibits intentionally attacking civilian populations. This provision is beyond doubt customary, it is implicit in Common Article 3(1)(a), Article 4 APII, and express in Article 13(2) APII. It was also declared customary (with adequate support) in *Tadić*.[307] Article 8(2)(e)(ii) prohibits (in a parallel provision to Article

303 Cassese, 'The Rome Statute', 152.

304 See generally, Lindsay Moir, *The Law of Internal Armed Conflict* (Cambridge: Cambridge University Press, 2002). On the Rome Statute, see Djamchid Momtaz, 'War Crimes in Non-International Armed Conflicts Under the Statute of the International Criminal Court' (1999) 2 YBIHL 177; Darryl Robinson and Herman von Hebel, 'War Crimes in Internal Conflicts: Article 8 of the ICC Statute' (1999) 2 YBIHL 193.

305 Kirsch and Holmes, 'The Rome Conference', 7.

306 Arsanjani, 'The Rome Statute', 32.

307 *Tadić*, Decision, paras. 100–102, 110–113.

8(2)(b)(ii)) intentionally targeting buildings, etc. using the Geneva Convention emblems.[308] As civilian objects, these are not legitimate targets, so this is uncontroversial. As in international conflict, UN personnel are protected so long as they are entitled to civilian status.[309] This can be justified as in international conflicts. Article 8(2)(e)(iv) is identical to Article 8(2)(b)(ix). Hospitals and 'places where the sick and wounded are collected' are not legitimate targets, so targeting them is unlawful.

Pillage is forbidden, by both the customary law of internal armed conflicts[310] and the Rome Statute (Article 8(2)(e)(v)). Sexual offences are dealt with in Article 8(2)(e)(vi) in a similar way to Article 8(2)(b)(xxii), the only difference being that the final part substitutes 'Article 3 common to the four Geneva Conventions' for 'a grave breach of the Geneva Conventions'. As the reference implies, this is little more than an elaboration of the customary standard in common Article 3.[311]

Given the universal condemnation of the practice of 'ethnic cleansing', in former Yugoslavia,[312] which was not an international conflict at all times, it is acceptable to claim that Article 8(2)(e)(viii), which covers '[o]rdering the displacement of the civilian population for reasons related to the conflict, unless the security of the civilians involved or imperative military reasons so demand' is based on widely accepted custom.[313] One of the more controversial aspects of the *Tadić* decision at the time of its promulgation was its inclusion of perfidy in its survey of the rules applicable to internal armed conflict.[314] It has, nonetheless been included in the Statute, in Article 8(2)(e)(ix) (which uses the Hague Rule formulation of 'killing or wounding treacherously a combatant adversary'). This was, in all likelihood, correct from a customary perspective.[315] Of almost certain customary status is the prohibition in Article 8(2)(e)(x). This is the prohibition of mutilations or non-therapeutic medical/scientific experimentation. This can be seen as an elaboration on Common Article 3(1)(a) (the prohibition of violence to life and person, mutilation and cruel treatment), not least as it is clearly covered by Article 4(2)(a) APII.

308 This is contrary to Article 9(1), 11(1) and 12 APII.

309 Article 8(2)(e)(iii).

310 The prohibition of pillage is expressed in Article 4(2)(g) APII, which Greenwood considers customary, 'Customary', p. 113.

311 Robinson and von Hebel, 'War Crimes', 202–3.

312 See Drazen Petrovic, 'Ethnic Cleansing: An Attempt at Methodology' (1994) 5 EJIL 342.

313 See *Tadić*, Decision, paras. 111–112, on GA Resolution 2675, UN Doc. A/8028, p. 75, which prohibits such transfers.

314 Greenwood, 'International Humanitarian Law', 129.

315 Rogers, *Law*, pp. 224–5.

Article 8(2)(e)(vii) prohibits 'conscripting or enlisting children under the age of fifteen years into armed forces or groups or using them to participate actively in hostilities'. It is probable that this article is reflective, if not of long established custom then of the emergence of a recent consensus, at the latest at the Rome Conference, that under-15s are not to be used in armed conflicts. As mentioned above, the Special Court for Sierra Leone determined that this provision was customary by 1996. Denial of quarter is criminalised by Article 8(2)(e)(x). The ICTY in *Tadić* alluded to this being the position under customary law.[316] 'Destroying or seizing the property of an adversary unless such destruction or seizure be imperatively demanded by the necessities of the conflict' is included in the jurisdiction of the court by virtue of Article 8(2)(e)(xii). There are few, if any, clear treaty-based precedents for this crime in internal armed conflicts, but the sub-Article is an application of the basic principle of military necessity, which was recognised as customary prior to 1998.[317]

What is more important in relation to the provisions covering internal armed conflicts, though, is what is not included. The *Tadić* Case devoted a large amount of space to displaying how the law on the means and methods of warfare had developed in custom for internal armed conflicts, with specific reference to the prohibition of chemical weapons.[318] None of this is included in the Rome Statute.[319] This is a serious omission, as it is in the case of international armed conflict, but here there is not even an analogous provision to Article 8(2)(b)(xx).[320] Finally, there is no provision relating to indiscriminate attacks or collateral damage. Custom is not silent on this matter,[321] and modern internal conflicts are replete with examples of civilians being caught up in fighting. These absences are exacerbated by the fact that most modern conflicts are internal.[322]

316 *Tadić*, Decision, para. 102.

317 Theodor Meron, 'The Continuing Role of Custom in the Formation of International Humanitarian Law' (1996) 90 AJIL 238, 244. Rogers, *Law*, p. 230, considers this crime to be customary.

318 *Tadić*, Decision, paras. 119–127.

319 For criticism, see Cassese, 'The Rome Statute', 152–3.

320 For a narrower view of the law, see David Turns, 'At the Vanishing Point of International Humanitarian Law: Methods and Means of Warfare in Non-International Armed Conflicts' (2002) 45 GYBIL 115.

321 See Rogers, *Law*, pp. 231–2, *Kupreškić*, para. 524, *Tadić*, Decision, para. 127.

322 For another list of absences, see Boot, *Genocide*, pp. 604–5.

The Special Court for Sierra Leone

The Special Court has jurisdiction over violations of Common Article 3 and Additional Protocol II by Article 3 of its Statute. Article 4 of the Statute grants the Court jurisdiction over three named violations of international humanitarian law:

> (a) Intentionally directing attacks against the civilian population as such or against individual civilians not taking direct part in hostilities;
> (b) Intentionally directing attacks against personnel, installations, material, units or vehicles involved in a humanitarian assistance or peacekeeping mission in accordance with the Charter of the United Nations, as long as they are entitled to the protection given to civilians or civilian objects under the international law of armed conflict;
> (c) Conscripting or enlisting children under the age of fifteen years into armed forces or groups or using them to participate actively in hostilities.

Article 3 of the SCSL Statute is clearly acceptable from the point of view of the *nullum crimen* principle, as Sierra Leone is a party to the Geneva Conventions and APII. Two of the three violations mentioned in Article 4 are clearly customary, as discussed in relation to the Rome Statute, from where they are drawn. Article 4(c) has caused controversy, in particular because the jurisdiction of the Special Court goes back to 1996. This caused Sam Hinga Norman to challenge the jurisdiction of the Court over this crime. The majority of the Appeals Chamber rejected the challenge, although the decision is based on accepting a relatively small amount of evidence that international law criminalised rather than merely prohibited the use of under-15s in conflict[323] (not significantly less than the ICTY was prepared to accept in *Tadić*, though). The Security Council was very certain about the existence of the crime as far back as 1996. The list of offences is closed, which has been criticised, on good grounds.[324] This could be because, as in the case of genocide, the Secretary General decided that there was no evidence of crimes that would not fall under Articles 3 and 4, or crimes under Sierra Leonean law in Article 5. On the other hand, this simply could be an example that runs against the trend identified in this chapter or evidence that Sierra Leone was able to convince the United Nations to accept a limited approach on war crimes.

[323] *Norman*.

[324] Amnesty International, *Sierra Leone: Recommendations on the Draft Statute of the Special Court*, AFR51/083/2000.

Other crimes

There were provisions on criminal organisations in the London Charter.[325] Any organisation declared criminal by the Nuremberg IMT was to be considered so by the signatories to the Charter, who then had a right to bring any person to trial and convict them purely for membership in that organisation (Article 10). It is undisputed that there was no precedent or basis for this in international law.[326] Its addition was a practical response to the large-scale criminality which surrounded the Nazi regime. The IMT itself accepted that this was new, and approached it with great caution, describing it as 'a far reaching and novel procedure. Its application, unless perfectly safeguarded, may produce great injustice'.[327] As a result, they tailored their findings so to ensure that proof of voluntary membership and knowledge of criminal purposes for a conviction was to be recorded in any national proceeding.[328] They also acquitted three of the six indicted organisations.[329] Despite the (arguably) analogous organisations in Japan (primarily the *Kempetai*, or secret police), no such provision was included in the Tokyo Charter. There was one proposal to include organisational criminality in Rome,[330] it received very little support.

The possibility of other crimes being included in the Rome Statute was on the table. The initial revival of the idea was by the Caribbean states looking for a court to act against large-scale drug traffickers.[331] The original ILC drafts all focused on other crimes, in addition to the core crimes, which at times seemed sidelined.[332] At the pre-Rome PREPCOMs the developing countries argued strongly for the inclusion of drug trafficking and terrorism in the jurisdiction of the court.[333] One

[325] London Charter, Articles 9 and 10. See Stanislaw Pomorski, 'Conspiracy and Criminal Organisations', in Ginsburgs and Kudriavtsev, *Nuremberg Trial*, 213; Woetzel, *Nuremberg Trial*, pp. 190–217.

[326] See John F. Murphy, 'Norms of Criminal Procedure at the International Military Tribunal', in George Ginsburgs and Vladimir N. Kudriavstev (eds.), *The Nuremberg Trial and International Law* (Dordrecht: Martinus Nijhoff, 1990), p. 61, pp. 68–9.

[327] Nuremberg IMT Judgment, 250. See generally, Lippman, 'Nuremberg', 35, Schwarzenberger, *International Law*, p. 506.

[328] Nuremberg IMT Judgment, 251.

[329] The SA, Reich Cabinet and High Command. They convicted the SS, Leadership Corps of the Nazi party and the Gestapo/SD, Nuremberg IMT Judgment, 268–271.

[330] A/CONF.183.C.1/L.3.

[331] Roy S. Lee, 'An Introduction', in Roy S. Lee (ed.), *The International Criminal Court: The Making of the Rome Statute* (The Hague: Kluwer, 1999), p. 1, p. 2.

[332] See James Crawford, 'The ILC's Draft Statute for an International Criminal Tribunal' (1994) 88 AJIL 140, 143.

[333] Boister, 'The Exclusion', 27.

reason for the non-inclusion of terrorism was fairly simple: there is, as yet no clearly acceptable definition of such an international crime in customary international law (or treaty law).[334]

The arguments on drug trafficking were different. The developed countries in general were strongly against the inclusion of drug trafficking in the Rome Statute.[335] The primary reason for its exclusion was probably not legal (although its opponents did phrase their arguments in legal form) but because the existing system of national obligations to extradite or prosecute enshrined in the 1988 Vienna Convention privileges their interests.[336] Because of the strength of support for them though, both drug trafficking and terrorism were included in the Final Act of the Rome Conference as possible additions to be considered at any Review Conference.[337]

Conclusion

Having considered the jurisdictional competence of ICTs, the trends suggested above are visible. It is important not to overstate the case. The evidence on this point is not sufficient to claim that this form of selectivity is an immutable law. But the basic point is that States tend to take a broader view of the applicable law and the extent to which courts may be permitted to interpret the law. Let us take the Tribunals in turn. First, the Nuremberg and Tokyo IMTs. For the offences included, with the exception of the war crimes charges, it can be seen that the Allies took a very broad view of the law. Crimes against humanity, although morally clearly justifiable, were at best an emerging principle during the Second World War, and it is very unlikely that crimes against peace were referable to existing international law. Discretion was left in the court to determine, for example, what the laws and customs of war entailed.

When the ICTY was set up, slightly different policies were afoot although, again, none of those involved in creating the ICTY thought themselves likely to be subject to its jurisdiction. Most decisions on the law

334 This remains the case despite the 1997 International Convention on Terrorist Bombings (GA Resolution 52/164, UN Doc. A/RES/52/164), which is not yet in force, never mind reflective of customary international law.

335 The United States was express about this, see Scheffer, 'The United States', p. 13.

336 Boister, 'The Exclusion', 36. Scharf claims that US opposition to the inclusion of drug crimes came at least partially from the US Justice Department, which did not wish to lose the revenue they received as a result of expropriation of drug-related moneys; Michael P. Scharf, 'The Politics of Establishing an International Criminal Court' (1995) 6 DJCIL 167, 171.

337 Final Act of the Rome Conference, C/CONF.183/10 Annex I Resolution E.

were left to the ICTY itself. This was done through short descriptions of the law of crime against humanity (although subject to the link to armed conflict) and the open-ended provision in Article 3.

With the ICTR, criminalising Common Article 3 and APII involved an enlightened view of the law and was probably thought exhaustive of the material prohibitions applying to non-international conflicts. Crimes against humanity were drafted with a limitation that is best explained as either an attempt to link the definition to the facts in Rwanda or an understandable uncertainty about the law. It could be argued that Rwanda managed to get in the requirement to exempt RPF killings from the ICTR, but there is no material in the public domain to support or undermine this idea. Rwanda voted against the ICTR Statute as it included crimes other than genocide, ostensibly on the ground that the ICTR should not waste its resources prosecuting such offences. In reality, this was more to do with the new government wishing to ensure that offences committed by them (as the RPF) which were thought to amount to war crimes or crimes against humanity were not included in the mandate of the ICTR. As Rwanda did not have the power to prevent the creation of the ICTR, its view was not taken up. The ICTR Statute does show some evidence of being the outcome of negotiations, however.

The drafting of the Rome Statute shows strong support for the thesis argued for in this chapter. States drafting the Rome Statute were not merely setting down law to deal with anyone else, but law that could be applied to both them and their allies. Also, this law is to be enforced by a court which is to be independent of the creating States. This meant that the way to rein in the court was by ensuring that all the law to be enforced was defined by the States themselves, leaving as little discretion as possible in the Court. This setting down of the law need not necessarily be unwelcome, primarily because parts of international criminal law had, at least up until recently, been rather open-textured, and without authoritative interpretations legitimacy was affected.

The problem with the Rome Statute is that definitions of crimes are sometimes narrower than customary international law permits (or, in some cases, requires). This is particularly the case for war crimes, with a closed list of crimes which are frequently defined in a limited fashion. Only in one instance, persecutive crimes against humanity, can it be claimed that the Statute clearly develops the law.

The Special Court does not provide a clear picture from the point of view of this chapter, as although crimes against humanity are broadly defined and, in accordance with custom, war crimes are contained in short closed lists. Only the child soldiers' provision in Article 4(c), back-dated to 1996, is possibly in excess of custom. It is difficult to determine whether or not the Court therefore provides support for the contention in this chapter. As with the other Tribunal in which there was negotiation between the territorial State and the United Nations, the position is slightly mixed. At most, the war crimes provisions are an exception which justifies caution, showing the critique in this chapter to be of a trend, not an inevitability.

6 Selectivity and the law: II – general principles of liability and defences

Introduction

In chapter 5, another aspect of selectivity was discussed, an aspect which is related to the scope of criminal liability. In short, when 'safe' ICTs have been set up, although there are some exceptions, the scope of liability tends to be broader than when 'unsafe' Tribunals are created. We saw that this tendency was identifiable with respect to the definitions of the core international crimes. This chapter is intended to complement chapter 5, by investigating whether or not the same process can be identified in relation to defences and the general principles of criminal liability, together sometimes known as the 'general part' of criminal law.[1] The case can be made that it can.

It should come as no surprise that the argument can be made for either the definitions of crimes or the 'general part' of international criminal law. They are, after all, part of the same process, that of determining the parameters of criminal liability. This can be seen from one of the negotiating documents for the Rome Statute, a proposed new text for the Article on superior orders.[2] After the document had set out a proposal for the defence of superior orders, which excluded crimes against humanity and genocide from the defence, a telling footnote recorded that 'Some delegations are willing to accept the inclusion of crimes

[1] M. Cherif Bassiouni and Peter Manikas, *The Law of the International Criminal Tribunal for Yugoslavia* (Ardsley: Transnational, 1996), p. 339, in a rather expansive definition, defines the 'general part' as '(1) definitions of the terms used in the special part of the statute; (2) constitutive elements of the crimes which include definitions of the material, mental and causal elements; (3) definitions of inchoate offences, such as attempt, solicitation and conspiracy; (4) conditions of exoneration, such as excuses and justifications; and (5) factors to be considered in mitigation of punishment, as well as additional remedies, such as compensation for victims.'

[2] A/CONF.183/C.1/WGGP/L.9/Rev.1.

against humanity in this paragraph subject to the understanding that the definition of crimes against humanity will be sufficiently precise and will identify an appropriately high level of *mens rea*'. The questions of definitions of crimes and the general part were thus clearly linked in the minds of the drafters at Rome.

Examples of selectivity in the use of principles of liability and defences at the national level can be given from Argentina and the United States. In Argentina, when prosecutions of the deposed military *junta* became politically inexpedient, two measures were taken: a time bar was imposed, then, to ensure that all ongoing cases were brought to a close, the *Ley de Obedencia Debida* was passed.[3] This created a very broad form of the superior orders' defence, designed to lead all the ongoing trials to acquittals or abandonment.[4]

The second example, that of the United States, is best shown by contrasting two decisions, the *Yamashita*[5] and *Medina*[6] cases. When dealing with command responsibility, it is unclear precisely which level of knowledge the Military Commission required to ground liability in *Yamashita*.[7] The Commission decided either that Yamashita did know of atrocities, or that he should have known.[8] This is probably the standard of liability in custom, even if the Commission's view of the facts and application of the law to those facts is contested.[9] Irrespective of the

[3] Law No. 23521, 4 June 1987, reprinted in (1987) 8 HRLJ 477.

[4] Kai Ambos opines that the *ley* 'perfected the policy of impunity'; Kai Ambos, 'Impunity in International Criminal Law: A Case Study on Colombia, Peru, Bolivia, Chile and Argentina' (1997) 18 HRLJ 1, 11.

[5] *US* v. *Yamashita* 4 LRTWC 1 (US Military Commission, Manila); 327 US 1 (US Supreme Court).

[6] *US* v. *Medina* (1971) 43 CMR 243. The *Medina* Case is the subject of an article written by the Chief Prosecutor in that case, William G. Eckhardt, 'Command Criminal Responsibility: A Plea for a Workable Standard' (1982) 97 Military LR 1. His defence to the charge (made by Telford Taylor 'The Course of Military Justice', *New York Times*, February 2, 1972, 37) that the United States was propounding different standards for itself to those it applied to others, is that the 'should have known' test is 'too broad and one that would subject the commander to after-the-fact judgments concerning what he should have known' (Eckhardt, 'Command Criminal Responsibility', 18). This does not refute Taylor's charge that differential standards were applied.

[7] W. Hays Parks, 'Command Responsibility for War Crimes' (1973) 62 Military LR 1, 22–38, esp. 30–2.

[8] Parks, *ibid*. This was the interpretation of the case by ICTY in *Prosecutor* v. *Delalić, Delić Mucić, and Landžo*, Judgment, IT-96-21-T, 16 November 1998 (*Čelebići*), para. 384.

[9] For opinions casting doubts upon the interpretation of the fact by the Military Commission, see M. Cherif Bassiouni, *Crimes Against Humanity in International Criminal Law* (The Hague: Kluwer, 2nd edn., 1998), pp. 427–31; Anne-Marie Prevost, 'Race and War Crimes: the 1945 War Crimes Trial of General Tomoyuki Yamashita' (1992) 14 HRQ

controversy over the disposition of the case, the *mens rea* considered applicable in the *Yamashita* Case was not applied when the US military justice system was evaluating the conduct of the US army in the Vietnam War. In the case of Ernest Medina, the instructions to the jury by the Presiding Officer required actual knowledge of violations of the laws of war rather than the *Yamashita* 'should have known' standard.[10] Not only was this contrary to existing jurisprudence, but also the US Army Manual, which embodies the customary rule of 'known or should have known'.[11] The Colonel giving the instructions may have been responding to the argument of the defence counsel in the *Medina* Case, who said that 'I don't think that what is done to a Jap in the heat of vengeance after World War II can be done to an American on an imputed theory of responsibility'.[12] Notwithstanding these examples, this chapter will follow the lead of chapter 5, by focusing mainly on the law as it has been developed by the founding documents of the ICTs. It is here that definitional selectivity is at its clearest.

Defences

Defences in the sense in which they are understood here are those which apply to exclude liability at the merits stage of proceedings. They do not include immunities from jurisdiction, which are not defences in this sense.[13] Immunities such as diplomatic immunity and State immunity

303, 318–19; A. Frank Reel, *The Case of General Yamashita* (Chicago: Chicago University Press, 1949), pp. 166–74. See also, *Yamashita* in the Supreme Court, Justice Murphy, pp. 39–40; Parks, 'Command Responsibility', 33–4, is more sanguine, but see at 62, where he implies that the heat of war may have affected the process.

10 Instructions to Court Members, *United States* v. *Medina*, Appellate Exhibit XCIII, p. 18. See Leslie C. Green, 'Command Responsibility in International Law' (1995) 5 TLCP 319, 353–4. From the quotation given in Green, it could also be that the formulation required a specific causation element, which is also controversial.

11 US Department of the Army, Law of Land Warfare, Field Manual, 27–10, 1956, para. 501.

12 Cited in Prevost, 'Race and War Crimes', 329. The racist term used in the defence counsel's statement gives some credence to her claim that the *Yamashita* decision was partly based on racial prejudice. For further critique of the case, see Mary McCarthy, *Medina* (London: Wildwood House, 1972); Roger S. Clark, 'Medina: An Essay On the Principles of Criminal Liability for Homicide' (1973) 5 *Rutgers Camden Law Journal* 59.

13 Dinstein deals with the two together; Yoram Dinstein, 'Defences', in Gabrielle Kirk McDonald and Olivia Swaak-Goldman (eds.), *Substantive and Procedural Aspects of International Criminal Law* (The Hague: Kluwer, 2000), p. 369, pp. 384–8, terming them 'defences based on official position'. Eser makes a similar distinction to that made here; Albin Eser, 'Defences in War Crimes Trials', in Yoram Dinstein and Mala Tabory, *War Crimes in International Law* (Martinus Nijhoff: Kluwer, 1996), pp. 251, 253. See also Ilias Bantekas, 'Defences in International Criminal Law', in Dominic McGoldrick, Peter

are waiveable by States irrespective of the views of the accused, which is inconsistent with the nature of a true defence, that is invocable by a defendant irrespective of the wishes of others. As has been pointed out so often that it is at risk of being seen as a cliché, immunity from jurisdiction does not translate to an absence of responsibility, it simply is a plea that the relevant forum is not competent to adjudicate that responsibility.[14] Defences are traditionally something which have not, with the exception of superior orders, received a great deal of attention in international criminal law.[15] The jurisprudence on them is also not overly impressive.[16]

Superior orders

The moral issues involved in pleas of superior orders are difficult,[17] although to read the Nuremberg IMT Charter on the matter those thinking them to be simple could easily be forgiven. The Nuremberg IMT Charter simply provides: '[t]he fact that the defendant acted pursuant to order of his government or of a superior shall not free him from responsibility, but may be considered in mitigation of punishment if the Tribunal determines that justice so requires.'[18]

Rowe and Eric Donnelly (eds.), *The Permanent International Criminal Court: Legal and Policy Issues* (Oxford: Hart, 2004), p. 263, pp. 263–4.

14 *Difference Relating to Immunity From Legal Process of a Special Rapporteur of the Commission on Human Rights* [1999] ICJ Rep. 62, pp. 88–9.

15 One of the few monographs on the subject is Geert-Jan Knoops, *Defences in Contemporary International Law* (Ardsley: Transnational, 2001). Other helpful treatments include Matthew Lippman, 'Conundrums of Armed Conflict: Criminal Defences to Violations of the Humanitarian Law of War' (1996) 15 Dickinson JIL 1; Kai Ambos, 'Other Grounds for Excluding Criminal Responsibility', in Antonio Cassese, Paula Gaeta and John R. W. D. Jones (eds.), *The Rome Statute of the International Criminal Court: A Commentary* (Oxford: Oxford University Press, 2002), p. 1003 and Elies van Sliedregt, *The Criminal Responsibility of Individuals for Violations of International Humanitarian Law* (The Hague: T. M. C. Asser Press, 2003), pp. 226–342.

16 The ICTY, for example, has had little to say on defences, and its largest foray into the area, *Prosecutor* v. *Erdemović*, has not been well received, see, pp. 302–3.

17 On orders generally, see Yoram Dinstein, *The Defence of 'Obedience to Superior Orders' in International Law* (Dordrecht: Martinus Nijhoff, 1965); Leslie C. Green, *Superior Orders in National and International Law* (Leyden: Sitjhoff, 1976); Lippman, 'Conundrums', 4–58; James W. Grayson, 'Superior Orders and the International Criminal Court' (1995) 64 Nordic JIL 243; Mark J. Osiel, *Obeying Orders: Atrocities, Military Discipline and the Law of War* (New Brunswick: Transaction, 1999); Mark J. Osiel, *Mass Atrocity, Ordinary Evil and Hannah Arendt: Criminal Consciousness in Argentina's Dirty War* (New Haven: Yale University Press, 2001).

18 Nuremberg IMT Charter, Article 8.

To evaluate the Nuremberg IMT Charter on superior orders from the viewpoint of the pre-existing law on the subject we need to look back to the start of the twentieth century. In 1906, Lassa Oppenheim took the view that superior orders remained a complete defence to war crimes.[19] As to the period after the First World War, Dinstein opines that although there is some evidence that the position was moving away from an absolute defence of superior orders, 'these traces are somewhat blurred and indistinct, and the trend is too uncertain to serve as a beacon in this issue'.[20] However, the case law from the pre-First World War and pre-Second World War eras tended to support the 'manifest illegality' test: that although superior orders may constitute a defence, this is so only when the order is not to commit an act which is manifestly illegal.[21] This was the position adopted by many States and academics in the pre-Second World War era.[22]

It was possible to raise doubts about the legal status of the defence by the end of the First World War. The 1919 Allied Commission on the Responsibility of the Authors of the War could not decide what to do, so effectively ducked the issue of superior orders by leaving it to any subsequent court to decide on the applicability of superior orders as a defence.[23] Twenty-three years before the Commission's report, the second edition of Winthrop's classic *Military Law and Precedents* viewed the manifest illegality test to be established law.[24] There is no evidence that by 1919 the defence of superior orders was excluded unless the orders were manifestly unlawful.

Late in the Second World War the United States and United Kingdom both altered their military manuals, as they had initially provided for the absolute protection of those acting in accordance with superior

[19] Lassa Oppenheim, *International Law, II* (London: Longman, 1906), pp. 264–5. This was very famously changed by Hersch Lauterpacht in 1944: Hersch Lauterpacht (ed.), *Oppenheim's International Law, II* (London: Longmans, 6th edn., 1944), pp. 452–3.

[20] Dinstein, *The Defence of 'Obedience to Superior Orders'*, p. 103. There was at least one case where the defence was refused during the First World War, the (in)famous *Fryatt* Case (see Dinstein, *The Defence of 'Obedience to Superior Orders'*, pp. 160–2).

[21] See *R.* v. *Smith* (1900) 17 SCR 561; *Commonwealth ex rel Wadsworth* v. *Shortall* (1903) 55 Atl. 952; *Riggs* v. *State* (1866) 43 Tenn. 85. The classic cases adopting this view are the *Dover Castle* Case (1922) 16 AJIL 704 and the *Llandovery Castle* Case (1922) 16 AJIL 709.

[22] See the survey by Lippman, 'Conundrums', 4–16.

[23] Report of the Commission on the Responsibility of the Authors of the War and Enforcement (1920) 14 AJIL 95, 117.

[24] William Winthrop, *Military Law and Precedents* (Washington, DC: Government Printing Office, 2nd edn., 1896), pp. 446–7.

orders.[25] They were altered in the British case to remove the defence,[26] while the US manual accepted that superior orders 'may be taken into consideration . . . either by way of defence or in mitigation of punishment.'[27] Against this background, it seems quite clear that the Nuremberg provision (which was largely repeated in Article 6 of the Tokyo IMT Charter) went beyond existing international law in refusing the superior orders defence in any situation.[28]

There is another way of seeing Article 8 which could bring it within the fold of the manifest illegality test, and thus pre-existing law. This is to see Article 8 as being limited to the situation being dealt with in Nuremberg, namely the major Nazi war criminals, and amounting to a predetermination by the drafters that any of the orders involved were manifestly unlawful.[29] If this view was right, it would help make the argument of this chapter anyway, as it would involve a preordained exclusion of a possible defence when prosecutions of non-nationals were involved. Yet it is still important to evaluate it, as the argument has risen again in relation to whether or not the manifest illegality test was an accurate statement of the law in the 1990s.

The proponents of the narrower understanding of Article 8 make a good case, one which has gained a number of supporters.[30] There is also one case in the post-war prosecutions of Nazi crimes that expressly supports this position. In the case of *in re Zuehlke*, a Netherlands Court said that 'as appears from the context of the wording, Article 8 only relates to major war criminals . . . not the other war criminals . . .

[25] Dinstein, *The Defence of 'Obedience to Superior Orders'*, pp. 46–8; Lippman, 'Conundrums', 21.

[26] Amendment 34 to the *Manual of Military Law* (London: HMSO, 7th edn., 1944).

[27] Basic Field Manual, Rules of Land Warfare, Change No. 1, 15 November 1944. See also Bassiouni and Manikas, *The Law*, p. 375, 'the military regulations of almost all States prior to the IMT Charter essentially had provided for an absolute or qualified defence of superior orders'.

[28] See Dinstein, *The Defence of 'Obedience to Superior Orders'*, p. 117; at p. 118 Dinstein describes the Nuremberg Charter as 'high handed and sweeping'. He is more friendly to the Tokyo IMT Statute (p. 157); there was a slight textual difference, but the Tokyo IMT read the two provisions as identical, and the evidence of the opinion of its drafters shows that the intention was to exclude the defence completely; see Joseph B. Keenan and Brendan F. Brown, *Crimes Against International Law* (Washington, DC: Public Affairs Press, 1950), pp. 132–6. For a contrary view, see van Sliedregt, *The Criminal Responsibility*, p. 320.

[29] Hilaire McCoubrey, 'From Nuremberg to Rome: Restoring the Defence of Superior Orders' (2001) 50 ICLQ 386; Charles Garraway, 'Superior Orders and the International Criminal Court: Justice Delivered or Justice Denied?' (1999) 336 IRRC 785.

[30] Van Sliedregt, *The Criminal Responsibility*, pp. 319, 322; Bantekas, 'Defences', p. 271.

Article 8 of the Charter is not an expression of a law of wider purpose, applicable to all war criminals, without exception'.[31]

The problem with this approach is that if the drafters had simply preapplied the law to the facts, this would have amounted to an unwarranted intrusion into the fact-finding powers of the Nuremberg IMT (although this does not mean the Allies did not intend that). Charles Garraway, in the course of an eloquent argument in favour of Article 8 being an application of the manifest illegality principle, makes much of a question by Nikitchenko in the London negotiations. Nikitchenko asked if with such major criminals it was an issue of principle.[32] But Nikitchenko was not the only person at the London Conference, and his views did not reflect the discussion surrounding superior orders in London. Nikitchenko's view was that the defendants were guilty, and that the duty of the Nuremberg IMT was merely to quantify that guilt and sentence the defendants.[33] There is no evidence that Nikitchenko's view was accepted by the other drafters.[34] They chose the route of declaring what international law was, rather than applying the facts to preexisting law.[35] Although the actions of the drafters were not always admirable, they did not quite write an act of attainder in London.

As with the prosecution when they argued before it,[36] the Nuremberg IMT itself showed some uncertainty about Article 8 of the Charter. But it seems that Nikitchenko's view was not adopted by the other members of the Nuremberg IMT.[37] The majority judgment gave the conclusionary declaration that 'the provisions of this article are in conformity with the law of all nations . . . the true test, which is found in varying degrees in the criminal law of most nations, is not the existence of the order, but whether . . . moral choice was in fact possible'.[38] The assertion that it is in conformity with the law of all nations is patently false. More difficult

[31] In *re Zuehlke*, XIV LRTWC 139, 149. The UNWCC commentary disagreed with this aspect of the case (p. 151).

[32] Garraway, 'Superior Orders', 787.

[33] Minutes of the Conference on Military Tribunals: London, 19 July 1945.

[34] See Minutes of the Conference on Military Tribunals: London, 23 July 1945. Dinstein claims that the position grants too much subtlety to the drafters' intent, *The Defence of 'Obedience to Superior Orders'*, p. 129.

[35] See, p. 234.

[36] See Paula Gaeta, 'The Defence of Superior Orders: The Statute of the International Criminal Court versus Customary International Law' (1999) 10 EJIL 172, 180.

[37] Justice Birkett, for example, seemed to think that the rejection of superior orders was long established in international law. Justice (Norman) Birkett, 'International Legal Theories Evolved at Nuremberg' (1947) 23 IA 317, 317.

[38] Nuremberg IMT, 'Judgment and Sentences' (1947) 41 AJIL 171, 221.

to understand is the seeming addition of the requirement that there was no 'moral choice' to the test relating to superior orders.[39] Dinstein gives the best explanation for this addition. He maintains that the Tribunal was accepting that superior orders were not, in and of themselves, a defence under the Nuremberg IMT Charter, but expressing their view that the existence of superior orders was relevant to other such defences as coercion (duress).[40]

Both Control Council Law 10 and the 'Nuremberg Principles' adopted the view that superior orders were not a defence (Principle IV).[41] Control Council Law 10 is probative: that law was for the prosecution of the non-major war criminals. The Nuremberg Principles are important as, whatever the intentions of their drafters, they are strong evidence of how States (and legal opinion) saw the Nuremberg precedent. On the question of whether Article 8 was an application of the manifest illegality test to the facts or a separate proposition of law, namely that superior orders were not a defence, Principle IV clearly plumped for the latter.

The rejection of superior orders as a defence was the 'Nuremberg Principle' around which most controversy has centred. A major reason for this has been the relatively low uptake of the principle in national laws.[42] This need not be fatal to the claim that Article 8 represents the law. The uptake of international criminal law in domestic systems has not generally been that high in any case. Equally, there is authority to the contrary. Such authority may be found in the Nuremberg 'subsequent proceedings', in which US tribunals in the *Einsatzgruppen*[43] and *High Command*[44] Cases seemed to use the manifest illegality test, as did certain other judgments in the direct post-war period.[45] There were other US cases, such as the *Sawada* trial, that rejected superior orders as a defence.[46]

39 See, for example, Maurice Greenspan, *The Modern Law of Land Warfare* (Berkley: California University Press, 1959), p. 493.

40 Dinstein, *The Defence of 'Obedience to Superior Orders'*, p. 152.

41 GA Resolution 177, UN Doc. A/1316.

42 Gaeta, 'The defence of Superior Orders', 179, cites Argentina, Austria, Iran, Romania and the United Kingdom. Also, to some extent, France, Norway and the Netherlands (*ibid.*, 179–80). The Israeli Law (on Nazi Crimes) also rejects the defence; Nazis and Nazi Collaborators (Punishment) Law 1950, 57 Sefer Hachukim, 9 August 1950, 281.

43 *US* v. *Ohlendorf* 4 TWC 411, 470–471.

44 *US* v. *von Leeb (The High Command Trial)* 11 TWC 1 88–89.

45 For example, *US* v. *Masuda (The Jaluit Atoll Case)* 1 LRTWC 71, see Lippman, 'Conundrums', 35. For more on such cases, see generally, Green, *Superior Orders*, pp. 283–348; Lippman, 'Conundrums', 21–34; Gaeta, 'The Defence of Superior Orders', 177.

46 *US* v. *Sawada*, 5 LRTWC 1, 19–22. For a British case rejecting the defence, see Colin Sleeman (ed.), *The Gozawa Trial* (London: William Hodge, 1948), p. 231.

Expressions of the manifest illegality test have continued in various cases up to the present day,[47] although the defence has been generally rejected on the facts.[48] In the sphere of international legislation, suggestions were made to include provisions relating to superior orders. All were rejected as they did not gather enough support.[49] Before the ICTY was created, the ILC wavered on the total exclusion of the defence,[50] and academic opinion has been split. The schism is between those claiming that the manifest illegality test reflects custom,[51] and those saying that superior orders are never a defence *per se*, but may be a relevant factor for other defences, such as duress.[52] In practice, the difference may not always be important, as the orders in cases coming to trial will probably be considered manifestly illegal.[53] That does not mean that the distinction will never matter, particularly in matters such as targeting, or where reprisals are at issue where the application of the law to the facts may be difficult. By the early 1990s, the simple fact was that either position could be asserted and receive a fair level of support.[54]

When the ICTY was created the only State's comment addressing the draft Statute's provision on superior orders which adopted the manifest

[47] See the US cases of *US* v. *Kindler* (1953) 14 CMR 742, *US* v. *Calley* (1973) 22 USCMA 534, and *Priebke*, Rome Military Court of Appeal, 7 March 1998. Lippman, goes as far as to say that the cases show 'coherence and consensus' on manifest illegality; 'Conundrums', 52.

[48] See Gaeta, 'The Defence of Superior Orders', 183–4. It is wrong, however, to consider this to be evidence of the rejection of the manifest illegality test; there is a conceptual difference between rejecting the application of a test and applying the test, but finding that the facts do not fall within it.

[49] In the Genocide Convention, a provision excluding superior orders was defeated (A/C.6/215/Rev.1). The vote was 28–15–6, see Lippman, 'Conundrums', 51–3. In both the Geneva Convention negotiations and those leading up to the 1977 Additional Protocols, no agreement could be reached, but ICRC proposals including a conditional liability (manifest illegality) approach were rejected. See Gaeta 'The Defence of Superior Orders', 187–8. See generally, Howard Levie, 'The Rise and Fall of an Internationally Codified Defense of Superior Orders' (1991) 30 RIDMDG 183.

[50] See the history of the ILC's approaches, in Otto Triffterer, 'Article 33', in Otto Triffterer (ed.), *Commentary on the Rome Statute of the International Criminal Court: Article by Article* (Baden-Baden: Nomos, 1999), p. 573, pp. 574–6. They latched on to the 'moral choice' aspect thus, if Dinstein's approach is followed, not accepting the defence.

[51] The primary proponent of this view is Green, *Superior Orders*; see also Steven Ratner and Jason A. Abrams, *Accountability for Human Rights Atrocities in International Law* (Oxford: Oxford University Press, 2nd edn., 2001), pp. 136–8.

[52] This view is almost synonymous with Dinstein's classic, *The Defence of 'Obedience to Superior Orders'*.

[53] Gaeta, 'The Defence of Superior Orders', 183–6.

[54] See, for example, Andreas Zimmerman, 'Superior Orders', in Antonio Cassese, Paula Gaeta and John R. W. D. Jones (eds.), *The Rome Statute of the International Criminal Court: A Commentary* (Oxford: Oxford University Press, 2000), p. 957, pp. 965–6.

illegality test was that of the United States.[55] The ICTY Statute, in Article 7(4), adopts the Nuremberg-type position that superior orders are not a defence (although it is now accepted that orders may be relevant for other defences).[56] The United States was unhappy about this, and in both the Security Council,[57] and in its draft Rules of Procedure,[58] it suggested that the ICTY be brought into line with its assertion of the manifest illegality test. As the proposals ran directly counter to the express provisions of the ICTY Statute, the US attempts did not work. However, the United States was not prepared to prevent the creation of the ICTY on the ground that its position was not generally accepted. The ICTR has an identical provision on superior orders despite the United States being the primary drafter, implying that its opposition to the exclusion of the superior orders defence was hardly entrenched when its nationals were not defendants.[59]

The 1996 ILC Draft Code of Crimes Against the Peace and Security of Mankind rejected the defence of superior orders unequivocally, on the basis of the Nuremberg, Tokyo, Control Council Law 10, ICTY and ICTR precedents.[60] In 1997, the Joint Separate Opinion of Judges McDonald and Vohrah expressly adopted Dinstein's approach of permitting evidence of superior orders only for defences of duress and mistake of fact or law.[61] President (as he then was) Cassese might be taken as having adopted the opposite view, given his *obiter* comment that 'if the superior order is manifestly illegal under international law, the subordinate is under a duty to refuse to obey the order'.[62] However, his extra-judicial writings clearly show that such an inference would not accurately reflect his view that superior orders are not, *per se*, a defence.[63]

55 S/25575, Article 11(a).

56 On this, see Virginia Morris and Michael P. Scharf, *An Insider's Guide to the International Criminal Tribunal for the Former Yugoslavia* (Ardsley: Transnational, 1995), pp. 101–3.

57 S/PV.3217, p. 16.

58 US Suggestions on Rules of Procedure and Evidence, IT/14, November 17, 1993, Rules 25.14(A).

59 Article 6(4). See Virginia Morris and Michael P. Scharf, *The International Criminal Tribunal for Rwanda* (Ardsley: Transnational, 1998), pp. 266–8.

60 Draft Code of Crimes Against the Peace and Security of Mankind, UN Doc. A/51/10 (1996), Article 5, Commentary, para. 4.

61 *Prosecutor* v. *Erdemović*, Judgment, IT-96-22-A, 29 November 1997, Separate Opinon of Judges McDonald and Vohrah, para. 34. Judge Stephen seemed to be of the same view; Separate Opinion of Judge Stephen, paras. 13–15.

62 Separate and Dissenting Opinion of Judge Cassese, para. 15.

63 Antonio Cassese, *Violence and Law in the Modern Age* (Cambridge: Polity, 1984), chapter VIII; Antonio Cassese, 'The Rome Statute of the International Criminal Court: Some

It might be thought that the rejection of the manifest illegality approach in two International Tribunals would have settled the issue for the Rome Conference. The onus must have been on the proponents of the manifest illegality test to prove its continued international relevance.[64] But, of course, the situations surrounding the creation of (and thus State concerns about being the subject of) these two Tribunals were very different to the circumstances and policies surrounding the creation of the ICC.[65] This is not to say that there was no support for the approach in the existing tribunals' statutes. A strong coalition of States (led by Germany) supported that position. Opposition came from another group led by the United States, which clung to the manifest illegality test, as the *lex lata* position.[66] The result was a compromise, and not a comfortable one.[67]

Article 33 reads:

'1. The fact that a crime within the jurisdiction of the Court has been committed by a person pursuant to an order of a government or of a superior, whether military or civilian, shall not relieve that person of criminal responsibility unless:

(a) That person was under a legal obligation to obey orders of the Government or the superior in question;
(b) The person did not know that the order was unlawful; and
(c) The order was not manifestly unlawful.
2. For the purposes of this article, orders to commit genocide or crimes against humanity are manifestly unlawful.'[68]

Cassese avers that: '[a]rticle 33 must be faulted as marking a retrogression with respect to existing customary international law'.[69] This may be right, especially after the creation of the two UN Tribunals in the 1990s,

Preliminary Reflections' (1999) 10 EJIL 144, 157; Antonio Cassese, *International Criminal Law* (Oxford: Oxford University Press, 2003), pp. 232–41.

64 Bantekas, 'Defences', pp. 272–3.

65 Gaeta, 'The Defence of Superior Orders', 178 admits that the possible reason surrounding the adoption of the Nuremberg-type approach in all international tribunals prior to Rome may well have been the result of them all being set up to try non-nationals of the creating States.

66 Gaeta, 'The Defence of Superior Orders', 188–9.

67 Per Saland, the Chair of the Working Group that drafted Article 33, describes the drafting as 'very difficult', Per Saland, 'International Criminal Law Principles', in Roy S. Lee (ed.), *The International Criminal Court: The Making of the Rome Statute* (The Hague: Kluwer, 1999), pp. 189, 211. At p. 212, Saland notes that 'the article is very difficult to read and is bound to be debated'.

68 On which see, Triffterer 'Article 33'.

69 Cassese, 'The Rome Statute', 157. See also Gaeta, 'The Defence of Superior Orders', 190, describing it as having departed from customary international law without reason.

whose Statutes adopted the opposite position. This is particularly the case insofar as Article 33 operates beyond the military context.[70] On the other hand, there is room for some doubt as to the precise customary position. Even if Article 33 is not a large retrenchment in substantive law,[71] it shows that in cases where States are legislating for themselves rather than for others they are either supporters of, or are prepared to accept, a more lenient corpus of law.

In addition, there are certain other problems. Although Article 33's acceptance of the manifest illegality test is (presumably) meant to be limited to war crimes (by Article 33(2)),[72] the wording is infelicitous.[73] 'Orders to commit genocide or crimes against humanity' is ambiguous. If it is taken literally it would serve to refuse the defence only where orders were to 'commit genocide' or 'commit a crime against humanity'. If so, the provision will be of little effect, particularly because of the euphemistic nature of many orders to commit atrocities.

It is highly unlikely that this was the intention of the drafters, but even dismissing this interpretation does not end the problem. The wording of Article 33(2) implies that the relevant *mens rea* relating to the nature of the order is that of the orderer. In the case of genocide, the special intent is of the essence of the offence. It is therefore possible that if the orderer can be proved to have genocidal intent, even if this cannot be shown for the subordinate, the order will be taken to be manifestly illegal. This could be the case even if the subordinate is charged with a war crime. Even if the Court does not adopt such an approach, Article 33 runs against the grain of the idea of a coherent set of laws which applies to all international crimes: it creates a defence applicable to only one sort of crime.[74] It also, illegitimately, assumes that every example of a war crime will necessarily be more opprobrious than every

[70] Leila Nadya Sadat, *The International Criminal Court and the Transformation of International Law: Justice for a New Millennium* (Ardsley: Transnational, 2002), p. 219.

[71] See Garraway, 'Superior Orders'.

[72] Admittedly Article 33(2) does not include aggression in this list, but this is as yet unprosecutable before the ICC. General principles issues remain undetermined for aggression.

[73] See Robert Cryer, 'Superior Orders in the International Criminal Court', in Nigel White, Richard Burchill and Justin Morris (eds.), *Essays in Conflict and Security Law in Memory of Hilaire McCoubrey* (Cambridge: Cambridge University Press, 2005) 49.

[74] On the principle, see Saland, 'International Criminal Law Principles', p. 208. That there are more defences for war crimes than the other crimes also may well be probative of governmental fears that they, while highly unlikely to be charged with genocide or crimes against humanity, may well see themselves, or their nationals, charged with war crimes. This is also implied by Gaeta, 'The Defence of Superior Orders', 189.

example of a crime against humanity, and (perhaps more legitimately) every example of genocide.[75] On a practical level, as the ICC cannot compel the attendance of witnesses, and it may be expected that States will consider orders given in times of conflict to relate to issues of national security (therefore under the special regime discussed above), evidence of any orders will be difficult to obtain.

To turn, finally, to the Special Court for Sierra Leone, Article 6(4) of the Statute of that Court returns to the rejection of the superior orders pioneered in the Nuremberg IMT Statute, and adopted by the ICTY and ICTR. The Secretary General's report which accompanied the draft Statute provides no explanation for this rejection of the Rome Statute approach to the defence of superior orders. Article 6(4) may be taken as providing some evidence that Article 33 was not considered customary by those drafting the Special Court's Statute.

Other defences

With the above provisions, we reach the end of the defences which were express in any of the statutes prior to Rome. It certainly gives pause for thought that, particularly in the London Charter, the only mention of defences was to exclude the application of those most likely to be asserted. It is unfortunate that this was the pattern that was followed until the Rome Conference. Equally when the ICTY was created, at least the Secretary General recognised that other defences would be relevant. In his report on the ICTY, he left decisions on the applicability and definitions of these to the ICTY itself, though: 'the International Tribunal will have to decide on various personal defences which may relieve a person of individual criminal responsibility, such as minimum age or mental incapacity, drawing on principles of law recognised by all nations.'[76] The same authority was granted to the ICTR. This amounted to a strong form of delegation of authority to those Tribunals to declare the law. Indeed, President McDonald has described the tribunal as a 'laboratory' for the law here.[77] Pursuant to

[75] Zimmerman, 'Superior Orders', p. 972.

[76] Report of the Secretary General Pursuant to paragraph 2 of Security Council Resolution 808, UN Doc. S/25704, para. 58. Leaving it to the ICTY has not gone uncriticised; see Christopher Blakesley, 'Atrocity and its Prosecution: The *Ad Hoc* Tribunals for the Former Yugoslavia and Rwanda', in Timothy L. H. McCormack and Gerry J. Simpson (eds.), *The Law of War Crimes: National and International Approaches* (The Hague: Kluwer, 1997), p. 189, p. 204.

[77] ICTY Press Release CC/PIO/272/E, 9 December 1997, cited in Peter Rowe, 'Duress as a Defence to War Crimes After *Erdemović*: A Laboratory for a Permanent Court?' (1998) 1

this mandate, both Tribunals have developed some, albeit not much, jurisprudence in relation to defences.[78] The Special Court for Sierra Leone has a similar discretion to that of the ICTY and ICTR.

States were not prepared to allow the ICC to act in such a fashion. Their nationals were not to be guinea pigs. For the ICC, States insisted on defining the substantive defences themselves.[79] This is not necessarily a bad thing, as it provides for the first time an express statement of the defences which may be presented in a trial of international crimes,[80] providing determinacy[81] and the possibility of a uniform corpus of law.[82]

A number of the defences in the Rome Statute are relatively uncontroversial. For example, mental illness, which is sufficiently serious that it 'destroys that person's capacity to appreciate the unlawfulness or nature of his or her conduct, or capacity to control his or her conduct to conform to the requirements of law', is clearly acceptable as a defence.[83] Such a person is not the voluntary actor assumed by criminal law. The Nuremberg IMT implied that such a defence existed,[84] and in the *Čelebići* Case the ICTY assumed such a defence to exist, as did the ICTY's Rules of Procedure and Evidence.[85]

Duress is perhaps slightly less accepted, primarily because of the split (3–2) decision of the ICTY in *Erdemović* the year before the Rome

YBIHL 210, 210. Knoops also notes the strong impact of judicial decisions here, Knoops, *Defences*, pp. 1–2.

78 The most famous of these must remain the *Erdemović* decision, which has been the subject of much criticism. See Suzannah Linton, 'Reviewing the Case of Drazen Erdemović: Uncharted Waters at the International Criminal Tribunal for the Former Yugoslavia' (1999) 12 LJIL 251; Robert Cryer, 'One Appeal, Four Opinions, Two Philosophies and a Remittal' (1998) 2 JACL 193; David Turns, 'The International Criminal Tribunal for the Former Yugoslavia: The *Erdemović* Case' (1998) 47 ICLQ 461; Olivia Swaak-Goldman, 'International Decisions: *Prosecutor* v. *Erdemović*' (1998) 92 AJIL 282; Rowe, 'Duress'.

79 Saland, 'International Criminal Law Principles', p. 206, notes that this was not an easy thing to do. On Article 31 generally, see Saland, 'International Criminal Law Principles', pp. 206–10; Albin Eser, 'Article 31', in Otto Triffterer (ed.), *Commentary in the Rome Statute of the International Criminal Court* (Baden-Baden: Nomos, 1999), p. 537.

80 See Cassese, 'The Rome Statute', 153.

81 In particular, determinacy; see Thomas M. Franck, *The Power of Legitimacy Among Nations* (Oxford: Oxford University Press, 1990), chapter 4.

82 Again, of course, we must remember that this is subject to the necessary qualifier that the quality of that corpus of law must also be investigated.

83 Rome Statute, Article 31(1)(a), see Eser, 'Article 31', pp. 545–6; Knoops, *Defences*, pp. 108–15; Peter Krug, 'The Emerging Mental Incapacity Defence in International Criminal Law: Some Initial Questions of Implementation' (2000) 94 AJIL 317.

84 In relation to Rudolf Hess, see Dinstein, 'Defences', p. 378.

85 *Čelebići*, paras. 1156–1157, Rule of Procedure and Evidence 67(A)(ii)(b).

negotiations which, while (correctly) noting the customary foundations of the defence of duress, excluded its applicability where the killing of innocents was at issue. Article 31(1)(d)[86] adopts the defence of duress without such a limitation. *Erdemović* has been almost universally rejected on this point.[87] Unlike the defence of superior orders, where there was the Nuremberg, Tokyo and (more importantly) ICTY and ICTR precedents, there was little clear authority on point. Only Judge Li in *Erdemović* asserted that there was a clear customary rule on duress where killing was alleged.[88] On the basis of this, the formulation of this defence should not therefore be taken as strong evidence in favour of the argument made in this (and the previous) chapter. It could be argued in favour of the thesis that, given the choice, States opted for the more indulgent formulation of the defence. That position is weakened by the fact that in doing so States were probably in accordance with the general principle of duress in most national legal systems. Thus on this point Article 31(1)(d) will not be taken as proof or disproof of the contention made in this chapter.

Next in increasing order of controversy is necessity, which may also be found in Article 31(1)(d).[89] The ICTY has been at times rather coy about such a defence, in all likelihood because of the fear of giving credence to claims of military necessity at every turn.[90] In *Aleksovski*, the Appeals Chamber did not feel the need to express an opinion on whether necessity was a defence in international law.[91] On the other hand, Cassese was willing to concede the applicability of the defence as an analogue to duress in the *Erdemović* Case.[92] There is post-Second

[86] On which see Eser, 'Article 31', pp. 263–5.

[87] See the literature cited above and Cassese, *International Criminal Law*, pp. 246–51. Dinstein is an exception, see Dinstein, 'Defences', pp. 375–6 and Yoram Dinstein, 'International Criminal Law' (1985) 20 Israel LR 206, 232–5.

[88] *Erdemović*, Separate and Dissenting Opinion of Judge Li.

[89] See Eser, 'Defences', pp. 261–3; Ambos, 'Other Grounds for Excluding Criminal Responsibility', in Antonio Cassese, Paula Gaeta and John R. W. D. Jones (eds.), *The Rome Statute of the International Criminal Court: A Commentary* (Oxford: Oxford University Press, 2002), pp. 1035–42; Eser, 'Article 31', p. 550 criticises Article 31 for mixing duress and necessity in one provision. Cassese, however, supports it on this ground, Cassese, *International Criminal Law*, p. 251.

[90] On which, see Hilaire McCoubrey, 'The Nature of the Modern Doctrine of Military Necessity' (1991) 30 RDMDG 215; Burrus M. Carnahan, 'Lincoln, Lieber and the Law of War, the Origins and Limits of the Principle of Military Necessity' (1998) 92 AJIL 213; William Gerald Downey, 'The Law of War and Military Necessity' (1953) 47 AJIL 251; N. C. H. Dunbar, 'Military Necessity in War Crimes Trials' (1952) 29 BYBIL 443.

[91] *Prosecutor* v. *Aleksovski*, Judgment, IT-95-14/1-A, 24 March 2000, para. 55.

[92] *Erdemović*, Separate and Dissenting Opinion of Judge Cassese, para. 14.

World War authority such as the *I. G. Farben* Case[93] to the effect that necessity may be a defence, and as such it is likely that Article 31(1)(d)(ii) represents a codification of custom.[94] So again Article 31(1)(d) proves neutral from the point of view of the claim made in these two chapters.

Mistake is dealt with in Article 32 of the Rome Statute, Article 32(1) recognising mistake of fact, Article 32(2) covering mistakes of law.[95] The latter provision has been the subject of a great deal of criticism. Cassese, for example, is hostile to the defence, claiming that it has never been a defence in national law, and has only the most tenuous claim to a place in international law.[96] As a result, he is of the view that Article 32(2) 'amounts to a serious loophole . . . and may eventually be misused for the purpose of perpetrating crimes clearly prohibited by international law'.[97] He is too harsh on Article 32(2). As Triffterer points out, there are very few possible situations in which this could apply.[98] The article does not apply to situations where the person merely does not know that the crime is under the jurisdiction of the Court.[99]

More fundamentally, both mistakes of fact and mistakes of law exculpate only if they serve to negate the mental element required for the relevant crimes.[100] This has led some to say that in fact Article 32 is superfluous, on the basis that it merely confirms the basic point that where there is no mental element, there is no offence.[101] Some would have preferred the Rome Statute to include the broader civil law

93 *Krauch and Others*, VIII TWC 1080, 1179. See also the review in van Sliedregt, *The Criminal Responsibility*, pp. 279–86.

94 See Cassese, *International Criminal Law*, pp. 234–44, 251.

95 See generally, Albin Eser, 'Mental Elements – Mistake of Fact and Mistake of Law', in Antonio Cassese, Paula Gaeta and John R. W. D. Jones (eds.), *The Rome Statute of the International Criminal Court: A Summary* (Oxford: Oxford University Press, 2002), p. 889, pp. 934–46; van Sliedregt, *The Criminal Responsibility*, pp. 301–16.

96 Cassese, 'The Rome Statute', 155–6. For interpretation of the provision, see Triffterer, 'Article 32', in Otto Triffterer (ed.), *Commentary on the Rome Statute of the International Criminal Court* (Baden-Baden: Nomos, 1999), pp. 568–9.

97 Cassese, 'The Rome Statute', 156. Cassese's later writings are more sanguine; Cassese, *International Criminal Law*, p. 256.

98 Triffterer, 'Article 32', p. 569. 99 *Ibid.*

100 Article 32(1), 32(2), or if the defence of superior orders applies; on this, see Cryer, 'Superior Orders'. In the latter case, the issues are those of superior orders discussed above.

101 Otto Triffterer, 'Article 32', p. 555, pp. 555–68. This was the view of some of the drafters; see Roger S. Clark, 'The Mental Element in International Criminal Law: The Rome Statute of the International Criminal Court and the Elements of Offences' (2002) 12 CLF 291, 308.

concept of mistakes of law.[102] Given that a number of delegations at Rome were dubious about any mistake of law defence,[103] and the fact that it is unlikely that customary law accepts any defence broader than that in Article 32, this would have been very difficult.[104] This provision is probably acceptable from the customary point of view.

Greater questions may be asked about the next ground of exclusion of responsibility,[105] intoxication, which is included in Article 31(1)(b). Some, including some Islamic States that do not permit the drinking of alcohol, were uncomfortable with the defence. A defence of involuntary intoxication was not too difficult to obtain agreement on; voluntary intoxication was the bone of contention.[106] In the end, it was excluded in most but not all circumstances. This 'had the benefit of not satisfying anyone'.[107] It is probably an innovation not justified by custom, and it may be doubted whether complete exculpation through voluntary intoxication could be considered a general principle of law.[108]

In national systems accepting voluntary intoxication as relevant, this tends to be accompanied by a concept of a less serious offence to which evidence of exculpatory intoxication is inadmissible. There is no such distinction expressly drawn in the Statute.[109] The Statute may move towards

[102] Eser, 'Mental Elements', pp. 934–5. Neil Boister, 'Reflections on the Relationship between the Duty to Educate in Humanitarian Law and the Absence of a Defence of Mistake of Law in the Rome Statute of the International Criminal Court', in Nigel White, Richard Burchill and Justin Morris (eds.), *Essays in Conflict and Security Law in Memory of Hilaire McCoubrey* (Cambridge: Cambridge University Press, 2005).

[103] Report of the Working Group of General Principles of Criminal Law, UN Doc. A/CONF.183/C.1.WGGP/L.4/Add.1/Rev.1, at p. 3.

[104] On the post-war cases here, see van Sliedregt, *The Criminal Responsibility*, pp. 313–14.

[105] Some doubts may be expressed about the nature of intoxication as such a ground, as it is conceptually usually seen as a question of whether or not evidence of intoxication may accompany a claim of absence of the mental element. See, for example, A. P. Simester and G. R. Sullivan, *Criminal Law: Theory and Doctrine* (Oxford: Hart, 2nd edn., 2003), p. 559. On intoxication generally, see Knoops, *Defences*, pp. 117–25.

[106] Saland, 'International Criminal Law Principles', p. 207; van Sliedregt, *The Criminal Responsibility*, p. 248.

[107] Saland, 'International Criminal Law Principles', p. 207, excludes it in most circumstances. See also Eser, 'Article 31', pp. 546–8.

[108] Van Sliedregt, *The Criminal Responsibility*, pp. 248–9, 254, although see, *contra*, Bantekas, 'Defences', p. 281. It is not included as a defence in, for example, Eser, 'Defences', a piece from 1996. Schabas goes as far as to describe the defence in the context of the ICC as 'absurd'; William A. Schabas, 'General Principles of Criminal Law in the International Criminal Court Statute – Part III' (1998) 6 EJCCLCJ 400, 423.

[109] Although some Arab States moved towards the view that such a defence is generally not applicable to genocide and crimes against humanity, it may be to war crimes, Report of the Working Group, p. 4.

this through the back door, however, through the exclusion of intoxication as a defence where the defendant 'knew, or disregarded the risk, that, as a result of the intoxication, he or she was likely to engage in conduct constituting a crime within the jurisdiction of the Court'.[110] This exclusion is narrower than the Anglo-American approach, which does not require recklessness to the specific risk of committing such a crime to exclude the defence. The provision also seems to allow for a complete acquittal from all crimes in the Statute which, as mentioned above, is not in line with the thrust of domestic law on the subject, where there is a back-up crime of which the defendant will be guilty when intoxication is shown to negate the mental element in an offence.[111] We therefore have here a show of a distinctly expansive approach towards the defence.[112]

Self-defence, although in itself clearly an appropriate ground for excluding responsibility, is defined in Article 31(1)(c) in a way that gives cause for concern.[113] That a person who 'acts reasonably to defend himself or herself or another person' should not be liable is not contested.[114] But Article 31(1)(c) goes beyond this, providing, for war crimes,[115] that a person acting reasonably to defend 'property which is essential for the survival of the person or another person or property which is essential for accomplishing a military mission, against an imminent and unlawful use of force' has a defence. The last part of 31(1)(c) is an innovation, and 'this extension is manifestly outside the *lex lata* and may generate quite a few misgivings'.[116]

Eser is a little more sanguine, trying to tie the rule back to notions of military necessity.[117] The problem with such a view is that international

[110] Article 31(1)(b). [111] See similarly, Ambos, 'Other Grounds', p. 1031.

[112] The defence may be appropriate from a criminal point of view, but that does not undermine this point, in that it is only with the Rome Statute that such a concern became notable.

[113] See generally van Sliedregt, *The Criminal Responsibility*, pp. 254–67; Knoops, *Defences*, pp. 73–127; Ambos, 'Other Grounds', pp. 1031–5. Most are at a loss to explain circumstances in which it could operate in relation to international crimes; see Eser, 'Defences', p. 263.

[114] The wording is from Article 31(1)(c). It is admittedly difficult to imagine where acting 'reasonably' could amount to an offence in the jurisdiction of the court, though.

[115] Again, we see a specialised regime being created for these offences.

[116] Cassese, 'The Rome Statute', 154–5. See also Julio Barboza, 'International Criminal Law' (1999) 278 RdC 9, 152. Saland, 'International Criminal Law Principles', p. 208, informs us that this was the most difficult provision in the Working Group, and it runs against the principle they tried to work to that the general principles were applicable to all the crimes.

[117] Eser, 'Article 31', pp. 548–50, esp. p. 549.

humanitarian law already takes such considerations into account, therefore to add another defence on the basis of such notions double counts their relevance. Eric David is highly unsympathetic to the inclusion of defence of property in the Rome Statute, believing it to be contrary to *jus cogens*.[118] The latter view is questionable. The former, that the rule is more generous than custom, is correct. It is notable that Belgium has made clear its view that Article 31(1)(c) is unacceptable bearing in mind pre-existing custom.[119] It is surprising that the ICTY was so willing to accept the defence as adopted in the Rome Statute in *Kordić and Čerkez*.[120]

On a practical level, this defence may also cause problems, as its terms are rather vague.[121] Interpretation will also be hampered by the fact that what is considered mission-essential property is frequently classified information, therefore the rules on national security information in the Rome Statute, with their limited duty to co-operate with the ICC, will be applicable. The formulation of the defence of mission-essential property is grist to the mill of this chapter's argument, that a narrower view of the range of criminal conduct is adopted when an 'unsafe' Tribunal is created, in particular when war crimes, the most likely charge against many States, are an issue.

These are all the exclusions of liability expressly provided for in the Statute. However, the Court, in an extraordinary provision, is entitled to refuse to apply a particular ground from Article 31 in the case before it.[122] This is one instance where the ICC is granted some discretion to work with the law. Saland reports that the article was necessary for negotiating purposes, primarily as delegations were unhappy with various formulations of the defences, so this discretion was necessary to get agreement.[123] As some of the definitions are more widely drawn than customary law, this may work to limit the problems, but it may raise important questions of *nullum crimen sine lege*.[124] On the other hand, the ICC will be constrained by Article 21, which will require it to work within the bounds of international law.[125] This stands as one example of delegation of authority to the ICC.

[118] See van Sliedregt, *The Criminal Responsibility*, pp. 259–60.
[119] Eric David, 'Belgium' (2000) 3 YBIHL 426, 427.
[120] *Prosecutor* v. *Kordić and Čerkez*, Judgment, IT-95-14/2-T, 26 February 2001, paras. 448–452.
[121] Cassese, 'The Rome Statute', 155.
[122] Article 31(2); see Saland, 'International Criminal Law Principles', 208–9.
[123] Saland, 'International Criminal Law Principles', 208–9.
[124] Saland, *ibid*. [125] Triffterer, 'Article 31', p. 553.

Article 31 does not dispose of all possible defences. These include reprisals, reports of whose death are greatly exaggerated.[126] Certain weapons offences are still subject to such a defence[127] and, *Kupreškić* notwithstanding, reprisals against civilians not protected by the 1949 Geneva Conventions may still be applicable.[128] Consent will also be relevant for some offences. The impossibility of getting agreement on such defences led to the inclusion of Article 31(3), which allows the Court 'to consider a ground for excluding criminal responsibility other than those referred to in paragraph 1 where such a ground is derived from the applicable law as set forth in article 21'. We can see a grant of a 'window'[129] of opportunity to the ICC in relation to defences to determine the law, and possibly to amend it. When compared, however, to the grant of authority to the ICTY and ICTR in this area to determine the law, it is clear that only a limited level of discretion has been delegated to the ICC.

Principles of liability

Principles of liability are the counterpart of defences as they, too, relate to the parameters of liability. They are traditionally an area of responsibility that has played a limited role in the statutes of international criminal courts. It is not that there was no law on the subject at all prior to the negotiation of the Rome Statute, it was just that little effort had traditionally been expended discovering such principles. The endeavours of the ICTY and ICTR in relation to the principles of liability were

[126] On reprisals see Frits Kalshoven, *Belligerent Reprisals* (Leyden: Sitjhoff, 1971); Christopher J. Greenwood, 'The Twilight of the Law of Belligerent Reprisals' (1989) 20 NYBIL 35; Françoise J. Hampson, 'Belligerent Reprisals and the 1977 Protocols to the Geneva Conventions of 1949' (1988) 37 ICLQ 818.

[127] See Robert Cryer, 'Hague Law Comes Home: Prosecuting Weapons Offences at the International Criminal Court' (2002) *Acta Juridica* 238, 247–9.

[128] *Prosecutor* v. *Kupreškić*, Judgment, IT-95-16-T, 14 January 2000, paras. 521–536, denies the continued validity of reprisals on this point. The reasoning in the case is effectively skewered by Christopher J. Greenwood, 'Belligerent Reprisals in the Jurisprudence of the International Criminal Tribunal for the Former Yugoslavia', in Horst Fischer, Claus Kreß and Sascha Rolf Lüder (eds.), *International and National Prosecution of Crimes Under International Law* (Berlin: Arno Spitz, 2001), p. 539. Kalshoven chose *Kupreškić*'s Presiding Judge's *Festschrift* to launch an all-out assault on the reasoning in the case; Frits Kalshoven, 'Reprisals and the Protection of Civilians: Two Recent Decisions of the Yugoslavia Tribunal', in Lal Chand Vohrah *et al.* (eds.), *Man's Inhumanity to Man: Essays in Honour of Antonio Cassese* (The Hague: Kluwer, 2003), p. 481.

[129] The term being Saland's, 'International Criminal Law Principles', 208.

beginning to make headway into the fog, not least because they were given the authority to do so.

The 'traditional' principles of liability

The Nuremberg IMT Charter included some rather terse provisions on the principles of liability. The Charter provided that 'leaders, organizers, instigators and accomplices participating in the formulation or execution of a Common Plan or Conspiracy . . . are responsible for all acts performed by any persons in execution of such plan'. This was complemented by Article 6(a), which stated that liability existed for 'participation in a common plan or conspiracy for the accomplishment of the above [crimes against peace]'. This latter phrase is absent from Article 6(b) and 6(c). As a result, it is difficult to see whether the final clause in Article 6 was intended to create a separate, free-standing charge of conspiracy, or if it was merely an aspect of the crime against peace charge in Article 6(a).[130] The reason for this vagueness is simple: the Charter was a compromise on this issue.

The concept of liability of conspirators for all conduct engaged in pursuant to their conspiracy is a creature of the common law. It was unknown in civil law systems at the time.[131] This fact is fatal to any claim of conspiracy being a part of international law by virtue of it being a general principle of law. In addition, there were no precedents for this type of liability in international law, so any claim for its customary status must also fail. The reason for its inclusion at all was US insistence. The entire US plan for dealing with Germany was based on the assumption that there was a wide-ranging conspiracy including a huge number of German politicians, militarists, industrialists and ordinary Germans. US plans for dealing with the large number of putative defendants began with the idea of this conspiracy. The idea was Murray

[130] See John F. Murphy, 'Norms of Criminal Procedure at the International Military Tribunal', in George Ginsburgs and Vladimir N. Kudriavatsev (eds.), *The Nuremberg Trial and International Law* (Dordrecht: Martinus Hijhoff, 1990), p. 61, pp. 68–9.

[131] Hans Ehard, 'The Nuremberg Trial Against the Major German War Criminals and International Law' (1949) 43 AJIL 223, 227; Murphy, 'Norms', 64; Stanislaw Pomorski, 'Conspiracy and Criminal Organisations', in George Ginsburgs and Vladimir N. Kudriavatsev (eds.), *The Nuremberg Trial and International Law* (Dordrecht: Martinus Nijhoff, 1990), p. 219. The French and Soviet delegates to the London Conference were said to be shocked by the idea of conspiracy when it was explained to them; Pomorski, 'Conspiracy'. Robert K. Woetzel, *The Nuremberg Trials in International Law* (London: Stevens, 1962), p. 215. See also Richard Minear, *Victor's Justice: The Tokyo War Crimes Trial* (Princeton: Princeton University Press, 1971), pp. 36–42.

Burnays', an American government lawyer in charge of developing the plans for prosecuting Nazi crimes who had cut his teeth prosecuting racketeering conspiracies in the United States.[132]

In the Nuremberg IMT Judgment on this count and despite the US Prosecutor's insistence that conspiracy covered all of the crimes in Article 6, it was determined that the conspiracy crime related only to the charges of crimes against peace under Article 6(a).[133] Even this was controversial. Both of the French judges and one of the US judges wanted to reject the charge in its entirety,[134] and even the charge that remained was limited. For proof of conspiracy, the Nuremberg IMT required that 'the conspiracy must have been clearly outlined in its criminal purpose. It must not be too far removed from the time of decision and of action . . . a concrete plan to wage war [must have] existed and [the IMT be able to] determine the participants in that concrete plan'.[135] The Nuremberg IMT was also quite strict on the requirement of actual knowledge of the plan.[136]

Despite this, the Tribunal did not define the acts that amounted to participation in the conspiracy, and was not entirely consistent in the individual judgments.[137] Conviction on this count seemed irrelevant in the sentencing,[138] perhaps that is indicative of the Nuremberg IMT's distinct antipathy to this charge. Article 5 of the Tokyo IMT had a provision for our purposes identical to that in Nuremberg, but its handling of the charge was far less subtle, and the majority did little to demonstrate any discomfort with this novel charge.[139] Although two of the judges in Tokyo expressly rejected the crime of conspiracy, saying that it had no basis in international law,[140] the majority proceeded to take an exceptionally wide approach, going far beyond the Nuremberg

[132] See Taylor, *The Anatomy*, pp. 35–6; Howard Levie, *Terrorism in War: The Law of War Crimes* (New York: Oceana, 1992), pp. 405–11.

[133] IMT Judgment, 223–224.

[134] Bradley F. Smith, *Reaching Judgment at Nuremberg* (London: André Deutsch, 1977), p. 129, Taylor, *The Anatomy*, p. 550.

[135] IMT Judgment, 222. [136] See Pomorski, 'Conspiracy', 234.

[137] See Ian Brownlie, *International Law and the Use of Force by States* (Oxford: Oxford University Press, 1963), pp. 196–9.

[138] Pomorski, 'Conspiracy', 235.

[139] The majority agreed with the Nuremberg IMT; see R. John Pritchard and Sonia M. Zaide (eds.), *The Tokyo War Crimes Trial, 20: Judgment* (New York: Garland, 1981), pp. 48, 439; Judge Bernard and Judge Jaranilla both expressly upheld the charge for all Crimes in Article 5 (*ibid.*, v. *21: Separate Opinions* (of Bernard and Jaranilla), pp. 4–7, 1–7, respectively).

[140] Judge Webb and Judge Pal (*ibid.*, vol. 21, pp. 475, 491).

limits, and disregarding 'even the bounds set by Anglo-American jurisprudence'.[141]

After the Nuremberg IMT's judgment, the ILC 'Nuremberg Principles' recognised that '[a]ny person who commits or is an accomplice in the commission of an act which constitutes a crime under international law is responsible therefor . . . [and liability may arise for] . . . Complicity in the commission of a crime.'[142] The problem was that although the Nuremberg principles recognised complicity, it was not clear what types of liability the ILC considered 'complicity' to entail at that time.

When the ICTY was created, more attention was paid to secondary responsibility. Almost all of the State comments dealt with principles of liability.[143] With respect to genocide, Article 4 gives the ICTY jurisdiction over the inchoate crimes listed in Article III of the Genocide Convention. This is customary, as a part of that Convention.[144] The main Article in the ICTY Statute (to which Article 6(1) of the Rwanda Statute is identical in all material respects) is Article 7(1). This provides that '[a] person who plans, instigates, orders, commits or otherwise aids and abets in the planning, preparation or execution of a crime incurs individual criminal responsibility'. This list is probably no more than customary. Not only did the State comments basically agree on this matter,[145] but the customary nature of the principles expressly included in Article 7(1) has also been confirmed by the Trial Chambers on several occasions with adequate support.[146] This was also accepted by the Appeals Chamber in *Tadić*.[147]

Debate has centred not on the express terms of Article 7(1) but on principles not directly referenced in that provision. In particular, there has been considerable discussion around the induction, from the terms

141 Brownlie, *International Law*, p. 203; John Piccigallo, *The Japanese on Trial* (Austin, TX: Texas University Press, 1979), p. 212 sums up their approach admirably, as showing 'a misplaced determination to force, after the fact, unrelated and fortuitous events into a preconceived thesis'.

142 GA Resolution 177.

143 See the summary of proposals in Morris and Scharf, *An Insider's Guide*, II, pp. 364–6.

144 Morris and Scharf, *An Insider's Guide*, I, p. 96.

145 *Ibid.*

146 *Prosecutor* v. *Tadić*, Opinion and Judgment, IT-94-1-T, 7 May 1997, paras. 663–669; *Prosecutor* v. *Furundžija*, Judgment, IT-95-17/1-T, 10 December 1998, paras. 193–216; *Čelebići*, paras. 319–321. On the crime of ordering international crimes, this crime was recognised far before that time, its genesis is traceable at least back as far as the Hague regulations; see Green, 'Command Responsibility in International Law'. On all the others, they are also present in similar form in the 1991 Draft Code (Article 3) (importantly predating the ICTY, unlike the 1996 Draft) and the 1954 Code (Article 2(13)).

147 *Prosecutor* v. *Tadić*, Judgment, IT-94-1-A, 15 July 1999, paras. 186–189.

of Article 7(1), of the concept of joint criminal enterprise.[148] The Appeals Chamber has said that with regard to this type of liability it does not matter that such a principle is not clearly referred to in Article 7(1) as the ICTY Statute, unlike the Rome Statute, does not purport to be a comprehensive code of principles of liability. Therefore, the Appeals Chamber claimed, it is sufficient to base liability on customary law and an implicit reference in Article 7(1).[149] As the Appeals Chamber accepted, such a route would certainly not be available to the ICC.

As the Rome Statute, for the first time in international criminal law, sets out in detail the various forms of liability, it has been said to 'undoubtedly constitute a major advance in international criminal law'.[150] In particular, it has made the Statute watertight from the point of specificity, and not subject to the criticisms levelled at the *ad hoc* Tribunals' Statutes. There was never any dispute that such specificity should be in the Rome Statute,[151] but full praise must be reserved until an examination of its provisions can be undertaken, especially as the point of such detailed provision was partly to rein in the ICC so that it could not engage in the divining of custom in the way the ICTY has.

Article 25(3) sets out all the principles of liability except command responsibility. It reads:

> A person shall be criminally responsible and liable for a crime within the jurisdiction of the Court if that person,
>
> (a) Commits such a crime whether as an individual, jointly with another or through another person, regardless of whether that other person is criminally responsible;
> (b) Orders, solicits, or induces the commission of such a crime which in fact occurs or is attempted;

[148] See, in particular *Tadić* Appeal, paras. 172–229; *Prosecutor* v. *Vasiljević*, Judgment, IT-98-32-A, 24 March 2004, paras. 87–132; *Prosecutor* v. *Krstić*, Judgment, IT-98-33-A, 19 April 2004, paras. 39–134; but see *Prosecutor* v. *Simić, Tadić and Zarić*, Judgment, IT-95-9-T, 17 October 2003, Separate and Partly Dissenting Judgment of Judge Lindohlm, paras. 1–9, esp. para. 5, 'the concept or "doctrine" has caused confusion and a waste of time, and is in my opinion of no benefit to the work of the Tribunal or the development of international criminal law.'

[149] *Prosecutor* v. *Multinović, Šainović and Ojdanić*, Decision on Ojdanić's Motion Challenging Jurisdiction – Joint Criminal Enterprise, IT-99-37-AR72, 21 May 2003, para. 18.

[150] Cassese, 'The Rome Statute', 153.

[151] See Christopher Keith Hall, 'The First Two Sessions of the Preparatory Committee for the International Criminal Court' (1997) 91 AJIL 177, 181; Christopher Keith Hall, 'The Third and Fourth Sessions of the Preparatory Committee for an International Criminal Court' (1998) 92 AJIL 124, 129–130.

(c) For the purpose of facilitating the commission of such a crime, aids, abets, or otherwise assists in its commission or its attempted commission, including providing the means for its commission;
(d) In any other way contributes to the commission or attempted commission of such a crime by a group of persons acting with a common purpose. Such contribution shall be intentional and shall either
  (i) Be made with the aim of furthering the criminal activity or criminal purpose of the group, where such activity or purpose involves the commission of a crime within the jurisdiction of the Court; or
  (ii) Be made in the knowledge of the intention of the group to commit the crime;
(e) In respect of the crime of genocide, directly and publicly incites others to commit genocide;
(f) Attempts to commit such a crime by taking action that commences its execution by means of a substantial step, but the crime does not occur because of circumstances independent of the person's intentions. However a person who abandons the effort to commit the crime or otherwise prevents the completion of the crime shall not be liable for prosecution under this statute for the attempt to commit that crime if that person completely and voluntarily gave up the criminal purpose.

A few points are worthy of note.[152] To begin, Article 25(3)(e) is drawn directly from the Genocide Convention, and raises no difficulties from the point of view of customary law.[153] Rather less simply, omissions are not separately dealt with in the Rome Statute. This has led some to question whether, outside of the express provisions relating to omission in Article 28 (on command responsibility), any responsibility for omission

[152] On this provision, see Albin Eser, 'Individual Criminal Liability', in Antonio Cassese, Paula Gaeta and John R. W. D. Jones (eds.), *The Rome Statute of the International Criminal Court: A Commentary* (Oxford: Oxford University Press, 2002), p. 767; Robert Cryer, 'General Principles of Liability in International Criminal Law', in Dominic McGoldrick, Peter Rowe and Eric Donnelly (eds.), *The Permanent International Criminal Court: Legal and Policy Issues* (Oxford: Hart, 2004), p. 233; van Sliedregt, *The Criminal Responsibility*, chapters 1 and 2; Kai Ambos, 'Article 25', in Otto Triffterer (ed.), *Commentary on the Rome Statute of the International Criminal Court* (Baden-Baden: Nomos, 1999) 475; Saland, 'International Criminal Law Principles', 198–200. More generally, see Kai Ambos, 'Individual Criminal Responsibility in International Criminal Law', in Gabrielle Kirk McDonald and Olivia Swaak-Goldman (eds.), *Substantive and Procedural Aspects of International Criminal Law* (The Hague: Kluwer, 2000), p. 1; Ilias Bantekas, *Principles of Direct and Superior Responsibility in International Humanitarian Law* (Manchester: Manchester University Press, 2002).

[153] See, for example, *Prosecutor* v. *Nahimana, Barayagwiza and Ngeze*, Judgment, ICTR-99-52-T, 3 December 2003, although this case also shows the complexity of prosecuting such offences.

may arise. If this were true, not only would the Rome Statute be behind custom on the point, but also seriously deficient from the point of view of criminal law. It is likely that the ICC has sufficient elbow-room to interpret the Statute so not to exclude omissions' liability.[154]

Although there is little doubt that Articles 25(3)(a) and 25 (3)(b) are unobjectionable from the point of view of customary law, Article 25(3)(b) is not as satisfactory. Solicitation and inducement are, as implied by that Article, probably crimes of complicity, but ordering is not.[155] The ICTY has erred towards the view that ordering is a crime of complicity, rather than a separate inchoate form of responsibility, for example in *Prosecutor* v. *Blaškić*.[156] This was based on a prosecutorial concession, the Trial Chamber decision of the ICTR in *Akayesu* and a misunderstanding, shared with that case, about Article 2(3)(d) of the ILC Draft Code of Crimes Against the Peace and Security of Mankind. Article 2(3)(d) contains the limitation that the ordered crime must at least be attempted. The Trial Chambers in both *Blaškić* and *Akayesu* thought that the ILC sought to exhaustively define liability for ordering offences, when the commentary to the relevant Article clarifies that they were not.[157]

Article 25(3)(b) provides that, for those ordering a crime, that crime must be at least attempted for liability to arise. The requirement is not present, for example, in either the ICTY Statute (although *Blaškić* accepted it was an aspect of the offence) or the Geneva Conventions. The Grave Breaches provisions of the Geneva Conventions provide that High Contracting Parties must prosecute those committing such breaches or ordering then to be committed.[158] In the post-war *von Falkenhorst* decision, it was made clear that an order need not be carried out for a conviction to be recorded.[159] The reconceptualisation of ordering offences as solely being a form of derivative liability is unnecessary, more limited than customary law requires and unjustified from the point of view of criminal law theory.[160]

[154] See Cryer, 'General Principles', pp. 236–40.

[155] Some see it as such; see, for example Bantekas, *Principles*, p. 51.

[156] *Prosecutor* v. *Blaškić*, Judgment, IT-95-14-T, 2 March 2000, paras. 281–282; see also *Kordić and Čerkez*, para. 388 and *Prosecutor* v. *Akayesu*, Judgment, ICTR-96-4-T, 2 September 1998, para. 483. As Bantekas, *Principles*, p. 51, notes, *Akayesu* also supported the proposition with reference to Rwandan domestic law.

[157] ILC Draft Code, Commentary to Article 2(3)(b), para. 9. See Cryer, 'General Principles', pp. 244–5.

[158] See, for example, Article 49 Geneva Convention I for the Amelioration of the Condition of the Wounded and Sick in Armed Forces in the Field.

[159] *von Falkenhorst* 11 LRTWC 18.

[160] See Cryer, 'General Principles', pp. 245–7.

Probably the most controversial of the provisions contained in Article 25(3) is sub-paragraph (d), which is basically a form of liability for conspiracy.[161] Although such an offence is probably (as a result of the Nuremberg and Tokyo IMTs' judgments) part of customary international law, its inclusion is still controversial, as it remains primarily an offence particular to common law systems.[162] Perhaps to sweeten the pill for those countries not having municipal crimes of conspiracy, the wording for the definition of the crime is taken directly from the International Convention on Terrorist Bombings.[163] Although the article is not easy to read and interpret, it may well be that the Rome Statute has defined this form of liability more narrowly than customary law. It requires the accomplice either purposefully to contribute to the criminal activity or purpose, where that involves a crime in the Statute (Article 25(3)(d)(i)), or know that the offence will be committed. This is more limited than the customary test enunciated in the *Tadić* appeal,[164] which includes liability where crimes are committed by others outside the common purpose where there is 'foresight that those crimes outside the criminal common purpose were likely to be committed'.[165]

In one situation, it might be argued that the Rome Statute casts the net of liability wider than customary law, for aiding and abetting.[166] Article 25(3)(c) gives liability when a person, 'for the purpose of facilitating the commission of such a crime, aids, abets, or otherwise assists in its commission or its attempted commission, including providing the means for its commission'. Customary international law may require the assistance to be 'substantial', although the ICTY has not taken the requirement as imposing a high threshold.[167] However, the Article also

161 Although not of the fully inchoate common law type found, for example, in section 1 of the Criminal Law Act 1977. On Article 25(3)(d), see van Sliedregt, *The Criminal Responsibility*, pp. 94–110; Cryer, 'General Principles', pp. 249–51.

162 Ambos, 'Article 25', p. 483.

163 GA Res, 52/164, UN Doc. A/RES/52/164. See Mahnoush H. Arsanjani, 'The Rome Statute of the International Criminal Court' (1999) 93 AJIL 22, 36.

164 Ambos also makes this point, referring to earlier jurisprudence, 'Article 25', p. 486, but distinguishes such cases on the grounds that they are dealing with responsibility under the analogue to Article 25(3)(c).

165 *Tadić*, Appeal, para. 229. On this point, see van Sliedregt, *The Criminal Responsibility*, pp. 108–9.

166 On complicity, see generally, William Schabas, 'Enforcing International Humanitarian Law: Prosecuting the Accomplices' (2001) 843 IRRC 439; van Sliedregt, *The Criminal Responsibility*, pp. 87–94.

167 See Ambos, 'Article 25', pp. 481–3. This has been confirmed by the *Tadić* Appeal, para. 229.

introduces a purposive, motive requirement that is not required by custom (under which knowledge suffices).[168] The crime is thus not defined in accordance with customary law, but in practice the addition of the purposive intent will render liability under the Rome Statute more narrow than in custom and many national laws.[169]

In line with the approach taken in its provision on superior orders, the Special Court for Sierra Leone's Statute follows the ICTY and ICTR's lead on the principles of liability applicable to international crimes. Article 6(1) is for all practical purposes identical to the provisions in the ICTY and ICTR Statutes, providing that 'A person who planned, instigated, ordered, committed or otherwise aided and abetted in the planning, perpetration or execution of a crime . . . shall be individually responsible for the crime'. Therefore, and consistent with the idea of the Special Court as one which was thought by its Sierra Leonean drafters to be essentially 'safe', a considerable degree of leeway was granted to the Special Court to interpret the principles of liability.

Our investigation so far has thus shown, perhaps more so than in relation to defences, that the Rome Statute takes a fairly narrow view of inculpatory doctrines, whereas other tribunals have either been mandated to apply broad principles in their Statutes (the Nuremberg and Tokyo IMTs), or have had the authority to interpret them into their jurisdiction (in particular, the ICTY). As we shall see, the fairly narrow approach to liability taken by the Rome Statute is also discoverable in relation to international criminal law's special form of incrimination, command responsibility.

Command responsibility

Command responsibility is the liability of superiors for crimes committed by forces not ordered by that superior, but tolerated or ignored by him or her.[170] Although its precise legal nature is controversial,[171] the

[168] Ambos, 'Article 25', p. 483; this, again has been confirmed by the *Tadić* Appeal, para. 229.

[169] See Cryer, 'General Principles', pp. 247–9; van Sliedregt, *The Criminal Responsibility*, p. 93.

[170] See generally, Green, 'Command Responsibility'; Parks, 'Command Responsibility'; Cameron N. Crowe, 'Command Responsibility in the Former Yugoslavia: The Chances for Successful Prosecution' (1995) 29 *University of Richmond Law Review* 191; Ilias Bantekas, 'The Contemporary Law of Superior Responsibility' (1999) 93 AJIL 573; Bantekas, *Principles*, chapters 3–4; Matthew Lippman, 'The Evolution and Scope of Command Responsibility' (2000) 13 LJIL 139; van Sliedregt, *The Criminal Responsibility*, chapters 3–4.

[171] See, for example, Mirjan Damaška, 'The Shadow Side of Command Responsibility' (2001) 49 AJCL 45; Timothy Wu and Yong-Sung Kang, 'Criminal Liability for the

principle is a vital one for ensuring that international criminal law is enforced by and against high-level officials.[172] In the *Čelebići* Case, the ICTY elaborated the threefold requirements of the concept. First, a superior/subordinate relationship; second, the 'mental element' and, third, a failure to take reasonable measures to prevent or punish violations of international criminal law.[173] This trio has since been adopted by the UN Tribunals and is a helpful list of the requirements.[174] The definitions of these requirements have been the subject of a large degree of debate, but discussion will be limited here only to those elements necessary for the theme of this chapter.

The principle of command responsibility was not directly mentioned in the Nuremberg or Tokyo IMTs' Charters, although the principle was relied on, if not widely at Nuremberg then certainly at Tokyo. The Nuremberg judgment dealt mainly with ordering of offences. However, at times, for example in the judgment on Frick, the IMT seemed to hold defendants responsible for not bringing to an end offences of which they were aware.[175] Mostly, though, it is as Green says: 'the Nuremberg Tribunal's findings were only concerned with command responsibility in the most indirect fashion.'[176]

The Tokyo IMT's judgment on war crimes, on the other hand, dealt almost entirely with command responsibility. Its discussion is particularly interesting because it dealt not only with military superiors (to whom it was generally accepted command responsibility in some form attached),[177] but also imposed liability on civilian officials under

Actions of Subordinates: The Doctrine of Command Responsibility and its Analogues in United States Law' (1997) 38 Harvard ILJ 272; Cryer, 'General Principles', pp. 257–61.

[172] See, for example, Bantekas, *Principles*, pp. 70–3; Yuval Shany and Keren R. Michaeli, 'The Case Against Ariel Sharon: Revisiting the Doctrine of Command Responsibility' (2001–2002) 34 NYUJILP 797, 829–37.

[173] *Čelebići*, paras. 344–400.

[174] See, for example, *Aleksovski*, Appeal, para. 72; *Prosecutor* v. *Kayishema and Ruzindana*, Judgment, ICTR-95-1-T, 21 May 1999, para. 209; *Blaškić*, Judgment, para. 294.

[175] Nuremberg IMT Judgment, 293.

[176] *Ibid.*, 333. William J. Fenrick, 'Some International Law Problems Related to Prosecutions Before the International Criminal Tribunal for the Former Yugoslavia' (1995) 6 DJCIL 103, 112. Some German war criminals were held responsible under this head though. See Green, 'Command Responsibility', 333–5 and, for example, the *Abbaye Ardenne* Case 4 LRTWC 97.

[177] IMTFE Judgment, 48, 443–448, 445. This was not uncontroversial; Pal was highly dubious of such an offence, keeping liability very narrow (Dissenting Opinion of Judge Pal 1,124-1,127) and Röling differed on its conditions of application (*ibid.*, Dissenting Opinion of Judge Röling, 54–61). Parks is clear that some such offence did

this head, which was, at least at the time, uncharted territory.[178] Until 1977, the development of the principle of command responsibility was primarily by means of jurisprudence. There have been various attempts to rationalise the various cases, in particular on the mental element. The most elaborate of those preceding the formation of the UN Tribunals, that of Major Parks, concluded that the requisite mental element was present if the commander 'failed to exercise the means available to him to learn of the offence and under the circumstances, he should have known and such failure to know constitutes criminal dereliction'.[179] This statement received judicial confirmation in the *Blaškić* Case.[180]

1977 saw the adoption of Additional Protocol I (API),[181] which provided, in Articles 86–87, for command responsibility, aspects of which some writers consider customary.[182] Article 86(2) reads,

> [t]he fact that a breach of the Conventions or of this Protocol was committed by a subordinate does not absolve his superiors from penal or disciplinary responsibility, as the case may be, if they knew, or had information which should have enabled them to conclude in the circumstances at the time, that he was committing or was going to commit such a breach and if they did not take all feasible measures within their power to prevent or repress the breach.

This has to be read together with Article 87(1), which requires commanders 'with respect to members of the armed forces under their command and other persons under their control, to prevent and, where necessary, to suppress and to report to competent authorities breaches of the

exist prior to 1945, Parks, 'Command Responsibility', 2–20. The 1919 Commission accepted the principle (121) (although the Japanese members dissented on this, 152).

178 *Ibid.* See Fenrick, 'Some International Law Problems', 117–18.

179 Parks, 'Command Responsibility', 90. For discussion of this case law see Parks, 'Command Responsibility', 22–77; Lippman, 'Conundrums', 77–83. See also *Čelebići*, paras. 359–378.

180 *Blaškić*, Trial Chamber, para. 322. But see *Čelebići*, Appeal, paras. 228–230; van Sliedregt, *The Criminal Responsibility*, pp. 125–8, considers the cases less consistent.

181 Protocol I Additional to the Geneva Conventions of 8 August 1949 and Relating to the Protection of Victims in International Armed Conflict 1125 UNTS 3.

182 See *Čelebići*, paras. 340–341, 390–393; Fenrick, 'Some International Law Problems', 119. Jia differs on this; Bing Bing Jia, 'The Doctrine of Command Responsibility in International Law' (1998) 65 NILR 325, 346–347. The Trial Chamber in *Blaškić*, para. 324, considered the mental element narrower than custom, if it was thought that the mental element included the requirement that there be specific information in the possession of the accused. The Appeals Chamber in *Čelebići*, on the other hand, considered the narrower view representative of custom, paras. 231–235.

Conventions and of this Protocol'.[183] This was the intention of the drafters of the provision. There is some controversy about the precise meaning of the provisions,[184] however, the authoritative ICRC Commentary on the provision the Protocol 'obliges them to be constantly informed of the way in which their subordinates carry out the tasks entrusted to them, and to take the necessary measures for this purpose'.[185]

The ICTY Statute, in a formulation differing from Articles 86–87 API,[186] deals with command responsibility in Article 7(3).[187] This states that 'the fact that any of the acts referred to in articles 2 to 5 of the present Statute was committed by a subordinate does not relieve his superior of criminal responsibility if he knew or had reason to know that the subordinate was about to commit such acts and had done so and the superior failed to take the necessary and reasonable measures to prevent such acts or to punish perpetrators thereof'.

As Fenrick says, this provision is unhelpfully worded, and leaves many of its terms undefined.[188] The approach of the ICTY has been to treat it as having imported the customary law on the subject into its jurisdiction, thus giving it the right to determine what that is.[189] The major controversy which has raged over Article 7(3) is over the mental element implied by the standard 'had reason to know',[190] although there has also been dissension over the question or the responsibility of commanders for offences committed prior to their taking post.[191]

[183] On the requirement that they be read together, see Yves Sandoz (ed.), *Commentary on the Additional Protocols of 8 June 1977 to the Geneva Conventions of 12 August 1949* (Dordrecht: Martinus Nijhoff, 1986), p. 1011. This was expressly adopted by the ICTY in *Blaškić*, Trial Chamber, para. 329.

[184] See, for example, Wu and Kang, 'Criminal Liability', 284–5.

[185] Sandoz, *Commentary*, p. 1022; Bantekas, 'The Contemporary Law', 589.

[186] See Howard Levie, 'The Statute of the International Tribunal for Former Yugoslavia: A Comparison With the Past and a Look at the Future' (1995) 21 *Syracuse Journal of International Law and Commerce* 1, 13, who claims it comes closer to the stand taken in the *Yamashita* Case than Article 86(2) of API.

[187] The ICTR Statute's Article 6(3) is to all intents and purposes identical.

[188] Fenrick, 'Some International Law Problems', 111–12. See also Bassiouni and Manikas, *The Law*, p. 344.

[189] *Čelebići*, paras. 390–393. On the ICTY jurisprudence, see Daryl A. Mundis, 'Crimes of the Commander: Superior Responsibility Under Article 7(3) of the ICTY Statute', in Gideon A. Boas and William A. Schabas (eds.), *International Criminal Law Developments in the Case Law of the ICTY* (The Hague: Brill, 2003), p. 239.

[190] The two major cases dealing with the question being *Čelebići* and *Blaškić*.

[191] This being decided by a bare majority in *Prosecutor v. Hadžihasanović, Alagić and Kubura*, Decision on Interlocutory Appeal in Relation to Command Responsibility, IT-01-47-AR72, 16 July 2003.

The Rome Statute is far more verbose (but not necessarily the worse for it). Article 28 is controlling on the ICC, imposing liability on:

1. A military commander or person effectively acting as a military commander . . . [for crimes] . . . committed by forces under his or her effective command and control, or effective authority and control as the case may be, as a result of his or her failure to exercise control properly over such forces where:

(a) That military commander or person either knew or, owing to the circumstances at the time, should have known that the forces were committing or about to commit such crimes; and
(b) That military commander or person failed to take all necessary and reasonable measures within his power to prevent or repress their commission or to submit the matter to the competent authorities for investigation and prosecution.

2. With respect to superior and subordinate relationships not described in paragraph 1, . . . [such superiors are liable for crimes] . . . committed by subordinates under his or her effective authority and control, as a result of his or her failure to exercise control properly over such forces where:

(a) The superior either knew or consciously disregarded information which clearly indicated that the subordinates were committing or about to commit such crimes;
(b) The crimes concerned activities that were within the effective responsibility and control of the superior and;
(c) The superior failed to take all necessary and reasonable measures within his power to prevent or repress their commission or to submit the matter to the competent authorities for investigation and prosecution.[192]

A difference in wording, at least for military leaders, is the mental element in Article 28(1)(a), which requires that the defendant 'knew, or, owing to the circumstances at the time, should have known' of existing or imminent violations. This removes the express requirement of having 'had information which should have enabled them to conclude' Article 86 of API. It might be thought, therefore, that the Rome Statute is broader than the ICTY and ICTR Statutes, by implying, through the 'should have known' standard, that there is a duty to collect information.

[192] See generally, William J. Fenrick, 'Article 28', in Otto Triffterer (ed.), *Commentary on the Rome Statute of the International Criminal Court* (Baden-Baden: Nomos, 1999), p. 515; Saland, 'International Criminal Law Principles', pp. 202–4; Kai Ambos, 'Superior Responsibility', in Antonio Cassese, Paula Gaeta and John R. W. D. Jones (eds.), *The Rome Statute of the International Criminal Court: A Summary* (Oxford: Oxford University Press, 2002), p. 823, pp. 848–71.

If this were the case, the argument of this chapter would be weakened. The position could be supported by reference to the decisions in the *Čelebići* Case. The Trial Chamber in that decision gave the impression that it viewed the Rome Statute as broader than their interpretation of custom in the early 1990s.[193] The Appeals Chamber expressly refused to drop the requirement of there being some information in the possession of the superior. The Appeals judgment reads in relevant part:

> Article 7(3) of the Statute is concerned with superior liability arising from failure to act in spite of knowledge. Neglect of a duty to acquire such knowledge does not feature in the provision as a separate offence and a superior is not therefore liable under the provision for such failures . . . The Prosecution's argument that a breach of the duty to remain constantly informed of his subordinates actions will necessarily result in criminal liability comes close to the imposition of criminal liability on a strict or negligence basis.[194]

There are a number of problems with the reasoning of the Appeals Chamber on this point. The first is the assertion that the drafters of API rejected a duty to be apprised of the actions of subordinates. Whether they did so or not is controversial. The Trial Chamber in *Blaškić* interpreted the provisions in API, insofar as they represent custom, as inferring that 'if a commander has exercised due diligence in the fulfilment of his duties yet lacks knowledge that crimes are about to be committed, such lack of knowledge cannot be held against him. However taking into account his particular position of command and the circumstances prevailing at the time, such ignorance cannot be a defence where the absence of knowledge is the result of negligence in the discharge of his duties.'[195] In this, they included negligence in the collection of information. The *Blaškić* interpretation has received considerable support in doctrine, partially on the basis that the *travaux préperatoires* for API do not clearly show the rejection of the duty to remain informed.[196] As

[193] *Čelebići*, para. 393. [194] *Čelebići*, Appeal, para. 226.

[195] *Blaškić*, Trial Chamber, para. 332. This formulation appears satisfactory, with one exception; the level of negligence is probably higher, at gross negligence. Bantekas is correct, as we are dealing with very serious crimes, negligence *simpliciter* should not suffice, Bantekas, 'The Contemporary Law', 590.

[196] See Maria Fiera Tinta, 'Commanders on Trial: The Blaškić Case and the Doctrine of Command Responsibility Under International Law' (2000) 47 NILR 293, 314–22; Bantekas, *Principles*, p. 112; Kirsten M. F. Keith, 'The *Mens Rea* of Superior Responsibility as Developed by ICTY Jurisprudence' (2001) 14 LJIL 617. Dinstein also appears to prefer this view; Yoram Dinstein, *The Conduct of Hostilities Under the Law of International Armed Conflict* (Cambridge: Cambridge University Press, 2004), p. 241. Support is not universal though, see Bing Bing Jia, 'The Doctrine of Command Responsibility: Current Problems' (2000) 3 YBIHL 131, 155–60.

we saw above, the ICRC commentary seems to support this view. It has also been contended that if API is more limited than custom, it did not overturn customary rule.[197]

The next problem may have arisen because the Appeals Chamber appeared to assume that the Prosecutor's argument was that they should presume knowledge on the part of the defendant where there was a failure to remain informed of actions.[198] They were understandably concerned about doing so, as it would look close to strict liability.[199] But the principle of command responsibility does not require the presumption of knowledge in this situation. Correctly understood, the principle is made up of at least two different aspects, although they are not always well separated. The first is where a person knew of the offences, a matter that may be proved by circumstantial evidence. The second, which is less culpable, but still appropriately criminal, is where a person is seriously negligent in failing to know of the offences.

This is perhaps implied by the commentary on Article 7(3) from the Secretary General (the OLA), which states that the principle is 'imputed responsibility or criminal negligence'.[200] The two should, for the sake of fair labelling, be separate, but if it is accepted that criminal (i.e. serious) negligence is the gravamen of the second type of command responsibility, it should not make any difference to the fact of liability *in abstracto* what form that negligence takes. In other words, there is no *a priori* reason for imposing liability when the negligence is a failure to investigate further when there is some information suggesting the need to do so,[201] yet refusing it for failing to obtain even that information when this reflects serious negligence in supervision of subordinates.[202] The statement of the drafters of the ICTY Statute that criminal negligence is a basis of command responsibility also confounds the statement by the Appeals Chamber at para. 226 of *Čelebići* that they were loath to impose liability on a negligence basis.[203] They were meant to. It is therefore unfortunate that the Prosecutor conceded the accuracy of the *Čelebići* Appeal on this point in the *Blaškić* appeal, and the Appeals

[197] See, for example, Robert Kolb, 'The Jurisprudence of the Yugoslav and Rwandan Criminal Tribunals on Their Jurisidction and on International Crimes' (2000) 69 BYBIL 259, 310.

[198] For example, *Čelebići* Appeal, para. 230.

[199] *Čelebići* Appeal, para. 239.

[200] Report of the Secretary General Pursuant to Paragraph 2 of Security Council Resolution 808, UN Doc. S/25704, para. 56.

[201] Which the *Čelebići* Appeal accepted formed the basis of liability, para. 238.

[202] Which *Blaškić*, Trial Chamber, accepted as sufficient for liability.

[203] See also *Prosecutor* v. *Bagilishema*, Judgment, ICTR-9-1A-A, 3 July 2002, paras. 34–35.

Chamber in that case considered that the earlier decision had settled the matter.[204]

Finally, the idea that Article 28(1)(a) necessarily implies a test imposing a broad duty to remain informed much in advance of that in *Čelebići* may be questioned. Article 28(1) requires that the defendant fails to exercise control over forces and that he or she knew, or, 'owing to the circumstances at the time, should have known'. Thus the additional limitations on the 'should have known' standard that it is 'owing to' not 'in' the circumstances, the defendant should have known, and that there be a failure to exercise control over the forces, mean that the conduct criminalised under either test is likely to be very similar because of the broad way in which the Appeals Chamber interpreted what information would put a superior on notice such that he or she needed to engage in further inquiry.[205]

The qualifying phrase that the superior is responsible for crimes only where they are committed 'as a result of his or her failure to exercise control properly over such forces' might be thought to introduce a new causation requirement. In the vast majority of cases, the requirement is not new, in that it is inherent in the 'failure to prevent' type of liability, as was recognised in *Čelebići*.[206] However, the relationship between such an element and responsibility for failure to punish liability is far more fractious.[207] It is possible that the inclusion of the phrase narrows existing law, at least in respect of liability for failure to punish offences committed prior to the commander coming into post. This was the position of the dissenters in *Hadžihasanović*.[208] Although they make a strong case,[209] the customary position is sufficiently unclear that it would be ill advised to make too much of this.

The final aspect of the Rome Statute that requires comment relates to the separate provision for civilian superiors. It has been generally

[204] *Prosecutor* v. *Blaškić*, Judgment, IT-95-14-A, 29 July 2004, paras. 59, 62.

[205] See also *Prosecutor* v. *Kvočka*, Judgment, IT-98-30-1/T, 2 November 2001, paras. 317–318.

[206] *Čelebići*, para. 399; Greg Vetter, 'Command Responsibility of Non-Military Superiors in the International Criminal Court (ICC)' (2000) 25 Yale JIL 89, 119 claims that the Trial Chamber hedged its bets a little in para. 399.

[207] *Ibid.*, para. 399. See generally, Otto Triffterer, 'Causality, a Separate Element of the Doctrine of Superior Responsibility as Expressed in Article 28 of the Rome Statute?' (2002) 15 LJIL 179.

[208] *Hadžihasanović*, Separate and Dissenting Opinion of Judge Hunt, Separate and Dissenting Opinion of Judge Shahabuddeen.

[209] See Christopher J. Greenwood, 'Command Responsibility and the *Hadžihasanović* Decision' (2004) 2 JICJ 598, 605.

accepted that civilian superiors can come under the concept,[210] but the extent of control that they need to exercise and the standard to which they are to be held has been a matter of controversy.[211] For civilian superiors to become liable, the crimes must concern 'activities that were within the effective responsibility and control of the superior'. This seems correct. No superior should be held responsible for activities outside their control or responsibility.

Despite the fact that the requirements of the superior/subordinate relationship are at least as onerous as for military personnel, the *mens rea* requirement for civilians is different in the Rome Statute. Whereas military commanders are responsible if they 'knew or, in the circumstances, should have known', civilians are responsible only if they 'knew, or consciously disregarded information which clearly indicated' that crimes had been, or were about to be, committed. This runs counter to the ICTY and ICTR Statutes, which do not make any such distinction (and were described by the Secretary General as describing 'criminal negligence'). The Tokyo IMT made no distinction between the standards applied to military and civilian leaders in its judgment. In the *Čelebići* Trial Chamber decision, it was decided that once the qualifications to become subject to the standard were complete, then the *mens rea* standard was the same.[212] It was only late in the Rome negotiations that the proposal to separate off civilian superiors was made, and the chair of the negotiations was clearly uncomfortable about the customary status of the distinction.[213]

Later cases, such as the *Čelebići* Appeal Judgment, have sometimes been bashful about Article 28's relationship to custom.[214] In one instance, *Kayishema and Ruzindana*, the ICTR used the Rome Statute standard for civilians, as an interpretation of the 'had reason to know' standard in Article 6(3) of the ICTR Statute.[215] It was wrong to do so.[216] There is a legitimate

[210] See *Čelebići*, paras. 356–363 and the cases cited therein.

[211] See, for example, *Prosecutor* v. *Musema*, Judgment, ICTR-96-13-T, 27 January 2000, para. 140 *contra Kordić and Čerkez*, paras. 415–416, 840, *Čelebići*, Appeal Judgment, para. 197 settled the matter, on effective control. For a critique of *Musema*, see Alexander Zahar, 'Command Responsibility of Civilian Superiors for Genocide' (2001) 14 LJIL 591, 601–604.

[212] *Ibid.*, paras. 379–393. See also *Prosecutor* v. *Krnojelac*, Judgment, IT-97-25-T, 15 March 2002, para. 94.

[213] Saland, 'International Criminal Law Principles', p. 204.

[214] The Rome Statute makes no major appearance in the decision's section on the *mens rea* of command responsibility.

[215] *Kayishema and Ruzindana*, paras. 227–228.

[216] Zhu Wenqi is less critical, 'The Doctrine of Command Responsibility as Applied to Civilian Leaders: The ICTR and the *Kayishema* Case', in Sienho Yee and Wang Tieya

concern that civilian superiors, who are by definition not in the stratified military system should not be subject to liability beyond the duties they have undertaken by accepting their post. It is just that the mental element is not the place to provide for such protection. The Rome Statute already ensures that civilian superiors are not subject to liability for matters falling outside the ambit of their responsibility. Not only must the offences occur owing to a failure to exercise control over forces, but also Article 25(2)(b) states that the offences must fall within the authority and concern of the superior. Once these tests are fulfilled, there is no further reason to raise the bar for prosecution. A clear and highly unfortunate retreat from the requirements of customary international law can be seen here.[217] This mistake is not repeated in the Special Court's Statute, Article 6(3) of which is practically identical to the ICTY and ICTR Statutes on this point.

Conclusion

Defences and principles of liability are often overlooked or treated as secondary to definitions of crimes. This is odd, as they are part of the same overall process, and similar policies come into play in this aspect of determining liability as do in the definition of crimes *simpliciter*. Both the Nuremberg and Tokyo IMT Charters did not deal fully with defences or principles of liability.

The only express provisions related to the creation of a legally insupportable liability for conspiracy (which later passed into customary law), and denying the defences liable to be raised.[218] When it came to the UN Tribunals, most problems were expressly left to the ICTY and ICTR, who could (and would have to) create a body of principles of liability. The controversies on international criminal liability were left to the Court. The Security Council was happy to allow this to occur, and leave the power in the ICTY and ICTR to do this, probably as the States on the Security Council thought themselves to be likely to come under the mandate of the Tribunal. The only State voting against a resolution, Rwanda, was one that saw the ICTR as 'unsafe'.

(eds.), *International Law in the Post-Cold War World: Essays in Memory of Li Haopei* (London: Routledge, 2001), p. 373.

217 See *Accord*, Vetter, 'Command Responsibility', 123–4; van Sliedregt, *The Criminal Responsibility*, pp. 191–2.

218 The best thing that can be said for the exclusion of the superior orders defence was that the defence would probably have been inapplicable even if correctly formulated according to international law.

Up until this time, and due to the absence of international legal instruments dealing with the issue of liability, the law was basically existent only in general principles and custom that had not been studied to any extent. In this respect, the granting of the power to determine this law to the UN Tribunals gave the law another form of legitimacy. As Franck notes, if a law is in itself vague, legitimacy is not denied to it if there is 'judicially supplied process determinacy',[219] i.e. a court which is authorised to authoritatively determine what the law actually is. In this way, then, the ICTY and ICTR, alongside the more recent statute of the Special Court for Sierra Leone, despite having Statutes which are generally less determinative of issues than may be ideal, are not totally inadequate.

When the Rome Statute came to be drafted, no such sanguine view of a court's competence was taken by States who, with the exception of the discretion granted in Article 31(2) and 31(3), insisted on defining the law themselves. In this way, the law did become more determinate, but along the way lost coverage in some places. The definitions of previously existing principles are at times wider where defences are involved,[220] and frequently narrower on inculpatory doctrines, at times in manifest contradiction to existing international law. This is because not only were States far more unwilling to grant the ICC any legislative power over themselves, but also were prepared to accept, if not a lowest common denominator approach towards the principles, a position close to it. Therefore the 'general part' of criminal liability in the Rome Statute may well lead to acquittals in the Rome Court which are not warranted by customary international law.

Customary international law was exceeded by the Nuremberg and Tokyo IMTs and is now the basis of prosecution of offences in Sierra Leone, former Yugoslavia and Rwanda, although whether those Tribunals have accurately identified that law is a matter of contention. So it seems that the Rome Statute's formulations of the 'general part', which were designed, unlike the previous Statutes of ICTs, to apply to the nationals of those States who defined the law, betray different policy choices by their drafters, the same policy choices that we saw in relation to the definitions of crimes. The Special Court for Sierra Leone returns to the model of the ICTY and ICTR. This could be used as evidence that the Court was seen as 'safe' by the negotiators, but as evidence of the attitude of the Sierra Leonean government is scant, little can be determined either way on the point.

219 Franck, *The Power of Legitimacy*, p. 64.

220 Although these are now subject to Article 30(2).

Conclusion

In the 1970s, there were confident assertions of another form of global justice, albeit of a distributive, rather than corrective, nature. This was the declaration of the 'New International Economic Order' (NIEO), associated with General Assembly Resolution 3821 (XXIX).[1] This was intended to redress the imbalance between developed and developing States, in particular by creating obligations on developed States to grant development aid to developing States. Because of the opposition of several developed States, the programme never moved beyond the realm of rhetoric and 'soft' law.[2] The NIEO is not discussed much today, and it might be thought that, although the international criminal law enforcement regime is more developed than the NIEO, it too might fall away, or be rendered impotent in the face of opposition. There are reasons to doubt that such pessimism is warranted, however, even if optimism must be tempered with caution.

There is opposition to the newly emerged International Criminal regime. The United States is the most vocal opponent of the ICC, and has used its predominant position in international society to attempt to ensure that its nationals will never appear before the Court.[3] While the Bush administration is perhaps the government most hostile to the ICC, there are other important countries such as India and China who are unsympathetic and happy to let the United States lead the charge against the Court.[4] For this reason, the regime this book has investigated

[1] (1974) 13 ILM 715.

[2] See Antonio Cassese, *International Law in a Divided World* (Oxford: Clarendon, 1986), pp. 366–7.

[3] See Dominic McGoldrick, 'Legal and Political Responses to the ICC', in Dominic McGoldrick, Peter Rowe and Eric Donnelly (eds.), *The Permanent International Criminal Court* (Oxford: Hart, 2004), p. 389.

[4] McGoldrick, 'Legal and Political Responses', pp. 437–41.

cannot be seen as a global one, nor is it likely to become global in the near future. There has already been talk of a 'post-Rome' world, in which developments in international criminal law have been retrenched not only by States such as the United States creating a network of Article 98 agreements, but also by decisions such as the *Yerodia* Case in the ICJ. Judge *ad hoc* van den Wyngaert noted that the majority opinion even shied away from the term 'international criminal law'.[5]

That said, it is nevertheless extraordinary that in some ten years a regime has been set up. Ten years is, in international terms, a very short time; it took nearly twice that time to move from the non-binding Universal Declaration of Human Rights in 1948 to multilateral treaty law in the International Covenants in 1966. It took a further ten years for the Covenants to enter into force. So it is far too early to write off the regime as doomed: a longer-term view is required. Soon after the Rome Conference, one of the NGOs which strongly supported the creation of the ICC, Amnesty International, issued a statement that:

> [t]he true significance of the adoption of the Statute may well not lie, not in the actual institution in its early years, which will face enormous obstacles, but in the revolution in moral and political attitudes towards the worst crimes in the world. No longer will these crimes be simply political events to be addressed by diplomacy at the international level which states have a duty to punish themselves, or if they fail to fulfil this duty, by the international community in accordance with the rule of law.[6]

There are elements of overstatement in this remark, in particular in the unqualified assertion of a duty to prosecute international crimes, and in the claim that moral and political attitudes have been revolutionised: any revolution which has occurred is an uneasy one.[7] But there is truth in what Amnesty International had to say, and not just that the ICC would not have an easy start. The focus on the normalisation aspects of the ICC is important, when compared to fifteen years ago, and perhaps more recently than that, prosecution of international crimes was not considered a serious possibility for the vast majority of such offences. Now the call for accountability has been far more broadly

5 *Case Concerning the Arrest Warrant of 11 April 2000* (*Congo* v. *Belgium*), ICJ List 121, Dissenting Opinion of Judge *ad hoc* van den Wyngaert, para. 6.

6 Quoted in William Pace and Mark Thieroff, 'Participation of Non-Governmental Organisations', in Roy S. Lee (ed.), *The International Criminal Court: The Making of the Rome Statute* (The Hague: Kluwer, 1999), p. 391, p. 396.

7 Leila Nadya Sadat and Richard Carden, 'The International Criminal Court: An Uneasy Revolution' (2000) 88 *Georgetown Law Journal* 381.

adopted. Although the Rome Statute has been ratified by fewer than half the total UN members (ninety-four), early suggestions that only comfortable Western States not likely to find themselves in the dock would ratify have not been borne out. The ICC has enough work to attend to, and the Prosecutor appears, at this early stage, to be adopting a sensibly cautious approach to his duties.

It is perfectly possible to find faults in the Rome Statute; this book has devoted a large amount of time to doing precisely that. However, what must be borne in mind is the improvement that the Rome Statute represents over what went before. As was noted in chapter 1, although the history of international criminal law is a long one, and prosecutions had occurred, these were the exception rather than the norm. As we saw in that chapter, where there were prosecutions many of the problems that have been noted recently have considerable historical resonance. Chapter 2 showed that although all States have jurisdiction over international crimes, whether or not there are legal duties to prosecute those crimes, apathy or practical difficulties have meant that most States have avoided even domesticating international criminal law norms. The fact that States undertook what prosecutions there were on the basis of their own law meant that the substantive law was far from uniformly applied.

The Rome regime, although not as strong as that created by the Security Council for the former Yugoslavia or Rwanda and far from perfect, has sufficient weight to do what the ICC was really meant to do: that is, encourage States to prosecute international crimes themselves. The ICC was not created to prosecute many international crimes. It is not a frontline forum, national courts still are. However, the ICC needs to prosecute enough international crimes to maintain a reasonable level of credibility to give teeth to the implicit threat contained in the complementarity regime. The threat of prosecution in the ICC will ensure that States party to the Rome Statute are not as apathetic as almost all States were prior to 1998. As time goes on, and more prosecutions are entered into, the normalisation of prosecuting international crimes may make prosecution appear the natural response, as Amnesty International suggests.

It is true that the Rome regime is not a global one, neither is it entirely free from a legitimacy critique. The role of the Security Council, and some of the limits in the Statute, ensure this. A Security Council Resolution could perhaps have created a global version of the Rome regime in a similar manner in which it legislated into being in Resolution 1373 global prohibitions on terrorist financing alongside an overseeing organ. Prior to that Resolution, it was not thought possible that the Security

Council could act in such a manner, but the waters are now muddied somewhat. For the Security Council to legislate into being a permanent ICC would be of dubious legality[8] and, given the unrepresentative membership of the Security Council, open to other forms of legitimacy critique.[9] Absent a change in the way international society is structured, the treaty method of creating the Rome Statute was the only possible manner of creating the ICC in 1998, and the limits of that method are the limits of international law creation itself.

The Rome regime certainly covers a larger area than any of the other ICTs did, and appears to be encouraging States to prosecute some international crimes. It should therefore be welcomed. But the creation of a regime with a broader temporal and geographical jurisdiction had a cost. That cost was a contraction in the substantive law the ICC is entitled to apply.

The ambit of international criminal law has never been apolitical. The distinction in protection between international and non-international armed conflicts is referable to no moral reason or legal necessity.[10] International criminal law is also largely blind to the issues of structural violence that cause misery around the world. Famine, a lack of clean water and basic medical care kill millions of people per year, yet remain for the most part outside of the criminal ambit of international law.[11] It has not been the purpose of this book to critique the overall corpus of international criminal law, but to make a narrower point. What we saw in Rome was a trade off: a choice between the creation of an ICC which could enforce some international criminal law and a system where the full ambit of international criminal law remained largely unenforced. The creation of the ICC was the right option to take, but this should not blind us to the fact that in decreasing selectivity over who was to be prosecuted, a selective attitude to the law was also taken.

8 See Matthew Happold, 'Resolution 1373 and the Constitution of the United Nations' (2003) 16 LJIL 593.

9 See Happold, 'Resolution 1373', 607–10; David Caron, 'The Legitimacy of the Collective Authority of the Security Council' (1993) 87 AJIL 552.

10 See Colin Warbrick and Peter Rowe, 'The International Criminal Tribunal for Yugoslavia: The Appeals Chamber Decision on the Interlocutory Appeal on Jurisdiction in the *Tadić* Case' (1996) 45 ICLQ 691, 698; Steven Ratner, 'The Schizophrenias of International Criminal Law' (1998) 33 TILJ 237.

11 For an attempt to use international criminal law to cover some of these issues, see David Marcus, 'Famine Crimes in International Law' (2003) 97 AJIL 245.

Select bibliography

Abi-Saab, Georges, 'The Proper Role of Universal Jurisdiction' (2003) 1 JICJ 596

af Jochnick, Chris and Normand, Roger, 'The Legitimation of Violence: A Critical History of the Laws of War' (1994) 35 Harvard ILJ 49

Akande, Dapo, 'The Jurisdiction of the International Criminal Court Over Nationals of Non-Parties: Legal Basis and Limits' (2003) 1 JICJ 618

'International Law Immunities and the International Criminal Court' (2004) 98 AJIL 407

Akehurst, Michael, 'Jurisdiction in International Law' (1972–1973) 46 BYBIL 145

Akhavan, Payam, 'The International Criminal Tribunal for Rwanda: The Politics and Pragmatics of Punishment' (1996) 90 AJIL 501

'Justice and Reconciliation in the Great Lakes Region of Africa: The Contribution of the International Criminal Tribunal for Rwanda' (1997) 7 DJCIL 325

'Can International Criminal Justice Prevent Future Atrocities?' (2001) 85 AJIL 7

Alvarez, José E., 'Nuremberg Revisited: The *Tadić* Case' (1996) 7 EJIL 245

'Crimes of Hate/Crimes of State: Lessons from Rwanda' (1999) 24 Yale JIL 365

'Trying Hussein: Between Hubris and Hegemony' (2004) 2 JICJ 319, 326 7

Ambos, Kai and Wirth, Steffen, 'The Current Law of Crimes Against Humanity: An Analysis of UNTAET Regulation 15/2000' (2002) 12 CLF 1

Amnesty International, *Universal Jurisdiction: The Duty of States to Enact and Implement Legislation* (London: Amnesty International, 2001) AI Index IOR 53/05/2001

Arbour, Louise, 'The Crucial Years' (2004) 2 JICJ 396

Arbour, Louise, Eser, Albin, Ambos, Kai and Sanders, Andrew (eds.), *The Prosecutor of a Permanent International Criminal Court* (Freiburg: edn. iuscrim, 2000)

Arendt, Hannah, *Eichmann in Jerusalem: A Report on the Banality of Evil* (Harmondsworth: Penguin, 1994)

Arsanjani, Mahnoush H., 'The Rome Statute for an International Criminal Court' (1999) 93 AJIL 22

Ascensio, Hervé, 'Are Spanish Courts Backing Down on Universality? The Supreme Tribunal's Decision in *Guatemalan Generals*' (2003) 1 JICJ 690

Ashworth, Andrew, *The Criminal Process: An Evaluative Study* (Oxford: Oxford University Press, 2nd edn., 1999)

Principles of Criminal Law (Oxford: Oxford University Press, 4th edn., 2003)

Askin, Kelly D., *War Crimes Against Women: Prosecution in International Tribunals* (The Hague: Kluwer, 1997)

Bantekas, Ilias, 'The Contemporary Law of Superior Responsibility' (1999) 93 AJIL 573

Principles of Direct and Superior Responsibility in International Humanitarian Law (Manchester: Manchester University Press, 2002)

Bass, Gary J., *Stay the Hand of Vengeance: The Politics of War Crimes Tribunals* (Princeton: Princeton University Press, 2000)

Bassiouni, M. Cherif, 'Crimes Against Humanity: The Need for a Specialized Convention' (1994) 31 CJTL 457

'The United Nations Commission of Experts Established Pursuant to Security Council Resolution 780' (1994) 88 AJIL 784

'From Versailles to Rwanda in 75 Years: The Need to Establish a Permanent International Criminal Court' (1997) 10 Harvard HRLJ 11

Crimes Against Humanity in International Criminal Law (The Hague: Kluwer, 2nd rev. edn., 1999)

(ed.), *International Criminal Law* (Ardsley, Transnational, 2nd edn., 1999)

'Universal Jurisdiction for International Crimes: Historical Perspectives and Contemporary Practice' (2001) 42 VJIL 1

(ed.), *Post Conflict Justice* (Ardsley: Transnational, 2002)

'World War I, "The War to End All Wars" and the Birth of a Handicapped International Criminal Justice System' (2002) 30 DJILP 244

Introduction to International Criminal Law (Ardsley: Transnational, 2004)

Bassiouni, M. Cherif and Manikas, Peter, *The Law of the International Criminal Tribunal for Yugoslavia* (Ardsley: Transnational, 1996)

Bassiouni, M. Cherif and Nanda, Ved, *A Treatise on International Criminal Law* (Springfield, IL: Thomas, 1973)

Baxter, Richard R., 'The Municipal and International Legal Bases of Jurisdiction Over War Crimes' (1951) 28 BYBIL 382

Bell, Christine, *Peace Agreements and Human Rights* (Oxford: Oxford University Press, 2000)

Benvenisti, Eyal, 'Judicial Misgivings Regarding the Application of International Law: An Analysis of Attitudes of National Courts' (1993) 4 EJIL 159

Benvenuti, Paolo, 'The ICTY Prosecutor and the Review of the NATO Bombing against the Federal Republic of Yugoslavia' (2001) 12 EJIL 503

Best, Geoffrey, *Humanity in Warfare: The Modern History of the International Law of Armed Conflicts* (London: Methuen, 1983)

Binder, Guyora, 'Representing Nazism: Advocacy and Identity at the Trial of Klaus Barbie' (1989) 98 Yale LJ 1321

Birkett, Justice (Norman), 'International Legal Theories Evolved at Nuremberg' (1947) 23 IA 317

Boas, Gideon A. and Schabas, William A. (eds.), *International Criminal Law Developments in the Case Law of the ICTY* (The Hague: Brill, 2003)

Boelaert-Suominen, Sonja, 'The International Criminal Tribunal for the former Yugoslavia and the Kosovo Conflict' (2000) 837 IRRC 217

Bohlander, Michael, 'Last Exit Bosnia – Transferring War Crimes Prosecution from the International Tribunal to Domestic Courts' (2003) 14 CLF 59

Boister Neil, 'The Exclusion of Treaty Crimes from the Jurisdiction of the Proposed International Criminal Court' (1998) 3 JACL 27

Boister, Neil and Burchill, Richard, 'The *Pinochet* Precedent: Don't Leave Home Without It' (1999) 10 CLF 405

Bolton, John R., 'The Risks and Weaknesses of the International Criminal Court From an American Perspective' (2000–2001) 41 VJIL 186

Boot, Machteld, *Genocide, Crimes Against Humanity and War Crimes: Nullum Crimen Sine Lege and the Subject Matter of the International Criminal Court* (New York: Intersentia, 2002)

Bosch, William, *Judgement on Nuremberg: American Attitudes Towards the Major German War Crimes Trials* (Durham, NC: North Carolina University Press, 1970)

Bothe, Michael, 'The Protection of the Civilian Population and NATO Bombing on Yugoslavia: Comments on a Report to the Prosecutor of the ICTY' (2001) 12 EJIL 531

Brackman, Arnold C., *The Other Nuremberg: The Untold Story of the Tokyo War Crimes Trial* (New York: William Morrow, 1987)

Brierly, James L., 'Do We Need an International Criminal Court?' (1927) 8 BYBIL 81

'The Lotus Case' (1928) 44 LQR 151

Broomhall, Bruce, *International Justice and the International Criminal Court: Between Sovereignty and the Rule of Law* (Oxford: Oxford University Press, 2003)

Brown, Bartram S., 'Primacy or Complementarity: Reconciling the Jurisdiction of National Courts and International Criminal Tribunals' (1998) 23 Yale JIL 383

'US Objections to the Statute of the International Criminal Court: A Brief Response' (1999) 31 NYUJILP 855

Brownlie, Ian, *The Rule of Law in International Affairs: International Law at the Fiftieth Anniversary of the United Nations* (The Hague: Martinus Nijhoff, 1998)

Principles of International Law (Oxford: Oxford University Press, 6th edn., 2003)

Brubacher, Matthew, 'Prosecutorial Independence Within the International Criminal Court' (2004) 2 JICJ 71

Burgers, J. Herman and Danelius, Hans, *The United Nations Convention against Torture: A Handbook on the Convention against Torture and Other Cruel, Inhuman or Degrading Treatment or Punishment* (Dordrecht: Martinus Nijhoff, 1988)

Burke-White, William W., 'A Community of Courts: Toward a System of International Criminal Law Enforcement' (2002) 24 Michigan JIL 1
'Regionalisation of International Criminal Law Enforcement: A Preliminary Exploration' (2003) 38 TILJ 729
'The Law and Politics of the Pinochet Case' (2000) 11 DJICL 415
Byers, Michael (ed.), *The Role of Law in International Politics* (Oxford: Oxford University Press, 2000)
Byron, Christine, 'Armed Conflicts: International or Non-International?' (2001) 6 JCSL 63
Byron, Christine and Turns, David, 'The Preparatory Commission for the International Criminal Court' (2001) 50 ICLQ 420
Carpenter, Allegra, 'The International Criminal Court and the Crime of Aggression' (1995) 64 Nordic JIL 223
Carroll, Christina M., 'An Assessment of the Role and Effectiveness of the International Criminal Tribunal for Rwanda and the Rwandan National Justice System in Dealing With the Mass Atrocities of 1994' (2000) 18 BUILJ 163
Cassese, Antonio, 'On the Current Trends Towards Criminal Prosecution and Punishment of Breaches of International Criminal Law' (1998) 9 EJIL 2
'The Rome Statute of the International Criminal Court: Some Preliminary Reflections' (1999) 10 EJIL 144
'When May Senior State Officials Be Prosecuted for International Crimes?: Some Comments on the *Congo* v. *Belgium* Case' (2002) 13 EJIL 853
International Criminal Law (Oxford: Oxford University Press, 2003)
'Is the Bell Tolling for Universality? A Plea for a Sensible Notion of Universal Jurisdiction' (2003) 1 JICJ 589
Cassese, Antonio, Gaeta, Paula and Jones, John R. W. D. (eds.), *The Rome Statute of the International Criminal Court: A Commentary* (Oxford: Oxford University Press, 2002)
Chandler, David, 'Will There be a Trial for the Khmer Rouge?' (2000) 14 EIA 67
Charlesworth, Hilary and Chinkin, Christine, *The Boundaries of International Law: A Feminist Analysis* (Manchester: Manchester University Press, 2000)
Charney, Jonathan, 'Progress in International Criminal Law?' (1999) 93 AJIL 452
'International Criminal Law and the Role of Domestic Courts' (2001) 95 AJIL 120
Cissé, Catherine, 'The End of a Culture of Impunity in Rwanda' (1998) 1 YBIHL 161
Clark, Roger S., 'Medina, An Essay on the Principles of Criminal Liability for Homicide' (1972) 5 RCLJ 59
'The Mental Element in International Criminal Law: The Rome Statute of the International Criminal Court and the Elements of Offences' (2002) 12 CLF 291
Clark, Roger S. and Sann, Madeline, *The Prosecution of International Crimes* (New Brunswick: Transaction, 1995)

Coombes, Mary, 'International Decisions: In re Surrender of Ntakirutimana' (2000) 94 AJIL 171

Cotler, Irwin, 'R v. Finta' (1996) 90 AJIL 460

Cowles, Willard B., 'Universality of Jurisdiction Over War Crimes' (1945) 33 CLR 177

Crawford, James, 'The ILC's Draft Statute for an International Criminal Tribunal' (1994) 88 AJIL 140

'The ILC Adopts a Statute for an International Criminal Court' (1995) 89 AJIL 404

The International Law Commissions's Articles on State Responsibility: Introduction, Text and Commentaries (Cambridge: Cambridge University Press, 2002)

Cryer, Robert, 'One Appeal, Four Opinions, Two Philosophies and a Remittal' (1998) 2 JACL 193

'A Special Court for Sierra Leone?' (2001) 50 ICLQ 435

'Hague Law Comes Home: Prosecuting Weapons Offences at the International Criminal Court' (2002) *Acta Juridica* 238

'Implementation of the International Criminal Court Statute in England and Wales' (2002) 51 ICLQ 733

'Witness Evidence Before International Criminal Tribunals' (2003) 3 LPICT 411

Cryer, Robert and White, Nigel D., 'The Security Council and the International Criminal Court: Who's Feeling Threatened?' (2002) 8 *International Peacekeeping: The Yearbook of International Peace Operations* 143

Dadrian, Vakhan M., 'Genocide as a Problem of National and International Law: The World War I Armenian Case and its Contemporary Legal Ramifications' (1989) 14 Yale JIL 221

Damaška, Mirjan, 'The Shadow Side of Command Responsibility' (2001) 49 AJCL 45

Danner, Alison Marston, 'Enhancing the Legitimacy and Accountability of Prosecutorial Discretion at the International Criminal Court' (2003) 97 AJIL 510

Davis, Kenneth Kulp, *Discretionary Justice: A Preliminary Enquiry* (Baton Rouge: Louisiana State University Press, 1969)

de Bertodano, Silvia, 'Developments in Internationalized Courts' (2003) 1 JICJ 226

de Mildt, Dirk, *In the Name of the People: Perpetrators of Genocide in the Reflection of their Post-War Prosecution in West Germany* (The Hague: Martinus Nijhoff, 1996)

Dicker, Richard, 'Issues Facing the International Criminal Court's Preparatory Commission' (1999) 32 Cornell ILJ 471

Dickinson, Laura A., 'The Promise of Hybrid Courts' (2003) 97 AJIL 295

Dinstein, Yoram, *The Defence of 'Obedience to Superior Orders' in International Law* (Dordrecht: Martinus Nijhoff, 1965)

Dinstein, Yoram and Tabory, Mala (eds.), *War Crimes in International Law* (The Hague: Martinus Nijhoff, 1996)

Doherty, Katherine L. and McCormack, Timothy L. H., 'Complementarity as a Catalyst for Comprehensive Domestic Penal Legislation' (1999) 5 UCDJIL 147

Donovan, Daniel Kempner, 'Joint UN–Cambodia Efforts to Establish a Khmer Rouge Tribunal' (2003) 44 Harvard ILJ 551

Dörmann, Knut (with Louise Doswald-Beck and Robert Kolb), *Elements of War Crimes under the Rome Statute of the International Criminal Court: Sources and Commentary* (Cambridge: Cambridge University Press, 2003)

Draper, Gerald I. A. D., 'The Modern Pattern of War Criminality' (1976) 6 IYBHR 9

Drumbl, Mark A., 'Looking Up, Down and Across: The ICTY's Place in the International Legal Order' (2003) 37 NELR 1037

Dugard, John, 'Obstacles in the Way of an International Criminal Court' (1997) 56 CLJ 329

'Dealing With the Crimes of a Past Regime: Is Amnesty Still an Option?' (1999) 12 LJIL 1001

Durham, Helen and McCormack, Timothy L. H. (eds.), *The Changing Nature of Conflict and the Efficacy of International Humanitarian Law* (The Hague: Kluwer, 2000)

Ehard, Hans, 'The Nuremberg Trial Against the Major War Criminals and International Law' (1949) 46 AJIL 223

Fawcett, James E. S., 'The Eichmann Trial' (1962) 38 BYBIL 181

Fenrick, William J., 'Some International Law Problems Related to Prosecutions Before the International Criminal Tribunal for the Former Yugoslavia' (1995) 6 DJCIL 103.

'Attacking the Enemy Civilian as a Punishable Offence' (1997) 7 DJCIL 539

'International Humanitarian Law and Criminal Trials' (1997) 7 TLCP 23, 35

'Targeting and Proportionality during the NATO Bombing Campaign Against Yugoslavia' (2001) 12 EJIL 489

Ferencz, Benjamin, 'An International Criminal Code and Court: Where They Stand and Where They're Going' (1992) 30 CJTL 375

Finkielkraut, Alain (Roxanne Lapidus trans.), *Remembering in Vain: The Klaus Barbie Trial and Crimes Against Humanity* (New York: Columbia University Press, 1992)

Fischer, Horst, Kreß, Claus and Lüder, Sascha Rolf (eds.), *International and National Prosecution of Crimes Under International Law* (Berlin: Arno Spitz, 2001)

Fletcher, George P., 'Against Universal Jurisdiction' (2003) 1 JICJ 580

Forsythe, David P., 'The United States and International Criminal Justice' (2002) 24 HRQ 974

Fox, Hazel, 'The Objections to Transfer of Criminal Jurisdiction to the UN Tribunal' (1997) 46 ICLQ 434

Franck, Thomas M., *The Power of Legitimacy Among Nations* (Oxford: Oxford University Press, 1990)

Fairness in International Law and Institutions (Oxford: Oxford University Press, 1995)

Frulli, Michaela, 'The Special Court for Sierra Leone: Some Preliminary Comments' (2000) 11 EJIL 857
Fuller, Lon L., *The Morality of Law* (Yale: Yale University Press, revised edn., 1969)
Gaeta, Paula, 'The Defence of Superior Orders: The Statute of the International Criminal Court versus Customary International Law' (1999) 10 EJIL 172
Gallant, Kenneth S., 'Jurisdiction to Adjudicate and Jurisdiction to Prescribe in International Criminal Courts' (2003) 48 Vil. LR 763
Gallavin, Chris, 'Article 53 of the Rome Statute of the International Criminal Court: In the Interests of Justice?' (2003) 14 KCLJ 179
Garraway, Charles, 'Superior Orders and the International Criminal Court: Justice Delivered or Justice Denied?' (1999) 336 IRRC 785
Gilbert, Geoff, 'The Criminal Responsibility of States' (1990) 39 ICLQ 345
Transnational Fugitive Offenders in International Law: Extradition and Other Mechanisms (The Hague: Martinus Nijhoff, 1998)
Ginsburgs George and Kudriavatsev, Vladimir N. (eds.), *The Nuremberg Trial and International Law* (Dordrecht: Martinus Nijhoff, 1990)
Glueck, Sheldon, *War Criminals, their Prosecution and Punishment* (New York: Knopf, 1944)
The Nuremberg Trial and Aggressive War (New York: Knopf, 1946)
Goldstone, Richard J., *For Humanity: Reflections of a War Crimes Investigator* (New Haven: Yale University Press, 2000)
Graditzky, Thomas, 'War Crime Issues Before the Rome Diplomatic Conference on the Establishment of International Criminal Court' (1999) 5 UCDJIL 199
Grayson, James W., 'Superior Orders and the International Criminal Court' (1995) 64 Nordic JIL 243
Green, Leslie C., *Superior Orders in National and International Law* (Leyden: Sitjhoff, 1976)
'Drazen Erdemović: The International Criminal Tribunal for the Former Yugoslavia in Action' (1997) 10 LJIL 363
The Contemporary Law of Armed Conflict (Manchester: Manchester University Press, 2nd edn., 2000)
Greenawalt, Alexander Kent A., 'Rethinking Genocidal Intent: The Case for a Knowledge Based Interpretation' (1999) 99 Columbia LR 2259
Greenwood, Christopher J., 'International Humanitarian Law and the *Tadić* Case' (1996) 7 EJIL 265
'The Development of International Humanitarian Law by The International Criminal Tribunal for the Former Yugoslavia' (1998) 2 MPYBUNL 97
'Command Responsibility and the *Hadžihasanović* Decision' (2004) 2 JICJ 598
Grotius, Hugo, A. C. Campbell, trans., *The Rights of War and Peace* (London: M. Walter Hill, 1901)
Gurulé, Jimmy, 'United States Opposition to the 1998 Rome Statute Establishing an International Criminal Court: Is the Court's Jurisdiction Truly Complementary to National Criminal Jurisdictions?' (2001–2002) 35 Cornell ILJ 1

Hafner, Gerhard, Boon, Kirsten, Rübesame, Anne and Hutson, Jonathan, 'A Response to the American View as Presented By Ruth Wedgwood' (1999) 10 EJIL 108

Hall, Christopher Keith, 'The First Two Sessions of the Preparatory Committee on the Establishment of an International Criminal Court' (1997) 91 AJIL 177

'The Third and Fourth Sessions of the Preparatory Committee for an International Criminal Court' (1998) 92 AJIL 124

'The Fifth Session of the Preparatory Committee on the Establishment of an International Criminal Court' (1998) 92 AJIL 331

'The First Five Sessions of the Preparatory Commission for the International Criminal Court' (2000) 94 AJIL 773

'The First Proposal for a Permanent International Criminal Court' (1998) 322 IRRC 57

'The Sixth Session of the UN Preparatory Committee on the Establishment of an International Criminal Court' (1998) 92 AJIL 548

Happold, Matthew, *Child Soldiers in International Law* (Manchester: Manchester University Press, 2005)

Harhoff, Frederik, 'Consonance or Rivalry? Calibrating the Efforts to Prosecute War Crimes in National and International Tribunals' (1996–1997) 7 DJCIL 571

Harmon, Mark B. and Gaynor, Fergal, 'Prosecuting Massive Crimes With Primitive Tools: Three Problems Encountered by Prosecutors in International Criminal Proceedings' (2004) 2 JICJ 403

Harris, David J., 'Progress and Problems in Establishing an International Criminal Court' (1998) 3 JACL 1

Harris, Sheldon H., *Factories of Death: Japanese Biological Warfare, 1932–1945 and the American Cover Up* (London: Routledge, 1994)

Hasenclever, Andreas, Mayer, Peter and Rittburger, Volker, *Theories of International Regimes* (Cambridge: Cambridge University Press, 1997)

Hawkins, Keith, *The Uses of Discretion* (Oxford: Clarendon, 1992)

Henkin, Louis, *International Law: Politics and Values* (The Hague: Kluwer, 1995)

Henquet, Thomas, 'Mandatory Compliance Powers *vis-à-vis* States by the *Ad Hoc* Tribunals and the International Criminal Court: A Comparative Analysis' (1999) 12 LJIL 969

Higgins, Rosalyn, *Problems and Process: International Law and How We Use It* (Oxford: Clarendon, 1994)

Hirsch, David, *The Law Against Genocide: Cosmopolitan Trials* (London: Glasshouse, 2003)

Horwitz, Solis, 'The Tokyo Trial' (November 1950) 465 *International Conciliation*

Hosoya, Chihiro, Onuma, Yasuaki, Ando, Nisuke and Minear, Richard (eds.), *The Tokyo Trial: An International Symposium* (Tokyo: Kodanasha International, 1986)

Jackson, Robert H., *Report of Robert H. Jackson: US Representative to the International Conference on Military Trials* (Washington, DC: Government Printing Office, 1945)

Jennings, Robert Y. and Watts, Arthur, *Oppenheim's International Law* (London: Longmans, 9th edn., 1992)

Jia, Bing Bing, 'The Doctrine of Command Responsibility in International Law' (1998) 65 NILR 325

'The Doctrine of Command Responsibility: Current Problems' (2000) 3 YBIHL 131, 155–160

Johnson, Larry D., 'The International Tribunal for Rwanda' (1996) 67 RIDP 211

'Ten Years Later: Reflections on the Drafting' (2004) 2 JICJ 368

Jones, Adam (ed.), *Genocide, War Crimes and the West* (London: Zed Books, 2004)

Jones, John R. W. D. and Powles, Steven, *International Criminal Practice* (Oxford: Oxford University Press, 2003)

Jørgensen, Nina H. B., *The Responsibility of States for International Crimes* (Oxford: Oxford University Press, 2000)

Joyner, Christopher C., 'Strengthening Enforcement of International Humanitarian Law: Reflections on the International Criminal Tribunal for Former Yugoslavia' (1995) 6 DJCIL 79

Kalshoven, Frits, *Belligerent Reprisals* (Leyden: Sitjhoff, 1971)

Kamminga, Menno, 'Final Report on the Exercise of Universal Jurisdiction in Relation to Gross Human Rights Abuses', in ILA, *Report of the Sixty-Ninth Conference, Held in London* (London: ILA, 2000), p. 403

Katz Cogan, Jacob, 'The Problem of Obtaining Evidence for International Criminal Courts' (2000) 22 HRQ 404

'International Criminal Courts and Fair Trials: Difficulties and Prospects' (2002) 27 YJIL 111

Kaul, Hans-Peter and Kreß, Claus, 'Jurisdiction and Cooperation in the Statute of the International Criminal Court: Principles and Compromises' (1999) 2 YBIHL 143

Keen, Maurice H., *The Laws of War in the Late Middle Ages* (London: Keegan Paul, 1965)

Keenan, Joseph B. and Brown, Brendan F., *Crimes Against International Law* (Washington, DC: Public Affairs Press, 1950)

Kelsen, Hans, 'Collective and Individual Responsibility in International Law with Particular Regard to the Punishment of War Criminals' (1942–1943) 31 Cal LR 530

'Will the Judgment in the Nuremberg Trial Constitute a Precedent in International Law?' (1947) 1 ILQ 153

Keohane, Robert, *After Hegemony* (Princeton: Princeton University Press, 1984)

Kerr, Rachel, *The International Criminal Tribunal for the Former Yugoslavia: An Exercise in Law, Politics and Diplomacy* (Oxford: Oxford University Press, 2004)

Kirk McDonald, Gabrielle and Swaak-Goldman, Olivia (eds.), *Substantive and Procedural Aspects of International Criminal Law, I: Commentary* (The Hague: Kluwer, 2000)

Kirsch, Philippe and Holmes, John T., 'The Rome Conference on an International Criminal Court: The Negotiating Process' (1999) 93 AJIL 2

Kissinger, Henry, 'The Pitfalls of Universal Jurisdiction' (2001) (July–August) FA 86

Kleffner, Jann K., 'The Impact of Complementarity on National Implementation of Substantive International Criminal Law' (2003) 1 JICJ 86

Knoops, Geert-Jan, *Defences in Contemporary International Law* (Ardsley: Transnational, 2001)

Kochavi, Arieh, *Prelude to Nuremberg: Allied War Crimes Policy and the Question of Punishment* (Durham, NC: North Carolina University Press, 1998)

Kolb, Robert, 'The Jurisprudence of the Yugoslav and Rwandan Criminal Tribunals on Their Jurisidction and on International Crimes' (2000) 69 BYBIL 259

Kopelman, Elizabeth, 'Ideology and International Law: The Dissent of the Indian Justice at the Tokyo War Crimes Trial' (1991) 23 NYUJILP 373

Koskenniemi, Martti, *The Gentle Civilizer of Nations: The Rise and Fall of International Law 1870–1960* (Cambridge: Cambridge University Press, 2001)

'Between Impunity and Show Trials' (2002) 6 MPYBUNL 1

Kranzbühler, Otto, 'Nuremberg Eighteen Years Afterwards' (1963–1964) 13 De Paul LR 333

Krasner, Steven (ed.), *International Regimes* (Ithaca: Cornell University Press, 1983)

Kreß, Claus and Lattanzi, Flavia (eds.), *The Rome Statute and Domestic Legal Orders, 1* (Baden-Baden: Nomos, 2000)

La Haye, Eve, 'The Jurisdiction of the International Criminal Court: Controversies Over the Preconditions for Exercise of its Jurisdiction' (1999) 46 NILR 1

Lamb, Susan, 'The Powers of Arrest of the International Criminal Tribunal for Former Yugoslavia' (1999) 70 BYBIL 165

Lattanzi, Flavia and Schabas, William A. (eds.), *Essays on the Statute of the International Criminal Court* (Teramo: il Sirente, 1999)

Lauterpacht, Hersch, 'The Law of Nations and the Punishment of War Crimes' (1944) 21 BYBIL 58

'The Grotian Tradition in International Law' (1946) 23 BYBIL 1

'The Problem of the Revision of the Law of War' (1952) 29 BYBIL 360

'Codification and Development of International Law' (1955) 49 AJIL 16

(ed.), *Oppenheim's International Law, II* (London: Longmans, 6th edn., 1944)

Lavalle, Roberto, 'A Vicious Storm in a Teacup: The Action by the United National Security Council to Narrow the Jurisdiction of the International Criminal Court' (2003) 14 CLF 195

Lee, Roy S., 'The Rwanda Tribunal' (1996) 9 LJIL 37

(ed.), *The International Criminal Court: The Making of the Rome Statute* (The Hague: Kluwer, 1999)

(ed.), *The International Criminal Court: Elements of Crimes and Rules of Procedure and Evidence* (Ardsley: Transnational, 2001)

Levie, Howard, 'The Rise and Fall of an Internationally Codified Defense of Superior Orders' (1991) 30 RIDMDG 183

Terrorism in War: The Law of War Crimes (New York: Oceana, 1992)
Linton, Suzannah, 'Cambodia, East Timor and Sierra Leone: Experiments in International Criminal Justice' (2001) 12 CLF 185
'Rising From the Ashes: The Creation of a Viable Criminal Justice System in East Timor' (2001) 25 MULR 122
Lippman, Matthew, 'Nuremberg Forty-Five Years Later' (1991) 7 Connecticut JIL 1
'Conundrums of Armed Conflict: Criminal Defences to Violations of the Humanitarian Law of War' (1996) 15 Dickinson JIL 1
'The Pursuit of Nazi War Criminals in the United States and in Other Anglo-American Legal Systems' (1998) 29 CWILJ 1
Mandel, Michael, 'Politics and Human Rights in International Criminal Law: Our Case Against NATO and the Lessons to be Learnt From It' (2001–2002) 25 Fordham ILJ 95
Maogoto, Jackson Nyamuya, *State Sovereignty and International Criminal Law: Versailles to Rome* (Ardsley: Transnational, 2003)
Martin, David A., 'Reluctance to Prosecute War Crimes: Of Causes and Cures' (1994) 34 VJIL 255
May, Richard and Wierda, Marieka, *International Criminal Evidence* (Ardsley: Transnational, 2003)
May, Richard, *et al.* (eds.), *Essays on ICTY Procedure and Evidence in Honour of Gabrielle Kirk McDonald* (The Hague: Kluwer, 2001)
Mayfield, Julie V., 'The Prosecution of War Crimes and Respect for Human Rights: Ethiopia's Balancing Act' (1995) 9 Emory ILR 553
McCormack, Timothy L. H., 'Selective Reaction to Atrocity' (1996–1997) 60 Alb LR 681
McCormack, Timothy L. H. and Simpson, Gerry J. (eds.), *The Law of War Crimes: National and International Approaches* (The Hague: Kluwer, 1997)
McCoubrey, Hilaire, 'The Concept and Treatment of War Crimes' (1996) 1 JACL 121
'War Crimes Jurisdiction and a Permanent International Criminal Court: Advantages and Difficulties' (1998) 3 JACL 9
'From Nuremberg to Rome: Restoring the Defence of Superior Orders' (2001) 50 ICLQ 386
McDonald, Avril, 'Sierra Leone's Shoestring Special Court' (2002) 845 IRRC 121
McGoldrick, Dominic, 'The Permanent International Criminal Court: An End to the Culture of Impunity?' [1999] Crim LR 627
McGoldrick, Dominic, Rowe, Peter and Donnelly, Eric (eds.), *The Permanent International Criminal Court: Legal and Policy Issues* (Oxford: Hart, 2004)
Megrét, Frédéric, 'Epilogue to an Endless Debate: The International Court's Third Party Jurisdiction and the Looming Revolution of International Law' (2001) 12 EJIL 247
'The Politics of International Criminal Law' (2003) 14 EJIL 1261
Meron, Theodor, *Human Rights and Humanitarian Norms as Customary Norms* (Oxford: Oxford University Press, 1989)

'War Crimes in Yugoslavia and the Development of International Law' (1994) 88 AJIL 78

'International Criminalization of Internal Atrocities' (1995) 89 AJIL 554

Bloody Constraint: Crimes and Accountability in Shakespeare (New York: Oxford University Press, 1998)

War Crimes Law Comes of Age (Oxford: Oxford University Press, 1998)

Mettreaux, Gunaël, 'US Courts-Martial and the Armed Conflict in the Philippines (1899–1902): Their Contribution to National Case Law on War Crimes' (2003) 1 JICJ 135

Minear, Richard, *Victor's Justice: The Tokyo War Crimes Trial* (Princeton: Princeton University Press, 1971)

Moir, Lindsay, *The Law of Internal Armed Conflict* (Cambridge: Cambridge University Press, 2002)

Morris, Madeline, 'The Trials of Concurrent Jurisdiction: The Case of Rwanda' (1997) 7 DJCIL 349

'High Crimes and Misconceptions: The ICC and Non Party States' (2001) 64 LCP 131

Morris, Virginia and Scharf, Michael P., *An Insider's Guide to the International Criminal Tribunal for Former Yugoslavia* (Ardsley: Transnational, 1995)

The International Criminal Tribunal for Rwanda (Ardsley: Transnational, 1998)

Murphy, Sean D., 'Progress and Jurisprudence of the International Criminal Tribunal for the Former Yugoslavia' (1999) 93 AJIL 57

Naqvi, Yasmin, 'Amnesty for War Crimes: Defining the Limits of International Recognition' (2003) 851 IRRC 583

O'Brien, John C., 'The International Tribunal for Violations of International Humanitarian Law in the Former Yugoslavia' (1993) 77 AJIL 639

O'Keefe, Roger, 'Customary Crimes in English Courts' (2001) 72 BYBIL 293

Oppenheim, Lassa (Ronald F. Roxburgh, ed.), *International Law – A Treatise* (London: Longmans, Green & Co., 3rd edn., 1920)

Orientlicher, Diane, 'Settling Accounts: The Duty to Prosecute Human Rights Violations of a Former Regime' (1991) 100 Yale LJ 2537

Osiel, Mark J., *Mass Atrocity, Collective Memory and the Law* (New Brunswick: Transaction, 1997)

Mass Atrocity, Ordinary Evil and Hannah Arendt: Criminal Consciousness in Argentina's Dirty War (New Haven: Yale University Press, 2001)

Parks, W. Hays, 'Command Responsibility for War Crimes' (1973) 62 Military LR 1

Paust, Jordan J., 'My Lai and Vietnam: Norms, Myths and Leader Responsibility' (1972) 57 Military LR 99

Piccigallo, John, *The Japanese on Trial* (Austin, TX: Texas University Press, 1979)

Politi, Mauro and Nesi, Guiseppe (eds.), *The International Criminal Court: A Challenge to Impunity* (Aldsershot: Ashgate, 2001)

The International Criminal Court and the Crime of Aggression (Aldershot: Ashgate, 2004)

Power, Samantha, *A Problem From Hell: America and the Age of Genocide* (London: Flamingo, 2003)

Prevost, Anne-Marie, 'Race and War Crimes: The 1945 War Crimes Trial of General Tomoyuki Yamashita' (1992) 14 HRQ 303

Pritchard, R. John and Zaide, Sonia M. (eds.), *The Tokyo War Crimes Trial* (New York: Garland, 1981)

Provost, René *International Human Rights and Humanitarian Law* (Cambridge: Cambridge University Press, 2002)

Randall, Kenneth C., 'Universal Jurisdiction Under International Law' (1988) 66 TLR 785

Ratner, Steven R., 'The Schizophrenias of International Criminal Law' (1998) 33 TILJ 237

'Belgium's War Crimes Statute: A Postmortem' (2003) 97 AJIL 888

Ratner, Steven R. and Abrams, Jason A., *Accountability for Human Rights Atrocities in International Law* (Oxford: Oxford University Press, 2nd edn., 2001)

Reydams, Luc, 'Belgium's First Application of Universal Jurisdiction: The Butare Four Case' (2002) 1 JICJ 428

'Belgium Reneges on Universality: The 5 August 2003 Act on Grave Breaches of International Humanitarian Law' (2003) 1 JICJ 679

Universal Jurisdiction: International and Municipal Legal Perspectives (Oxford: Oxford University Press, 2003)

Rittberger, Volker (ed.), *Regime Theory and International Relations* (Oxford: Clarendon, 1993)

Robinson, Daryl, 'Defining Crimes Against Humanity at the Rome Conference' (1999) 93 AJIL 43

'Serving the Interests of Justice: Amnesties, Truth Commissions and the International Criminal Court' (2003) 14 EJIL 481

Rogers, Anthony P. V., *Law on the Battlefield* (Manchester: Manchester University Press, 2nd edn., 2004)

Röling, Bernard V. A., 'The Law of War and the National Jurisdiction Since 1945' (1960-II) 100 RdC 329

Röling, Bernard V. A. and Cassese, Antonio, *The Tokyo Trial and Beyond* (Cambridge: Polity, 1992)

Röling, Bernard V. A. and Rüter, C. F., *The Tokyo Judgment* (Amsterdam: Amsterdam University Press, 1977)

Ronzitti, Natalino, 'Is the non Liquet of the Final Report by the Committee Established to Review the NATO Bombing Campaign Against the Federal Republic of Yugoslavia Acceptable?' (2000) 840 IRRC 1017

Rowe, Peter, 'Duress as a Defence to War Crimes After *Erdemović*: A Laboratory for a Permanent Court?' (1998) 1 YBIHL 210

Rubin, Alfred P., 'International Crime and Punishment' (Fall 1993) 34 NI 73

Ethics and Authority in International Law (Cambridge: Cambridge University Press, 1997)

'The International Criminal Court: Possibilities for Prosecutorial Abuse' (2001) 64 LCP 153

Sadat, Leila Nadya, *The International Criminal Court and the Transformation of International Law: Justice for a New Millennium* (Ardsley: Transnational, 2002)

Sadat-Wexler, Leila, 'The Interpretation of the Nuremberg Principles by the French Court of Cassation: From Touvier to Barbie to Back Again' (1994) 32 CJTL 289

'The Proposed International Criminal Court: An Appraisal' (1996) 20 Cornell ILJ 665, 679–83

Sandoz, Yves (ed.), *Commentary on the Additional Protocols of 8 June 1977 to the Geneva Conventions of 12 August 1949* (Dordrecht: Martinus Nijhoff, 1986)

Sarooshi, Danesh, 'The Powers of the United Nations International Criminal Tribunals' (1998) 2 MPYBUNL 141

Schabas, William A., 'Justice, Democracy and Impunity in Post-Genocide Rwanda: Searching for Solutions to Impossible Problems' (1996) 7 CLF 523

Genocide in International Law: The Crime of Crimes (Cambridge: Cambridge University Press, 2000)

'Prosecutor v. Barayagwiza' (2000) 94 AJIL 563

An Introduction to the International Criminal Court (Cambridge: Cambridge University Press, 2nd edn., 2004)

Scharf, Michael P., 'The Jury is Still Out on an International Criminal Court' (1991) 1 DJCIL 135

'Getting Serious About an International Criminal Court' (1994) 6 Pace ILR 103

'Swapping Amnesty for Peace: Was There a Duty to Prosecute International Crimes in Haiti?' (1996) 31 Texas ILJ 1

Scheffer, David J., 'The United States and the International Criminal Court' (1999) 93 AJIL 12

'A Negotiator's Perspective on the International Criminal Court' (2001) 167 Military LR 1

'Staying the Course with the ICC' (2001–2002) 35 Cornell ILJ 47

Schimmelpennick van der Oije, Pita J. C., 'A Surinam Crime Before a Dutch Court: Universal Jurisdiction or a Post-Colonial Injustice?' (2001) 14 LJIL 455

Schraga, Daphna and Zacklin, Ralph, 'The International Criminal Tribunal for Yugoslavia' (1994) 5 EJIL 360

'The International Criminal Tribunal for Rwanda' (1996) 7 EJIL 501

Schwarzenberger, Georg, 'The Problem of an International Criminal Law' (1950) 3 CLP 263

International Law as Applied by International Courts and Tribunals, II: The Law of Armed Conflict (London: Stevens & Sons, 1968)

Schwelb, Egon, 'Crimes Against Humanity' (1946) 23 BYBIL 178

Sewell, Sarah B. and Kaysen, Carl, *The United States and the International Criminal Court* (New York: Rowman & Littlefield/American Academy of Arts and Sciences, 2000)

Silving, Helen, 'In re Eichmann: A Dilemma of Law and Morality' (1961) 55 AJIL 307

Simma, Bruno and Paulus, Andreas, 'The Responsibility of Individuals for Human Rights Abuses in Internal Conflicts: A Positivist View' (1999) 93 AJIL 302

Sluiter, Göran, *International Criminal Adjudication and the Collection of Evidence: Obligations of States* (New York: Intersentia, 2001)

'The Surrender of War Criminals to the International Criminal Court' (2003) 25 LLAICLR 605.

Smith, Bradley F., *Reaching Judgment at Nuremberg* (London: André Deutsch, 1977)

Stahn, Carsten, 'The Ambiguities of Resolution 1422' (2003) 14 EJIL 85

Stromseth, Jane E. (ed.), *Accountability for Atrocities: National and International Responses* (Ardsley: Transnational, 2003)

Sunga, Lyal S., *The Emerging System of International Criminal Law* (The Hague: Kluwer, 1997)

Tallgren, Immi, 'We Did It? The Vertigo of Law and Everyday Life at the Diplomatic Conference on the Establishment of an International Criminal Court' (1999) 12 LJIL 683

Taylor, Telford, *Nuremberg and Vietnam: An American Tragedy* (Chicago: Quadrangle Books, 1970)

The Anatomy of the Nuremberg Trials (London: Bloomsbury, 1993)

Teitel, Ruti, *Transitional Justice* (New York: Oxford University Press, 2000)

Tinta, Maria Fiera, 'Commanders on Trial: The *Blaškić* Case and the Doctrine of Command Responsibility Under International Law' (2000) 47 NILR 293

Tolbert, David, 'The International Criminal Tribunal for the Former Yugoslavia: Unforeseen Successes and Foreseeable Shortcomings' (2002) 26(2) FFWA 7

Triffterer, Otto (ed.), *Commentary on the Rome Statute of the International Criminal Court: Article by Article* (Baden-Baden: Nomos, 1999)

'Genocide: Its Particular Intent to Destroy in Whole or in Part the Group as Such' (2001) 14 L JIL 399

Triggs, Gillian, 'Australia's War Crimes Trials: A Moral Necessity or Legal Minefield?' (1987) 16 MULR 382

Turns, David, 'The International Criminal Tribunal for the Former Yugoslavia: The *Erdemović* Case' (1998) 47 ICLQ 461

'Prosecuting Violations of International Humanitarian Law: The Legal Position in the United Kingdom' (1999) 4 JACL 1

Tusa, Anne and Tusa, John, *The Nuremberg Trial* (London: Macmillan, 1983)

van Alebeek, Roseanne, 'From Rome to the Hague: Recent Developments on Immunity Issues in the ICC Statute' (2000) 13 LJIL 485

van Elst, Richard, 'Implementing Universal Jurisdiction Over Grave Breaches of the Geneva Conventions' (2000) 13 LJIL 815

van Schaak, Beth, 'The Crime of Political Genocide: Repairing the Genocide Convention's Blind Spot' (1996–1997) 106 YLJ 2259

van Sliedregt, Elies, *The Criminal Responsibility of Individuals for Violations of International Humanitarian Law* (The Hague: T.M.C. Asser Press, 2003)

Vetter, Greg, 'Command Responsibility of Non-Military Superiors in the International Criminal Court (ICC)' (2000) 25 Yale JIL 89

Vohrah, Lal Chand, *et al.* (eds.), *Man's Inhumanity to Man: Essays in Honour of Antonio Cassese* (The Hague: Kluwer, 2003)

von Hebel, Hermann A. M., Lammers, Johan G. and Schukking, Jolien (eds.), *Reflections on the International Criminal Court: Essays in Honor of Adriaan Bos* (The Hague: T.M.C. Asser Instituut, 1999)

Warbrick, Colin, 'International Criminal Law' (1995) 44 ICLQ 466

'The United Nations System: A Place for International Criminal Courts?' (1995) 5 TLCP 237

Watson, Geoffrey R., 'The Humanitarian Law of the Yugoslavia War Crimes Tribunal: Jurisdiction in *Prosecutor* v. *Tadić*' (1996) 36 VJIL 687

Wedgwood, Ruth, 'Fiddling at Rome: The United States and the International Criminal Court' (1998) 77 FA 20

'The International Criminal Court: An American View' (1999) 10 EJIL 93

Weller, Marc, 'Undoing the Global Constitution: UN Security Council Action on the International Criminal Court' (2002) 78 IA 693

White, Nigel D., *The United Nations System: Toward International Justice* (Boulder, CO: Lynne Reiner, 2002)

White, Nigel, Burchill, Richard and Morris, Justin (eds.), *Essays in Conflict and Security Law in Memory of Hilaire McCoubrey* (Cambridge: Cambridge University Press, 2005)

Williams, Paul R. and Scharf, Michael P., *Peace With Justice: War Crimes and Accountability in the Former Yugoslavia* (London: Rowman & Littlefield, 2003)

Wirth, Steffen, 'Immunities, Related Problems and Article 98 of the Rome Statute' (2002) 12 CLF 429

Woetzel, Robert K., *The Nuremberg Trials in International Law* (London: Stevens, 1960)

Wright, Quincy, 'The Law of The Nuremberg Trial' (1947) 41 AJIL 38

Young, Simon N. M., 'Surrendering the Accused to the International Criminal Court' (2000) 71 BYBIL 317

Zahar, Alexander, 'Command Responsibility of Civilian Superiors for Genocide' (2001) 14 LJIL 591

Zappalà, Salvatore, *Human Rights in International Criminal Proceedings* (Oxford: Oxford University Press, 2003)

Zegveld, Liesbeth, *The Accountability of Armed Opposition Groups in International Law* (Cambridge: Cambridge University Press, 2002)

Zimmerman, Andreas, 'The Creation of a Permanent International Criminal Court' (1998) 2 MPYBUNL 169

Index

CAMBRIDGE STUDIES IN INTERNATIONAL AND COMPARATIVE LAW

Books in the series

Prosecuting International Crimes
Selectivity and the International Criminal Law Regime
Robert Cryer

Great Powers and Outlaw States
Unequal Sovereigns in the International Legal Order
Gerry Simpson

Reading Humanitarian Intervention
Human Rights and the Use of Force in International Law
Anne Orford

Local Remedies in International Law
Second Edition
C. F. Amerasinghe

Conflict of Norms in Public International Law
How WTO Law Relates to Other Rules of Law
Joost Pauwelyn

The Search for Good Governance in Africa
Making Constitutions in the States of the Commonwealth
Peter Slinn and John Hatchard

Transboundary Damage in International Law
Hanqin Xue

European Criminal Procedures
Edited by Mireille Delmas-Marty and John Spencer

The Accountability of Armed Opposition Groups in International Law
Liesbeth Zegveld

Sharing Transboundary Resources
International Law and Optimal Resource Use
Eyal Benvenisti

International Human Rights and Humanitarian Law
René Provost

Remedies Against International Organisations
Basic Issues
Karel Wellens

Diversity and Self-Determination in International Law
Karen Knop

The Law of Internal Armed Conflict
Lindsay Moir

International Commercial Arbitration and African States
Amazu A. Asouzu

The Enforceability of Promises in European Contract Law
James Gordley

International Law in Antiquity
David J. Bederman

Money Laundering
Guy Stessens

Good Faith in European Contract Law
Reinhard Zimmerman and Simon Whittaker

On Civil Procedure
J. A. Jolowicz

Trusts
A Comparative Study
Maurizio Lupoi

The Right to Property in Commonwealth Constitutions
Tom Allen

International Organizations Before National Courts
August Reinisch

The Changing International Law of High Seas Fisheries
Francisco Orrego Vicuña

Trade and the Environment
Damien Geradin

Unjust Enrichment
Hanoch Dagan

Religious Liberty and International Law in Europe
Malcolm D. Evans

Ethics and Authority in International Law
Alfred P. Rubin

Sovereignty Over Natural Resources
Nico Schrijver

The Polar Regions and the Development of International Law
Donald R. Rothwell

Fragmentation and the International Relations of Micro-States
Jorri Duursma

Principles of the Institutional Law of International Organisations
C. F. Amerasinghe

To Susie
Keep.
Edward

It Takes Time

A JOURNEY TO ULTRAMARATHON GREATNESS

First published in 2023 by Uplift Press

Introduction

You may think it a little bold for an old guy who started running late in life and never won a single race to give his book a title that has more than a passing likeness to one written by one of the great ultra-runners, Scott Jurek. My journey has been vastly different from his and is the life of an ordinary person with no extraordinary talents other than the ability to just keep going. And in doing just that I created my own place in the history of ultra-running. Not an impressive list of first places like Scott, but something that has not been achieved by any other person. I can proudly say that more people have walked on the moon than have done what I have done. A journey like mine can be travelled by anyone irrespective of their genetic abilities, it just takes time. Running, unlike most other sports, which require skill, allows ordinary people to achieve extraordinary things if they have the vision and determination. A lack of natural ability or skill are not limiting factors.

I hope my story inspires you to find your own unique greatness. I also hope it provides you with some useful information, advice and tips. It will also probably help you avoid making some mistakes. But most of all I hope it makes you want to be active and enjoy life, which I believe only really begins at the edge of our comfort zones.

I will not keep you in suspense, what I have achieved is to finish the Kalahari Augrabies Extreme Marathon more times than anyone else. I achieved this completing it seven times; however, I haven't stopped and in 2019 I notched up twelve completions. In doing this I have had a wonderful time and met some lovely people, both on the event and when I have been training for it. This is my story, a journey from non-runner to ultramarathon greatness.

It is a rough road that leads to the heights of greatness.
--Seneca

CONTENTS

An inauspicious start

I was not having a good day, it was hot, my brain was fried, I was lightheaded and felt sick. This was Day 1 of the 2007 Kalahari Augrabies Extreme Marathon, a 250km 7-day self-sufficiency race through the Kalahari Desert in South Africa. I had travelled over 8,000 miles and spent a lot of money to get here. I had been training for this event for a year; it was something that was to be the pinnacle of my 17 years as a runner.

I wasn't a rookie, I had lots of ultra-marathons under my belt (a belt that I had to let out a bit) and had completed the Marathon des Sables, described as the Toughest Footrace in the World. This was not good, this shouldn't have been happening, unfortunately it was. I slowed to an easy walk, although it just wasn't easy, every step was a struggle and things were not getting any better. A few of the other competitors passed me and asked if I was okay. "Fine thanks, just taking it easy for a bit" was my cheery reply. I don't think I fooled them. The heat was relentless, and my temperature was rising. This was going to be embarrassing, I had a reputation for always finishing, which had given rise to one of my nicknames, Big Man. That was probably part of the problem; I was a big man and was carrying too much weight. Not the 10kg plus of the rucksack containing my food and equipment for the week, but the not insignificant weight of the extra inches around my waist. I plodded on dejected and considering how best to explain this defeat when I got home. Then I rounded a corner and there was hope.

Beside the track was a small vineyard and beneath the rows of vines was some lovely welcoming shade. The Orange River runs through this part of the Kalahari and, where conditions are right, some enterprising farmers use this water to irrigate small vineyards growing grapes for raisins. They are an amazing sight, one minute you are in a barren and desolate environment, then as you near the river you see these lush green fields of vines. I took my pack off and crawled in amongst the vines.

It wasn't much cooler in the shade, but it was enough and at least I was away from the relentless sun. I just lay there feeling very woozy; then I vomited. That's not a good thing when you are in the heat of the desert, you need all your liquids and food inside you, and you need to be able to put more in. I moved a little further into the vineyard not for more shade, I wanted to make sure other competitors did not see me. I just lay there and have never felt so bad, both physically and mentally. Then there was another glimmer of hope, Gloria Gaynor came to the rescue - these words came into my head, "Did you think I'd lay down and die? Oh, no, not I, I will survive."

I thought about it, I will survive, just hold on to that thought. I worked out a plan and set about getting myself back into the race. Cool down first, dampen my buff, wave it around a little so the evaporating water cools it down (never thought I'd get such a graphic demonstration of school physics), pull it over my head and enjoy the cool material against my skin. Pour a little water over the backs of my hands and on my wrists. The evaporating water would help cool the skin and the blood that is close to the surface there. It would only have a small effect; however, the difference between success and failure is often exceedingly small, you just need to be the right side of the red line. Repeat several times. Okay it's working. Now mix up some rehydration drink. I learnt from my experiences in the Marathon des Sables that the sachets of rehydration powder you get from the chemists for treating children when they have had diarrhoea are worth their weight in gold. The hard bit would be keeping this down, so very, very small sips with a big wait in between. After keeping half a cup full down, I was starting to feel hopeful. "Did you think I'd crumble? Did you think I'd lay down and die? Oh, no, not I, I will survive."

Stage two of the recovery process was to get some food inside of me. Muscles can use fat as an energy source and I had plenty of that, but the brain needs glycogen to function. I was probably low on that and definitely would be later on in the day if I didn't eat. I slowly chewed on a couple of sun-dried bananas as I finished off the rest of my rehydration drink. I still didn't feel great, but Gloria was with me "And I grew strong, and I learned how to get along." I crawled out from under the vines and started walking. I walked at a steady pace sipping water and chanting my new mantra "I will survive, I will survive, I will survive." That was a close thing, but I'd got through it, the Big Man was on his way, life was good. However, there is a saying in the ultra-marathon world. "If you feel good in an ultra, don't worry, it will pass." That was going to be so true that day.

That particular year the course went through a long canyon that functioned very nicely as an oven. Ever since that day it has been referred to as 'Death Valley'. The hot rocks and the canyon walls radiated heat which made the trapped air almost unbearable. The only way to cope was to make a little progress, pushing as far as you dared then rest, hopefully in some shade. The other competitors were doing the same, so you would come up to people resting ahead of you, if there was any shade left you would join them for a while until they moved on. Or, if there was no shade you would move on until you found some and, perhaps a little later, they would come past and someone else would join you. There was not a lot of talking, there was no energy for that, but everyone understood what everyone else was going through. This was a shared experience in its rawest form.

I eventually made it out of the canyon; others were not so lucky and needed medical help. It was a very tough day and a dramatic introduction to the Kalahari. The course was only 27km long that day, yet 5 trained athletes didn't make it to the finish and there were still over 200 kilometres to go. What had I let myself in for? The Marathon des Sables had lost its Toughest Footrace in the World title and it was only day one. When I arrived in camp that afternoon, I felt nauseous again, this was not good especially as the medics were around and I thought throwing up in front of them would not be a good idea. I've since learnt that on this event they are your best friends, not the enemy. They will do everything that they can to keep you in the race until the point is reached where you are likely to do yourself some permanent damage. They will help you take it right up to the line, but they will not let you step over it.

Under the camp gazebos it was sweltering hot, even though they did provide some shade, so I went off in search of a cooler spot, which I found in the shadow alongside the massage tent and there was a little bit of a breeze there. I stayed there for a long time, sipping another rehydration mix, then water and nibbling on snacks, only moving occasional to keep in the shade as the sun moved. Eventually it started to cool as the sun dropped behind the hills and I headed back to the gazebos to try and get some substantial food inside me before watching the Rugby World Cup final. Estienne Arndt, race director, had somehow managed to fix up a screen and a satellite link in a derelict building near the camp.

England had made it through to the final and would face South Africa. The South African's were confident that they would win and there had been some great banter between the English and South Africans on the 11-hour coach trip from Johannesburg to the Augrabies Falls where the Kalahari Augrabies Extreme Marathon starts. The day before we had been on a short game drive when Phil Waudby (South Africa) spotted a Springbok and delighted in teasing us that Bryan Habana, the South African wing, would use a similar turn of speed to leave our team flat-footed. Unfortunately, I cannot tell you whether he did or not as I just didn't have the energy to make the short walk up the hill to see the match. Instead, I tried to sleep, but the level of cheering sweeping down the hill left me in no doubt that we were losing.

The South Africans were in particularly good spirits the following morning, I, on the other hand, was very pensive wondering how I was going to make it through the day. The results show that I did, however, I remember nothing of it, other than the sheer drudgery of just putting one foot in front of the other until I reached the camp.

The next few days were just the same; a struggle to survive and keep going, although I did have time to take in the awesome scenery and become totally enchanted by the magic of the Kalahari. I also developed some very unpleasant blisters, although after my Marathon des Sables experience, I knew I could cope with these. By day 4 the temperature had dropped, although it was still hot, I was feeling good and started to think that I could finish even though this stage was 45 miles.

By the end of the day a total of 13 of the original 33 starters would have withdrawn. I saw some of the runners at the point when they realised that they could no longer go on, those were very emotional times and I can still today see the haunted look on their faces, unable to fathom why their bodies had let them down and their dream lay in tatters. It is a huge testament to their character that a few days later they were out on the course helping at checkpoints and encouraging the runners still in the event. I cannot put into words how much I appreciated that and how much respect I have for their strength of character.

"Character cannot be developed in ease and quiet. Only through experience of trial and suffering can the soul be strengthened, ambition inspired, and success achieved." - Helen Keller

The long day was good for me, and I enjoyed running and walking in the moonlight alone in Africa watching the stars, except when I missed one of the markers and went a considerable way up a track the wrong way before realising my mistake. That was a big panic moment, my big fear was getting lost then getting timed out.

I've since learnt that the course is always well marked and as long as you pay attention it's 'impossible' to get lost. Every year some runners do, normally because they are in a group chatting and no one is paying attention or because they are following people in front, and they have got lost.

It was also that night that I had one of many wonderful animal encounters in the Kalahari. I stopped to have a pee at the side of the track and was startled by a big Kudu coming out onto the track from behind the bush I was peeing into. I think he was more startled than I was. He kicked out his hind legs then crashed through the bushes opposite and ran off. Seen up close they are majestic, but frightening creatures.

I don't remember much of the rest of the race, I think this was because I was in my own world of pain and suffering, one of my feet was swollen and this was causing even more blistering. I later learnt I had a spider bite that had become infected. I do remember on the penultimate day being slightly behind Jean, a French competitor who also had badly blistered feet. As we were going down a hillside on a track he was ahead out of sight around the twisting bends; however, I knew he was there and what the conditions were like underfoot because of the loud and frequent "Merde, Merde".

By then I knew I was going to finish and started the final day in great spirits, it was only about 18km; easy. That was until the Kalahari threw us a curve ball, it started raining. We were subject to an incredible storm with a massive amount of electricity in the air which discharged to the ground with spectacular lightning strikes. We were in no danger; the lightening is attracted to the nearby hills rich in iron and manganese. I didn't know that at the time. The storm caused me to have two problems. I had thrown away the plastic bin bag I had kept my gear in inside my rucksack to keep it dry in case of rain, as per the race director's advice. Great timing Edward. I had also taken my sleeping bag out of its sack and stuffed it, unrolled, into my rucksack to stop the few items left from bouncing about. The rain was soaking into the sleeping bag and my pack was getting heavier and heavier. By the time I realised this it had reached saturation point and it was not worth doing anything about it.

The second problem was that I was getting incredibly woozy and feeling faint. Slowing down didn't help, even resting had no effect. I think all the electricity in the air was getting to my brain. I had visions of collapsing and waking up later not knowing whether I had finished or whether I had been picked up by the medics and brought in by vehicle. This became a complete obsession until I could see the finish line and even then, I could not relax until I'd crossed it. The immediate feeling was one of relief that it was all over, it was some time before it started to sink in that I'd done it. Then started my love affair with Castle Lager; that post race beer tasted so good and has come to symbolise all that is good about the Kalahari Augrabies Extreme Marathon and the haunting beauty of the Green Kalahari.

What does not destroy me make me stronger - Friedrich Nietzsche

The following evening, I had what was probably my most bizarre beer drinking experience. The doctor was concerned that the antibiotics he had given me were not working so decided to administer some intravenously. An Australian competitor had just gone to the bar to get some beers, when he returned the doc asked him to squeeze the top of my arm to make it easier to find a vein. Once he had got the needle in, he handed the drip bag to the Aussie to hold above my head and started to drink his beer. We drunk our beers chatting about the Kalahari, two of us sitting comfortably and the poor Aussie guy standing with his arm in the air. Fond memories.

I have thought long and hard about what happened on that first day, it so nearly went horribly wrong, so I wanted to learn as much as possible from that experience. You could say nothing went wrong as I finished and almost 40% of the field didn't. I think at one point the race organiser was getting worried that no one would finish. My body copes well with the heat, it just needs time to figure out what it should be doing, and I didn't give it that time until it was almost too late. It's a bit like attempting a record breaking 100 metre sprint without warming up; your lungs won't cope, your circulation won't cope, and you'll probably tear a muscle as they are too cold and stiff.

Why didn't it happen on the first day of the Marathon des Sables? Well actually I think it did, but I had reached the camp by the time it did and was resting so didn't notice so much, I just thought I was tired. The heat on the first day of the Marathon des Sables was not as bad and, in the Sahara, it is a very dry heat, so easier to deal with (that's a comparative term). Even though the humidity in the Kalahari is quite low, that small amount makes a significant difference and that first day did get hot very quickly. I was also a lot warier of the heat my first time in the desert so went slower on the first day in the Marathon des Sables and made it into camp before experiencing any adverse effects. I think I was probably a little bit over-confident at the start of the Kalahari Augrabies Extreme marathon and went out too fast (another comparative term). The important thing is I listened to my body, but obviously not early enough, took the right corrective action and survived to face another day without having totally depleted the reserves.

I've come to learn over the years, from my own experiences and from observing and talking to other competitors, that succeeding in extreme multi-day events requires a special mix of factors. You have to train well, prepare well, have the right kit, get your food right, look after your feet, manage your body, manage your hydration, have determination and you must want to succeed. You would have thought that last one to be a given, but some people just don't want it enough, so when the going gets really tough there isn't that motivation to carry on. Your reason for taking on a big challenge must be personal and deep, otherwise you will buckle when things get really tough. Not every one of those factors has to be spot on, having great kit doesn't guarantee success, the latest superfood isn't going to get you to the end, training needn't be perfect, but these events are too extreme to tough it out without having done sufficient training. But what you do need is a magic mix off lots of things and even if everything is right that's no guarantee.

If the hottest and toughest part of the day coincides with you feeling good, there might be a completely different outcome from if it coincides with when you are going through a low patch. You also need to have a history of facing adversity and succeeding, so you have positive things to reflect on and then you can convince yourself that you can conquer* the challenge. You can survive! You need to know that your body will help your mind come up with lots of good reasons why it is all right to give up and be prepared for that and have a big toolkit full of all the reasons why it's not all right to give up. With a history you know that when things are bad, they will not stay that way forever, things will get better. You know just to focus on taking the next step because after one of those next steps it will either get better or you will have got to the finish. You also need that history, so you know that when things suddenly go bad it doesn't come as a complete surprise; it's happened before, and you coped. It does not have to be a running history; you just need to have done plenty of stuff outside of your comfort zone. I know one runner who, on a tough mountain stage, found the strength to continue from the fact that she had endured, then escaped, from an abusive relationship.

"Even when you have gone as far as you can, and everything hurts, and you are staring at the spectre of self-doubt, you can find a bit more strength deep inside you, if you look closely enough." – Hal Higdon

Hal is a runner and writer regularly contributing to the US editions of Runner's World with articles on training for marathons and shorter distance races. Had he been an ultra-runner I am sure he would have said '*you can find a lot more strength deep inside you*'.

I continue to build on my history of having done plenty of stuff outside my comfort zone as this post from my blog in 2015 shows.

Making deposits in the fortitude bank.

When you are out on the moors your mind can do strange things. On Christmas day 2015 I went for a run over Bodmin Moor, it was very windy and wet, the visibility was poor, and the ground was waterlogged. I decided it would be sensible to stick to a route I knew and one that didn't offer the opportunity of falling into any bogs. I set off with the plan of running south along the east side of Davistow Moor, skirting around the bog to pass to the north of Buttern Hill and Bray Down, then heading towards Leskernick Hill, where there are the remains of a Bronze Age settlement, before heading back along a fairly straight line north north west. Or, if the wind had died down, climb up to the top of High Moor and head back from there.

On the way the weather cleared briefly, and I spotted a valley in the distance ahead that I had not been along before. Not the time to go exploring I said to myself, I'll stick to my planned route. Twenty minutes later I was well on the way to the valley, it was lovely and did afford some shelter from the wind, the bad weather had closed in again by then. When I reached the head of the valley, I wasn't quite sure where I was and did wonder how I had got there when I quite clearly didn't intend going there. I knew I couldn't be far from somewhere I'd recognize so I just kept running. That is one of the great things about being an ultrarunner, if you are lost you can just keep running until you find yourself, that applies both physically and mentally. Eventually I spotted some trees ahead that I recognised, I have a great affinity with trees I'm better at recognizing trees than remembering people's names, so I knew where I was. Or rather I didn't, but I knew how to get somewhere where I would know where I was. I was a little further south than I had intended going, but it wouldn't take long to get to Leskernick Hill, so I was soon back on course.

I love running over Leskernick Hill among the remains of the Bronze Age settlement, there are no signs there to say what it is, but you can clearly make out the outlines of houses and boundary walls. I ran along thinking about what it must have been like all those thousands of years ago and wondering what the moor looked like then. I was navigating on autopilot, it's not difficult, up over the hill then bear left at the bottom. I realised I'd probably gone too far left so corrected by going right. Unfortunately, I didn't recognise where I was. The map case was splattered with rain so I couldn't read the map clearly, the sensible thing would have been to stop get my glasses and the compass out of my rucksack (that's why I carry them), but I didn't. I ran around for a bit not really knowing where I was until I realised that instead of coming down the north side of Leskernick I had somehow come down the east side and was heading in the wrong direction. A quick about turn and I was soon heading in the right direction although I was a little nervous until I was on top of a hill when the gloom lifted and I could see the radio mast near the Davidstow cheese factory; yes, I was heading in the right direction.

When you are heading over fairly featureless ground it's difficult to get the navigation spot on and I drifted too far north so had to head back south again to get around the end of the bog which is just above the source of the river Fowey. Not what you really want to do at the end of a long run, but then there is nothing you can do about it other than run that extra bit.

I do think these sorts of run are great mental training. To start with you learn that if you switch off it is very easy to go the wrong way without realising it, so in a race concentrate on making sure you know where you are going. But more importantly it increases your fortitude (noun 1. mental and emotional strength in facing difficulty). I went wrong and had to run a few extra miles when I didn't really want to, but I had no choice there was no other way out of it. Okay it was only a relatively minor thing, but it added to that bank of experience. Things go wrong, you arrive at a checkpoint in a race thinking you have almost finished only to discover that you have got quite a few more miles to do, what are you going to do? You can either sit down and cry (doesn't look good on the CV) or think I can handle that; I've done that sort of thing loads of times before. Sometimes I get lost on purpose so I can add a little more to the balance in the fortitude bank.

I get lost in a safe way and would suggest that you do. I discovered the technique by accident early on in my trail running career thanks to Runners' World. There was a description in the magazine of a route, called the Rhinefield Roundabout, in the New Forest. A few weeks later I had to go to a conference in Bournemouth so thought that on the way back to Sussex I would stop off in the New Forest and run the route which was mainly on tracks around Rhinefield House. There was a sketch map of the route in the magazine and a warning not to rely on it and to take the appropriate Ordnance Survey map. It didn't look complicated, so I ignored the advice and just took the page out of the magazine.

I got lost and after a while had absolutely no idea where I was on the sketch. I did notice that the area was enclosed on all sides with roads that formed a square, so I ran in a straight line until I found a road, ran along it until I knew which road it was and worked out how to get back to where I had parked my car. A 14-mile run turned into a 22-mile outing. Now when I plan a getting lost exercise, I look for somewhere that is boxed in by obvious features. I'll say it again, the great thing about being an ultra runner is that you can just run until you find yourself both physically and mentally. I have also learnt that in some places that are featureless you can find yourself going around in big circles, Dartmoor is good, for that so I always carry a map and compass (at the very bottom of the bag on getting lost exercises). I also have the OS Locate app on my phone, which works on GPS so doesn't need a phone signal, it gives you a fully accurate grid reference; great for finding where you are on the map.

As well as all the things you can control, training, equipment, mental attitude etc you also, at times, need another element - luck. I had plenty of that in the 2018 Kalahari Augrabies Extreme Marathon. The legendary ultra-runner, Bruce Fordyce, (9 times winner of the 56-mile Comrades Marathon in South Africa) often says it is better to start a race slightly undertrained and slightly overweight than the other way around.

Unfortunately, I arrived at my race very undertrained and considerably overweight. Not ideal. I will spare you the details of the things that transpired to get in the way of my training. They are not important – they are just excuses.

I wasn't feeling confident when I arrived at the Augrabies Falls Lodge for the race briefing and kit check. Not a good place to be not feeling confident that is – the Augrabies Falls Lodge is a wonderful place to be. By the time I reached the start line I had turned things around. I was in a positive frame of mind; you have to be to succeed at these types of events. I knew what challenges lay ahead and had heaps of experience of overcoming challenges, this book is all about those. My active lifestyle means that I have a particularly good level of fitness at any time. So, why am I talking about luck when I was going to rely on my knowledge and experience? An account of how the week unfolded will explain.

Day 1 - 25km. This is usually the day I feel the worst; my body likes to protest about what I am putting it through. It gives up protesting on day two as it realises the mind is not listening. This year day 1 was wonderful, it was like a stroll in the park. It was relatively cool, and I went very conservatively. It was a stroll in the park, the Augrabies Falls National Park.

Day 2 – 35km. This is when the serious work starts, but it is just a question of managing things well, so you stay hydrated and in good condition. That happened to an extent this year, but I started to get severe back pain after about 25km and the temperature rose to over 40°C. I finished the stage in some distress.

Day 3 – 38km. I had recovered well overnight and developed a series of stretches to help ease the back pain. The day was relatively cool with a nice breeze. I had a good day and got into camp in a reasonable condition.

Day 4 – 78km. This is the big one, the day everyone fears. This was the day that I thought was going to be my biggest problem. However, I had heard that it was forecast to be unusually cool which gave me hope. It was cool for most of the day and I got through without any problems except the back pain. I don't like taking pills, but I sought out the medics and was happy to take some painkillers to ease it a little. Being in the Kalahari in the moonlight is a wonderful experience.

That was the lucky bit – having a cool long day. Had it been hot I probably would have been toast.

Day 5 – rest day. Rest and refuelling for the marathon+ stage.

Day 6 – 48km. The temperature had shot back up and reached 44°C. I took it steady and was please to get through it.

Day 7 - 26km. This should have been a formality, it is only 26km, however, the temperature was high right from the start. It was tough, but finishing was in no doubt. I think the Kalahari just wanted me to know that I had been extremely lucky to have finished after having been stupid enough to turn up ill-prepared.

The Kalahari was kind to me, we have been friends for a long time. Those hot days were thrown in to let me know, in no uncertain terms, that I will not get away with it again if I have the temerity to disrespect her and turn up in an unfit condition.

*A word of warning; conquer is probably the wrong word to use in extreme environments, particularly in deserts. Being macho and going all guns blazing is asking for trouble, you need to be in harmony with your environment. Push hard when the conditions allow, then back off when things get more extreme. Respect the desert and she will look after you. Disrespect her and she will crush you.

The beginning

The beginning for me was in the back bedroom of my grandfather's house, 39 Eltisley Avenue, Cambridge on the afternoon of 26th June 1954 when I was born. My mother was going to have strawberries and cream that afternoon; however, severe contractions put paid to that; strawberries have been a birthday tradition ever since. My running adventures did not start until forty years later, which was sometime during the early summer of 1994. I do have some earlier vague memories of egg and spoon races at primary school and some more vivid and painful memories of cross-country runs at grammar school. During my final years at school I was fairly successful at avoiding these causing my PE teacher to state in my school report "Edward's spasmodic appearances leave little room for comment." I think his comments would have been more forthright had he known that on the rare occasions I could not avoid the ordeal I, and a few others, stopped in the woods and smoked cigarettes until the rest of the class returned and we joined the back of the group for the short run back to school. My avoidance of all forms of vigorous exercise, except for the occasional dash to catch a train, lead to an increasing girth and deteriorating health until a visit to the doctor's surgery in 1994 and some chilling words from my appropriately named GP, Dr Stern; "Edward, change your diet and get some exercise, or you may not get to see your children grow up". That was a seminal moment for me, and I set about improving my lifestyle; fruit & vegetables and wholefoods became my new friends replacing saturated fats, biscuits and pastries. Unfortunately, I have not been blessed with an athletic body, for me just looking at a biscuit puts on a couple of kilos. Mesomorph in spades tending to endomorph is my body type, not ideal for a runner and definitely not ideal for an ultra-runner. The change in my eating habits was the start of my journey towards becoming vegetarian and eventually following a vegan diet. Unfortunately, it took a lot longer for exercise to be embraced with affection and it was a rather painful journey. Fortunately, I had given up smoking a few years earlier before my first daughter was born.

Despite the dreadful memories of cross-country running at school I decided that running would have to be my exercise of choice as it didn't involve being part of a team or finding a partner to play against or booking a court, and it didn't require any skill. It was simple, but it certainly wasn't easy.

Running is real and relatively simple…but it ain't easy.
--Mark Will-Weber, author and runner

More importantly it was something I could do on my own, in secret and away from any critical eyes. I did not know then that running, unlike most other sports which require skill, allows ordinary people to achieve extraordinary things. I bought a pair of trainers and a track suit and headed off with the dogs to Great Wood near Battle, which was close to where I was then living. The plan was to walk into a quiet part of the woods, where I could do some running unseen, then walk back to car. That plan almost worked; I did find a quiet part of the woods where I would be unobserved, but the running didn't amount to much as after only a relatively few steps a shortness of breath and a racing heart forced me to stop. It was at that point that I fully realised it was absolutely vital to pursue an active life and get fit. I also realised that it would take time, a lot of time. I did not realise at that point what a totally life changing journey I was embarking on or that it would eventually lead me into the Kalahari and ultra-marathon greatness.

Even the longest journey starts with a single step. [This saying appears in many forms and is usually attributed to Lao-tzu, a Chinese philosopher -The Way of Lao-tzu (604 BC - 531 BC). A more accurate translation from the original Chinese would be 'The journey of a thousand miles begins beneath one's feet'; even more apt.

I returned to the car with my enthusiasm a little dented, but my determination strengthened, which was fortunate as the next visit to Great Wood also only produced a few steps of running, as did the next and the next until gradually those few steps became a whole circuit of the woods and I felt confident to run in parts of the wood where I'd be seen by other dog-walkers. I also discovered that track suits are not designed to run in, non-runners and actors running in TV series wear track suits, real runners wear shorts or leggings, some even wear shorts over leggings. About three months later I started to feel like a runner, well at least like a jogger, and went to a specialist running shop and bought some running shorts and proper running shoes. Newly kitted-out I hit the road with a fresh enthusiasm and soon ran into a problem; Achilles Tendonitis (now more commonly called Achilles tendinopathy). I knew it was that because I had now skimmed through the running books I'd bought, and they told me that a dramatic increase in training could result in injuries, such as Achilles Tendonitis. The symptoms matched precisely.

When it comes to injuries there are two words that are very well known to runners: rice and peas. No not Jamaican cuisine, but R.I.C.E the mnemonic for Rest, Ice, Compression and Elevation, the treatment for many running injuries and a packet of frozen peas which are an ideal way of applying the Ice part of the treatment. The tendonitis only required rest and ice plus some gentle stretching. Stretching was something I'd been neglecting. The tendonitis was a good thing, because it made me read more about running, work on a sensible training plan and consider a stretching and strength training regime. This, and the fact that I then built up my training and fitness gradually, has, I believe, lead to a fairly injury free running life. A mistake many runners make is to do too much too soon and not give their bodies time to adapt to the more active lifestyle. This often results in injuries which they ignore for far too long before resting and many runners start training again too soon, so the injury occurs again, and they are then in a vicious circle. Recovering from the tendonitis also told me that I was a runner, I was incredibly grumpy when I wasn't running.

The books I was reading, such as The Runner's Handbook by Bob Glover and Jack Shepherd, had all sorts of good advice; perhaps too much as I found it all very confusing. They also contained magic between their covers and one word enchanted me more than any other: 'marathon'. Wikipedia describes a marathon as "*a long-distance running event with an official distance of 42.195 kilometres (26 miles and 385 yards) that is usually run as a road race*". But it is more than that, it is history, it is human endeavour, it is drama, it is accomplishment. Emil Zatopek, one of the greatest runners of all time, in my opinion, said "*If you want to win something, run 100 metres. If you want to experience something, run a marathon.*" Wikipedia goes on to say that the event was instituted in commemoration of the fabled run of the Greek soldier, Pheidippides, a messenger from the Battle of Marathon to Athens, who died after delivering his message. There is a fair amount of controversy surrounding the Pheidippides story, but the commonly held version came about because of a poem by Robert Browning and is the version most people believe. The poem goes on a bit; these are the key lines:

> *Run, Pheidippides, one race more! the meed is thy due!*
> *'Athens is saved, thank Pan,' go shout!" He flung down his shield,*

Ran like fire once more: and the space 'twixt the Fennel-field
And Athens was stubble again, a field which a fire runs through,
Till in he broke: "Rejoice, we conquer!" Like wine thro' clay,
Joy in his blood bursting his heart, he died--the bliss.

The distance of 26 miles and 385 yards, is not based on the distance Pheidippides ran between Sparta and Athens but is derived from the 1908 marathon course that went from Windsor Castle to finish in front of the Royal Box in White City Stadium. Before then the distance was approximately 25 miles. I have run a marathon of that shorter distance, when my club, Hastings Runners, ran the 1908 Hastings Marathon route. I did not count that 'short race' when totting up my marathons to see if I qualified to join the 100-marathon club. I am more than eligible but have never joined. The Hastings Marathon was put on again in the centenary year covering the original route plus a little extra to make it the full 26 miles and 385 yards. I ran that year, somewhat slowly as I had finished the Round Rotherham 50 miles the day before.

I'm getting ahead of myself, at this point in the story I haven't even run any races let alone a marathon. Although it wasn't long before I was planning to enter one. On one of my training runs I ran a distance I'd measured in the car to be 3 miles and that gave me the confidence to think about entering the Hastings 10k. That 3-mile run day was a fantastic achievement for me and I still remember it very clearly, I'm sure no one has been as pleased as me to see the traffic lights at Flimwell on the A21, which was where the run ended. They have now been replaced by a roundabout. Training then began in earnest for the 10k which was in about three months' time. I followed a training plan from a booklet enclosed in a Runner's World magazine and all went well. It felt good to be mixing with real runners on race day and even better to finish the event in 48 minutes and 44 seconds; nowhere near last as I had feared. The next month I ran the Ashford 10k just over a minute faster and followed that the following month with the Hastings Half marathon which I ran in 1 hour 42 minutes and 46 seconds. I was now hooked on racing and chasing PBs (personal bests). The great thing about being relatively new to running is that PBs are reasonably easy to achieve as fitness levels improve. Almost every race saw a new PB unless it was a particularly hilly course. I now view 'personal bests' as strange things, they are something you try extremely hard to achieve then, when you have it, you do not value it, you want something better, even if that is only by a few seconds. Of course, my PB days have long gone now, unless I run a distance I've never tackled before.

I was still relatively new at all this and had only just joined a club, Hastings Runners, a very friendly bunch, from whom I learnt a lot and received a great deal of encouragement. I loved the club events like the Pier to Pier (Eastbourne pier to Hastings's pier) and the Rye to Hastings. I did not get to training nights very often due to working late and commuting, but it was good to belong to a group of like-minded people. I was starting to feel that I was becoming a runner.

I remember very clearly the exact point at which I became a runner, which is strange because my memories of most things in my life are at best unclear, but mostly non-existent. I can remember the first kiss with Vanessa, my now ex-wife. I know it is a cliché, but it knocked my socks off. I remember very clearly the vision of her on our wedding day. And I can remember seeing both my daughters being born as if it were yesterday, but most of the rest of my life is very unclear. So, it seems strange to me that that I remember the precise point when I became a real runner.

It was on the train from Charing Cross to Etchingham, I can remember the seat I was sitting in, that it was sunny and that I was reading The Runner's Handbook. I had reached chapter 6, The Beginner Marathoner, and these words inspired me "The marathon is the longest and most difficult race most runners ever attempt." I thought marathon runners are real runners; I can do that. I would never sprint 100 metres in under 10 seconds, I could not set the mile record, I was too old and didn't have the right genetic make-up, but for marathon running I just needed true grit. It was a presumptuous assumption, but at that point I was committed, the desire to prove myself as a runner was born. I had taken on the rigours of training as a Chartered Accountant and stood the test of tough professional examinations, so I knew I could take on big challenges.

Since then I had not really thought about that seminal moment until November 2008 when a conversation during the Cornish Marathon brought the memory flooding back. The Cornish is my favourite road marathon (I've run it at least 6 times), it has a relatively small field, is well organised and very friendly. It is a tough event that has a lot of hills in it. Although the hills are not as big as those you will encounter in the Snowdonia Marathon there are a lot of them, and the cumulative height gain is greater.

About five miles into the race there is a nice downhill section that is a welcome relief. I caught up with another runner and commented that it was great to be running downhill. She replied, "Yes, I like the downhill bits because I can go faster and feel like a real runner." "You are a real runner," I said, "you are running a marathon therefore you are a runner." "Compared to the people up front I am slow," she replied, "I am not like them, they are real runners." I again said, "You are running a marathon therefore you are a real runner, only a very few people can run a marathon even at a very slow pace; amongst runners you are one of the elites." We ran on chatting about various races, running in general and the Cornish marathon. I soon realised that there was something special about this person and that I had not got the full picture. "How many marathons have you run I asked." "This is my 78th" was the stunning reply. Not a real runner indeed.

'*O would some power the giftie gie us to see ourselves as others see us.*' Robert Burns,

The Cornish marathon has always thrown up surprises. In 2007 just after the start I was running along chatting to a stranger when we reach the first climb. "You go on" he said, "with my chest I find hills difficult." Thinking that perhaps he had asthma or was suffering from an infection I said, "What's the problem?" "I have lung cancer" was his reply. He was starting another course of chemotherapy the following day and wanted to get a good run in while he still had the chance. What a great positive approach to life that guy had, there was no way I could have pulled out that day. No matter how sore and tired my legs felt I had to keep going, I would have been ashamed to do otherwise thinking about him struggling up all those hills in what is probably the toughest road marathon in the UK.

But I have digressed, more about marathons later. On that train I decided to change my life entirely. At the time I did not realise how dramatic that would be, but I knew it would be a definitive change. The fact that I wrote this section in Mossel Bay, South Africa, in the sunshine overlooking the bay with the mountains behind illustrates the point: a long way from the commuter land of East Sussex and office life of London. Other parts of the book were written in different locations in

South Africa, in Cornwall and Singapore, in an old mill in Spain, in my tent on Dartmoor, in Scotland and on a boat moored on the Fal estuary.

Although the change was dramatic it took a long time to come into effect, on the train something in my mind changed like a switch, but it took a long, long time for my body to adapt and catch up. Years of idleness, poor eating, lack of exercise and generally being a slob cannot be reversed overnight just because you have read a book and said yes, I can do that. The body needs time to heal and to adapt.

Like with most things I had to serve my apprenticeship, start with small steps and build upon each one. It was tough to start with, but I loved it, I loved feeling fitter, being part of a healthy crowd of positive people. I loved being out in the wind and the rain when almost everyone else was slouched in front of the TV. I think I was becoming a little bit addicted.

"Setting a goal is not the main thing. It is deciding how you will go about achieving it and staying with that plan." -- Tom Landry

I used to keep a record of all my races and proudly displayed the medals, but by the end of 1996 I was running about one race a month, sometimes two, recording them didn't seem important and the medals were consigned to a drawer. I now only keep medals and mementoes for marathons and races beyond that distance. The marathon medals are in a drawer, but the medals for ultras are proudly displayed and the mementoes from multi-day races have pride of place. Now to me recording race times seems to miss the point, what is more important is the depth of the experience. That might be the stunning scenery, an interesting conversation, a word of encouragement, someone helping you or you helping someone else. So much happens in a race that to reduce it just to something that can be measured by a stopwatch I think is wrong. To paraphrase Lisa Jackson author of *Your Pace or Mine?* and the proud finisher of 25 marathons in last place. It is not a good time that is important, but the good time you had. Lisa is a member of the 100-marathon club; her book is a great read.

My training at this point just consisted of running and trying to go a little further or faster. That was enough to start with because, as I was getting fitter and slimmer, I was setting new PBs quite regularly, but eventually they became hard to come by. Now that I'd lost a lot of weight, I felt a little bit more confident about going to a gym. Although I still found it daunting when I went for my induction session; everyone looked so fit. There were some machines I preferred to others, but the instructor who gave me my initial programme seemed to instinctively know to avoid the ones I liked. I persevered and started to enjoy it, but it wasn't the same as being outside. However, I do think those gym sessions helped to improve my overall fitness, particularly core strength, and this has helped me have a relatively injury free running life. Footballers do strength and conditioning training, tennis players do strength and conditioning training, rowers do strength and conditioning training, and sprinters do strength training, but road and trail runners just run and run and wonder why they are always injured.

Those gym sessions also had another benefit. The treadmills all faced a window that looked out over the bowls green, as I jogged along on the treadmill during my warmup, I could look out on the type of life I wanted to avoid and have a very powerful vision of where I did not want to end up in my old age.

My first marathon

After I had been running in earnest for about nine months, I was quite unexpectedly offered the chance to take up a place on an organised trip to run the Boston marathon in its centenary year, 1996. Someone I met through work had booked a place on an organised trip to the Boston Marathon, however she had sustained a serious injury and knew she would not be recovered in time, so I bought her place from her. As it was its centenary year, there was no qualifying time needed to enter, I doubt I would have ever met the qualifying requirements. The Boston Marathon is the world's oldest annual marathon and ranks as one of the best-known road racing events. I couldn't let this chance slip away, but the thought of tackling a marathon so soon was rather daunting. I immediately dug out the Runner's World's booklet and was pleased to see there was a 'get you round' beginner's marathon training plan and looking at it I had plenty of time to train for Boston. It built on the half-marathon training plan and took 12 weeks. I had completed a half-marathon by then and had a lot more than 12 weeks before the event, so I was feeling extremely optimistic. I couldn't believe it; fat, unfit me was going to run in one of the most famous marathons in the world. Runner's World magazine was having a big impact on my life, little did I know then that it would also, a little later, set me on my ultra-marathon course.

Training went well for Boston, although I had a little secret, I was actually training for the New Forest marathon in September 1995. I was aiming to raise a lot of money for charity running the Boston Marathon, I wanted to make sure I was up to the job. I set my sights on running a marathon six months before Boston, so I had time to recover and train some more if things didn't work out. The New Forest Marathon was easy, for the first 20 miles, then I discovered that not all miles are created equal. Mile 21 is at least 50% longer than any of the preceding 20 and by mile 26 things have doubled. And that final 365 yards is pure torture, except for about the last 50 yards where all of a sudden sprinting is the order of the day. I finished in a time of 4 hours 11 minutes and 54 seconds which I was pleased with; my target had been between 4 hours and 4 hours 30 minutes. I was not pleased with the thought of running another marathon in 6 months' time, marathons were hard work, they hurt, you walked funny for a few days afterwards and stairs were a big challenge. Also, your nipples bled; I've now learnt Vaseline or tape will prevent that. But now I knew I could finish the Boston Marathon so set about getting pledges for my chosen charity knowing that, unless there was a disaster, I would be collecting those pledges on my return to the UK. That was in the days before online giving platforms; you asked people to pledge how much they would give on a physical form then, after the event, chased them for the cash. Sometimes collecting the cash was harder work than doing the event.

I was extremely excited about flying to Boston as I hadn't travelled internationally since my early 20s; my wife had a fear of flying so we holidayed in the UK. That trip back in 1976 was to the United States and included a visit to Boston so it was good to be going back. I loved every moment of the Boston trip except for about an hour after the race, but I'll come to that later. I travelled with a group made up of Blackheath Harriers, Bromley vets and a few odd bods like me. I'd run with Bromley Vets a few times, so they weren't complete strangers. I'd also had one outing with Blackheath Harriers which was quite memorable. They have some exceptionally good runners and on the whole are extremely competitive. I was paired up with a young woman who was considered to be my standard. I think she took this to be a bit of an insult and ran like the wind. I didn't know that part of London very well and my only option for finding my way back to the starting point and my car was to not let my 'guide' runner out of my sight, even though she seemed determined to disappear out of view. I wish Strava had been about then, I am sure I would have recorded my fastest speed ever and it would have shown that I maintained it for a long time. The only time I might have bettered it was when I was staying with Phillip Howells, who I had met through the charity Comrades of Children Overseas, and he suggested we go to a local race that evening, only a 5k. When we arrived all I could see was very thin people in singlets warming up at a pace that was as fast as my race pace; it was the county championships and I had to run as hard as I could not to come last. I was third from last.

I don't remember very many details about the trip to Boston, because I was so nervous, except visiting an American Diner and tucking into a big plate of waffles with maple syrup. Great carbo-loading. I do remember marathon day very clearly. We were transported from Boston to Hopkinton, where the race starts, on those iconic yellow American school buses, snow was piled up alongside the road in places, even though it was forecast to be a warm day. When we arrived in Hopkinton, which is a very typical New England town, we were herded into a field for the long wait until the start. I had come prepared and laid out a couple of bin bags on the damp grass and rested. When I opened my eyes, about half an hour later, the field was cram packed with runners all nervously waiting just like I was. When it was time to go, I stripped off my track suit and was then just in my Hasting Runners' vest and shorts which caused the guy next to me to exclaim "I don't believe it! Whatever race you go to there is always a Hastings Runner." He was from Horsham another town in Sussex. You'll find that often in the running world, when you are in amongst many thousands of complete strangers you will be right beside someone that has a connection with you.

The start of the race was incredibly slow, because it was centenary year the numbers of runners was a great deal bigger than usual and the narrow streets at the start were crammed. It took me 25 minutes to reach the start line after the gun went off and when I did it was still a long time before I could start running. It was fortunate that it was a chipped timed race, so my race time would be recorded from when I crossed the start line. Once we were clear of the houses all the men flocked to the side of the route to have a pee. A little while later, when there were some bushes beside the road, the women disappeared for the same reason. We then went about the serious business of running a marathon. There was a party atmosphere and lots of support, so the early miles went past very comfortably indeed. I was starting to take a little bit of strain as I neared the infamous Heartbreak Hill, but the Japanese drummers at the bottom were a massive lift and I was soon at the top and from there it would be a simple run into the finish. It was on this hill, in 1936, defending champion John Adelbert "Johnny" Kelley overtook Ellison "Tarzan" Brown, giving him a consolatory pat on the shoulder as he passed. This gesture renewed the competitive drive in Brown, who rallied, pulled ahead of Kelley, and went on to win—thereby, it was said, breaking Kelley's heart. If you didn't know the story you would wonder, why it was called heartbreak hill because it is not very daunting. Incredibly Kelley last ran the Boston marathon in 1992 aged 84.

"I'm afraid to stop running. I feel too good. I want to stay alive."—Kelley at age 70

The sight of the magnificent Boston buildings was like a magnet and I was fascinated to be running under the type of overhead railway tracks you see in films, passing American diners and seeing yellow cabs. I was pleased with my finish time of 4 hours and 7 minutes and felt as if I could have gone quicker, but that didn't bother me. I'd set out with the intention of enjoying this unique event and enjoy it I did. There was a small fly in the ointment; the baggage truck with my kit in had broken down and had not yet arrived at the finish. Although I was wrapped in a foil blanket, a specially printed Boston marathon one which I still have, I was getting cold. A kind local spectator bought me some soup and gave me his jacket to wear until my bag arrived and I could put on some fresh clothes and my track suit. On the subway ride back to the hotel I felt very tired, but happy and was looking forward to a slap-up meal that evening. I ordered a starter of nachos with cheese and a steak (I wasn't vegan or vegetarian then) but wasn't even able to finish the nachos. American restaurants serve massive portions.

There was very little time for sight-seeing (although I did get to visit the bar that was used in the TV series Cheers) as we flew home on Wednesday (the marathon takes place on Patriots' Day, a Monday) because some of the group wanted to get back with time to rest before running the London marathon on the Sunday. This was when I first realised that there were among the running fraternity some people doing extraordinary things. I thought myself amazing for having completed two marathons in just over six months, here were people running two marathons in a week. I was to discover later that people ran three marathons in three days. A few years later I became one of those people. It used to be possible at the end of October to run the Beachy Head marathon on Saturday, the Snowdonia Marathon on Sunday and the Dublin Marathon on Monday. Unfortunately, this is now not possible as they have changed the dates of two of those marathons. Although it was possible in 2009 to run Beachy Head, Greensands and Dublin; I took full advantage of that opportunity. Things always move on and now we have witnessed feats like Eddie Izzard running 43 marathons in 51 days and then 27 marathons in 27 days and Ben Smith running 401 marathons in 401 days.

I was extremely pleased to have completed the Boston Marathon and even more pleased to have raised a significant amount of money for the charity One World Action. They had organised for a cardboard cut-out of me in running kit to appear at various conferences to aid my fund-raising efforts, which probably put more people off than encouraged. After the marathon this was stored in their offices in the entrance to the ladies' toilet. What a sad end to an illustrious career.

I felt as redundant as the cardboard cut-out. I'd run the most prestigious marathon, so what was left to do? I felt that I had achieved all that I was capable of. What other people were doing (running Boston & London) was beyond me. I have since learnt that it is only your beliefs that can limit your achievements. I moped about for a bit, did a few training runs, half-heartedly, put on some weight, then moped about even more. I lost a lot of my fitness so decided that I should enter a race to have a focus. Nothing ambitious, my Runner's World training booklet was strangely silent on what to do after a marathon, but I'd heard from fellow runners that you need to take time to recover and not do any significant distance for a few months. So, I entered a 10k, the Downland 10k, which started at Lancing College, West Sussex. If you've ever driven past Lancing College, you will know that it is a lovely location and the buildings are beautiful. That wasn't the case on race day, it was tipping it down with rain and you couldn't see much. This was a 10k off-road race, which I and all the other runners slipped and slithered around, the only supporter on the course was a man and his dog. I loved it and realised there was a running life after Boston. Just over a week later I was in Blackpool for a conference and noticed that on one of the evenings there was a 10k race in Poulton-le-Flyde. It wasn't too far to drive so I entered and achieved a personal best, my running mojo was back.

The other significant event that happened that week was going on the Big One, the roller-coaster at Blackpool Pleasure Beach. One of my colleagues at the conference was a huge fan of roller coasters and wanted to go on it, she didn't want to go on her own, so I said I would take her if she couldn't find anyone else to go with. I was desperately hoping she would find someone. She didn't, so on the final day we went down to the Pleasure Beach to ride the Big One. It was drizzling and as we were approaching the funfair, I couldn't see any carriages going around the ride. I was hoping that they didn't operate in the wet. No such luck, we had arrived just before the first ride of the day. As the carriage was slowly going up the first big climb, Emma asked me what other rides I had been on. I had to reply "none" to which she responded, "You idiot." At that point we crested the summit and plunged down the other side. I realised why she thought I was an idiot. The Big One is the UK's tallest & fastest roller-coaster. Had I looked at the brochure I would have read 'Prepare yourself for the first drop which boasts an incline angle of 65 degrees and speeds of up to 87mph; this roller coaster is an experience like no other!' and decided not to experience that thrill first hand thereby avoiding the Pleasure Beach's biggest, fastest and scariest coaster. The information also says 'The Big One is one of the longest roller coasters measuring over a mile in length. Don't forget to smile for your picture near the end of the ride!' The photo shows Emma with a massive smile and me gripping the bar in sheer terror; you can clearly see why it's called a white-knuckle ride.

1996 saw more pbs at 10k, 10-mile, half-marathon and 20-mile, but no more marathons – they were hard work. Well there was one, but that was a club event, as mentioned earlier, Hastings Runners organised a running of the 1908

Hasting Marathon as a handicap event. I couldn't miss that. I was surprised at my handicap start time as I was starting after some of the faster runners in the club and queried it. I was told that those speedsters would struggle with the distance whereas I would maintain my steady pace throughout. The handicap worked well, and we all finished fairly close together, I even overtook some of those speedsters. It's all about horses for courses and choosing your sport. There was a young personal trainer in the gym I used who used to swagger about, impress the ladies, and make us less fit members feel inadequate. He entered the Hastings Half-marathon one year and finish a long way behind me. On my next visit to the gym, I couldn't resist going over to him when he was chatting to a group of women "Hi, Wayne, how did you get on in the half-marathon? You were looking good when I passed you." Petty perhaps, but it felt oh so good. Too much muscle to be an effective runner.

I learnt a lot that year. I learnt that I could achieve big things and there were joys to be had in smaller runs. I also learnt that it is not much fun running a half-marathon in the blistering heat having drunk too much the night before at a wedding. I might have learnt that, but the lesson didn't sink in because I was to do similar things quite a few more times. I have a deep appreciation of the Spanish proverb 'The second time you get kicked by a donkey you learn nothing.'

The Luton marathon, which no longer exists, was best run with a hangover. It was a popular event in its day, possibly because it was the final marathon in the calendar every year, so the last chance to get a fix. It was a three-lap course, mainly though housing estates, so not pleasant. If you were running for a time (no hangover) the first lap was easy, the second a little harder and boring and the final lap hard and tedious. With a hangover the first lap is tortuous and you are totally unaware of your surroundings, the second lap is not too bad and you start to notice your surrounding and on the third lap your hangover is gone, you are feeling great and the finish line comes all too soon. The Luton marathon was also the scene of the bald head incident which led to me buying several wigs as training aids. More about that later.

Memory is very selective and with time the memories of pain and difficulties fade, and the memories of joy and pleasant things grow richer. Perhaps it is because you have paid a high price in terms of pain and suffering that those joys have great value.

"If you want to win something, run 100 metres. If you want to experience something, run a marathon." Emil Zatopek

I didn't realise it then, but immediately after the Boston marathon a little seed had drifted into my brain and was slowly starting to germinate. Those runners who headed back from Boston to run the London marathon kept popping into my thoughts. They seemed, on the outside to be ordinary people, but they were doing extraordinary things. That seed was going to grow into the belief that I too could go beyond the limits of the possible to the impossible.

The only way to discover the limits of the possible is to go beyond them to the impossible.
Arthur C. Clarke

That quote is on the back of the commemorative t-shirt for the 75th Comrades Marathon which took place in the year 2000. I still have that t-shirt.

Moving on

1997 saw me doing lots more running and loving it. I got a place in the London marathon (my third marathon), which was relatively easy to get into then unlike now, and loved the experience, although I will probably never do it again; far too many people and, of course, it is on road which I now try and avoid as much as possible. It is an event that has so much going for it that it should be on most aspiring marathon runners' bucket list. The atmosphere is wonderful, the organisation is exceptionally good, the other runners and the crowds make it an incredibly special experience and to run past such iconic landmarks as the Cutty Sark, Tower Bridge, the Tower of London and the Houses of Parliament, is something to remember for a long time. I have since been back to spectate, support friends and let my children experience the magic. On one occasion I was close enough that I could have reach out and touched Paula Radcliffe as she ran past, there was no barrier.

That is the wonderful thing about running, you can be in the same race as the elites. I will probably never play tennis on Centre Court at Wimbledon, and certainly not in the same tournament as Roger Federer, but I have run in the same race as some of my sporting heroes; Kelly Holmes, Paula Radcliffe, Steve Cram and the legendary Bruce Fordyce, and I have beaten two of those. More about that later. My tally of beating Olympians is two. One of those was in the Kalahari. Before you get the wrong idea of my prowess, I should mention that in 2007 I finished a few places above Burger Lambrechts who represented South Africa in the 2004 Olympics at shot put. At 135kg he is the heaviest competitor to finish the Kalahari Augrabies Extreme Marathon. On the rest day we had a rock throwing contest, my effort was puny compared to Burger's.

Again, after London I was on a bit of a down and was not enjoying my running. My wife and Runner's World came to the rescue (this is the start of it setting me on my ultra-marathon course). Even though she is not a runner Vanessa had been leafing through the most recent edition of Runner's World and said 'This looks like a nice event and passed the magazine over to me. There was an idyllic picture of a couple of swans beside some reeds on a canal. Nice and flat I thought, then I read the caption. Grantham Canal Run – 33 miles." It's 33 miles I can't do that." "You've done marathons," my wife replied, "It's only 7 miles more." I ran the Sevenoaks 7 in 1995 three weeks after the Reading Half, it was tough. Add 7 miles on to a marathon and it's going to be very, very tough. But the marathon seemed a massive challenge once and I conquered it, so why not 33 miles, after all it would be flat. I signed up and started training with enthusiasm; I was loving my running again.

To quote Dizzee Rascal being interviewed on TV by Jeremey Paxton:

You've gotta believe it to achieve it innit

The race started in Nottingham and followed the canal all the way to Grantham and finished in the centre of the town. I was right, running 7 miles after having completed 26 already is very, very tough. Oh, and those swans were not idyllic, they were nesting and aggressive, so we had to give them a wide berth. Never mind the pretty scenery, I just wanted it to end. I was so pleased to see the A1 (how many of us can say that) because I knew, once I'd past under it, there were only two miles to go to the finish. Three years before I couldn't even run a mile, now it was 'only two miles' after having already run 31. What was once an extraordinary achievement was now ordinary.

I learnt a few things that day; I like running off-road, if you keep going the suffering does eventually end, beer tastes wonderful after a long run and I learnt the benefit of having things to motivate you. Seeing the A1 in front of me lifted my spirits and I just worked at getting closer to it, when I passed under it I was so happy - almost home. I did learn a little later that some motivational targets can get you into trouble.

After the Grantham Canal run I didn't suffer the loss of my running enjoyment that I had after the marathons. That extra 7 miles had changed me, I was now a confident runner and knew I'd always be a runner. When I gave up smoking it was a long time before I knew I'd never go back to smoking and considered myself a non-smoker. This was similar, I'd crossed the Rubicon. I was not a fat bloke trying to get fit, I was now someone who just enjoyed running rather than someone who needed to finish races and improve on pbs. I was a runner and a runner for life.

I still entered races, and I still trained to get better times, but I also just went out to run for pure enjoyment. I finished off 1997 by running the New Forest marathon again in September improving on my time and having a much more comfortable run than 2 years before. I've since learnt that when my sister saw me finish the New Forest marathon in 1995 she thought I was about to die. I always look bad when I am running, which is why people are always asking me if I'm all right. I ran the New Forest marathon one more time in 2000, that year I didn't finish, and I was pleased that I didn't. It was a training run in preparation for the London to Brighton race, I wasn't feeling on form and was struggling. I could have finished, but at what cost? It was a training run designed to build me up not break me down, so I stopped at 16 miles and waited to get picked up. I was pleased with my running maturity.

1998 was a year of enjoying club races and a few others with the Shakespeare marathon near the beginning of the year, the Luton marathon at the end and another run along the Grantham canal in between. It was also the year that I learnt that some motivational targets could get you in trouble. I was determined to get a pb for the Pier-to-Pier run (Eastbourne to Hasting Pier, about 16 miles), but was a bit concerned when I caught up with club mate Arlene as she was always a lot faster than me in training. Had I gone out too fast? I stayed with Arlene and told her that I was aiming for a pb, but felt I was going a bit too fast. “Stick with me” she said and “I'll get you there.” And that is what I did, it was hard work and I was running better than I had ever done before; it felt good. We didn't talk much, I could only manage one-word answers, but Arlene chatted a bit and offered words of encouragement. Running through Bexhill was good because there was fair bit of support there, but I kept worrying about Galley Hill, the only real climb on the whole course. I worked out a plan, if Arlene pulled out a lead on the hill, I'd drop in behind her concentrate on her shapely backside and that would drag me to the top. It worked like a dream and I was only a few paces behind her at the top, When I caught her up going down the other side she said, “That was nice of your wife to turn up and support.” I had to admit to her that I'd been too focused to notice. I didn't admit what I had been focused on. When we neared the finish, Arlene said she was going to go flat out and urged me to try and stay as close to her as possible. We flew over the line and I had smashed my pb, I was so happy. When my wife arrived in the car to take me home, I apologised for not saying hello on the hill and explained I was totally focused. She gave me that look and said “Yes, I know what on” before smiling at me. Both my daughters have inherited ‘the look’.

Many female runners also use this technique, I'm reliably informed by female friends that male triathletes have more shapely bums than men who only run. My physio, when treating me for an ankle injury, left me in doubt that I was lacking in the gluteus maximus department. She was much more complementary about my quads.

1998 was also the year I first heard about the Comrades marathon in South Africa. It's not a standard marathon, it is 56 miles long. I was enchanted and once again thought "I can do that". At that point I didn't realise that it was such an amazing event with a rich history and so many inspiring stories. I also didn't know that it would change my life forever and for the better. Back in those days ultra-running was not well known, there were very few events and it was something done by gnarly types with beards who wore skimpy shorts and singlets or Americans with no shirts on. There were no Runners' World training plans for ultras, so I had to search far and wide for training information. I eventually found a booklet produced by the Road Runners Club called 'International Ultra Training'. It consisted of 90 pages of small type and was made up of chapters by ultra notables such as Hilary Walker, Bruce Fordyce and Bernd Heinrich. His book 'Why we run – A natural History' is well worth a read. Each chapter of International Ultra Training consisted of each individual's views on training and for different events. The chapter written by Bruce Fordyce, the Comrades King, was called 'Preparation for racing the Short Ultra'. I chose to ignore the advice in this chapter as I wasn't aiming at racing, I just wanted to finish. I did ponder over the title, 56 miles – a short ultra? I read the book from cover to cover and descended into deep despair. Each chapter started with words like "I'd run 54 marathons in six years, winning 28, coming second in 11 ... or ... has a formidable record over the ultra distance in the United States. In his first ultra he set a new US 100km best.'

Eventually I looked at the book again and seized on the chapter by Gary Cantrell. In the introductory paragraph were these magic words, "Unlike the majority of the other contributors to this booklet he is not an elite performer.'

Gary's approach to training was quite simple "...beginning ultramarathoners need only make two adjustments to their normal running program. Firstly, they need to adapt to a slower pace. Second, they must consider the weekly "long" run as the core of their preparations." I thought I can run slower and my long run was the core of my marathon training. So, I took Gary's advice and adjusted my marathon training plan. Gary also said, "The runner going for a first-time fifty-miler should have done at least two or three runs in the 35-40-mile range over the preceding couple of months." I measured back three weeks from the date of the Comrades and pencilled a 40-mile run into my diary, I then pencilled another one in three weeks before that. The final thing was to work out when to start training if I was going to add 10% to my long run distance each week. I had plenty of time and the Luton marathon at the end of the year would provide my qualifying time for Comrades, so I was all set. To be allowed to start the Comrades Marathon you have to have run a sub 5-hour marathon within twelve months from the start of the race. I knew the time would not be a problem, I just needed to make sure I ran a marathon in that period. Your qualifying times dictated whereabouts you start. The fast runners near the front and the slowest at the back.

This quote from William Hutchinson Murray has always resonated with me.

"Until one is committed, there is hesitancy, the chance to draw back, always ineffectiveness. Concerning all acts of initiative (and creation), there is one elementary truth that ignorance of which kills countless ideas and splendid plans: that the moment one definitely commits oneself, then Providence moves too. All sorts of things occur to help one that would never otherwise have occurred. A whole stream of events issues from the decision, raising in one's favour all manner of unforeseen incidents and meetings and material assistance, which no man could have dreamed would

have come his way. I learned a deep respect for one of Goethe's couplets:

Whatever you can do or dream you can, begin it.
Boldness has genius, power and magic in it!

When I find a quote I like to do some research into it and you usually find some interesting background material. W H Murray was a Scottish climber and the quote comes from his 1951 book The Scottish Himalayan Expedition. He was an active campaigner to protect wilderness areas of Scotland from ill-considered development. In 1961, a major success was the defeat of plans to build a hydroelectric scheme in Glen Nevis. 55 years later I enjoyed the unspoilt beauty of Glen Nevis during my wild camping trip in 2016. Thank you, W H Murray and the others that joined in that campaign. The adage 'Blessed is he who plants trees under whose shade he will never sit' in action.

Once I had committed to running the Comrades marathon all manner of incidents and assistance came my way. I discovered that the Shakespeare marathon was on the same weekend as I was due to do a 26-mile training run, and that the Compton 40-mile Downland challenge event fitted in with one of my planned longest runs. I found that the road from my house to Pevensey Bay and then on into Eastbourne had a pavement almost all the way, and where it didn't there was an old, little used road running parallel to the main road, so I had a safe long run route. I did get to know the early miles of that route very, very well. I also found a club member, Brian Kirkdale, who had run Comrades before and was running it again in 1999. Unfortunately, he had moved away from the area, so we couldn't train together, but I did get some great advice from him. More about Brian later, he played a significant role in my ultramarathon journey.

By the end of 1998 I had gone from a non-runner in 1994 to having completed six marathons and two ultras so I was feeling confident that if I stuck to my training I would be ready for Comrades in 1999, although I knew there was no guarantee that I would finish. When you have knocked out quite a few marathons you know you can finish, with Comrades a finish is always in doubt. I was in the right place mentally; excited and nervous in equal measures and had a great deal of respect for the challenge.

Training went well, there was an inevitability about it, Run in the evening Monday, Tuesday, Wednesday & Friday, gym on Saturday morning then a long run during the day on Sunday. One of the midweek runs was a speed session, normally a tempo run. I had read that it was important not to neglect speed work when training for distance. Distance makes you slow, at least one speed session helps arrest that process. The words of Emil Zatopek would pop into my mind *"Why should I practice running slow? I already know how to run slow. I want to learn to run fast."* I kept reminding myself that I was a completer not a competer so slow running was okay. Every Sunday I'd run a little further than I did the week before. I ran races when they fitted in with the schedule, most notably the Shakespeare Marathon, Luton Marathon and the Compton 40. I just stuck to the plan and eventually the plan said "taper"; which meant reduce the amount of running so that I would be rested and fresh for the race.

Another great Hal Higdon quote; "*Rested, Refreshed, and Ready to run, the three Rs of peak performance.*"

That sounds as if everything was easy, it wasn't. Work and family commitments got in the way so that running plans had to be changed, I had off days when I had to give myself a good talking to and I missed a few sessions. However, there are two sayings that I think are particularly relevant to running.

You can have
results
or
excuses
you can't have both
If it is important, you will find a way

If not, you will find an excuse

For many years those saying were written large and fixed to my office wall, now they are fixed in my head. They were on the wall because I remembered something from school; a passage from Belshazzar's Feast - And a finger of a hand came forth and wrote upon the wall 'You have been weighed in the balance and found wanting'. I didn't want to be found wanting.

The Comrades Marathon

I tried to read as much as I could about the Comrades marathon, but there was little material available at that time. Now there are lots of books, including one with my name in; 'Comrades Marathon – Highlights and heroes 1921 - 1999' was published in 2000 and is a history of the race in the 20th century. The first half of the book is an account of the race from its humble beginnings in 1921 when there were 16 finishers to 1999, by which time the number of finishers had grown to 11,275 and Comrades had become established as the world's greatest ultra-marathon. The second half consists of an alphabetical list of all the people who have finished the Comrades marathon in those years. I feel honoured and humbled to be listed alongside such great runners as Arthur Newton, Wally Haywood, Bruce Fordyce, Alan Robb, Frith van der Merwe and Lindsay Weight. There are about 65,000 names in that list, when you think that in the mid-80s the number of finishers was close to 10,000 each year and slightly over that in the 90's you can imagine how many people have run it many times.

So, other than the advice I'd received from Brian Kirkdale, my knowledge of the race was limited, as was my knowledge of South Africa. It was the start of a great adventure when I boarded the plane at Heathrow to fly to Johannesburg. I very soon learnt that South Africa is a country of massive differences after I visited Sandton, an expensive shopping area and Soweto, where I was taken to a shanty town. I then flew to Durban to rest for a few days, pick up my number at the Expo and get into the right frame of mind to tackle this enormous challenge. Brian had been very insistent that I take the bus trip along the route the day before the race, he was adamant that it was something every novice should do. He was right. It was a long drive in an old school bus that sometimes struggled on the hills. The enormity of the task became truly clear which would make me cautious in the early part of the race, going too fast early in the race is the downfall of many runners. Presumably, they had not had the benefit of the bus trip. Even though 1999 was a 'down' run there were still some noticeably big hills to climb. Each year the run alternates direction, one year it goes from Durban to Pietermaritzburg' which is about 650 metres above sea level, so an 'up' run and the next year it starts in Pietermaritzburg and finishes at sea level in Durban, the 'down' run. The bus trip was also an opportunity to talk to other 'novices' and learn that they were just as nervous as I was.

The next bus trip was at 3am the next morning, when we were taken to the start. Fortunately, the pick-up point was just at the back of my hotel, so I didn't have to go far as I'm sure I would have got lost in the dark. It was warm and humid in Durban, but by the time we had arrived in Pietermaritzburg it was cold and still dark. Brian had advised me to wear extra clothes over my kit that I wouldn't mind throwing away, so I didn't feel the cold and to take a plastic bin bag in case it was raining. That was good advice, although it did seem strange standing in the dark, in the cold layered up putting sunblock on. The sun would soon be up, and I would be out in it for a long time.

The atmosphere at the start of the Comrades is something quite exceptional, everyone is jostling to get into the relevant start pen and dealing with nerves and excitement in their own way. Some people are talking loudly to their friends, other people are singing, the Zulu songs are particularly moving, announcements are blaring out over the sound system and all this is mixed in with the smell or wintergreen, arnica and other ointments. We shuffled forward occasionally as people press towards the front, then the dividers between the pens were removed and we all surged forward then came to a stop. As is the tradition Shosholoza, Chariots of Fire, the South African

National anthem and Max Trimborn's recorded cockcrow were played before the gun was fired for the start of the race. We all shuffled forward, and it was some time before we could start jogging, I tried to go carefully as it was still dark, and I did not want to trip, but I was getting carried along by the crowd.

It wasn't long before I started getting warm, I took off my long-sleeved shirt and handed it to one of the children lining the road waiting for all the discarded gear. I had heard that there would be a lot of congestion at the first couple of water stations, so I'd taken a water bottle with me which I would give away to someone along the way; water stations are at approximately every 2km, so I would not need it once the field had thinned out. I was running comfortably and now that I was moving the nerves had died down, it was a lovely warm morning and I was enjoying running through Africa. A completely different experience to running either Boston or London because of the views and the multi-cultural make-up of the field of runners. One very emotional point was passing the Ethembeni School for children with disabilities. The children line the route outside their school and shout encouragement to all the runners, high fiving those passing near them. It brought tears to my eyes and I ran a considerable way crying. Every year it has been a very emotional experience and every year I have cried. On my fifth running I was determined not to cry and almost made it except I spotted a young girl in a wheelchair who was at the back of a group of children who had moved forward to greet all the runners and to get the pennants that a radio station had given to the runners just before that spot. I went over to her and gave her my pennant; she looked at me and said, "God bless you sir". I ran on crying freely.

The first significant hill, Inchanga, wasn't until almost halfway, but I was still feeling fresh and just chugged up it to be rewarded with stunning views of the Valley of a Thousand Hills. The halfway point at Drummond has a big gantry over the road with a massive sign saying 'halfway' it is a wonderful thing to see and that part of the course is lined 6 or more deep with noisy spectators. Their enthusiasm almost lifts you off your feet and propels you forward. There is a small climb out of Drummond before reaching Arthur's Seat. This is a niche cut into the bank of the cutting at the site of the wall of honour and is reputed to have been a favourite resting spot of the legendary Arthur Newton, 5 times winner of the Comrades Marathon in the 1920s. Legend has it that runners who pay tribute to Arthur as they pass by placing flowers in the niche and greet Arthur with "good morning sir", will enjoy a strong second half of the race. I'm not at all superstitious, but I was not going to take any chances, I picked a flower well before I got there (a wise precaution because the roadside near his seat had been picked bare by all the runners before me – thanks for the advice Brian) placed it in the niche and said "good morning sir" loud and clear.

I ran on feeling very relaxed and enjoying the experience, the camaraderie of my fellow runners and the support of the crowd was fantastic. The water points were absolutely brilliant, staff by enthusiastic people handing out sachets of water or Powerade with flat coke also available and all sorts of food, bananas, biscuits, chocolate even salted boiled potatoes. I would take extra and give some to the Africa children waiting up the road just for such handouts. Running doesn't get better than this, but soon I was starting to get hot and tired; I made copious use of the sponges they had and the big troughs of iced water to soak them in. Things were still okay, it was tough, but I was in control and keeping to my schedule. Then suddenly the world changed, everything was different; I was deeply tired, completely empty, my body just wouldn't work. All I wanted to do was stop. Having run several marathons, I was used to being tired and wanting to give up, I knew that my mind would think up loads of reasons why it was okay to stop, and I knew that I needed to have an arsenal of good reasons why I should keep going to counter those negative thoughts. But this was nothing like a marathon; this was the big time, big pain, big despair, and big trouble. In the marathon people hit the wall at about 20 miles, in an ultra like Comrades the wall is at about 40 miles. You do not hit it, it falls on you; one minute I was okay the next I was flattened, I had no idea how I was going to make the next few steps let alone run 20 more kilometres.

I forced my way onwards, my joints felt like rusted-up hinges, it was a Herculean effort just to take one step and I had to take lots of them. It was then that I realised that the Comrades Marathon, with a field of thousands of runners and hundreds of thousands of spectators is a very lonely place. At that point on the road between Pietermaritzburg and Durban at a place called Fields Hill I had to look deep inside myself to find the answer to the question "Can I carry on?" It was about 30C and the sun was relentless, but I remember it being a very dark and lonely place. I found my answer, I was going to go on I was going to finish the Comrades Marathon; all I needed was a plan.

I was now at the 19k to go mark. In South Africa they show the distance left to go not how far you have come like they do in the UK. My plan was to make it to the next kilometre marker then the next and the next until I reached 10k to go. I knew that I had lots of time, I would be well within the 11-hour cut off, (the cut-off has now been extended to 12 hours) and that I had run many, many 10k races; I could manage 10k. If I had to, I would crawl that last 10k. Very gradually the kilometre signs got closer and closer to the 10k marker, then I was there. What a fantastic relief to see 10k to go. The euphoria was short lived as the realisation hit me that I had to actually run those 10 kilometres, each and every one of them.

They were a little easier than I had expected, and I eventually reached the Kingsmead Stadium and crossed the finish line. I did not feel anything, no joy, no relief at finishing, no sense of achievement, just nothing, a complete emptiness. Later a deep sense of fulfilment, satisfaction and contentment would grow within me, getting stronger as each day passed.

Making that decision to keep going changed me forever, I moved into another world where I would expect more from life and expect more of myself. It gave me a rock-like confidence that would help with all sorts of things from public speaking to taking on sporting challenges. Yes, I am still nervous, unsure and a little shy on the outside, but deep down I know I am an ultra-runner that had to look deep inside and found the answer. I found the fact that when it was tough it was me alone, no one else that could decide to go on or give up very empowering. I was totally in control of my life. Life might throw all sorts of things at me, but it was up to me and me alone to decide how I reacted to them. I might be dealt a bad hand of cards; however, I could still win if I played them well. No one else could mess my life up. The Comrades Marathon has become a colourful thread running through my life, which has opened up many rewarding experiences and relationships. It would not be too strong a metaphor to describe the Comrades as my spine.

It was also my entry into the ultra-runners' world where there is a special understanding between people. I know that they too have been in a dark, lonely place, looked deep inside themselves and found an answer. I know in a way that only someone who has been there themselves can know. Those are my words and my thoughts; I was surprised therefore to find the following extracts on the Comrades Marathon website many years later. They may have been there earlier, but I only found them recently.

"This then is the point each runner, from the first to the last, must pass if he is to arrive in Durban on his own feet. It is here, stripped of any of society's false privileges, that he finds no hiding place, no shelter of convenience. Face to face with himself he must look deep inside." "These miles," wrote George Sheehan, "will challenge everything he holds dear, his value system, his lifestyle. They will ask nothing less than his view of the universe."

'Later I join my friend Tim Noakes as he reflects: "I know why this is all necessary," he says "what common bond unites all Comrades runners. It is the need to look for the mountains in life. Skill, you see, is not our requirement, nor has your race got anything to do with winning or losing. These are the spoils of other lesser games, unable to transport you to the places we have been."'

When I finished that Comrades down run, I had to do almost a lap of the ground to reach the finish line and once I had crossed it was led into the middle of the stadium. To get to the changing areas and other facilities I had to pass over a scaffolding bridge that have been erected over where the finishers were running, or I had to complete a circuit almost all the way around the outside of the stadium. I stood at the bottom of the bridge totally lacking in energy and with legs that were so stiff they would not move. I was holding on to the handrail trying to pull myself up when I heard the announcer say "Give a warm welcome to Steve Cram* "I thought he was coming to the microphone to give an interview, but the announcer continued "he's just coming into the stadium to finish" I sprinted up the stairs and watched my sporting hero run underneath me. It was an incredible moment I, an ex-fat bloke, had beaten an Olympic Silver medallist, Word Championship Gold medallist and someone who in a magical 19-day period in 1985 broke 3 World Records.

Comrades 1999

Edward Chapman 9:38:42

Steve Cram 9:47:02

A little while later I met Brian Kirkdale in the international hospitality area; he congratulated me and said, "You realise that you are not a complete Comrades runner until you have also finished an up run." I won't tell you what I said to Brian, it wasn't very polite. I had absolutely no intention of ever running Comrades again; that one finish was to be the pinnacle of my running career, but Brian and Steve made it otherwise.

Brian's words kept running through my mind as did all the fantastic memories I had of Comrades day. I wanted to go back and run an up run, but how could I break the news to my wife that she would have to suffer many more months of my ultra-marathon training. Later that year there was an article in a running magazine about why Steve had run Comrades and about the charity he co-founded with Jim Panton. It ended by saying 'Why not join Steve's team and run the Comrades marathon to raise money for his charity Comrades of Children Overseas (COCO)?' I left the magazine, open at the relevant page, on the sofa and hoped. I was not disappointed, later that day my wife said "Why don't you run as part of Steve Cram's team, it's an opportunity not to be missed.

The sensible thing would have been to complete the 2000 up run and end it there having got an up and down under my belt. I wasn't sensible, I got the up run under my belt, but I didn't stop there. I was starting to identify with Buzz Lightyear from Toy Story and his catchphrase "To infinity and beyond"

Moving on and up

Unfortunately, due to an injury, Steve could not run in the 2000 Comrades, but he was at the side of the road encouraging the runners and handing out bananas and other treats to the COCO team. I finished the up run in 9:43:25, only a few minutes slower than my down run time the previous year. I have found over my 8 finishes that my time for the up and down runs are remarkably similar. You just hurt a lot more after a down run due to the pounding your quads take towards the end and that is why you walk like a penguin and avoid stairs after the down run. Bruce Fordyce gives a talk to new international Comrades marathon runners; when it is a down run, he says that they are lucky that it is a down run. He points out that after a down run you walk strangely and that last for many days and that is why they are lucky. He says, "When you get back to work people will ask why you are walking like that and you can tell them."

We had stayed in Durban before the start of the race but arranged rooms in a hotel in Pietermaritzburg for after the race and our luggage was transferred while we were running. We arrived at the hotel, tired and very stiff, to discover that our luggage was in a room on the ground floor and the bedrooms were on the first floor; there was no lift. The stairs were going to be a problem without luggage, but with they were going to be a nightmare. Steve stepped forward and told people to go to their rooms and he would carry the luggage up. They say you should never meet your heroes because you will be disappointed. Steve didn't disappoint, not only is he a great athlete, he is also a nice guy.

After one night's stay in Pietermaritzburg, we went up into the Drakensberg mountains for a few days. It was a good opportunity to relax and get to know the other runners better.

Two were to have a big influence on my ultra-running career. Ian Little and Gary Jackets. As the coach got near to our hotel, Ian turned to me and said, “I have just got to go out for a run in that beautiful scenery.” I was thinking the same thing, so we agreed to dump our bags in our rooms, get our kit on and meet up for a run. It was as good as we expected it to be, but a lot harder, not because we had run Comrades the day before, but because we were at altitude. I learnt that day that a few gentle runs after an ultra followed by a week of rest is better for recovery than resting straight away. Someone, I think it was Gary, came up with the idea of a 10-minute post Comrades run the day after the race. That tradition was maintained by COCO runners and one year, when Comrades was on a Saturday, there was a 5k fun run starting on Durban seafront on the Sunday morning. Three of us decided to take part in the that race, me, Peter Bullock and Ian. As we shuffled slowly towards the back of the group of runners lined up for the start the commentator spotted us and could tell what we had been up to the day before by our shuffling gait. “Ah we have some Comrades runners joining us at the back” he announced. All the onlookers turn to look our way and at the point the gun went for the start, everyone sprinted off leaving us to shuffle along watched by the crowd of supporters. It took a long time to get our seized-up bodies to move at anything near a reasonable pace.

Ian and I became friends and had a few running adventures together, including a trip to Winschoten, in the Netherlands to take part in their oldest ultramarathon, *de RUN* which started in 1976. It is a 100km race that often incorporated the European and World 100 km championships. That translates to 62 miles so a little further than Comrades, distance was no longer a barrier. And it was through Ian that I met one of the Comrades greats, Lindsay Weight.

I shared a room in the Drakensberg with Gary, and we took it in turns to read a report about the Marathon des Sables that a club mate of one of the other runners in our group had written. We both agreed that it was a completely stupid thing to do. Running 250km through the Sahara Desert carrying a heavy pack was not for us, especially when we read the lurid accounts of people's badly blistered feet. I was therefore surprised to receive an email from Gary about 18 months later saying he wanted to tackle the Marathon des Sables, did anyone want to go with him. I was even more surprised when I emailed back to say yes, I did. We would enter the 2003 Marathon des Sables – the toughest footrace in the world. My belief in myself and my ability to take on big challenges had grown during those 18 months thanks to my Comrades finishes. And that is how my multi-day desert racing started.

That second Comrades trip was the start of my deepening involvement with the charity Comrade of Children Overseas which led to me becoming a director and trips to rural Tanzania and townships in South Africa to visit schools supported by the charity. On one visit, to a transition home run by a South African charity, iThemba Lethu, in the Cato Manor area of Durban, which placed orphaned and abandoned children in permanent homes, I had an experience that started my journey away from the corporate world and has resulted in me fundraising and volunteering for children's charities ever since. A few weeks before travelling out to South Africa I had been to a corporate event at the Royal Academy Summer Exhibition. Some of the exhibits were a bit whacky and we had a laugh at one, a cardboard box. To this day I can still visualise that moment, the men in black tie and the women in summer dresses, all of us drinking champagne and saying amusing things about the exhibit. It is frozen in my mind because of what happened a few weeks later. I visited iThemba Lethu for the first time and as we were being shown around one of the babies woke up. We were told that children were all given their bottles at the same time and I was asked to hold and pacify the child until the rest woke up for feed time. The baby was quite content in my arms held close to my chest. I also found it comforting, the child's story was not. It was the time of the height of the HIV epidemic in South Africa and children were being orphaned or abandoned at an alarming rate. This little baby had been found abandoned at the side of a dirt road in a cardboard box. The contrasting images of those two cardboard boxes haunted me for a long time. A few years later I was at a fundraising event for One World Action and a painting by Jon Snow, the newsreader, was one of the raffle prizes; it had been rejected by the Summer Exhibition. That night lady luck smiled on me and that painting is now on the wall beside my desk. It's a reminder of the Summer Exhibition I attended and the two cardboard boxes,

One more significant thing happened at the 2000 Comrades marathon. When I met Brian Kirkdale in the International tent after I had finished his first words after "Well done" were "Do you want to be in the Hastings Runners Team for the London to Brighton road race?." The London to Brighton race is like Comrades in respect of the distance but is nothing like it when it comes to number of competitors, spectators or atmosphere. Brian had for some time had the ambition of Hastings Runners being the first Sussex club to have a team finish the London to Brighton race. Brian had been right to encourage me to run Comrades for a second time, so I put my trust in him and said yes. With me on board all he needed was one more victim to complete a team of three. I ran gently for about a month then started training in earnest for the London to Brighton race. My job was to finish inside the 10-hour time limit, which is stricter than the 11 hours set for Comrades which it was when I first ran it but is now 12 hours.

The London to Brighton race was a spectacularly understated affair, with little publicity and no razzmatazz. About a hundred of us assembled on the pavement on Westminster Bridge and just before 7am got into a starting line then, when Big Ben bonged for the 7th time, we headed off on our way to Brighton. It's not too bad while you are on the pavement, but at some points you are running along the side of a main road with trucks thundering past. The water stations are few and far between, so most people rely on family and friends as seconds and they are about the only supporters. There is only one big hill on the course and that is Ditchling Beacon, I struggled to get up that and suffered until I started descending into Brighton and finished on the seafront in 9:48:43. Job done. Brian had finished about 25 minutes before me and Paul Eickert, the other member of our team, 20 minutes before him so we had achieved Brian's dream of being the first Sussex club to have a team finish the London to Brighton.

Strangely it was during this uninspiring event with no scenery, no support and no atmosphere that I became infected by the ultra-running bug; I have no desire to find a cure. It is easy to be charmed by the majesty of the Comrades marathon; but when a low-key event, with little support and bad weather, makes your heart sing you know you have found your passion. For me there is beauty in solitude and disquiet in crowds; I know for others that the reverse is true. Running is a broad church and can accommodate everyone.

Things settled down into a regular pattern for a few years. The Luton marathon in December to get a qualifying time for my Comrades entry, the Compton Downland Challenge, a 40-mile event, in April as a good training run for Comrades which was at the end of May, it has now changed to the second Sunday in June. And around that schedule I fitted in as many marathons and shorter races as I wanted. Life was changing during this time, we moved to a Cornwall (although I stayed in London during the week), the children started school and all the normal changes affecting family life happened. The Comrades marathon and my training schedule was my stability. Mostly I managed to fit it around family life; however, I'm sure it must have impacted it just like golf, football or nights out with mates does in other families. I hoped I was setting my children a good example and found out later that they were proud of my exploits which made me different from the other Dads. I had learnt not to jump to conclusions about what your children say about you. Charlotte once said I reminded her of Flik, the hero ant in the movie *A Bug's Life*. The conversation was interrupted before I could ask why and assumed that it was because of his perseverance in the face of adversity. A few months later I asked her why and she said, "You know that bit where he is trying to explain something to the young ant that doesn't understand and he starts shouting – that's how you explain things to me." I now use edwardflik in my personal email address to remind me not to assume. I do have evidence that my children are proud of my exploits because often when I used to give their friends lifts back from parties, they would congratulate me on a recent race having heard all about it from my daughters.

Sometime in 2002 Ian Little, who I had met via the Comrades marathon, suggested entering a 100k in the Netherlands I agreed. I have a bad habit of doing that when people suggest races; longer than Comrades, but at least it would be flat. In fact, the course in Winschoten is certified as canal flat. Winschoten is a delightful town in the far north of the Netherlands which is quite easy to get to despite the need to change twice on the train journey from Amsterdam. The Dutch train system works. When we went to the sports hall to register the day before the event, it was almost as if the event wasn't happening, there was just one man and a small table, at which to register and he had trouble finding a pen to mark us off the list. However, the following day was completely different, there was a carnival atmosphere, the town was decorated with flags and bunting and lots of runners were there for the 10 X 10k relay, the marathon, the 50k and 100k, which was the IAU European Championships. I had travelled out with a heavy head cold, and only turned up so as not to let Ian down. The previous evening, we had an interesting time trying to explain to a local chemist, who's English was as good as our Dutch – non-existent, that I wanted something to clear my nasal passages. I think he thought that we believed the Netherlands' liberal approach to cannabis also extended to cocaine and that we were trying to buy some. Anyhow I was not feeling too bright at the start and had to make an emergency visit to the bathroom, when I got back, I couldn't find Ian because unbeknown to me our race had started. It wasn't until I noticed that everyone around me was wearing different colour numbers to me that I realised something was up. After a hurried conversation with the nearest person that spoke a little English, I realised that my race had started and climbed over the crowd barriers to get to the start line and set off. After a little while a motorcycle rider explained that I was going the wrong way because the start had been altered for the marathon. I raced back onto the right course and tried to catch up with the tailenders. The race consisted of 10 laps around a ten-kilometre route; I completed the first lap in a personal best time. Not good when you have 90 more kilometres to go, but at least I had caught up with some other runners.

The support during the race was fantastic, the local people decorate their gardens and are either in them supporting or standing by the roadside cheering runners on. Each runner's number and name were printed in the race programme which meant people could look up your name, which explained why so many people were shouting "Go Edvard". I seemed to attract some very loyal groups of supporters and each time I passed their houses the shouts would get louder. After the panic of the first lap I'd settled down into a pace that I felt I could maintain for the rest of the race and I started to enjoy the experience. Ian had to drop out due to injury and told me he was going back to the hotel but would come back to see me finish. I felt sorry for him, he'd trained hard for this race, I felt even sorrier for myself. I had trained hard for the race, but my cold was making it a big struggle now that I'd reached 60km, unfortunately I didn't have an injury so had no reason to quit. It became a war of attrition as my body started closing down and seizing up, would I get to the finish before it packed up completely? I had one important thing going for me, the supporters, they could see my pain and their support was now becoming frenetic. One group even shouted out "Edvard we love you – keep going" and on my last lap, when I must have looked at my very worse, they shout "Edvard don't give up we will be coming to the finish to see you". I just had to keep going. I crossed the finish line in 11:16:18. My local supporters, true to their word, had made it to the finish to see me cross the line and so had Ian. For years after he would tell the story of how he had dropped out at about 60km, had time to walk back to the hotel, take a bath, have a meal, watch a movie and still have time to make it back to the finish to greet me.

The following day my cold had miraculously gone, but my legs just would not work; the problem with a canal flat course is that you use the same muscles in the same way without any variation for a long time. I have since learnt to vary my stride length and knee lift on those sorts of events. Later I took a walk in a local park to try and ease the legs out before the trip home, I had the unenviable experience of being overtaken by a toddler who, judging by his erratic gait had only just learnt to walk. I didn't care, despite the pain I was an incredibly happy and contented ultrarunner. I would visit the town of Winschoten again, but that is another story. I think the next time I ran in the same race as Ian other than comrades was the 2006 Two Oceans marathon in Cape Town.

I now knew that for me distance was not a problem so the long day in the Marathon des Sables was not going to be an issue, it was all the other days, the sand and the heat that were going to be the problem. I couldn't afford to take too long recovering from the 100km before starting training again. This time I was quite happy to have a period of not running, rest is an important part of training. I have some long walks and gentle runs to keep ticking over until I had got over the exertions in the Netherlands then I started on my training for the big adventure in the desert.

The Marathon des Sables

The Marathon des Sables is invariably described as the toughest footrace on Earth and that is how it is described on the event's UK website as well as being 'an extraordinary race for extraordinary people in an extraordinary place'. It was once probably the toughest footrace on Earth, as it was the only extreme multi-day self-sufficient race, but now there are many contends for the crown and I think I have taken part in the winning event the Likeys 6633Ultra. However, the extraordinary is accurate. For me, at that point, it was the toughest race I was going to attempt, and I was treating it with a huge amount of respect. In ultrarunning a mix of excitement and fear is a good thing.

When I started training for the Marathon des Sables there was not a lot of information about it available, my trusty guide, International Ultra Training, did not have a relevant chapter and at that time it wasn't something that appeared in Runners' World. All that has changed now, there are books on training for MdS and other multi-day races, MdS specific seminars and lots of articles in running magazines now that Ben Fogle, James Cracknell, Ranulph Fiennes and a few other celebrities have completed it. And now there is also the internet.

I did find a couple of runners who had done it before, Mimi Anderson and Rory Coleman, and was able to pick their brains. Mimi had some great advice about the mental side of things, whereas Rory offered advice on equipment; I still have the rucksack he recommended and have used it on all my multi-day races and the training runs for them. The more modern equipment is much lighter but doesn't last; as I'm never going to win, I don't see the need to get rid of it and spend hundreds of pounds on a new one just to save a few hundred grams on my back. You can read about Mimi's exploits during the Marathon des Sables in her book *Beyond Impossible*.

With the scant knowledge I had I set about training, which consisted of running a lot with a heavy pack and a little bit of gym work, not very scientific, but that is how we did it back then. Yes, I know it was only 17 years ago, but with the way ultrarunning has developed in recent years it was the dark ages then. I had moved to Cornwall a few years earlier, well the family had, I was renting a flat in Banstead and going back home at weekends, which I normally made into three-day affairs. This meant I had the coastal path to run on and Braunton Burrows, the largest area of sand dunes in the England, were a 45-minute drive away so I could get some of my training done on sand.

The flat in Banstead had been carefully chosen, it was seven miles away from where I worked so just right for running in to work and back and the route had very few side roads to cross so I could keep the pace going. There were showers in our offices so all I had to do was make sure I had clean clothes and a suit in the office. I'd run into work twice a week and the important thing was, even if I did not want to run back to the flat, I had no choice I had to run back. This was great use of time as the last few miles of the route in were quite congested and would take some time in car, it was faster on foot. Sometimes I'd passed one of the women who worked in the office on her drive into work and would be at my desk showered and changed before she arrived. Sometimes a Ferrari would pass me on the faster section of the A217 and it would give me great satisfaction when a few miles later I would overtake it as it sat in traffic at the approach to a junction.

When I was in Cornwall I'd head out along the coastal path, often passing the local farmer leading her cattle out to the fields after the morning milking and would see her again on my return, when she was bringing the cattle back for the evening milking. I think I became known as the Mad Marathon Man of Morwenstow. The staff at the garage where I had my car serviced viewed me with a mixture of awe and suspicion. The garage was in Barnstaple, so I would drop the car there and head off to the Burrows for sand dune training. The first time I did this the guy checking the car in said "Sir, it is a major service your car won't be ready for at least 5 hours." Don't worry" I replied, I'm planning on running for about 6 hours". He looked at me very strangely and things got even worse when I said, "oh I need to get my rucksack out of the back." He fetched it for me and, when he felt how heavy it was, asked what was in it. "Rocks" I replied. I had exceptionally good service from the garage after that, I think they thought I was a bit unstable and didn't want to risk upsetting me. The plastic covers mechanics put on the driver's seat are great for protecting the fabric from a smelly runner.

Training went well, but with a few incidents. I changed from running with rocks in my rucksack to running with plastic milk bottles filled with water as I felt these were less likely to damage the pack or be uncomfortable on my back. Unfortunately, one of the bottles burst when I was running on the Burrows, which is used by the army to practice desert warfare. I wasn't particularly worried about the fact I'd got wet, but I was concerned about the loss of weight. I decided to fill the bottle with sand and wrap a plastic bag around it. I did wonder whether it was a wise idea to be digging a hole in the sand beside a tank track on an army training ground. I kept looking around to make sure I wasn't going to get shot. Shortly after that the British joined the US in the Iraq war. A week later I had my dress-rehearsal, with full Marathon des

Sables kit, running through the Burrows. I came charging over the top of a sand dune and surprised the tail guard of a TA unit out on manoeuvres, he got quite a fright; I'm glad they do not use live ammunition when on exercises in public places.

The day eventually arrived when it was time to set off for Ouarzazate in Morocco for the start of my adventure in the Sahara. I flew there on a charter flight with Monarch airlines, it was easy to find the right check-in desk; there was a big queue of healthy-looking people with rucksacks in front of it. When we arrived in Morocco, we were bussed to a luxury hotel for an overnight stay, before a six-hour coached ride the following day into the Sahara Desert. We transferred into the back of some big open trucks for the final mile or so to the camp. This was our first experience of our accommodation for the week. Eight-man tents consisting of black threadbare hessian material slung over some sticks held up by flimsy ropes and pegs. The floor was covered with thin mats that did little to protect you from any stones. The first night we had our luggage with us, so it was fairly civilised. The following day after kit checks and having our medical certificates examined, we said goodbye to our luggage and then had only the kit we would carry with us for the next seven days. That evening we were provided with a final meal, which as you would expect from the French, was particularly good and then everyone tried to get some sleep before the early start in the morning.

Every morning you must get up early, not because the race start is particularly early, but because the local Berbers start taking the tents down so that they can be packed away, transported to the next camp and erected before the first runners arrive. If you are still in the tent, they will just take it down around you and they are not particularly careful about how this is done. The start each morning follows the same pattern; you line up at the start ready to go then have to wait in the blazing sun while Patrick Bauer, the race director, makes a speech, usually at great length, explaining how the race acts as a great metaphor for life. There is then a very brief translation from French into English which leaves out the flowery stuff (usually drowned out by the sound of the helicopter which has moved in closer to film the start) before we all head off at various speeds and in various states. I found the first day quite dramatic, I never knew the world could be so hot, or that a breeze could feel as if someone had just opened the oven door. The first day was relatively short, 28km, which was fortunate as I doubt I could have coped with much more. My pack seemed to have doubled in weight and my running ability halved, although it was still an awesome experience to be out there in the Sahara Desert and to get into camp with everything intact. A few people had already got blisters.

I didn't sleep well that night and vomited just before dawn; I had an upset stomach and could not keep my breakfast down or any water. I had visions of having to retire on Day 2 only 10s of kilometres into the 250km race – not something to boast about. I worked on a plan, which was to get to the first checkpoint, see how things were, then work on another plan. I stood on the start line, in the heat listening to Patrick blather on desperately hoping I wouldn't throw up in front of a medic. I needn't have worried there was nothing left to come up. Eventually we were off, and I put my plan into action; stay just in front of the three camels. These are led along at the back of the field and if they catch you up you are pulled out. I took tiny sips of water and used some of my ration to wet my head, neck and wrists to help me keep cool (a relative term). This strategy worked, and I started to feel slightly better, especially when I passed a few people. Eventually I arrived at checkpoint 1, ten kilometres into that day's stage of 38 kilometres. It was a great relief because I then felt I could continue on that day, but of course that meant I had to actually do it, not easy when you are dehydrated and hungry.

I filled my bottles up at the checkpoint and continued for about 1 km before stopping to mix up a rehydration drink, which I was please to find stayed down. I could do this. I just needed to look after myself and grind the kilometres out. Just before the next checkpoint I came across someone bending over another person lying on the ground, he explained that his friend was recovering from an epileptic fit and that, although she was ok, he was concerned because she had had several fits that morning. I volunteered to run to the checkpoint and find a doctor. I was able to run at quite an impressive speed, which was amazing considering that a little while earlier just shuffling along was a major effort. It took a fair bit of gesticulating, broken French and shouting to get a medic to head off to help, but once he was on his way, I filled my bottles and set off. The rest of the day was pretty much as I had expected, a long, slow, hard slog, but now I felt better and started to think I can do this. Of course, I still had the dreaded long day to come, but I had trained for that; I'd run comrades 4 times by then, the London to Brighton and a 100km race. Distance wasn't a problem; the heat and sand were. I finished that day in good spirits, with my feet intact and was able to get a good amount of food inside me. Panic over.

The following day was yet again hot and sunny; I enjoyed it even when a sandstorm blew through and I was forced just to stand there because I could not see anything. We had been advised to stop in these circumstances as the possibility of wandering off course is extremely high. It was soon over so I got to see what a sandstorm was like without suffering too much. I was pleased to have experienced it. The other high point that day, if that is the right word, was the salt flats. Almost 10km of a pancake flat white surface reflecting the heat back at you. I almost cooked, but that was the whole point of the exercise; taking on something extreme. Unfortunately, my feet blistered very badly towards the end of the day and I had to spend quite some time that evening sorting them out. I didn't sleep well because of the pain and worrying with how I'd cope with the long day. I needed to go to the toilet a few times in the night and the short shuffle I did was extremely painful. For a particularly good account of toilet matters and other practical things during the Marathon des Sables read the e-book by Graeme Harvey, 'Running the Highway to Hell'

I took me an age in the morning to get one trainer one over my swollen and blistered foot, then I needed fifteen minutes to recover and build up the courage to attempt to put the other one on. Eventually I was able to shuffle over to the start and roast in the sun while Patrick described how our international group banded together to struggle against the desert was a metaphor for the countries in the free world co-operating to oppose tyrannous regimes, or some such guff. The English translator just said Patrick said, 'Have a good day.'

I was alarming to see how fast most of the field set off, however there were some shuffling along at my pace and I was quite pleased that after about 20 minutes I started pulling away from the tail-enders and after a while was setting a reasonable pace, the pain in my feet had subsided to a manageable level and I was starting to enjoy the awesome views. Then I stepped on a small stone and the searing pain in my foot was back. The day progressed in this pattern, pain for half an hour then some sort of reasonable running/shuffling until my foot landed awkwardly and the pain was back. However, this was one of the best days I've had in my life; I felt so alive, aware of my surrounding, aware of my body and I knew that I would finish 'The toughest footrace in the world,' unless I died.

Gary and I had decided to run our own races rather than stick together, it is difficult to run at someone else's pace, so we thought we would do better going at our different paces. I think at that point in time my overall time was faster than his because he had been suffering from blisters early in the event, but on the long day, he was ahead of me. I caught him up just before nightfall and he was not a happy bunny. His Achilles heel was causing him problems, his blisters hurt and to add insult to injury there was a thorn in his trainer that he couldn't remove and was pricking the bottom of his foot with each step. When we reached a checkpoint a very brave French guy stuck his hand in Gary's smelly trainer and eventually managed to get a grip on the thorn with a small pair of fliers and remove it. We refuelled and left the checkpoint to plod our way through the night. It was a surreal experience walking through sand dunes towards a massive green laser beam shining up to the sky which never seemed to get any closer. I decided to stay with Gary; I was concerned about him and thought that he might pull out, if I was there beside him he never would. It was a long night, near the end Gary would take a few steps then have to rest to get over the pain before taking a few more. A blister on his heel was badly infected and the Achilles inflamed.

About 5km from the end of the stage Gary was convinced that we only had about 500 metres to go; I didn't tell him otherwise. Then a medic came past on a quad bike, I didn't want him getting too close and seeing what a state Gary was in, he might have pulled him out. I gave a cheery wave and said we were fine. As he drove off the medic said "Only 5k to go lads – keep going". Gary collapsed to the ground and let out a series of expletives which if repeated here would cover a few pages in asterisks and other strange characters. It took me half an hour to get Gary off the floor and walking again although that is a rather grand description of the progress we were making. Eventually we came over a small rise and there was the camp just a little way away, unfortunately it was across a piece of land scattered with lots of small stones, not good for blistered feet. I added my page of expletives to Gary's. We arrived at camp a little after sunrise, which was spectacular. Before we started my ETA had been 2am at the latest.

The best laid schemes o' mice an' men
Gang oft a-gley.
An' lea'e us nought but grief an' pain

Tae A Moose - Robert Burns

I steered Gary towards Doc Trotters, the medical tent, then found my tent and collapsed. With the benefit of hindsight, I don't think staying with Gary was an altruistic act; I needed company and a distraction from my own problems to see me through the night and safely into camp. When you are in trouble I think you marshal all the resources that you need and sometimes you trick yourself into believing that you are not doing that because you don't want to admit to yourself that things are bad.

I awoke a few hours later hot and very, very smelly. That was a mistake, I should have got some food inside me and sorted my feet out before sleeping. It was good that I had all of the rest day to sort things out. Now I always do my 'admin' before anything else, it was a valuable lesson I learnt that day. I ate then made my way over to Doc Trotters, my feet were too far gone for me to sort out, I needed professional help. Doc Trotters is a team of medical professionals, which now numbers about 50, many of whom volunteer to get valuable experience. By the time I got there a big queue had formed and I had to wait a long time before I got seen. Fortunately, there was shade, but it was still blooming hot. There was no banter and only a little other conversation taking place, I think we were all immersed in our own pain and contemplating the horrors to come. You hear terrible horror stories about Doc Trotters before you arrive at the Marathon des Sables. I'm told it's a little more civilised now.

My time eventually came to enter the chamber of horrors, it was like a very well organised field hospital with people lying in two rows with their feet resting on stools pointing to the sides of the tent. Medics were sat on camp chairs lancing blisters, cutting of dead skin, and doing other gruesome things. I could tell from his accent that the chap lying with his head near me was a South African, so I started up a conversation about the Comrades Marathon. He said he would never do anything as extreme or as stupid as that. I was about to point out that given his current circumstances that statement was definitely false when we were distracted by a guy crawling past us towards the next vacant spot; his feet had totally lost all their skin and were like two very raw pieces of bloody meat. I didn't feel too badly off after seeing that until the doctor put iodine on my feet where he had just cut large patches of skin away: that stung a bit.

For the rest of the day I just dozed in the tent, trying to stay hydrated and snacking to restore my energy levels. The view out of the back of the tent was just a vast expanse of sand. Gary and I played i-spy for a while but as there was only sand and sky it soon turned into. I spy something beginning with s. Sky? No, the other one. Towards the end of the afternoon we had to go and collect our ration of water which was in the middle of the big circle made by our tents. As I shuffled towards the supplies I experienced a small act of kindness that will stay in my memory forever. A member of the French crew had been standing out there in the sun for a long time supervising the handing out of the water rations to about 600 runners, when he saw me emerge from my tent and start to shuffle towards him, he held his hand up gesturing for me to stop and came to me with my water bottles; he knew my pain. Ben Fogle, an adventurer and broadcaster, has completed the Marathon des Sables. In the documentary film about it there is a poignant moment. He is extremely tired, and his feet are badly blistered. Trying to describe how he feels he realises that even though he is a professional communicator he cannot find the words to describe how he feels. He looks at the camera, confusion in his eyes shakes his head slowly and says, "you have no idea". Those of us that have been there understand exactly what he was saying.

All too soon the following day came, and it was the daunting marathon day, but it turned out to be relatively undramatic. Gary went off like a steam train; he'd had a cortisone injection in his Achilles, the infected skin on the back of his heel had been removed and a dressing put over it, the antibiotics had started working and he was dosed up on strong painkillers. He was a completely different person from the crumpled heap he'd been 24 hours before. I felt pretty good as well, knowing that getting through this day would mean that it was almost all over; the final day was less than a half-marathon.

And then it was all over Patrick Bauer, the race director was hugging me and kissing me on both cheeks, and I had my medal. I had completed the toughest footrace on Earth, I had done something amazing and could now go back to being normal. Except for the fact that in the desert in the night I had looked deep inside myself to find what I needed to keep going and I now knew that there was a lot more in there to be discovered during other adventures.

My feet were in tatters and when I got home, I removed the bandaging applied by the Doc Trotter's medics, not a pretty sight. I tidied things up applied a few dressings and wanted to bandage my feet again, the only thing we had in the house that was suitable was some strapping used for binding up our pony's leg. That had to do; not the sort of treatment you expect as a conquering hero.

I ran the Shakespeare marathon a week later; there was the small matter of getting prepared for the Comrades Marathon. Probably not the best idea; however, it did add to my crazy reputation when several people saw my bandaged feet when I changed after the run.

Comrades 2009 DNF

Ten years after my first Comrades run in 1999, I posted a DNF (did not finish). Strangely, I was not disappointed to miss out on a medal and being one more run closer to my ultimate goal of achieving ten finishes and getting the coveted Green Number status awarded for ten finishes. (I did not run in 2004 & 2005 due to injury so 2009 would have been my 9th finish.) I was not disappointed because I had given it my best, evidenced by the fact that I spent an hour and a half in the medical tent and had two intravenous drips. If you have given the best you have then there is no disgrace in not finishing, just the incentive to come back fitter, better trained and better prepared. It also gave me an opportunity to see a different aspect of the race I love so much. Even though I had run the race eight times, read lots about it and talked to countless Comrades runners I was fascinated to see more Comrades magic unfold in front of me at the back of the event.

In the early stages of the run all went well. Estienne Arndt, race director of the Kalahari Augrabies Extreme Marathon, accompanied by his friend Peter Marklew (who very kindly put me up when I was in Durban) had driven me to the start. As usual I had spent a few days being on the Kalahari Augrabies Extreme Marathon stand at the Comrades Expo. We arrived in Pietermaritzburg early enough to be able to park close to the start area. It was just a short stroll to my start pen so I was able to arrive relaxed and have time to visit the toilet, apply Vaseline to parts that might chafe, apply sun block and do all the other necessary things without rushing.

As usual the music and singing before the start created a great atmosphere before the playing of the traditional "Chariots of Fire", the cockcrow and the firing of the starter's gun. It took me five minutes to cross the start line and even longer after that before I could get into a comfortable running pace. The first 30km of the race were relaxed and comfortable while I chatted with numerous friends and acquaintances that I met along the way.

Then I felt a twinge in a muscle deep in my left buttock and running became a little less easy. As time and the kilometres passed by the pain became worse and started to slow me down significantly as my stride pattern was affected. At that point I was not unduly worried as the pace was still all right for a finish. I had over the last few years perfected the technique of finishing with about fifteen minutes to spare. When the 12-hour Runners World pacing group passed me, I was a little concerned, but thought that if they came in 20 minutes early I could still be behind them and finish in less than 12 hours. When the second group came past, led by Roy Tolfts, a very experienced pacer who I had met in the Kalahari Desert, I was concerned. I increased my pace as much as possible and was pleased to see that Roy was hardly pulling away from me at all. A few kilometres later I could no longer see Roy ahead of me and I started to worry, that was the first time that it occurred to me that I might not make it.

About five kilometres before the halfway point at Drummond the crowd were starting to warn us that we should keep the pace up because we were in danger of missing the 6-hour cut off at Drummond. With a kilometre to go it was starting to get a close call. The crowd were becoming frantic, urging us to go faster; it worked. I crossed the halfway point with just under two minutes to spare, and probably only managed that because of the support and encouragement of the crowd and other runners. Sadly, many runners did not make it in time, and I heard the commentator announce that the halfway point was closed, and the crowd fell silent. It was an incredibly sad

moment. I felt so sorry for those runners left behind, but incredibly pleased for myself.
It was clear that I had to pick the pace up to avoid missing the next cut off, but this was going to be difficult particularly as the sprint, which is what it felt like, to get through Drummond had taken a lot out of me. I walked up the hill to help me recover, and then gently jogged down the other side. The first few kilometres of the road after Drummond were littered with runners for whom the effort to get past halfway was too much. Some sat on the side of the road waiting for the rescue bus dejected while others had a resigned look on their faces. Some were even smiling; I can only assume that it was because of the relief that they did not have to endure any more pain.

I counted myself lucky that I was not one of the runners collapsed on the side of the road especially as I watched some of them being physically lifted into the rescue vehicles. My task now was to get through the next cut off point and try and gain some time. The tactic was to walk strongly up the up hills, try and run well down the hills and maintain a good pace on the flat. I also had another tactic, I was as usual going to place a flower on Arthur's seat, but this time I was going to say, "Please help me out Arthur".

Every other time I have run Comrades there has been a crowd of runners around me and a great deal of banter. Now I was virtually on my own, those that were behind had missed the cut off and some of the runners that were with me had fallen by the wayside, some quite literally. In the areas where there were no supporters it was eerily quiet. Where there were supporters it was very noisy and personal. With very few runners to support the crowds had time to read the name on your number and shout out to you personally. They knew you were struggling and were determined to do their bit to get each and every one of the stragglers to the finish. In their enthusiasm to support they often abandoned common sense, "Looking good Edward" was a phrase I heard often despite the very visible evidence to the contrary. By this point I was running with a very definite lean to the left, a hobbling gait and a grimace.

It is hard to describe the passion, commitment and energy of the supporters. I was moved by how fervently these people wanted to help a complete stranger reach his goal; at times I was moved to tears. This was in sharp contrast to the fact that everything was being cleared away, the refreshment tables were being packed up with only a few items left out for the stragglers, all the club tents were being dismantled after the last club member ran past and people were going about their normal business. It seemed abnormal, almost wrong, to be running Comrades in these surroundings. It was definitely wrong to be taking so long to catch up old ladies strolling along with their shopping balanced on their heads. Then I would encounter another group of committed supporters who had stayed to offer their encouragement until the bitter end or pass a restaurant where people would shout their encouragement from the terrace or be asked by a concerned supporter "Did I need anything, ice, deep heat, food" then the madness that is the Comrades marathon would be restored.

About this time the medical support vehicles and runners rescue buses (called bail busses by runners) started to show an unhealthy interest in me. All I could think about was jackals pestering a wounded wildebeest. "Are you OK?" they would ask. "Yes, I am fine" I would reply despite being far from it. It was also about this time that the shouts from the supporters changed. It was no longer "You are looking good" but now "keep on going" and "you can do it" were the order of the day interspersed with "man so much pain you are an inspiration" and my favourite "Edward you are my hero".

I made the 2 o'clock cut-off at Hillcrest with a more respectable eight minutes to spare, according to the announcer there were three people behind me. Logic should have told me that I had no hope of finishing, although the cut off time is 2 o'clock the E.T.A of the last finisher is given as 13.18 in the route guide. I was 44 minutes off the finishing pace with only about 31 kilometres to make it up in. I still believed it was worth continuing but was amazed when I passed other runners who also felt it worth going on. In reality I was now engaged on a quixotic quest, it was obvious that I was not going to finish, it was obvious that I was not going to make the next cut off in Pinetown. Obvious that is except to one small part of my brain, or was it my soul, which refused to give up.

The support became even more amazing; people would run out and say, "I am going to run with you Edward come with me" and we would run together for a while and I would pick up speed as they jogged with me in their dresses and sandals or shorts and flip-flops. "Keep going Edward," they would say as they dropped away. I would run on alone, occasionally passing a runner who could not go on any longer sitting on the side of the road waiting for a rescue bus. Even more occasionally I would pass another runner, usually walking, and we would exchange encouragements and continue on with our pointless task.

I was suffering a lot at this stage and the bail busses were closing in for the kill. To start with they would ask "are you ok" and when I said yes, they would go away but soon they would say "well you do not look it" and I had to repeat "I am ok" before they would go away.

In Kloof a man ran beside me, obviously a Comrades veteran, and said "Edward you must maintain your focus, I want you to shuffle on the flats for three minutes, no less, not two minutes fifty seconds but three minutes then walk for a minute, no more and keep doing that. Run all the down hills and walk up hill. Don't bother wasting energy running up the hills. But whatever you do keep going." That seemed like a good plan, so I did it. The good thing was that there was a long downhill section ahead. The bad news was that I was finding it particularly difficult running downhill. Going down Fields Hill I was passed by two runners who had been behind me for some time. We had a brief chat and decided that no matter what the only thing to do was to keep going and not get in the bail bus. We were almost certain not going to make the cut off but getting in the bail busses was not an option.

At this point I was considered to be the last runner on the road, the man I had passed sitting on the crash barrier at the side of the road must had succumbed to the bail bus, and the rescue vehicle was driving beside me. "You might as well get in because I am going to keep beside you until you do" the driver said. I was emphatic "I am keeping on the road until I fail to make a cut off"; he kept driving beside me. There was a police vehicle in front and a medical car behind. Eventually the inevitable happen, cut off time came, and I had to get in the minibus. A little later we picked up the two runners who had passed me earlier. The bus was full and silent; obviously, no one felt like talking, we were all coming to terms with what had happened.

As we drove towards Durban, we could hear over the radio buses and medical vehicles being directed to pick up runners ahead who either had medical problems or were too tired to continue. It was an incredibly sad thing to hear. When we were on the outskirts of Durban we could see a long line of runners progressing towards the finish, fortunately given the time most of those we could see would make it.

Approaching the Kingsmead Stadium, I started to feel dizzy and faint. I had to be helped out of the bus and onto a stretcher to be taken to the medical tent. I have never seen this part of the Comrades operation before and found it fascinating. It was a mixture of chaos, order, Heath Robinson arrangements and professionalism. Strung across the large marquee that housed the medical teams were lines of red and white hazard warning tape. Attached to the tape at intervals were numbered boards and below the boards were camping style cot beds. Runners, in various states of distress, occupied most of these beds. Hanging above many of the beds were bags for intravenous drips. It appeared that each two-person medical team was assigned several cots to look after and a supervisor oversaw several teams.

I was placed on one of the cots and was soon seen by a medic who asked me how I felt, what I had drunk during the race and when I had last been for a pee, if I had any medical conditions, if I had any chest pains and was I on any medication. My pulse and blood pressure were checked, and a pinprick blood sample taken. At this point I started shaking so was covered with a blanket, this was later to be increased to a space blanket and two wool blankets. All my relevant information was noted on a clipboard, which was placed on my chest and checked at intervals by a doctor and administrators. Having established that there was nothing seriously wrong and that I had not drunk too much water I was given some coke and a bottle of water to drink while they attended to the runner in the next bed. Hyponatraemia, low levels of sodium which can be caused by drinking too much water when exercising and sweating is a serious condition which can be fatal, so it is important for the medics to establish this is not present before administering intravenous fluids to counteract dehydration.

My shaking did not improve so another blood test was ordered; the results came back remarkably quickly and were stuck to the notes on the clipboard. When the medic came back he explained the results to me. Nothing to worry about, I was informed, mild acidosis and slight dehydration, not unexpected given the circumstances. He went on to explain that I had exerted a great deal of effort and that now it was over I was in shock. "A couple of intravenous drips and a little rest and I would feel like a million Rand. Make that a million pounds as the Rand is not worth very much," he said.

So, I lay there observing, as best I could, what was going on around me. People were arriving all the time: some on foot, helped by friends, others on stretchers. The process was always the same, careful questioning, noting down the relevant information and deciding on a course of action. All this was done in a very calm and sympathetic manner; however, it did seem like bedlam in the tent. People shouting out which area the stretchers should go to, people calling out for assistance or equipment, runners with severe cramp screaming out in pain and the general hubbub of people talking. The scene reminded me very much of the old TV programme MASH, particularly when people wandered past on their way to the toilet holding IV bags above their heads with the tubes hanging down.

The person in the next cot to me had been stretchered in feeling nauseous and looking very pale. After some coke and water and a rest he was cleared to leave and was replaced by a guy looking very bad. Apparently, he had been suffering from the flu earlier in the week but still chose to run and managed to finish. He was given some oxygen then transferred to hospital after a stern warning not to do it again. His place was taken by a lady who was looking ashen, but after a short while was feeling better. In the meantime, another lady was placed on the floor on the other side of me almost filling the aisle. She was suffering from severe cramp and cried out, in either pain or relief as the physiotherapists worked on her.

After the drips had finished, I was cleared to go once I had been for a pee. As the medic was removing the needle from my arm, checking my notes and generally tidying up we chatted. Surely it can only happen at Comrades that the medical team after treating you ask if you are coming back to do the event next year and are fully expecting and hoping you will say yes. Thankfully after the drips I needed a pee but had to be helped up from the bed as I could not get up myself and if I had tried I would probably have fallen on the lady suffering from cramp on the floor beside me. After the toilet I came back to thank the people who had looked after me and to let them know that I would try and avoid the medical tent next year.

I shuffled from the tent to the tog bag collection point to get my bag, decided not to change except for putting on a clean top then phoned Estienne to come and pick me up. Overall, a very good Comrades. Arthur Newton had helped, he showed me a part of the Comrades marathon that I had not seen before and made my experiences even richer.

The following year I decided to discover what it was like to be a spectator. I could have entered the race, but I made a conscious decision to be a spectator. I wanted it to be a deliberate choice and not one forced upon me by injury or other circumstances. Again, I stayed with my friend Peter Markew and did all the normal pre-Comrades things. I worked on the Kalahari Augrabies Extreme Marathon stand at the expo, chatted to fellow runners, walked along Durban seafront, had a few Castle Lagers and general drank in the Comrades atmosphere. This visit to South Africa was extra special because my daughter Holly was with me.

We were up early on Comrades day, but not as early as the runners, to get to our spot on Fields Hill and set up. We had tables and chairs, coke and snacks for the runners and beer and snacks for ourselves to carry to the chosen spot and get ready before the runners started arriving. It was a lovely warm day, well it was for us, it was probably a little bit hot for the runners. I had a wonderful day. For the first time I saw the lead runners and the media circus that went with them. I saw the good club runners and then the rest of the field. I applauded them all, extraordinary athletes all of them. It was great to spot friends and to run with them a little way to offer my support. I stayed until the final runner came through, then rushed to the finish to see the struggle to beat the cut-off. I found that extremely emotional and was in tears when the gun went, and they closed the finish line and turned away the runners who hadn't made it.

I thoroughly enjoyed the day and was pleased that I made the decision to experience this magical race from a different viewpoint. For a change it was my hands and arms that hurt the following day rather than my feet and legs. I had clapped so much that my hands stung and my arm muscles, unused to all the exercise, ached so much that I found it extremely hard in the morning to raise them enough to turn the shower on.

I think I have now experienced Comrades enough to let it go. If you complete 10 you get to keep your number in perpetuity and are awarded a special Green Number, but I am content to stay at 8 finishes, one did not finish and one spectated. That is my ten. Nowadays I am a trail runner and the thought of running a race on tarmac doesn't appeal at all. But you never know.

A few words about DNF. For many people DNF (Did not Finish) has negative connotations, most of the time I don't think it should. Claire Maxted, trail runner, blogger and writer gave an interesting talk at the Bloggers' Forum Award event about her experience in the Cape Wrath Ultra. Claire did not finish hence the DNF, however she learnt a lot of lessons. I know what she went through as I was on the crew for that event. On reflecting on her experiences Claire decided that this time she had taken on something that was slightly beyond her reach. Not finishing was not failing but a learning experience which made her stronger and more capable for future events, so she decided to reclassify the DNF as Did Not Fail.

That started me thinking about other possible meanings of DNF. I ran the Likeys Beacons Ultra as part of a team of three once, approximately 46 miles with 8,000ft of elevation in the cold and wet of Wales in November. I finished slightly after the first member of our team got in, but we waited in vain for the third and final member. Eventually we went to the pub and there she was, slightly drunk and very chatty. The race is over a two-lap course and after the first lap she had popped into the pub to use the loo. She got chatting had a drink and things went downhill from there. She had completely forgotten that she was part of a team. So DNF = Distracted No Finish or Discovered New Friends. Another friend told me that she had dropped out of a race because it was boring, and she was not enjoying it; she was quite capable of going the distance; DNF = Definitely Not Fun. When I pulled out of the New Forest Marathon a training run for the London to Brighton which wasn't going well, I classified it as Definitely Not Foolhardy.

To adapt a line from Bachman-Turner Overdrive "I think that any love is good lovin' "(You Ain't Seen Nothing Yet) 'Any running is good running' so I have never had a DNF – Definitely Not Fun. The Brent 10k came close; however, it was saved by the finish in the old Wembley stadium. You finished running a little way alongside the pitch and entered the stadium through the players' tunnel. The finishers medal was place around your neck once you climbed the same steps that championship and international match winners climbed to get the trophy. Even though there were only a few supporters in the stadium I could hear the Wembley roar in my head. That is the best finish of any short road race I have ever run.

There was a run where I wished I could have posted a DNF (Did not Finish) because it was DNF (Definitely Not Fun) there was a training run which I just had to see through until the end. It was during the Foot and Mouth outbreak of 2001. We had only recently moved to the southwest renting a house in Bradworthy, Devon until we could find a house to buy in the location we wanted just across the border in Cornwall. I had found lots of lovely new off-road routes to run; however, all footpaths across farmland were closed during the outbreak so I could only run on the road, cattle and sheep rearing was a big thing in the area. One Sunday I had planned a long run of about 18 miles finishing in the Old Smithy in Welcombe where I would meet the family for lunch. I had become known in the pub by then, if I arrived before the family they were happy to give me a pint of water followed by a pint of beer which I would pay for when my wallet arrived along with my clothes allowing me to change in the toilets. I set off from Bradworthy heading west aiming to cross the A39 near Meddon, it wasn't long before I passed a farmyard close to the road. In the yard was a pile of dead cows their bodies bloated with legs sticking out at the four corners, I cried. I ran on feeling miserable crossed the A39 and started to head across Bursdon Moor, it was there I saw a JCB scooping up cow carcases and dropping them into a pit. A short while later there was the acrid smell of burning flesh as smoke drifted across the moor. I wanted to turn back and go home;

however, I did not have my key with me and the family had set off for Bude before arriving to meet me in the pub, the only thing to do was to carry on as planned. I left the moor and the smoke behind, but not the smell, it was still in my nostrils and seared into my mind, as I headed to Tosberry then Wagery before heading south. I was thoroughly miserable and dejected. At Elmscott I met the army setting up a roadblock, there had been confirmed cases on a nearby farm, if I couldn't get through it would mean a very long detour to get to the Old Smithy. I explained that to the two soldiers setting up the roadblock and they let me through saying if anyone stopped me later, they were not there when I passed through. That was the worse running day ever. I was a vegetarian then (vegan now) and a big animal lover, to see them being destroyed on an industrial scale was heart-breaking. Living in a farming community I knew that not only were the animals the source of the farmers income they were also their heritage and future. Many had built up their herds over many years, sometimes generations. I felt so sorry for those farmers. I learnt later that my neighbour, a policeman, had the job of visiting farms and persuading the farmers to give him their shotguns. Facing financial ruin, being isolated from family and friends and being in possession of the means to kill yourself is not a healthy combination.

Two Worlds

Running has taken me into a completely different world, but sometimes I need reminding of that fact. A friend said to me "Edward you live in two entirely different worlds". And although I knew what she meant I did not truly understand its meaning until a few years later when I got two contrasting text messages. Jackie, a club mate from Sutton Runners, made the statement and the text messages were from Eva, who I met when crewing for the Marathon of Britain, and Vanessa, my wife.

At that time, I was living in Banstead, London during the week and returning home to Cornwall for the weekends. I worked in Wimbledon, so this arrangement meant that my family could enjoy all the benefits of Cornish life and the benefits of a London income. I would work long hours so that I could have three-day weekends and take the children to school on a Friday morning, something that I had missed out on when working a normal 9 to 5 five-day week. It also meant that I could run and go to the gym to my heart's content during the week without any moans from the family. I joined a local running club, Sutton Runners, and enjoyed training with them during the week.

I had invited Jackie to a training weekend in Cornwall for some of our club mates and some others as part of their preparations for the Comrades Marathon. It was a great weekend, the weather was perfect, and everyone enjoyed the running, each other's company and the countryside. The weekend got off to a flying start when we followed a badger along the last part of the country lane to my house as I drove my London friends down for the weekend. Everyone enjoyed the hilly 10-mile run on the Saturday, once it was over, and it set them up for the challenge to come the next day. Sunday was the key session of the weekend, a long, long run. They started on the beach in Bude and headed south along the coastal path to Boscastle before turning around and coming back past Bude to end at Gooseham a distance of about 40 miles. My wife and I set up water stations along the way. For many in the group it was the furthest they had ever run so, although tired, they were happy when they finished. Jackie was an absolute legend, she had initially planned to run with her friend Lisa for about 20 miles, which she thought was her limit, but stayed with her for the whole 40 miles. On the Bank Holiday Monday, we had a very pleasant recovery run along the beach followed by a delicious Cornish cream tea at the Rectory Tea Rooms in Morwenstow, (the best cream teas in Cornwall and therefore the world are served there) before driving back to London. As we were driving through south London in the drizzle Jackie, moved by the contrast between the lush green Cornish countryside and its clean air and the grey, drab and dirty streets of London, turned to me and said, "Edward you live in two entirely different worlds."

As I said earlier, I knew what she meant but did not realise how profound a statement it was until the two text messages arrived a few seconds apart a couple of years later. I was in Tesco, Barnstaple doing the weekly shop when a text arrived from Eva. We had spent ten days together virtually 24/7 in Transylvania six months earlier, researching running routes and had had a fantastic time running in the mountains, eating wild berries and having encounters with bears. She was texting to say that she was back in the UK after a holiday on Ascension Island. It said "Good morning and a Happy New Year! I am now back in the land of the living sporting a great tan! □ Eva". Memories of running in the Carpathian Mountains in wonderful sunshine came flooding back as did memories of the day we treated ourselves to the spa baths in Budapest on the way back to England. That certainly cheered up the detergent aisle in Tesco's.

Then came a text from my wife. "Could u also get some tuna 4 tatties and cat biscuit. Ta Xx." Back down to earth again. Yes, I do live in two entirely different worlds, one full of joy, excitement and sunshine, the other the humdrum realities of life. That is in no way intended as a criticism of family life, that world is vitally important to me. I was married for 28 years, which I think says a lot. I purposely did not say happily married, as like all couples we had some ups and downs, but all-in-all it was a good 28 years and I am extremely proud of the two wonderful girls we raised: Holly and Charlotte. Both have joined me in the Kalahari, Charlotte as part of the support crew on several occasions and Holly is a regular on the film crew. It is wonderful to have shared some of my most memorable moments with them. I'm pleased to say that both are now runners, without any pressure from me. I hope they get as much pleasure from running as I have. They have supported me in so many ways, this blog post illustrates one of them.

I was having supper with my younger daughter, Charlotte, at the Bay View Inn a few weeks ago and was surprised by what she said. Now that I live at the other end of Cornwall from her, we do not see each other as often as we used to. This was the first time I had seen her since completing the Kalahari Augrabies Extreme Marathon in October.

We chatted and caught up with each other's news and then inevitably the conversation turned to the Kalahari event. Charlotte is knowledgeable about it; she has crewed on it three times and grown up listening to her father talk about it. I said that I had struggled this year and thought it was my slowest ever. "No, it wasn't Dad" she immediately replied, "I was following your progress via the website and there are a couple of years that you were slower". I knew that she knew how I was doing because she had sent me a lovely email of support during the event, which I got on the rest day. The organisers print emails out and deliver them to the overnight camps the following day. What I had not realised was the depth of her interest and that she would look back at the history to see how I was doing compared with previous years. It gave me a nice warm feeling inside.

Our conversation was interrupted by the start of the pub quiz on gin. The Bay View Inn has good range of speciality gins; many of them from Cornwall. We did not do very well in the quiz, but we didn't come last. Just before we left Charlotte asked if I was going back in 2019. I replied that I wasn't sure. Completing 10 was my big aim and I achieved this in 2016. I had always planned a year off after that. Going back in 2018 had been wonderful, but I now felt that I can pick and choose when I go back. Charlotte, who is always direct, said "Don't be too picky, if you want to do another 10 you haven't got a lot of time to play with." (I am 64).

Later, when I was lying in bed and reflecting on the evening, still enjoying the rosy glow from the fact that Charlotte had shown so much interest in what her dad was doing, I thought about how useful her feedback was. She had observed what was happening and looked at the data so knew it wasn't my slowest performance. I had been relying on emotion and been subjective about my performance labelling it my worst. Charlotte helped me put it in context. And when it came to thinking of the future, I was looking at it from an internal aspect, I would pick and choose. She had an external view and saw the whole picture; I do have limited time. If I do not miss a year, I will be 73 when I complete my 20th, not a too ambitious a goal as the oldest finisher so far is Harry Hunter aged 70. But miss a few years and the goal will become much tougher and possibly out of reach.

Thank you, Charlotte, for providing clarity.

I used to inhabit one fairly normal world with the occasional daydream. I was a Chartered Accountant so that fairly normal world was very humdrum compared to most peoples', but I enjoyed it. When I was a young idealistic teenager my idea of hell was to be married, with two children, an office job, a Volvo estate and a Labrador. Later when I was married, with two children, an office job, drove a Volvo estate and had a Springer spaniel I was in heaven. I don't think it was the breed of dog that accounted for the big difference. How we change with time. I enjoyed that life, but the office work no longer has the same satisfaction and driving a Volvo is not a pleasure, just a necessity.

Fortunately, I now have the other world, travel, exotic locations (this piece was written in Mossel Bay, South Africa) big running challenges, friends throughout the world, uncertainty, drama, big highs and the occasional big low. The world that most of this book is about.

I know the exact point at which this other world opened up when I decided to cross over into another existence. It was in 1999 during the Comrades marathon. I must have been laying some ground work before then, but, as described in an earlier chapter, there was a point during that race when I had to make a decision; to do one thing would have left me as ordinary, the Volvo driver, the office worker, the weekly shopper in Tesco's and nothing else. To do the other would make my life extraordinary. I am so glad that when I looked deep inside myself at that point on Fields Hill, when everything was so dark, I found what was needed. Had I not carried on, I would have regretted it, I would have got over it and I would have never had known that another magical world existed where I would feel so much more alive.

The two worldness of my life and that of other sportsmen is skilfully dealt with in Ed Smith's book 'What Sport Tells Us

About Life'. To answer the questions; 'what keeps the proven champion going. Where can his motivation possibly come from? Surely, he has nothing more to prove?' He examines the motivations of actors, artists and other creative people and draws parallels with sportsmen and concludes. "To creative temperaments, the imagination, once inhabited, makes living merely in the 'real' world seem bland. Once summoned 'the hunger of imagination', as Samuel Johnson called it, is hard to satiate. Retreating back into normal life sometimes proves harder than escaping it once had been. I can certainly identify with that.

I am constantly reminded about this other worldness and not just by text messages. Sometimes when I am running on Dartmoor I will answer my phone (I carry it for emergencies and tend to answer calls in case it is my daughter, Charlotte, needing something) and if it is someone with a query that is quite mundane, perhaps concerning some committee I sit on, I look around at the bleak beauty of the moor or see a group of ponies or a pretty, stunted tree and feel a massive sense of relief that this other world exists for me to retreat into. Before I had a fairly conventional view of what was beautiful. I would have described a woman as beautiful if she was like all the models you see in glamour magazines. Furniture would have had to be highly polished with classical lines to be bestowed the description beautiful and gardens well-laid out and manicured. This has all changed now I have that other world to escape into. There I look at things from an altered perspective; I look at the misshapen, the broken and the damaged and see their beauty. I now find beauty in differences and not conformity to norms. Beauty is everywhere.

As an accountant I didn't fully appreciate the beauty of nature and the joy to be found in simple things; my real world was bland. In my running world I am more aware of my surroundings and find joy in them. The following is blog posts written after a local run.

Running smells

Yesterday I wrote about running being a sensuous thing involving all the senses and that on Sunday my auditory senses got the lion's share. Today it was the turn of my olfactory senses.

As I left the house there was the smell of baking coming from the nearby supermarket, but this was soon wafted away by the breeze and there was nothing remarkable smell-wise until the scent of the massed daffodils in the council flower beds reached my nostrils. I then turned onto the canal towpath where the air has its own smell, which is hard to pin down and describe; it is just different. It's not a strong smell like you get by some canals in cities, the water in our canal is clean and has a reasonable flow. I was still pondering how to describe it when I turned off across the fields towards the coast. There was a boggy patch with a dank, unpleasant smell of rotting vegetation. Later this was to be outdone by the foul smell of slurry, but not before my nostrils had experienced the sweetness of haylage as I passed some stables.

When I reached the coast the sea breeze, heavy with salt and with a slight hint of seaweed, cleared away the unpleasant smells. I ran along the cliff tops where there are stubby bushes and some old dead long grass, when the breeze dropped a musty smell rose from it as it was bathed in sunshine. I came down off the cliffs and back to the edge of town past the graveyard behind St Michael & All Angels church. There was a confused perfume smell from the flowers laid on the graves, then there was the clear and strong smell from patches of bluebells on the bank beside the track. I could taste it at the back of my throat.

It was then just the smell of traffic fumes until I got home and was assaulted by the smell of my own sweat. That was soon replaced by the citrusy zing of my Lemon & Lime shower gel followed by the wonderful spicy warm smell of Lynx Africa antiperspirant.

The final notes in this scent symphony were provided by the aroma of freshly ground India Gems of Araku Organic coffee beans.

I do find it hard to hard to retreat back into normal life after a big running adventure like the Kalahari Augrabies Extreme Marathon. My way of coping is to plan another adventure. It used to be another big challenge where I would have to test myself and look deep inside to be transported to that other world. But now, having tested myself enough, it is sufficient for me just to be involved with things that are not part of the bland ordinary world. I volunteer at big running challenges. There is a great buzz to be around people challenging themselves to the limit and sometimes, when you know that it was your words or support that got them to the finish it is enormously satisfying. One of the best instructions I had as a volunteer was '*Drive to checkpoint 1 then run to the top of Snowdon where your checkpoint is located*'. The table, water and food had been taken up on the train the day before and left in the café. After the last runner had passed through, I left the equipment in the cafe to go down on the train the next day and ran back down again picking up the race markers on the way. Volunteering does have other challenges; you can be getting up before the athletes and going to sleep after them so sleep deprivation becomes an issue on multi-day events. Add to that the fact that you are standing around either in the cold and wet or searing heat for long periods of time waiting for people to arrive at a checkpoint it can be difficult to maintain a good spirit. But maintain it you must because the athletes need you to be cheerful. I have always been grateful for the support of volunteers at events. I am even more appreciative now that I know what they go through.

The hunger of imagination is hard to satiate; to try and satisfy that hunger I have instigated a yes/no approach to life. Saying no to negative people and saying yes to positive ones. No to the normal and yes to adventure. No to voluntary jobs I used to feel obliged to do and yes to ones that will make a big difference and add to my experiences. This approach is working well as a couple of examples will show. Someone I had not heard from for about two years, perhaps more sent me a message saying "I am running an event at the Eden Project on 22nd January and I need some helpers. Cannot give you any details, only that you will have to be there all day. It will be hard work, but fun. Can you help?" I immediately checked my diary and sent a text back to say yes.

Jeannie is an artist with lots of energy and enthusiasm; I had no doubt that the experience would be worthwhile. The event was the creation of a mural and consisted of over 400 small canvasses painted by the Eden Project's staff which were then put together to make the big picture. It depicts the Eden Project's plans for more venues across the globe. My job was to help with setting things up, refilling paint when necessary, clearing up mess, giving encouragement, help and guidance and then helping clear up when everyone had finished. It was a fantastic day and a great thrill to see the finished art installation.

We had been encouraged to take photographs but were not allowed to publish them on social media until the Eden Project had issued their press release. I was therefore checking their website regularly and spotted that they were hosting the Indoor Gig Rowing Championships. There was a solo category and within that a super vet category, so I entered, using the logic that I'm fit and have rowed in the past (45 years ago). I was a bit dismayed to learn that a super vet was anyone over 50, but I still gave it a go; I was 63. The result is that once again I had a fantastic day and can now say that I have been in the final of a World Championships – great bragging rights.

The other example was when I spotted the Say Yes More community on Facebook. I signed up straight away and saw that they wanted volunteers to ride a water bike along canals and pick up litter. That sounded like fun, so I signed up for two legs to make it more fun by having a night's camping in between and a run back along the canal to where I had left the car when I handed the bike over to the next volunteer. I was right it was great fun although arduous work, my section had a flight of 22 locks in it. At times I felt like a celebrity, people on the passing boats had never seen a waterbike before and would take photographs and call out greetings to me. I loved it. On the run back I met two guys sitting by the canal drinking beer, one lived on the rundown barge moored nearby the other had been camping in the nearby woods for the last two years. The boat owner had suffered brain damage and some other injuries in a recent accident and found it difficult to manage the boat through locks. The Canals and Rivers Trust had given him permission to moor his boat in one place. Normally boats are only allowed to moor in one place for a short time. They had also provided him with a letter to show to anyone who told him he should move on. It was heartening to know that there is compassion in some organisations, not just rules. I enjoyed a few beers and listened to their fascinating tales before setting off on my run again. It was too late to make it back to my car before dark and running on a beer filled belly was difficult, so I stopped and camped beside the canal. I was rewarded with a wonderful sunrise as I prepared to set off on the final leg back to the car.

The two worldness of running is probably more experienced by trail runners who habit both the built and natural environment. Driving out of London on the A3 one day I turned off and discovered the Wey Navigation. It is one of the oldest river navigations in the country, the River Wey Navigation was created between 1651 and 1653 to offer Guildford merchants a magic highway to London; a series of canals replaced the difficult to navigate parts of the river to make it the A3 of its day. Now it is owned by the National Trust and only used for leisure purposes. After the cut and thrust of London traffic then hurtling down the A3 dual-carriage way at 70 miles an hour I was running along the tree lined canal admiring the shimmering water and electric blue kingfishers in almost total silence.

This almost instant transformation can occur in the heart of a city. Several times I have stayed in a hotel in the west of London near the Hanger Lane Gyratory system (if you have been there you will know how crazy and busy it is), the Paddington branch of the Grand Union Canal runs passed the rear of the hotel so it doesn't take long to escape the madness for a quiet run. Not as idyllic as the Wey navigation but still a transformation. The other end of the canal in Birmingham offers similar city centre escapes.

It's not just canals that provide escape, the New River Path performs this function in busy Islington, it is a green ribbon oasis through the borough; it starts about 40km away in Hertford. The time of day can also be a transformation, I've run through the Canary Wharf area in the late evening when it has been deserted and a calm urban desert; running along the same streets that are filled with runners during the London Marathon. In the morning, I took the DLR into the city and had a glimpse of our dystopian future, when we have felled all the trees to make way for the car, trapped behind the glass walls of the Bank of America building stressed executives were getting their morning exercise on treadmills. Running but not as I know it.

I don't know whether running was responsible for my marriage coming to an end, my wife never said why she decided it was all over. We did grow apart and I assume that I changed from spending time in the 'other word' of adventure and endeavour, I was no longer the person she married, I took a different path.

Nicknames & silliness

Over the years I have acquired a number of nicknames, some of the most enduring are, the bear, big bear, big man (a certain trend appearing) I.H.E. and Mr TT. These last two will require some more explanation than the first three. I am sure there are some other things people call me that I have not heard about, but these are probably best left unknown to protect my self-esteem.

The bear came about because of the way I walk and lumber along running, people say I move like a polar bear. I'm fairly confident that the name is based on the way I move and not that my attitude is like a grizzly bear. The big man is fairly obvious, I'm not built like a whippet, I'm a big man so friends and strangers often call me that. Ian Little often uses the term and one year before a race, when I was feeling nervous and low, his simple text 'Go well Big Man' gave me a massive boost. Thank you, Ian.

When I ran the Belfast marathon, I loved hearing the local people call out 'Fair play to you Big Man'. The Belfast Marathon was a wonderful experience. I had previously visited Belfast for work during the troubles and that was not a good experience. In parts Belfast was like any other city in the UK, however, there were also areas that were unlike anywhere else; checkpoints, armed troops, fortified police stations looking like something from a sci-fi movie and an air of uneasiness. I was shown around the city by a Fire Brigade officer who took me to places that I could not have gone to be myself, such as the Falls Road and the Shanklin Road and saw the murals. He pointed out where they had attended incidents and gave details of the body counts, sometimes with graphic details. That was rather unfortunate as I had drunk a lot of beer the night before, finishing up in the Europa Hotel and I was not feeling very well. Fortunately, I had declined more drinks there when I was told it was the most bombed hotel in Europe. So, my first visit left me with the impression of a city in turmoil and tearing itself apart. It was therefore lovely to return to a peaceful, friendly and vibrant Belfast to run the marathon and enjoy some beers and a meal afterwards. My stay was extended by the volcanic events at Eyjafjallajökull in Iceland when an ash cloud prevented air travel across many parts of Europe. EasyJet were brilliant and organised a transfer to a local hotel and paid for food and non-alcoholic drinks until flights could resume. It must have cost them more than I paid for my budget airfare.

Mr TT came about in May 2007 during the Addo Elephant Trail Runs. For reasons that will become apparent it will take the longest to explain why it came about so I will deal with it first even though in the chronology it comes last. Unfortunately, it does not mean that I am twice the man that B A Baracus is. For those of you too young to remember, Mr T was a larger-than-life character also known as B. A. Baracus in the 1980s hit TV series The A Team. No, the TT refers to Tree Talker, a name given to me by Estienne Arndt, race director of the Addo Elephant Trail Runs and the Kalahari Augrabies Extreme Marathon.

I first met Estienne and his wife, a fellow conspirator, sorry business partner, in Cape Town in 2006 thanks to the miracles of modern communication, email and text messaging. I had arranged to meet them at the Two Oceans Marathons Expo a few days before I was to run the event. At the time I was looking for advice on organising an international event and Estienne had come highly recommended. Apparently, Estienne would be easy to spot as he is tall and only has one foot. Whilst a missing foot may well be very apparent to Estienne and Nadia it was not to me due to his prosthesis. Fortunately, a mobile phone call quickly established that we were standing about 6 metres apart. Over a cup of coffee, a bond was established and a whole new rich chapter in my running life began. The story goes that Nadia, of Italian origin and a travel agent, met and fell in love with Estienne, a draughtsman and ultrarunner, veteran of many Comrades Marathons, when she arranged his travel when he entered the Marathon Des Sables. That was the start of a long loving marriage and the conception of the Kalahari Augrabies Extreme Marathon.

I met them again in 2006 during the Marathon of Britain where they were competitors and I was part of the support crew. It was at this event that I also met Eva Wheeler, which added another colourful thread to the running tapestry. Eva, originally from Romania, was in the British military and had many tales of adventure, and woe to tell, we instantly became friends. Estienne and Nadia suggested that I should come over to South Africa and run the 50-mile Addo Trail Run. It was put in such a way that it was difficult to refuse or perhaps I am just gullible.

When I pitched up in South Africa to compete in the Addo Trail run I was completely in Estienne & Nadia's hands and I had only met them twice. The arrangements were 'just turn up we will sort out everything else'. I arrived at Port Elizabeth airport, which is about 60 miles away from the Addo Elephant Park, about mid-day on Thursday with instructions to meet Charl Malherbe, the race doctor, who would give me a lift to Addo Elephant Park. Nadia had kindly provided me with a photograph of Charl, presumably because he still had all his limbs. Everything went smoothly, except that Charl's navigational abilities are limited and we took several wrong turnings before eventually finding the Park. Fortunately, during events Charl has a driver to take him places; he is a superb doctor for endurance events and has tremendous experience and knowledge when it comes to looking after people pushing themselves to the limits. If I ever have a serious problem during an event, I'd want Charl looking after me, I do not want him as my navigator.

On Friday morning Estienne suggested that I came with him in the 4 X 4 while he marked the last part of the course for the 100-miler so that I could see some of the scenery. The scenery was certainly impressive, and I envied, briefly, the guys doing the 100-miler until I remembered the distance involved. At about 10.00am Estienne received a call on his mobile phone informing him that there was a potential problem with the race and that he should contact the Park Rangers' office. The problem was that there had been severe storms in the mountains overnight and certain areas of the route could not be accessed by vehicle so there could be no medical back-up for the runners in the case of an emergency. Given those conditions it was decided that the race could not go ahead over the original course. There were two options, cancel the race or find a new course. The race briefing was due at 3.00pm so it seemed pretty obvious that the race could not go ahead. For Estienne nothing is impossible, the safety of the runners is paramount to him, so the original race was off, but finding a new route was a possibility. There was a large map on the office wall and following much discussion with the head ranger and a few others a new route was planned and plotted on the map. The route was then drawn onto smaller scale maps which I photocopied for handing out to checkpoint staff, runners and others while the large map was taken down from the office wall and whisked away to Kirkwood for the briefing.

After the briefing came all the hard work. Nadia and her crew had to rearrange all the checkpoint provision boxes as checkpoints were in different places and would need different amounts of food and water. Originally many of the checkpoints were for both the 50-mile and the 100-mile race, this had now all changed. Estienne and I set off to mark out the new course fortified with some bread & cheese and a Castle lager. That is why I found myself in an old Toyota Landcruiser, in the dark, in the middle of nowhere, in a strange country, with someone I barely knew in a stressful situation.

We were marking the course with signs on metal posts at major junctions and by tying hazard tape on trees and bushes for the rest of the course. We did most of this driving along dirt roads or 4x4 tacks at high speed, stopping and leaping out of the car or leaning out of the window as appropriate before speeding off. At one point, just after narrowly missing a Kudu that leapt onto the track, Estienne stopped the car leant out of the window and said, "Excuse me tree do you mind if I tie this tape on you?" So now I was in an old Landcruiser, in the dark, in the middle of nowhere, in a strange country with a mad man.

I decided that the only thing to do in a situation like this, which was completely new to me as it was not something Chartered Accountancy prepares you for, was to join in. At the next stop the most convenient tree was on my side of the road. I leaned out of the window and said, "excuse me tree do you mind if I tie this tape on you." I then waited a few seconds and continued with "what do you mean you are not sure, your friend down the road said it was okay" We continued through the night chatting to the trees as we marked out the course. Amazingly we completed it before sunrise, and I was able to get a few hours' sleep before the start of my 50-mile race. It was a superb event; the best single day trail race I have ever done. When I got into camp at the end of the race, I discovered that there was a story going around that during the night I had surprised Estienne by talking to trees.

From that point on I was known as Mr Tree Talker which became shorten in emails to Mr TT. Strange that Estienne started the thing, but I ended up with the nickname. The name has stuck and become a regular feature of the Addo Trail runs and the Kalahari Augrabies Extreme Marathon. I did once overhear Estienne telling the story and he completely left out that he talked to the trees. I wonder if he is aware that he did it. Special friends call me Treeman as a term of endearment.

I.H.E. was acquired in a gentler manner and has nothing to do with me acting strangely. It is connected to the London to Brighton road race, not my running of it, but the more impressive efforts of a group of friends. They wanted to become the first ladies' team to complete the London to Brighton Road Race and had asked me to organise some training runs for them. On one of then I was unable to run so was supporting on a bicycle, meeting them when the trail crossed a road to provide sustenance and encouragement. Late in the afternoon, as they were approaching me across a field, I heard chanting and rhythmic clapping. As it got closer, I could make out the words, "If you all hate Edward clap your hands". Apparently, Karen Hills had created this little chant to keep the group motivated during the final stages of this gruelling training session. It was a good way of defecting attention away from how their tired bodies were feeling. And that gave rise to I Hate Edward, shortened to I.H.E, the title the group members and a few others still use today. I'm pleased to say that they did become the first ladies' team to complete the London to Brighton although that year two teams finished and as the other team had more points they took the trophy. Our team had all their members across the line before the last person in the American team finished so they were the first ladies' team to complete the London to Brighton. It was a very emotional day for the team, and I am extremely proud to be associated with that wonderful achievement. I was very touched when I attended Karen's wedding, a few years later, and discovered the place name on the table at the rather fine reception in a Cambridge College said 'I.H.E.'

Karen and David's wedding day started with runs, there was a ladies' one for the bride and a men's one for the groom as tradition dictates that the two could not see each other that day before the wedding ceremony. I was given special dispensation to attend the ladies event. We were instructed to 'dress accordingly'; I chose my long black wig and tied some tin cans behind me in line with the wedding theme. The run was early in the morning and went through some of the colleges, the cans made an awful lot of noise, so I'd like to apologise to all the students I woke up that morning.

I should perhaps explain why I had a wig readily available. It was a training aid. When the group were training for the London to Brighton, one of them, Lisa, was rather competitive and would run races too hard, even when they were supposed to be training runs. To stop her doing this I made it clear that if she overtook me during the Luton marathon she would be off the team. Lisa crossed the finishing line a few minutes behind me and told me that she kept seeing my bald head bobbing up and down in front of her. I stored this little gem away and then used it later to provide her with a boost when I knew she was going to need it during training.

I had organised a training weekend in Cornwall and there was going to be a 40-mile run along the South West coastal path. I would provide the water stations at various points, getting there by a combination of driving in my 4 X 4 (essential for the green lanes) and running. At the top of one particularly steep climb I set up the water station and put on a long black wig I'd bought for the occasion and waited for Lisa to arrive. As she came panting up the cliff and before she could say anything I said, “You can’t see my bald spot now”. She burst out laughing and it lifted her spirits as it did for the rest of the group. At every checkpoint after that I appeared in a different wig, it seemed to do the job. Although it was a little bit embarrassing when I had to run from the car park in Clovelly to the coastal path with a rucksack full of water bottles wearing a wig because on the way there I met a group on ramblers coming the other way. I often wonder what they thought, I never stopped to explain.

I have run with Karen a few times since her wedding and she is always good fun to be with. On the first occasion we were both training for Comrades and as I was in the Cambridge area we met up for a long run. Her husband David was very kindly meeting us at various points with food and water. At one stop he had obviously been chatting with a dog walker as when she met me in a field she said she was so impressed with what I was doing especially as I was ‘no spring chicken’. I replied with ‘what do you mean I am 35’. The look of embarrassment on her face was a picture until I put her out of her misery and admitted I was 53 and teasing her. Karen obviously overheard the conversation because at the next stile and every stile or obstacle after that she offered me a helping hand saying, “Remember you are no spring chicken” Banter helps you get through tough runs.

The other occasion was when she was staying in Salisbury and I was working in Southampton. There was a footpath close to where the Salisbury road joins the A303 that I had always wanted to run on. So, we arrange to meet up and go running. It was towards the end of winter, so a cold day and I had forgotten two important things. Karen hates puddles and hills; the route had those in excess. She started out trying to avoid all the puddles but eventually gave that up as a hopeless task and ran through the centre of one. Unfortunately, it was the deepest one we had encountered, not quite as bad as the puddle in the television programme *The Vicar of Dibley*, where the vicar jumped in a puddle and disappeared up to her neck, but it came close. After that Karen constantly moaned about her feet being cold. I was trying out a pair of waterproof socks and my feet were nice and toasty. I mentioned that fact a little too often and Karen stopped, pointed and said "You see that telephone wire? If you don't stop saying how *$%*&** good your socks are they are going to find you hanging from that wire by your *$%*&** socks. Sometimes banter can go a bit too far.

One of the other I.H.E contingent, Jackie Smith, had endeared herself much earlier. She had come with a friend to meet me for a run on Ranmore Common and did not have any way of carrying water easily. I had a spare water belt in the boot of my car so offered that to her. She adjusted it to the smallest size, but it still slipped off her slim waist, so she handed it back saying, "sorry Edward I'm not fat enough". Sometime later I mentioned winning on the lottery (it was only £2.60) her response was "are you going to spend it on liposuction?".

Comrades training and the trips to South Africa have created some special moments. When you have shared the same hardship, the same doubts and been in the same very dark places a bond is forged that is special and that others cannot fully be a part of. In 1999 I travelled to Comrades on my own, but since then I have always been with other people either as part of the Comrades of Children Overseas group or with other friends. One year one of the group, Peter Bullock, had arrange to meet a relative of the person who arranged his travel insurance. I never understood why. They were meeting in the hotel for lunch and Peter invited me along. I was surprised to discover that she was in fact the Mother Superior from a local convent and arrived looking like Mother Teresa. She was a very entertaining and energic woman from Ireland who had spent a lot of time in Africa. She told us about the sardine run, an annual event on the coast where huge shoals of sardines are driven onto the beach by predators and offered to drive us to the beach to see if it was happening. It wasn't, as we were probably a little too early in the month. Mother Superior hitched up her habit and invited us to join her for a paddle. A surreal experience. She extracted from us a promise to visit the convent after our Comrades run as she was sure that the old people they looked after would be thrilled to meet some Comrades finishers from the UK. We did just that accompanied by another runner Mike Gaunt. After visiting the elderly residents in the home and a tour of the convent we were treated to afternoon tea in Mother Superior's office; an impressive high-ceiling room adorned with paintings of the Last Supper, the Madonna and Child and the Crucifixion. Tea consisted of cups of tea, Mother Superior liked hers 'strong enough so that you could trot a mouse over the top', slices of melon and sandwiches served on the finest china. After we had eaten Mother Superior said she had some chocolate biscuits as a treat, it seemed rude not to accept. She pulled out a box from a drawer and started placing a few biscuits on a plate. The name of the biscuits on the box was Love Bites. It was hard keeping a straight face. How many people can say they have had a love bite from a Mother Superior.

Later we travelled to the Hluhluwe Umfolozi Game Reserve for a few days' relaxation before the flight home. I had been there in 1999 so knew we would have an enjoyable time and have good sightings of wild animals. We signed up for a night-time game drive and were taken out on an open truck that had been converted to have bench seats and search lights at the side to illuminate any game that was about at night. We hadn't seen any when the driver stopped the truck and said there was a rhino close by in the bush and proceeded to tell us the difference between black rhino and white rhino and how the reserve had help preserve the numbers of black rhino. At that point the rhino emerged from the bush and looked at the truck that was in its way. Don't worry said our guide that is a white rhino it is the black rhinos that are aggressive, white rhinos are passive. At this point we had our search lights trained on the beast and it didn't look very passive. The guide reassured us it was a white rhino and wouldn't charge. At which point the rhino lowered its head and charged the truck. The guide shouted turn the lights out, turn the *$%*&** lights out. Everything was dark, there was a loud crunch and the truck jolted backwards then a moments silence before there was the sound of the rhino pulling its horn out of the front of the truck and the vehicle shook from side to side as it barged its way past and on up the track behind. There was another eerie silence as the sound of its heavy footsteps stopped, was it thinking of having another charge? Then there was relief as the sound of the steps moved away up the track. Mike Gaunt captured it all on video, although there was only sound after the lights went out. By the time we got back to camp we were all in high spirts and marvelling at the rhino's timing. "Don't worry it's a white rhino it won't charge" - bang. Although at the time it had been a frightening experience,

The following year we went to Cape Town to relax after Comrades and it was penguins that provided the amusement. The tour guide at the hotel took us to Boulders, just up the coast, to see the penguin colony on the beach and found it highly amusing that we all were walking like penguins. After a Comrades down run when your quads take a battering your legs are stiff, and you do in fact walk like a constipated penguin. The day after visiting the penguins we wanted to go up Table Mountain; conditions were ideal. Unfortunately, the cable car was out of action for routine maintenance. That small detail wasn't going to stop us, we were Comrades heroes. There are a number of walking routes up the mountain so a group of us got a taxi to the start of the route up Platteklip Gorge where we met up with Ian Little and Lindsay Weight who lived in Cape Town. Platteklip gorge is a steep, large stair like route so was not easy going at first but our legs soon eased out. We had a wonderful time wandering across the mountain and descended via Skeleton Gorge to the Botanical Gardens where there was a restaurant serving ice-cold lager. When we phoned for our taxi driver to come and pick us up, he could not understand how the passengers who had trouble getting in and out of his cab could have travelled so from where he left them. Back at the hotel the tour guide could not believe that the penguin impersonators from yesterday had climbed the mountain. We had to show her the photographs we had taken from the top to convince her.

The Kalahari Augrabies Extreme Marathon

The Kalahari Augrabies Extreme Marathon (KAEM) 2014 was always going to be difficult, I just didn't realise how difficult. This account is going to be relatively short, I've no desire to relive the pain. I have almost managed to erase it from my memory. There is no benefit to be had from it remaining there.

When you have done something before, and I had completed the event 7 times before by then, people think it is easy for you. In some ways they are right, you know what equipment you need, what food to take and how to prepare, but the physical things are only part of the equation. In a multi-day event, they are a small part of the equation. The biggest element is mental, and this aspect tends to get harder when you do events more than once. Motivating yourself to do the training required is hard, after all you know you are capable, you are not staring at some huge mountain which you are unsure about whether you can climb. You've been on the summit, enjoyed the exhilarating view and lived in that land on the other side of the mountain.

I learnt the danger of being complacent and not training enough from one of the ultra-running greats and at the same time earned some bragging rights. In 2002 I was running the Comrades marathon and was surprised to catch up with Bruce Fordyce (9 times winner) who can still put in a good performance even though he gave up competitive running years ago. We chatted for a while about football, he is a mad keen Manchester United supporter, before I started to move ahead. The support Fordyce gets is phenomenal and it was good to hear the cheers of the crowd getting quieter, meaning I was extending my lead, then unfortunately I heard the noise getting louder as he started to catch me up. I was about 7 km from the finish by then and I vowed that the only way he would pass me was if I collapsed and perhaps died. I finished in 9 hours 45 minutes and 35 seconds, Bruce Fordyce's time was 9 hours 48 minutes and 46 seconds, an hour more than his time the previous year and his time the following year.

When he was interviewed and asked what happened he told the truth, he could have said he was unwell or injured, but he said, "I got cocky, I thought I'm the great Bruce Fordyce I'm aiming for 9 hours I don't need to train, how wrong I was." Bruce's best time for an up run is 05:27:42. That day my admiration for Bruce went up a notch because of his honesty. I was not to speak to him again until 2016 when he gave a talk at an ultra running festival in the UK. He was very motivational when he spoke and endeared himself to many of the runners when he joined a group of us when we headed off to do parkrun on Saturday morning. The record will show that Bruce beat me that day, what that record will not show is that I and some of the others enjoyed a coffee and a chat with him after the run.

Even though I remember that interview like it had been given yesterday, and therefore the dangers of not training are very much in my mind, I still find it hard to motivate myself to train enough. Particularly this year because there was no competitive element. The previous year I needed to finish to take the record for the most number of completions, which I did. In 2014 there was no one entered who could take the record away from me. So, I decided not to train for the KAEM; what I would do was concentrate on other events so that by the time KAEM arrived I was trained enough to take it on. The plan was to train for a full-on June, recover in July, do more in August recover in September, keep ticking over in early October, by exploring new routes, and taper towards the end of October. So, in June I ran a 24-hour track race then the next weekend ran the Round the Isle race - 2 days of 31 miles a day around the Isle of Wight (hilly). I was incredibly pleased to be awarded the over 60 trophy, the only age group trophy I have. The following weekend it was the North Devon AONB Marathon (off-road and very hilly) a lovely event with magnificent views and a wonderful friendly atmosphere.

The Gloucester 24-hour race was a special event, it was my first, and only 24-hour track event. I had previously run for 12 hours on a track at Crawley; an event organised by Pam Storey, who had very kindly said a prayer for me during the 2003 Comrades marathon when I was struggling. The fact that it was my first 24-track event was not what made it special, it was who else was there. In 1982 local runner Dave Dowdle, aged 27 at the time, ran around the oval track 686 times setting a world record distance of some 170 miles (274km). He was on the refurbished Blackbridge Jubilee Athletics Track to commemorate that feat. Geoff Oliver, aged 80, was also there trying to set a new age group world record. He didn't manage it, but he did beat me. The event was also special because my friend Greg Pretorius had come to be my support crew and had brought some Castle Lager with him. Castle is what I drink to celebrate crossing the finish line in the Kalahari; the beer is hard to find in the UK. Greg and I crossed the finish line of the Kalahari Augrabies Extreme Marathon together later in the year and enjoyed a Castle.

August was the 32-mile Roseland August Trail (off-road even more hilly than the North Devon AONB Marathon), followed by my own invention a 24-hour run around a short loop taking in a very steep part of the Coastal Path. In those 24 hours I climbed (and descended) the equivalent height of Kilimanjaro, Africa's highest mountain and the highest free-standing mountain in the world. I took it easy at the beginning of September then I ran locally during the week exploring new routes with a trip to Bodmin Moor midweek and Dartmoor at the weekend to explore and have fun. The plan worked, and I arrived in South Africa feeling good, but a little apprehensive as always.

The other mental problem with having done an event before is that you know what pain you are going to go through. You also know that you have no excuse to let it beat you, after all you've done it before, but the prize is not so motivating as achieving your goal for the first time. Getting to the start line can be a battle, as can crossing it. In 2003, when I ran the Marathon des Sables a competitor, who had run it the year before and come back in 2003 with a film crew to make a documentary, suddenly remembered how much it hurt, walked away and didn't start the race. He wasn't prepared to put his body through all that trauma again despite the protestations of a bewildered film crew.

> *Mind is everything; muscles, mere pieces of rubber. All that I am, I am because of my mind.*
>
> . -Paavo Nurmi, Nine-time Olympic gold medallist

Paavo's running CV is amazing this is the first part of his Wikipedia entry:

Paavo Johannes Nurmi (13 June 1897 – 2 October 1973) was a Finnish middle-distance and long-distance runner. He was nicknamed the "Flying Finn" as he dominated distance running in the early 20th century. Nurmi set 22 official world records at distances between 1500 metres and 20 kilometres and won nine gold and three silver medals in his twelve events in the Olympic Games. At his peak, Nurmi was undefeated for 121 races at distances from 800 m upwards. Throughout his 14-year career, he remained unbeaten in cross country events and the 10,000 m.

I was able to get to the start line for KAEM 2014 and cross it. Day 1 went pretty much as expected, badly. In most of my multi-day events Day 1 has always been a disaster and a massive struggle to finish. I think my body is saying "Don't do it!". My muscles and organs are saying "We don't want to play this game." If I ignore them and keep going at the end of Day 1 they realise that I'm not going to stop and start co-operating. I finished near the bottom of the field but being 60 and a big guy I was never going to challenge for the top honours, although I did finish in 10th place one year.

Day 2 went according to plan and I ended that day moving slightly up the rankings, with the expectations of moving up several more places in the days to come particularly during the long day where you run some of it in the cool of the night. I knew what I was doing and what to expect, most of the other runners didn't. Then on the morning of Day 3 disaster struck. Normally I sleep out in the open, partly because I love solitude and love looking at the stars and partly because I hate bending over under the low gazebos that make up the accommodation. However, for the first two nights it rained (it never rains in the Kalahari according to race director Estienne Arndt) so I was under the gazebo. Bending over I twisted to get something out of my rucksack and felt a sharp pain in my back. I've had back problems in the past and knew this wasn't going to be good. Previously I had hurt my back putting the duvet on the bed, don't laugh, and was off running for several months. Fortunately, this wasn't as bad as the previous occasion; then I'd been totally immobilised, at least now I was still able to move, but I was in a lot of pain.

The rest of the week was going to be incredibly simple; I was going to disappear into a world of pain with just one thought, no surrender. There were just two possible outcomes, I'd either cross the finish line or they'd have to bury me on the route; I wasn't leaving it. There was no place for fancy motivational techniques, no visualisation, no carrots, no sticks, no association, no disassociation. Those types of things are based in rational thought, to go on was irrational. There was just one thought; keep going.

There were some good things that happened in the following days, painkillers that worked for a few hours. Patrick Hobbs, a fellow Brit and long-term Kalahari friend with one more start than me but fewer finishes, said he could tell how well the medication was working. A little while after I took the pills, I would pull out a lead on him then a few hours later as it wore off, he would catch, then pass me until I was allowed some more and the process would be repeated. Patrick is a tough competitor who suffers badly when it gets extremely hot. I love what someone said when I posted some photos of the 2018 event on Facebook (one of the years when Patrick finished) 'Julian Paterson - I won't ever forget, Edward, you were a bit in front of me when Patrick passed me and with a crooked yet determined grin muttered " right, Chapman, you're next". Special moment.' There were incredible views that made me forget my troubles. One view, which is the best I think I have ever seen, made me stop, stand and stare and cry. I'd like to tell you where it was and what it was like, but details of that year's Kalahari experience have disappeared in the fog of the pain. I don't want to remember it; I don't think I can bear to remember it. And there was the kindness of my fellow competitors who, when I got into camp each day, helped me get my rucksack off, carried my water, found me some shade and on one occasion took my shoes and socks off when I was too tired and in too much pain to do it myself. I can remember all of those; they were very touching simple acts of kindness. There was a beautiful moment when the race doctor, who knew I was in a lot of pain when I got into camp but could not give me any more medication for a few hours, just sat and held my hand. An exceptionally beautiful moment indeed.

Finally, day 7 arrived and I knew I had only a short distance to go. My friend Greg Pretorius, who I'd met while he was training for KAEM and who very kindly was my second earlier in the year when I competed in the 24-hour track race, caught me up then stayed with me so we could finish together. On the final day there is a staggered start with the faster runners leaving later than the slower ones. The idea being that everyone finishes within a short space of time and so that everyone is there before the overall winner. All the racing has been done in the days before, so the final day is a celebration run just like the last day in the Tour de France. Finishing crossing the line with Greg was incredibly special indeed. Greg had been full of doubts about his ability to complete the event, I never had any doubts; I knew he would finish.

KAEM number 8 took more out of me than any of the previous 7 and I probably had less to gain, but the Kalahari and the event always gives you so much. Yet again I came away enriched in so many ways by the experience.

Always in my mind were the words of the KAEM song composed by Simon Kelly

I want to go where the sun shines
Where the river flows and the quiver trees grow.
To a place I know my soul will be revived.
I want to go where the rocks and cliffs rise up from the trail
I want to run through the space into the setting sun.
It's here I feel alive with a challenge to survive.
Even though I sometimes wonder what's on my mind
The sand is like the sea – rough and yet serene
And the sky runs up as far as the eye can see
I know I feel the pain as the sweat drops from my brain
Runs into my eyes as I cross this hot terrain
I have overcome my fear and I know the end is near
I will leave this place as I know I'll be back again

The finish line is near – I can almost taste the beer
As I forge towards the end with quickened pace
And when all this is done – I'll be happy that I've run
Now I yearn for rivers rocks and sand and space
Cause it draws me back again when I cannot feel the pain
Yes, the sunsets, rivers rocks and sand and space
Yes, it draws me back again to the desert and the sand
To sunsets, rivers rocks and sand and space …

Even in 2014 when I suffered so much this line is absolutely true:

It's here I feel alive with a challenge to survive.
You forget the pain and remember how good it was to be alive.

Yes, it draws me back again to the desert and the sand
To sunsets, rivers rocks and sand and space …

As I said earlier, 2014 wasn't the year for fancy motivational techniques it just needed pure stubborn grunt. Other years I have relied on mental tricks to see me through, some derived from Neurolinguistic Programming (NLP), for example visualisation and anchoring, others I have learnt from fellow runners. Despite having a whole arsenal of techniques, I have sometimes had to be inventive. Normally I visualise the beer I have at the finish and wrap all sorts of other stuff in with it to make a compelling vision. One particularly tough year I had to adapt that and swap the tasty carrot for a big stick. The deal I made with myself was that if I didn't finish that year, I would not be allowed to have a beer until I finished the race the following year. That worked. Another time, when things were very tough, 2015, I was trudging up a sandy riverbed in extreme heat and nothing was working, I had used every tool in the box. Then I had a flash of inspiration, a few days earlier someone had mentioned that you should never eat a polar bear's liver, it is highly toxic due to massive levels of Vitamin A. And there it was, my fortunes had suddenly turned around, what a blessing I was probably the furthest away from eating a polar bear's liver than I would ever be. I continued on with a spring in my step as I carried on trudging up the riverbed chuckling at my good fortune. That might sound crazy until you analyse what is going on. I was in a bad frame of mind and needed something to change that, it needed to be out of the ordinary to be effective, I'd already tried normal. Polar bears are very easy to visualise and when you do it brings up the images of the cold and ice-flows; that takes you away from thinking about the heat and makes you feel cooler. You are also thinking positively and away from the current problems. I used the polar bear liver thing later in the event to distract me when I was just grinding out distance along an easy to navigate boring section. I tried to think if there was ever a situation where I might accidentally eat a polar bear's liver. I did think of one, if we ever meet, I will tell you about it over a beer.

Other multi-day events

Running the Kalahari Augrabies Extreme Marathon leaves little time, energy or money for other multi-day events. I have managed to squeeze a few in over the years. The first was in 2009 as part of a Minus 40 to Plus 40 challenge Phillip Howells and I set ourselves; entering the 6633Ultra in the Arctic with temperatures of minus 40, it doesn't matter which scale, Fahrenheit and Celsius are the same at that point, and the Kalahari event where temperatures reach plus 40 C or more. Likeys, who organise the Arctic race, had offered us a discounted entry; it was still expensive. Then there was the kit we needed to buy to keep us safe during the 350-mile non-stop self-sufficient foot race which is regarded by many as the toughest, coldest, windiest ultra distance footrace on the planet. The price of a sleeping bag for the minus 40 conditions was almost as much as I paid for my car and I got 250,000 miles out of it. I did think that at least I wouldn't have to buy sunglasses as I had those for my desert trips. I was wrong the strength of the glare coming off the snow and ice meant I need an upgrade.

Training went well, although the winter weather in the UK was too hot for training in full kit, and I flew to Vancouver, then to Whitehorse in the Yukon, with a mixture of excitement, confidence and dread. My luggage including the pulk (sledge) and most of the equipment didn't arrive in Whitehorse with me which caused some panic. Fortunately, it arrived the following day in time for the 500-mile drive to Eagle Plains where the race started. Fans of the TV programme *Ice Road Truckers* may recognise that name; it is one of the truck stops. On the way we stopped for a coffee and I had the biggest cinnamon bun I've ever seen; I was enjoying being in Canada. We broke our journey in Dawson City and took the opportunity to join the Sourtoe Cocktail Club, with a visit to the Downtown Hotel. It is easy to become a member of the club, you just need to follow these simple steps.

Step 1 – Come down to the Sourdough Saloon and ask for Captain River Rat
Step 2 – Purchase a shot (most club members prefer Yukon Jack)
Step 3 – Pledge the 'Sourtoe Oath'
Step 4 – Watch as a (genuine) dehydrated toe is dropped in your drink
Step 5 – Drink your Sourtoe Cocktail

Be sure to remember the most important rule: "You can drink it fast, you can drink it slow, but your lips have gotta touch the toe."

And yes, it is a real amputated toe. There is an advert on the hotel's website:

WANTED

TOES FOR SOURTOE COCKTAIL

Got frostbite? The Downtown Hotel in Dawson City,
Yukon is currently seeking toes for its
World Famous Sourtoe Cocktail

Donors will forever be immortalized
in the Sourtoe Hall of Fame.

The hotel has a stock of about 10 toes which are kept in salt and used in rotation, being retired when they start getting worn, usually after about five years. One toe was swallowed, and a couple have been stolen. Fortunately, there is a steady supply due to the harsh conditions in the area, a recent one came from a British Marine who lost it to frostbite during the Yukon Arctic Ultra marathon.

It was good to eventually get started in the race pulling our pulks along the frozen dirt road which is the Dempster Highway towards the Arctic circle. It is extremely hard to describe how cold minus 40 degrees is because most people have nothing to compare it with. Minus 40 isn't just twice as cold as minus 20 it is a lot more extreme. It was quite mild when I reached the Arctic Circle; only about minus 27C. I decided to push on that day and into the night; I was rewarded with a stunning display of the Northern Lights. Being on my own in the middle of nowhere seeing that display is something I will remember for ever; it was a very spiritual experience. The technical explanation for the Northern Lights (aurora borealis) is relatively simple, it is caused by particles in the solar wind hitting the atmosphere and emitting light at different wavelengths. I knew that, but it didn't prepare me for what I saw. Every day of my life the night sky has been similar, either cloudy, clear with stars or a combination of the two. Sometimes when viewed from dark areas, Dartmoor, the Kalahari, Bhutan etc., the stars have been amazing. The sky that night started out like any other night then things started to change, there were thin arcs of colour, greens and blues, in the sky which seemed to be dancing. They thicken and the green became darker coalescing into curtains that appeared move as if in the breeze from an open window. I stood there with my head torch off watching spellbound for what appeared to be hours. I could not have been, I would have become dangerously cold not moving for that length of time. When the curtains dissolved, like the Cheshire Cat in Alice in Wonderland, I realised I was cold and moved on knowing I had experienced a wonderful spectacle of the natural world that few others will ever see. I have watch videos of the Northern Lights since and they just do not capture the full majesty of the spectacle or the emotion that goes with it. To see the Northern Lights while you are on foot, alone in a vast wilderness is a magical blessing.

Disaster struck the following day; it was partly bad luck and partly my inexperience. I was feeling good and powering up a hill, going too well because I started to sweat, which is not a good thing in those conditions. I slowed down to cool down and at about the same time a fierce cross wind started blowing. I still felt okay; however unbeknown to me the sweat on the inside of my left thigh froze. Every time I stepped forward with my left leg the thigh was exposed to the wind which pushed the fabric of my thermal leggings hard against the sweat. Had I been more experienced I would have stopped and put an extra layer of leggings on, but I didn't feel cold. One of the crew, Murray, was at the top of the hill in a vehicle checking everyone was okay, I got in the vehicle for a chat and a little rest and that is when I discovered things were not okay, the inside of my leg felt like giant bubble wrap and I started shaking uncontrollably. With the skin broken and frozen it was easy for heat to escape from my body and I was entering the early stages of hypothermia. I was driven to the next checkpoint, a snow-plough barn and then it was decided I needed to go to the hospital in Inuvik. My leg was a mess and very painful, fortunately the doctor didn't think there would be any permanent damage. Had I stayed out any longer the outcome would have been hugely different.

I was given the option of staying in hospital at $250 a day where they would change my dressings or I could leave the hospital, they could give me the dressings and I could change them myself. There was a dire warning that if I didn't thoroughly abrade the wounds to remove dead skin gangrene was a possibility and I would be back in hospital possibly for an amputation. I opted for the do-it-yourself option as that meant I could follow the race with the crew and get to the

Arctic Ocean at Tuktoyaktuk. To cope with the pain of abrading the wound I was prescribed a cocktail of four different painkillers.

I'm glad I started the event, got the opportunity to cross the Arctic Circle, see the Northern Lights, experience a vast wilderness, walk along the froze McKenzie River (the Ice-Road) and stand on the frozen Arctic Ocean. I have no desire to go back; the cold is not for me. You have layers and layers of clothes on and are strapped into a harness to pull the pulk. You are wearing a balaclava, a hat, mask and goggles which freeze up so you can only see out of the small spots where you had wiped away the ice. Most of what you could see was just a lot of white stuff. For me that was not fun and it was not being free. A pair of shorts and t-shirt for me does it every time. I am also glad I was not in a position to be immortalized in the Sourtoe Hall of Fame. I just have the certificate to say I had the cocktail and the toe touched my lips.

There were some other benefits of the trip; Andy Murray (the GP and ultrarunner not the tennis player) in his book describes winning the 120-mile version of the race and to illustrate how tough conditions were he says, 'even a gnarly competitor like Edward Chapman was forced to withdraw'. Mimi Anderson, who won the race in 2007, uses a photograph of my leg, with my permission, when she gives presentations about her running exploits which are legendary. Again, she uses it to illustrate how tough the event is. My leg is more famous than I am. At the 2020 National Running Show I was chatting to another runner about various races when she suddenly said "Oh, my God that was your leg in Mimi's talk". I'm quite happy for my leg to steal the limelight. Any publicity is good publicity.

My next big other multi-day race wasn't until 2011 and the Al Andalus Ultimate Trail a semi-supported 5-stage, 230km ultra-marathon race in Andalusia, southern Spain. The event takes place in July so can be extremely hot with temperatures over 40C. Much more my thing. The area is close to the only real desert in Europe which lies in the barren interior of the Costa de Almería. It is described as semi-supported as you have to provide some of your own food, but you are also able to pop into villages at the end of the day for a pizza, something more substantial or even a cold beer. On the nights when there are no villages near the camp paella and pasta are provided.

It is not an event to be taken lightly, the course is hilly and on varied terrain. The event starts from the town of Hoja and you very soon get a good idea of how things are going to be with a big climb out of the town over the Sierras (mountains) Loja. I had recently been diagnosed with peripheral neuropathy, a painful condition caused by my immune system attacking my nervous system causing pain in my hands and feet. The diagnosis was a relief because, apart from a very gradual loss of feeling in my extremities, there were no serious long-term outcomes. Originally there was a concern that it could be the start of Multiple Sclerosis. The medication I was on affected my running making me slow. However, I was enjoying being out in the stunning countryside even though I was at the back of the field. One of my favourite memories was running along a track where we would brush against wild herb plants; the smell was wonderful. On Day 4 the race director judged that I would not make the cut-off at the next checkpoint so moved me up the course in a vehicle. I thought he was wrong, however when you sign up to an event you agree to a abide by the race director's decisions. They know the complete picture and have the safety of the runners and the crew and the success of the event to think about. That decision meant that I would not be included in the list of finishers even though I was allowed to complete the rest of the event. It was some consolation that I would get to see all the course when 20 of the 65 entrants had had to pull out at some stage. It is a great event, well organised and friendly so I knew I would be back.

In 2013 I heard about a new event taking place in Bhutan, a country I have never heard of until I did an internet search and found that it was the least visit country in the world having only recently being open to foreigner visitors. The event was the Last Secret, 200 km over six days. Each stage is roughly 30 km long with one stage over 50 km and the final day a relatively short 15 km but with a massive climb. Tourists have to be part of an organised tour with an inclusive price of at least US$250 a day. That made the cost of the race look very reasonable, so I signed up. This was an event that went well and far exceeded what I expected, Just getting there was a mission, a flight to Delhi, a long wait, then a flight to Paro in Bhutan which provided a view of Everest and a long wait in Kathmandu until the winds at Paro dropped to allow for a safe landing. The approach to the airport is along a valley and I'm sure the wings were only metres away from the valley sides; only a few pilots are licenced to fly into Paro. From there it was about a two-hour bus trip to Thimphu the capital; the only capital in the world not to have any traffic lights.

The race started in the Punakha Dzong, the second largest dzong in Bhutan and one of its most majestic structures. Stefan Betzelt, the race director likes his events to start and finish in dramatic locations. We crossed the bridge from the temple over the river and out into the countryside after listening to local school children singing. That first day was wonderful, suspension bridges across gorges, big climbs, lovely view, pretty houses and prayer flags everywhere. The overnight stops were all different with wonderful food provided for us at everyone. One night we were treated to a traditional hot rock bath, where rocks are heated in a fire then placed in the end of a wooden bath to heat the water, it gets extremely hot. The rocks release minerals which are supposed to be good for the body. I certainly felt good after the bath. Another evening we were allowed to sit in on a Buddhist prayer ceremony. We even had a football match against some young monks. The terrain varied every day, seldom flat except for a run around the perimeter of the airport before heading into the hills again.

For me there was a slight hiccup in what was, except for that, a perfect event. When I reached the end of stage 3 at the Phajoding Monastery which is at an altitude 3,600 metres it was cool and my bag with a change of clothes had not arrived. There is no road access, so our kit bags were transported to the monastery on packhorses; my bag had been mistaken for one belonging to the crew who were not with us at this overnight stop. To make matters worse I was beginning to feel very unwell. This was diagnosed as altitude sickness, I was whisked away to a monk's room, given his bed and an electric fire put in the room to keep it warm. The unfortunate monk slept on the floor so that he could monitor my condition in case it got any worse. In the morning I still felt terrible and wondered how I was going to make it through the next stage described as "38km, ups and downs, mainly through forest and villages. Crosses a mountain pass of about 3500m, last section is a descent to the camp at 2280m". Fortunately, the first part was down and after I had descended a little bit, I felt a lot better and ended up having the most wonderful run. A day I remember as the best piece of trail running I have ever encountered.

The finish of this event must be the best of any event in the world, you climb up what at first seems an impossible route to finish at the entrance to the Tiger's Nest Temple, the most sacred place in Bhutan. The temple hangs off the side of a mountain and when you look up at it you can only wonder about how it, was built, how the material was carried up the mountain and how the temple stays there rather than toppling down the mountain. The only way up there is on foot so that also means the only way back down again after you have finished is on foot. We stopped at a restaurant halfway down for a celebration meal. As I said earlier, one stage of the race contained the best single track running I have ever done, it was stunningly beautiful and as we descended from altitude we passed through all sorts of vegetation from pine forest to jungle and out into what looked like alpine meadows. This is the testimonial I left on the event website.

'Thanks for a fantastic event; it exceeded my expectations by a long way. The running was absolutely wonderful with some great single-track sections; I particularly enjoyed the technical downhill sections and weaving through the paddy fields on the narrow paths. The organisation of the event was excellent, as was the course marking, particularly in view of the fact that children kept removing the orange tape. I also liked that fact that care had been taken to select interesting overnight stops and to allow us to experience some of the culture of Bhutan. I have absolutely no hesitation in recommending this event to others.'

The children removed the tape, not to be troublesome, they were fascinated by it. You would be running along wondering which way to go and a dog would trot by with some tape attached to its collar. The race organisers somehow manage to find some eco-friendly spray paint to solve the tape problem.

I'd also entered the Al Andalus Ultimate Trail again that year, when I entered, I did not expect to be doing another multi-day race a few weeks before hand. Still, I had paid so I was going to turn up and give it ago. When I started, I knew things were not going to go well, I'd been feeling under the weather the week before and I was still not right. I took a sanguine view and decided not to push things. I could have finished on the first day in a state, instead I found some shade, sat down and sent the organisers a text saying that I was stopping, I was okay had plenty of water and was quite happy to wait until a vehicle was passing to be picked up. In camp that night the doctor checked me over, found that my blood pressure was low so gave me a drip. After a good night's sleep, I felt marvellous so chose to help on checkpoints the next day, then after that I re-joined the race to soak up the scenery. So again, I didn't get a medal, I was in good company 12 of the 50 entrants didn't finish that year.

I might go back and give it another shot sometime however there are some other events to tick off before then, Cape Wrath Ultra (400km in 8 days in remote north west Scotland), Ultra Race Romania (250km on 6 stages through the Transylvanian section of the Carpathian Mountains) and, possibly the Dragon's Back (380kn in 6 days across the Welsh mountains – considered to be the toughest mountain race in the world). With the Grand to Grand in the USA and a race in Namibia waiting in the wings.

People often ask me why I love multi-day races as a competitor and a volunteer. That is a hard question to answer because there are so many reasons and many of them are hard to put into words in a way that those that don't know can understand. One of the reasons is that I meet real people. That may need explaining.

When you run with someone for a long time on a difficult stage, or you are a sweep and spend time with someone who is grinding it out until they get to the finish, the talk often revolves around what the race does to you. Most people talk about it stripping them down to the basics, removing the layers that we allow other people to see and that hides the true us. They talk about being deconstructed, of looking into very dark places to find answers: Do I have what it takes? Can I go on? Do I want this enough? It is then that you see the real person: the barriers, the defences, the glossy exterior is stripped away. Stripped to the core, there is no black or white, no man or woman, no boss or employee, there is just a person. These are incredibly special moments; moments when you really know each other, and a bond develops that is deep and profound.

Sometimes you can help, but most of the time the individual has to find their own answers and if they share that with you it is a very humbling experience. I have had many such moments and will share just one with you. I was talking with someone towards the end of a tough multi-day race, the long day was over and the end was in sight, it was then that she shared with me what had got her through when it got very, very tough and she wanted to quit. She had been in a relationship where her partner belittled and beat her. She told herself that she had survived that and that what she was going through in the race was not as bad as that; she could keep going. It angers me that someone so gentle and so strong should have been so badly treated. Unfortunately, I have heard similar accounts from several people. Yes, multi-day events strip you down, but they also reconstruct you into a much better person, more able to cope with whatever life throws at you. They build you up, put you in control. You see yourself in a different light and want to go through that rebuilding process again to continually improve, to live life, to know yourself and to be with beautiful people.

A few of my favourite things

There are some events that have that special something and you want to keep going back while there are others that are great fun, but I have been content to do only once. Obviously, Comrades is one that fits in the former category; I have completed it eight times although I doubt I will ever run it again now that I am a trail runner rather than a road runner. You have to train specifically for events and the thought of all the necessary train on the road doesn't appeal even though the event does.

Firmly in the do once category is the Streak for Tigers. This was an event dreamt up by London Zoo to raise awareness of the plight of the Sumatran Tiger. The collective noun for Tigers is a streak so, they decided to get some runners to streak around the zoo to raise money and attract lots of publicity. I was one of those runners. The event was well thought through and designed to put us all at ease as much as possible. Getting your kit off and running naked in front of a lot of strangers is not easy. We arrived after the Zoo had been closed to the public and undressed in some rooms set aside as male and female changing rooms. Everyone was provided with a space blanket to cover up with and we were shown into a garden where drinks were available. The trees and bushes were decorated with bras and colourful pants. The drinks were black and orange and arranged in alternate rows to look like tiger stripes. Everyone chatted nervously while we waited for the event to start. It was good to realise that most people were just as nervous as I was, although there were some naturists there who were standing around totally naked and totally unperturbed. Family and friends who had bought tickets were admitted to the zoo and were waiting on the route to witness the spectacle. At the appointed time we all lined up at the exit to the garden took our space blankets off, putting them in the baskets provided, and ran.

Even though the run was only a few hundred yards it was still the hardest thing I have done. It was a very liberating experience and most of us decided to run extra laps to enjoy the occasion. We didn't see many animals, but those that we did pass seemed quite disinterested in what was going on. I am glad I did my bit for the tigers; I hope one day to see one in the wild. The event was a great success and raised a lot of money for poacher patrols, but more importantly it got a great deal of publicity. London zoo had invited a lot of press to attend and the unusualness of the event meant most turned up and wrote about it; fortunately the photographs used were not revealing.

There are a few Long Distance Walkers Association (LDWA) events that are on my favourite list. The Long Distance Walkers Association is welcoming of runners, have cheap events and excellent food at the checkpoints. You can put on weight running their events. The ones I would single out (this is purely from the ones I have done, there may be others that are far better) are the Surrey Tops, a 50-mile route that takes in all the high points in Surrey. The Wellington Boot a 100km route that goes via the Quantocks, the Brendon and Blackdown hills, rising to 1000ft on 3 occasions. It takes place every three years. And the Three Rings of Shap, a 100km route which as the name suggests consists of three different but roughly equal length routes based on the village of Shap. After each loop you return to the village hall for a meal. I don't think the event is held any more, however the route details are available from the LDWA website. My favourite is the Winter Tanners which takes place in January near Leatherhead and is a 30- mile loop. The event has been going for over 40 years. I think these stand out and are favourites because they all involve hills, therefore views, and showcase the countryside in different areas of England.

I am always pleased when serendipity throws up a lovely running experience, this one also served up a humbling experience as well. I had been on a sales trip in the north of England with the last visit on Friday afternoon in Penrith. I decided to stay up there for the weekend and looked for a race. The only one I could find was the Haweswater Half – a road race, not my thing but needs must when the devil drives. It was cold, but beautiful, an out and back course mostly alongside the lake. I'd forgotten how much fun small races organised by a local club, in this case Eden Runners, could be. There was a great atmosphere at the start, good facilities and good organisation. The course was on almost traffic free roads. The organisers' claim that "the hilly course offers an exhilarating run in unique surroundings" was not unfounded. It was certainly hilly, and I think it is the most scenic road half-marathon I've ever run. Throughout the race I kept passing a lady on the downhill sections and she would then pass me on the uphill sections. She eventually finished just in front of me, I desperately tried to catch her on the relatively flat last mile into the village, but she finished very strongly. As we waited in the queue for tea to go in our race-memento mugs I politely asked her how old she was, I thought she was possibly in her early 60s. 73 was the reply – oh how humbling running can be. Until then I had been feeling good about passing quite a few runners a lot younger than me. The Haweswater Half is probably on the do once list; however, if I was passing at the right time, I'd do it again.

Another firmly in the do once category is 24-hour track racing, despite the nice things I said about the Gloucester 24hr in an earlier chapter. A 12-hour track race is also in that category, although I do have very fond memories of the Crawley 12-hour race. Someone had brought the torch from the 1948 Olympic Games to the event and we were each allowed to carry it around the track for a few laps with the flame lit. I cannot explain why, but I found carrying the torch to be a deeply moving experience. The 1948 Olympics in London were the first to be held after a twelve-year hiatus caused by the outbreak of World War II; these were the first Summer Olympics held since the 1936 Games in Berlin. Those Olympics became known as the Austerity Games, because of the difficult economic climate and rationing imposed in the aftermath of World War II. There were no new venues built and no Olympic village. They probably embodied the Olympic spirit more than any other games. It was also the first Olympic games for my biggest athletics hero, Emil Zatopek, who won silver at 5,000m and gold at 10,000m. In the 1952 Olympics he became the only person ever to win gold at 5,000m, 10,000m and the marathon at the same Olympics. It is possible that the torch I carried was also carried by him during the 1948 Olympic opening ceremony. I was a fan of Zatopek before my running days thanks to a school project on the post war Olympics and my father being a big fan of his. There is an excellent biography of Zatopek, 'Today we die a little' written by Richard Askwith, author of the iconic running book 'Feet in the Clouds'. I am a great reader of biographies, most of them are of runners, but I also find other sports people interesting. Most that I have read are about current people, some are about athletes that are now dead and one fits into both categories.

On June 30, 2007 Alberto Salazar had a heart attack and his heart stopped beating, he was dead for 14 minutes before his heart was started again. He only recovered without permanent brain damage because of the excellent CPR he received before the ambulance arrived. He was overseeing a training session at a sports ground when he had the heart attack and was fortunate that there was a doctor nearby who was with an American Football team training on the same ground. Alberto Salazar made it onto my heroes list in 1999 when I ran the Comrades marathon for the first time and discovered that in 1994, he became the only top-class international marathon runner to win Comrades. He ran Comrades because of a love of running and for the challenge, not for money or to advance his career. In fact, it was the last competitive race he ran.

The book is a fascinating read, not just because of the running stories, but also because of his background. Alberto Salazar originally came from Cuba, his father José fought alongside Fidel Castro and Che Guevara in the Cuban revolution. Salazar's father become disillusioned with Castro and left Cuba to live in exile in the United Sates leading an opposition movement against Castro. Alberto Salazar and I have several things in common, the Boston Marathon, Comrades and Medjugorie (a Catholic pilgrimage site in Bosnia); he deals with his experience of Medjugorie in the book - it was a religious experience for him. My link with that place is more tenuous. In the chapter Nicknames & Silliness I mentioned meeting a Mother Superior, she gave me a small medal that she had brought back from Medjugorie, I think she brought back many. The medal has allegedly been blessed by the vision of the Virgin Mary. I am not religious or superstitious so didn't think about the medal when I got home until I had an accident on the busy M6. My Ford Ranger span across all three lanes and ended up facing the wrong way on the hard shoulder, it was incredible that I didn't get hit by anything especially the big lorries thundering along the inside lane. When I pulled on the handbrake, I noticed the medal in the tray between the two seats. As I said I am not religious or superstitions; however, I'm also not foolhardy so I now keep the medal in my wallet.

The world of ultra running is a relatively small one, although it is growing fast, so it is often possible to find a link with an ultra running book or even to find your name in there. The excellent book by Adharanand Finn 'The *Rise of the Ultra Runners – a journey to the edge of human endurance*' is scattered with the names of people I know, both the well-known and the ordinary ultra runners, if there is such a thing. The race that was his first ultra is one that I know well; I have run it a few times and been a volunteer on it more times. It is one of the events in the Endurancelife Coastal Trail Series, a series of events with 10k, half-marathon, marathon and ultra options along stunning sections of the England and Wales coastline. I have run and volunteered at most of their events and would put the South Devon and Exmoor events firmly in the do several times category. They also organise the Classic Quarter, 44 miles along the South West Coastal Path from the southernmost point of England (Lizard Point), to the western most tip (Land's End). This translates to running 90 degrees of the compass, hence the name, Classic Quarter. The innumerable steep climbs and descents, plus the varied terrain make this a tough event; however, as well as the solo option it can be entered as a relay with teams or two or four, so accessible to most club runners not just ultramarathoners. This is definitely on the do more than once list; different weather and sea conditions make it a different experience each time.

Another event that is changed significantly by the weather is the Cornish Marathon because it takes place in November and goes over Bodmin Moor. I've run it when it has been cold and sunny, when it has been relatively warm and when it has been cold, sleeting and blowing a gale. It is a road race, so I no longer enter; between 2002 and 2008 I ran it 5 times.

But most of all I just like to run. My favourite places are the South West Coastal path (sometime soon I plan to run it all), Bodmin Moor, Dartmoor, the Pentland Hills, the North Downs Way and Groenkloof Nature Reserve, Pretoria, South Africa – I had a close and scary encounter with an angry giraffe there once. I like cliffs, hills and mountains; however, I think when I get old, I will explore routes in East Anglia, they will be nice and flat.

I also like to great my own challenges, the first was my 24-hour challenge which I have already mentioned, running around a short loop which included a section up a cliff. Two years later I created my parkrun challenge. My local parkrun at the time, Tamar Lakes, takes place around a reservoir and consists of almost a full lap; the 5k is about 200m short of a full lap. For some reason, best left unfathomed, I decide to run the parkrun and then complete the route 99 more times before the next one and then take part in that; 500k (310 miles) in a week. There was a campsite beside the route with toilets and showers, so I set my tent up with food and off I went, running about a marathon and three quarters each day. It was a wonderful experience, friends came and ran with me for several laps, I was interviewed by the local radio station then strangers came and ran with me. I met lots of interesting people; a local artist, a retired policeman who had been in the Diplomatic Protection Group, someone who had cycled from Land's End to John 'o' Groats and people with local stories to tell. I also inspired children to come and cycle alongside me, mothers to run with their children in buggies and people who wanted to be part of my adventure. I even met a tortoise, which I felt a strong affinity with. A local man came walking around the reservoir with his tortoise most days so that it could enjoy the views. He carried the tortoise, holding it so that it could look around; the tortoise seemed very attentive. All-in-all a rewarding experience. I raised money for the children's charity CHICKS (now renamed Go Beyond) both online and with a collection box in the site café. Handing the cash over to the charity led to another rich thread in the tapestry of my life. Mick, the fundraiser, an ex-navy man, thought I would be a good role model and should volunteer on the breaks they ran. CHICKS organise respite breaks for disadvantaged children where they get the opportunity to try out a variety of activities, many outdoor. It is a tremendous boost to their self-esteem and helps them cope with the challenging conditions they are facing. The thought of spending a week with difficult teenagers filled me with dread; however, applying my Say Yes More principle (Saying yes to things outside my comfort zone and no to boring stuff) I agreed. I was nervous about the first break, I didn't need to be, the children were great, and I had a wonderful time. I have now volunteered on seven breaks and enjoyed everyone, I am particularly good at encouraging the more timid children to try new challenging things without putting them under too much pressure and letting them feel comfortable about not doing it should it be too big a step for them. I also helped with a four-week scheme that ran over the summer holidays called Fit & Fed that catered for children from Plymouth who were at risk of going hungry. They came to the centre in Cornwall for fun outdoor activities (going to the beach, team games in the fields, den building and more) and were provided with snack when they arrived and a healthy lunch. I was trained in safeguarding, first aid, food hygiene and how to deal with conflict between children before being let loose on organising daily activities for a group of about twelve to fourteen children with the help of another volunteer. It was hard work and stressful particularly when we took the children off site, but it was also fun and extremely rewarding. My endurance background was helpful.

My last fundraising event definitely comes into the never again category. I decided that to celebrate my 65th birthday in 2019 I would run every day in June (my birthday month) with the mileage each day equalling the day number. The first week was easy 1 mile, 2 mile, etc. with the last seven days being a bit testing starting with 24 miles and ending with 30 miles so 189 miles in the last week and a total of 465 miles in the month. To keep route selection simple I decided upon out and back runs from home turning around when I had reach halfway for the day. Originally, I used a variety of routes locally then as the distances needed to be longer, I settled on running to the coastal path and turning right one day and left the other. I soon decided to always turn left due to the set of steps on the way to Portreath if I turned right. It wasn't boring covering some of the same ground every day because the weather and the changing sea always makes the views different. I would also meet different people each day, very often German tourist attracted to the area because of the Rosamunde Pilcher books set in the area and serialised on the national television station ZDF. With the benefit of hindsight, it would have been better to decide to run for 26 days and use kilometres for the distance.

The last never, never do again event was a virtual 10k. In a moment of madness, I decided to do it running around my office chair. 1,695 laps of a 5.9 metre circle. Before the event I had a little practice and decided to change direction every 10 laps to prevent myself getting dizzy. That worked for a while; however, I eventually found it was better to keep going in one direction as my body adapted to it. I did change direction occasionally in case always going in the same way on a tight loop would affect knees or hips or both. Keeping track of laps was a problem because Strava did not record any distance, so I settled on counting to ten then using an old-fashioned tally sheet and a pencil.

Parkrun is a big favourite thing for all sorts of reasons. Parkrun organise free, weekly, 5km timed runs all around the world. They are open to everyone, are safe and easy to take part in. These events take place in pleasant parkland surroundings and people of every ability are encouraged to participate. However, they do have their dark side. For me it is embodied in my nemesis, Ben.

Ben was 11 and a regular at my local parkrun. He always finished before me and I had been trying for a long time to beat him. In a rare moment of self-flagellation, I posted on

Facebook about trying to run faster than a boy who looked about 10 (I didn't know his name then) and taking comfort that I could beat his younger brother. One of the Race Directors commented on my post, tagged a friend and said, "I think Edward is talking about your boys". That is how at parkrun the next week I met the family and learnt the boys' names and ages. It was also when Ben learnt that I was trying to beat him. It obviously spurred him on as he was faster that week than ever before and kept improving every week, but so was I. Never have I thrown myself into speed training and hill reps with so much enthusiasm and determination. I was going to beat him, before he got too fast and age slowed me down.

A few weeks later, as we lined up for the start, Ben said to me you will probably beat me today because I had a full day of training at rugby academy yesterday. A wise lad to get the excuse in early, but we all have our own issues. I'd had a tough few days at work, you have just got to soak it up and perform the best you can. I set of at a cracking pace and was glad to see that Ben was not in front of me. I was feeling rather good at the prospect of beating Ben at last. It was at this point that he silently cruised past and started to pull away from me. I could do nothing; I'd gone out too fast and was starting to tire. I struggled to the finish line an almost broken man.

I missed several parkruns after that, things got in the way, but if I am honest with myself, I probably let them. Then one Saturday there was nothing to prevent me going, so I had to turn up. It was one of those mornings when it was difficult to decide whether to wear a jacket or not. I decided not to, I would not be running for long and being a bit cold would not matter. I noticed that Ben was wearing his Hi-Viz one; he would be easy to spot in front of me. As we listened to the safety briefing the wind dropped and the sun came out, then we were off. Ben quickly pulled out a lead and soon disappeared around one of the bends. A little while later I spotted him ahead slowing down as he tried taking his jacket off. I sped up and started catching him, but just as I got close he was out of the jacket and speeding up. He wasn't pulling away from me though because he was distracted by carrying the jacket. You and I would have tied it around our waists; he obviously hadn't learnt that yet. It annoyed him, and he shifted it from one hand to the other, glancing behind all the time looking for his father who runs with Ben's brother. I think he was hoping to throw the jacket to the side of the track, so his dad could pick it up. Adam was obviously having an off day because he and his dad were nowhere in sight, so Ben struggled on distracted by the jacket.

This was my chance, I sped up and passed him, I didn't say anything, just ran strongly and built up a significant lead. I could have told him to tie the jacket around his waist, I could even have offered to carry it for him, but this is a tough old world, he'd soon learn. When I had a big enough lead to be confident that Ben wasn't going to catch me I had a little internal celebration; I'd beaten him! At this point two girls, who looked about 14, passed me chatting away and sharing their sweets. Oh, how my bubble burst. Shortly after that I moved away from the area, so I never ran against Ben again (that wasn't the reason for the move).

For me parkrun is a great leveller and it gives me a chance to connect with all sorts of runners at their level; talking to a beginner I can talk about parkrun as a goal for them and it doesn't seem too far away, often they are on a couch to 5k programme. With half-marathon and marathon runners I can talk about parkrun for speed work and with ultra runners I can sympathise about how hard they are and how our times always look bad for experienced runners. I love that parkrun is a place where children and adults can mix in a shared experience and it is a place where people of all ages and abilities are welcome.

Another event that caters for people of all abilities, and one I would definitely do again was the 50-hour non-stop run in Singapore which took place while I was visiting my daughter who lives in Singapore. She ended up there we she went with her boyfriend to Indonesia, where he had got a job teaching English. Unable to get a work permit Holly went to the nearest country where she could get work, Singapore, and ended up with her dream job, working for the World Wildlife Fund. Although it is called the 50-hour non-stop run, you do not run for 50 hours and you do not need to run non-stop; the course is open for 50 hours, which allows you to fit your run in when you want to and around whatever else is going on. The event takes place in the Bedok Reservoir Park and consists of laps around the reservoir on a dirt path. 3 laps (12.9 km) earns you a bronze medal, 6 laps (25.8 k), a silver medal, 10 laps (43 km) a gold medal and 15 laps (64.5 km) a special oblong medal. It is a non-competitive event and times are not recorded, just the laps you clock up. Participants go at their own pace and time within the 50 hours duration. I managed to earn 4 medals over the two and a half days. On Friday, which was a public holiday in Singapore, I completed 3 laps with my daughter, the first time running in an event with her so special. We then did some tourist things and met some of her friends for dinner. On Saturday morning I headed off to another reservoir, MacRitchie, to meet Stephen Lee, who I knew from the Kalahari, and run with a local group. Afterwards I made my way to Bedok to put in more laps; two more medals before my daughter collected me to take me to a restaurant for dinner with Stephen and Kian Hwee Tan, another Kalahari friend. I refrained from drinking so that I could go back to Bedok that night and knock out the last laps to get the final medal. My daughter and her boyfriend, Dan, watched me from a nearby bar and bought a beer for me before the bar closed so that I had something to celebrate with. A great event that allowed people to fit running around their commitments, whether that was work, family or religious events.

For me the joy of running is that it takes you to different places, allows you to meet inspiring people and presents you with amazing opportunities, if you are open to them and prepared to take them on. It provides experience at both ends of the spectrum and all that way along. I have experienced the brain-addling heat of the Sahara and the mind-numbing cold of the January 2005 Tring to Town run along the Grand Union canal into London, both great experiences, but after they were over. The sheer agony of grinding out the last ten kilometres of a 100k race when I was unwell and the relaxed run I had in the Hastings 10k as I helped a slower friend run her first ever race. The majestic solitude of running through the African bush in the Addo 50-mile Trail Run and the excitement and joy of running with thousands of other runners in the 100th Boston marathon. All of these are my favourite things.

KAEM Training

I am often asked by people who have signed up for the Kalahari Augrabies Extreme Marathon if I would send them my training plan. The answer is always no, not because I am unhelpful, I will gladly give them all the information and advice I can, but because I have many different plans and not all of them are written down. Also, they would probably not be appropriate for their circumstances. Generic plans work reasonably well for half-marathons and marathons and can be quite easily adapted to suit individual circumstances, but multi-day events are a little more complicated than the standard marathon and people entering them usually have a running history with differing strengths and weakness that need to be considered.

If you look at the training for my first ten Kalahari Augrabies Extreme Marathons it has always been different because I was starting from a different fitness level each time. Sometimes I was starting my specific training having a great endurance base, in other years I was coming back from an injury or had just not done much running or occasionally too much.

2007

For my first Kalahari Augrabies Extreme Marathon I adapted my Marathon des Sables training plan adding in some back-to-back long runs. I had nine more marathons (including 3 in one long weekend) and four ultramarathons in the bag before the end of 2006 so I felt I was starting from a great point. I put in two big runs before Comrades, the Tring to Town (45 miles) and the Addo Elephant Trail Run (50 miles) with a couple of marathons in between so I didn't need to do much training for Comrades. After recovering from that race, I commenced specific training for KAEM, putting in some back-to-back long runs over the weekends and running with a rucksack. I gradually increased the weight until I was carrying about 12kg, a little over the 10kg starting weight of the pack in the event. I was living full-time in Cornwall by then so getting out on the South West Coastal path was no problem. I didn't enter any races between June and October I just wanted to concentrate on my training. I was well-trained for KAEM in 2007, but a little overweight.

2008

For 2008 I knew what I had to do, nothing very different from 2007. My training had been good it was my race strategy and blisters that let me down. I finished 2007 strongly with a tough off-road marathon the Endurancelife Pembrokeshire event (cold and wet) and a tough road marathon – the Cornish which goes over Bodmin Moor and passes close to the famous Jamaica Inn. My build up marathons in 2008 for Comrades were the South Devon Coastal, Portland and Exmoor marathons, all off road events, the Gloucester, Duchy and Cork road marathons and the Compton 40. I avoided longer races because I was saving myself for the Addo 100. Comrades went well, I recovered quickly and soon got into a training rhythm. I had even started to find novel ways to fill my rucksack. On the coastal path just over the border in Devon is Ronald Duncan's Hut (he was a poet and author). His family started leaving copies of his books in the hut with a message saying please help yourself. I used to pick a few up and then carry on with my run (normally about 20 miles) with the weight in my pack. One of those books, The Tale of Tails, has inspired some of my creative writing. Sometimes I would find other things to add weight; once it was apples from a road-side tree, another time it was coal I found on a steep hill, obviously fallen off the back of a lorry. The coal went on the fire one cold evening.

I think 2008 was my best performance, it is hard to compare years, because the distances change, the terrain varies, and the weather makes a massive difference. I finished in 10th position albeit out of 20 starters. The previous year there were 33 starters and the following year 73. Why the numbers were so low in 2008 I don't think anyone knows. My average time was also the fastest that year and my time as a multiple of the winner's time the most favourable, so I think it fair to say 2008 was my best performance. I needed something to get over my disappointment of not finishing the Addo 100 trail race earlier in the year.

2009

I had finished 2008 off with a couple of marathons followed by the Round Rotherham 50 and the Centenary Hastings marathon on the same weekend ready for a big year in 2009. The early part of 2009 was all about final training for the 6633 ultra in the Arctic in March. Training went well, but the event didn't; I was pulled out with frostbite early on and had a trip to the hospital at Inuvik. At least that meant I was well rested by the time I got back home and could concentrate on Comrades training. That went well, but again the event didn't I posted a DNF – chapter 8.

I had a long hard think about what training I needed to do for KAEM 2009, after the disappointments earlier in the year I wanted something to go right. I dialled the training right back. I knew I had massive endurance; I just needed my body to be strong. I ran without a watch and without any targets, just enjoying being out in the fresh air. The big focus was on strength and mobility exercises in the gym. If I felt good, I would run the 10 miles to the gym, do my workout and run home. If I didn't, I would drive to the gym, do a slightly longer workout and drive home. I did a few races, including the Classic Quarter (44 miles) and the Moray marathon because it was a friend's 100th marathon and I used to live in Elgin where it started. It took it easy in all those events, they were training runs. It worked I arrived at the start line of KAEM 2009 feeling relaxed and as confident as you can be when facing running 237km in the searing heat. It was a good event for me, I loved it and in terms of average speed and time relative to the winner it was my second-best performance. Having the confidence not to run big distances in preparation was what got me through, my body needed a rest.

2010

The 2009 KAEM was early in October which meant that I could do the triple again at the end of October, this time the Beachy Head, Greensands and Dublin marathon over a long weekend. If you love running there is nothing better than getting three events in three days. I finished 2009 with the 40-mile Likeys Brecon Beacons Ultra. I was feeling strong.

My training for the 2010 KAEM was remarkably similar in nature to what I did in 2009, I just enjoyed running in the Cornish countryside and occasionally venturing out of Cornwall to run in a race. The most memorable was the Belfast City Marathon because I had previously visited Belfast during the troubles working on a tax case for a client. It was lovely to see the city at peace after the very stark and frightening images from my previous visit. Our return flight to England was cancelled due to the Eyjafjallajökull volcanic eruptions. My travel insurance company were useless saying it was an act of God, however EasyJet were brilliant organizing transport to a hotel and paying all our expenses except for alcoholic drinks. For me the travel disruption ended too quickly; I enjoyed the extra time in Belfast.

This was the first year that I was not training for the Comrades marathon; I had decided to spectate instead and see a view of the race I had not seen before. I also had a holiday in South Africa with my older daughter, Holly. I didn't run any races over marathon distance and only ran three marathons that year. Almost all of my running was done on the Cornish coastal path, although I did stray across the border into Devon sometimes. I didn't follow any particular plan other than to increase the long run on Sunday and sometimes get long runs in on consecutive days. I did some hill work, but mainly by running hard up the hills I encountered on my route. As usual I started to get used to carrying a pack a few months before the event and gradually increased the weight until I was carrying about 12 kilograms. I went into the 2010 Kalahari Augrabies Extreme Marathon feeling strong and relaxed. The event went well.

2011

I thought I would find it hard to train properly for KAEM, because I had now finished the event 4 times and without any drama in the last two years; I had now found an effective strategy to prevent blister. Two pairs of socks; a thin pair of toe liner socks and Wigwam Terrain Trax Pro socks on top. To avoid being complacent I decided to train for another event, the Al Andalus Ultimate Trail (AAUT) in Spain and just maintain fitness from that event in July until October.

The AAUT is a semi-supported 5-stage, 230km ultra-marathon in Andalusia, Spain which means that you do not have to carry a heavy pack. The event should not be under-estimated. In July Andalusia is extremely hot; the course is very hilly and there are cut-offs to beat. I needed to be fit to finish and that gave me the incentive to train hard with several marathon and ultras completed early in the year including a 12-hour track race in April. I also followed Paul

Bateson's, the race director, advice and did more speed work and cut out some of the long slow runs. The plan worked I was very motivated and trained well.

Unfortunately, my peripheral neuropathy, which had been developing over the last five years, caused me problems during one day of the race and I had to be moved up the field by vehicle otherwise I would have been excluded. I managed to finish all the other stages, but, of course, I didn't appear in the results. After AAUT I felt fit but was worried about the peripheral neuropathy so just kept things ticking over. 2011 KAEM was my slowest, I just wanted to finish.

2012

I had planned to go back to basics in 2012 and follow a plan similar to 2007 with a touch of 2011; focus on the 100-mile Ultra Trail South West. I would train hard and do well. I was aware that a finish in 2012 would mean that I would equal the record for the most number of completions. Both Geoff Hilton-Barber and Lynne Simpson had completed the event six times. Geoff, who is an amazing blind adventurer, had not entered the event in several years and Lynne dropped out the previous year. She had recently become a mum and just wanted to be back home with her family. 2012 would be my opportunity to be equal to those incredible people.

The plan was torn up when 2012 became the worst year of my life. On the 5th March, while on a sales trip, I received an email from my wife saying our marriage was over. Just before I left the matrimonial home with my younger daughter Charlotte I hurt my back while straightening out a duvet. Doesn't sound much but I was totally incapacitated and in pain for many months. Running was out of the question and it looked like the Kalahari Augrabies Extreme Marathon was too.

But I hadn't allowed for the great support you get from ultra runners and in particular from the great KAEM 'family'. I posted on my blog about the back problem.

TIME TO MAN UP

The blog title was inspired by the Rudyard Kipling poem 'If', particularly the lines,

If you can fill the unforgiving minute

With sixty seconds' worth of distance run,

Yours is the Earth and everything that's in it,

And—which is more—you'll be a Man, my son!

It is inspired by those words because I can't fill the unforgiving minute - I'm injured and cannot even run for 30 seconds. You are probably thinking pulled hamstring during a tough hill sprint or inflamed Achilles due to overuse or perhaps ITB problems, but no; it's my back. I leant over the bed to straighten out the duvet and suffered an intense pain in my lower back; I couldn't move. After a while I managed to get myself on to the bed and just lay there waiting for the pain to go; it didn't. It has now, many days later, but I have pains and muscle cramps in my left leg. These have been very slow to improve.

A good friend, Te, responded to the emergency and drove miles to give me some treatment; she is a horse chiropractor, so I was in good, but firm hands. Her view was that the problem had been building up for some time and that bending over to straighten the duvet was the last straw. I'm also fortunate that another friend, Eva, has arrived and she is qualified in sports massage. Unfortunately, both agree that it is going to take some time to remedy something that has been gradually building up. This means I will have to pull out of the 100-mile Ultra Trail South West on the 23rd June 2012.

So back to the Rudyard Kipling poem.

If you can meet with Triumph and Disaster

And treat those two impostors just the same:

……..

Yours is the Earth and everything that's in it,

And—which is more—you'll be a Man, my son!

So, it is time to man up as I'm not coping with the disaster very well. The 100 Ultra Trail South West has been my focus for some considerable time; I've trained hard, I've lost the weight I needed to and was confident I've done all I could to ensure success. What a cruel twist of fate to have it taken away from me at the last minute. I could just conceivably make it to the start line, but I know there is truly little chance of that and none of finishing. I also know that course of action could lead to more serious and longer lasting injury.

It's not easy to stay positive, but Kipling does have a line that may help;

If you can dream—and not make dreams your master.

So that is what I'm going to do. UTSW was my big dream, it is gone now so it is time to find a new one, but before then I'm going to rest and when I run again, I'm going to try some short orienteering events. As this will be my first venture into this world, I will not be tempted to match my previous performances. I understand that accuracy is more important than speed, so I can take it slowly to start with until my navigation skills improve.

The dream is dead long live the dream. Watch this space for details of the new one.

I received lots of emails and messages of sympathy support and advice. This one from one of my KAEM friend, Laura

Bannatyne, hit the spot.

> *"Well, this may sound very trite, and advice is always SO satisfying to dispense (I feel wiser and more venerable with each word), but you need to be as dedicated about recovering as you usually are about training.*
>
> *You quoted the poem "if", and here are some other "ifs":*
>
> *if you can work on the basis that you are NOT "doing nothing",*
> *if you can keep in mind that you are healing yourself over the next few months,*
> *if you can remember that this requires more, not less, discipline, and that*
> *if done properly and thoroughly, it will give you the results you need, you will be putting money in the bank for a back-pain free future!"*

I look Laura's advice and applied my usual training discipline to my recovery and allowed myself to heal. I also followed to the letter what the hospital physio told me to do. At the beginning of September there was a glimmer of hope that I might be able to take part in KAEM 2012. I wasn't going to get any significant training in, the only thing I could do to improve my chances of finishing the event was to lose weight. I always carry extra weight and rely on my fitness to overcome that handicap. This year had to be different. 2012 wasn't my best result, but it wasn't my worst. It was another finish.

2013

I was worried about setting myself a challenge for 2013 to

motivate me considering what happened in 2012. Irrational I know, but the mind is a strange thing. I got over it and decided to lay the ghost of AAUT so entered that again and as a treat the 64-mile Plague event on the Roseland peninsular in Cornwall organised by Mud Crew. I then had the opportunity to enter the first stage race in Bhutan; I jumped at that, so I needed to be on top form. Training went well, I was focused by these challenges. I ran a few off-road marathons in the early part of the year and enjoyed those outings very much.

Bhutan went well, and I had just enough time to rest before flying to Spain. I arrived in Spain well rested and well trained, but on day one I didn't feel well, far from well. Not wanting to do any damage, 2013 could be the year I set a record for the most number of completions of the Kalahari Augrabies Extreme Marathon, I sat down in the shade with about 6 or 7km to go and sent a text to the organisers asking them to come and pick me up when they had time. I worked on a check point the following day then re-joined the race. Again, I was not to feature in the finishers list.

Shortly after the Spanish event I travelled to South Africa with my younger daughter Charlotte for a holiday. She was a teenager at the time and liked a lie in, so I was able to train in the early mornings. This was fortunate as I was coming to the end of attempting a 365-day running streak so had to run every day. After the holiday I stayed on for a friend's wedding, Laura who sent the supportive email, and took the opportunity to enter the Num-Num Challenge in Mpumalanga. The course is 32km long with 1700 meters of ascent and over some of the toughest, most variable terrain at high altitude on the African Escarpment. I flew back to the UK just in time for the Plague and was pleased with my performance, about one third of the field missed the tight early cut-offs and failed to finish. I finished. A short recovery and some gentle running and I was ready for my record-setting run at KAEM 2013 – 7 completions. This was becoming a habit.

2014

I covered my training for the 2014 KAEM in the chapter about that year's event. In case you skipped over it or do not remember what you read I will summarise. I ran a lot of races.

2015

I thought long and hard about how to train for KAEM 2015, I was finding it hard to motivate myself, I didn't want to do lots of races like I had done before. I couldn't afford to enter big overseas challenges and I didn't want to churn out lots of hill reps or long Sunday runs. I was tired of training and tired of races; I still loved running and when I looked back on 2014 the things that stood out the most were being on Bodmin Moor and Dartmoor. So, I decided to run on Bodmin on a Tuesday or Thursday - Wednesdays I ran with a local group BUDEiful Runners Powered by cake (easy paced runs of about 6 miles) and explored routes on Dartmoor at the weekend. I wouldn't train I wouldn't run, I would explore and running would be my means of getting around.

It is difficult to compare my performance in 2015 with other years due to the extreme heat that year and the fact that one of the stages was cancelled and everything rearranged. But I think the 'not train' plan worked.

2016

This was going to be the big one, number ten. My experiences on Dartmoor led to a desire to immerse myself in nature and I came up with a plan to hike most of the Scottish

National Trail wild camping on the way. I had met its creator, Cameron McNeish, a few years early when I was asked to present an award at the National Adventure Awards in Glasgow. It seemed fitting therefore to pick up the trail near Glasgow and follow it to its end at Cape Wrath, the furthest northwest point on the Scottish mainland. I did do some running early in the year, including running part of the course to check the marking for Endurancelife at their South Devon and Exmoor events. Then in June, after the Ultra Festival and a parkrun with Bruce Fordyce I headed off to Scotland for my great adventure.

I returned at the end of August very fit but underweight, a first for me. All I needed to do to get fit for KAEM 2016 was to run a little and eat a lot. The Way of Legends race in Spain gave me the perfect opportunity. Manu Pastor, a Spanish runner whom I'd met in Bhutan and obviously impressed, was the race director and he asked me to crew on the race; the Way of Legends is a fully catered six-day stage race in northern Spain in September. The food is prepared from local ingredients by cooks from an organic vegetarian restaurant; there was lots of it, so I ate well. My crew duties consisted mainly of working on a checkpoint then running to the next one as sweep once the last runner had passed through. Perfect training for me. I felt particularly good for KAEM 2016 and think if I had tried I could have put in my best every performance, however, I did not want to push hard and risk not finishing so I went round with my foot firmly off the pedal. The record shows that it was my 4th best time so I think it quite fair to claim it could have been my best time had I tried.

Sometimes I have strayed

Running is what I love, but occasionally I have looked elsewhere for fulfilment. I have dabbled with mountain-biking, adventure racing and triathlon. I even trained as a triathlon coach; I thought I would learn more from that than taking an athletics course although I have since trained as a run leader. Those other disciplines were fun for a while; however, they could not keep my attention and I always reverted to running, now almost exclusively off-road.

My first big fling was in 2001, but it was brought about by something that took place earlier. My old accountancy firm used to provide services to the charity One World Action and I was impressed with the work they did helping disadvantaged people by providing practical support to organisations that were committed to strengthening the democratic process and fighting discrimination. When I left the accountancy world I became a trustee of One World Action and was involved in boardroom decisions about the projects they supported. In 2001, through a third-party organisation Three Hands, they organised a 5-day 200km cycle ride through the stunning mountains and valleys of North West Nicaragua' visiting several projects the charity supported. I wanted to visit those projects and to raise money for the charity. The only problem was that you had to be an experienced mountain biker and I hadn't ridden a bike since my teenage years, 30 years ago, and that was a 'sit up and beg' road bike. I did meet one of the requirements, a good level of fitness to tackle some arduous mountain cycling. I signed up then asked my neighbour's 16-year old son, who seemed to be rather good on a bike, how to train and what sort of bike I should buy to practice on. His advice was good, I had a fantastic time in Nicaragua. There is nothing better than cycling 4km up a hill on a rough track, in the hot sun, getting to the top, sitting in the shade of a tree, eating a juicy mango waiting for people 20 years younger than you to catch up. Most of them beat me on the way down the hill as their technical skills and lack of fear were better than mine.

I learnt a lot on that trip about poverty and how democracy at all levels can help people implement their own solutions. It had a big impact on me and the way I think. It is probably the one event that shaped me more than any other. It also provided me with an opportunity to climb an active volcano. Looking down from the rim of the crater and seeing the smoke rising from deep below was just how I imagined looking into hell to be. It was also the only time I have been in the Pacific Ocean.

Training for the Nicaragua bike ride started in the summer of 2000 and as I was also doing some swimming, as cross-training for running, I thought I would enter an off-road triathlon. I had completed a sprint aquathon at Morden Park, South London closed to where I worked, so adding the bike element made sense. There was one in September near Minehead that looked good, Olympic distance so not too demanding. A swim in Minehead Bay, a cycle ride across Exmoor and a run that started and finished at Dunster Castle so in a beautiful part of Somerset. The event was called Xterra.

There were a few things that conspired to make my first venture into triathlon less than successful: I had seriously underestimated how much more difficult open water swimming was than pool swimming, (my only experience was when they turned the wave machine on at the Kingston indoor pool) it was the British Championships and a qualifier for the Worlds therefore the standard was high and finally there was a storm in Minehead Bay. The conditions were so bad that swimmers were given the option of getting into the safety boat, incurring a penalty and still be allowed to start the bike leg. Normally if you do not complete the swim that is it you are out of the race. The penalty was that they were not allowed to get on their bikes until the last swimmer had left transition. I was that swimmer; there was a large number of competitors waiting for me to leave the transition area.

I was told that given how tired I looked after the swim that I was unlikely to make the cut off about halfway into the bike ride. There was a major road crossing being looked after by the police, once they left I would not be allowed to cross the road. I cycled like crazy, threw caution to the wind on the downhills and made the crossing with just a minute to spare. The second half was tough with some big hills and patches where you had to carry the bike over fallen trees. My bike was not light like those of the other competitors who had paid thousands of pounds to buy their bikes. Mine cost £300 from Halfords; I struggled.

Unfortunately, I finished the bike leg a few minutes too late to be allowed to start the run. I was led away in tears, momentarily broken. But after the post-race party, fortified with a few beers, I was determined to come back the following year and finish. Which is exactly what I did, the conditions in Minehead Bay were not as bad as the previous year and I had practiced a lot, so I exited the water middle of the pack, had a good bike ride and an excellent run so I now have a certificate that says.

Finisher

Edward Chapman

Successfully completed the 2001 **XTERRA** Great Britain Championships
At Dunster Castle, Minehead, Exmoor, Somerset, England
On September 8th, 2001
within the allotted time...
Congratulations ~ you survived!

I was also presented with a Lei (the event has its roots in Hawaii) for having the determination to come back and do well after being defeated the year before. This resulted in my younger daughter crying because a strange woman kissed Daddy as she put the Lei around my neck. So, both years resulted in tears.

Flush with success I decided to enter a local duathlon in January of the following year, the Stinger in Newnham Park, Plymouth. It consists of a 5km off-road run, followed by a 20km mountain bike route before you head out on a 3km run consisting of the deepest mud and steepest hills Newnham Park has to offer. I loved the muddy running, but the downhills on the mountain bike terrified me.

I should have done it again so that I was completely put off mountain biking, but I didn't so when a friend I had met running Comrades in 2003 asked if I would be her partner in a series of short adventure races I said yes. I have a bad habit of doing that. They were good fun and consisted of a 3-hour run where you collected points for visiting various controls and a 5-hour bike ride again collecting points for visiting various controls. Different controls had different points so there were decisions to be made about whether to go for low point easy to get to and find ones or the harder higher point controls. Good navigation and route choice were key. You also lost points for returning to base after the allotted time. We were last in the first event, mainly due to a navigation error made by me, but we got better. Margaret's dreams turned to Ironman, so road cycling became her focus and we stopped the adventure racing. That was the end of my mountain biking.

Another deviation was to take part in the UK Backward Running Championships. I know it is running, but it is in the wrong direction. Running backwards for a mile, the championship distance, was hard. Training for it resulted in some very strange looks from passers-by fortunately my years as an ultrarunner mean that I no longer care about that sort of thing. Once was enough for me to realise backward running is not for me. I do still do some backward running in training; it is great for your posture and for running on your toes. It is also a great way to run barefoot (and I mean bare feet - no expensive contradiction in terms barefoot shoes for me) as you cannot heel strike running backwards, something that is quite painful in bare feet.

Bare foot running has helped me empathize with the artistic temperament. I met an artist, Rosemary Goodenough, in a running shop trying on trainers. She didn't run but found the support in running shoes helped when she was standing all day painting or working on a sculpture. I looked her up online and was fascinated by her work. I bought a piece as a present for one of my daughters (one of her less expensive pieces). I found these words on her website:

"The colour and smell of the paint, the sounds of the charcoal on board or paper, the feel of clay on my hands, music and silence, all these are triggers and every mark is a decision... As an artist I am viscerally aware of the absolute straight-line connection between me and the artists who made their marks with such verve on the walls of the Chauvet Caves approximately 35,000 years ago. We don't know their names or motivations but the drive and passion to make marks is a primitive and inescapable human need and this straight-line connection between artists across millennia will never be broken. For me, being part of a link in this past and future chain is fundamental to my life as artist."

I knew exactly what she meant. A few evenings before I had run barefoot and felt the texture of the road under my feet, enjoyed the warmth of the tarmac where it had been in the sun and noticed the cool contrast where it had been in shade. My feet made a gentle pattering noise and my step was light, I was in tune with my environment. Then suddenly the prick of a small sharp piece of gravel would interrupt my peace and I would be viscerally aware of my feet before eventually reaching a smooth patch of tarmac and returning to peace again. Running is a primitive and inescapable human endeavour; I was connected to my ancestors who ran freely across the plains of Africa.

I thought I'd done with all that silliness and straying; however, in 2017 I entered a competition to win an entry into a Tough Mudder event, I've no idea why, I think I just wanted to win some Trek bars. Instead, I won an entry for two people in the South London event, as I was travelling up to London that weekend for the Shine Walk, a marathon walk around London at night to raise money for breast cancer awareness, it was ideal. A post on Facebook and I soon had someone to take the second slot, Jackie Waterman. I first met Jackie when she accompanied her husband on a trip to the Comrades marathon and we have become good friends. We lost contact for a while after Comrades, but reconnected after we saw each other in London, I was dressed as a nun and she was a marshal for The Sister Act Nuns Run. Jackie also joined me in Scotland for a week of walking and again for my walk up Cader Idris.

I was amazed at how many people attend these events and was pleased at how well organised it was. It was basically 10 miles of mud with obstacles of all sorts to get over and under. Early on there was the Arctic Enema – a slide into a big tank of water with ice in it, then having to duck under the water again to get to the other side to get out. Then there were things to crawl under (nets and barbed wire), things to climb over, logs to carry, water to wade through (and fall in) and at the end you had to run though loads of dangling electric wires. There was no way to get through that without getting several shocks, well there was you could walk around it if you wanted to wimp out. I enjoyed, and coped, with some obstacles more than others, water and mud were no problem; however, anything requiring a lot of upper body strength I struggled with. Fortunately, fellow competitors were incredibly helpful and pushed or pulled the less able up and over the obstacles. The free cider at the finish was very welcome as were the hosepipes to clean the mud off. It is not something I would pay to do again; however, if another competition comes along, I'll be entering.

My last act of silliness in the non-running world, until the next one comes along, was on 24th February 2018 when I entered the World Indoor Gig Rowing Championships. Gig rowing is a part of Cornish history; a gig is a six-oared rowing boat that used to take pilots out to incoming vessels off the Atlantic Coast. The fastest gig crew who got their pilot there first got the job. Nowadays gig rowing is a popular sport in Cornwall and elsewhere with a World Championships taking place in the Isles of Scilly every year. The Indoor Championships were just a bit of fun, took place at the Eden Project and used indoor rowing machines. There was an individual category, I had rowed in an eight on the river Camb for one season when I was 17 and had occasionally worked out on an ergo machine so thought I would enter. I was particularly interested in the super vet category, although disappointed that it was for anyone over 50. I'm pleased to say I didn't disgrace myself and can now proudly say that I am listed as an age group finalist in a World Championship, unfortunately no podium place though.

I have also embraced walking on occasions, not because I was forced to in a race, it was because I wanted to hike and wild camp or take part in a walking event for a special reason.

One year, for a charity challenge, my business partner, Phillip Howells and I came up with the idea of a fun, fun run sandwich, two fun events sandwiched in between two bigger events, One of the fun events was the Sun Walk in Southampton, it is a fundraiser for Breast Cancer charities, mainly for women however men can also enter. To take part you wear a decorated bra, men included, and walk a 10k route through the city. Phillip's wife died from breast cancer, so it seemed a fitting event to include in our charity challenge. I think we were the only men; we were definitely the only ones in bras, so we attracted a lot of attention from the ladies. There was an awkward moment at the beginning of the event, I had decorated my bra (a Playtex one supplied by the organizers a few weeks before hand) with flowers from a Hawaiian outfit I had bought from a fancy-dress shop. The woman standing next to me had on the exact same outfit – we pretended to be mortified.

It was a very humbling event, most of the women had a friend or relative who had died of breast cancer or who undergoing chemo; some of the women on the event were undergoing chemo. I was impressed with the quiet, but strong solidarity they showed for each other.

Never one to miss an opportunity to publicise fundraising or the business I wrote an article for a running magazine about the event and sent a photograph of Phillip and me in our bras and pink caps standing in front of a cruise liner (the event was sponsored by Celebrity Cruises). Unfortunately, due to a late change the article wasn't printed just the photo and our names with no explanation. My younger daughter was deeply embarrassed by that photo of her dad being in a popular running magazine, my older daughter didn't care, she has a thicker skin having grown used to her dad's unusual exploits. I think Charlotte has caught up with her older sister now.

Another walk I entered was the Shine Walk which raises money for Cancer Research UK; it's a marathon walked through the streets of London at night. I was invited to take part by the event's PR agency who contacted a number of running bloggers and asked them to take part and write about it both before and after. There were no decorated bras this time, although we were given coloured glow bands to make us stand out. It was a fun night; however, all us runners agreed that walking a marathon is a lot harder than running one.

My big hiking expedition was in the summer of 2016, (briefly touched on in the training chapter) I had heard Cameron McNeish talk at the National Adventure Awards in Glasgow a few years earlier when I presented one of the awards and was captivated by his tales of the Scottish National Trail. I did a little bit of research and loved that some sections were described as Extreme Wilderness. The early sections seemed a little tame so I started my hike from Milngavie which would take me along the West Highland Way, the Rob Roy Way and the Cape Wrath Trail to Cape Wrath the furthest north west point on the Scottish mainland. A journey of 400 miles which I would do on foot avoiding roads as much as possible and wild camping on the way.

The early stages were reasonably gentle with a few encounters with people and frequent places to buy supplies. When I got to the wilder parts it was five days walking between shops and seeing only the occasional person; I went for 3 days without seeing anyone – wonderful. To start with I was frustrated about not running; my pack when it was full with 5 days of food weighed 18 kg, so it was impractical and unwise. However, after a little while I welcomed the slower pace and the chance to fully appreciate the environment. On warm sunny days I would stop for a day, do some washing and lazy about soaking up being in the wild. On a couple of days when the weather was extreme, I stayed in my tent. It rained a lot that summer which made crossing rivers interesting as most had no bridges and when they did they were not substantial structures; one was just two ropes, one to walk on and another a little higher to hold on to. There was one river that was too wild to cross resulting in a five-hour detour. I loved every minute of the trip, the good weather, battling the elements, the solitude, meeting fellow kindred spirits, sighting of deer, eagles and badgers the occasional night in a bothy and the odd beer in a pub.

Another walk of note was a relatively short one that was a repeat of something I had done 50 years earlier. I had been on a school trip to Wales as a young teenager which included a walk up Cader Idris a mountain in North Wales at the southern end of the Snowdonia National Park. I hated that walk and the whole trip. Fifty years later I was in north Wales to help with a race which started in Porthmadog, crossed over Snowdon and finished in Conwy. Jackie Waterman was also on the crew and we decided to have a few days afterwards walking and camping. Revisiting Cader Idris was a wonderful experience, the weather was perfect, which meant wonderful views. We sat at the top eating peanut butter sandwiches; I was blissfully happy, a lot different from fifty years earlier. On the way down I stopped and swam in the lake; cold but wonderful.

There are plenty of running challenges for me to do that will keep me away from being tempted to try other sports. None seem to have the simplicity and purity of running, although sea kayaking and stand-up paddle boarding look good.

Music, mates & merriment

I never run with music, however, as you can see from chapter one, sometimes songs can be extremely helpful. Studies have shown that music can help running performance on many different levels. It reduces the perception of exertion, making running feel less strenuous. Music can enhance positive aspects of mood, like happiness and excitement, while reducing negative aspects, such as anger and confusion. By engendering a more positive mindset, it inspires people toward higher levels of performance. When it comes to the type of music there is no Holy Grail. Music is very personal. Preferences will depend upon your social-cultural upbringing and the type of musical influences you had during your formative years. During my formative years there was no music, my soundtrack was nature, so I prefer to hear the natural sounds.

> *The Earth has music for those who will listen* – Reginald Vincent Holmes

This blog post after a local run identifies me as one who will listen.

The Sound of Running

Running to me is not about exercise, muscle and sinews; it is a sensuous thing involving all the senses. My auditory senses were the main beneficiary on Sunday. I ran from home and had to pass through a small housing estate, along a footpath to the local primary school and then out into the fields and woods. As I passed through the estate there was the sound of children playing outside, how wonderful to hear children enjoying the open air and being sociable. Along the footpath I caught up with a woman pushing a child in a buggy. She was chatting away to the child, pointing out all the things to look at, primroses, a starling, a dog. There can be no more heart-warming sound than a mother talking lovingly to her child.

As I neared the fields, I could hear sheep making quite a din and as I got closer the noise got more frenetic. Then I saw why, the farmer had just arrived with a sack of feed. I stopped and chatted to her for a while then ran on. As I got further away the noise died down and for a moment all I could hear was my breathing and the sound off my feet of the tarmac drive. That soften as I turned on to the muddy track, however my breathing got louder as it was uphill.

Then came the sound of the church bells from the nearby village, which got louder as I approached. I love churches and I love the sound of bells. I'm not religious at all, but I think churches are a great link with the community and the past; a constant thread stretching back hundreds of years. The bells fell silent and I stayed a while enjoying the peace and looking out over the cemetery. It is well maintained and many of the graves have fresh flowers on them. I don't see it as a place of death, but a remembrance of lives once lived.

My route took me towards the sea and the evocative cries of seagulls. For me that sound conjures up memories of holidays on the coast; sunshine, paddling in the sea, sand between your toes, ice-cream and drifting off to sleep tired and contented. Then I turned inland across a stream and into the woods. I find the sound of running water relaxing, unless it's a raging torrent, then I find it invigorating. In the woods small birds were calling out, either to mark their territory or to attract a mate. All too soon I was out of the woods and back into the fields where the only sound was my breathing. When I passed them again the sheep were silent, presumably their hunger was satisfied.

It was then back through the estate where my contemplative mood was rudely interrupted by the strident beeping of a lorry reversing. My magic running world was gone, but I will be back there again soon.

That is not to say that music is absent from my running life there are many songs that weave a thread through my running adventures. Ever since hearing Chariots of Fire being played in Pietermaritzburg at the start of Comrades 1999 I have goose bumps whenever I hear it and memories of Comrades come flooding back, always the good ones never the pain and suffering.

Another feel good piece of music is Believe by Cher. It was playing in all the cafes on Durban seafront as I was shuffling along with a huge post-Comrades grin on my face in 1999. Hearing it always reminds me of the sunshine and warmth and the immense feeling of satisfaction I had at completing my first Comrades. Soaking in the sunshine and the relaxed atmosphere little did I know that it would become a regular part of my life. I was also perhaps wondering if there was '*Life after love',* words from that song. I had fallen in love with the Comrades marathon, would life at home be good enough? Would I find running the pleasure it had been? It was also the first time I had heard the distorted vocal effects and it resonated with me as my view of life had been distorted by completing the Comrades marathon. A line from this song became my mantra until Gloria came along "*Well, I know that I'll get through this 'cause I know that I am strong*".

Writing about music here has reminded me of when I posted a link on social media to a song and video, run. The responses I got demonstrated to me what a wide church running is. The first comment was from a young German woman who runs about 3 miles a few times a week. The second was from a retired English woman who regularly runs

24-hour races. I don't think you could get two runners farther apart than that.
That threw up some interesting memories. When I was training for a 100km race I met someone who had been a sprinter and now wanted my help and advice to prepare for a 10k event. She was going to take on something 100 times longer than her normal race distance. I on the other hand was only taking on something that was about 10% further than I had run before. We talked about the training she used to do, which was tough and took up a lot of time. I couldn't understand how anyone would want to work so hard preparing for a race that would be over in seconds. Then she described what it was like and how she felt when she was racing, there was magic in her eyes. Her words were like music; I understood.

We ran the 10k together, which meant I posted a personal worst by a long, long way, but she was pleased to have finished a 10k. She was doubly pleased by the finish, it was on an athletics track and when she came off the last bend and saw the finish line that was it. Minutes earlier I had been nagging, almost bullying her to keep going, now she was flying and I just couldn't stay anywhere near her. That was a great day.

Quite a few months after the 100k, I was in my local pub chatting to a group of young lads, one of who had just won the Duchy 20-mile race in an obscene time; I would have taken at least twice as long as him. I was surprised therefore, but very flattered, when someone congratulated him on his win and he said, "Thanks, but I am nowhere near good enough to do what Edward does". Interesting that he envies my endurance and I envy his speed.

Those two events made me think 'what makes a runner?' as did a blog post I saw a little later, it started:

"Wanna know what makes me a runner?

I run!
Wanna know what makes me a writer?

I write!"

There wasn't much more after that. It had an eloquent simplicity (except for the wanna) and its logic could not be faulted, but I think it lacked so much. A meal is a meal, but there is a huge difference between a vegetable stir-fry and boeuf-en-croute, especially if you are a vegan. So, I think to understand what makes someone a runner you have to consider the type of running and who they are. If the two are in harmony you have a happy runner, if they are not, you have a tortured soul.

I love to run and explore the countryside, to be in the fields and the forests, seeing animals and birds, smelling different smells. I like to go fast sometimes, or what is fast for me, but I also like to have time to take in the view, to relax, to unwind and to grow. I do enter races, but not to compete, sometimes it is to explore new places and sometimes it is to challenge myself. I'm not very competitive, but I am immensely proud that through my running I have achieved something unique; finishing the Kalahari Augrabies Extreme Marathon more times than anyone else and I will do all I can to defend that record for as long as I can. But ultimately success for me is measured in how much I have enjoyed the experience - good times.

Others love to race on the road or track, they train to race and then they race. It is all about the competition, the test. Do you live up to the standard you have set yourself? Fields and forests are seen as obstacles that slow them down and get in the way of a fast performance. Satisfaction is measured in trophies, minutes and seconds – good times.

I love to run long distance, others like to sprint, but ask us to describe what it feels like and you will see the same look in our eyes.

Do you want to know what makes a happy runner? They run how they want to run.

> *There are as many reasons for running as there are days in the year, years in my life. But I run because I am an animal and a child, an artist and a saint. So, too, are you. Find your own play, your own self-renewing compulsion, and you will become the person you are meant to be.*
> Dr. George Sheehan

Running partners can be a great source of inspiration and support. They can urge us on when things are tough, help us through bad patches, calm things down when nerves get the better of you and loads, loads more. Occasionally they can bring you down to earth with a bump. On 2nd May 2009 I was running the Addo Elephant Park 100-mile trail race near Port Elizabeth, South Africa with a friend. We were chatting with a couple of other runners during the early stages of the race in the cool, early morning conditions. As so often happens in these situations in South Africa the conversation turned to the Comrades Marathon. I recounted the story of how I once beat the Olympic athlete and mile world record holder, Steve Cram, during the 1999 Comrades.

On hearing this story my friend said, “What was wrong with him, was he injured” That was my bubble burst, my running partner couldn’t believe I was capable of great feats and could only triumph if the other guy was injured. Interestingly when I tell my friends the story of my victory in 1999 they often say “Ah, but Steve was a 1500 metre runner not an ultra runner.” They do not seem to take into account that I was a couch-potato in the past, not a trained athlete. There is of course a lot of difference between ultra running and normal athletics. Only one top international marathon runner has ever won the Comrades Marathon and that is Alberto Salazar. Track athletes often struggle at the marathon distance, I once heard Roger Black (silver medal in 400 metres, Atlanta Olympics,1996 – Michael Johnson took gold) talk about being left in the wake of a 60-year old lady during the London Marathon. I also know someone who was a contemporary of Seb Coe who used to beat him sometimes in junior races; his half-marathon personal best is a minute slower than mine and mine is not that good. Horses for courses I suppose. Incidentally, Steve Cram once called me a donkey when referring to the athletes he was training as thoroughbred racehorses. I was staying in Newcastle and came back from a run with a few other ultrarunners when I bumped into Steve with a group of young runners he was training. He asked, “Are there any good grassy hills that way suitable for hill reps?” I replied, “There is one just around the corner; however, there are a few dips in it from cows’ hooves”. Steve commented, “That is okay for you donkeys but not for my thoroughbreds.” I don’t mind, this donkey had his day in 1999.

Someone with the same name as my ‘unhelpful’ Addo 100 friend gave me a great boost when I came in almost last in the North Devon AONB marathon and made me feel like a king. She said I was an “inspiration”. Bemused I asked why, fearing a bubble bursting response, but this is what she said. “You ran a tough marathon with a bad cold, struggled to get around, were out there the longest but crossed the finish line with a big smile saying that you had really enjoyed it. Most of the people who finished before you looked miserable. I want to be like you, I want to enjoy my running."

Yes, I enjoy my running, I set big challenges which means I have to keep running, train a lot, do different things, meet different people, face triumph and disaster. I never know whether it is going to be a tough slog that has to be endured or whether something will come along to make it something to be treasured forever. One day when I was running a buzzard flew out of a tree and gently glided above the road in front of me and then a little later, I saw a tiny wren fly out of a bush and flitter off. The contrast in size between the two birds started me thinking about the contrasts in my running life and I soon realised why I set myself challenges. It is to experience contrasts. I remembered the brain-addling heat of the Sahara and the mind-numbing cold of the January 2005 Tring to Town run – both great experiences.

We never know how tall we are

Until we are asked to rise

And then if we are true to plan

Our statures touch the skies

Emily Dickinson

I remembered being lost, tired, hungry and cold in the Cotswolds, cursing the local farmer for obliterating all trace of the footpath as I struggled through the long grass. Then a few seconds later being elated as several deer jumped up from the grass in front of me and bounded off. I recalled battling against the wind on the Cornwall Coastal Path and moaning about it always being a head wind. Then being grateful that it was when I came across a badger rummaging about for food because being downwind meant that I got remarkably close and watched its antics for a long time without being detected.

Animals have often lifted my spirits stags, foxes, badgers, hares, rabbits, jays, kingfishers, herons, a goldcrest, wrens, buzzards, peregrine falcons, woodpeckers and many more. In Africa they have been more exotic giraffes, baboons, kudu, springbok, dassies, zebra, vultures and on one very memorable occasion a leopard.

The stag appeared towards the end of a long training run in Sussex when I was being blasted by strong winds and sleet. I had my head down trudging miserably along when a noise made me look up and there was a stag with a wonderful set of antlers. He had come onto the track from a field through an open gate. Startled he ran off along the track rather than returning the way he came and was stuck on the track due to the thick hedges on either side. I ran after him, I don't know why, although his pace was fairly leisurely, I was flying along no longer miserable and dejected. Eventually the stag found a gap in the hedge and disappeared across the fields, I carried along the track at speed laughing to myself at the futility of trying to chase the animal down.

Having pointless chases is a recurring theme in my running, see the chapter Comrades DNF for an example. Another happened during a 40-mile training run for the Comrades Marathon. I was about halfway into the run when I meet some young kids on a farm track. One of them asked where I had come from, when I explained he didn't know where I meant until his sister said, "It's near where we stop for McDonalds when we visit Nan." "Cor that's miles away" he said "you must be knackered. Do you want to race me on my bike?" I have never understood why he thought I would want to, but I accepted the challenge. He pedalled furiously, and I ran as fast as I could. Fortunately, the track was muddy making cycling hard and I just managed to beat him to the gate at the end of the track. The kids went off for their tea and I had the prospect of 20 miles more running after exhausting myself in a pointless race. I chuckled to myself most of the way back at the stupidity of it, but it had been fun.

The next bit of fun was post Comrades on a recovery run. I was jogging along at a comfortable pace on a narrow path in a wood when I disturbed a pheasant. He decided to run away from me by running straight ahead along the path rather than dodging to the side into the wood. I sped up to see how fast he was, he sped up, I sped up some more. He was more than a match for me. I tried even harder and he resolutely refused to fly or escape to the side. I was determined to beat him. Then there was a sudden urgency as I realised that we would soon reach a busy road and I was probably chasing him to his death. I put in a lung-bursting effort and started gaining on him before he casually flew off to the side and into the woods. What a great speed session that was.

I have chased deer, kingfishers, hares, herons, outrun lippy kids on housing estates, played aeroplanes running down hills, raced cars (not that difficult in London), run to beat the breaking waves on Hastings seafront and on one occasion chased a shoal of fish up a stream. Making running fun is a great way to train without the strain.

Sometimes running and training isn't fun and that is when tough love from people is what is needed. There are lots of people who will say 'missing a training run doesn't matter' or 'never mind the run come down the pub for a few beers' and even 'you don't want to go out running it's raining'. We can think of those excuses ourselves; we need people who can point out that they are just that, excuses! We need tough love.

We also need people to hold us back when we are overdoing it. Those people are hard to find.

Vanessa, my ex-wife, has probably made the biggest contribution. She has no interest in running whatsoever, but has been incredibly supportive and, having listened to me and all my running mates prattle on, knows a great deal about distance running. Early on in my running career I came home one day and said, "Do you think I would be crazy to want to run a marathon". She could have crushed my emerging passion for running then and there by saying yes, but she didn't she just said, "If you put your mind to it you can achieve anything."

Years later, when I was lying in bed making excuses for not getting up for an early morning run, she gave me a withering look and said, "You know how to use the door handle". A few weeks earlier I had written a blog post about how getting out of the door was sometimes difficult and that learning how to use the door handle was essential for runners. She had obviously read my blog.

Vanessa is a great coach; she knows how to inspire and when a withering look is needed. She knows when I am malingering and need tough words and when a softer approach is needed. I remember vividly, even though it was 15 years ago, a time a when I had been injured and had not run for some time and I was going through a tough time at work; I was in a very dark place. Vanessa, through gentle but persistent persuasion, convinced me to run the Tunbridge Wells half-marathon, she knew that the outing would do me good and I would meet up with lots of my running club mates. About 3 miles into the race I was going to give up, my knees felt like rusty hinges and every step was a massive effort, but another runner started talking to me and suddenly we were at 5 miles and I was feeling good so I continued. We parted company and I ran alone quite contented and happy then at 9 miles the wheels came off big time. I was going to drop out, but again someone started talking to me and I didn't stop. I think I was embarrassed to stop because this was his first half-marathon and I'd run quite a few. This was repeated a few times over the last few miles, and I finished feeling very pleased with myself. I had a great time catching up with people I hadn't seen for some time and when I got home, I was tired, but happy. I arrived at work on Monday morning ready to take the world on. It is amazing what a run and the love of a good woman can do.

Other people have also played a big part in my running successes, some of whom have been complete strangers. Some of those strangers have since become good friends, others have been like ships passing in the night, they have given a word of encouragement and then gone on their way. They all have something in common, a positive attitude and the strength to do what is right, encouraging when necessary, giving positive criticising when appropriate and support when required. When you find friends like this cherish them.

Running can be emotional

In the chapter on the 2014 Kalahari Augrabies Extreme Marathon, where my back gave me a great deal of trouble, I mentioned a quote from Paavo Nurmi to illustrate how important mental strength is to succeed.

Mind is everything; muscles, mere pieces of rubber. All that I am, I am because of my mind.

Exertion in races, particularly extreme races, affects our pieces of rubber, our muscles and if we are very unlucky, or unwise, our joints. We walk stiffly and try and avoid stairs after a long race, we need recovery time and massage to get the body back to where it was before and hopefully a little stronger.

What doesn't destroy me makes me stronger – to paraphrase Friedrich Nietzsche.

Races also affect the mind; they produce all sorts of emotions. This was particularly the case with the 2011 Kalahari Augrabies Extreme Marathon. It was characterised by emotions, highs and lows. As always, the event was friendly with a great family atmosphere. This was demonstrated very clearly at the award ceremony when both the winner and the person who finished in last place received the same enthusiastic applause. But it was the emotions I will remember the most.

There was great sadness at the passing of JJ who had been a member of the support crew for many years. He could not come to the event that year due to the ravaging effects of cancer. He died on day two of the event and I shed a few tears when I heard the news. After the event we stood around a tree planted in his memory, drank a brandy & coke, his favourite drink, then poured some of our drink on the ground at the base of the tree. This was a good way to remember a great, fun-loving man.

There was joy from meeting old friends and making new ones. From enjoying the stunning scenery of the Kalahari, swimming in the Orange River, lazing in the shade and swapping stories.

Meeting one old friend again was very emotional. Phil Waudby, who I first met during KAEM 2007, had run from Johannesburg to Augrabies before competing in the event. It was good to see him again and great that he had completed the run from Johannesburg. He looked strong and I knew that he would complete KAEM to finish his 1188-kilometre fundraising run. Sadly, Alison, his wife and a key member of his support team, died a few months before the event so there was also sadness. It all became too much for Phil at the award ceremony and I hugged him and held him close as he cried his heart out. Later that evening I held Carmon close as we danced to the song Lady in Red. Carmon is a nurse who has worked on the medical team at KAEM and ADDO and we had become good friends.

A few days earlier it had been Nadia, one of the race organisers and a dear friend, who had held me close when I was near to the end of day 6, exhausted and overcome by my own emotions. I cried for a while, and then we both ran to the finish line hand-in-hand.

Tough events can be tough on the mind and when that mind gives way things can get exceedingly difficult and dark. This is an example of that in its rawest form. I was a volunteer on a multi-day race over 250km in 6 days where my role was to look after a water station then when the last competitor had passed through continue along the course as ‘sweep’, either with them or slightly behind them to the next water point. It was their choice whether we chatted, or I stayed quietly behind them; some runners like the company, some do not. The role of the sweep is mainly a safety one to make sure those at the rear of the course get help if they encounter problems, to let the next waterpoint know they can pack up and, where necessary help motivate the tailender to finish.

At the event I’m talking about on the second day when the sweep I was taking over from arrived at my waterpoint she took me to one side and explained that the person in last place was having problems and what they were. The sweep was an experienced runner, a doctor and a friend; she said to me “I’m trusting you to get her to the finish”.

The problem was that the runner had entered the perimenopause and waves of hormone fuelled symptoms were washing over her They manifested themselves about 20-minutes later when she sat down on the course and started sobbing. I had met her a few years previously in a desert race so knew she was a tough cookie; this was not her. I have a great deal of experience in motivating people during extreme challenges, I trained a group of women to become the first women’s team ever to finish the 56-mile London to Brighton road race, I have helped people finish tough ultramarathons in the cold and wet and I have helped people finish tough multi-day desert races. None of those skills prepared me for what was facing me now, this was way outside my experience.

The only thing I could think to do was sit down beside her and hold her. Men like to solve problems, which would not be appropriate here, support and perhaps diversionary tactics might help along with talking and more importantly listening. I have never known anyone who has not been bereaved sob so much and so hard. After about half an hour she felt a little better and stood up saying she wanted to go back to the water point and quit; that was easy to deal with, there was no point they would have already have packed up and been well on the way to the finish so we might as well just keep walking. I didn't tell her I could have phoned for them to come back. As we walked, incredibly slowly, she talked and told me about some of what she was going through. That was a conversation way outside my comfort zone; however, I knew that it was nothing compared to what she was going through. I knew from our previous encounter in the desert that she was a cancer survivor, a strong woman, with many adventures under her belt; she was a fighter able to take on big challenges. That was not the woman I was seeing now; I was seeing someone almost broken about to give up. I could see a tiny glow of the old her, could she nurture that and make it bigger, could I help in that process. I did not know; I just knew I had to try my best.

She started to walk faster then started running before again collapsing to the ground. I help her up and led her to a pile of rocks to sit on. Again, I just held her; I was operating completely in the dark here. Again, she wanted to give up and again my response was simple; not happening because they cannot get a vehicle here, we will just have to keep walking. We continued in this fashion, walking, the occasional jog, talking, (her mostly), stopping, crying until we could see the finish for the day in a small village. There was a group of runners, mostly women, waiting to welcome her in, so we walked in with purpose, she was crying, I was crying and the people waiting for her were crying. There are tears now as I am writing this. I was pleased that her fellow runners rallied around it gave me a chance to slope off and recover.

The following day when my doctor friend handed over to me, she said, hang back so she has to spend time on her own and work through it, let's see how she copes. So that is what I did, at least initially, I had to hide behind trees and take long breaks lounging in the grass, so she didn't see me when she looked back; she was looking back often. Then I heard my phone ping, I was in an area with signal, I had a Facebook message 'Edward, I need you'. Damn someone had told her we had mobiles with us for emergencies or she had worked it out for herself. I trotted along the course and soon found her sitting beside the track crying. "Thank you, Edward, I'm sorry, my mind is my strongest asset. I am not a fast runner; I am a completer because I am mentally strong. My mind has turned to mush, it's deserted me what am I going to do? I hadn't got a clue what to do, yesterday had drained me emotionally, the prospect of another session was not something I wanted to contemplate. Unfortunately, I had to, she was a runner in need, I was a runner, she had told me so much about herself and ask for help, I could not refuse. That day was remarkably similar to the previous one.

The following day was the mountain stage and I had a different role, clearing away the markers after the last runner had been through, someone else was the sweep for that section. I was close behind and could see that the chemistry was not working between them, so I suggested to the sweep that we swapped roles. The mountains were beautiful, but challenging at the best of times, normally runners would be finished just before dark, or slightly after, therefore head torches were compulsory. We needed ours because we were going so slow that we finished after midnight. We talked a great deal in the dark hours about all sorts of intimate things, conversations that I had not even had with my wife. We saw a wonderful sunset.

"You would not have seen that but for me Edward' I'll send you the invoice later" Things were looking up if she could make jokes. We saw an amazing star filled sky, there was no light pollution in that remote area. "You would not have seen that but for me Edward' I'll send you a second invoice later." Things were definitely looking better, the second part of the day had generally been good, except for the part where I had to hold her hair back when she was sick. It all fell apart when we hit a very stony part in the dark, her feet had blistered so she was in a lot of pain, which distracted from her other problems, but did result in a lot of swearing. I heard more swearing in those few hours than I had in my life up until then, well that is how it seemed.

I was so pleased when she finished the event, some of the male runners thought she was a drama queen and received too much support and attention from the crew, most of whom were female. I know different, none of those men could have coped with what she did and succeeded. I am so in awe of her achievement. The experience left me a bit traumatised; it was a very intense experience. Now looking back, I remember it as the most rewarding experience I have had as a race volunteer.

***

If you look at most of the records of races emotions and experiences are not recorded. The London Marathon weekend is a wonderful time in the running calendar. World class athletes battle it out to win this prestigious event and their times are recorded in the annals of history. Club runners have been training for months and are looking for good times, perhaps bettering last year's. These will be recorded on the club website for all to see, compare and perhaps try to emulate or better the following year. First-time charity runners will have their times permanently recorded in their minds along with the memories of the pain of the journey and the joy of crossing the finish line. Perhaps we runners record the wrong things, we record races run and the time it took, but there is probably something else far more important that we should be noting down.

Just over a week before the marathon I invited a friend from London to come and stay for a few days to enjoy the Cornish sunshine. She had been through a rough time and I thought the change of scene and pace would do her good. Friend was possibly the wrong term to use; we became 'friends' on Facebook a few years ago through our mutual interest in several online running groups and I met her once at a race and we ran a few miles together. When I explained who it was that was coming to stay my daughter (17) gave me a lecture on 'stranger danger' and was concerned that I might have invited an axe-murderer into the house. Things were not improved by our guest announcing that she always travelled with her Swiss Army knife. Fortunately, there was no blood shed during her stay and we all survived.

She joined me for my regularly Wednesday morning run with the 'Caked in Mud' group, now morphed into BUDEiful Runners - Powered by Cake. This is a group of mainly ladies, who meet up for a muddy off-road run then have tea and cake afterwards. We take it in turns to bake. The sun shone and we had a beautiful run, my guest fitted in well and soon made friends with several members of the group. It was a lovely few hours, but because it was not a race and not officially timed there will be no record of it on a spreadsheet or results listing. I was introduced to the group by Bridget Funnel who I had met in the local gym when she was training for one of her adventurers. She knew of my love of the countryside, mud and cake and thought I would fit in well. Bridget is a few years older than me but shows no sign of slowing down. She spends a lot of time running on Dartmoor and the Coastal path when she is not on overseas adventures.

I wanted to show my friend her my special running place, Marsland Valley, so we ran again that evening. It is where I go when I need to find peace, healing time or just some space to escape from the pressures of life. Old stunted sessile oaks grow in this deep valley, with a beautiful babbling stream and pretty wildflowers; it's impossible not to feel at one with nature there. I could feel the peace flowing into her, driving out the pain of the recent past. She was relaxed and content as we watched the sunset from the beach at the end of the valley. Again, there will be no record of this magical run, it was not a race, there was no first, second and third place, no times, no lists.

***

Running is a great restorative however sometimes you have to work at it. I remember one particular run that didn't start well; it was tough going, it felt like I was plodding through treacle. This annoyed and frustrated me, I should have been running much better. I plodded on in a bad mood, probably muttering to myself, then suddenly realised I'd passed the Gunnera without noticing it. They are like massive rhubarb plants with leaves which can be twelve feet wide, so hard to miss. I love that plant and the way its massive leaves grow so quickly. What is the point in running outdoors if you don't notice things? You might as well be on a treadmill in a characterless gym.

I gave myself a bit of a talking to and decided that I should accept how things are, not keep thinking that they should be better or like they were the other day. Just accept it, deal with it, get over it and enjoy. I decided to change my route, I was going to head to the coast, turn right and come back through the woods in Tehidy Country Park. Instead I was now going to turn left and head to Godrevy; a strange decision because this would be a longer route; an extended plod. There was method in my madness. There are often seals at Godrevy, I would have a count and pass the information on to the

Cornwall Seal Group Research Trust. They always like data about seal sightings. I would plod with a purpose.

It made me think about some advice I had given a woman a few weeks before. She had been fit when she was in the military, but since leaving and having children that fitness had ebbed away. She asked my advice about getting back into running. She had tried a couple of times and been disappointed with her performance. I told her to forget about the past. She was a different person now with different circumstances; consider it a new beginning. I advised her to join a couch to 5k group that was starting up locally. I told her that she might find it a little too easy, but it would be good to have a goal and to mix with people who would keep her motivated. She would make new friends and perhaps be able to motivate and help the others in the group. Once she had reached her goal she could then reassess and consider what type of runner she wanted to be. She would have some running experience that was relevant to her new life, not her old military one. I am pleased to say that she did contact the Couch to 5k programme organiser and sign up. Achieving goals is not necessary about doing tough stuff, most of the time it is about having a plan and taking small incremental steps.

Now back to my run. I was now enjoying my plod it was a reasonably pleasant day, although my right cheek was cold from the wind and my left one hot from the sun. That would soon change when I turned for home. I had one moment of negativity when I thought 'knowing my luck there will be no seals there'. After another talking to, I banished that thought and enjoyed the views and wildlife, noticing the first flowering Foxglove I had seen that year. I love those plants they were the start of my love of nature. As a child I spent a lot of time in Cambridgeshire, one of the few counties where Foxgloves do not grow. On a trip to Durdle Door and the Blue Pool in

Dorset, while walking in a forest, I saw my first Foxglove which was standing looking magnificent in a small clearing. It looked like a plant that would have existed at the time of the dinosaurs. Strange how a child's mind works.

When I got to Godrevy the seals where there and so was a lady from the Seal Group recording the numbers, so I didn't fulfil my purpose, but I did see the seals and my spirits were uplifted. I'd like to say that on the way back I ran with the speed and elegance of a gazelle, but life is not like that. I plodded; however, the sun had warmed the treacle and it was slightly easier to plod through. I had a wonderful run enjoying the fresh air, the sea breeze, the sun, the views, the brightly coloured gorse, all the flowers, the sound of the gulls and the sight of two jays on the way back.

'Running really isn't about the time you do, but the time you have." – Lisa Jackson author of Your Pace or Mine? and other books.

***

Running has been a big part of my life for over 25 years, and hopefully for many years to come; however, I could live without it. I realised that one very eventful Sunday morning a few years ago. In a little over a second my life changed; my view of the world was altered forever. I estimate that the number of beats my heart had made before that day is about 1.8 billion and I have not given them a second thought. My heart has just continued beating away without me thinking about it. Then one day it didn't and I noticed; something that was constant suddenly wasn't. That was scary.

When I wake up in the morning and think I will not run today, even though I'd plan to, I check my resting pulse rate, if it is normal, I give myself a good talking to and go for a run. If it is elevated, I know it is right to rest. One morning, a little while ago, I took my pulse. 1, 2, 3, 4 .... 25, 26 - pause - 27,

28... Wow that was scary, you cannot image how much space that pause filled even though it lasted for a little over a second. Okay calm down try it again 1, 2, 3, 4 .... 10, 11 – pause - 12, 13.... The silence from those missing beats filled the room. Even though I had no pain, no dizziness, in fact no symptoms at all, my thoughts were: 'This is not good, definitely not going for my Sunday run. Doesn't seem serious enough to dial for an ambulance or to call the out of hours doctor, I'll just have a quiet day in, but I'm going to the doctor first thing Monday morning.' I spent the day considering my own mortality, something I haven't done before. Previously I had some vague notion that at some point in time I'd have to give up running and I would die. I assumed that those two things would happen pretty much together and if I was lucky at exactly the same moment in time. But now there was the possibility that a heart problem might stop me running before I was ready to die. Would life be worth living without running? Almost as soon as that question popped into my head the answer popped up right beside it. Yes! I didn't know why the answer was yes, but I was absolutely sure it was yes. Which was strange as before that point I was convinced the answer was definitely no!

I spent the rest of the day thinking about this and decided it was because running has been good to me, I have some wonderful memories, and we have an extraordinarily strong and committed relationship. I have heard that people in strong relationships cope better when their partner dies than people in shaky relationships do. Presumably, there are no regrets, no if only, no thinking of how things could have been. Yes there are races I'd still like to do and places I'd still like to run, just like I'm sure a loving couple would like to spend more time together, visit places and do things, but there is always going to be an end; if what you have now is good then that end is easier to bear.

My running life has been good, a steady progression from short road races to marathons and ultras followed by lots of off-road racing and running. I've run on my own, in a group, with friends, in races with thousands and in races with only a few entrants. I've run every day for a year, I've run for 24 hours, I've had non-running days, non-running weeks. I've run some races only once while others I've run many times. I've only ever been awarded one trophy, but with every race and on every run I've won a prize; a little something to strengthen the relationship and to put in the memory bank for that time when I might not be able to run.

In the morning I saw my doctor (who is a runner as well) and she said it was probably an ectopic heartbeat which occurs when the heart cells fire off an electrical impulse outside of the normal, coordinated impulses which make the heart contract. After an extra beat, the heart rests a little longer than usual and this feels like a missed beat. This is apparently quite common, and the extra beats are harmless. She could see I wasn't convinced or calmed by this explanation, so she arranged for me to have a 24-hour ECG to rule out anything else. I dropped the kit back into the surgery at the end of the 24-hours and was told to phone in the morning for the results. When I phoned the first thing the practice nurse said was, "It's lucky I know that you are that mad ultra runner otherwise I would have sent an ambulance, your average heart rate for the 24 hours was way below the resting heart rate for a normal person". She told me that the pattern was fine there had been a couple more ectopic beats but that was all so I could stop worrying, which is what I did. Since then I've not noticed any further missing beats, although I have started worrying about what they say about me in the doctor's surgery; up to that point I had never spoken to the practice nurse, how did she know about running exploits and how had she formed the opinion that I was mad?

How to have a running life

You may remember this quote from chapter two.

Running is real and relatively simple…but it ain't easy.
--Mark Will-Weber

Running is simple; however, making sure you keep running in your life is far from simple (unless you make it so), there are lots of things that will get in your way if you let them and therein lies the answer. Don't let them; simple to say not so easy to do. There is one person I wish I had met early on in my running career; it would have made things a lot easier. I had been running for about 18 years when I met him. It was at a trade show for running and outdoor brands, he was on the stand next to mine and was a lapsed triathlete, having done a few sprint triathlons and one Olympic distance one before, as he put it, work got in the way. He complained that as a salesman he travelled around a lot, so it was hard to train and having to attend shows didn't help. I found that strange because I was a salesman who travelled a lot, attended shows and still found time to train for ultras and multi-day events. He was employed and I was self-employed, perhaps that was the difference.

After the show closed on the first day, I went to my hotel room, changed and headed out for a run. It was only a short distance on road before I could pick up a footpath across some lovely countryside and up some challenging hills. I had checked for routes on an Ordnance Survey map as soon as I knew I would be attending the show. When I got back, I showered and headed for the bar to hydrate before dinner. The guy from the next stand was in the bar chatting to another exhibitor. I think they had gone there straight from the show, they were still wearing the lanyards with their badges on. As I was ordering my drink, beer, I had downed plenty of water in my room, I heard the lapsed triathlete say he had seen all the episodes of *Sex and the City*; I vaguely knew it was a long-running romcom – I have never seen an episode. That is when it struck me that it is simple for people to make things part of their lives. Up and down the country millions of people tune in everyday to watch *EastEnders, Coronation Street,* other soaps and reality TV programmes; nothing gets in the way of their viewing. That is how it can be with running, a healthy habit.

Of course, running requires more effort than sitting watching TV but it does not require more time unless you are an ultra runner. Then again, I suppose there are binge TV watchers performing amazing feats of static endurance. TV just requires you to flop down in front of the TV at the required time, running requires some preparation, you need to make sure you have kit available and not churning about in the washing machine or hanging wet on the line. I did once run in wet leggings. My daughter was back from university and my kit was in the wardrobe in her old room, she was sleeping and there was no way I was going to disturb her early in the morning. I ran in a pair of work socks, a casual t-shirt and wet leggings grabbed off the washing line (they had been left out overnight and it had rained). Fortunately, my smelly trainers were banished to the garage, so they were accessible. Failing to plan is planning to fail.

There is no catch-up facility with runs, and you cannot record them, well you can using Strava, Garmin, etc but you have to still do them at the time so scheduling is important as is flexibility. Some years ago, after I had finished the Luton marathon and had a chat with friends I was walking back to my car when I met someone I hadn't seen for a long time. I asked how she had got on and this produced floods of tears. I gave her a hug then asked what was wrong. She had been extremely disappointed with her marathon time and explained that training was not going well and she was struggling fitting training in around her new job. We were getting cold standing on the street in Luton so I suggested we met up a few days later for a curry.

Over the poppadoms I learnt all about her new job, then things went a little quiet while I tucked into my vegetable biryani. Afterwards, as we had another Kingfisher lager, she told me about her marathon training plan, which was similar to the ones in Runners' World that I had followed so successfully. And there was the problem, she had a chaotic working life, jetting off all over the world to attend conferences and meetings then having periods working from home or commuting into London and was trying to fit a very regular training schedule into that life. It was never going to happen. If you have a regular work pattern, working the similar hours every week in the same place, a regular training plan where you do the same sessions on the same day each week, week after week will work providing unexpected events, procrastination and a lack of motivation don't get in the way. If you have a regular shift pattern it will need some adjustment, if there is no regularity it needs to be ripped up and something else worked out. A week is an artificial construct, your training doesn't have to have a regular weekly pattern. Over another pint in a nearby pub we worked on a new plan one that was infinitely flexible. We worked on essential elements, what could be done to maintain fitness when running was not possible (security concerns in some locations for example) and how not to cram too much in when she was working from home and had lots of time to train. I'm pleased to say it worked; she was a lot happier with her running. They were tears after her next marathon, tears of joy because she had achieved a pb.

On your journey towards a running life you will get lots of advice. In the song Ironic by Alanis Morissette is the line:

"It's the good advice that you just didn't take."

Not following good advice is annoying but listening to bad advice is even worse and can be disastrous. How can you tell the difference between the good, the bad and the indifferent? Fortunately, there are some simple questions you can ask yourself to judge how good the advice you are being offered is likely to be.

Do you know the person? Can they be trusted. If you don't know them do some research to see if they have the relevant knowledge and experience.

Are they just displaying their knowledge or are they applying it to your circumstances?

Here is some advice I received from Comrades Winner, Lindsay Weight, about running the Two Oceans marathon. She knew I was an experience runner so didn't say any of the normal stuff, I could see her thinking 'What does Ed not know?' Then she said "Run in the middle of the road. There is a very severe camber, if you run at the side you risk having knee problems." That was good advice that I did take along with 'don't trip over the cat's eyes'.

Are they similar in nature to you or at least sympathetic to your goals? If they always want to win and you just want to complete' then their advice may not be appropriate.

Is the advice supported by other people's opinions? But remember Copernicus and later Galileo were lone voices and they were right.

Does it feel right. Sometimes we instinctively know when something is wrong because we have unconsciously processed important information.

As a general rule the more emphatic someone is that you should do something the more likely it is that you should not.

The best advice will come from you with the benefit of experience. Don't let it be the good advice that you just didn't take. The second time you get kicked by a donkey you don't learn anything (Old Spanish proverb).

A little bit of Bon Jovi is always good; It's my life May 2000 (I've changed a few words)

It's my life
It's now or never
I ain't gonna run forever
I just want to run while I'm alive
(It's my life)
My heart loves an open highway
Like Frankie said I did it my way
I just want to run while I'm alive
It's my life

And that is the point I am making; it is your life and if you want running to be part of it permanently you need to make sure it fits into your life, both emotionally and practically and the life of those people who are dear to you. Other people's training plans are useful, some will work as they are, others need to be adapted. Other people's achievements and goals can be very motivational if they align with your aims and motivation. It is the same with advice; we are all an experiment of one, so it is no surprise one size doesn't fit all. Running is a broad church.

I read a lot of running books, more recently the biography type, and they illustrate the huge range of adventures and achievements. Two of my favourites are *Beyond Impossible* – Mimi Anderson and *Your Pace or Mine?* - Lisa Jackson. I know Mimi and have been in several races with her, in the same event not against her. Her list of achievements is staggering, I was worn out reading the list in the back of the book which includes; female 7 day treadmill record, the fastest crossing of Ireland on foot, first person to complete a double Grand Union Canal Race (145 miles x 2) and first female to complete the double Spartathlon (153-miles X 2). You could say Mimi doesn't do things by halves or even in full, she doubles them.

Lisa, I didn't meet until after I had read her book *Your Pace or Mine?* Her main claim to fame is that she's come last in 25 marathons. Both runners are inspirational and have in common a love of running and a willingness to encourage others. As you can see there is a vast difference between their aspirations and motivations. I recommend both books.

I have listed the books that have had an effect on my running at the end of this book; however, I would just like to mention two more here, both written by Kelly Holmes. *Black, White and Gold: My Biography* is the story of her running life and Olympic success. Even though I knew how her Olympic races turned out I was willing her on to succeed when I was reading the book. The other book is *Running Life: Mindset, fitness & nutrition for positive wellbeing*. It is the Haynes manual (the iconic car maintenance books) for beginner runners and something the more experienced should dip into from time to time.

You can find other motivational people at the back of the field at parkrun. I often volunteer as a Tail Walker so I can hang out with the people at the back and hear their stories. One man was a Guinness World Record holder, he had been part of the group that set the World Record for the largest gathering of cardiac arrest survivors – 127, Basildon, Essex, UK, on 9 June 2018. He had a voluntary role encouraging other cardiac arrest survivors to exercise. A lady one week told me how running kept her sane, she was a single Mum of three children, and this was her first week back after a series of health problems. Her Mum was looking after the children. There are a lot of people with health issues at the back, it makes me realise how lucky I am to have good health. It also makes me glad I have been first aid trained. Fortunately, I wasn't the Tail Walker the week someone collapsed, the local GP was which was lucky and the marshal near the spot where it happened was an intensive care nurse.

There was one occasion when I found Tail Walking a little demotivating (although I am only saying that in jest). I was joined by Chloe, aged 11. She was keen to cover all the volunteer roles at parkrun so, even though she was not old enough to be Tail Walker, I gave her the vest and accompanied her. We chatted about all sorts of things. She had an interest in English so I introduced her to the concept of spoonerisms (inadvertently switching the first letters of words) and that we were therefore Wail Talkers and I explained that I thought one of the best spoonerisms could be made from the running club where I used to live Bude Rats. This swiftly moved the conversation on to her running and the discovery that her parkrun PB was better than my current time was, fortunately my pb set a few years earlier was just a little bit quicker than hers. That is what I love about parkrun it is for all ages and all types of people.

And therein lies the secret to a running life, variety and finding motivation wherever you can, whether that is from an older man who is a cardiac survivor or a young girl starting out on her running adventure. It is finding joy in a 5k and a 50k, on the road and on the trail, in competition and in recreational runs.

Everything has beauty, but not everyone sees it. – Confucius

See the beauty in running and it will be yours for life. I think you also need a child-like fascination with things to find that beauty., well I do. For years just the sound of the Dursley Dozen in Gloucestershire appealed to me, initially I didn't do anything about it, I was too busy doing other things; I just rolled the words around in my brain. Then I looked up details of the event, "A challenging race of twelve miles over hillsides, roads, woodland, open country, mud, more mud, and solid rock. The course sets off steeply up a road for 200 metres and then ascends a woodland track to the top of Stinchcombe Hill." ... "For the final climb, "THE PRECIPICE" ropes are provided." That did it I had to do that race. It was a few years before the timing was right and I entered, I was right it was tremendous fun. It is another great example of a club organised race. Thank you, Dursley Running Club.

Talking of being a child you may have noticed that comic book and cartoon characters have alliterative names; Bigs Bunny, Peter Pan, Micky Mouse, Betty Boop, Desperate Dan etc. Race directors use that technique to great effect. I have been enticed by the Broadclyst Bimble and the Bicton Blister in the South West and further afield there is the Steyning Stinger, the Sodbury Slog, the Bungay Black Dog Marathon and the Causeway Crossing which allowed me to experience the amazing Giant's Causeway near Belfast. The Poets Path Potter is perhaps the best use of alliteration, it is also a very scenic and friendly event. I have managed to avoid the Arc of Attrition; it takes place along a section the coastal path in Cornwall that is familiar to me, so I don't see the point. It takes place in January which means you are very unlikely to see the stunning views given the short amount of daylight and the bad weather prevalent at that time of year.

Although there is no alliteration another race title that attracted me was the Osmotherly Phoenix in North Yorkshire, a fascination that was also shared by my business partner, Phillip Howells, so in 2011 we organised a sales trip to coincide with the race date. Unfortunately, the event is no more, it was a beautiful off-road marathon starting and finishing at the Village Hall, Osmotherly, with a choice of distance involving some 4000 feet of climbing on the 33-mile route and 3500 feet of climbing on the 26.2-mile route. Which of course meant stunning views and a big thirst for the particularly good and cheap beer afterwards.

Sometimes competition can help keep you motivated, and I create my own in races competing against people that probably don't know what is going on. The first time was quite early in my running career during the Brands Hatch half-marathon, a wonderful event that starts and finishes on the grid and consists of laps of the race circuit and the track perimeter roads. It was a great treat to be standing on the start line I'd seen so many times on TV smelling the evocative aroma of rubber and fuel rising from the track knowing I'd be going along Clearways, through Dingle Dell, around Sheene Curve, Hawthorns, Paddock Hill Bend etc. It was a surprisingly hilly course and I was struggling a bit; running behind me was someone whose feet made a loud slapping sound, as I tired, I could hear the sound getting closer. He overtook me on a downhill section, slapping like mad, and I was surprised to see he was a lot older than me. I overtook him on the next uphill section, but he came passed going again on the next down section. This cat and mouse game went on for a long time I just couldn't pull away from him. I didn't want to be beaten by this old guy so worked out a strategy on the final downhill I would keep as close as possible when he came passed, run as strongly up the final hill to open out as big a lead as possible then keep running as fast as I could along the finishing straight until I reached the chequered flag. It worked; a pointless victory as we were both a long way behind the winner; however, it kept me motivated.

I've used that sort of technique in may events to good effect and it would often result in a PB, so thank you to all those unknown opponents. It has on a couple of occasions caused me problems. The first I can remember is the Wellington Monument Race, in the Blackdown Hill, Somerset. It's a 10k (actually 10,090m) that starts at the Catherine Wheel Public House in the village square at Hemyock, finishes at Hemyock County Primary School and takes you out of the village on a relatively short flat section, up a big climb until you turn off the road for about 800metres of flat to the Wellington Monument, around the monument then back to the road for a dash down the hill and the short run in to the finish. On the downhill I focused on staying with the guy ahead who was running well then, just before the finish, I would put a spurt on come flying past him and across the finish line. Unfortunately, I had not read the bit about finishing at the school which meant going past the pub along the road around a corner then into the school, which of course meant maintaining a fast pace a lot longer than I had expected to keep my adversary at bay. Even though we did not know each other, and he probably did not know we were racing he shook my hand at the end and said, "Well done, I just couldn't catch you".

The other memorable occasion was the Endurancelife Exmoor Trail Marathon, I was still new to trail running and it was only the second Endurancelife event I had taken part in. I didn't know then that trail race organisers are more concerned about having a good finish area than a precise distance race, provided it is not shorter than the stated distance. The Exmoor marathon courses encompass stiff climbs and long descents, open moorland, thickly wooded combes (valleys), dizzying cliffs, and a stretch of coastline that is unsurpassed. The organisers say "*We are confident that there is no course in Britain that offers such a variety of terrain within such a compact area. This truly is trail running territory at its best. The Exmoor course is widely regarded as the toughest course in The Series and is definitely a gruelling test of endurance for even the very hardiest trail and fell runners.*" What they didn't say then but do now is that it is longer than a marathon. I was using a runner a little faster than me as motivation, hanging in behind him and getting pulled along, when I judged we were about a quarter of a mile from the finish I spotted that the path ahead narrowed along a dizzying cliff section and there would be no overtaking so I sprinted ahead of my 'opponent' to get to that section first. It went on forever because the race was longer than the marathon distance, I felt bad about possibly holding the other runner up so ran as fast as I could. The upshot was that I dropped him and finished about a minute ahead of him totally exhausted and unable to speak for a while as I gulped down great lungs full of air. That was a great day out.

I find quotes and lines from songs motivational and extremely helpful in tough times. At the start of this book I described how the words from Gloria Gaynor, 'Did you think I'd lay down and die? Oh, no, not I, I will survive', rescued me now that I have survived that ordeal and more these words from Labi Siffre are my mantra.

"Something inside so strong
I know I can make it"

I once wrote a running anthem to keep me motivated, as you can see it is very heavily influenced by the Calvin Harris song *Girls*.

I like them road runs

I like them trail runs
I like them muddy runs
I like them mixed terrain runs
I like them training runs
I like them fun runs
I like the recovery runs
And I like steady runs
I like them long runs
I like them short runs
I like them hot runs
I like them cold runs
I like them slow runs
I like them fast runs
I like them carrying a little bitty weight runs

If there is nothing in there that floats your boat, then perhaps a running life is not for you. If it is it takes commitment, determination, ingenuity, perseverance, sacrifice and perhaps a few tears. It is worth it, it's only very occasionally that I have experience the runners high, most memorably in the Hastings Half coming down the hill towards the seafront when I felt I was running two feet off the ground; however, there are a myriad of magical moments and memories of the most wonderful kind thanks to a running life. There haven't been many lows, or dark moments and those are even highlights, when looked back on from a distance, things to make me grow and to make the special moments even more special.

The bard knew the benefit of being a runner.

> *Now bid me run,*
> *And I will strive with things impossible.*
> Ligarius – Julius Caesar, William Shakespeare

There's a proverb, normally described as being an old African saying however I think it may be a modern construct:

"If you want to go fast, go alone. If you want to go far, go together."

This would seem to be at odds with the phrase 'The loneliness of the long-distance runner'. This was the title of a short story written by Alan Stillitoe published in 1959 which was later adapted for a film with the same title released in 1962. The story and the film have received plenty of analytical comment. The running in the story is cross-country running, so is not particularly long, and the main character uses it as a method of both emotional and physical escape from his situation. With the character using running as a way to mentally reflect this allows the author to comment on the class divisions in society.

I think a lot of runners get a great deal emotional and physical escape from long distance running and find clarity, but I would not describe it as a lonely sport. Yes, there are long runs alone, but there is also the camaraderie of races, clubs, training groups etc. In the UK, the long Sunday run is often done in isolation, but in South Africa, where many runners are preparing for Comrades, the Sunday run is a social, early morning affair followed by brunch at a cafe (they start very early). And nowadays there is all the friendly banter on social media. It is only a lonely sport if you want it to be.

Seeing things from the other side - volunteering

Volunteering isn't a one-way process; you get a lot back. I've learnt a lot from the runners I've talked to and from fellow crew members, normally very experienced runners. I first volunteered at a race in about 1995, my club, then Hastings Runners, expected members to marshal the club 10k. I did so willingly and was rewarded with a smile from Kelly Holmes as I indicated to her which way to go. Earlier I had had a rather nasty run in with a motorist who was moaning about the road closure. His aggressive attitude to me drew the attention of the police and his continued rant and bad language led to his arrest. I saw the extremes of human nature that day.

When I was running half-marathons and marathons I didn't volunteer very much, I was keen to race, but I did my bit. Now I volunteer a lot, some of it involves running part of the course to either check the markings or clear them away, sometimes both so I get a run in and am helping others. On other occasions I am on a checkpoint handing out water, encouragement and, when needed, hugs. Sometimes when you are unsure which words of encouragement will help a hug will do the job. A tough job if it is hot and a long race; runners can get very sweaty and smelly. I learn a lot from observing how runners manage themselves both physically and mentally. I mostly volunteer on long-distance events; with a short race, runners are concentrating on a fast time so there is little interaction between volunteers and runners. Your duties are over quickly, which for many will be a plus, for me it is not, given where I live it is usually a long journey to get to the events, so I like to get my money's worth. In a long-distance event many runners are just hoping to finish so time is not as important, and they can stop for a chat. Sometimes your words of encouragement can be the thing that helps them carry on. If they cannot continue your words can also be of great benefit making them feel better about pulling out. Runners can be very hard on themselves.

To make running a permanent part of your life you must be committed and consistent. Being obsessive is not the same thing. Yes, I know that obsessed is what the lazy call the dedicated, I don't subscribe to that. I have come across a lot of runners who have had to give up doing what they love doing because they have done too much. Bruce Fordyce is one such person, he now says:

"*'If you love running you want to be able to run all your life. So, it is best to run less now if that means you run for longer. That way over the whole of your life you will run more.*"

It is okay not to run sometimes. Volunteering is a great way to have a break from running while still getting the buzz, and you will come back motivated by the experience. Here is how one two-week break panned out for me.

For the first week I volunteered on a CHICKS (now renamed Go Beyond) respite break for disadvantaged children. I knew my time would be fully committed so made no plans to run. It was a highly active week as the volunteers get to participate in all the activities with the children. I played cricket, table tennis, football, visited an indoor climbing centre (where I went on the aerial walk, climbing wall and abseiled) went swimming, river rafting and did lots more. Great cross training.

For the second week I was volunteering on the legendary Berghaus Dragon's Back Race which follows the mountainous spine of Wales from north to south. This incredible 5-day journey is 315 kilometres long with 15,500 metres of ascent across wild, trackless, remote and mountainous terrain. It is said to be the toughest 5-day mountain running race in the world. I am not qualified to comment on whether it is or not, but what I do know is that of the just over 400 starters 154 did not finish. Some were friends and I know that they are very experienced, determined runners so it must be very, very tough. Being on the crew isn't easy either, but it is great fun. I knew we would get breaks so there would be the possibility of a run (I packed my kit), but I decided I would not be running so I would not be disappointed if it didn't happen and pleasantly surprised if it did. In the end I didn't run, not due to a lack of time, but a lack of showers. I did go for walks (less sweaty) and one lovely river swim (not sweaty at all).

I was one of 120 volunteers that helped make up the 132-event crew. I have crewed for the event organisers, Ourea Events, before so knew to expect long hours, hard work, good food and appreciation from the event staff and the runners. I knew I would have a wonderful time among liked-minded people. The crew is split into a number of teams, Checkpoint, Wrangling, First Response, Admin, Camp, Catering and Medical. There are also a couple of special people who look after race control, monitoring the runners via their trackers and co-ordinating any emergency response. I was part of the camp team and within that on the early shift of the bag drop team. Our main job, when not on other duties, was getting the big blue competitor tents down, packed away, transported to the next camp and erected before the runners arrived. Most of the camp team had volunteered before so we soon developed into a very efficient, happy group. Shane Ohly, Race Director, has a great management style which filters down throughout the control structure. He gives good, detailed instructions of what he wants to achieve, how to achieve it only where this is important for safety, then leaves people to implement their own solutions to achieve the desired results. It is a system he has developed over the years, and he knows who he can depend upon.

I was team leader on my shift for a subset of the camp team working on bag drop. The team leader part was easy, about all I had to do was make sure people took their breaks, everyone was super keen and motivated. Bag drop is a fantastic job as you get to interact with the competitors, although it does mean an early start. Runners are allowed a 60-litre dry bag which is transported between camps. Typically, it will contain a sleeping bag, sleeping mat, spare clothes, extra shoes, food for each day on the mountain (breakfast & dinner plus snacks at the finish are supplied) wash kit, spare food, power bank to charge GPS devices and whatever else they think they will need. One competitor had 8 bottles of beer in his bag – he had only drunk one by day 4. Moving those bags about was great strength training. They are also allowed a 5kg dry bag that is transported to a support point (about halfway) each day. Each morning competitors drop off their bags to be loaded on to vans to be transported to the support point or finish as applicable. When they do there is a kit check to ensure they have the compulsory items with them. Some don't and have to mess about in their bags to find them. There is a large group of runners on the early start, after that some of the bag drop team transfer to taking tents down then, when the last runner has left, we all switch to that task. The last thing we do before leaving the site is to have a mass litter sweep; we find almost nothing and what we do find seems to have been there before we arrived.

As soon as we arrived at the next camp the bag drop team unload the overnight drop bags and sort them into number order for when the runners arrive, we then switch to help putting the tents up. When that is completed, it is time for lunch, then a short spell helping with whatever is needed before the first runners arrive and we carry their bags to the tents. The runners really appreciate this because, as you would expect, they are very tired. After a few hours we get a break and that is the time to go for a run, a walk or as I did on that one occasion a swim in the river. We were normally back on shift about 6 of 6.30 pm for three hours of bag carrying, checking the toilets, emptying bins and keeping the washing up area clean. Glamorous stuff. Often some of the team would be diverted to other duties, looking after a road crossing, helping in the canteen at busy times etc. At 9.30pm we would finish for the day and head to our tents to get some sleep ready to be up for a 5:45am start.

Walking with the runners to carry their bags to the tents was a great chance to interact with them, although at times diplomacy was needed if they had missed a cut off or had to withdraw for another reason. I loved this interaction with the runners, it was a chance to understand what they had been through during the day and hopefully provided words of encouragement or succour. Our team was a joy to be part of and I am sure people felt the same in the other teams. When you do different adventurous things, most ordinary people are not interested in hearing about them, but when you are with like-minded people the conversation flows. Being with like-minded positive people makes volunteering pleasant even though at times you are tired, cold and wet or have to do strange things like the time we had to clear a field of sheep's poo before we could erect the tents. We had to use our hands, fortunately there was a supply of gloves.

Volunteers at Ourea events are given a credit equal to the value of the event they crew on which they can use towards any Ourea Event. So, I have a free entry to the Dragon's Back race. I did have no intention of ever entering the Dragon's Back race, something I have always thought was beyond my abilities, plus I'm frightened of heights; the thought of going over Grib Goch terrified me. I have now been inspired, by the children on the CHICKS break and by the Dragon's Back athletes. Helping one of the children overcome her fear of heights at the climbing centre helped me conquer my fears. When I expressed doubts to one of the competitors, he mentioned this quote from Eleanor Roosevelt:

> *You gain strength, courage, and confidence by every experience in which you really stop to look fear in the face. You must do the thing which you think you cannot do.*

I came back from those two weeks physically tired (knackered is the technical term) and lacking in sleep (good multi-day race training), but mentally refreshed and looking forward to some great running over the weeks ahead. I also came back with the desire to do something I thought I never would. Dragon's Back here I come.

Never set limits, go after your dreams, don't be afraid to push the boundaries. And laugh a lot - it's good for you! – Paula Radcliffe

I think for me volunteering is a pleasure because I have reached the stage where I am runner rather than someone who runs. The difference between a runner and someone who runs probably needs some explanation. On one race I helped with my job on Friday afternoon was to run part of the course to make sure the markings were clear and still there. One of the organisers showed me on a map which section he wanted me to check and when he got to the point where the route joined a road he said. "You will remember that bit from last year, it's that long steep hill where I came past you in the van and said do you want a lift. You looked at me as if I had two heads and said, "Why would I want a lift?" and ran on." He was someone that ran, I am a runner. Someone who runs looks out of the window to check the weather so they can decide whether they will go for a run or not. A runner looks out of the window so that they can decide on what kit to wear.

Volunteering can be simple and easy, for example standing at a junction pointing the way to go like I was at the Hastings 10k. Or simple and hard like many of the coastal events I help with, long hours in tough weather conditions and perhaps with some strenuous running. Or it can be complex depending on how you approach it. I cannot be passive; I get involved and love to encourage the runners and, if they need it, provided some personalised motivation. Sometimes that involves taking risks. I was helping on a coastal event that had a range of distances including a marathon and an ultra marathon. Before setting out on the final section of the ultra competitors came through the marathon finish area. I was there when a friend came in moaning about the weather and saying how tough the course was and saying that she was going to stop, I knew she was training for a big event and that stopping was not a good idea for her. I gave her a stern talking to and packed her off out on the final leg. A little while later another friend came in with similar complaints and intentions, she was also training for the same big event. I gave her a hug, some sympathetic words of encouragement which would have sent her on her way except, because she had not expected to be so slow, she did not have a headtorch and would need one; simple, I gave her mine and off she went. The weather was atrocious, and I did wonder whether I had been right to send them on their way, I also wondered whether the first friend would be upset with me for the harsh words. I waited on the finish line with quite some apprehension, When, they came in both smiled when they crossed the finish line, and both gave me a hug and said the same thing. "Thank you, Edward, that was just what I needed." Fortune favours the brave. I hope I have never got it disastrously wrong; my I.H.E. nickname and wig collection indicate that I can be tough in an effective way and inventively supportive. I hope I have always chosen the right tactic each time. On one occasion I just had to do nothing. I was asked to help a friend of a friend running the 145-mile Grand Union Canal Race (145 miles). The friend had organised a group of people to help, and I was allocated a 30-mile section towards the end of the route in Paddington central London. When the runner arrived, I was told he didn't want anyone to run with him but did want to know there was someone behind if he needed any help. My job was to run behind unseen ready to help if necessary. Help wasn't needed so I just ran, I could have done with some company it is not the most inspiring section.

Fuelling the machine and keeping it running

Following the health warning from my doctor in 1994 I started to take more of an interest in what I ate. Before then I ate what I always ate and what everyone else was eating and never really gave it any thought. The more I ran the less I wanted meat, particularly red meat and I ate more rice, pasta, vegetables, and chicken. What I read about modern farming and food production methods lead me towards thinking about becoming vegetarian for a variety of reasons; animal welfare concerns, health considerations and because it just felt like the right thing to do. I made the decision a few summers later. We used to drive down to Welcome in Devon for our summer holiday overnight. There was less traffic, and our young children would sleep in the car. That particular year we drove down in two cars because I had to leave before the end of the holiday to go to a business meeting. Overnight I made the decision to go vegetarian and decided to tell my wife the following morning on the beach. The conversation went something like this "Vanessa I have something I want to tell you." That was probably a bad choice of words I very seldom used my wife's name when speaking to her. A rather tense 'what' was her response. "I am going to go totally vegetarian." "Oh, thank God for that I thought you were going to say you were having an affair." My decision to become vegetarian was very much a personal thing, I didn't want to protest or try and convert people I just wanted to live my life my way. My wife and two children remained meat eaters. My wife was very accommodating and would plan meals so that we could all have similar things. Friends were also quite accommodating, although one local farmer's wife did serve me with a vegetable pie with 'veggie muck' written in pastry letters on the crust. I think the children just thought it was part of their dad being a strange runner type. I tried not to influence them in any way towards any particular food choices. Although I did encourage then to try new things, particularly vegetables.

After a while I started to feel a little bit of a fraud eating dairy products and eggs; there are animal welfare issues connected with dairy herds and egg production. However, I never made the switch to a totally plant-based diet, it would have been too disruptive for family life. The family were happy to join me in a vegetarian meal, like vegetable lasagne, pizza and cauliflower cheese, but I think if all my meals were vegan then it would have been a case of always cooking two meals on every occasion and that would have been just too complicated and disruptive. If I had gone vegan it would have probably ended in divorce.

In 2012 my marriage ended after 28 years, and I moved out of the family home; this seemed the perfect opportunity to turn vegan. I had also just read Scott Jurek's book, *Eat & Run,* and thought 'if it is good enough for him then it is good enough for me'. For those that don't know about Scott he is an ultra-marathon runner and a vegan with an exceptional record of success:

.

> Won the Western States Endurance Run seven consecutive times (1999–2005),
> Won the Spartathlon 153-mile (246 km) race from Athens to Sparta, Greece three consecutive times (2006–2008).
> Won the Badwater Ultramarathon twice (2005, 2006)
>
> Plus, lots of other race wins setting records along the way.

On April 14, 2014, (the year I met him) Jurek and Rickey Gates became the first North Americans to complete the Bob Graham Round in under 24 hours. Had he not come over to the UK that year I doubt we would have ever met.

Set the speed record for completing the Appalachian Trail (approx. 2,200 miles) in 46 days, 8 hours, and 7 minutes in 2015

I was happy that switching to a vegan diet would not undermine my running, in fact I thought it might even improve it. Unlike Scott I have not got a record of success, although since turning vegan I have won my first trophy - the male over 60-category in the Extreme Energy Events Round the Island race on the Isle of Wight. 65 miles over two days on the coastal path around the island's perimeter.

Again, the vegan thing is what feels right for me, I'd like other people to take the same approach but I'm not going to berate or condemn them if they don't. My younger daughter lived with me after the marriage break up; my older daughter had already left home. I am so glad she chose to stay with me, I don't know why she made that choice, but her comments during an argument a few years later give a clue "Dad you annoy the hell out of me, but I know it is because you care". The youngster passionately believed that 'a meal without meat was not a proper meal'. So, I cooked two meals, I do not believe that I should force my beliefs upon her, especially as they were different when she was born and growing up. My elder daughter has recently turned vegan after participating in Veganuary. It was very much for her own reasons.

My first few months as a vegan were not easy, I tended to try to find substitutes for dairy products and missed cheese a lot. Then I had a seminal moment, why try and find things that were like the things I did not want to eat? From that point on I just tried lots of new things, creating meals from fresh ingredients and enjoying experimenting with different combinations of herbs and spices. The advice I wished I'd had when I first became a vegan is this 'don't think in terms of giving things up, instead crowd them out by trying lots of new things. You won't like everything you try, but there will be more than enough that you do to keep your thoughts off of what you are not having'. I love my food more now than I've ever done and feel a lot healthier. I used to get lots of colds, both in the winter and the summer, but since following a vegan diet I've had one in eight years. A vegan diet can be an extremely healthy one; however, I often get asked 'how do I get enough protein' to which I usually answer, "go and ask the same question to a gorilla or a bull, they seem to get enough". Now I can tell them to go and ask heavyweight boxer, David Haye, he went vegan in 2014. A vegan diet can also be an unhealthy one, particularly nowadays when there are so many ready meals and meat and cheese substitutes that are highly processed.

Being vegan and running presents no challenges at all, except that you cannot use many of the commercial gels and energy drinks. Not really a bad thing. It is really annoying when you find a protein shake based on a vegan protein source like pea powder then find it is not vegan because they have added Vitamin D from an animal source. The vitamin D probably doesn't provide any additional benefit. Entering long-distance races does offer up some challenges. You do not know whether the checkpoints will have food suitable for vegans. Some races do, some try, but do not get it right because they do not know for example that Jelly Babies contain gelatine, an animal product, and some just don't think about it. My simple solution is to always make sure I take my own food. For shorter races that will be whole dried bananas and for longer ones those plus vegan flapjack or peanut butter and jam sandwiches. I am not one for fancy solutions. There is at least one race that is vegan, the V3K in Wales where competitors have to agree to follow a vegan diet for the duration of the race.

In multi-day races which are catered there is normally good provision for vegans due to the higher proportion of vegans in the ultra-running community than in the wider population. Of course, in many foreign countries a no meat or low meat diet is the norm. When I was in Nicaragua (I was vegetarian then) we were staying in poor rural communities and the staple fare was rice & beans with tomato for breakfast, rice and beans with avocado for lunch and rice and beans with cheese for dinner. I loved the flavours and was in epicurean heaven, my meat-eating friends suffered, although one day a scrawny chicken was served up; they were in raptures,

When I first started entering self-sufficiency multi-day races there were virtually no vegan options among the commercially available dehydrated meals, so I used to make my own with couscous, dried fruit, seeds and nuts. Dehydrated food is really the only option in these events as you will be carrying up to a week's worth of food on your back, often in extremely hot conditions. Now I take a more practical approach; Pot Noodles have some flavours in the range which are vegan, so I take these. I remove them from the pot and crush them up before putting them in ziplock bags. One and a half pots are sufficient for my evening meal. I am lucky I can manage on the 2,000 Kcals minimum that most races state you must have per day. I know many other runners need more. For breakfast I take Ready Brek to which I have added a little sugar and some ground almonds to boost the calories and taste. Extremely easy to make up in the morning and great tasting with some agave nectar on. During the day I nibble on some whole dried bananas and liquorice and my absolute favourite treat in the desert, Hula Hoops.

Over the years I have watched what other people do and when I see something I like I add these in as treats; a plastic tub of peanut butter and some crackers, a little olive oil to add to the pot noodle and vacuum-packed olives for a treat.

As well as providing energy food is great for keeping your spirits up. I start the morning with fresh coffee, using ground coffee from Sabins Artisan Coffee Roasters in what is called the dirty coffee method. Stir some grounds into a cup of hot water, allow to settle and cool then drink, taking care not to drink the last bit. It would be a grim experience if I didn't have good coffee. The grounds are excellent used as a scourer to help clean the Ready Brek out of the breakfast bowl. In the evening I have a cup-a-soup, it might seem a strange choice for the desert, not for me it helps me sleep, my Ovaltine.

Food can be great for motivation and focus. During the Crawley 12-hour track race I set up a small table beside the track just after the start/finish line with my snacks and drinks laid out on top. Every half an hour I would have a piece of flapjack and every three hours I would have a rice pudding (I was veggie then) eaten walking around the track and the empty pot put in the rubbish bag beside the table on the next lap. That was a great way to break up the event into manageable chunks with a treat at the end of each completed chunk of time. All went well for the first three hours, and all went well for almost all of the next three before disaster struck. At 6 hours we changed direction by going around a traffic cone place on the finish line, my table was a few yards beyond the turn so my rice pudding was out of reach. It was only 400 metres before I could have that rice pudding but that change affected my mental state and I didn't enjoy the treat when I got it. Silly I know but a tired and bored mind is a fickle beast.

In his book '*Eat & Run my unlikely journey to ultramarathon greatness*', which was the inspiration for this book, Scott Jurek finishes each chapter with a recipe. I have not copied that, instead I am finishing off a few recipes. Both of the meals I make often because I can quickly prepare them when I get back from a run and then shower and change when they are cooking. I also have a lot of soup; a great way to keep hydrated and get a dose of antioxidants.

Roasted Cauliflower with Chickpeas and Tofu

This is a very quick and easy recipe. It can be adapted to meet nutritional needs. Long run planned for the following day; increase the amount of potato. Need more protein after a tough training session increase the amount of chickpeas or tofu.

Ingredients for one

1 medium potato cut into cm cubes
1 small cauliflower cut into small florets
120g cooked chickpeas (1/2 large can)
120g firm tofu cut into cm cubes
1½ tablespoons olive oil
1 tablespoon curry powder
Salt and freshly ground pepper

1. Heat oven to 200°C/400°F/Gas 7

2. Put everything in a bowl and mix together
3. Spread on a non-stick shallow baking tray.
4. Bake in the oven for about 25 minutes until vegetables are soft. Turn occasionally.
5. Serve sprinkled chopped fresh parsley or coriander.

Puy lentil, carrot and almonds

I get this simmering away, pop the almonds in when I get out of the shower then it is ready by the time I have dressed and grabbed a beer.

150g puy lentils or red split lentils
2 medium carrots, thinly sliced
1cm piece of root ginger, peeled and finely chopped
50g whole almonds
½ tsp ground cumin
½ tsp ground coriander
½ tsp celery salt
600ml vegetable stock
A little olive oil
Salt & pepper

1 Heat olive oil in saucepan over a low to medium heat and gently fry the ginger, cumin, coriander and celery salt for about 1 min, stirring all the time to avoid burning.
2 Add the sliced carrots and continue cooking for another 2-3 minutes
3 Add the lentils and stir in the stock. Bring to the boil then reduce the heat, cover and simmer for about 10 minutes.

4 Add the almonds and continue cooking for about 10 more minutes until almost all the liquid has been absorbed.
5 Season to taste.

Serve with fresh coriander garish for a light meal or flatbread for something more filling.

Butternut squash and sweet potato soup

An easy to make soup that can be enjoyed hot or cold. Packed full of antioxidants. Lovely as a post run treat.

1 tbsp olive oil
1 medium onion – peeled and diced
2 cloves garlic – peeled and crushed
1 tsp curry powder
300g sweet potato – peeled and diced
250g butternut squash (peeled weight) – diced
2 tbsp torn basil leaves
750 ml vegetable stock
250ml soya milk
Pinch of salt

1. Heat oil in a large saucepan, add onion and garlic and cook until soft, add curry powder and cook for a further minute stirring.
2. Add the sweet potato and butternut squash and cook for 3 minutes.
3. Add the stock, basil leaves and salt, bring to the boil, reduce heat and simmer for 20 minutes or until the sweet potato is soft.

4. Allow to cool slightly then whizz the mixture in a blender until smooth.
5. Return to the pan, add soya milk and re-heat gently
6. 6 serve with a swirl of vegan cream or yoghurt on top.

Note; If you are serving the soup cold you may wish to add more soya milk to improve the consistency. It can feel a bit like eating baby food without the extra milk.

Ed's dairy-free cream of broccoli soup

1 tbsp olive oil
1 onion, coarsely chopped
1 clove garlic, crushed
1 large head of broccoli, washed and chopped (you can use the stem as well provided it is not too tough)
800 ml vegetable stock
2 tsp mild curry powder
1 tbsp creamed coconut or one 50g sachet (Patak's do a box of 4 x 50g sachets)

1. In a large saucepan heat the oil and sauté the onions and garlic until translucent
2. Add chopped broccoli. Cook over medium heat, stirring until broccoli turns bright green.
3. Add the vegetable stock, bring to the boil and simmer until the broccoli is tender, but not overdone. About 10 to 15 minutes depending on how finely it was chopped.
4. Allow to cool slightly then transfer to a food processor or blender and process until smooth.
5. Return to the pan, add the creamed coconut and a little water or stock to thin the soup if necessary. Heat

gently, stirring regularly until the creamed coconut is mixed in.

6. Serve with some tasty bread. This soup is good with sliced avocado floated on top.

You can boost the wholesomeness of this soup by adding kale or spinach just after the stock is added to the broccoli.

In the weight-lifting world they say they say, muscles are made in the kitchen, not in the gym. That principle carries over into the running world; you cannot run well unless you are eating well.

Happy healthy running.

Printed in Great Britain
by Amazon

39676108R00126